God The Artist & Other Poems

Sammy Oke Akombi

Langaa Research & Publishing CIG
Mankon, Bamenda

Publisher:
Langaa RPCIG
Langaa Research & Publishing Common Initiative Group
P.O. Box 902 Mankon
Bamenda
North West Region
Cameroon
Langaagrp@gmail.com
www.langaa-rpcig.net

Distributed in and outside N. America by African Books Collective
orders@africanbookscollective.com
www.africanbookscollective.com

ISBN: 9956-792-55-1

Table of Contents

Forward

The author of this collection of poems, within the Cameroonian landscape of literary creativity, is very well known as a novelist, short story writer, and essayist. What is probably not known about him is the fact that he is equally a poet of very considerable powers. This work, ***God the Artist and other poems***, a collection of over fifty poems, justifies that claim. For lovers of poetry, they will find in his collection not only a wide range of themselves/ subjects, but also poems whose style is reminiscent of great poetry in the English Language. The title of this collection requires a special comment.

God the Artist, is the first poem in this collection. It expresses the poet's contemplation over and an admiration of God's creativity, acknowledging human procreation process as God's greatest artistic work. This poem is one of my favourites in the collection. The theme of man's endless and largely unsuccessful attempts to find happiness by trying to ape His master/creator is powerfully and skillfully conveyed by evocative imagery - God the blacksmith or goldsmith working with a furnace, transforming under very high temperatures molten matter into his artifacts, man being the ultimate. This poem like a few others in the collection is concerned with God and expresses a religious sentiment. The poet is not a bigot and there is no suggestion here or anywhere in the book that we are to be presented with a collection of religious poetry.

One interesting thing about this collection is that, it escapes characterization either in terms of its themes/ subjects and their treatment or in terms of its style. In reading through the work, the reader is deceptively moved to assume with the author many different roles, adopt several perspectives and attitudes, and moods. As regards the roles, for example, in the poem, The First, second and Third Saturday after my Death, the poet appears as an uncommitted narrator, naively recounting the sad events from the points of view of the innocent child and the victims of the traffic accidents now lying as corpses in the mortuary. In some of the poems he is a philosopher, questioning the very essence of life. I find the role of the poet as a social critic both interesting and intriguing. Several poems in this collection definitely express the poet's dissatisfaction with the state of affairs in our society, for example, arbitrary arrests and detentions, corrupt practices, abuse of power etc. What is interesting about the poet's social criticism is his gentle attitude toward the object of his criticism/denunciation. The poet might criticize his society for its failings but does so, knowing that he is also part of that society. This attitude of the poet makes a reading of his collection different from ***Bate Besong's*** collection, ***DISGRACE***. In Disgrace, the author is also concerned with the failings of society but his attitude is completely different. He is angry and totally disappointed with society, especially people in authority. His intention is to denounce and castigate society. His tone is aggressive and his voice spits out fire. He takes a stance outside society, as if he arrives from Mars. In this collection, the poem, ***Casualties,*** is one of the poems in which the author expresses his strong criticism of society. The poem is the poet's reflection and recollection of the period the society is passing through, a passage from a period of relative prosperity, happiness and hope to one of uncertainty, anxiety and insecurity, where the concern is with the individual survival rather than the collective good. The poet's condemnation of the leaders is obvious but as characteristic of him, he does this in a lighthearted way and tagging his criticism at the end as if it were an after-thought:

> A reign, a reign that dupes even rain
> The very rain that waters its grain

To the reader, what we have tried to do above is to give a foretaste of the sumptuous banquet the author has prepared for us. We have not done justice to it remembering that the taste of the pudding is in the eating, no reviews, no forewords, no introductions or prefaces can replace your actual reading and enjoying of these well written poems.

Chief Professor Samson. N. Abangma
Registrar / Professor of Linguistics & English Language
University of Buea

God The Artist

Inordinate imagination!
Towering creation!
A stupendous void churned and turned concrete.
The loud wailed and got discreet.
And then the ugly and the good
the beautiful and the bad
all shuffled and thrown into a furnace.
An incredible furnace of art.
And then man was made
and made to plunge into the centre.
The centre of the furnace.
He started a search, a toilsome search.
The search for solace.
So he's in continuous apprenticeship to the artist
God the artist
in His eternal creative endeavours.
One of which stands out as tall
as a pinnacle of art:
There's no greater display of art
than when He made the gents' *gens*
fit so cozily in mam's *gens*.
No greater display of art.
I bet, no greater display of art.

The Written Word

The word made the world.
And the written word has sustained
and will forever sustain God's word.
It's sustained the likes of Shakespeare
The likes of Achebe, Bebe, Kafka,
Soyinka, Bate Besong, Moliere
and the like and the like and the like.

The written word is the only means
by which men, and of course women's
minds can clearly be read
The unbreakable mirror of the mind.
The written word that makes the world.

Silent Scribbles

The truth, says the drunkard,
resides in the cup.
The truth, says the soldier
resides in the gun.
But the truth, insists the writer
resides in the pen.
The pen, many would agree,
has far greater might.
Mightier than the cup
and of course the gun.
So, the truth I swear, lies in:
The silent scribbles of a pen.

Blackness in Darkness

Blackness is God's creation
Being the artist He is, He sure knew why.
Like every creation, there's evolution
whose limit must touch the sky.
But ours, the black evolution
has been much marred, marred by
Much dejection and interruption
So, so much interruption and dejection.

Should we then fold up and invade the parks?
The parks of civilization,
thick blankets or duvets under our armpits,
telling everyone who cares to listen,
we're a homeless and hopeless lot
fit for nothing to change the world,
eager to accept the spare coins
that may grudgingly drop out
of both bountiful and spiteful pockets.

No! No! Blackness isn't so much poverty as it's dignity.
It is integrity, morality, and so much respectability,
It's also so much humility that turns around humanity.
Blackness sure has the will, courage and power
to change itself and the whole wide world.

Give the dejections and abject interruptions.
that have kept blackness in darkness, a positive touch.
Let them become the bearers of our torch
a mighty torch that'll lead us through
through and out of the depths of darkness.

In it we've lived for a long, long time.
It's time we got out of it, this time!
Blackness must forge a divorce, divorce from darkness.
to enjoy the light, even if it takes a revolution,
that the creator - God, provides for all creation.

Magnanimous Mandela

From a screen, I watched him emerge
out of Verster premises.
All the eyes in the mammoth crowd widened
And surged for glimpses.
Glimpses of the pedestal
that holds: Nelson Mandela.
My mind slipped into past ages
My fingers flipped through pages,
hoping to find that man, born of woman
who braved the devil's noxious temptation,
for two decades and a half and more
and conquered!
I stumbled on just one: Nelson Mandela.
Magnanimity, thy name is Mandela.

Winsome Strength

What strength!
He's been able to stand erect
in spite of the weight
The crushing weight of problems
of our problem world
resting on his ageing shoulders.

What a man!
Able to man
every single mission
for peace to all troubled spots
of our problem world.
Taunted and sometimes abused
he remained undaunted.
Focused, only on the peace of the world.

What a man!
Who the man?
Only an African
Born an Annan
Called Kofi
though counts not on coffee
for his winsome strength'
to find peace, only peace for the world.

Ode To A Leader

Only the scum and bums believed you'd fallen
No, Gorby you hadn't fallen, you'd risen
Your people have aptly proved it so.
For when a people love their leader,
it's hard to ruin their trust, and even harder
to rub their peace and their pride in mud.
When a people love their leader,
it's hard, so hard to ruin their privileges and rights.
And even harder to have justice denied.
When a people love their leader,
they're wont to sacrifice the sweat of their flesh
and also, the blood in their veins.
When a people love their leader,
their will towers tall against guns and bombs.
When a people love their leader,
there's silence on strangulation, damnation and perdition.
Finally, when a people love their leader,
Coercion is bound to lose itself in a maze of cohesion.

Some Showers Of Peace

A knot tightly tied, one day sure unties
The fate of our world for long remains,
Tightly tied to a stiff, stiff stake.
A stake bearing ruin, blood and thorns.
Too much for Mathias Rust, too much for sane man.

Have the sane, cause today
to heave a glossy sigh?
Now that some showers of peace
promise to bathe the globe:
Washington today receives a Gobatchev.
Even we too, we too in this part of the cusp
are much assured, as today
Yaounde is sizing up bouquets for Badamosi Babangida.

Have the sane, cause today
To heave a glossy sigh?
Yaounde 8/12/'87

The First Saturday After My Death

On the first Saturday after my death
My six-year-old boy
Thirsty for an answer
To the many questions
That boggled his kid mind
Went down his knees in prayer:
Papa God
Nobody has got round
To tell me when my father and my mother
Will arrive with the car,
The car they'd gone for.
They'd call to tell me, they were on the road.
On the road with my aunty.
I was to see them and my aunty
Come back in the glittering car, last Saturday.
And today is another Saturday.
Instead my grandmother has come
Carrying toad-like eyes full of tears.
Many more aunties and many more uncles
Have filled our house.
Everyone with bulging eyes, ready to explode in tears.
When I see their tears, I no longer want
The things that make me want to live
Not even my Fanta, after a wholesome meal.
And my mummy doesn't like it like that.
Please, Papa God, where are they?
Even if they don't bring the car
I want to see them. Them, and my aunty too.
Please, O please send them to me quick.
I don't like to see all these people,

With eyes bulging like those of toads and frogs.
I want to embrace, I want to laugh, I want to smile.
Smile with my daddy, mummy and aunty.

The Second Saturday After My Death

The confusion has only settled to a grave plight, so grave
That no head stood still to deal
With it, such a plight, so grave.
My mortal remains were in the outer chamber of the morgue.
And so were those of my better half.
As if it wasn't grave enough,
The corpse of my sister-in-law, my son's aunty,
Was also at our side, waiting to thaw.
Three corpses to deal with, and so many questions to answer.
Our boy needed, so badly, even if it's just an answer.
Two weeks have gone by, with no pleasing morsel between his jaws.
He's yet to know what happened to his daddy mummy and aunty.
There has been none with an answer
The only one with one should have been
Papa God Himself, whom he's been taught to respect, love and count on.
But in this grave plight, he's too little to find Him. He can't be seen.

The Third Saturday After My Death

On the third Saturday after my death
The nakedness of it all dawned on my six-year-old.
And he couldn't help but speak to himself, indeed, he did:
I'd always known tears to translate my wants.
Now I know they can also translate my sorrows.
No doubt the many bulging eyes like a toad's full of tears.
My daddy mummy and aunty have all been fatal victims.
Victims of that road. That road that rips apart body and soul.
Robbing the innocent like me, of their spring of happiness.
I'd seen their faces as they were laid lifeless.
All void of the usual bloom, bustle, grace and smile.
How could they smile, when they'd been mangled.
So badly mangled, I could hardly believe, the faces were theirs.
Even then, the mangled remains strained before they got there.
There, where they were buried.
At some points it wasn't a road, it was a mount of rubble.
Churned rubble – mud, pebble, granite and rock
Through which the *hiluxes* ached, roared and groaned
As they fought their way to get there.
There, where they were buried.
The coffins, jostled, rattled and even cracked
littering the whole place with splinters and bits and pieces of glass.
The mourners got muddled, and then shuffled and jerked violently.

As for the occupants of the coffins, for once ever since, I was glad
They were spared the pain and the shame.
It seemed a journey of a million miles but alas we got there.
There, where I saw them dipped back into earth
And covered for good, never to be seen again.
I then realized I too had come there for good, never again
To go back to where I was born, where I knew warmth and love.
I'd have to be content with a grandma, so broken and so worn.
Papa God! Please Papa God, forbid that it happens again.
Lest anyone else feel what I feel.

Images Of A Time

Naked women in fervent protest
Big buttocks rolling behind them
As they went by pressing a point.
Ragged students running riot.
Gun-totting soldiers pouring in the street.
Some drunk, some drugged
And some just trigger-bombo.

Jackbooted truncheon-bearing men wreaking havoc.
And grenade-thirsty ones in the alleyways.
Scarified arms, backs, fronts and faces
Even scarified hearts.
Horror-stricken eyes with tears and blood
Intermingling as they ran down sagged cheeks.

The young and the old, the short and the tall
Tearing up one another, letting the pieces fall
Buildings bursting and going up in flames.
Others crumbling and going down in rubbles
And bodies stout and firm
Roasting like fatty beef in a grill.

And there's no remorse, not a pinch of it
In the eyes and faces of the perpetrators.
None! Because timorous cheats had made them taut.
And the gods of evil had plucked their souls.
And made colonies of them – poor human souls.

Corruption, injustice, blatant and foul
Did conjure up this invasion
Invasion of souls – the poor human soul
By alien gods – alien gods of evil.

Children of ages, both reasonable and unreasonable
Peeped out through any openings they're able
To reach for – rotten rafters, cracked walls...
Some were crying out for attention
But who's there for mere pretension.
Father with a slashed nose
Is slowly bleeding towards his end.
Mother's lying prostrate, swooned
Because of the horrors of the time.

The air's foul with smell.
The smell of human flesh and blood.
Bloating bodies embracing swarms of flies.
And they littered every compound
That hitherto bustled with human life.
Charred bodies made the charcoal and ashes of the time.

For the children peering through rafters and cracks
Life is a huge heap of nonsense.
It's so bleak and hopelessly bleak
The derailment had been crushing, so crushing.
Even their doleful voices had been drowned in the brawl.
Their weary eyes got bled by the images – images of a time.

My God, I guess
This time is a time, in the past tense.
So at least the kids, can make sense
Of the images, images of a time.
A time they can't wait to forget.
So they can pick up the courage
To look forward to, better images-images of a time.

Casualties

No longer do I see potbellies roll away
to gallivant about on street corners.
No longer do I see shined cheeks
smile at giggling flowery faces.
No longer do I see confidence radiate
from the faces of my countrymen.
No longer do I see anyone
offer booze in celebration
of some success. Success!
Success's gone asleep on the lips
of everyone that comes my humble way.

Ours must be on arrival
a thoroughly cursed generation,
Casualties of a damned devious reign
Keen on reigning misery on
both friend and foe.
A reign that dupes its own voice
and crooks the hoe, the very hoe
that tills the deeply endearing soil,
plunging into a sham pool of shame
a nation whose glory remains unsung
A reign, a reign that dupes even rain.
The very rain that waters its grain.

Douala, December 1992

Cameroon

An unusual triangle in the heart of Africa
Wedged between ebullient Nigeria
And the remnants of the crumbled empire of Bokassa.
Other neighbours include: the battle weary Chad,
Happy-go-lucky Gabon and their cousins Equatorial Guinea.
Africa's soccer darling, before and after
Italia nineteen ninety carnival.

Cameroon
Blessed land, with quite a large body of water
Splashing at its base and yet another at its tip.
The Manyu, Ndian, Shari, Nyong. So'o and Sanaga
The wouri, Logone, Benue and Mungo
Meander, in a dire desire
To nurture life by serving man and plant.
Amongst its many peaks, there's a great grand one
That stands in all majesty above cape Limbo.
Displaying the grandeur that is Cameroon.

Cameroon
Opens out, wide at its luxuriant base
And narrows in at its Sahel tip.
It's Africa's wonderland, having all that obtains
In different parts of the continent.
So a truism it is,
When called: Africa in miniature.
Counts ten score and more cultures
For a bare twelve million people.
The language code can switch with ease

Be it French, English or another.

Cameroon
A part of the world would wish
It was just Cameroon, plain and simple
But another insists on Le Cameroun
An accident turned to reality, which the people
Now embrace and keep like a religion.

Cameroon
When cynics talk, they call it a reference
in the gospel according to bacchus.
There, however, seems a chance, a veritable chance
to belie them- the cynics.
A crisis called economic, has since taken control
and have been on patrol
to ensure a landslide backslide from the baneful gospel.

Cameroon
When the world talks soccer, it talks Brazil
When Africa talks soccer, it talks Cameroon.
And when Brazil talks soccer, it talks Pele
When Cameroon talks soccer, it talks Milla
Soccer gods sure know, where the legends should hail
So it was no omission Albert Roger Milla, should hail
from that unusual triangle – Cameroon.

Cameroon
Has all it takes to make a nation
rich, powerful, proud and
always in constant motion.
Like a spectacle full of emotion

because skill, land and water abound.

Cameroon
Must wake up from slumber
and impregnate its land and water
to bring to fruition
a nation that's neither an omission nor illusion.

Douala , July 1993

Genesis

Long, long before anyone knew,
God had written His will.
A country shall emerge
Out of the ashes of colonialism
And its name shall be called
Cameroon.

So the Portuguese came to trade
and were enchanted by the prawns
they saw in the Wouri
And then in their hurry
to give the place they found a name:
They gave it Cameroes which later grew up
to be Cameroon.

The Portuguese had come along for trade
But Germans came along for good.
Then the scramble for Africa began
winding up in a partition
that gave Cameroon away to them.

They built their plantations
and set up administration
Their culture they brought
Their language they taught
And called the country, Kamerun.

Then came the first world war
which the Germans fought to win
But fate never let them on

They lost the war and lost Kamerun
to the English and the French.

The winners shared their booty into two.
A part for England, a part for France.
So at once Kamerun became Cameroon
And also Le Cameroun.
Their cultures they brought
Their languages they taught.

But as none can put asunder
what God has put together
The two at independence
decided it was immense
pride to reunify.
And so decided to defy
all odds to stand again, as one nation.

The nation has been bathed in peace
so it has moved on thorns with ease.
We might not have life abundant
but we've got food abundant.
Being a bread basket for many
in its surroundings.
It keeps its place in Africa.
It keeps its pace in the roles it plays.

Many more will come and go
And Cameroon forever stays
One big proud nation
That counts so much on things
always getting better

for the betterment of a virile nation.

Yaounde, November 1995

I Wish I Wore Your Shoes

A

I wish I wore your shoes.
They're absolute dust jackets for your toes
And they fit just right.
Looking quite creamy white.
Look! They glitter under the rays of the sun.
I dote on the gloss and fragrance of your skin.
It mirrors; you dine well and drink well.
At table your food is served course after course.
First course, and then second and third in a meal.
You eat omelette, spaghetti, steak, green beans…
You sleep on a bed with immaculate white sheets,
in a cozy room with flowery curtains.
A radio set at the head of your bed
And a TV set at the foot, also a computer at the side.
How I wish I wore your shoes.

B

How I wish I wore your shoes.
They expose and relax your toes.
You walk freely in mud and dust,
Having no fear they'll pick up dirt.
You can wear them even when there's rain.
Thus, you're no prisoner of restriction.
At table you're tied to no rituals and courses.
You crack the bones of chicken
and suck out the marrow as you feel.
You swallow your 'fufu' until you're bellyful,
not expecting any desserts to crown the meal.
I tell you, my mom and pop are so keen

on some magic of a thing they call honey,
that flows out of hives in their farm.
How I really wish I wore your shoes

A
You wish you wore my shoes!
I wish you'd never try it,
To keep out of the headache I've got

B
Your headache can't be keener than mine.
My headache is a headache of a kind.
I honestly wish I wore your shoes.

West Cameroon Brother

My West Cameroon brother
In a dark khaki suit and a red beret
Who feigns not to understand what I say
because I say it not in French.
Sorry, I speak some French
But I'll say nothing
in that language.
For I know you're just feigning.

Look brother, look!
A black man
no matter how much metamorphosis
he's undergone
never is denuded of his blackness.
So my West Cameroon brother
no matter how much metamorphosis
you might have undergone,
You've got no right, to let anyone
denude you, of your culture.

Victoria, June 1978

It Was Our Choice

It was our choice, our glowing choice.
Be it a leap in the dark
Be it a leap into the ark
It was our choice, our glowing choice
to defy the odds and reunify
with our kith and kin whom
together we had succumbed to the whip.
The malicious German whip.
Together we had bowed to the effigy
The effigy of the Kaiser.
Together we'd been taught to greet in German.
Together we'd watched Germans choose
the choicest of mother earth's places – Buea
and made it the place to be – in Kamerun.

It was our choice, our glowing choice.
Be it a leap in the dark
Be it a leap into the ark
It was our choice, our glowing choice
to reunify and identify
with our kith and kin
who had been taught to speak French.
We had been taught to speak English.
The blend has made us specify and modify
huge issues to magnify and edify
an image, our image.
Fifty years have quietly gone by
and together we've made things happen
Happen in our cherished nation - Cameroon.

So, our choice, the glowing choice we'd made
hadn't been a leap in the dark.
It was, in fact, a leap into an alluring ark,
reinforcing our oneness - one people, one nation.

Buea, 11th February 2011

Guests At Dawn

It was a usual Thursday
My mind was getting set for the drudgery of the day.
Then an eerie cry of a child downstairs
Came ringing in my ears.
Papa, papa, ne va pas.
Ne va pas avec eux.
Before I could come to terms
With what the matter was downstairs
Footsteps were trudging upwards.
As I paid attention to the trudging steps.
Big bangs invaded my door.
Frightened kids kept to their room.
My shivering wife urged me not to open.
But the bangs were loud and deafening.
I couldn't help but open.
Four heavy booted policemen immediately stepped in.
"Police control" they thundered.
"You mean police check, please" I said politely.
"Police control" they insisted.
"Search warrant then, sirs".
"Are you of this land? Ask that again
And you'd swallow the teeth in your mouth".
"In that case sirs, I'd rather the teeth stay where they are".

The apartment was turned inside out.
My wife and kids watching in despair.
Satisfied, they asked me to pick up my I.D and follow.
"How about going to work?" I dared asked.
"When we are at work, no other work matters,"
they said with so, so much conviction.

Liberty Unveiled

Showers poured on them, coerced Cameroonians
In the northwest town of Bamenda.
They poured and then poured into the streets.
Delighted they'd found their voices
After decades of dumbness.
The voices burst out in a shrill:
Our freedom, freedom, freedom!
Or we choke and choke and die.

Bazookas, bayonets and bullets
Stealthily found their way among them.
And a spring of blood sprang alight.
Six souls fell, giving up the ghost against their will.
Thousands others drenched in sweat and blood
Left for home to nurse, their bruises and their wounds.

When the dead had been buried
And the tears had been dried
The people were amazed
Their voices were yet not lost.
They cried out to ascertain they're in fact
intact. The voices were intact.
Thus, in our country, liberty was unveiled.
Its showers still pour down on us all
Like corn flour from the open mouth of a mill.

Era Of Demagogues

How I hate to count my days
each time a new day dawns.
I'd rather make each day count
But as each day dawns
My fingers tremble, my lips tremble
Counting my days.

Counting my days, I tremble to count each day
In spite of myself, in spite of my will
I tremble to count them for I'm ruffled,
Rifled and stifled, and hear but swill,
Swill all over the place, each time a demagogue
Opens wide their mouth.

I hate to count my days
Each time a new day dawns
But I can't, O I can't make them count
Because I live in a sad era
an era where only demagogues count.

Deception

While the showers of liberty still poured on us all
tyrants whom by mischance ruled us all
Came to grips with a stark reality:
a desperate call for democracy.
A call they couldn't help but answer.
In poverty or in wealth, democracy cleans the wall.

These tyrants in a bid to keep their grip
had agreed to the terms in place.
But soon made a demon of it – democracy.
Incumbents know in advance how the goals
would be scored.
So they always made it seem plausible
their way to the keys of power – demoncrazy.

Cry Of Distress

In hordes of years gone by
No country other than mine
had really caught my envy.
I've had love, I've had joy
And above all, I've had peace.

Today, I worry at the flurry
I worry, really worry at the flurry
about my country, my beautiful country
for love, joy and peace
are slipping by in much haste.

In the wake of liberty
my country folk had dared
to open their mouths too wide:
Let's talk national
in a national conference.

Since the voicing of this request
an innocuous request,
even suckling babies
have known no love, no joy
nor the ease of peace.

There've been killings and still there are.
There've been battering, and still there is.
There've been burnings and still there are.
People are day by day, having their
Bodies and of course their souls emptied of morale.

Amidst these odds, the shepherds
Seem to go dumb. Seem to go blind.
They get into a kind of jingoism
Once in the safety of their homes.
And don't care less at others' smouldering homes.

Bully at His Best

Never have a people hungered for words.
Words from the soothing lips of their leader.
They were all hope and optimism.
For the preceding days had seen them
through harassment, deprivation, arson and murder.

Never have I seen, an entire nation
Come to a halt, just to listen
to their leader talk.
Expectations ran riot in view
of the assurances, the leader would give.

But the people, bruised and jaded
got but bullshit from the harsh lips of their leader:
My faithful subjects, faithful as always,
so far, my struggles to revive the economy
haven't started their fruitful yields yet.
In fact, the worst is yet to come.
It's already on its way, creeping steadily along.
The entire world economy is crumbling
so too are we crumbling along.
Therefore your belts, your belts I tell you
should be tightened, further.

I have for a pretty time been the object
at which all rotten eggs are thrown:
Gossip and despicable insults
all in the name of a nonsensical request.
Even my family and close collaborators have
had these rotten eggs thrown at.

I tell you, leave them out of this.
Is it democracy, when I give you
a mouth and you open it too wide?
Is it democracy when I give you teeth
and you bite and wound your own tongue?
Is it democracy when I give you
a stick of match and you strike it
to put your house aflame?
Is it democracy when I give you
my keys and you use them
to despicably invade my privacy?

I must tell you, and will keep telling you
democracy isn't putting me under any kind of pressure.
Democracy is watching me in peace and reverence,
do the things I've got to do at my own pace,
in my own way, and at the time I think is better.
My time, I must tell you, is God's time - period.

The Optimist

Sometime ago, in nineteen ninety-one
In the place where I had the grace to be born,
It was a long odd year.
The human brain took refuge in the anus
Whilst the anus took refuge in the skull.
Consequence: a whittling nation
in a whirlwind of confusion.

Nineteen ninety –two
Do we stand a chance, even a murky chance,
The anus will quit the skull
To let the brain, take up once more
Its avowed place and worthy function?
Consequence: a hopeful nation
back on the wheels of action.

Postscript: a score and one year have gone by
Yet to get on the wheel of action.
Thanks anyway, it's still a nation, our nation.

Launched Into The Labyrinth

I sat in the crowd watching tense
The performance of intellectuals
As they used words to polish words.
I simply moaned, at a point.
Thank God. All isn't lost yet.
Our country is still quite hot.

Then I listened to the brevity of the one
Who had just given birth to ***Disgrace***
I'd rather it was Grace.
Yet I yearned that his life
Won't be as brief
as the brevity of his brief.

But the very next day
In the wee hours of that day.
It was all over the place. He's gone.
Launched into a labyrinth of the unknown.
No more tumultuous ululations of BB, BB.
Never again shall a BB book launch be.
Thank God he's already got many on the hook.

BB's so spectacular, he couldn't do it alone.
How could he? Such an artistic don.
Hilarious, hilariously escorted him.
And Kwasen too, artfully did the same.
An able driver they had with them.
To drive them through the labyrinth of the unknown.

A Million Thanks For Listening

How much time before the next bus?
"Twelve minutes I suppose"
We won't wait long then.
Look! You see, you see those hedges over there?
"Yes, I do. I think they enclose the graveyard."
There lies the other part of me.
It sought refuge there, not quite twelve months.
It was unfair. That was unfair.

I spoke to him at six minutes to twelve
And at six minutes past , he was gone.
It wasn't anything to believe, when I found him
Stiff and cold.
Stiff and cold he was and I was oddly alone
I garnered all that was left in me
To shake off the stiff coldness in him.
But nothing triggered to pay me back my effort.
So I turned to frantic phone calls.

And today, I stand here and see there
There at that place , that place
The graveyard, you just called it
He was dipped away, dipped deep down
Not quite twelve months.
It was unfair. That was unfair.

Six times twelve years of partnership
Six times twelve years of common courtship
Six times twelve years of shared fortunes
Six times twelve years of shared misfortunes

Six times twelve years of shared anxieties
Six times twelve years of a shared dread
Six times twelve years of a shared bed.
Now my light has fused into darkness
And emptiness has given me a hand of friendship.

My heart starts breaking each time I stand here
And my eyes take me over there
To those hedges that enclose the graveyard.
It was unfair. That was unfair.

"How old was he?"
Ninety-six.
"Ninety-six! Far beyond the biblical six score and ten."
Yes beyond but you needed to see him.
Still strong and full of dreams.
"It's a pity, you're left to bask, nay freeze in the coldness of life.
With no quilt to spare you some warmth".
What can I do but gather the remnants
Of my pierced heart and do him honour.
His grave deserves a tombstone,
On which an epitaph should attract every passing eye.
Here lies the other part of a woman's breath.
Gladly shared everything but death
Which isn't fair. Not fair.

Quite true. Even true , through and through.
Sharing breath, and not sharing death
Is cruelly unfair.
And the creatures that prowl and crawl this earth
Make things more cruel and unfair.

They make the cruelty of the act
Sting like an angry wasp.
Hardly any words of cheer for the dispirited.
Nor consideration for the disabled and the aged.
Not even a silent moment for the desolate.
Nor a glass of water for the thirst-stricken.

Here, here we are. The bus is here.
"Thanks, thanks a million. Thanks for listening".

Coventry, UK May 1990

Bird Watching

Such a glorious hobby that always is in boom
When vibrant trees are in gigantic bloom
None needed to lobby to get its fans.
I was one of such lofty fans.
For I saw in it nature in full bloom.
The birds flying and perching in reckless abandon
The trees luring in reckless abundance.
Such a joy to watch and share the exuberance.

For some time I've been away from the exuberance
I hungered so much and only dined with perseverance.
One day, at the sight of trees in the horizon
on my fleeting feet I stayed,
bird watching from a window
on the tenth floor of Sheraton at Clayton.

It took me two hours
To know I was in the wrong place.
As I hate to waste precious time
I cashed in for other things:
Sunset was artfully marvelous,
Seeing the entire sky turn gold.
By and by the sun slowly faded,
Timidly disappearing behind tall trees.

Soon after darkness set in, street lights
Sprouted like mushrooms, to save the city a blackout.
My view went past the towers
And landed on a nearby highway
Where lights were speaking threateningly.

They spoke a language that only had three words:
Green, red and amber.

The city was still in motion
Gathering speed until the motion went a blast.
My bird watching turned head watching.
Heads carrying, blonde, dark, red and even blue hair.
Others carrying caps, scarves and hats.
Interesting, this lot shall come to pass
and another lot shall take the queue.
It went on into the night until two words
dropped off the language of the lights.
And my eyes told me the watching was enough.
My tired feet concurred.

St. Louis, Missouri, USA November 2004.

It's Just Too Much

It's just too much for a single generation
To enjoy so much veneration
In reliving a John the Baptist
Heralding the coming of a Jesus Christ,
Who indeed has come to fulfill his pact
Behold, this time, the protagonists are black.

It's just too much for a single generation
To enjoy the luxury of living a Mandela era,
Seeing probity and nobility work wonders
for the blacks and whites of a nation.
Also a grey-haired Annan era, in which there was
So much shuttling out of breath, throughout
The length and breadth of this wide world, in a bid
to troubleshoot and bring about peace to each a nation.
Behold, this time, the propellers of the eras were black.

It's just too much for a single generation
To wake up one fine morning and watch live
The devil in man, make him use man-made wonder
To cripple a skyscraper- another great wonder,
squeezing out of thousands of his kind, the gift of life.
Behold, the victims were both whites and blacks.

It's just too much for a single generation
For millions of millions of pairs of eyes
In their different corners
Watch live a man-made giant of a bird
Get so distressed by a God-made bird
That it nose-dived into an open-mouth river.

All aboard the giant bird, who were feared dead
came out with their breaths intact – such a wonder.
Behold the survivors were whites and blacks.

It's just too much for a single generation
To enjoy so much veneration
In watching with amazing adoration
the crowning of a president.
A president from whom so much expectation's rife.
The world in all its corners think he's the life
The kind of life that makes sense to mankind.
And Behold! This crowned prince is black.

Yes, it is. It's just too much for a single generation.
A generation which we each have the privilege to be a dweller.
Like the wise from the east, we can't ask for anything better.

Lessons from America

Lesson one

Two of their best minds are slugging it out
As they yearn for the most exalted seat.
The two parties got out of the primaries
without a broken tooth, nor a battered face.
Money for their deeds, they didn't fetch from the state pond.
Nor did a state Minister stop work for the campaign trail.
Nor did anyone find a stray state car on the trail.

A black boy with white tint
Who once smoked *ganja* in a back street
has been accorded acclaim and inspiration
by blacks and whites alike.
The poor and the rich alike
with no-one, shouting out: how dare you! How dare you!
He's disbanded and banished the clannish bar, nay the colour bar.

Let's watch out for what November shall fetch.
Already, it stands out clear: the wretched can be much fetched.

Lesson two

Politics is only a game, no huger than football.
It can be fierce and brutal but rarely fatal.
Losers dolefully lick their wounds
And like humbled dogs,
Lower their tails between their hind limbs
As they watch the winners run riot in celebration.

Change is such a vital element for virility.
And so, there are a mighty lot who yearn for it.
It doesn't matter who and what brings it.
I t could come even from a most unlikely bit.
Keep then, your heads, hearts and eyes open for change.
Booker Washington, Du Bois, Malcolm x, Marcus Garvey
Rosa Parks, Martin Luther King, Louis Armstrong, James Brown
Langston Hughes, Ralph Ellison et al are smiling in their every corner
Waving and saying it loud: GIG! GIG! God is Great! Alas, alas!
The invisible man has become visible.

Lesson three

Voters greatly feel they count as their votes are counted
They watch the counters do their jobs feeling well trusted.
Then it takes hours and not days to get the verdict out.
Defeat is conceded without resort to arms, crime and courts
And victory is so sweetly accepted with exceptional humility.
All seem to clearly say: It is the country first.

Democracy is no demon when practised in fairness
It strangulates the apathy in minds
and stimulates the prodigious hope in them.
Making them burn for love, for their country
So we saw amongst the youth, American youth
Who had been dying for change.
And change they got on the altar of democracy.
All hands are on deck, to row and not rock the boat.

Every great mind is called upon to give their bit,
caring not who the victor was or the vanquished.
The Key protagonists of the political saga, sit side by side
Mapping out a way for ward for a country
They both love so much.
So indeed, for they each shall quit the scene.
Their country never shall. Indeed Country First.

Lesson Four

It was a country in ecstasy that I saw in America.
Never have I witnessed such unanimity
in an expression of magnanimity.
It was so chivalrous as an entire world stood still
to watch a dream come through.
For once in a life time man has evinced oneness.
An indication that he's always yearned for thc one
Who'd trigger in him that virtue.
The all exalting virtue of oneness.

Democracy has done great in America.
It has pulled out a source of inspiration
That a country needs when spirits are down.
It has given them the kind of leadership
that occupants of a ship in distress would love to have.
America has pulled up shoulder high to face the odds.
And the rest of the world is happy for them.
There's no fear! There can't be any when hope dominates.
Change has brought that hope.
Great lessons from great America.

Lesson Five

America's just gathered much momentum
From a momentous event on the altar of Washington mall.
Millions braved the bitter winter to be part of it all.
And even greater millions, the world over, watched it live.
Some let loose themselves and were betrayed by their tears.
Others held their breaths to allay their fears.
The world and America were unanimous
It was an extremely great height of democracy
Making it a huge shame for demagogy
They applauded, ululated and even fainted in celebration.
They were right, very right to celebrate an era in motion.

And then the walk, the majestic walk to the white house.
They walked amidst the crowd rather than ride on a white horse.
Exuding so much assurance, radiating so much confidence
That the vicious, simply dropped their guns
and wearily walked away in shame.
All and sundry who lined the snowy pavements
Surged and surged forward for the genuine handshake.
And thank God, that handshake they were gloriously obliged.

She

She
Is
The most wonderful
Creature
That creation
Has created
And placed to plod on
The surface of mother earth.

She
Is
Not only the roses
But also
The catharsis
And
The very spring of life

Yet
She stands accused
Of lots and lots of faults:
Frailty
Perfidy
Adultery
And finally the fall of man

So
On her head
Is placed a crown
Despicable crown
With piercing prongs that hurt bad

She turns to man for help
Sometimes it comes, sometimes it doesn't

But
Like every messiah
She's bound
Firmly bound
To suffering and enduring
In order for mother earth to stay afloat.

The Pearl Spell

Steinbeck's Kino lived in consummate harmony
afore he dived out the pearl that ruined his family
A land east of Africa was dubbed the pearl
By a Briton called Winston. Since then all
of Africa boosted it as her jewel.
Like Kino's pearl denied him peace
This land with keenness denudes its dwellers of ease.

The spiral of unease surged in the virgin rule of a Milton
Who smelt plenty of rats in a kabaka. Hence befriended a baton
To cover his folk and ease his throne.
Hoisted with own petard, an Idi took Milton over.
The folk hurrahed, at last some easement in view.
But no, non was nigh. Terror! Terror rather terror
Was the dish the people got served by Idi.

Milton flexed! Flexed muscles and fought
aided by friends and foe. Got back the throne he thought
Was his by right. Again he sat on it.
The folk felt, he'd learnt from Idi's hotch potch.
But he grew more hoodlum than the hoodlum his mum did hatch.
Where Idi maimed he murdered, and where Idi murdered he massacred.
Such is the plight of the land of the pearl. The pearl spell indeed.

An Okello has come rumbling in.
Any chance peace for his folk he'll bring?
There's a yearning for the pearl to fit the pearl.

O! Nigeria

O! Nigeria, Africa's husky conundrum.
Fought a bloody civil war of doom
Just for greed, corruption and nepotism.

Killed a very fine soldier on a bloody Friday noon.
For fear he would bring about a new moon.

Drugged a big, big man and crated him up
Despite the watchful eye of Scotland yard.

Got rid of a very distinguished man with a pen of gold
By simply handing him a letter sealed with a bomb.

Silenced a multi-billion business magnate
For daring to get himself elected president.

Destroyed many a well-meaning nationalist
For expressing views that were viewed in bad taste.

Went into small and large scale kidnapping for ransom
Misleading into the creation of Boko Haram.

Boko Haram! A hazard for many a neighbourhood:
Maiming and murdering men, women and even children
With machetes, clubs, guns, grenades and bombs.
All in the name of Allah – our Almighty God.

Then lately, as the world wondered at what happened to over 200
occupants of a Malaysian Airlines flight MH370

Boko Haram harassed and *'haramed'* Chibok, abducting over 200
vulnerable secondary school girls, holding them hostage.
Which act amounts to taking an entire democracy hostage.

And now the nation, Africa and the world want their girls back.
They want them back in good state, with none having a backache.

I see them, I see Nigeria, O! Nigeria, Africa's husky conundrum.
Going far, to create a hurricane Katrina a typhoon and a snow-storm.

Oke Akombi, 22/05/2014

Black September In The U.S.

Hatred got hold of the hearts of some humans
And they chose a horrible path of death
for themselves and for thousands others.
Thousands others who had no pressing business with death.
Rather they had much business to ditch poverty.
O! Where's the love? The love that made
God Almighty create man. The love that made
God make man lord and governor of all that's this world.
Where's the love that sinks mountains
That breaks rocks apiece
That has reduced an entire planet
to only a comet.
Where's the love that's crushed the lethal war
Between capitalism and communism
Bringing down and turning into rubble the Berlin wall.
Where's the love that sinks differences
between nations, between religions and races.
Where's the love that swallows Semitism, Zionism, Arabism
and many other isms that ache the world.
Man is born to love and not to hate
for love cleanses where hatred messes.
O! Where's it? That love that our world so badly needs
for man is born to love and not to hate.

Black Saturday At Nsam

One time too many, our nation
Went for her mourning garment
Jumped into it and stooped to mourn.
To mourn her seed, caught in an inferno.

It was on a Saturday, a black Saturday
Like the ageless scriptures say
An inferno will consume the condemned.
As if to get these words fulfilled
The inferno like a hungry hawk swooped
Over Nsam and consumed the condemned.

They had been condemned. Condemned by their sins-
The awful sins of poverty.
From these sins they were striving for repentance.
Too late they couldn't have the luck, the luck to repent.
The gruesome inferno swept each one off their feet
Skinned them, roasted them and charred them.

Kindred, their kindred watched in horror
But none could deal the inferno a deadly blow
They rather took its blows, its ghastly blows
While questioning with their tearful eyes
Shall repentance ever come?
Repentance from the awful sins of poverty.

Innocence

In the little corner,
Where I was born, in the heart of Africa
Nothing, nothing, nothing good is said of a snake.
When you see it, kill it before it bruises your heel.
Be it small, be it medium or be it big and long.
It's such a big, big bigger danger.

There was this day,
I was looking, desperately for my one-year-old,
adventurous little boy.
I went round, round and round the yard
But I couldn't find him.
I called out loud, loud and loud
but I couldn't hear him.

So I went out, out of the yard, down a brook
And there he was, quietly playing
with none other toy, than a snake.
My God, what a sight: the head of a snake
snaking in my boy's hand.
I was stunned, so stunned, I couldn't shout.
I got into a shock and then into a trance.

By the time I recovered, my boy was by me.
And his toy – the snake, had gone
I looked at my boy and I wasn't sure of him.
He must have been filled with venom
And any minute, off his chest, his heart will fly.
But I've since waited, even for years, he's yet to die.

Dry Season

Ha! How the green is browned by the sun
When sprinkles cease to sprinkle
The browning green plead with parched throats
as the fires rush in with a relish
licking them up, with huge anxious tongues.
Rats and rabbits are smoked out of their hearths.
Helter-skelter they run for fresh ones
which stand out well for strangeness.
Strange like the bowels of men.

Good for cows and sheep that never cease
to thirst for green.
They're garnered and guided down to the vales
Lucky fellahs they are: blessed with care
for the care of the bowels of men.

The rats and rabbits quaintly feel good.
They're glad, vengeance has sauntered
As imperious snakes that had ' *homelessed'* them
are made to cry it out in turn.
The smoke draws out tears
From their tyrant lurid eyes
Compelling them a sinuous groping out
To unknown hearths that may stand out strange.
Strange like the bowels of men.

Season Of Green

Grudgingly, the bright searing rays yield
to a dark gathering cloud.
Conceding the first drops, a trip to thirsty earth.
There's a stir as dust and ashes rise in horror.

With arms outstretched the farmer bows
On the hard handle of his hoe
Straining with tilling and sweating with ploughing the earth
in a race with the rains.

Gradually the plain earth takes a lumpy phase
As it shapes in beds, paths, ridges and furrows
Also it's heaped in mounts big and small
in readiness for seeds and seedlings.

Then the down pouring grows in strength and gait
as the dark clouds gather above every day
offering the seeds and seedlings enough to drink
nodding an accord for them to sprout in perfect green.

It's green! Green everywhere, green on every farm
The infant maize plant sprouts out green, so does the yam.
The sprawling bean, sprawls cautiously green.
Groundnuts or peanuts, they broadly smile green.
So do all the plants, so does the entire land
'Green! Season of green', hails the chameleon.

A Bush Fire

Turmoil jostled me from the depths
Back to surface I rubbed my eyes
like a miner freed from earth's bowels.
The shrieks and shouts made me prance.
In a minute I was outside.
Cases edged out through smoky doors.
Suits too were ebbing away on their hangars.
Books leaped and landed into safety
Like noisy frogs surprised in a pool.
My puzzled mind took the hint
As a huge tongue in majesty surged
Towards our bungalows,
like the Manyu on a new course.
I turned and looked at my bungalow
and noticed it was gapping in horror.
Soon it too would be in action
like the fauna and flora were.
Flashes of thoughts like lightening
Invaded my hazy mind.
Finally, I settled for my manuscripts.
As I kept watching in horror
a friendly gale from nowhere came
and changed the course of the deadly flame.

Something From Nothing

My tummy grumbled with a rumbling
A yawn forced its way out and I got the hint.
I looked around and saw around
Nothing.

I frisked all pockets in the wardrobe
No sound nor weight of a miserable coin.
Then the grumbling tummy will simply go on
a rumbling.

I bowed my head and turned pensive
When it, I took up again,
I saw through my window, the slim snaky stems
of yams, snaking on tall stakes.

I pulled down one of the stakes and dug out the root.
Twitching my eyes, I saw pumpkin leaves
I cut them lush and tender, one after one after one
Through and through, I jerked to go

But the ripened fruits of the pepper plant
Beckoned pitifully to me
Even so did those on the tomato plant
My time I took to pick the fruits, one after one after one.

With very thirsty wood I made a fire
that boiled the roots, bowling me a weighty fufu lump
And the fruit plants gains, dishing me a tasty sauce.
Lucky me, winding up with a marvelous dinner
That indeed came, from nothing.

A Costly Regal

The cold dry harmattan has pined thin
The sweat stirring heat is soaring tense
Unconditioned rooms rivaled active ovens
Sending its occupants out on exile.
Misty breeze blew gently from the lagoon
Soothing and cooling the heat-ridden sphere
While the neon's bravely fought the pitch dark night.

The arena for sports innocuously lay flat and wide
unresistingly invaded by the dark.
Perched on a nearby pear tree was a bumptious owl.
Cozily carrying out its eerie hooting.

Of places far and wide, a lad and a lass
Found this arena of sports, the plushest of all
To settle and pamper their burning lust.
The lagoon kept fanning on the misty breeze
As the baby couple sleekly swept into ecstasy.

Unknown to them their ecstasy was the grief
of another mortal:
A reposing snake that had taken on their weight.
The weight dilated with each added beat
Almost shattering its fragile spine.

It widened its transverse mouth and had a loathsome bite.
To signal the lovers, its burden was hard to bear,
It abandoned its fatal venom in the frame of the she,
Shivering and gasping beneath the hissing he

The she jerked in sudden pain and then it dawned on them
They'd been taking liberties with the long crawling one.

Like hemlock fired into an artery of a vibrant being
The venom paused not in tainting, the circulatory stream
shortly ripping vital breath off the chest of the lass.
Wow! The costliest of prices to pay for an evening regal.

'Able' Captain Camara

The man behind the indulging camera
Was none other than the 'able' Captain Camara
The Camera that shot the abhorrent scenes
With so much craze and craving.
Whitish matter stained with blood
Oozed out of broken skulls like hot, hot gravy.
Ears bled as flying pellets eagerly burst through.
Hearts stood at a standstill
As fiery pellets hit rib bones and pierced them.
The bearers couldn't stay standing still
And so, they in their numbers fell
Forelimbs desperately dangling as they seemed
to say their byes to the country and to the world
they so much have loved.

More and more shots fell on scenes obscene, the victims:
vulnerable women, being watched by their unable men.
And then more pellets, plucked eyes out of their sockets.
The sockets become fountain pipes
through which blood from the victims poured out.
The camera zoomed, and so pleased was Captain Camara.
Many are, who shall be pleased to see the scenes.
They are, true-to-type – scenes from the dark.
Ah Guinea Conakry, the country of the Toures and Camaras.
Such a pain, you've always lived in pain.
Alas! ***On va faire comment?***
Such is the fate of many a sibling from Mama Africa.
Hundreds and thousands, every other day, die of thirst.
The thirst for liberty and for peace.

Reagonophobia

Shrills of fear scurried down spines
When a sliding land assured Reagan
He'd stay within again.

Many thought the globe would crack
Forgetting it pays to flex muscles
Which his people acclaim it's right to do.

Like the sane shepherd he's wont to be
He's apt to comply with the bidding of his flock
Which for him their succour must premier be.

Reaganophobia hence has no cause to alarm
for the septuagenarian's wits still kick
and he's astute about the caprices and whims
that dominate men's lives.

Reaganophobia has no cause?
When the scared minority down south: apartheid
Have their boon from Reagan and his flock?

'tis the globes greatest plague: minors lording majors
Down the catchment of the plague, reagonophobia's
Raging high and the reagonophobic dying numberless.

Why? Reagan can save the world this pest, which root
His name engenders by effacing from lexicons
The nauseating lexeme: apartheid.

His able hands have got a grip of the yam
And of course the able knife that can. Yes it can.

The Monster Down South

There was an awful monster down south
That used to keep in misery, the lives of humans
who numbered in their millions – twenty and four.
Each time it reared its horrible head
Great numbers sank down, into its ugly mouth.

It reared it bastardly once
In the infancy of the glorious nineteen sixties
Six days after the brutish ides of March
and *Sharpevilled* sixty and nine vital souls.

Again it swung into a horror-struck action
On the sixteenth day of the sixth month of the sixth
Year of the nineteen seventies
and *Sowetoed* a mere child: Hector Petersen
signaling death for hundreds and hundreds of others.

Again! And again, it emerged with much mischance
In the pubescence of the dreary eighties
Six days after the brutish ides of March
and brutishly *Langaed* ten and nine virile souls.

Since then it had been blood, blood!
Blood, flowing out of dark skins

It got so much distaste, this monster, so much distaste
For blood that flowed in the veins covered by skin white.
But had poignant and voracious taste
For blood that flowed in the veins covered by skin black.
Hence the bulky burden of the black man!

But I did ask!
Was black blood for free?
Ought not someone stop the monster's spree?

I was told it had tentacles
Like those of the ugly octopus
It was fed from the West
And even from the East
North and South, not left out
I did ask again!
Had those who fed the monster
No strength to withhold their fodder?
So that it starved to death
before its damage swelled in such great depth.

Those millions down south, twenty and four
Tired and battered didn't need such air, so foul.

Alas! Alas! The monster's swooned and it's down with no limb.
Enfeebled by a De Klerk and a Mandela
Two men who stood tall to ensure easement down south.
And easement there is and the wide world without shame jubilates.

Africa Welcomes The World

What a dawn? A mighty dawn for Africa!!
Africa that many an ignorant think is only a country
No! It's not a country, it's a continent! Superbly huge.
The only that exported humans like modern economies export goods.
One of the continents where humans are still
transported in *goods-only* trucks and carriages.
The only continent that created and harboured apartheid.
One among those that produce deadly dictators and carry out deadly deeds.
The only where hunger, disease indigence and dumping are rife.
The only whose pristine concepts of God have been crushed, so bad.
The only whose history is inordinately painful to listen to.
Africa! whose love for music and dance, sports and games is gigantic
Then of course the only continent blessed with a Mandela.
And it's dawn today, Africa welcomes the world to the celebration
of the English game at the centre of which is the *Jabulani*.
Jabulani! The African name for the ball that twenty-two
men of the world will at each time, kick and run after,
giving joy to the billions that make the world alter.
See how today, all roads lead to Johannesburg.
And of course other cities, including Rustenburg.
How all minds steer away from boredom, need and evil.
How all minds stir and gear towards love.
Love for the individuals that play, love for their teams

Love for their nations and love for humanity.
Today, that love radiates from the rainbow nation: South Africa!
Africa! No longer is trusted only with the bad and ugly.
Africa is also trusted with the good and lovely.
Yes! Africa can. Can make the world stir and go into a frenzy
because of much joy, inspiring love and peace.
See how Zuma zooms to shake hands with the entire world.

The Report Card

Excellent in all aspects. Proof of hard work,
and ingenuity. Keep it up!!
You've belied all misgivings
You've made Africa proud
And of course, the entire world.
Other comments:
The jabulani flaw was floored.
The vuvuzela flaw was also floored.
And even the crime flaw was floored.
You can be trusted with anything
Anything, but apartheid.

Lessons Of Madiba's Demise

Black is power ! Again came alive!
in a live celebration of a life.
Mandela's demise brought to life
A redefinition of a black man.
A black man can also stand tall and proud,
making humanity feel good and proud,
and learning lessons of much import from him.
His life told us:
Always bend low to thank your Creator
for what you are and submit to what you are
teaching others to stop faking and be what they are.
Money, which's much in pursuit, should only be incidental.
Use the blessings of power for the edification of humanity.
As you can see, the spill of blood only gets yours spilled.
The rape of fellow man only gets an entire world raped.
We all are just one, nourished by the same red, red blood.

Oke Akombi, 10/12/2013

Money! Money!

It pined down the barter days and then swept them away
Like floods do, green plants that flood the bay.
Good barter days that soared products
as products dealt in products, not these days that cash addicts.

Money! It's been 'a big bigger brain bother' since
Its trajectory jostled through the commerce
of the universe, making humans stoop for it, bow for it
and even die for it. Others for it trip and slide and sink in a pit.

Pity! The misery enshrined on faces that go around
without it. White haired and wrinkled raw, haggard
and senile raw, allowing death to sweep them raw.
No qualms, the relay for money is a race to watch with awe.

The furious race is persistent and run with much determination.
Some falsely hand their batons. Others, fellow racers trip their motion
in a bid to vitiate. Some, their tracks, they jump but the judge a blind eye
turns. At the end of it all, some are tops, others bottoms but what's the joy?

The joy, the joy, the joy of it all is the fairness displayed.
Money! It's beaten all goals and now assumed
the ultimate goal of eager ambition, for without it,

lots of things stay undone, including the house that stays unbuilt.

Even plants weep, whittle and wither without money.
Without money we may make no friends and drink no beer. Like honey
money soothes the bitterness in our mouths, giving a meaning
to our lives and daily we wish life was such a business unending.

Ah money! Some have it big
Some have it small and some not even a pfennig.
But it's given lots and lots of attention
and products are made with so much pretention.
Love and learning are damned, so are honesty and patriotism.
So that, the joy, the only joy in its quest is apt fairness in the game.

Stakes Of Love

Unlike yam stems that twine and twist
Around firm and stout stakes,
Love twines and twists
Around fake flimsy stakes
that stir and rustle even at
light short sniffs and mostly abound
in purses, wallets, safes and sometimes bras.

Though flimsy and supple
They stoutly stand up to
Cyclones and hurricanes
that stand out as threats
to the twining and twisting stems of love.
They tend and nurture love
to the lusciousness of palm maggots.

Like yam stems creep away
when their stakes are blown aground
so too does love creep away
When aground their stakes are blown
They creep a wild
developing desperate tendrils
desperate to grab new stakes.

Like farmers foray dense forests for their yam stakes
Randy boys foray dense safes and banks for the stakes of love.

Man's Body's Sacred

Until death has had the last laugh
Man's body's a great work of art.
The symmetrical patterns of the frame can only be divine.
And the strokes and curves of the artist are simply sublime.
Man on their knees should thank the artist
And on their feet should celebrate art.

Not much on earth compares this art so wonderful..
The human body in its abundance of beauty
beauty that's built up to become sacred.
Whether in procreation or in creation
Every single element stands out strikingly proud.
If anyone loves art, the one should celebrate art,
In profound acknowledgement: man's body's in fact sacred.

The anus in all its beauty discharges waste
Fingers in their charm make man write.
Legs in their grace take man for a walk
Tongue in its comeliness makes man talk
Eyes in their radiance make man see
Ears in their excellence make man hear
Teeth in their brilliance make man bite and chew
The nose in its fairness makes man smell
and palms in their splendour make them feel.
With all this bounty, man on their feet should celebrate art.
In profound acknowledgement: man's body's in fact sacred.

But there can be a blemish when gaiety turns into arrogance
Making man tend to: walk on their head rather than their legs.
See with their ears rather than their eyes
Smell with their tongue rather than their nose
Bite with their fingers rather than their teeth.
Or shit through their mouth rather than their anus.

Forlorn Sparrow

Up on a topmost twig of an eucalyptus tree
perched a forlorn sparrow
watching the furrows of a vegetable garden
sink under the burden of water.
And then whole fields sank.
Fields that had been laboriously attended to.
Fields that had had many a mouth depend on.
All gone! All gone under the burden of water.

The perching sparrow stirred, flapped its wings
as if to fly off, but it saw it surge,
the dirty brown liquid, turn into furrows and eat up
human homes, as they crumble under its force.
There was desperation, as far as the sparrow
could see. A family uncannily clings on a floating trunk,
hoping for the indulgence of hope
even when all's gone, gone under the burden of water.

It was too much, far too much for the forlorn sparrow
on the twig. It tries to whistle a dirge
but it's drowned in the noise of a strange bird.
It flies just above the family on a floating trunk,
making such a disturbing noise as it swings its wings.
The forlorn sparrow can't stand the noise.
It stretched out, flapped its wings and flew into space
wondering why man that boasts big brain
Should be so vulnerable to the caprices of rain.

Kid Brother Ayukepi

Born in severe seizures that gave birth to fissures
Lived with the fissures begotten by the seizures
And yet he loved life and strode hard to live.
He loved all those he could talk to
He loved all those he could look at
He loved, he loved, all those he could count on
And even those that he couldn't even sit by.
Whether his love was returned, he couldn't care.
All he cared was love, love and love
with a heart as clean and clear as crystal.
Every single kolanut he offered bore a disarming smile.
No qualms, no grudge. No tears: The likes of you are eternal.

Dark Tuesday, 18th Jan 2011.

Pushed To The Wall

In absolute peace and calm, lived a porcupine
inside a deserted anthill.
The procreation law caught up with her
And she settled to nurture her young.
Sturdy young porcupines, vivacious like palace princes
in their considered castle.
A hunter in his avowed duty was passing by once,
a furtive glance at the castle, he felt the pinch to go ahead.
But his legs dragged him down.
And then his two greyhounds dog trotted by and stood,
their transverse mouths agape with panting.
They looked at his face and saw he was musing
But at what? They couldn't know.
His rolling eyeballs rolled on to the serene castle.
The dogs bounced and went a sniffing,
sniffing at every available opening.
It took them not long a time to know,
life existed within.
Growling and barking then caught the air.
Down, down the castle, the young porcupines
got caught in fright, as the noise to them made no sense.
It thundered on and on and they felt their safety faltering.
So they started out turn by turn.
Armed with a cutlass, a razor at its edge, the hunter
Played the serial killer. The pretty necks of the sturdy breed
Went down in turns as he kept an acute eye
On the gate that let them out .
None was spared and nineteen of them went down that day.

What ruin for a generation.

Their mother dear, didn't do as much as budge, until the turbulence
did die down. She looked around in discomfort
and saw she was all by herself. Left alone to grope along alone.
She knew, never to her will those sturdy kids make a run again.
She broke down to weep their loss.
Up above the castle, the hunter was far from peaceful
He put twigs together and lit a fire
to fire out that which stayed still within.
Anon, all the rooms were a cloud of smoke.
Smoke that drew out tears from eyes and coughs from chests.
'cause it was spiced with onions and pepper.
Sneezing, choking and suffocating mother porcupine
gradually groped her way out.
Close to the outlet, it shot out like a bullet from a darn gun.
Before hounds and hunter knew it, she was gathering speed far ahead .
The pursuit took off as the flora gave way.
She vamoosed into a hole but behold deep in it
a snake was hissing in its sleep, in all majesty. So out again she scrammed.
Letting sleeping snakes lie in their perfect ease.
Retracing her trail, out she shot again and the chase at once ensued.
Pushed to the wall, mother porcupine stood out of breath,

arched out and took the form of a bow
and then its quills began to fly, flying off like arrows
from the bow of an artful archer.
Abashed, by the twirl of things the chasers lost their bearing.
They got blinded as the quills hit their targets
Blood oozing out red from six burly eyes.
The barking whirled to a whine, the shouting yielded to yells.
So it was, greyhounds and hunter hoisted with their petard.

For Esong I

My succour I obtain by bleeding my pen tense
because all by myself I wrestle your absence.
The bungalow in which I live haunts me hollow
as bedrooms, garage, bath and even kitchen bow
in my presence with emptiness.

Each morning the sighs on my lips unveil
as bleak ideas surge for me to muse upon and avail
myself of my pen , and also her mate- the paper
to process and build, varnish and furnish, to cater
for the minds that care to care.

Then I go to school to build not ideas this time but souls
that gulp down all that I proffer like bustling fowls
would the grains from the hand of a concerned farmer.
I return in the forenoon tired and consumer
conscious for food prepared not by your hand.

And then I slump on a bed in want of sleep.
Poor me, instead of much needed sleep, thoughts start to slip
into my fretting mind, all bothered on you and my plans
By and by the sun runs low allowing free lance
for the construction of my hazed up fancies.

You may wish to ask if I'm void of friends
to busy my time and let it fly the wilds
leaving none to give a thought to you
and the plans I presage for the future too.
Esong dear, no friends as such: male nor female.

The male are damn bored to listen to me and
my cares. Care not a hoot about what my hand
scribbles. They get stressed, really stressed by the antics
of a literary mind: doctors, engineers, lawyers and soldiers.
They believe hard in the craft of writers.

I try hard to let them know, the basis of life lies in culture
And this is realized and preserved by literature.
So whether it's a flying man or medicine man, culture's at the fore.
Their interest thus in literature I strive to make them ensure.
This they hate to like and so, away they keep from me.

The female I had as friends got scared, their ogling
I tended to ignore. Never having a wish to listen to my ranting
about this great mind or that, this honoured feat or that. Rather
they wished me engage in constant prattles, foibles and flatter
like an ever-go-gay Casanova.

But there's one or two who longed to have my love.
How could I give them unless to cheat my dove.
So all are gone the friends I had. They've got nothing
to gain by palling up with me: no endearing concourse nor dating.
I'm glad it leaves me with much freedom
to concentrate and contemplate on a blithe future.

Also to give a thought to and scan my album for your picture
which each time it's looked at my heart a tango dances
and I long for that day which when I think about, my frame prances
with a loud report of my heart.

Esong, Esong, does that instinct akin to your kind
a rousing future presage for you and the things on my mind?

For Esong II

Another dawdling day has slovenly yawned into life
seeming to be heavy with boulders, unlike a sprightly wife
who's heavy with an astute baby. I walked to the calendar
to blurt the day gone by and realized it was a Saturday. In temper
I shook my head as I counted the months that still stayed.

Like the dawdling day, I paused for a yawn thinking, what's up
for the day. I lumped back to bed and let thoughts pop
up like polluted fish desperate for life. Then I remembered
the dream. I'd dreamt last night, I from school returned tired
you from nowhere ran for my case, planting on my cheeks

a kiss and walked me home, settling me at table
titillating my countenance with sweet soft smiles. Unable
to hide my surprise, I asked, but how? How did it happen
that you're here with me, or am I mistaken
I've been expecting you?

"No time for questions ok, all is set for a sumptuous dish
prepared by a hand that you greatly love and with much relish
do feed from." Anon, it soared, it soared and towered, anon.
That was my stormy appetite that had lain
low all the while.

The food was in elegant dishes and china plates.
Unlike the plastics I use for plates. Oh! The Hades
that I've been in. I'm glad you've come to take me
out. I ate like a hungry worm, drank like a fish, my tummy
outgrew its resilience and I was full of food and of course
joy.

For once these five months, I felt more like a man.
True! They say, each a man of success has for a fan
a woman he loves. Ah! My siesta this time, with you by
my side.
My thoughts this time to share with me. My worries, like
a high tide
You swept away.

And then I stammered, I want, I want, I want all of you.
You took it in immediately, I trust your wits. "But it's too
Soon" ran the sweet whisper. "The food needs repose,
your body needs it too . And then you'll be quite fit I
suppose.
I simply nodded in concord.

I slept off awhile, and when I lifted my drowsy eyes
they fell on an exquisite form, garnished by peeping rays
that ran away from the setting sun. I stretched out my left
arm
longing for a touch, but it shrank as if I had meant to
harm.
I tried the right, much better. But each spot touched
melted away.

The nose melted away, an ear I touched melted, and even her hand melted.
My heart sank and I felt very insulted.
Then my right hand found courage to run down the navel,
which in turn melted like clean wax on a glowing piece of charcoal.
Fright ran up to rescue me. It was a dream! But I've been hag-ridden since.

Esong, It's hard, so hard to live in someone else's nation
All the same , I'm glad, so glad for our separation
It sure promises a sweet, honey sweet return.
There's so much healing, soul healing that's firing on
really firing on here, in me.

Out and out here, I've come to know, man's one.
The colours of man , the cultures of man and man's languages are all done
done for man's good. They bring about a blend, a superb blend.
There may be hatred, there may be arson and killings but the trend
the moving trend's that these hurtful deeds are narrow paths leading to one.

Esong, Esong, carry no-one as a burden in your heart.
That'll do the good of keeping you free from evil and hate.
And love in its pure sense will on you descend in depth.
Imagine! Just imagine the joy that'll be on my return. You and I shall bathe.
Bathe in an enormous bath of love, thanking God for all the glory.

A Chimpanzee In Tears

What are they up to? These beings called humans!
They hunted me down and got me out of my nature.
Out of my nature, where I'd been nurtured,
nurtured in glee and absolute freedom.
And then they caged me in a place surrounded,
by a forest- a forest of concrete, not of trees.
Here I spend my time in absolute boredom,
grudgingly but silently watching humans slaughter us,
not only for their food but also for their sport.

I've given up my feeble fight to return, back to freedom.
Being only a chimp, one of the doomed in human kingdom,
there's been no way, I can make way for progress.
I'm only waiting and counting my days.
As I wait and count them – these days,
The sound of jackboots, guns and bombs deafen my ears.
The stench of disruption, corruption, shit and death stuff my nose.
I tell you, they litter everywhere, shit and die every day.

They detonate themselves amongst themselves.
They're so jealous, they blow up their kin who fly like birds.
They hideously butcher the ones who think in a way positive.
They sink vessels that dare to transport their kind to glory.
They're simply 'murderageous' for want of a better adjective.

And yet, they shout out, the freedom for which they labour
is greater than the freedom that we animals harbour.
I'm in tears, not even for us but for them – these humans.

What are they up to? These beings called humans!
They've got all, all it takes to create a paradise. But they got me caged.
And I remain cruelly caged.
Yet for thanklessness, greed, opportunism and mercilessness,
they're getting the entire life on earth, and themselves caged.
In my tears, I see a murky return, a return, back to chaos!

Oke Akombi, Buea, 30th July 2014

Common Enemy

The quarrels keep tumbling in, on and on.
The wars are raging, and raging on and on.
Artillery is grumbling and rumbling.
Grenades and bombs are exploding.
Friends are fighting furiously against foes.
One enemy pounding on another's nest,
emptying mother earth of its content.

There's so much inattention:
- inattention to child welfare.
- inattention to social welfare.
- inattention to moral welfare.
- inattention to animal welfare.
- inattention to environmental welfare.
There's so, so much inattention!

Energy, sweat, brain, brawn and blood
are like a lamb on the altar of warfare.

Suddenly, out of a dark, dark cloud
emerged a mysterious virile enemy.
An enemy common to all who are enemies.
This enemy destroys, mangles and kills,
using no guns, no grenades nor bombs.
Gives not a damn about enmity nor amity.
It simply puts down any life on its path.

Too abrupt to be true; quarrels halted, wars stopped.
Guns, grenades and bombs all dropped.
Enemies turned allies, united to confront the enemy.

They all woke up to the reality of the virile enemy,
the common enemy, beckoning for much attention.
Its origins have been traced, incidentally traced to Africa
and invariably been given an African name – Ebola.

Oke Akombi, Buea, 08/08/14.

To My Brother The Thief

Life's like that. Full of tricks, tricks so difficult to beat.
I keep wondering how my brother's my brother, a brat so different.
So different from me, his elder brother.
When he was growing up, he would lie, and sting like a bee.
And wouldn't want anyone else to stay fit and be the one to be.
He could steal and conceal, stealing like a rat
in a peanut barn. Does nothing but steal and eat.
He's full, so full of tricks that make even angels fall out,
which makes him laugh and brings him so much fall out.
It's been my lifelong wish he weren't my brother!

One dull day he came ranting:
I've done it! I've done it!
Don't you see! Can't anyone see, I've done it!

Done what again? I asked him.

The operation brother, the operation has come through.
And the customer too brother, the customer came along
So I'm smiling, I'm smiling home with three strong
hundred thousand francs worth of clean banknotes.

Operation, operation, what operation?

I operated in the darkest of nights, last night
At a neighbourhood called Sandpit.
Right in the very depth of the pit.

There I broke into a fenced yard
And found the right car saintly parked
Its parts sell like *maïs chaud, maïs chaud.*
First, I demobbed the alarm system
Then I ripped open the boot and then the bonnet.
Systematically I dismembered it of its worth:
Control system, dashboard, wipers, windscreens,
Loudspeakers, side lights, rear mirror, head and back lamps.
By the time I finished dismembering, the car was a carcass.
While the meticulous operation proceeded
The *mugoos* in the comfort of their rooms slept like logs of wood.
Some breathing heavily, others snoring sonorously
I picked up everything clinically and squeezed myself away
unperturbed, not even by a mosquito, nor cockroach
even though it was cold, lonely and rainy.

At exactly ten o'clock, my client was on hand.
Anxious to have his promised goods placed in his hands.
And to me he handed the strong, sleek notes.
Brother, I tell you, life's good, so, so good.

So good indeed, you think. Kid brother, I rather pity you.
Operations worth the name are carried out for common good.
Yours is carried out for common ruin.
Feeling so good on the theft of someone's sweat's an aberration.
What a shame! Imagine me , your brother , as the victim.
Me, your own blood brother, a victim of your nefarious deeds.
How do you think I'd have felt?

How you'd have felt brother? I can't imagine that.
We thieves never think how others feel. We do, we fail.
There's no sentimentality brother, in our deals and deeds.
All we think is success. Success in deeds is what we feel.
Not minding whose cow or horse is gored.

Pouah – pouah! I wish I could spit on you, kid brother
I would have spat and spat on you for proudly running to me
Priding on:
I've done it! I've done it!
An exclamation that should come out of the mouths of those
Those who have achieved noble feats or even those
who have passed exams, have won medals or prizes
I have wished every day you were not my brother
but here you are, telling me about an abhorrent operation.
One that's rattled and would for a long time sadden a family.
And why not? It may cripple an entire community.
For all that brother, you stuff your pockets
With only thirty dirty notes of ten thousand francs.

Brother, any operation worth its salt
aims to heal and not to kill humanity

Tell you what? Once there was the like of you
Who lived his life only on crime.
He one day dared to steal from a home.
The home was four floors off the ground
He got a rope and tied to it a short rod.
He managed to fling it on to the balcony of the home.
A flat on the fourth floor of the house.
The rod got entangled between the balusters.
And so it served as a hook.

With the rope in hand the thief started an upward climb.
Halfway up the climb, the home owner noticed the climb.
He imagined it was an ominous way to gain entrance.
He thus picked up a knife, sharp and clean
and went to the balcony to receive the climber.
So he watched the tedious climb come on and on.

Just before the climber could place his foot
on one of the balusters of the balcony, his host
lifted the sharp knife high and with one giant blow
The rope separated from the rod
Causing a really great fall
which ended down on a concrete surface.
And so badly shattered was a human body and face.

And yet there was this other case.
A fabulous man who lived on cases
was returning home after a dinner out
hoping to rest from the day's woes.
But before he had stepped on his door step
A hoodlum of a thief had stalked him and his wife.
When he noticed the hoodlum, coming at them with a knife
He knew that was bad news, but he calmly asked:
'What is it you want from us sir?'
'Your money or your life,' the hoodlum answered.
'Not our lives of course, nothing compares with human life.
'So your money then,' the hoodlum requested.
'of course all of it. Take everything,' man and wife said.
'Everything! Will you grant me an appointment?
For I bet, everything can't be on you.'

'Well, if you wish to take an appointment,
so we can clear the banks of all that we've got as money
and even sell all our property and keep the money for you.
Provided the life of my wife and my own too
are not squeezed out by your lethal tools.

'Ah, ah, ah, well said, well spoken, but I'll be a big, big fool
If I take you for your words. I thrive on distrust.
So man and woman, I'll be content with what's on you now.
And so now be quick, hands on your heads place. No procrastination.'

On his head the man placed his hands and let himself be mugged
while his wife helplessly looked on. In her hand her precious handbag.
As the mugging went on she knew her turn to be mugged was on hand.
She looked at her precious bag as if to bid it bye, flung it at the mugger
but it landed with a thud on the grounds near his feet.
At that point, the mugger's accomplice who had been lurking by, ran up
out of the shadows, a brutal knife in hand, held high up.
But luck ran against him as he tripped on the handbag
and went aground violently, his knife flying out of his hand.
The gun totting man thought he should pay attention to the precious bag

before the woman developed second thoughts.
As he gave away his attention, the fabulous man saw it as an opportunity.
Like a flash of lightening, he grabbed the hoodlum's gun.
Weakened by this act, the mugger's desire for the precious bag surged.
He rushed towards it but too late the trigger had been pulled.
Before his accomplice got his head cleared, it had been cleared by the gun.
In one, two short steps, two fallen daredevils.

Brother, tell me if life, precious as it is should be risked in crime.
No kid brother I tell you, you had better risk it in things sublime.

Sometimes they, people like you
run into an angry mob, who because of their anger have no qualms
in transforming rejected car tyres into necklaces
placed on their necks to decorate them before they're set ablaze.
They get bloated and roasted like beef on a barbecue.
Brother, remember, the voice of man is the voice of God.
And I tell you, no man has any voice for you but a curse.
Also note that there's no way and nowhere a thief can hide.
If they're not fished out, they fish themselves out.
You thieves are not only hateful but also very deceitful,
negative , hurting others and atrociously ungrateful,
which can only make you sink into grave ungainliness.

Why? Why brother shouldn't that be?
When your deeds do nothing but stink and sting like a bee.
If the head is sane, that's above your shoulder,
then now's the time to turn about, in prayer
and thank the many desolate voices that sincerely say:
Father forgive them, for they know not what they do.
Listen to these voices and then tell yourself:
Henceforth, I'll always be **truthful, positive** and **helping others**.

When you make an about turn, adopting this as a daily affirmation
You'll be the kid brother I'd like to have, for the good of our nation.

Thank you brother, your words have hit me like lightening,
enlightening me to think , think of Saul who later became Paul.
An indication, I can turn around and not be different
considering that you and I are one womb's product.
And also that we're wonderful creations of one artist - God the Artist.

Printed in the United States
By Bookmasters

TARNISHED HEISMAN

TARNISHED HEISMAN

Did Reggie Bush turn his final college season into a six-figure job?

DON YAEGER

AND JIM HENRY

POCKET BOOKS

New York London Toronto Sydney

To my sister, Nani:
I am proud of you and have loved watching
the passion for life you bring every day.
Mom & Dad are smiling down on you!
—DY

To Dawn, Bryan, Brooke, and Brittany:
A man couldn't ask—or hope—for a better wife and children.
Thanks for your love and support. I am blessed beyond words.
—JH

Pocket Books
A Division of Simon & Schuster, Inc.
1230 Avenue of the Americas
New York, NY 10020

First Pocket Books trade paperback edition December 2008

POCKET and colophon are registered trademarks of Simon & Schuster, Inc.

For information about special discounts for bulk purchases,
please contact Simon & Schuster Special Sales at 1-800-456-6798 or
business@simonandschuster.com.

Designed by Jessica Shatan

Manufactured in the United States of America

10 9 8 7 6 5 4 3 2 1

ISBN-13: 978-1-4165-7756-0
ISBN-10: 1-4165-7756-4
ISBN-13: 978-1-4165-7819-2 (pbk)
ISBN-10: 1-4165-7819-6 (pbk)

Contents

Author's Note

As authors, our goal in taking on this project has been to recount an exceptionally newsworthy story in as accurate and balanced a fashion as possible. We believe we have achieved that goal to the extent possible, notwithstanding the impediments we have encountered that should be clearly understood.

Reggie Bush has generally denied the charges recounted in this book. However, despite our persistent efforts, we were unable to obtain any specific response to the detailed allegations the book recounts, either from Reggie Bush, his family and their representatives, or from the University of Southern California, its athletic department, and coaching staff. Also, on the ground that their inquiries and investigations are still pending, we have had only limited access to representatives of the NCAA and the Pac-10, who could not comment on the substantive charges. As a result, this book is unavoidably based on claims and information provided by those primarily on one side of the story. As far as our sources are concerned, we have attempted in the book to be transparent in identifying their backgrounds, involvement, and possible motivations in leveling or commenting on such serious charges.

A primary source of the allegations against Reggie Bush is Lloyd Lake, a co-founder of New Era Sports & Entertainment. Lake's allegations against Bush had already been extensively reported before this project was undertaken as was the fact that Lake had tape-recorded conversations with Bush and his stepfather, portions of which are reproduced in this book for the first time. The reader should be aware that Lake has been

compensated in return for his full cooperation, including his provision of the tapes. However, Lake had no editorial control over how he, his tapes, or Reggie Bush and his family have been presented in the book.

Although they did not respond substantively to our inquiries, representatives of Bush and his family have already publicly questioned Lake's credibility, based on his checkered background, including criminal convictions and incarcerations—a history that is fully laid out in the pages that follow. Of course, every writer would love to have Mother Teresa as a corroborating witness. But, for better or worse, in the real world you can't pick your sources—especially when the issues involve claims of questionable activities and possible law or rule violations.

In any event, as reported in this book, multiple sources have corroborated the key allegations against Bush and his family. Lake and many others have also provided extensive physical evidence—not only the tapes but also bank and credit card records, phone bills and logs, emails, etc., whose detail also appears to corroborate and document Lake's charges and the charges of various other sources and witnesses. [Much of this documentation is available for the reader to review on the website www.tarnishedheisman.com.]

ONE

Thanking All the Wrong People

Reggie Bush stepped to the podium, flashing one of the most electric smiles in all of college sports. Past Heisman Trophy winners served as a historic and humble backdrop. An adoring audience stood and cheered as an elated yet poised Bush beamed with pride.

Bush, a junior running back from the University of Southern California, did what had never been done in the history of college football: He won the Heisman Trophy by beating out a teammate who had won the prestigious award the year before and was in the front row with him. It told the world that Bush was a young man whose future knew no limits.

The Nokia Theatre Times Square, a 2,100-person venue that had officially opened three months earlier, was wired as ESPN televised the 2005 Heisman Trophy presentation live to the country from New York City. An elegantly dressed, energized crowd had waited in anticipation for this exact moment during the sixty-minute broadcast.

Sitting next to each other in the second row near the center aisle were Bush's parents, Denise and LaMar Griffin; Bush's younger half-brother, Javon, was also in the audience. The group was dressed to the nines:

Denise in a spectacular long silk brocade jacket with a mandarin collar, offset by gold chandelier earrings that brushed her shoulders; LaMar and the fourteen-year-old Javon in stylish, striped suits with color-coordinated pocket silks.

The Heisman Trophy—a bronze statue that depicts a football player sidestepping and straight-arming his way downfield to a mythical touchdown—sat handsomely on a stand to Bush's right. The framed, lighted canvas portraits of past Heisman Trophy winners, including Bush's USC teammate Matt Leinart, would soon make room for Bush on its hallowed walls.

Chants of "Reg-gie, Reg-gie" reverberated off the theater walls moments after Bush climbed six quick steps onto the stage. One past Heisman winner could be heard saying "Welcome back" to Bush, a finalist for the award a year earlier in 2004, as he approached the wooden podium that featured a bronze plate on front for all to read: The Heisman Trophy Award.

As Bush began his acceptance speech, it became an instant ESPN Classic. By all accounts, it was one of the most well-received acceptance speeches in the history of the Heisman. Everyone in the room recognized this twenty-year-old man didn't have just football talent. Soon the appeal, the flash, and the dash that were good for him on the field were going to take their course off, and he would be a significant endorser of major products, rivaling the very best in the NFL, even as a rookie.

Dinner was being prepared three time zones away on the West Coast on December 10, 2005. Lloyd Lake was sitting in his television room with buddies at his home in Southern California, watching the Heisman Trophy presentation to his friend Reggie Bush. But it wasn't a sight that Lake enjoyed as he shifted uncomfortably on the couch and muttered to himself. Actually, he couldn't believe what he had seen and heard. About everything that Bush owned at that point, Lloyd Lake had helped pay for. And yet, as Bush was accepting college football's most prestigious award and getting ready to play in the most important game of his career—the national championship against Texas in twenty-five days—Lake realized that Bush had turned on him.

It had become obvious to Lake just days earlier that several promises he thought Reggie had made to him were suddenly not going to be honored. Lake, his family, and his business partner had provided Reggie Bush and his family with nearly $300,000 in benefits as Reggie was finishing up his career at USC. They did it all with the complete understanding that Reggie was going to be the face and part owner of a company they intended to build around him, a sports marketing firm called New Era Sports & Entertainment.

"We were happy for him, but I knew at that time it wasn't the same," said Lake, who cofounded New Era Sports along with San Diego businessman Michael Michaels in late 2004. "I knew everything was unraveling, but I still wanted to see Reggie win, him being from San Diego and all that. I never knew at the time that we would be in the position that we are right now. I thought anybody with common sense would say, 'I'm wrong, I did this, let me make it right,' and shake hands and go on our separate ways. But it didn't happen like that."

Michaels, meanwhile, also had to feel betrayed as Bush accepted the Heisman.

More than a year earlier, in October 2004, Lake and LaMar Griffin had approached Michaels, a friend of Lake's and a business development officer for the Sycuan Indian tribe, in the tribe's luxury suite in Qualcomm Stadium after a San Diego Chargers football game. It was suggested to Michaels that he, Lake, and Griffin could be partners in a sports and entertainment agency, along with the Sycuan tribe.

While Lake and Michaels had no history as agents before being with Reggie and starting New Era, the opportunity seemed too good to pass on. Since Michaels had money available, he became the financial cornerstone of the agency. Michaels immediately paid off $28,000 in debt for Bush's parents so they could concentrate on helping the fledging agency sprout wings and fly.

New Era wouldn't stay in the air for long.

Larry Pierce—who played high-school football with Bush at Helix High in La Mesa, California—intended to watch the Heisman presentation with Lake. Pierce considered Bush a good friend, and Bush had actually introduced Pierce to Lake at a USC football game months earlier. Pierce attended all but one of the Trojans' home games in 2005. Reggie

had left Pierce's name on the team's pass list for recruits—even though Pierce had played college baseball for two years and had been recently hired at the San Diego Gas & Electric Company. Larry often mingled with Bush in the locker room following the games.

By hanging with Lake and Bush, Pierce quickly learned of the wide array of benefits that Lake had provided Reggie and his family. "I know there was money involved," Pierce said. "I never knew the total amounts. But I knew it was money given to help [him] out personally—things he needed personally. Like any struggling kid in college, you might need some money to go buy a couple things here and there."

As Lloyd Lake sat and watched, his blood pressure began to rise. He knew this was all a charade. Reggie Bush didn't meet the criterion on the Heisman ballot that reads any winner of the award "must be in compliance with the bylaws defining an NCAA student-athlete." In fact, Reggie was probably the highest-paid amateur in college football in 2005.

AUTHORS' NOTE

Believing it was the best way to protect his financial investment, Lloyd Lake, at the urging of his mother, Barbara Gunner, secretly taped with a digital recorder hidden in his front pocket more than two hours of conversations with LaMar Griffin and Reggie Bush over a two-week span beginning December 5, 2005.

Lake's two conversations with Griffin were face-to-face. The first was on December 5 before the Heisman presentation when Lake met Griffin in the parking lot at Morse High School, where Griffin is a security guard. Lake's former girlfriend, Maiesha Jones, accompanied Lake but remained inside Lake's Mercedes Benz as Lake and Griffin talked outside the car.

The second conversation between Lake and Griffin followed the Heisman ceremony and was in the parking lot of a Rally's Hamburgers near Griffin's home in Spring Valley, California. There were also two telephone conversations recorded with Reggie. The conversations between Lake—at his home in El Cajon, California—and Bush took place after he returned from the Heisman ceremony in New York City. Agent David Caravantes also joined the second conversation near the end after being called by Lake. Lake could not recall the specific dates when he talked to Bush.

Excerpts of these transcripts appear throughout this book. In a select few instances, a clarification is provided in brackets to establish context.

In this first excerpt, Bush indicates that he intends to repay Lloyd.

Lloyd: Okay, let me ask you this. Why would I have to mention something I think you know? Get your dad on the phone right now if you want to. We can get it out in the open if you want. I'm not going to lie to you. I have no reason to lie to you, chief. I'm thinking you know your dad told me, "I told Reggie, you know. Reggie said thanks, and he appreciates the way you're looking out for us." Man, that's what he told me, so what am I supposed to do? Why am I supposed to tell you something I think you know? You know what I mean?

Reggie: I'll make sure you get all that back. I don't know how much it is, I am not going to say it, but I'll make sure you get it all back.

Lloyd: What about the time and the effort, Reg?

Reggie: What do you want me to do? You all got to [inaudible] get a decent chance just like all the other agents.

William J. Dockery, president of the Heisman Trophy Trust, stood to announce the recipient of the seventy-first Heisman Trophy. The ESPN cameras focused on the three candidates in the front row—Texas quarterback Vince Young was on the end seat near the center aisle, Reggie Bush was next to him, and Matt Leinart was to Bush's left. The trio, impeccably dressed in dark suits, sat expressionless, each with his hands clenched together as if in prayer. Denise and LaMar Griffin sat directly behind Young and Reggie, their eyes centered on the stage and Dockery.

Dockery finally said, "And now without further delay, the Heisman Trust is proud to announce the winner of the 2005 Heisman Memorial Trophy, the winner is . . . Reggie Bush, USC." Bush immediately lunged forward in his seat as the crowd exploded in celebration. A grinning Leinart leaned toward Bush and extended his right hand in congratulations; Young, reacting as if surprised by the announcement, stared straight ahead and graciously applauded.

In the second row, LaMar Griffin, holding a small, white towel in his left hand, leaned back in his chair as if to gain momentum, then stood and thrust his arms triumphantly skyward. To his right, a smiling Denise Griffin stood at the same time and clapped. As the revelry spread throughout the theater, the two turned away from each other when it came time to share in the moment.

LaMar looked left and shook the hand of Bob Leinart, Matt's father, and hugged him, while Denise reached out for Javon, who made his way up front. Following a hug from Leinart and handshake from Young, Reggie walked around and hugged LaMar first, then his mother. Denise could be heard saying, "Oh, my God, Oh, my God," as the two embraced. Reggie reached around and pulled Javon close to him as they shook hands.

A smiling Reggie then made his way to the stage to receive the most prestigious individual player honor in American college sports.

Darryl Hartzog, nicknamed "Bandit," was relaxing in his suite at the Doubletree Guest Suites Times Square early Saturday night. The Heisman Trophy presentation had just started, and Hartzog was excited for Bush and his family. A night earlier Hartzog had partied with Reggie, Denise and LaMar Griffin, Vince Young, and others—including veteran marketing agent Mike Ornstein, who, like Lake, was positioning himself to work for Bush when he declared for the NFL.

Hartzog said the group ate a late lunch at the ESPN Zone on Broadway and arrived in limousines that evening at the trendy 40/40 Club, owned by hip-hop mogul Jay-Z and partner Juan Perez, in Manhattan. As could be expected, Bush was in great spirits as evening rolled into morning.

"Reggie and I were sitting there and he was asking about the music industry—what it takes to get in the music industry," Hartzog said. "He said he also wanted to open up a soul food restaurant in San Diego, and we talked business ideas concerning my clothing line. He was fine, kind of nonchalant. If he was nervous about the Heisman, you certainly couldn't tell."

Hartzog, thirty-four, first met Reggie in 1999 through a younger cousin who attended Helix High with Bush. Hartzog, in the music and designer business in San Diego, said he and Bush immediately connected. Their friendship quickly flourished, and Hartzog said Bush even went as far as to introduce him as his cousin. In turn, Hartzog helped Bush get a summer job at Boogaloo Records in Los Angeles before Bush's freshman season at USC.

When the Heisman Trophy Trust announced Bush as one of the three

finalists for the Heisman on December 7, Hartzog knew he wanted to be in New York City that weekend to support Bush. Plus it was New York City, which has long been a mecca for music and the arts. One of the first things Hartzog did when he arrived in the city was take a horse-and-buggy ride around Central Park.

Lloyd Lake, who also is a good friend of Hartzog, was being taken for a ride, too. Lake could only wonder what was going on in New York City during the weekend of the Heisman presentation.

"When I really knew we were in trouble was when at the Heisman, when a friend of mine [Darryl Hartzog] was in the room with them," Lake said. "We go way back. Bandit was telling me how [Mike] Ornstein was running around and out there saying, 'Yeah, I do all of Reggie's marketing.' Reggie wasn't saying nothing. I knew then you are not going to let somebody make this presentation and represent you like this if you are really not considering or already locked in to doing it. So I was like, 'Okay.' At this point I am just trying to sit down with Reggie now to figure out what we're going to do about my time and my money. It's no big deal, but you are going to compensate me for my time. At this time, I am trying to sit down and talk with him. Now he's playing hard to get. This is when all the arguing starts.

"LaMar told me that Reggie said that when he goes to the NFL he's going to forget about you [friends] and not deal with you. LaMar was telling Reggie, be careful of the people you get around you. He was like, 'Oh, Dad, when I go to the NFL, I am going to leave all those people alone and get rid of them.' But you don't play with people like that. You don't get people to run around and do things for you and then you just abandon them because you go to the NFL."

Lloyd: I get with Reggie when he took money from other people, that's going to get ugly. Somebody doesn't get him, it's going to get ugly if they can prove it.

LaMar: It's hard to prove they gave cash, it's hard to prove. You can't prove cash. Somebody give somebody cash, because I can say right now you gave me something, no you didn't. I got cash, you can't prove nothing.

Lloyd: Just because it's cash, don't mean you can't prove it. I'll give you an example. Say when we bought the car, I gave you the $12,000, right, you go give it to Reggie when he bought his car and then look at my bank account right then. How would I know the $12,000 that came out my bank account was what he put down on his car. You see, that's how you can prove it, circumstantial evidence.

LaMar: Well, that was so long ago, you must have kept a receipt or something.

Lloyd: No, I went to the bank, and the bank always keep records. When I went to the bank and pulled out the $12,000—like your bank, if you go pull out money, it never go anywhere. You pulled out $12,000 this day.

LaMar: When did Reggie say he'll pay you the $12,000 back?

Lloyd: I never talked to him about it. I wasn't even looking for it back. I just wanted him to come to the company. I told him everything we did for you, because right now it's about two hundred grand. He can keep that or give it to you. If we get Reggie, he can keep that $200,000 we spent over the year and a half, whatever, see what I'm saying? He can just say, "Okay, pay that back to my dad," or he can give it to us, and we'll give it to you.

LaMar: I'm not going to say that I talked to my wife about this, because if I do, she's pissed.

Lloyd: She pissed off with me already. But she shouldn't be mad at me.

LaMar: She's mad at everybody. She's mad at the whole situation.

Lloyd: I wish I never got involved, too. The same way you're feeling, I told Maiesha [former girlfriend] today, I wish I had never got involved in this shit. I thought it was going to be good, and it should have been good.

LaMar: It might still be good, but you see what I'm saying, and I'm going to say this and then I'm just going to leave it, if we're friends and it doesn't go out there like the way it should be, it just should be left alone. Everybody get together, pay the money back that was

> for me this year. Gave me an opportunity to go out there and do what I do, to make moves and I love you guys for it. To Matt, man, I mean, what more can I say? The decision to come back this year has changed my life so much, thank you. To Coach Carroll, Coach McNair, the rest of the coaches, man, I love you guys so much. You guys are the best coaches, the best coaches I've ever had, I ever wish for. Trying to make sure I get everybody. And finally, to the Heisman voters, my new fraternity brothers, members of the sports media, thank you for your votes. Appreciate it greatly. Thank you.

Lloyd Lake's mother, Barbara Gunner, and sister, Lisa Lake, also watched the award presentation from their homes in the San Diego area. They had been pulled into the business venture by Lloyd, who was looking to straighten out a life that often landed on the wrong side of the law. Like Lloyd, Barbara and Lisa, a morning television news anchor in San Diego, knew the agreement with Bush was deteriorating.

Lisa Lake received a telephone call from Denise Griffin in New York City soon after her son won the Heisman. Lisa and Barbara often talked by telephone with Denise—so often, in fact, that Denise's name and number were programmed into their cellular phones. "She told me, 'I am so proud of him.' I was too because I told her, 'We're watching and we saw you guys,' and everything was great," Lisa Lake said. "That was the last time I remember thinking things were great."

And in these next three recorded excerpts, things had turned bizarre as Lloyd Lake weaved in the writings of Italian diplomat Niccolo Machiavelli (1469–1527) and LaMar later reminded Lake the importance of Scripture. Lake said he first read Machiavaelli's book *The Prince* in his early twenties.

> **Lloyd:** Hold on. Machiavelli book, man. Now tell me if this is true. This gets fucked up, Big Dog. I tried to call Reg, like you said. He don't call me back.
>
> **LaMar:** He don't call nobody back, man. He don't call nobody. The only time I see Reggie or talk to Reggie is when I see him for five

minutes in the evening, or when I see him last night at the banquet. He don't call nobody back.

Lloyd: I'm trying to figure out what's going on with the money, and how we're going to work that out?

LaMar: What money? What are you talking about? We already talked about this.

Lloyd: No, that's not what I'm talking about. Remember you told me we need to sit down, me and him, and go over everything?

LaMar: But not now, Lake.

Lloyd: When do you do it, Big Dog?

LaMar: Why are you panicking so much, Lake?

Lloyd: Because I'm panicking, shit.

LaMar: But why?

Lloyd: Because he could easily say, "I ain't giving you shit back."

LaMar: Why would you think Reggie would do that? Reggie told you, he already told you he's going to give it back. He told me he's going to give it back to you. He said, "Whatever I put in, whatever Lake gave me, I'll give it back." Why do you think Reggie would go against that?

Lloyd: Because he went against everything else he said. Look, it [Machiavelli] says, "Since the Prince must know well how to use the nature of the beast, he must choose the fox and the lion from among them. For the lion cannot defend himself from traps, and the fox cannot defend himself from wolves. Therefore it's necessary to be a fox to recognize traps, and a lion to fight the wolves. Those who live simply by the lion do not understand this. Therefore a prudent ruler cannot and must not keep his word. When keeping it will work against him and when the reason were made and the promises have been removed and men were all good, this precept would not be good. But since they are sadly wicked and would not keep their words to you, you do also do not be keeping to them." Do you see what he's saying with that? He's saying we are deceitful from the beginning.

LaMar: But see you were deceitful from the beginning too.

Lloyd: How?

LaMar: The motive that you was at.

Lloyd: I told you the motive, we're eating together. It's a business. Before I talked to you and it's different if you're being deceitful.

LaMar: Lake, hear me out, man.

Lloyd: I'll hear you out.

LaMar: We discussed this about the money way before I left to go to New York City. Whatever you gave Reggie, Reggie's not going to turn it back and not give you—if he don't come to the business, he's not going to say, "Oh, Lake, you know, thank you but no thank you." Reggie's not going to do that to you because he told me himself, he said, "Tell Lake if I don't come to this business or whatever, I'm giving him every penny that he gave me from the car, to the little money that you've given him before." He's not going do you like that.

LaMar: Like I said, I'm not in it because if anything happens, it's going to happen to Reggie. It ain't going to happen to me because he's the one been doing the stuff behind my back. I told him not to, I said, "Whatever you do, let me know, I got your back, but let me know." See, if he took money from you like that and I didn't know nothing about it, and shit falls on his head, what can I do? I love him, but . . .

Lloyd: I don't want to get in any of that, I just want to pull it off.

LaMar: I understand that, but if it's not pulled off, we're going to have to get together and figure out how we're going to get the money back to everybody and everything else like that that money was taken from. But see that part he took, that's between you and him. And I'm worried about my part with Mike. I'm not worried about that shit I didn't know. So I had nothing to do with it. That's between you and him. If you wanted to go do all that and then come call and tell me, did you tell Lake? Then I'd say, "Well, shit, I didn't say anything, you did." I'm going to have to have a talk with Reggie

and tell Reggie, "Man, you didn't tell me what's going on, man. Shit I need to know. You need to tell me if you took money from anybody anywhere. I don't care who, you need to let me know. Because if you don't let me know, it's still not being true, he's not helping me out. But if I just say okay, I'll just let it go, I can't let it go because he's not telling me the truth. I told him, "If you do anything with anybody. . . ."

Lloyd: What I'm afraid of is he took money from other people and probably did like the same situation.

LaMar: I don't think he'd do nothing like that.

Lloyd: I hope not. Right now, I'm telling you right now, if it was one of them white boys he did that to, they would bribe [blackmail] him right now. They would bribe [blackmail] him, period. Period. Look, your mom and them got the house. My partner paid for that. You know, they would bribe [blackmail] him no question. You want the Heisman, you want to finish this out? They would bribe [blackmail] him. I'm not that type of person. I just want to pull it off. I'm not going to try to bribe [blackmail] no one or threaten nobody with certain things, I just want to pull the thing off like everybody said together when we started. If we can do, the best way to do something is clean all the time. If we can pull it off and keep it clean, that's the best thing to do.

Lloyd: I don't want to argue either, but this is what I'm saying.

LaMar: I'm not going to allow you to blackmail Reggie or myself.

Lloyd: How am I blackmailing anybody?

LaMar: I'm just saying, Lake.

Lloyd: Blackmailing is when you—I'm just trying to figure out how to get my money back.

LaMar: You'll get your money back.

Lloyd: It's not like that, Big Dog. You can't say that for all the time and effort you put in, I'm going to just give you your money back. Why the fuck would I give you my money just to get the same amount of money back?

LaMar: But see, another thing is too, Lake.

Lloyd: Why would I do that?

LaMar: I'm going to tell you about yourself.

Lloyd: Tell me about myself, I want to hear it. And I'm going to tell you about yourself.

LaMar: You got a hustle mentality. You know what? You still got to come up there and present the agency to Reggie.

Lloyd: Reggie don't want to hear that because JC [Pearson, Bush's cousin and former NFL player with the Kansas City Chiefs] is up there telling them foolishness.

LaMar: JC hasn't even talked to Reggie, what are you talking about? He ain't even talked to Reggie. Reggie don't even return JC's calls. He was trying to call him and congratulate him for the Heisman. He's not talking to nobody. I couldn't even talk to my own son. What are you talking about? You're out here playing and acting a fool because you thinking about someone is going to fuck your money.

Lloyd: I got to think about my money that I put in that I'm going to lose behind people's words.

LaMar: But see no, sometimes it happens that way.

Lloyd: No, it doesn't happen that way.

LaMar: I have lost a lot of things by people saying they're going to do something for me. They're going to do this and they're going to do that, and it don't happen. You know what? Put that goddamn Machiavelli book down and pick up the Word and read the Word and see what the Word say about people promising. People don't promise. Jesus died on the cross behind crap like that. He died. I don't care about no Machiavellian. I care about the Word of God.

Lloyd: I understand that, Big Dog.

LaMar: Pick up the Bible and read that, and then come back and tell me some Scripture, about stuff like that.

Over the course of nine months, from March 2005 until the month he won the Heisman, phone records obtained by the authors show that Reg-

gie Bush and LaMar Griffin exchanged phone calls with Lloyd Lake on his cell an astonishing 484 times. But on this night, there was no call.

Reggie's acceptance speech was gracious, classy, articulate.

Reggie Bush thanked everyone.

Except Lloyd Lake and Michael Michaels.

TWO

Reggie

Anyone curious about the writing on the antiglare strips Reggie Bush wears under his eyes during games need only look to his childhood for the answer. Almost always emblazoned with one of two messages—"S.E." to represent Southeast San Diego, or "619" in tribute to the area code at that end of the town—the black tape serves to remind others where Bush came from and as a salute to the people who helped to get him there. He was driving down the field before he could drive a car, and he moved quickly from Pop Warner phenomenon to hometown hero to collegiate gridiron giant.

Born in San Diego on March 2, 1985, Reginald Alfred Bush, Jr., was a ball of energy almost from day one. An elementary-school teacher pressured his mother, Denise, to medicate him in an effort to calm the child, who was constantly on the go. The teacher was convinced that Reggie, while an obviously bright and enthusiastically curious child, was suffering from attention deficit disorder, as he seemed unable to stay seated, popping up every few minutes to run around the classroom.

This energy and need for movement was complicated by the fact that Reggie suffered from childhood asthma. His family remained unaware of

this condition for quite a while, chalking up his wheezing and gasping for breath to the fact that he was always running and jumping with unceasing intensity. The problem persisted, however, and eventually landed him in the hospital several times. His doctors were able to determine fairly quickly the cause of his breathing complications, but Reggie could not be convinced to lessen his activity. His lungs eventually recovered, and his energy finally found an outlet when he was introduced to Pop Warner football—the activity that would rapidly launch him into the local spotlight as a pint-sized sensation.

On September 3, 1994, a nine-year-old Reggie made his football debut and earned a series of statistics in that game that would eclipse even his outstanding college career numbers ten years in the future. He carried the ball six times, scoring five touchdowns against the Grossmont Warriors. A few weeks later in a game against the Kearny Mesa Komets, he amassed an even more impressive set of stats, racking up eight touchdowns, three extra points, twenty-seven carries, and a total of 544 yards, with two tackles, one recovered fumble, and one catch.

The coaches used to laugh about the fact that they often had to bench him during games in a sort of "mercy" move for the other team. It seems unlikely that an elementary-school-aged student could have material for a highlight reel, but that's exactly the sort of player Reggie was. The games attracted people from all over the area who wanted to see him in action, with many feeling his plays already had merited him a nickname: "The Cutback King." Among those fascinated fans was his estranged father.

Reggie Bush, Sr., was twenty when his son was born, and Denise was only nineteen. Bush Sr. has admitted openly to the press that he just "wasn't ready for a child" and thus chose to abandon Denise and Reggie Jr. They had met in the California Conservation Corps, a jobs-creation organization, in the mid-1980s. He had been a standout running back and basketball player at L.A.'s Hawthorne High from 1982 to 1983, but he dropped out of high school. The couple broke up shortly after Denise discovered she was pregnant, and she returned to San Diego to be close to her mother.

Accounts vary about Bush Sr.'s involvement in Reggie's early life. He claims that despite his fear of parenthood, he was as much a part of his

son's life as he was able to be, showing up at the hospital the day after his namesake was born, videotaping many of his son's early football moments, and spending weekends with the boy throughout his childhood. Bush Sr. maintains that his contact was heartfelt but limited, owing to his professional and, later, medical, circumstances. He worked both in construction and as a truck driver before he was seriously injured in a car accident in 1990 and required surgery on his back. He has been living on a small disability check ever since.

Reggie Jr. does not give as favorable a reflection on his biological father's presence in his life, though. His mother had to go to court in 1989 to get his father to pay child support; in fact, Reggie Jr. does not even refer to his biological father as "Dad." Instead, he reserves that title for his stepfather, LaMar Griffin, who married Denise when Reggie was two. The couple has a son together, Reggie's half-brother, Javon, who is six years his junior. This is the family unit that Reggie recognizes as his own, and in which he takes pride, despite the long financial struggle that colored Reggie's childhood. LaMar worked as a security guard at a local high school and as a minister at a church in San Diego; neither position paid much in relation to the high cost of living in Southern California. Denise spent as much time as she was able to at home with her sons, but also worked long hours first at the Humane Society and later as a correctional officer and deputy sheriff.

Despite Reggie's growing reputation as a power player, he was known as a quiet kid from a quiet family. The Griffin family was friendly and involved in Reggie's young football career, but they were not pushy parents demanding special treatment for their talented son. LaMar and Denise, while supportive, could not afford to invest all of their time and attention in Reggie's games; they were working-class people making a living and doing their best to make ends meet in the competitive, fast-paced world of Southern California. Parental support was important, but Reggie seemed determined to become a star no matter what.

It's no wonder that Reggie Bush likes to honor his hometown—there's something about San Diego that seems to produce and foster incredible tailbacks. Marcus Allen, the USC tailback who won the Heisman in 1981, is a native; so is Rashaan Salaam, who won the Heisman in 1994. The 1998 Heisman winner and 1999 fifth-overall draft pick, Ricky Wil-

liams, also hails from the city, while Denver Broncos tailback and all-time leading rusher Terrell Davis grew up in the same part of the town as Bush. Michael Pittman, running back for Tampa Bay, is one of San Diego's sons; Marshall Faulk was running circles around the opposing players at San Diego State all throughout Bush's childhood; first-round draft pick LaDainian Tomlinson, who, in 2007, would win the ESPY Award for Male Athlete of the Year, Best Record-Breaking Performance, and Best NFL Athlete, began training with talented young local sensation named Reggie Bush when Tomlinson joined the San Diego Chargers in 2001. While some of these players struggled in their off-field lives, their talent on the field was remarkable, and Bush had incredible athletic role models surrounding him in his formative years.

In 1999, Reggie started at Helix High, a charter school in the San Diego suburb of La Mesa. Kennedy Pola, a former USC running-back coach who now coaches that position for the Jacksonville Jaguars, considered the high-school Bush a better player than many NFL tailbacks. As a freshman, Bush was already racing the senior varsity athletes on the track and holding his own. He was already viewed as a player with the potential to become the best to ever come out of Helix, itself an impressive high-school athletic powerhouse.

According to Larry Pierce—a high-school friend of Reggie's—despite his natural ability, many people were shocked by how well Reggie's talent translated to the higher level of play at Helix. "I always thought he was a good athlete. I could see it," he said. "Some people just don't have it and they try to work on it. And some people just don't really have to work on it, they just have it. That's kind of like how he was. . . . He was a good Pop Warner football player. People knew he was fast, he was good. But it wasn't like, 'Oh yeah, wait until Reggie comes here.' It wasn't really like that. It was kind of like, 'Oh, here he is, that guy can play a little.' "

His football career continued to rise and continued to amaze as he matured as a varsity player for Helix. One teammate was quarterback Alex Smith, who would go on to play for the University of Utah, would be a Heisman finalist (along with Bush) in 2004, and was the overall number-one draft pick in 2005, selected by the San Francisco 49ers. The pair made a formidable combination on the field. They lost just one game during Smith's senior year in 2001, but went on to win the California

Division II championship. Smith recalled those days in a 2004 *New York Times* piece about his high-school teammate. "All I did was pretty much hand off to Reggie. . . . We'd be up by so many points that I wasn't in much after halftime. If I threw ten times in a game, that was a lot."

Reggie's senior year had a slightly more disappointing finish; he was out for four games with a fractured wrist, but still helped to advance his team to the Interscholastic Federation San Diego Division II finals. Regardless, scouts, coaches, and fans alike were amazed by his tenacity in running and tackling despite the cast on his arm.

Even with his injury, his high-school career produced an amazing list of game statistics. He scored 450 points, ran for a total of 4,995 yards, and averaged twelve yards per carry. At the end of his senior season in 2002, he was named to the *USA Today* All-USA first team and as a *Parade* All-American as well as their top running-back pick. But his success was not limited to the football field. Reggie also was an outstanding track star, placing third place in the state of California in the hundred-meter dash, and his finishing time of 10.42 also placed him as the fastest senior football player in the country that year. His time in the two-hundred-meter dash also made him the third-fastest in California.

His coaches were always amazed by his work ethic and dedication to improvement, even when he was far and away the top player. Donnie Van Hook, another Helix coach, told *USA Today* in 2005 about Bush's impressive determination to become stronger: "Reggie can bench four hundred pounds because his work ethic is awesome We had an early coaches meeting the day before practice started his senior year, and we heard the weights clanging in the weight room. It was 6:00 A.M., and Reggie was already in there. He'd snuck in through an open window that was ten feet above the ground."

Gordon Wood, one of Bush's high-school coaches, said that it was clear from the start that Bush was a different kind of player. "When Reggie was coming out of high school, everyone thought he'd be a guy who'd be up for the Heisman someday," he told the *New York Times* in 2004.

Pam Smith, Alex Smith's mother, echoed a similar sentiment in the same article. "If you'd taken one hundred people from Helix, myself included, and asked them who would be a Heisman candidate, one hundred people would have said Reggie. . . . He's been a star from the moment we

first watched him." Her husband, Doug, is the principal of Helix and has said many times to the press that the talent during the early 2000s at such a relatively small school (twenty-two hundred students in four grades) was remarkable and always incredible to watch as a proud parent, a proud principal, and just as a sports fan.

When college recruiters first watched his highlight tapes, many of them thought they were doctored. No one seemed able to believe that a high-school student could move so fast and with such agility as Reggie demonstrated on film. Those who did accept the validity of his tapes didn't need much convincing to recognize his potential as a college standout. Mack Brown, head coach for the Longhorns, spoke to the *Boston Globe* in 2006 about his first impressions of Bush's playing style, when he was thinking of bringing him down to the University of Texas: "When I worked for Coach [Barry] Switzer at Oklahoma and when we were watching film, he would say, 'There's a three-play guy and a five-play guy. If I watch a guy for five plays and I don't see whether he's good enough, turn it off.' Reggie is a one-play guy."

Offers came at him from all sides—Washington, Stanford, Notre Dame—but Reggie based his ultimate decision on two factors. First, he wanted to go somewhere with a strong premed program, which was his intended major at the time; and second, he wanted to be able to run track. Despite the number of major programs courting him, Reggie made his decision quickly—even before he'd finished all of his recruiting visits. He announced his plans on the sidelines of the All-American Bowl on January 5, 2003, as the first of many players to make their intentions known at the game that year. Chris Leak confirmed what was already suspected—that he was headed to Florida. Prescott Burgess revealed his plans to go to Michigan, and LenDale White—a star running back out of Colorado—insisted that he was not afraid of the competition posed by Reggie Bush and would be joining him in USC's backfield.

When Reggie graduated from Helix with a 4.0 GPA in 2003, he had impressive high-school statistics to back him up: 2,220 yards and thirty-four touchdowns during his senior season alone, and—as if his numbers as a running back weren't enough—he was a double threat, also playing as a punter, averaging forty yards per punt. His awards were numerous, and it looked as if it would only keep growing. He was tapped for the

All-State, All-California Interscholastic Federation, and All-American teams, just to name a few. The hometown hero was becoming a statewide superstar and was poised to become a national sensation.

As he joined the men in cardinal and gold in fall 2003, Reggie was about to help one of the most dynamic football teams in recent memory achieve one of its most exciting seasons ever. And despite his remarkable high-school career, his best was yet to come.

THREE

USC Dynasty

It is impossible to talk about the University of Southern California without a discussion of its long and distinguished history . . . in football. Established in 1888, just eight years after the university itself opened, the football program quickly rose to national prominence, even at a time when the sport was considered an Ivy League and East Coast specialty.

Of course, that's not to say that Trojan football didn't face challenges in its early years. The team, known first as the Methodists, played just one home game a year for its first few years and the school didn't even have a team in 1890 and 1892. Football also faced competition from other older, more established sports, as was evident when USC football was replaced by rugby between 1911 and 1913. The popularity of the gridiron and the intensity with which the football team played, though, soon cemented the team's place in USC athletics and on the national scene as a powerhouse.

They became the Trojans in 1912, and *Los Angeles Times* reporter Owen R. Bird reflected on the significance of this title, writing: "The term Trojan, as applied to USC, means to me that no matter what the situation,

what the odds, or what the condition, the completion must be carried on to the end, and those who strive must give all that they have." And strive they did, embodying the Trojan warrior spirit that would be incorporated ten years later into the lyrics of "Fight On!"—one of the most widely recognized collegiate fight songs in the country. "Fight on! for ol' SC/Our men fight on to victory," the song charges. "Our Alma Mater dear,/looks up to you!/Fight on and win for ol' SC/Fight on! to victory/Fight on!"

The Rose Bowl is almost synonymous with USC's postseason, and has been played for more than eighty years. Though the first Rose Bowl game was played in 1902, the event did not move to its historic stadium until 1923, when USC made its first Rose Bowl appearance—a matchup against Penn State that ended with a 14–3 victory for the Trojans. The Trojans went on to win their next eight bowl appearances, seven of which were in the Rose Bowl. In fact, USC did not lose its first Rose Bowl until January 1, 1946, when Alabama won 34–14.

As the traditional bowl for the Pac-10 champions to challenge the winners of the Big Ten, it is no surprise that USC has made thirty-one Rose Bowl appearances, winning twenty-two times. The most common Rose Bowl matchup has been USC versus Michigan, which has happened eight times as the two traditional powerhouses have battled it out, USC winning six times. Southern Cal has encountered Ohio State nearly as often, in seven bowl games, and a closer win-loss record of 4–3, still in the Trojans' favor.

The program could hardly have enjoyed the success it has over the past century, however, were it not for the legendary coaches that have made USC into a national powerhouse.

The most notable of the early coaches was "Gloomy" Gus Henderson, who headed the program from 1919 to 1924 before leaving for the University of Tulsa. Under his leadership, the relatively young USC program became a household name among college football fans, owing in large part to his incredible .865 career winning percentage, the highest of any USC football coach to date.

In 1960, USC hired a new head coach by the name of John McKay to try to reclaim the glory days of Henderson's program. McKay delivered. In the 1960s and 1970s, USC won five National Championships and produced three Heisman Trophy winners. The Trojans continued their

dominance into the early eighties, but the program was clearly declining as the decade wore on. Throughout the nineties, they enjoyed limited success, while the university sought to bring in a coaching staff and players who would return USC to her glory days.

USC's football program boasts an impressive social history, as well. It has enjoyed a long history of inclusion and diversity, going back to Brice Taylor, one of the first African-American players for USC. A descendant of the Native American hero Tecumseh and freed slaves, Taylor was a remarkable player not only for his aggressive playing style at offensive guard, but also for the fact that he was born without a left hand. He was selected to the All-America team in 1925—the first black Trojan to achieve this honor, and one of the earliest in the country.

The university attracted numerous athletes of color for many years while they were still forbidden to play in other regions of the country. The program garnered recruiting strength because of this policy, providing an opportunity for talented players who might otherwise have a limited choice of colleges—or no choice at all—to play serious football and gain a quality education.

USC also played an interesting role in changing the face of football at other college programs. In 1969, Alabama was still a segregated team. There were efforts to recruit African-American players, but they had yet to lead to an integrated varsity team. When the NCAA approved the addition of an eleventh regular-season game for the 1970 season, Alabama coach Paul "Bear" Bryant seized the opportunity to schedule a game against the Trojans, headed by his longtime friend McKay. The game was to be played in Birmingham, rather than Tuscaloosa, as usually happened once a season, and it was slated as the season opener for both teams.

What made USC an unusual choice for the Crimson Tide was that the Trojans had a record of 10–0–1 with a Rose Bowl defeat of Michigan in 1969, while Alabama had been on a steady decline from its wonder years in the early 1960s, with a disappointing 6-5 record for the 1969 season that ended with a loss to Colorado in the Liberty Bowl.

The 1969 Trojans also boasted a very intimidating feature: a group of defensive linemen known as "The Wild Bunch," and coached by Marv Goux, himself a Trojan gridiron legend. Composed of seven players—Al Cowlings, Jimmy Gunn, Gary McArthur, Bubba Scott, Tody Smith, Tony Terry, and Charlie Weaver—the men of the Wild Bunch were feared by

offensive lines throughout the country and have widely been considered the greatest defensive line ever to play for the university. A famous picture featuring six of the seven members of the bunch was dubbed the "gunslinger" photo and helped to heighten their reputation as a group of tough outlaws straight out of the western movies Southern California was churning out at that time.

Many fans wondered why Bryant would bring in such a dominant team considering Alabama's recent down years. There was another aspect of USC that made it an unusual choice to take on Alabama—it had the only all-black backfield in NCAA Division I football at the time.

The end result was a 42–21 victory for the Trojans, with all five touchdowns scored by African American players—two by a scrappy sophomore named Sam "Bam" Cunningham. Many sports historians now believe that the game was intentionally arranged to help grease the wheels of athletic integration for the Crimson Tide. Wilbur Jackson, the first African-American to be signed to the Tide, was a freshman in 1970, and according to NCAA rules at the time prohibiting freshman from playing, watched the game from the stands. The following year, he and a new recruit from the junior-college system named John Mitchell joined the Crimson Tide and helped to march the team back to the Bear's second Golden Age. The pieces were all in place for the change to occur, but Bryant was looking for a team to help ease the transition, and make it something that the fans wanted, rather than something that just happened as part of the march of progress.

Probably not coincidentally, Alabama won the next game of the series in Los Angeles in 1971—its first game played with an integrated team.

A special part of Southern California's storied history is its impressive collection of titles. USC has a remarkable record of National Championships, with eleven titles, making it second only to archrival Norte Dame in all-time championships. Even in the years that it hasn't been top-ranked, it's still had an impressive postseason record. Winning twenty-nine of forty-five bowl games, USC is second only to Alabama—and only by one victory—in all-time bowl game wins.

It can also boast of thirty-six Pac-10 titles since it joined the conference in 1922, more than double the number of any other team in its

conference. The Trojans have also enjoyed an incredible winning streak, suffering only three losing seasons since 1961, and can lay claim to the highest number of first-round draft picks; the highest number of top overall draft picks (5); most Pro Bowl players (200); and most Super Bowl players (92).

Much of USC's success can be credited to the legendary McKay, head coach from 1960 to 1975. Recognizing the need for speed and agility as well as superior judgment, dexterity, and an ability to block, McKay set out to develop some of the most formidable tailbacks on any gridiron. This rather demanding set of requirements meant that the number of highly successful all-around tailbacks was limited, but such demands did not stop McKay from producing players such as O. J. Simpson and Charles White, who redefined the position as the Trojans rolled through the 1960s. Mike Garrett, who won the Heisman in 1965, was the school's first winner of that prestigious award and one of the early breakout tailbacks in a program that would come to be known for them. When John Robinson inherited the program in 1976, after McKay's move to the pros, the legacy continued. In the twenty-two years of top-flight competition, spearheaded by the shrewd coaching styles of these two men, the school earned the nickname "Tailback U" for its unstoppable players who dominated that position. They helped to popularize the trend of players who were both big and fast, a dangerous combination. They brought a new focus to the running game, adding opportunities for track athletes to bring their skills to the forefront on the football field and adding a dynamic level of uncertainty to their plays.

The reputation for a strong backfield also created yet another legacy for a program full of them. Tailback U would dominate the position in college football throughout the sixties, seventies, and into the early eighties, upping the ante and redefining the way the game is played.

In a city where everyone wants to be a star, USC football is a legitimate starmaker. John Wayne suited up in cardinal before a body-surfing injury forced him off the field and onto the red carpet. The program is full of other notables, though, who have made and are continuing to make a lasting impression in professional football. There are currently more Trojans in the National Football League's Hall of Fame than athletes from

any other school—including Frank Gifford, O. J. Simpson, Ronnie Lott, Lynn Swann, Ron Yary, and Marcus Allen. The program has produced other professional standouts, as well, in players like Anthony Muñoz and Keyshawn Johnson, not to mention a current crop of forty-five players on professional rosters. USC also has seven Heisman Trophy winners among its alumni, tying it for the most wins with Ohio State and Notre Dame.

And the men of Troy are not active merely on the field. A number of former USC athletes have made a successful crossover into coaching, with three currently working as head coaches in the NFL. A USC cornerback in the early eighties, Jeff Fisher is now the head coach of the Tennessee Titans and has established his record as one of the winningest active NFL head coaches. Jack Del Rio currently heads the Jacksonville Jaguars and has helped to build the relatively young franchise into a serious and respected program. Mike Holmgren played quarterback for the Trojans in the late sixties and now is head coach of the Seattle Seahawks. Previously the head coach of the Green Bay Packers, he led them to two Super Bowl appearances and one Super Bowl victory during his tenure. When the Seahawks reached the Super Bowl in 2005, Holmgren became one of only five NFL coaches ever to bring two different teams to the NFL's ultimate game.

The USC football program has produced more than just great athletes, though. It has been a launching pad for countless professionals to begin successful careers in a variety of fields. In its earlier years, many Trojans left the football field for the red carpet. Ward Bond, a teammate of John Wayne, also launched a successful film career spanning three decades. Nate Barragar, a first-team All-American in 1929, played professional football before returning to Southern California as a producer and director. Aaron Rosenberg played for USC in the 1930s before hitting Hollywood, also as a director. His most notable film was the 1962 version of *Mutiny on the Bounty*, starring Marlon Brando; the first film credited as having been shot in the Ultra Panavision 70 Widescreen process. Irvine "Cotton" Warburton also played for USC in the 1930s and later went on to win an Academy Award for his work on editing the classic film *Mary Poppins.* Mike Henry, who played for the team in the midfifties, played Tarzan on the silver screen in three films. More recently, Patrick Muldoon became a soap opera star after joining the Trojans as a walk-on in the eighties.

Despite his current star status, Pete Carroll's initial reception at USC was less than friendly. He was not the first choice to replace fired coach Paul Hackett; he was not the second or third choice, either. It was not until Dennis Erickson of Oregon State, Mike Bellotti of Oregon, and Mike Riley of the San Diego Chargers all declined the position that the offer was extended to Carroll. The alumni were outraged when the new appointment was announced on December 15, 2000. Carroll had been fired as the New England Patriots' head coach in 1999, following their lackluster performance late in the season and their overall 33-31 record under his command. He hadn't coached a college program for more than twenty years. What could a man like Pete Carroll do for the illustrious Trojan football dynasty?

The answer seemed, at first, to be "very little." USC's 2001 season ended with a 6–6 record, capped by a loss to Utah in the Las Vegas Bowl. With four years remaining on his contract, it looked unlikely that Carroll was going to outlast the calls for his resignation and the whispers that the days of USC football dominance were really gone for good.

Los Angeles is a city famous for its zero-to-hero stories, and Carroll quickly provided another of those stories. Tapping the legacy of Tailback U, he developed an offense that not only dominated the Pac-10, capturing the conference title in 2002, but also earned them a 38–17 Orange Bowl victory over Iowa and a number-four overall finish in both the Coaches and AP national polls.

The following season promised to be an exciting year for the recovering program, as well, but very few could have anticipated just how quickly USC would assert its dominance. It had been thought that 2003 would be a building year for USC; it was facing a tough schedule with a roster that contained thirty-one true and red-shirt freshmen and was facing the loss of its Heisman Trophy–winning quarterback Carson Palmer to the NFL, while replacing him with a sophomore named Matt Leinart who had never started for USC before. The season opener—a road game against sixth-ranked Auburn—was highly anticipated. The Trojans were placed at eighth on both the AP and ESPN polls, so the matchup was sure to be a good one, but Auburn was definitely the favorite. That game proved to be a turning point for the men in cardinal and gold.

The Tigers never managed to push beyond the Trojan's thirty-three-

yard line and sacked quarterback Jason Campbell six times. The end result was a 23–0 victory over the Tigers and a renewed sense of victory as they moved to number four in the AP polls the following week. The charge was on, and the Trojans seemed virtually unstoppable. The only blemish on their record that season came from a heartbreaking 34–31 overtime loss to rival Cal. The other games, though, seemed marked by notable wins, including a 45–0 blowout at Arizona. Perhaps the two sweetest victories for 2003 came against the Trojans' biggest rivals: a 45–15 win at Notre Dame and a 47–22 home victory over UCLA. The men of Troy found themselves in the middle of a golden season. Following a 28–14 Rose Bowl win over number-four-ranked Michigan, USC was ranked second by the *USA Today* poll and first by the AP. The young team had a national championship in hand. It was the start of something big.

Carroll was well on his way to rebuilding Tailback U and returning USC to its former glory—and possibly even launching it to new heights of notoriety. His recruiting was focused and aggressive, bringing in some of the most sought-after young talent in the nation. Carroll recognized the potential of his team and his coaching staff, and the rest of the country soon caught on, too.

During the 2003 season, USC managed an end-of-season net yards gain of 2,027, while allowing its opponents only 782 the entire season. And it showed no signs of slowing down. On October 7, 2004, the *New York Times* ran a headline proclaiming, "Tailback U Is Making a Comeback." Sophomore Reggie Bush told reporters, "We're trying to put the tailback back in Tailback U." The effort seemed to pay off. By the end of that season, the Trojans had amassed 2,306 rushing yards, more than double what their opponents had against them. The points reflected this disparity: USC completed the season with 496 points scored (an average of 38.2 per game), while allowing their opponents only 169 points (an average of 13.0 per game). Their success continued in 2005, when USC chalked up 3,380 rushing yards, while its opponents only managed 1,697.

There seemed to be no question that the reputation and the nickname of the team's legendary backfield were restored. Tailback U was back in session once more and showed no signs of letting up.

Despite his slow start and rocky reception, in the years that followed

Carroll's hiring, he led the Trojans to remarkable statistics. Winning a record five consecutive Pac-10 championships, they gained back-to-back national championships in the 2003 and 2004 seasons and played in the championship game against Texas in the 2005 season. The Trojans also ended the season ranked in the AP top four in 2002 and 2006. In that same five-year span, they always finished with at least eleven wins each season—one of only four schools ever to do so—and made a BCS bowl appearance every season. In 2003 alone, Carroll won seven national Coach of the Year Awards, including the American Football Coaches Association Division I-A Coach of the Year, the All-American Football Foundation Frank Leahy Co-Coach of the Year, and the Pac-10 Coach of the Year, which he would go on to win in 2004, 2005, and 2006, as well.

The players themselves also stood out—during the first five years of Carroll's tenure, twenty-four USC players were named All-Americans and twenty-five entered the NFL Draft. Perhaps most remarkable, though, were the three Heisman Trophy winners that the program produced: Carson Palmer in 2002, Matt Leinart in 2004, and Reggie Bush in 2005. At the beginning of the 2007 season, USC's all-time record was 743-300-54, which comes out to an impressive 70.2 percent winning record—making it one of the all-time winningest college football programs in the nation. There is no question that the Trojans of Southern California have not only matched their former glory days, but are threatening to eclipse them with a new era of team brilliance, fan enthusiasm, and gridiron dominance.

By the start of the 2007 season, it seemed as if USC was on top of the world. It started out at number one in all of the major preseason polls and looked poised for another dominant season. But by midseason, USC had slipped out of the top ten as it suffered losses at the hands of both unranked Stanford and fifth-ranked Oregon. Several major sports publications, including *Sports Illustrated*, began to question whether USC's dream decade was beginning to come to an end.

Even so, the legacy of the program is undeniable. Unfortunately, so are some of the allegations.

FOUR

Lloyd Lake

Lloyd Lake was influenced by fast, easy money at a young age.

Like the time a well-dressed gentleman, an investor by profession, visited Lake's family home in San Diego and asked thirteen-year-old Lloyd to put his garment bag in the closet. "And, by the way," the gentleman said, "there's $50,000 in the garment bag so don't screw with it." Lloyd did what he was told, but not before unzipping the bag to see what $50,000 looked, felt, and smelled liked.

"I am like, 'Damn, this is a lot of money,' " Lake remembered. "I zipped it back up, but seeing all that money was a powerful feeling."

When Lloyd returned the garment bag—yes, every penny was in place—the visitor thanked him with a million-dollar smile and $200 in twenty-dollar bills. He also told Lloyd to go buy himself hamburgers and french fries at the local In-N-Out Burger, and not to worry about the change. That may well have been chump change, since there were other nights when Lloyd returned home to find adults in high-stakes card games such as Tonk with as much as $100,000 in cash on the dining-room table. Lloyd watched and learned, and the grip of fast money was

much like a cowboy's lasso that tightened around his waist and pulled him toward trouble.

Lake didn't resist.

Although he was considered an exceptional young athlete, it wasn't long before gambling was Lake's favorite sport. Lake and his friends rolled dice, bet on PlayStation football games, and dealt cards. This escalated further during his teenage years, highlighted by weekend trips to Las Vegas, where Lloyd pulled on slot machine levers until security ran the underage gambler off.

One scheduled weekend trip to Las Vegas lasted nearly two weeks, giving new meaning to losing track of time. Lake missed both his school classes and his team's basketball games and landed in school suspension. And there was another journey to Las Vegas when Lloyd, who had just turned twenty years old but had his older brother's ID stuffed in his pocket—the legal age for casino wagering is twenty-one—won $25,000 playing blackjack. Lloyd, a good sport, gave most of the winnings to his mother. She was a few blackjack tables away—and $21,000 in the hole.

"It's hard to explain. When you are young and you get influenced by a lot of people and a lot of money, you kind of take wrong paths in life and don't even realize it," Lake said. "That's when the seeds were planted. I was into women, gambling, and I made bad decisions. But I can't blame anyone because everyone is responsible for their own actions."

Many young athletes dream of playing sports at the collegiate and professional levels one day. Lake wasn't any different—at least early on. He figured he would follow his father's footsteps and play basketball at San Diego State. Lake's hopes were not far-fetched.

Lake was a standout player in basketball, baseball, and football youth leagues in San Diego before deciding to concentrate solely on basketball at age thirteen. Lake attended the Cliff Livingston Camp in Santa Barbara and the Bobby Cremins Camp at Georgia Tech in Atlanta. Lake also played with a local travel team that journeyed to tournaments in California, Arizona, and Nevada. In these tourneys, Lake often squared off against other budding prep stars such as Jason Kidd, who attended St. Joseph Notre Dame High School in Alameda, California, and is now the starting point guard and captain for the NBA's New Jersey Nets.

Lake attended Helix High School in La Mesa, where he grew into a

six-foot-three bruising forward who could shoot and crash the boards. Lake, a varsity starter as a sophomore, often registered double digits in rebounding and scoring. He eclipsed the thirty-point mark against rival Mount Miguel. While recruiting letters for Lake arrived at his home, they remained unopened or landed in the trash, exactly where Lloyd was headed.

It was a destiny that Lloyd Lake could not, or did not, stop.

"It all started just with gambling and before you know it, you don't even see it happening," Lloyd said. "I guess you could say it's kind of like a person who does drugs. Let's say a coke addict. At first they don't realize what this is doing to them until way down the line, [and] then they can see it. It might be something that made them hit rock bottom where they finally realize what this shit has done. But you don't see it at the time."

Lloyd's mother and father are both business people. His mother, Barbara Gunner, sixty-four, runs a privatized social services center and his father, Louis Lake, sixty-eight, is marketing a sports balm that he said will soon be available nationally and has been used by players from the Miami Dolphins. Both also share a keen interest in real estate. Barbara at one time owned more than ten properties, including a beach house that she still has in Rosarito, Mexico. One of her San Diego homes is nestled majestically on a hill and overlooks the city and the Pacific Ocean. On a clear night, one can see the Mexican landscape from her front porch. While Lloyd's parents are divorced, they remain on friendly terms, support each other's business ventures, and are extremely close to their children.

Lloyd is the third of four siblings. The oldest is Lisa (forty-one), a graduate of Spelman College in Atlanta and a strikingly beautiful morning news anchor for San Diego television station KGTV-Channel 10. Louis Jr. (thirty-eight) is employed by his mother at her Crossroads rehabilitation center in San Diego, while Leslie (thirty-two), a graduate of Grambling, was an elementary-school teacher in Houston, Texas, before she returned to San Diego to work with her mother at Crossroads in 2005.

At thirty-three years old, Lloyd Lake says he is finally determined to

realize his mother's expectations. But that means Lloyd must stay on the right side of the law, which has been a struggle since his teenage years.

Lloyd: Who said something about me in New York?

LaMar: There's rumors going on around you. "Man, Little Lake, he ain't . . ." See, I don't want to talk it.

Lloyd: Talk it, I'd rather you do.

LaMar: See I don't want to believe little stuff.

Lloyd: What did they say though?

LaMar: That you ain't shit. You're a hustler, you ain't shit. You're after yourself and yourself only.

For all the privilege and opportunity he was given through his parents, the high road was not something Lloyd was going to take. If there was a fork in the road, Lloyd took the wrong path. He developed a gambling habit at an early age. Several things came of it—quick money, questionable relationships, and, at times, significant debts. Despite his athletic talents and opportunities, Lake suddenly found himself in a life of crime.

"I *really* didn't get sidetracked until after high school," said Lloyd, who graduated from Helix High in 1992 with a grade-point average of 1.87 and then took six general and business courses at Grossmont Community College in El Cajon, California, from 1993 to 1994. Lake has one child, fourteen-year-old Jalen. "The power of those streets and the money, you really don't even realize it," Lake added. "You are like, 'I will do this and then go back and play basketball in six months.' But you never go back."

If Lloyd looked over his shoulder during this time, it was because the police weren't far behind. Lake can be a contradiction. He's an imposing figure, at six-foot-three and 250 pounds, and he lifts weights regularly. He braids his hair in cornrows, has a tattoo of a panther on his right forearm, and wears baggy, hip-hop, urban-style clothing. Lake also has a bright smile, an engaging personality, and a quick hug for friends. It might be twisted and bizarre, but Lloyd often talks of loyalty, character,

and integrity—this from a guy who has been arrested seven times, has spent several years of his life behind bars, and is categorized as a career offender in a United States District Court Southern District of California Presentence Report that he gave to the authors of this book.

The twenty-four-page report, submitted by David J. Mudd, Senior U.S. Probation Officer, offers a chilling look at Lake's life of crime, which started at age eighteen, and details related activities of individuals associated and arrested with Lloyd. It states Lake has a history of domestic violence offenses, narcotic distribution, and weapon possession. The report says that after Lake joined the Emerald Hills Blood Gang in the mid-1980s while still in school, he began to flourish in the drug-trafficking trade. Lake was identified as having the ability to purchase or finance $150,000 to $200,000 in drug transactions, specifically marijuana.

The report also revealed that Lake was known to carry handguns and at one time had an Uzi submachine gun in his residence. Jail medical records indicate that Lloyd also reported a history of marijuana addiction, though he swears he's now clean. Lake's drug-related activities involved people in California, Michigan, Minnesota, and Georgia. Lake said he often cleared $200,000 a month and made more than a million annually at least once.

"I'd like to think I was pretty good at what I did," said Lake, who is nicknamed "Tata" because his family says it was the first word Lloyd uttered as a toddler.

Lloyd was raised by his mother and grandmother after his parents' divorce. Lloyd says his mother worked full-time and his maternal grandmother played a significant role in his upbringing. Barbara Gunner stresses that, despite his later actions, Lloyd had "good training and had been taught the right way." In fact, Barbara often wonders if her actions and beliefs influenced her youngest son. Gunner says prostitution and marijuana should be legalized because law enforcement officials simply don't have the power to stop either activity. As an owner and operator of a drug rehabilitation center in San Diego, Barbara has witnessed the destructive behavior, specifically of women, brought on by illegal narcotics.

"Prostitution is the oldest profession," Barbara said. "It has been around since the biblical days. I wouldn't do it, and I wouldn't recommend any-

body to do it, but they are not going to stop it. The marijuana they are not going to stop. It's just like alcohol in the Al Capone days. They saw that they could not stop it, so they legalized it. I'm saying that to say that Lloyd had told me, 'Ma, I've never sold any kind of drugs but marijuana. I swear to you.' He was in court once, and the prosecutor was saying, 'No, Lloyd's thing is not hard drugs, he's the marijuana man.' So I'm thinking, 'Oh, my God, did I send him this message early in life that it was okay?' But it's not legal. I think when they legalized it here for medical purposes, Lloyd just thought, it's okay, it's cool. But if it's not legal, it's not cool."

Lloyd's Presentence report, which was filed with the clerk of the court on November 10, 2004, with the United States Probation Southern District of California, shows Lloyd made many decisions that were "not cool."

The report stated the information was obtained from a review of the investigative material and discussions with the assistant U.S. attorneys and case agents following a one-count indictment that was filed on June 26, 2002, in the Southern District of California, charging Lloyd Lake, friend Brandon Sanders, and nine other defendants with conspiracy to distribute more than one hundred kilograms of marijuana and more than five hundred grams of cocaine. Additionally, defense counsel was contacted to discuss the facts of the offense. On January 6, 2004, the indictment was dismissed without prejudice. However, a one-count indictment had been subsequently filed in the Southern District of California on December 23, 2003, charging Lake and one of the others with conspiracy to possess and distribute more than one hundred kilograms of marijuana. Lake stayed in jail for two years without bail.

Here is the word-for-word content of that Presentence report and a look into Lloyd's world at one time:

> The investigation centered on the controlled substance distribution activities of the Emerald Hills Bloods criminal street gang, which operates in San Diego, California. The gang was formed in the early 1980s and has been involved with an array of criminal activities including: narcotics, trafficking and sales; money laundering; weapons violations; prostitution; robbery; shootings; assaults; counterfeit currency; and vehicle theft.

Timothy Patrick was identified as one of the most influential members of the Emerald Hills gang and he acted as a "trendsetter" for the gang's criminal activities. His role in drug sales and trafficking expanded and in the late 1980s, Patrick became successful in dealing crack cocaine in San Diego. He also began conducting "rip-offs." Specifically, he would steal the drugs or use counterfeit money to pay the suppliers for the drugs. Reportedly, regarding one such rip-off, Mexican drug dealers took retaliatory action against Patrick. These drug dealers "shot-up" Patrick's Lexus automobile while it was being driven by another Emerald Hills Blood gang member (the driver sustained no injuries). Additionally, Patrick began to entertain the idea of robbing another Mexican drug supplier by using a gun. (The investigation provided no information to suggest that Patrick actually engaged in violence during the instant conspiracy to further his drug activities or caused injury to another.)

Further investigation into the Emerald Hills Blood gang revealed that in the mid-1980s, Patrick recruited Lloyd Lake to join the gang. After Lake joined the gang, he too began to flourish in the drug trafficking trade. He was identified as having the ability to purchase or finance $150,000 to $200,000 drug transactions. The investigation also revealed that Lake was known to carry handguns, and at one time had an Uzi submachine gun inside his residence.

Patrick and Lake developed a close relationship and often worked together on drug-trafficking activities, but worked separately as well. Together, in the late 1990s, they became involved in interstate trafficking of marijuana and cocaine. Their drug-related activities involved people in California; Detroit; Michigan; Minnesota; and Georgia. In furtherance of their illicit activities, Patrick and Lake used other individuals to transport drugs for them, both intrastate and interstate.

The investigation revealed that Patrick and Lake used Carlos Rodriguez as their main narcotics source of supply. Rodriguez would often supply them with loads of 100 to 300 pounds of marijuana. Additionally, when Patrick would set up drug transactions between Rodriguez and others, he would receive a profit of $100 for every pound of marijuana successfully delivered to Detroit. . . .

As previously mentioned Patrick and Lake have been identified as

two leaders of this drug conspiracy, who have recruited and used others to transport drugs. Rodriguez is the organization's main source of drug supply from Mexico. He provided large quantities of both marijuana and cocaine. . . .

In July of 2001, agents assigned to a multi-agency drug task force based in Tucson, Arizona, received information from an employee of a local steel business (Bonita Steel) that the two men ordered metal boxes and had provided a sample box which was "kilo size." The men indicated they did not care how much it cost to make the duplicate boxes. The individuals were later identified as Lake and Sanders. An employee of Bonita Steel noticed that the box that Lake and Sanders wanted duplicated was unusual in its construction. Also, the sample box smelled like marijuana and contained marijuana debris. Consequently, the employee suspected that Lake and Sanders were involved in illegal activities and contacted law enforcement officers.

On July 26, 2001, officers responded to the business and conducted surveillance at the location. The surveillance officers observed Sanders and Lake pick up the original box and two duplicate boxes and loaded them into a 1999 GMC Suburban, bearing Arizona license plates, and drive to Sanders' residence. While driving from the business to the residence, surveillance agents observed Sanders and Lake using countersurveillance driving techniques. At one point during the surveillance, Lake got out of the Suburban and "challenged" one of the surveillance officers, asking him about his identity. Due to the countersurveillance driving techniques used by Sanders and Lake, agents temporarily lost sight of the Suburban. However, after a short while, the vehicle was located at Sanders' residence located on Silverstand Drive in Marana, Arizona.

Agents contacted Sanders and Lake outside the residence. While speaking with Sanders and Lake, officers smelled the odor of marijuana emanating from the vents of the residence. After Lake and Sanders refused consent to search the residence, agents asked Lake and Sanders to stand by while they attempted to obtain a telephonic search warrant. While waiting for the warrant to arrive, Lake stated that he had to go to the store and left the scene. Lake returned to the residence a short time before the warrant was executed.

Numerous items were seized during the execution of the search warrant, including eight bales of marijuana weighing approximately 100 pounds (charging documents reflect 39 kilograms), the metal box molds, a 25-ton hydraulic log splitter (used to compress marijuana for shipment), two scales, numerous articles of packaging material, a table saw with marijuana residue, two Glock semiautomatic pistols, $1,090 in U.S. currency, and cellular telephones in the names of Sanders and Lake. The firearms were found in the master bedroom of the residence.

Wiretap surveillance revealed several telephone calls between Lake, Sanders and Ruben Gay prior to this seizure. Investigating agents concluded that the telephonic communication between the parties was to facilitate the delivery of the marijuana in question. Agents noted that Lake and Sanders have a well-documented drug trafficking relationship. Investigative material also outlines a Wells Fargo Bank wire transfer request which reflects that Sanders wire transferred $10,000 to Lake at First National Bank in San Diego on August 21, 2001. The wire transfer request was seized during the search of Sanders' residence. Agents believe that the money was derived from the sale of narcotics.

All of the defendants were arrested by federal agents on June 14, 2002, except for Rodriguez who remains a fugitive and Henderson was arrested by officers of the San Diego Police Department on March 7, 2002. Lake was arrested at his residence located on Windridge Drive in El Cajon, California. Arresting agents found a small amount of "personal use" marijuana, several firearm boxes including a Tech 9 semiautomatic machine pistol, M11 semiautomatic pistol, Colt 45 semiautomatic pistol and a Walther P38 pistol. Also found at the residence was a bulletproof vest, numerous rounds of ammunition, gun holsters and spent shell casings.

During subsequent questioning by FBI, Lake was advised that he was being charged with conspiracy to distribute marijuana and cocaine. Lake wanted to know who else was arrested along with him. Lake was advised of several other individuals, including fellow Emerald Hills Blood gang members, who were also arrested that morning. He was also advised that individuals in others states were arrested, including Arnold Gay in Detroit. Lake insisted several

times that he did not deal cocaine. Agents then asked him about dealing marijuana. Lake stated that he messed around with marijuana but hasn't lately. Lake said the "weed" is a different story.

The AUSA indicated that Lake and Sanders are only being held accountable for the amount of marijuana (39 kilograms) which was seized from Sanders' residence in Marana, Arizona. The prosecutor noted that there were indicators that Lake may have been involved in other narcotic distribution activity during the government's ongoing investigation; however, that conduct is not readily provable by the U.S. Attorney's Office. The AUSA added that Lake may have been a member of the Emerald Hills Blood gang at one time, but there is no proof that he was an active gang member during the course of the investigation herein. The prosecutor noted that he does not believe Lake should be categorized as a career offender under USSG 4B1.1(bo). He explained that the charging documents in case No ECR-7315 in which the defendant pled to 236-237-PC, False Imprisonment, do not specifically indicate that the offense involved "the use of force" which is predicate of a "crime of violence."

The case agent commented that Lake is undoubtedly a documented and high-ranking member of the Emerald Hills Blood street gang. The agent reported that the FBI has several photographs of Lake "throwing up" Emerald Hills Blood gang signs and dressed in Emerald Hills gang attire. He noted that the FBI as well as local law enforcement officers are very familiar with Lake and his ties to the Emerald Hills Blood gang. The agent noted that Lake and Timothy Patrick are leaders within the gang and have been heavily involved in narcotic distribution, money laundering and weapons. The case agent also noted that Lake has been involved in "drug rips" in which Lake and other members of the Emerald Hills Blood gang arranged to purchase or sell narcotics and proceeded to steal drugs or money from the other party.

The agent commented that Lake is very familiar with law enforcement and their investigations. As such, Lake typically has lower members of the organization committing criminal acts at his direction to avoid culpability. The case agent added that Lake has a history of avoiding detection and prosecution and has not yet been

> subject to significant custodial sanctions for past criminal behavior. The agent noted that Lake's claim to operate Breakbread Records, Inc. is a cover for his illegal narcotic distribution activities. The case agent noted that there is no evidence the company ever earned any income and no taxes were ever paid.
>
> The agent noted that (Brandon) Sanders was also a member of the Emerald Hills Blood gang as he grew up in San Diego. He views Sanders as "Lake's boy" who would follow instructions from Lake. The agent mentioned that on September 22, 2001, Sanders was stopped by the West Tennessee Violent Crime and Drug Task Force while driving a rental car near Memphis, Tennessee. Officers located $58,940 inside the trunk of the vehicle, which the agent is confident was narcotic proceeds.

In Lloyd's statement of the offense, the report read, "The defendant was interviewed on October 27, 2004, at the U.S. Probation Office in San Diego, California. He was interviewed in the English language and in the presence of defense counsel. Lake followed the advice of defense counsel and limited his statements to the information outlined in the 'factual basis' of the plea agreement. As such, Lake admitted that on or about July 25, 2001, in the Southern District of California and elsewhere, he knowingly used a telephone to help bring about a conspiracy to distribute approximately 39 kilograms of marijuana. The defendant explained that he became involved in the instant offense at the request of Sanders. Lake explained that he and Sanders are like brothers and he typically provides Sanders with assistance when requested. Lake stated that he planned to assist Sanders in packaging marijuana which would be picked up by another unknown individual for distribution. Lake stated that he was not paid for assisting Sanders, and that he (Lake) was not otherwise involved to this offense. Lake stated that he was very sorry for becoming involved in the offense and vowed not to become involved in criminal activity in the future."

According to the Presentence report, Lloyd's first brush with police occurred as an eighteen-year-old in 1992 when he was arrested for excessive

noise audible over fifty feet and fined fifty dollars. Six months later, on November 13, 1992, Lloyd was arrested and spent his first days in jail for driving with a revoked license, operating an unsafe vehicle, and failure to appear in court. Lloyd was convicted on January 14, 1993, and spent five days in jail.

Lloyd's troubles mounted during the following two years, when he was arrested twice for domestic violence against his then-girlfriend Shaunieele Street, who is also the mother of his son, Jalen. The first incident occurred on March 17, 1993, when Street told detectives that Lake struck her with a closed fist, then brandished a semiautomatic pistol and pointed it at her head. Lake told the San Diego County probation officer that he did not point the gun at Street nor did he hit her with a closed fist. However, Lake admitted that he hit Street four or five times with the back of his hand. Lloyd spent 267 days in jail on four counts—kidnapping, false imprisonment, terrorist threats, and battery of former spouse/cohabitant.

On February 13, 1994, the San Diego County probation report indicates that Street reported to sheriff's deputies that Lake had kidnapped, hit, and threatened her the previous night. Street explained that she was at Lake's residence, and she asked if he would take her home. Lake refused, locked all the doors, and would not let her leave the residence. After several hours, she attempted to call her grandmother. When the defendant discovered Street had attempted to call her grandmother, Lake took Street and their child against their will and drove around for approximately one hour. She tried to leave the car, but Lake struck her and pulled her hair every time she tried to do so. Lloyd spent 180 days in jail.

Lake was first arrested for possession of marijuana at the age of twenty-two on June 24, 1996. Investigative materials indicate that San Diego sheriff's deputies observed two individuals (one later identified as Lake) fighting in front of a residence in Spring Valley, California. After a trained narcotic dog began sniffing a vehicle parked nearby, officers searched the vehicle and found fifteen pounds of marijuana. A postarrest search of Lake resulted in the seizure of $8,500. Lake told deputies that he and his associate were fighting over the $8,500. Lloyd spent 365 days in jail.

Lloyd stayed clear of police for five years until he was arrested on July 26, 2001, for unlawful possession of marijuana for sale and possession of

drug paraphernalia in Arizona with Sanders. Lloyd was again arrested, for possession of marijuana and fighting in public, on November, 27, 2001. The investigative file alleges that Lake was driving a rental car and was accompanied by an Emerald Hills Blood gang member. While Lake was looking for the registration documents, the officers noticed a small quantity of marijuana in the glove-compartment area of the vehicle. A record check revealed that Lake was operating the vehicle without a driver's license. A search of the vehicle revealed a bag containing $20,000 in cash. A search of Lake revealed that he was in possession of $2,479 in his wallet.

In January 2006 Lake was sent to prison in Victorville, California, for a year for violating probation in an incident of domestic violence with his live-in girlfriend in November 2005.

Lloyd's father, Louis Lake, has led an interesting, eccentric, life. Lake has lived in San Diego since 1960, when he arrived from Washington to play basketball at San Diego State. "I could shoot and take it to the basket," said Louis, wirily built at six-foot-three. "That was my game; that was Lloyd's game." After two years at San Diego State and nearly four years in the Marine Corps, where he also played basketball and was a squad leader who "was fighting everybody," Lake took a state job in San Diego that focused on counseling.

Lake and Barbara married in 1968, and it was during this time that Lake rekindled his lifelong interest in boxing. Lake said he helped former light heavyweight world boxing champion Archie Moore, who made San Diego his adopted home and counseled youth following his boxing career. Lake said he remained in boxing as a promoter—he said he helped promote the Ken Norton–Muhammad Ali fight in 1973—and said he also worked with promoter Bob Arum. The versatile Lake said he also helped start an affirmative action group at the University of California, San Diego, and built a real-estate portfolio that made him one of the largest black landowners in San Diego in the late 1970s and early 1980s. "I would buy land and hold on to it," said Lake, whose first purchase was a four-unit apartment complex.

Louis Lake's latest venture, however, is the one that connected Reggie Bush with his family, specifically to Lloyd. Louis has been involved in

distributing Zen Sports Balm for more than seven years. The balm is distributed as a topical pain reliever and a safe and effective over-the-counter topical analgesic. Made in Malaysia, the balm is advertised as "a herbal combination of essential botanical extracts and natural ingredients that helps reduce swelling and speed recovery."

"Zen will take you away from the doctor," Louis Lake said.

Twelve testimonials on the insert that's packaged with each eight-ounce bottle include Rashaan Salaam, 1994 Heisman Trophy winner and NFC Rookie of the Year; Angelika Castaneda, gold medalist, ESPN Extreme Games, Adventure Racing; and Ken Norton, former world heavyweight boxing champion and member of the Boxing Hall of Fame.

Louis Lake said he first used the balm on his hip, which he injured when his Rottweiler dogs knocked him to the ground. He also applied it to his left foot, which he said was badly burned by boiling water in 2006. "Nobody believes it but here's what happened," the elder Lake said. "After I put Zen on my foot, five minutes later I had no pain. I was walking around in my wingtip shoes, with only a piece of gauze and Zen." While Lake said Zen's distribution has been mainly free and local in San Diego over the years, a pending deal with Wal-Mart could spread the balm nationally. Lake said Wal-Mart will purchase the balm for $7.75 and sell it for $9.97. The product is packaged in a small, colorful box that features a white lotus flower, which grows in muddy water and rises above the surface to bloom with remarkable beauty.

Louis Lake also thought the family's relationship with Reggie Bush would bloom into something special. Louis Lake's introduction in 2000 to Bush's stepfather, LaMar Griffin, didn't occur by chance. "It was my intention of meeting him because of Reggie," Lake said. The two met during one of Bush's varsity football games at Helix High School, and Lake provided Griffin with Zen Sports Balm to give to Reggie. Lloyd was quickly recruited by his father to deliver Bush the sports balm. But Lloyd ended up giving Bush more than sports balm over the years, starting with small cash payments for clothes and food while Bush was still in high school.

Louis Lake is proud of all his children, but he's quick to admit that it's Lloyd who most takes after him. "I know Lloyd and I are just alike," Louis said.

The elder Lake is also well aware of his son's struggles with the law but says, "Lloyd has to think for himself, do things for himself." Lake said his advice to his son was in the form of a question. "I asked him what kind of bird doesn't fly," Lake said.

The answer: "A jailbird."

In November 2007 Lloyd said he was helping his mother, Barbara, in her real-estate ventures, concentrating on land development in San Diego. Lloyd lives in a four-bedroom home owned by his mother in El Cajon and drives a 750 BMW. In his presentence report in 2004, Lloyd reported no assets or liabilities and was being financially supported by his mother. Barbara Gunner also has made child-support payment's on Lloyd's behalf. Lloyd also admitted to police in 2004—that at that time—he had not held a job in which he has paid taxes.

Before his dealings with Bush, Lloyd worked in the rap music recording industry for approximately ten years. He said he operated a recording company known as Breakbread Records, Inc., in San Diego, California. Barbara and daughter Lisa purchased nearly $30,000 worth of equipment for Lloyd. Lake said the company was barely breaking even financially but nearly had a "big break" by signing an artist known as "Relatiz" just before Lloyd was arrested for possession of marijuana in 2001. Due to Lloyd's arrest, "Relatiz" signed with another company. Lake then reportedly obtained employment at Loan Shoppers Mortgage Company in San Diego following his bond release on October 6, 2004. Lake said he was a real-estate agent's assistant and was paid on a commission basis. Lake indicated he had assisted on two real-estate sales but had not been paid for his services.

Lisa Lake said she has always looked out financially for her youngest brother.

"I gave the money to him because I've always tried to help him," Lisa said. "Lloyd was a phenomenal athlete. I had him down at Bobby Cremins's basketball camp when he was in the ninth grade for their summer-league camp. They were calling every year to try to get him to come down. And all these, 'You can do this, you can do this.' What does he want to do? He wants to follow that street life, he wants to be a

gangster. So then he wanted to get in the record business. I lent him a lot of money for that.

"Then this [New Era] came along when he got out [of jail]. I was amazed like, 'How do you do this? How do you get out and get connected with all these people.' He was like, 'No, this is it. This is going to be the thing where I can finally help Mom and help you. You have always helped me.' He was just so into it. So here we go again. I encouraged him because it was something he really seemed passionate about again, just like the music, and he really wanted to do. I wanted to see him do something that was legal, and on the straight and narrow, and I supported him."

Lloyd, ever the opportunist, recognized that Reggie Bush, a young stud running back, might be headed to greatness. Bush became somebody Lloyd wanted to spend time with, delivering him sports cream, giving him money, keeping in contact.

As Reggie blew up, Lloyd saw his opportunity to be part of the explosion.

LaMar: I understand all that. JC [J. C. Pearson] said himself, "Now the idea of the agency is great, 100 percent great." The only thing he didn't like about it was [sports agent] Dave [Caravantes].

Lloyd: That's why we got Bus [Cook].

LaMar: . . . but as far as the press on you, he said, "Lake's a hustler." That's the first thing he thought about you. So now I'm hearing all these people. What JC saying is just rumors.

Lloyd: What did JC say about me honestly?

LaMar: He thought you were a hustler and all you thought about was yourself. I said, "No, JC, he done come with the business." He said, "Oh, I thought Mike [Michaels] did." He said, "Now, I can look at it a different way." Because I said, "Lake is the one who thought up the business." He say now he's going to Mike [Ornstein]. He says, "Okay, now it's different. But when you first look at Lake, you think he's a hustler."

Lloyd: I am a hustler.

LaMar: No, I'm talking about a different hustler.

Lloyd: Oh, on the street?

LaMar: Yeah.

Lloyd: Oh, no.

LaMar: See, that's the person that they get.

Lloyd: I'll have to cut my hair, man.

LaMar: No, don't cut your hair.

Lloyd: My mom is like, "Cut that damn hair off."

FIVE

The Indians:

Michael Michaels

Michael Michaels couldn't get over the total contradiction of it all.

On a wall in the living room of his ranch-style home next to a golf course in El Cajon, California, Michaels had a signed copy of the *Sports Illustrated* commemorative issue cover from after USC's victory in the National Championship game on January 4, 2005, against Oklahoma in the Orange Bowl, capping an undefeated season.

The lone person pictured on the cover was Trojans running back Reggie Bush, practically leaping off the page in full stride against a USC cardinal background with gold lettering complementing it. Inscribed by Bush was the message: "To Michael, thank you for all your support! Reggie Bush." The cover of the magazine was nicely framed and in a spot where a guest would see it immediately. It also stood alone on the wall. There were no other framed pictures, let alone any sports memorabilia in the living room.

But in a case of cruel juxtaposition, Michaels looked at that message and then looked down at his cell phone. In small block letters was the text message that had left Michaels in disbelief.

"You're a joke," Bush wrote to Michaels, a man who had spent

more than $200,000 to help Bush and his family while Bush was in college.

This was in August 2006, months after Michaels had finally been forced to evict Bush's family from a new $757,000 home he had bought for them to live in, a home they promised to buy after Bush turned pro. Between the down payment and the fact that the family hadn't paid a dime of rent, Michaels was out more than $86,000. On top of that, there was another $28,000 Michaels gave Bush's parents to pay off a credit card. There were luxury hotel stays, restaurant bills, donations to Bush's family church, straight-out cash payments, and even some heartfelt counseling Michaels did for the parents when their marriage was in crisis.

Michaels was a man who operated on faith and hope in other people. In this case, his kindness had been repaid with scorn.

That's when the doorbell rang and Michaels met two reporters from *Yahoo! Sports* and opened the door on an investigation of one of the biggest scandals in college sports history. According to friends who know Michaels well, he didn't open the door out of spite as much as out of sheer disbelief. While it is true that Michaels saw the partnership with Bush as an opportunity for his beloved Sycuan Indian tribe, much of what he did for Bush, he said, was based first on kindness and generosity.

"He wasn't trying to be the slick agent that people see in the movies or in the sports pages," said a person who knows Michaels well. "That's not it at all. . . . This is not some Jerry Maguire–type guy trying to sell ice to Eskimos. He's an honest, forthright guy who was trying to help and saw a chance to build a really good business." Said another friend of Michaels: "Once you meet Michael, you tend to gravitate to him. He's not the rah-rah, he's not an attitude [guy], he's not confrontational at all. He's just a very gentle giant. Fun-loving. Considerate. He tells me to this day to lighten up because I am somewhat serious at times. Lighten up, relax, enjoy."

Michaels's life has not always been the picture of serenity. According to the *San Diego Union-Tribune*, Michaels was arrested under his Pettiford name in October 1999 on felony charges of making terrorist threats and discharging a firearm in a negligent manner in an incident involving current Sycuan tribal chairman Daniel Tucker. Charges were dropped in 2000 for lack of evidence, records show.

Jordan Cohen, the lawyer who represented Michaels in a March 2007 settlement with Bush, said in a written statement to the *Los Angeles Times* on January 27, 2007, that Michaels "was not out there looking to start a sports marketing agency. It was the [Griffin] family coming to Michaels because Michaels had the financial means."

Eventually, Bush and Michaels reached a settlement, according to a report by *Yahoo! Sports.* Sources said Bush paid Michaels between $200,000 and $300,000 and both sides agreed never to discuss the matter publicly. The only statement Cohen made on the matter at the time was that Michaels had decided to no longer pursue any legal action against Bush.

As the authors of this book were reporting the details of Michaels's interactions with Bush and his family, Michaels agreed to a casual meeting at the Hilton Hotel on the Avenue of the Stars. He wouldn't—actually said he couldn't—provide more details of how much money he provided Bush and the Griffins, alluding to the confidentiality agreement. The previous week, Bush had told ESPN that Michaels and Lake had attempted to "extort" from his family. Still, Michaels wouldn't discuss Reggie. After the meeting, Michaels sent a text message offering encouragement: "I sure hope everything works out towards the 'real' truth and not the 'Hollywood' truth!:)"

The relationship with Bush scarred Michaels in many ways. At the time the story broke in April 2006, Michaels was running for chairman of the Sycuan tribe. He eventually lost the election to Daniel Tucker by a single vote, the bad publicity being used against Michaels within the hundred-member tribe. The odd part is that Tucker and other members of the tribe were just as interested in getting the business started. Yet it was Michaels who paid for the embarrassment.

Michaels was born Michael Pettiford, the son of a Sycuan mother and a black father. In an interview with reporters from *Yahoo! Sports*, Michaels said that he was abused by his father and eventually changed his name to distance himself from a man he couldn't respect. Michaels, who is also nicknamed "Chief" by many associates, is a regal, imposing figure. He is roughly six-foot-four and 250 pounds with a broad shoulders and an athletic frame. Still, he has an obvious kindness that belies his physical image.

In that August 2006 interview, he was described as calm, anything but angry or abrupt. He talked about Bush with compassion. "He went through a lot of things. We shared stories about his real dad, all that situation, LaMar, his mom," Michaels said of Bush during the interview with *Yahoo!* "I think he really has a lot of pain inside of him and now he can be his own self and say, '[expletive] it.' But I think he's going about it the wrong way because he's turning that pain into the bad side of their character."

Michaels said that when he and Bush initially were talking about going into business, it was far more than simply about making money. "When we talked, he had a lot of dreams, a lot of ambitions and goals and we were going to help him realize some of those dreams . . . I think what happened is that as that superstar aspect of his football career started to materialize, I think he got sucked into the wrong group. I think I can help him in that regard, without the Cornwells and without the Ornsteins, and help him realize his dreams on a bigger level, untainted."

Michaels was referring to Bush attorney David Cornwell and Bush marketing agent Mike Ornstein.

Michaels had dreams as well, most of them related to growing and maintaining the tribe.

The Kumeyaay Nation dates its history in what now is the southern end of California and the northwest portion of Mexico back more than a thousand years. The Sycuan band of the Kumeyaay Nation sat in a small section just east of what is now San Diego. At one time, the territory was a sprawling expanse of land from the Pacific Coast at the west end going east over the low-lying mountain and then into the desert.

Over hundreds of years, the territory shrank during battles with the Spanish, the Mexicans, and finally the Americans. In the 1870s, a series of orders and acts by the U.S. government gave the Sycuans and other bands of the nation reservations. The Sycuans ended up in what is now primarily known as El Cajon. Over the next hundred years, the tribe battled back and forth with government intervention and economic problems.

In 1975, the Indian Self-Determination and Education Assistance Act gave tribal governments independent power rather than being purely

under the direction of federal policy. On November 23, 1983, the Sycuans parlayed that power into the establishment of a bingo hall, which looked more like a warehouse. The Sycuans had officially tapped into gaming as a financial foundation. In 2000, the band opened the Sycuan Casino complete with slots, blackjack, pai gow, and poker. The casino expanded in 2001 and bills itself as "the friendly, neighborhood casino where people come to play slot machines." Tribal spokesman Adam Day told *Yahoo! Sports* and the *Miami Herald* in April 2006 that the tribe had $800 million in gross revenues from its operations.

The casino-generated revenue has allowed the Sycuans to diversify beyond gaming. In May 2001, the tribe closed on a multimillion-dollar deal to purchase Singing Hills Resort and Country Club. The resort offers two championship eighteen-hole golf courses and an eighteen-hole par three course visited by two hundred thousand players a year. In addition, the resort boasts one hundred rooms, eleven tennis courts, fine dining, and banquet facilities.

In February 2000, the Sycuans paid a reported $1.5 million to become a sponsor of the San Diego Padres' season. They had sponsored the Padres' Opening Day since 1996. According to an article in the *San Diego Union-Tribune,* Sycuan tribal business manager John Tang said he sponsored the baseball team for reasons other than improving casino business. Tang wanted to "create a different kind of image for Native Americans and sports." The sponsorship campaign, titled "Padres 2000 Presented by Sycuan," was "crafted to avoid references to the Sycuan Gaming Center, although the casino was heavily advertised during Padres radio and television broadcasts. To this day, the Sycuan tribe has a large ad on the scoreboard at Padres games.

The sponsorship deal also gave the tribe negotiation rights for naming a planned downtown ballpark. Commissioner Bud Selig ultimately rejected the deal, reportedly saying, "I would reject any ballpark name which could be linked to casino gambling."

In 2001, during the Sycuans' second year of sponsorship with the Padres, they removed all references to their casino from their advertising campaign. The Sycuan tribe did not "market its East County casino in TV and radio ads before or during Padres games" and instead highlighted "the tribe's history, its government and its charity work in the community."

Their next venture into sports was a move into the boxing business with Sycuan Ringside Promotions. The first boxer to sign with them was Joan "Little Tyson" Guzman of the Dominican Republic. "We're diversifying," Tribal Chairman Daniel Tucker said of the deal. "Like anything else, we see it as a money-making project."

The Sycuan band donated $5.47 million to San Diego State University to create the Sycuan Band of Kumeyaay Nations Institute on Tribal Gaming in order to investigate the implications of the gaming industry for Native Americans. The university said the institute will focus on three areas: "Training students to work in the gambling industry, providing a public policy resource and clearinghouse on gaming, and doing research on tribal gaming issues."

The tribe has also developed numerous land holdings outside the reservation. That includes the purchase and sale of the Hotel Solamar in downtown San Diego and the purchase of the historic U.S. Grant Hotel in downtown San Diego, which the tribe refurbished. The hundred-member tribe is now thriving and powerful. Aside from the $5.5 million donation to San Diego State, there have been numerous other donations. The tribal offices, while hardly impressive in structure, feature armed security and require clearance before anyone can enter. Said one person with knowledge of the Sycuans, "They're extremely powerful in San Diego now and they're not going away."

Michaels still had his concerns about the extended financial health of his tribe. He wondered about how the state of California would react long term to allowing the tribe to get rich off gaming. He yearned for diversification, including building a casino in Las Vegas and buying an NBA team. To a smaller extent, the tribe felt the same and had formed Sycuan Promotions as part of a foray into boxing. But the boxing was really only to provide entertainment at the casino. Michaels wanted his bigger ideas to get more attention. That's why the association with Bush looked attractive to him. A sports marketing company would help raise the profile of the Sycuans. Even the money itself wasn't a key issue, which is why Michaels was willing to give Bush, his mother, Denise Griffin, and his stepfather, LaMar Griffin, a 20 percent stake in the company. Michaels was thinking beyond just New Era.

In 2004, when LaMar Griffin approached the Sycuans initially to run security for the tribe and later returned to pitch the idea of a sports mar-

keting company, Michaels was in. Bush further cemented the deal by giving Lake his assurance that he would join the company. Michaels and Lake quickly agreed to fund Bush and his family, and Michaels set up more meetings with the Sycuan Tribal Council, which had the wherewithal to make the idea a success.

That relationship is clear from taped conversations between Lake and LaMar Griffin from December 2005. The conversation includes a tacit admission by Griffin that he took money from Lake:

Lloyd: And see from him telling me that, I'm telling [Sycuan Tribal Council chairman] Danny [Tucker], "Yeah, Reggie's coming. We got Reggie." And [Michael is] in the middle of that, but if Reggie don't say that, I don't put my foot in my mouth like that with Danny and them. That's what I'm saying. The things that he was saying and doing made me react and put my credibility on line with some people that are big time that can open doors for us. And see what I'm saying, that's why I'm saying it's big, because if Reggie wasn't telling me this stuff and taking that, I would have never told Danny that.

LaMar: Yeah.

Lloyd: I wouldn't have been up there with Danny, "Reggie's coming, trust me," all in his ear, we're going to get Reggie.

LaMar: See, Reggie got to hold up to that. I hate to say that, but Reggie's got to hold up to what he said, and I didn't—that's why I really didn't say anything. You know, that's up to Reggie. But I didn't know about all this money and stuff that was being given. I didn't know nothing about that.

Lloyd: One time he came down, we came down here, remember, we were in front of the house and him and Javon left. I met him down at the 7/11, he sent Javon in the store, I had to give $5,000, right there. I've been giving him nice amounts the whole time.

LaMar: That's hard for me, that's why you wouldn't give me no more money, huh?

According to Lake, the plan was for him to supply cash and benefits for Bush, while Michaels did the same for the family. But Lake said, Bush

didn't want his stepfather to know what was going on. Meanwhile, Lake and Michaels said they received promises from the Sycuan Tribal Council to fund New Era Sports & Entertainment to the tune of $3 million, which created a problem when the deal started to fall apart:

Lloyd: But you know, he's like, "Don't tell my dad." No, me and [Michaels] worked it out. I got to take care of Reggie, Chief [Michaels] takes care of you guys.

LaMar: Oh, okay.

Lloyd: So everything Chief [Michaels] was doing, he was doing out of his pocket. Everything for Reggie, I was doing out of mine. So whenever Reggie needed money, because we're looking at it like we're partners and we are going to prosper together with the business. We all got our own money without Reggie's and Sycuan is putting up $3 million if we get Reggie. So now I'm under like, damn man, not only am I not going to get Reggie, I'm not going to get the $3 million Sycaun give me.

LaMar: See I don't know.

Lloyd: We might get $500 of it, but what's $500 when you could get $3 [million] with Reggie? And I wouldn't have been telling people that if Reggie wouldn't have been telling me that.

The Sycuans talked about giving that money after many meetings, including ones that Griffin attended while wearing a Reggie Bush jersey. During the taped conversations, Griffin confirmed he attended the meetings:

Lloyd: If that was my son, I would tell him you can't play with people's money because I know . . .

LaMar: That can be paid back, Lake.

Lloyd: You can't, Big Dog. You think money can just get paid back from people's time, all this shit I've been doing, all those damn meetings?

LaMar: I was sitting in those meetings, Mike was sitting. You know, I'm going to tell you something, Mike is the only one I ain't worried

about this crap because he knows the business aspect of this thing. Everything that fall the way everything went, Mike, how many people told me they were going to do something and they didn't do it. And he's still friends with them right now. He can call them right now and say, "Hey look, I know you didn't do it, but I need you." Right there. Mike's been political, they talked about him like a dog.

Lloyd: Come in. Let's go inside, the police are coming. I don't even want to have them think we are out here arguing.

LaMar: No, no. We ain't here arguing. If we was out here fighting, I could see. And I hate to say this, because Mike—I keep using Mike because he's been through this already—he's been through the time somebody say they are going to do something, and made a promise to them and they didn't do it. But see, Mike said, "I'll shake their hand and I kept on moving. I didn't try to do anything to the guy, because I know that if I shook his hand, if I need him again, he'll be there." You know what I'm saying? That's the way you know that's how business goes. I'm not here trying to hustle nobody's money.

Lloyd: That's how it seems to me, honestly.

LaMar: It don't seem like that. And the true honest thing that Reggie could do if he doesn't come, is say look, Lake, can I shake your hand? I apologize but here's the $40,000 that you loaned me, the money for the car, and that's all I can do.

Lloyd: But see, that shouldn't be all you could do with something like that.

LaMar: But see, but what Mike says, that's just the way it is sometimes.

Lloyd: Mike doesn't make me move, because when Mike says something, Mike ain't God. This is how I'm looking at it. Sycuan right now, behind all the work we did, is giving us $3 million.

When the idea fell apart and then later turned into a story investigated primarily by *Yahoo! Sports*, the *Miami Herald,* the *Los Angeles Times*, and

the *San Diego Union-Tribune,* the tribe distanced itself with a series of contradictory statements.

For instance, on April 17, 2006, tribe spokesman Day sent the following email to reporters Jason Cole (then working for the *Miami Herald*) and Charles Robinson of *Yahoo! Sports.* In addition, Day sent a copy of the email to sports editor Jorge Rojas and managing editor Dave Wilson of the *Miami Herald.*

> Please attribute this quote to Tribal Chairman Daniel J. Tucker:
>
> Neither the Sycuan Tribal Government nor any of its affiliated business enterprises have ever had or has now any relationship(s) with any current, former, or potential professional football player, their families, or their agents. There is not, and never has been, any relationship between the Sycuan Tribe or any of its affiliated business enterprises and New Era Sports. No representative of the Tribe, including our Tribal attorney, has filed or has threatened to file any lawsuits with any current, former, or potential professional football player or their families or agents. To suggest otherwise is baseless and defamatory. Printing any allegations contrary to the facts as stated above would be considered libelous, and will subject the newspaper and its reporters to suit.
>
> Thanks, please call with any follow-up questions or other information.
>
> ADAM DAY

By October 2007, Day had backed off that statement during an interview for this book. Day said that the tribal council was merely investigating the idea, but never had that much interest. "There were meetings, there's never been any dispute of that," Day said, contradicting his April 2006 statement. "Tribal members, and Mr. Griffin and others—I don't have all the dates and such—but they approached the tribe to become an investor. There's no question. And the tribe said no. The tribe said no, the developmental corporation said no. There's no involvement, there never has been any involvement. The end result speaks for itself. The tribe gave courtesy visits to Mr. Griffin and others. They listened . . . we get approached with literally dozens and dozens of investment opportunities

every month, literally every month. And 99 percent of them are rejected. This is one of them that was rejected."

Day said that Michaels was the person who brought the idea to the council. "That's why the courtesy visit was extended," Day said, referring to Michaels. "Yeah, he's a tribal member. But lots of tribal members have their own interests and businesses that are no part of the tribe's business whatsoever and the tribe doesn't even know about them.

"I don't know how you quantify the term 'interest.' We, the tribe—when I say we, the Tribal Council, development corporation, board of directors—extended the courtesy to both Mr. Michaels as a tribal member and Mr. Griffin to listen to their proposal. I mean if someone is classifying that as interest, then, you know, you could say that was interest but it was a courtesy visit. A proposal was made and the tribe rejected it. So, there's no partnership. There was never any partnership, there was never any financial interest, there was never any agreement."

Regardless of that, from Michaels's statements and what friends close to him have said, it's clear that Michaels believed there was an agreement. There was hope for one of Michaels's dreams. Michael "trusted Reggie," said a close friend of Michaels. Michaels is "a karma guy. I think when he's attacked, he goes on the defensive. I don't think he's really comfortable being very defensive. He's a very positive person. I mean to this day, he probably thinks one day he and Reggie may do something. That may well be."

Michaels told *Yahoo! Sports* he doubted that. "It can never be the way it was," Michaels said. To Michaels, all the things that have been done to make Bush appear to be a kind and giving person, such as Bush's charitable contributions in New Orleans, are part of the marketing efforts of Ornstein.

"Ornstein, I'm pretty sure, orchestrated most of that to make him look good," Michaels told *Yahoo! Sports*. "They probably said to him, 'There's this dark side of your character, you have to do some things to offset that.' I think if you're a naturally good person, then some of the good and righteous things will compel you to do things right. So I kind of don't blame him.

"It's kind of weird. I don't know what to think of him."

SIX

The Seeds of Relationship and Scandal:

How Bush, Lake, and Michaels Got Together

Reggie Bush and Lloyd Lake stood on the second-floor balcony of Lake's family home at 743 South Sixty-first Street in San Diego. From this vantage point, overlooking an expanse of suburban homes, the two could see all the way to downtown and beyond to the Pacific Ocean.

For Bush, just a sophomore at USC, the view was slightly different. He was already seeing the dollar signs associated with his stunning football ability. Everything he had worked for over the years was beginning to pay off, at least figuratively, on the field. In a sport where players are normally nurtured for a year or two before getting significant action in college, Bush was a prodigy. He played from the minute he got to USC as a true freshman in 2003. In 2004, he was on his way to joining the storied USC running backs.

Bush opened the season against Virginia Tech with three touchdown receptions, becoming the tenth player in school history and the first running back to do so. He also finished that game with 258 all-purpose yards. By the end of the season, he had 2,330 all-purpose yards, had scored fifteen touchdowns, and even threw a fifty-two-yard touchdown pass. His all-purpose total was the most by a Trojan since Marcus Allen had a

school-record 2,683 yards in 1981 on the way to winning the Heisman. Bush averaged a staggering 10.1 yards every time he touched the ball, including a stunning 6.3 yards every time he rushed it.

Bush was about to see his dreams of living a better life pay off financially with Lake's help. In turn, Lake was going to see his dreams of finding a way out of the drug-dealing, gangster life become a reality. It was a dream he shared with his family and friends, all of them wanting him to stop the cycle of chasing the easy dollar all the way to prison.

The odd part is that as they stood there, at least according to Lake, Bush was the one who had to convince Lake, a street hustler with a lengthy criminal history. Bush, a man capable of running zig-zagging lines like few ever in the college game, had to convince Lake that the best road for Lake to go straight was to start a business with him. "I brought him up here [to the house] because we had a proposal from Olson Construction for $3 million on some contingencies," Lake said of the meeting in 2004. "I was like, 'Reggie, look, man, we don't have to do this sports agency. Let me know before we get in too deep. I could go to this right here with my family, you know, I can do this with Olson.'

"My business partner at the time had a mortgage company. We'd be the first lender, preferred lender. Make Olson put that in the contract and that's another $2 or $3 million I could make, just off of loans. I was like, 'Reggie, I don't have to do this [sports agency].' "

According to Lake, Bush sold him on the idea.

" 'Oh no, let's do it, let's do it,' " Lake recalled Bush saying. "That's what pisses me off more than anything. We were right here on the balcony, looking out, in conversation, and I had the contract so he read it. So he wasn't thinking I was pulling his leg. And he looked me right in the eye and said, 'Let's do it,' and shook my hand. See, I operate on honor, integrity. That was new to me. I have friends doing twenty years . . . one of my best friends is doing twenty years right now because he wouldn't lie on me. And you come tell a lie over nothing and it kind of gets you sick. [Bush] has no dignity . . . it pisses you off."

Lake told Bush's stepfather, LaMar Griffin, about those feelings in taped conversations from December 2005 as the deal was starting to unravel:

Lloyd: I know, but it's the way you do it and go about it. He didn't have to manipulate or be deceitful with me. If he would have said,

"Look, just loan me the money," I would have loaned him the money with a little interest on it. He didn't have to get me all in this with my time, and everything telling me stuff to get money. He told me stuff in order to get money.

LaMar: Is that good or bad? What's wrong with that?

Lloyd: It's bad if I tell you, "LaMar, do this and do that, and we are going to do this, and I'm going to give you the money and I need this and I need that." And you bring it and then at the end you might not have said in so many words, but you know what you were saying to get the money, I'm saying. So Reggie was like being manipulative, because the situation—I don't want him to have no ill feelings with me or think I got any ill toward him. I'm trying to pull it off where it doesn't come to anything like that.

LaMar: If it's not pulled off, it shouldn't come to anything like that, that's what I'm trying to tell you.

Lloyd: Well, what would you do?

LaMar: I wouldn't do anything.

Lloyd: So you would just say I wasted all my time and energy.

LaMar: That's what I would do because being in a position I'm in, I cannot turn around and say, "OK, this didn't work out, so what I'm going to do is I'm going to try to find out a way to get my time back and get my money back and this and that." He can pay your money back, I'm not saying that. But I'm not going to go out and try to swindle.

Lloyd: Swindle? How do I try to swindle?

LaMar: I'm just saying, if the situation don't go good the way it's supposed to go.

Lloyd: I kept my word on everything.

LaMar: And you probably did, you know what I'm saying? But still you can't, if Reggie goes with somebody else, that's his life.

Lloyd: I understand, and I'm not saying that I don't understand. But what you guys aren't paying attention to, is the things that Reggie said.

LaMar: Well, see, that's Reggie.

Lloyd: I know.

LaMar: That's between you and Reggie.

But even Griffin said during the taped conversations that he would have warned his stepson not to take money from Michaels and Lake:

Lloyd: He told me don't tell you, that's what I'm saying. What am I supposed to do? I'm like you're my partner and his dad, but at the same time, it's tricky with business and family because if I tell you, then he's mad at me. You see what I'm saying? And it blows our chances to sign him. So I didn't know what to do, he just had me in an awkward position when he said, "Don't tell my dad."

LaMar: Right, because he knew what I was going to tell him. I told him that, "You take anything from them, then that means something and you can't do that. If you're not going to give them a chance, and go with them, then don't be taking nothing from them." I told him that, so that's what I told him. So I'm hoping everything goes fine, but like I told Reggie, I said, "You said the decision is yours. That's what you told me. You wanted me to support you, and that's what I'll do."

Lloyd: The only thing I don't like, and you're right about everything, and tell me if I'm wrong about this: Would you be mad if Reggie was out taking from everyone? He didn't have to do that with us, right? He could have just said, "Loan me the money," right? That's what I be mad about. You know if asked for the money, I would have loaned it to you and you'd just paid it back. But just don't be deceitful about it, like being slick. You hear what I'm saying? Like if you're taking money from everyone else.

Barbara Gunner and sister Lisa Lake both had openly hoped, for years, that Lloyd would find another path. Then came this idea for a business with Bush.

"I didn't even know who Reggie Bush was," Gunner said. "I had heard them talk about him. I'm really not a sports person. I watch tennis and

golf. But football, I just know the major parts of the season, the playoffs. But I didn't know who Reggie Bush was, but they had known him from [the time they were] kids because all of my children went to the same high school he went to. They were telling me about this guy. [Lloyd said], 'Ma, I think I've come up with this great idea with this guy Reggie in college and his parents, and I think it's something that we could do that we could all live comfortably, everybody. It's a good business that's a legal business.'

"That's all I wanted was for him to just do the right thing and do something. He introduced us, I met the family. They came over and they seemed like they knew what they were talking about. We talked about the Bible and they were Christians, and I sort of took to them and thought they were nice people at the time."

Still, Gunner had her daughter Lisa Lake check out the idea. Lisa talked to Michael Michaels, a longtime friend of Lloyd who was going to be a partner in the business with Lloyd, Bush, and Bush's family. It all sounded legitimate.

"Mike talked to my daughter and she had a better understanding of it than I did. She said, 'They might have a good idea, it might work.' So they kind of formed the corporation and started to talk to others. I wasn't at the meetings or anything. Lisa was because they had chose her to be [part of the company as a] spokesperson or something."

The seeds for the business had been planted years before.

Bush and Lake first met when Reggie was a star football player at Helix High in San Diego. Lake had played basketball at Helix High years before and was helping his father, who had developed a sports cream that Bush liked to use. Lloyd Lake would deliver the sports cream and, over time, developed a friendship with Bush. Lake even started to feel compassion for Bush at the time because his family was barely squeaking by.

"I knew the guy was going somewhere," Lake said. "But I felt bad for him in his situation. Genuinely, I felt sorry for him because I could tell he wasn't doing too good as far as finances with his family. So I told him when I met him, I was like, 'Look if you ever need anything, just let me

know. This was when he was in tenth grade. I dropped him off some [sports cream] and I could tell from his situation, so I felt kind of sorry for him."

Bush was "just a hungry kid who had a lot of ambition. You could tell he was serious about his football. I remember how it used to be with me [when Lake was in high school], so I didn't want him to get sidetracked and . . . I was trying to let him know if you need anything, let me know. Yeah, money. Help, period. He was at a point where you might not have food in the house. I never had it like that. That's a different severity. That's severe. I've never been like that, there was always money around. He was living in La Mesa. I didn't go inside [the Bush apartment]. It was a little apartment off Fletcher Parkway . . . I could tell from conversations with his dad they weren't doing too good. Reggie, I could just tell from looking at him he wasn't doing too good. I could tell with working, and football, it was taking a toll on him. I was trying to give him some extra help if he needed it. I saw him a couple more times . . . one of them [meetings], I gave him like $50 or $100. He used to come down here. We would ride around."

During the taped conversations, as Griffin was getting upset with what he perceived as manipulation by everyone involved, Lake reiterated that he had tried to help Bush long before Bush was a star:

LaMar: And all this sorry ass that you're throwing me about this and that other thing, I could care less.

Lloyd: You know why?

LaMar: I don't trust none of y'all, none of y'all.

Lloyd: You know what? You see, that's the problem. You don't trust none of us.

LaMar: All y'all got motives, every last one of y'all got motives.

Lloyd: I told you my motive in the gate.

LaMar: It don't matter if you told me or not. Mike told me his motive, you told me your motive, everybody's got a motive.

Lloyd: What's JC's motive?

LaMar: This big-time football player, that's all y'all after, you don't care about me, you don't care about my wife, you don't care about my son, it's all motive.

Lloyd: Big Dog, that's bullshit. Before your son was who he was, I came by your house . . . and I told your son, "Anything you need, just ask me and I'll give it to you." Before I even knew who the hell or what he would do.

LaMar: OK, so what you're saying is . . .

Lloyd: You say I only care . . .

LaMar: It's motive time, it's motive time.

Lloyd: But what about then? Was it motive time then? This was when he was in tenth grade. "Reg, I hook you up."

LaMar: I didn't know about that.

Lloyd: You did, you were there. I said, "Can I take him to train with [LaDainian Tomlinson]. My boy [Adrian] Dingle said he'll hook it up?"

LaMar: Okay.

The friendship with Reggie stalled because Lake was indicted in June 2002 for conspiracy to distribute marijuana and cocaine. Lake stayed in jail for two years without bail.

But when Lake got out of prison and started to make plans to straighten his life out, he eventually came back to the idea of working with Bush. For each of the main characters—Bush, Lake, Michaels, LaMar Griffin, and even small-time agent David Caravantes, who joined the operation much later—the company was going to be a way to make it big.

Griffin, Bush's stepfather, had toiled for years as a high-school security guard, fighting to make ends meet with his wife, Denise, who also was a guard at the San Diego County Courthouse. LaMar Griffin had an idea to break out of living week-to-week, which had put the family more than $25,000 in credit-card debt by the fall of 2004. He wanted to start his own security company. One of the first ideas he had for a client was the Sycuan Indian tribe.

The tribe ran a casino and golf resort on its reservation in nearby El Cajon, about ten miles from where the Griffins lived in Spring Valley.

Amid the desert brush and rocky hills of El Cajon, the Sycuans had built an oasis for themselves, a plush operation that grossed approximately $800 million a year.

With only one hundred tribe members, the Sycuans had parlayed the business into a foundation for wealth beyond the confines of the reservation. Many of them had built or purchased homes on the golf course around the resort.

Griffin's idea was to run the security for the entire operation, and he approached the tribe in summer 2004 about the idea. While Griffin's security idea was rebuffed (the tribe already had its own armed security force), he wasn't completely dismissed. One thing attracted some high-level members of the tribe to him: LaMar Griffin was Reggie Bush's stepfather, and he didn't hesitate to tell people that. He dropped Bush's name as easily as some people give out business cards. To members of the Sycuan tribe, an association with Bush could be profitable. Such an association would be the next logical step in expanding their sports interests. Bush was viewed as a great draw for the resort and golf course, and for the casino. Having Bush attend and host events on the property would have been a boon for business. With the Sycuan tribe indicating interest, Griffin needed an idea that would appeal to them. At one point in fall 2004, he was brainstorming with Lloyd. "LaMar expressed that he wanted to get involved in something and I knew it would be a good thing," Lake said. "So we just put the pieces together and went from there and it looked like it was going to be something good . . . I talked to LaMar about the things he was doing and he said, 'Let's do a sports agency.' "

In October 2004, Lake took LaMar and Denise Griffin to a San Diego Chargers game to meet with Michael Michaels, a Sycuan tribe member. The three of them met at the tribe's luxury box at Qualcomm Stadium.

"Michael was into it," Lake said. "I was really excited. I just came home from prison fighting a case where [the federal authorities] were trying to [give me] a lot of time for something I didn't do. [The business with Bush] was like a chance where you don't have to even take any chance of ever going back to prison, legit. It was something that I liked. I liked sports, it would have been good. A lot of good athletes come out

of San Diego, especially football. So it would have been a good spot to have a good agency base. Everybody was excited. Sycuan was excited. LaMar was excited. Everybody looked good until the end."

This was Lake's chance to have the life he had known as a child. The only drawback was that the tribe was not fully on board. At least not right away. But Michaels was. Lake and Michaels had known each other for almost a decade. Lake said he met Michaels for the first time at a restaurant called Elaine's, where Michaels was playing cards with another friend. Lake was invited to play, striking up a friendship.

The idea of a sports agency also appealed to Bush. Throughout his college career, Bush had become increasingly cognizant of his marketability. He was flashy as a player, had a warm, bright smile, and was well-spoken. Beyond that, he was a star in Los Angeles, the nation's second-biggest market and one without an NFL presence.

Bush had a built-in niche just waiting for him to take advantage of. In fact, not only did Bush agree to go in on the sports agency by late 2004, but he also did an internship with Los Angeles–based sports marketing agent Mike Ornstein in the summer of 2005, before his final season at USC. Bush was doing everything he could, not only to be part of the business, but also to know it. By the end of his sophomore year in 2004, Bush knew his potential was going to be vast. He was already a favorite among the autograph hounds who hung out around the USC locker room and practice field.

It was around that time when Bush probably started to understand how running his own marketing company would help him. Bush knew that he would have to hire an agent to handle his marketing opportunities. That agent would take anywhere from 10 to 20 percent of the money Bush got on a deal.

For every $1 million in endorsements and other off-field ventures, the agent would take anywhere from $100,000 to $200,000. To the money-conscious Bush, there had to be a way around that, or at least a way to make someone think he wanted a way around it. As Bush's family kept hobnobbing around Southern California on Michaels's and Lake's dime, his stepfather was explaining the main reason why Bush was ready to do business with them. Michaels was going to let them keep more of the marketing money rather than lose it on commission.

The plan was that Bush, his family, Lake, and Michaels were going to be equal partners in the agency, each owning 20 percent. Essentially, Bush would be his own marketing rep and would keep a percentage of the commission rather than pay it all to a marketing agent.

Bush's role as a partner in the business would be as the high-profile recruiter for the company, convincing other players to sign up with New Era Sports & Entertainment. As Bush was finishing the 2004 season, his sophomore year, the seeds of his ideas about how to capitalize on his fame were starting to sprout. Bush met with Michaels and Lake twice in November 2004, the first time at the Friday's restaurant in the Mission Valley area just east of downtown San Diego. The second meeting was at the Bonita Plaza Shopping Mall in National City, just south of San Diego. In addition, Michaels and Lake again met with LaMar and Denise Griffin that month.

This was just a start.

Reggie Bush and LaMar Griffin agreed to start the sports marketing agency with Lake and Michaels. Upon agreeing to the partnership, Bush demanded a monthly allowance of $3,000 as an advance on future company earnings. Lake and Michaels obliged, with Lloyd delivering the cash each month to Bush in Los Angeles, Lake said. Bush eventually moved with USC teammate Thomas Williams into a higher-end apartment near the USC campus at 123 Figueroa Street, where Lake would drop off the money.

Around December 2004, LaMar and Denise Griffin demanded $28,000 to continue with the sports agency, threatening to pull out of the deal if they weren't paid. "When Michaels and everybody agreed, when Reggie gave his agreement that he wanted to do it, Michaels gave LaMar and Denise [$28,000] in cash that day and tons more after that," Lake said. The demands came before USC played in the Bowl Championship Series national title game against Oklahoma on January 4, 2005, in Miami. The Trojans rolled to a 55–19 victory in that game, completing an undefeated season for USC that had people talking about the squad as one of the greatest teams in college football history.

In February 2005, Bush asked for and was given $13,000—by Lake—for the purchase of a car, a 1996 black Impala SS. The car was considered trendy in the neighborhood where Bush grew up because of the powerful stock engine it was equipped with from 1994 to 1996. The engine was similar to the type put in higher-end cars such as the Corvette and

Camaro. The car was so hip that on a website (Universityofthesoutheast .com) Bush was sponsoring—to help kick-start a clothing line for a friend—Reggie was pictured with the grill of a late-model Impala superimposed behind him.

Bush wanted to upgrade the car and received another $4,000 from Lake to "pimp" the car with a new stereo, tinted windows, and high-performance tires and rims. "He went and picked it out. It was in [Los Angeles]. I gave the money to Reggie and LaMar," Lake said. "Then he wanted the rims, the music, the alarm system, all that stuff. . . . [It was in] cash because at the time I'm trying to cover our tracks, too. I am not trying to do anything to get him [Reggie] in jeopardy of losing everything he worked so hard for. And I still wasn't really trying to put him in this position now, even with all this. He forced my hand. [Now], you don't want to give me back my money?"

When Bush had the car customized, he called Lake to come deliver the money to pay for it.

"He was calling me all the time for money. I remember he just got his rims. It was about 9:30 [A.M]. He was like, 'Man, can you ride up here? I don't have any money and the guy has my car.' . . . He put the rims on it and he put an alarm system in and some music and he owed the guy like $5,500, [the guy] that installed everything. And the guy was at the apartment over there [at the Promenade]. So I rolled up there and gave him the money and talked with [Bush] a little while and left. It was always things like that happening."

Lake's mother remembers meeting Bush when he was asking for the initial $13,000 for the car.

"I met Reggie once," Gunner said. "He came to the house. . . . He came for money that night and I think that's the night that Lloyd gave him the money for the car because he was going crazy about this car. He just had to have this car. Every day he was calling."

Lake also discussed the car with Griffin during the taped conversations:

> **Lloyd:** I don't know it again, because he called me a couple of times like for the alarm, and the lights under the car, I went and paid for that.

LaMar: Oh.

Lloyd: So I think if he needed something, he'd call me, "Bring this, I need this to get my alarm and everything fixed." So I'd ride up there, I'd take it to him, and then he needed his rims or something fixed or something happened, I took some more up to him.

LaMar: See, he didn't inform me of that stuff.

Lake: Yeah, we're talking business the whole time.

LaMar: See, he didn't tell me that stuff.

Lloyd: Yeah, I mean we're going up there and we're talking. I'm giving him money.

LaMar: See, that's why I said . . . now see, I'm way out of this matter now, because if that's what was going on, I don't know nothing about it. That's why I said, I'm way out of it because if you talk to him and he said something, I can't come back and say, you know what I'm saying? If he was doing that, hey, I'm out of it.

Lloyd: Right, but I still need your support, is all I'm saying.

LaMar: All the stuff he was doing and stuff, all them lights and stuff, I didn't know. If he had told me, it would have been a different ballgame. But see, he told you not to tell me. Now you're doing this and doing that, that's something I have no control over. . . .

Lloyd: But what am I supposed to do? But you see what I'm saying? I'm sitting up here every time he needs something looking out because you're my partner.

LaMar: But see, like I said before . . .

Lloyd: If you tell me I'd be pissing out . . .

LaMar: No, but I'm going to tell him, "Man, have you made any deals with anybody about this agency? Because if you did, you got to hold up to what you said." Because he ain't told me nothing.

Lloyd: I know but don't tell nothing, he told me not to. So if you say that, he's going, "No, Big Dog."

LaMar: I have to say, "Have you done anything that I need to know, or have you done anything?" See, OK, you're coming to me tell-

ing me that everybody's depressed and everything like that because the deal might not go through, but on the same token, y'all have been doing some stuff behind my back and I don't know nothing about it.

Lake, Griffin and Bush talked so often during that time that Barbara Gunner got her son's phone records to prove the relationship. She said she handed the phone records over to her attorneys.

"I had to get all the attorneys that because, at the end, [Bush's family] had said that they barely knew Lloyd when the deal went sour," Gunner said. "I had to go to Nextel and get all the phone bills for a whole year. I had to go through it and every day Reggie calling Lloyd, Lloyd calling Reggie [or] Reggie's parents. The attorneys have them all. All those documents show that it's not somebody you don't know calling."

By the time Bush was done with the car, he was asked by *DUB* magazine to do a photo shoot with the car. *DUB* is a hip magazine that features athletes, musicians, and actors posing with their cars, discussing the high-end equipment used to update them.

A photo of Bush sitting on the hood of the car ran in the June/July 2006 issue of *DUB*. It was shot at International Motoring Incorporated in Pasadena, California, where Bush apparently had the car updated (the front license plate holder featured a face plate for International Motoring). Bush was dressed in a Troy Polamalu Pittsburgh Steelers jersey with a Pittsburgh Pirates cap on, a Rolex watch, baggy gray-black shorts, and shiny high-top shoes. Another photo from that shoot was used for a mockup of the cover of the November/December 2006 edition of the magazine.

On the weekend of March 4, 2005, Bush visited San Diego to attend the birthday party of star NFL running back Marshall Faulk, who had played his college ball at San Diego State. The party was held at the exclusive On Broadway club.

Bush had Michaels get him a room at the posh Manchester Grand Hyatt, a few blocks from the club. Bush stayed two nights in room 477, a $639-a-night suite. Hotel employees confirmed to *Yahoo! Sports* that Bush stayed in the hotel that weekend and documents showed that Bush charged $1,574.86 to the room that was paid for by Michaels.

USC running back coach Todd McNair came to San Diego, as well, and met Bush at the room. "We [paid for] the rooms at the Hyatt suites . . . [McNair] was in Reggie's suite," Lake said. "It was Marshall Faulk's birthday party. [Bush] rolled with us to the club, to Marshall Faulk's party. It was me, my sister [Lisa Lake], Tony Gwynn's wife, Michael, Reggie, in the limo. We went to pick up Reggie from the Hyatt, him and his buddies. It was like two or three of his friends."

Before picking up Bush, Lake, Michaels, and the rest of their party went to dinner. "We were at Morton's Steakhouse eating. After we got done eating, we went and picked up Reggie in a limo and we all went to the Faulk party," Lloyd said. Lisa Lake was with her brother and Michaels that night. She wondered how the then-underage Bush was going to get into the posh party.

"I remember the second time I saw Reggie," Lisa said, "he came down and we all went out to that club [On Broadway]. We picked [Bush] up in a limo with Michael and Alicia Gwynn was in the car. . . . We all went out to dinner at Morton's . . . we went and picked [Bush and his friends] up at the Hyatt after. I kept saying, 'How are we going to get in the club because he's not twenty-one?' [Lloyd Lake] said, 'Trust me, they'll let him in.' "

For Lisa Lake, it was probably a sign of things to come, but one of many she chose to ignore. Eventually, she started loaning her brother money as he tried to keep the business going. By her estimate, she loaned Lloyd between $25,000 and $30,000 in increments of $2,000 to $3,000.

Lake and Michaels went to Los Angeles and met with Bush again at his apartment. "Me and Michael rode up to L.A. just to talk with him. Michael left that meeting so happy and excited just because the way Reggie led him on. It was all lies. He basically [said] everything he was going to do and he wanted Michael to do this and do that and he wanted to get into acting."

The weekend after Bush went to the Faulk party, Bush took a date to Las Vegas, where he stayed at the Venetian, an upscale hotel and casino. Hotel documents obtained by *Yahoo! Sports* showed that Michaels filled

out a credit-card authorization form naming Bush as the person who would stay at the hotel under his credit card and authorizing the hotel to charge the room fee of $564.62 for two nights to Michaels. Another document obtained by *Yahoo! Sports* showed Bush signed his name to an electronic signature pad upon checking into the hotel. Finally, another $59.01 in incidental charges for the room were paid with VISA card ending in 0853.

Lake said he and Michaels purchased an airline ticket for Bush to go to Atlanta to visit a girl he was interested in. Bush "paid for the ticket, but we gave him the money for his pocket. Amazing." In addition, Lake's girlfriend at the time, Maiesha Jones, once wired $500 to Bush's bank account, according to Lake. In an interview for this book, Jones, who broke up with Lloyd and asked the court for a restraining order against him, acknowledged making the wire transfer. Jones also said she had many conversations with Reggie and was aware of payments that Lloyd made to Reggie and his parents.

There was also a shopping spree Bush had one night with some friends on Lake and Michaels's dime. "Yeah, I remember we went to the mall," said Lake, who called the owner of the clothing store to open it after hours. "We all went out, Reggie's friends, me, and Mike took them to the mall. He spent like $1,500 in there, Reggie did. Maybe $2,000. Yeah, [it was] during the [2005] season. We would go up there for some games, go eat after the game at Reggie's favorite Chinese place."

At the same time, according to several people close to the situation, Bush's family had to leave an apartment they lived in. They needed a place to live and were ready for their biggest demand. Lake's mother said, "After a while, [once the business] started getting off the ground, Michael was supposed to do his part for the family and Lloyd was supposed to do his part for Reggie. But after a while, every week it was money, money, money and it never stopped." Lake's mother wondered, "How could they spend that much money? And then Reggie came and told the guys that his parents—they weren't getting evicted I don't think—he said the [owners] were selling . . . and they had to move. I guess they didn't have first and last security deposit, so they asked them to help them find a place to stay. Michael decided with his good credit and all [to help]."

At the end of March 2005, Michaels bought a house for Bush's family to live in at 9715 Apple Street, a main thoroughfare running along the side of a steep hill in Spring Valley. It was a new home, sitting at the apex of the street with a direct view of Sweetwater Reservoir to the south. The three-thousand-square-foot home cost $757,500. LaMar and Denise Griffin helped pick out the home, and the family moved there in April.

The agreement was for Michaels to pay for the home until Bush was drafted the following year. (Bush planned to skip his final year of eligibility at USC.) Reggie could buy the home outright for his family with his signing bonus. Michaels put down $38,000 for the house and began making the monthly mortgage payments. He also paid the utility bills. Said Gunner, "The deal was that Michael was going to let them rent the house and when [Bush] turned pro and got his signing bonus, he was going to purchase the house. Once they got in it, they never paid, not one month's rent, no electrical, no nothing."

Bush's family's dreams of a better life were starting to come true and they didn't even have to wait for Reggie to turn pro. They were so ecstatic that they put a permanent touch on the moment. After moving in, a member of the family etched THE GRIFFINS "05" in the wet concrete of the driveway.

Lloyd Lake said he never flinched at having to spend the money as Bush and his family made demand after demand. "I look at it like this: Any type of business you are in, there are certain criteria that the best people are doing. If you don't do it like that, you are not going to win. You see what I am saying? I will give an example because it's easier to relate to. . . . If you get into drug dealing, then you know that violence can come with it, prison can come with it. But you have to be able to deal with those things if you are going to get in that business. That's the same [with sports]. All of them do it. It's just a business where they all do it for those types of athletes. If you are not going to do it, you are not going to get those athletes.

"It's kind of like you know this is what you have to do to be in this business, to compete, and that's it. That's the bottom line. If you have an athlete you are trying to recruit, let's say you are following all the [NCAA] rules and you have an agent over here who's not and you have a kid over here who doesn't have too much. You're recruiting [that athlete], you

take him out, take him to eat, and follow the rules. He's like, 'Hey, man, you know, I don't have any money.' You know it's not right and you're like, I can't do that because of the NCAA. Now, here this [other agent] takes him out and he [gives] him $5,000 when [the athlete] asked. Who do you think [the athlete is] going to be more inclined to go with? The one that's looking out for him.

"That's why that business is like it is. You've got people that are broke, you have people who have nothing and are so close to getting some money they can't wait. I feel like schools should maybe give athletes a little more money with all that money they're making because it's not right that somebody is making a lot of money for the schools and the networks but they don't make anything and they are sitting around there without a penny. If you ever ran across any of those talents, they are so broke it's ridiculous. Like damn, treat your athletes a little better and maybe that will eliminate this part of the [problem]."

SEVEN

Reggie Breaks Out:

The Heisman Year

USC proved to be the best place for Reggie Bush's aspirations. He had to give up track because of its conflict with spring football, but his decision to be a Trojan seemed to be one Reggie never questioned. Bush also changed his major from premed to political science—a move that, coupled with his last name, earned him the nickname "the President." USC's coach, Pete Carroll, saw what many others did, too—an obvious parallel between Bush's style and that of University of Kansas great Gale Sayers, the "Kansas Comet." One of the first things Carroll did after Bush enrolled at USC was to have him watch some video clips of Sayers in action to get a deeper understanding of maneuvers and techniques perfected by Sayers that Bush could easily make his own.

And as his career at USC progressed, it became clear that while Bush might not be the leader of the Western world, he was one of the most powerful men in West Coast football.

Quarterback Matt Leinart enjoyed a tremendous season in 2003, emerging from Carson Palmer's dominating shadow to establish himself as an extremely talented quarterback in his own right and his team as one of

the most formidable college gridiron opponents in recent memory. Leinart's first career pass for USC resulted in a touchdown against Auburn in 2003, and he finished sixth in the Heisman voting that year. Matt would take it all the following year, and even come up for the prestigious award a third time in 2005. However, there was another young star emerging who would win the voting that year, and with Leinart's blessing. Anybody who backed away from the line of scrimmage could see that while Leinart had all of the makings of a future professional quarterback, there was also the other half of that magic equation: He had talent behind him.

When Reggie Bush began as a true freshman in 2003, he was joining a rapidly ascending team that was just beginning to enjoy the prestige and excitement of their newly rediscovered notoriety. Donning the number five uniform, Bush charged the field in 2003, proving to his coach, the fans, and his teammates that he was not to be taken lightly. He demonstrated incredible skill in both catching and throwing the ball, and his running game was remarkable. By the end of the season, he had accumulated 1,331 all-purpose yards, positioning him as the Pac-10 leader in kickoff returns (USC's first since Anthony Davis in 1974) and setting a USC freshman record for yardage. He scored three touchdowns (including a kickoff return), caught fifteen passes, and amassed ninety carries. Bush's freshman season was crowned with his being named ESPN's Newcomer of the Year for the Pac-10.

At six feet and two hundred pounds, Reggie's stature wasn't small, but it was hardly intimidating, either. Bush had to depend on things other than size to make his reputation. During his sophomore year, Bush started getting noticed; he was named Southern Cal's MVP and finished fifth in Heisman voting despite not starting in a single game.

The 2004 Trojan football team was a gridiron powerhouse. They started the season as number one in the AP polls and were never ousted from that position. The Trojans became the only team—other than Florida State in 1999—to gain a wire-to-wire National Championship, and the tenth school to win the title in back-to-back seasons.

Opening against Virginia Tech—in a sold-out FedEx Stadium in Landover, Maryland—USC defeated the Hokies in the first ever matchup between the two schools. The Trojans were facing some obstacles: Mike Williams had been declared ineligible by the NCAA due to his efforts to

enter the NFL. Some worried that losing Williams could upset the team's morale. Sophomore Reggie Bush scored three of USC's four touchdowns, caught five passes, and racked up a total of 258 all-purpose yards. Bush's scoring tied the school record of three touchdown catches in a game, the tenth Trojan and first running back to reach that mark. Reggie's performance in that game got him noticed. He was named the Pac-10 Offensive Player of the Week. The camera was starting to notice him, the football seemed to love him, and perhaps most important of all, the fans were fired up about him. The Trojans' 24–13 victory was just the start of an exciting and historic season.

The following week, USC had another first-time matchup, this time taking on the Rams of Colorado State. Bush once again impressed with his eighty-four yards, one touchdown, and three punt returns, which contributed to the Trojans' 49–0 shutout of their guests. Next, against Brigham Young, both Bush and teammate LenDale White broke one hundred rushing yards, with Bush racking up 124 yards and White 110. Bush also managed to score a twenty-one-yard touchdown, and gained thirty-eight yards on a kickoff return. The Trojans won easily, 42–10.

When the Trojans took on Stanford, Bush had an especially strong game in USC's closest matchup of the season. Perhaps his two most remarkable plays were the seventeen-yard touchdown in which he slipped and skirted his way through several tackles, and the thirty-three-yard punt return that almost looked like acrobatics as he traversed the field. This play put USC in scoring position to take the game in a 31–28 nail-biter.

Bush continued to shine as the Trojans took on California, and went on to Arizona State, where he managed to score a touchdown on a ten-yard pass. The Washington game saw him score a fifteen-yard touchdown and catch a career-high six passes. Against Washington State he got two touchdowns and a fifty-seven-yard punt return—in all, he had 143 all-purpose yards, including seventy-eight yards on three punt returns.

It was in the Oregon State game on November 6, 2004, that Bush really made jaws drop; eighty-eight yards on eleven rushes, eighty-two yards on three kickoff returns, and seventy-three yards on three punt returns wowed the crowd. When the dust cleared, Bush had a total of 249 all-purpose yards—he'd gotten six more on two receptions—and another

touchdown on a punt return, topping the previous week's run by eight yards. This sixty-five-yard return in the fourth quarter helped to push the Trojans to a 28–20 victory over the Beavers. His performance in this game merited Bush a Pac-10 Special Teams Player of the Week award.

Coming out strongly against both Arizona and Notre Dame, Bush broke out again in the UCLA game with a set of impressive numbers reminiscent of his Pop Warner days. The UCLA game was especially important because a win there would ensure USC an invitation to the BCS National Championship game at the Orange Bowl that year, and Bush helped to seal the deal for the Trojans. On the second play of the game, he made a sixty-five-yard run that criss-crossed the field as he sidestepped blocks and maneuvered deftly through the defensive line to score a touchdown. Later in the first half, he topped his own performance with an eighty-one-yard carry, the longest of his career and a play that drove the crowd wild. In the end, Bush had gained 335 all-purpose yards, including 204 running yards, both career records for him. He made six catches for seventy-three yards, racked up thirty-nine yards on two kickoff returns, and managed to get nineteen yards on two punt returns. The hard-fought game ended with a 29–24 win for the Trojans. A trip to Miami was the team's reward.

In a matchup that was sure to result in a knock-down, drag-out gridiron battle, the wire-to-wire number-one-ranked Trojans were facing the wire-to-wire number-two-ranked Sooners of Oklahoma. Not only were both teams undefeated, with something to prove, but the game would mark the first time that two Heisman Trophy winners would face each other in a college game. Oklahoma's quarterback, Jason White, had won the award in 2003, and was now pitted against his newly crowned successor, Matt Leinart. Three other 2004 Heisman finalists were on the field that night, all slugging it out in the backfield: Oklahoma's Adrian Peterson, USC's LenDale White, and, of course, Reggie Bush, who would go on to take top honors in the Heisman voting the following year.

The game opened with a drive from USC, but Oklahoma managed to stop it and ended up scoring the first points of the game. The Trojans then scored the next twenty-eight points, bringing the halftime score to an intimidating 39–10 lead over the Sooners. USC scored an additional sixteen points in the second half of the game, while Oklahoma managed to score only nine more. Leinart's Orange Bowl record–breaking five

touchdowns confirmed in everyone's mind that he deserved the trophy he'd just been awarded. The final score of 55–19 (coincidentally, USC's highest-scoring bowl game ever) left little room for doubt about which team was the dominant one that year after a season full of fierce competition and aggressive play.

There would be fierce competition over who would be the Trojans' star running back in 2005 as Tailback U made its triumphant return. There were several rising stars, but it was becoming increasingly apparent, in the minds of many, that the best running back to play at Southern Cal, the most electrifying player ever to pull a cardinal and gold jersey over his pads, was number five, Reggie Bush. Like all USC running backs, Bush had to wait his turn, but it happened that his turn seemed to line up perfectly with the building of college football's latest dynasty. He made other players look silly with his all-around talents—as a sophomore—and as the 2005 season loomed, many Trojans fans braced themselves for some incredible football.

Despite facing some coaching changes before the start of the season—including three new offensive and one new defensive assistant—the Trojans started out ranked at number one and rode that wave all the way to the BCS Championship game at the Rose Bowl. The hype surrounding the team was unbelievable—many said it might be the greatest college football team ever assembled. Leinart had decided to bypass the NFL and finish out his college career in the hopes of leading his team to three consecutive National Championships. Reggie Bush was ready to storm the field with two full years of college playing time under his belt and a thirst to prove his dominance.

The 2005 season opened with a bang. In a 63–13 road victory against Hawaii, Leinart took on Colt Brennan—his high-school backup—and Bush took on the Warrior defense, running in two touchdowns. The victory didn't just start out the season on the right foot—it also stretched USC's winning streak to its twenty-third game.

The following week the Trojans were at home, hosting the Arkansas Razorbacks, but they were hardly gracious. On the opening drive, Bush rushed seventy-six yards for a touchdown. This was immediately answered by an Arkansas touchdown pass, but the reciprocal scoring didn't

last long. By the close of the first quarter, USC had added three more touchdowns. The Razorbacks didn't fare much better in the second quarter, when LenDale White rushed in another touchdown and Leinart passed for his fourth of the game. Arkansas managed to hang on with a field goal, making the score 42–10 at the half. White rushed in another touchdown and Leinart passed for another one during the third quarter. The second string took the field, continuing the scoring until the 70–17 victory left Arkansas wondering what had hit them.

Against Oregon—in Eugene the next week—Bush rushed for a touchdown, helping the Trojans score forty-five unanswered points after the Ducks pulled ahead 13–0 in the second quarter. The rally was remarkable, and the Trojans did not allow Oregon to score again. With that victory, the Trojans' winning streak reached its twenty-fifth game—an impressive milestone and an impressive record.

USC stayed on the road, traveling next to Tempe to take on Arizona State. The Sun Devils were ranked at fifteenth in the polls and were projected to put up a good fight, and the game did not disappoint. At halftime, the Sun Devils were leading by eighteen points, but the Trojans came out swinging in the third quarter and took the lead briefly in the fourth with a quarterback sneak by Leinart, before Arizona State stole it back. Finally, scoring two touchdowns in a minute and a half, USC was able to hold on to the lead for a 38–28 win, breaking the Pac-10's consecutive-win record with twenty-six games. Both Reggie Bush and Len-Dale White had run for over 150 yards during the game, which didn't just help USC win the game, but also helped to close the deal on the school's revitalized "Tailback U" status.

In a game that most programs would love to have for their record books, the Trojans couldn't help but feel a little let down after beating Arizona the next week 42–21, after originally being a 38.5 point favorite over the Wildcats. Once again, Bush and White each rushed for over one hundred yards, marking the third consecutive game in which the pair had done so and setting a new school record.

Bush continued to enjoy his breakout season during the Notre Dame game, in which he made one of the most dramatic plays of his college career. During this seventy-seventh matchup between the historic rivals, the Irish came in with a grudge, having lost the last three games, each by thirty-one points. However, they were ranked ninth and seemed deter-

mined to dethrone the Trojans. As the lead changed through the first half, Bush helped to bring the score to 21–14 in favor of USC at the half. During the second half of the game, the Trojans pulled ahead 28–24 with five minutes left in the game, when Bush ran in his third touchdown. They lost the lead when Brady Quinn managed to score another touchdown for the Irish. The final moments of the game were marked by confusion—Leinart fumbling the ball out of bounds, the play clock running the wrong time, and Notre Dame fans rushing the field prematurely. On the final, winning play, Leinart and Bush shone. As Leinart tried to cross into the end zone, he was stopped and looked ready to fall until Bush literally shoved him past the line and into the end zone, in a move that would come to be called the "Bush Push." The result: a 34–31 victory for the Trojans. There had been no question of Bush's inherent talent, but now it seemed unrivaled, uncontested, and unstoppable.

Bush continued on his tear with another commanding performance the following week on the road against Washington. One minute into the second quarter, Bush ran in a touchdown and just two minutes later, caught a Husky punt and returned it eighty-four yards for another touchdown. Leinart threw four touchdowns before the second-string quarterback, John David Booty, was called in to finish the game. The final score was 51–24. Against Washington State, with a 55–13 victory, the Trojans reached the thirty-game mark with their winning streak. There was certainty that Bush, White, Leinart, and kicker Mario Danelo were part of the best team ever to take the college gridiron.

The next game, a grudge match against Stanford, was one of the most highly anticipated of USC's 2005 season. The Cardinal were the last team to hand the Trojans a defeat at home in 2001—and although they weren't ranked this year, there was a lot of recent history that might set the right conditions for a slugfest. It didn't happen. The game opened with five touchdowns, including a rushing score from Bush, and a field goal before the Cardinal managed to get on the scoreboard. The end result was a 51–21 loss for the Cardinal. USC was now at thirty-one straight victories. One more and they would be tied with the sixth-longest streak in history.

The thirty-second win came in the form of the California Golden Bears the very next week. The milestone was made all the better by the fact that Cal had been the last team to defeat the Trojans—back in 2003—the last time the Trojans had traveled to Berkeley. With the 35–10 victory, the Trojans were guaranteed at least a share of the Pac-10 title, and their National Championship dreams were inching closer and closer to reality as they held on to the number-one spot for another week.

One of the most challenging games of the year was the matchup between USC and the Fresno State Bulldogs. Fresno State, a small, scrappy team, had built its reputation on its willingness to duke it out with much bigger competitors. This year they were enjoying a David-and-Goliath season, climbing steadily up the rankings. They would roll into the Los Angeles Coliseum ranked at number sixteen, making them one of the more competitive teams the Trojans would face in regular season play. Like their mascot, the Bulldogs were a stubborn and pugnacious bunch. The Bulldogs were the first to make it on the board. After ending the first quarter tied, Fresno State managed to hold the Trojans to two field goals while racking up two more touchdowns of their own, closing the half with a 21–13 lead. The Trojans collected themselves in the locker room and reemerged ready to do battle in the third quarter. Leinart ran for a touchdown, as did Bush, and then Leinart passed for yet another TD. Bulldog quarterback Paul Pinegar responded by throwing a third touchdown pass for Fresno State. That was followed by Bush's fifty-yard touchdown run, which pulled the Trojans back ahead. Fresno State wasn't done, and they made it to the end zone twice more in the fourth quarter, and with the clock showing just nine minutes left, the Bulldogs were ahead by one point. However, Bush seemed unstoppable. He made a sixty-five-yard run, setting up White to finish the scoring drive. A field goal by Danelo set the score at 50–42, and after intercepting a pass from Pinegar in the final minute of the game, the Trojans celebrated a hard-fought and very sweet victory. Bush was able to celebrate a personal victory, as he set a new Pac-10 record with a total of 513 yards in the game—294 of them rushing. Many fans and commentators felt that if there was any question left in the minds of Heisman voters about who should take the trophy that year, Bush's performance in the USC–Fresno State game settled the matter.

The final game of the regular season was against their hometown rivals, the eleventh-ranked UCLA Bruins. Opening with a field goal by Danelo, the scoring just never seemed to end for the Trojans, as their passing and rushing games continued to rack up the points. Bush ran for two touchdowns in the first half, setting up the Trojans for a 31–6 lead after the second quarter. After halftime, the drives continued, with two touchdowns scored only thirteen seconds apart, thanks to a Bruin fumble. Once again, the starters left the game early and the second string continued the push, scoring another touchdown and finally bringing the score to 66–19. The win brought the Trojans the Pac-10 title and a bid to the BCS National Championship game at the Rose Bowl and tied them for the fourth-longest winning streak ever in college football at thirty-four games. And they were still ranked number one as they set their sights on the Rose Bowl and the Texas Longhorns.

The Heisman buzz had been growing around Reggie during the entire season. As regular-season play drew to a close and the voting ceremony in early December approached, the discussion of Reggie's career plans intensified—and so did the debate between the two men regarding the money Lloyd had supplied to Reggie. As the recordings tell:

Lloyd: Okay, getting his neck on the chopping block is doing what he was doing before that. Risking everything, losing all the money.

LaMar: Well, that's true.

Lloyd: But he did that and so now all of a sudden, everybody's worried about the money Reggie's going to lose. If I wanted to be nasty, I could fuck him out of a whole bunch of money.

LaMar: Go ahead. Do what you think is best.

Lloyd: I said if I wanted to be nasty, like if you think I'm trying to take money from him, I'm just using an example. If I wanted to be nasty . . .

LaMar: But see, I don't need that. That I don't need to hear.

The football world was still focused on Reggie's public concerns—the looming National Championship game that would determine once and for all which team deserved to have the crown for the season. Even before the opening kickoff, the 2006 Rose Bowl was being hailed as one of the greatest college football games of all time. The number-one, undefeated Trojans were taking on the number-two, undefeated Texas Longhorns, led by their quarterback, Vince Young. On January 4, the teams assembled in Pasadena and the sparks started to fly from the opening seconds. The Longhorns only allowed USC three yards on the opening kickoff, but then fumbled the ball on the punt return, allowing the Trojans to recover and eventually score. Both defenses had brought their "A" game, though, and the scoring was held at 7–0 in favor of USC through the first quarter.

Things really heated up in the second quarter. During the second play, Bush made a dramatic move, catching a pass from Leinart and running thirty-five yards to the Texas eighteen-yard line. This provided one of several controversial moments in the game, as he attempted a lateral pass to a teammate, but the ball was recovered by Michael Huff, a Texas strong safety. There was some question—in the replays—about whether USC should have retained control of the ball, since the fumble might actually have been a forward lateral, but no review was called for, so the Longhorns took possession and eventually scored on a forty-six-yard field goal. When the Trojan offense took the field again, they progressed to the twenty-five-yard line before a pass from Leinart was intercepted by Texas free safety Michael Griffin. The Longhorns then marched back down the field, scoring a touchdown in another of the game's controversial moments, when it appeared that Vince Young's knee might have made contact with the ground before he executed a successful lateral to Selvin Young, who carried the ball twelve yards for a TD. Again, no call was made for review, so the score stood. The Longhorns missed their extra point and pulled ahead of the Trojans by the slim margin of 9–7. They then scored again, capitalizing on a defensive stop on USC and fifteen-yard punt return, with a thirty-yard touchdown and successful kick this time, bumping up the score to 16–7. Leinart appeared to throw an interception, caught by Texas safety Drew Kelson. Despite video evidence that seemed to indicate that Kelson was down before the ball flew out of his hands, a review was not called, and it remained USC's ball as the nail-

biting and scrutinizing continued. Trojan wide receiver Dwayne Jarrett caught a pass from Leinart, then Bush made a twelve-yard rush to the thirteen-yard line, but the Texas defense attacked, pushing USC back thirteen yards and forcing a forty-three-yard field goal from Danelo, setting the score at halftime at 16–10 in favor of the Longhorns.

After halftime, the Trojans forced a punt on the Longhorns' opening scoring drive, then scored a touchdown on their next possession—putting them back in the lead by one point, 17–16. Vince Young rushed fourteen yards for a touchdown and kicker David Pino made the extra point to shift the score again, this time to 23–17 in favor of the underdog Texas team. Before the third quarter wrapped up, the Trojans managed another touchdown, throwing the score back in their favor. It was the fifty-seventh career touchdown rushed by LenDale White—his third in this game alone, and a new USC record. There was no time for celebrating. Vince Young carried the ball forty-five yards on a run up the field toward the goal line, but the Trojan defense held firm and forced a fourteen-yard field goal attempt in the first play of the fourth quarter, which proved unsuccessful, keeping the Trojans in the lead by one point.

As the fourth quarter started, the intensity reached an unbelievable level. Bush ran twenty-six yards for another Trojan touchdown, but Texas answered with a thirty-four-yard field goal, closing their deficit to only five points. Leinart made a thirty-three-yard pass to David Kirtman in the next possession that was plussed-up by a penalty against Texas for roughing the passer. Leinart punctuated the drive with a twenty-two-yard pass to score the touchdown, which was followed by the extra point—and USC pulled ahead by twelve points. With less than seven minutes to go, Texas was down by two possessions. A thirty-fifth Trojan victory looked inevitable.

In a remarkable drive that took only 2:39 to complete, Vince Young completed five passes and gained a total of twenty-five yards rushing—including seventeen yards running the ball into the end zone. With the extra point, Texas was now within five points of USC. After a midfield struggle for downs—USC gained one first down but couldn't secure a second—Pete Carroll went for the fourth-and-two conversion at the Texas forty-five-yard line, but the offense only managed to gain one yard, turning over the ball to the Longhorns with 2:13 left to play. The Longhorns

charged down the field. With a fourth down on the eight-yard line and five yards to go, Young racked up his third rushing touchdown of the game with nineteen seconds on the clock. A few moments later, he crossed into the end zone for the two-point conversion and Texas pulled ahead 41–38. With eight seconds remaining, Leinart and the Trojans made a last-ditch effort to win the game, but play ended on the Texas forty-three-yard line as time ran out.

The game was a heartbreaker for USC in more ways than one—not only had they lost the National Championship title and broken their winning streak, but for most of the younger players, it was their first college career loss, and for many of the older players, this was only their second one. The Trojans weren't used to defeat, and it weighed heavily on them as they watched Texas celebrate both the National Championship title and the historic and aptly timed eight hundredth victory of the school's football program.

Southern Cal's football program still had an impressive set of titles behind it for the 2005 season. Pete Carroll was named the Pac-10 Coach of the Year for the second time, and was a finalist for the Eddie Robinson Coach of the Year award; twelve players were named to the All-Conference team and ten were named to All-America teams; Dwayne Jarrett was a finalist for the Biletnikoff Award; Matt Leinart won the Johnny Unitas Golden Arm Award and was a finalist for the Davy O'Brien and Maxwell awards, placed third on the Heisman ballot, and was *Sporting News* Sportsman of the Year. Then there was Reggie Bush.

Bush was named the Pac-10 Player of the Year, won the Doak Walker Award, was a finalist for the Maxwell Award, was named both the Walter Camp Football Foundation Player of the Year for the nation's top running back and the AP Player of the Year, and won the Heisman Trophy with the seventeenth-largest margin of victory and was second only to O. J. Simpson in first-place votes. Reggie Bush had made an indelible mark on USC college football during his junior year and, as he looked ahead, the future became clear. As much as he loved being a Trojan, the NFL beckoned, and Bush was willing to answer the call.

EIGHT

A New Era:

Business Plan Takes Flight

By April 2005, the plans for New Era Sports & Entertainment were building momentum. In that month, Michael Michaels and Lloyd Lake contacted California business attorney Phillip Smith to start the paperwork for the company, which was being called Aggressive Integrity Sports Management, Inc.

At that point, Lake and Michaels funded the company to the tune of $100,000 in startup costs, according to documents obtained from Lake's attorneys. Smith billed the company $1,043.32 on April 5, 2005, for his initial work. On July 9, 2005, LaMar and Denise Griffin, Lake, Michaels, and Barbara Gunner met with Smith to incorporate the business. It was one of several meetings the group had.

As the summer turned to fall, Lake and Michaels started gathering more people.

Agent David Caravantes, who was certified by the NFL Players Association to negotiate contracts, was brought in to be a negotiator. Caravantes brought his assistant, Matt Cohen, a social gadfly and runner who got to know players at the clubs in San Diego and was on the front line of recruiting. Cohen went by the nickname "Hater Proof Homie" on the

Internet. The nickname was a knock on the type of people players often call "Haters," such as reporters and other critics.

Bringing in Caravantes was part of a plan to expand the interests of the agency beyond just marketing. The agency could now be a single-source shop for players who wanted both marketing and contract assistance.

But Caravantes was a small-time agent, representing primarily second-level players. While he had worked with prominent agents such as Joel Segal and Bus Cook during his career, he rarely worked with the top clients. He worked out of his suburban San Diego home and dressed in Tommy Bahama shirts and shorts most of the time when meeting clients.

But when Caravantes heard the rich and powerful Sycuan tribe was involved with Bush and his family, he was quickly hooked. For Caravantes, this kind of backing was what could vault his career as an agent. Bush could put him on the map with the big agents like Segal, Cook, and Tom Condon.

Reggie Bush could fulfill Caravantes's dreams.

Beyond Caravantes and Cohen, the firm brought in James Choe, to handle the organizing and development of the business. Lisa Lake was going to work in public relations and do media training. Lemuel Campbell—Lisa Lake's ex-husband, who had also worked with NFL athletes—was going to be vice president. Other adjunct employees would include Walter Josten, who was going to head the agency's Hollywood productions, Andy Schroeder for postcareer planning, Victor Ross for financial planning, and David Reyes for tax services.

It was all part of Lake and Michaels's grand plan.

"What people don't understand is they think I was trying to be an agent," Lake said, describing the makeup of New Era. "No, I was putting the right people [together]. Say you own a company. . . . That doesn't mean you are actually participating in every aspect of the company. I am not going to be your agent. We got you an agent. But your agent is going to work for this company."

Furthermore, Lake said he and LaMar Griffin started to form a personal bond. Part of that was born of Lake, his family, and Michaels often socializing with Reggie's family. Lake, his sister, his mother, and Michaels went to the Bush family church in San Diego. The church is only a short

drive from where Barbara Gunner ran one of her businesses. Lake and his group also made thousands of dollars in donations to the church, where LaMar Griffin would preach.

In turn, LaMar Griffin started to share family secrets with Lake, even going so far as to discuss his and his stepson's sex lives.

Griffin "was in, he was all partner. That's why he would tell me so much. He was very comfortable. We talked every day," Lake recalled. "Unless you are comfortable with a person, you don't tell him those type of things about your personal life, unless you are really, really, comfortable. That's why I don't understand why he would do that to me, when he told me everything like that. Why would you betray me like that? You don't let somebody get that close to you and then you stab them in the back because they got ammunition now. So it would have been better just to settle the situation and get it over with. You want to sit here and say this all to me. I'm the bad guy, I'm this and that. I don't feel bad telling what I know about him. Sometimes you've got to fight fire with fire. That's just the nature of the whole thing."

On October 7, 2005, the group, along with LaMar Griffin, but not Bush, held a planning and strategy meeting. On November 14, Michaels sent an email to Caravantes (by this time, Caravantes was also using a "New Era" email address) titled "Building New Era's Business Plan."

The plan listed an address for the company and identified eight people as "key personnel" for the company. Among the key personnel were Michael Michaels, David Caravantes, Lloyd Lake, Lisa Lake, and LaMar Griffin.

Still, Michaels and Lake had one major player left to add to their lineup: the Sycuan tribe.

As the business was building momentum, the Sycuan tribe became more interested. Several meetings were held with the tribal council, including Chairman Daniel Tucker. Michaels was there as the conduit to the tribe. During at least two meetings, LaMar Griffin was there to assure the tribe that Reggie Bush would be involved.

"LaMar came in with his Reggie Bush dad jersey on and he told everybody how Reggie was coming to the company for sure," Lake said. "There was no doubt about it. Basically that was it, Sycuan was told."

Lisa Lake, who also attended the meetings, confirmed, "All those meet-

ings at the Sycuan [tribe] that LaMar went to wearing his Reggie Bush jersey. I can't tell you how many times we had those meetings at Sycuan . . . LaMar spoke, 'Reggie's on board.' "

At one point, when Michaels and Lake were having financial problems and couldn't pay Caravantes, Lake said the tribe advanced New Era $10,000. Lake said he delivered the money to Caravantes himself.

But that was only the tip of the iceberg for what Sycuan wanted to do. Again, Sycuan saw Bush as another link to legitimacy for their growing casino and resort operation. While the tribe already had a boxing promotions company, Bush was a different level. He could give the operation a golden face to promote, and he was also a celebrity athlete.

As all this was going on, Bush's stock was soaring. He was leading USC to an undefeated regular season and the top spot in the polls. He was on the cover of magazines and newspapers across the country, being touted as the favorite to win the Heisman over teammate and defending Heisman winner Matt Leinart.

He confirmed the hype with another stellar season following up on his stunning 2004 season. Among his many achievements, he had more than two thousand all-purpose yards for the second consecutive season, which tied an NCAA record. He had five straight games with at least one hundred yards rushing and then had a staggering 554 yards rushing combined in back-to-back wins late in the season against Fresno State and UCLA.

His sixteen touchdowns scored came on plays that averaged 31.6 yards. He tied fellow Heisman Trophy winner Marcus Allen as the only USC back ever to rush for more than 260 yards twice in a career. He also became the first USC back to ever twice rush for more than two hundred yards against archrival UCLA.

As the season was unfolding, the excitement was growing for people planning the company. Lisa Lake was hoping for her brother's sake that Sycuan would act quickly.

"It was getting down to how much they were going to give, what percentage, and where they would get started," she said. "They had gotten to that point. And I said, 'Whatever you are going to do, you gotta hurry up and do it.' That was my little contribution. I kind of sat there and listened. I just kept looking at the calendar. It's getting late in the year

and everybody is going to start coming out of the woodwork [to recruit Bush as a client]. Little did I know he was already in everybody else's pockets. That was what really turned me off to the whole thing. Once you start finding out that Denise and LaMar were getting money when they were in New York [for the Heisman Trophy ceremony in December]. I kept saying, 'Wow, that's a really nice outfit.' "

The bottom line, Sycuan was in, according to Lake.

"Upon Reggie signing [a representation agreement, Sycuan] was going to cut a check for $3.5 million to the company for their percentage," Lloyd Lake said. "We had gotten an agent we were paying a salary to, David Caravantes, and Matt Cohen, David's assistant. This is before we did any of that and I knew that's where we were going next. So I asked Reggie [again], 'Just tell me if we are doing this or not because I got other things I could be doing for sure.' This was something that was cut and dried. It was done. Done deal. All we got to do is sign and we could get the $3.5 million."

It was just what the group needed to hear to proceed. The company became more aggressive about its plans for Bush. According to documents, Caravantes contacted Jay Schulthess, the president of Mercury Sports Management, for advice on marketing for Bush.

On December 8, 2005, Schulthess sent a letter to Bush that actually reads more like an attempt by Schulthess to recruit Reggie away from New Era:

> At the request of your advisors and Dave Carravantes [sic] I am writing to you on behalf of my company Mercury Sports Management. Mercury Sports Management has engaged in and has been very successful in the marketing of our clients. However, most professional athletes never realize their marketing potential, because they sign with agents that either fail to recognize their clients' true talents or fail to have the necessary connections in the marketing industry. We have achieved tremendous successes in the field of sports marketing with our corporate sponsors investing over $45 million in sponsorship dollars and promotions in our clients this coming year.
>
> We will endeavor to exceed the successful marketing goal we have previously achieved for other Mercury Sports Management clientele.

Therefore, you will have the benefit of connecting with sponsors who are currently sponsoring or have sponsored our clients in the last three years. These sponsors include, but are not limited to: Kodak, Sony, Pepsi Cola, EA Sports, Ford, Mountain Dew, Press Pass, Valvoline, Nestle, NesQuik, NEXTEL, Mobil, Puma, Gatorade, Tide, Toyota, Proctor and Gamble, Centrix Financial, Dodge, Line-X, Sirius Satellite Radio, Nestea, the US Army, Zerex, All State and Eagle One.

We plan to contact many of these corporations in order to set the stage for your potential endorsement opportunities upon being drafted. Your endorsement potential will be somewhat determined by the results of the draft, including your future team and your draft selection. However, our goal is to have several endorsement deals completed for you by draft day.

I look forward to meeting with you in the near future. If you have any questions or comments, please feel free to contact me at [—].

Best Regards,
Jay Schulthess
President

On January 3, 2006, the day before USC played in the National Championship game, Schulthess sent an email to Caravantes discussing a promotion Schulthess had set up for Bush at the Super Bowl involving Roger Penske's company.

Schulthess wrote, "This is an article on the gentleman that has invited Reggie to the Super Bowl. I hope that we can all attend as a team."

In another communication, dated December 28, 2005, Caravantes received a reply email from Michael J. Radcliffe, the president and chief executive officer with Image Sports & Entertainment. In the email, Radcliffe wrote:

Dave,

Happy Holidays! After reviewing the brief term sheet, what exactly would you like Image Sports & Entertainment (ISE) to do?

As discussed in past conversations, ISE would bring offers to Mr. Bush, very similar but not limited to the opportunities offered to the Colts superstar Peyton Manning.

Please explain what form of proposal would make for a deal closing package.

Michael J. Radcliffe
President & CEO

All of these communications were before Bush was scheduled to play in the Bowl Championship Series title game against Texas on January 4, 2006 in the Rose Bowl. Although it's not against NCAA rules for agents to line up potential marketing agreements for players who may come out for the draft, it's clear that Bush had given every indication to New Era that he was coming out.

Lake said that the Roger Penske company "was ready to get into business with Reggie. We had the best marketing people that does all the business with NASCAR, that's who we were going to partner up with and get money Reggie would never get from different avenues outside of football. Then with Sycuan, it would have been real good . . . he would have made way more money with us, there's no doubt about it. He would have made way more money if he would have went with us. Sycuan is a billion-dollar company. They open a lot of doors that other companies [can't]. They are mixing and mingling with a lot of people."

To Lisa Lake, the Sycuan involvement made it more stunning that Bush would eventually accuse her brother of extortion, a charge Bush made after *Yahoo! Sports* broke the story about Bush receiving benefits from Michaels and Lake.

"Sycuan, they were contemplating how much to get involved with because they needed money to make the agency work and they even had other players that they had recruited. For [Bush] to turn around and then to start saying all this stuff [about extortion], I was shocked," Lisa Lake said. "Especially because they had professed to be these Christians. I was shocked by that . . . that [Bush] looks at the camera and lies and that he does it so well."

By October, business plans and a brochure were being put together.

On October 7, 2005, the group held a meeting, according to an agenda put together by James Choe. Among the topics for discussion were website development, logo design, business identity (including both personnel and a stationery package), and goals.

Choe identified "website development" as the "flagship" of the opera-

tion. He defined it as the "first extension to those seeking information regarding the agency and its clientele. Must have a professional, sharp, clean image. Not too fancy, basically allowing for the highlights of [New Era] to speak for themselves. Image is everything."

Under "Communication of Desired Image, Representation," Choe wrote: "Who are you? What do you represent? What do you want your clients to feel? Socio-visual strength. What type of presence? Strategy—slowly develop or immediate? Who are your agents? What have they done? What image do we want to give them with your new management group?"

On October 11, Caravantes wrote an email to Choe saying that New Era Sports & Entertainment "will sign at least 10 players this year to the new company. I will ask Chief [Michaels] for more info and photos that will need to go in the brochures. We then need to start it asap."

Choe was then charged with putting together brochures highlighting the business plan of the company. The glossy brochures were detailed and sharp, discussing everything from a summary of career-related services such as contract negotiation to draft preparation to media relations and marketing.

Beyond career counseling, the brochure discussed how the company would help players make the crossover into Hollywood and its entertainment possibilities. It showed that the firm would offer financial planning, tax services, and legal advice. The brochure had biographical information on "The New Era Management Team," with Caravantes listed as the chief executive officer and Cohen as the director of player operations.

The brochure featured a detailed look at preparation for the NFL scouting combine, including plans on how to improve physical and mental performance and even samples of the Wonderlic Personnel Test and the infamous New York Giants four-hundred-question personality exam.

The brochure also discussed the idea of the company helping athletes cross over into the entertainment world. It talked about the company's commitment to charity. Finally, the brochure featured pages and pages of analysis of NFL players and their contracts that Caravantes had helped negotiate.

In early November 2005, Caravantes had Choe put together brochures for the likes of Wisconsin left tackle Joe Thomas (the number-three overall pick in the 2007 draft), San Diego State wide receiver Jeff Webb (a

sixth-round pick by Kansas City in 2006), and Nebraska defensive tackle LeKevin Smith (undrafted because of knee injuries, but signed by New England as a free agent).

Bush was one of the first to receive the brochures, a copy being sent to him through LaMar Griffin. During an interview with the *San Diego Union-Tribune* that month, Griffin showed off a copy of the brochure.

On November 14, Michaels wrote a detailed email to Caravantes titled, "Building New Era's Business Plan." In it, Michaels identified an address for the company at the Aventine Building at 8910 University Center Lane, Suite 660, in San Diego.

More important, Michael Michaels identified eight people as "key personnel" in the email. The eight were he himself, Caravantes, Lisa Lake, Lloyd Lake, LaMar Griffin, Lemuel Campbell, David Reyes, and Walter Josten.

The aggressive building of the company continued into December. Early that month after finishing its regular season, USC was preparing to play Texas for another national championship. Bush began coming through on his end of the bargain to recruit players, at least that's how Lake and Michaels viewed it.

USC teammates Frostee Rucker, a defensive end, and Winston Justice, an offensive lineman who many analysts thought had a chance to be a first-round pick, both went to San Diego. Rucker stayed at the tribe's resort in El Cajon and Justice stayed at the Hotel Solemar, according to a receipt uncovered by *Yahoo! Sports.* Both used limousines to party around town during their weekend stays, Michaels and Lake picking up the tab.

Neither Rucker nor Justice signed with New Era Sports & Entertainment, although Caravantes thought that even in January he had a chance to sign Rucker. Both were eventually drafted. Rucker was taken by Cincinnati in the third round in 2006. Justice was taken by Philadelphia in the second round that year.

Said Lake of Bush's efforts to bring players to the company: "I went to a couple of [USC's] practices. [Bush] introduced me to Winston Justice. He was basically telling me that's who we should go recruit, too. He's playing along the whole time like he's in."

To most people involved with New Era Sports & Entertainment, the plan seemed to be progressing. That is, to everyone but Lake. The streetwise Lake began to see how the plan was going to unravel because of

things he was reading about Bush and the double-talk he was getting from Bush and LaMar Griffin starting in late November.

During the taped conversations in December, Lake started to question the logic he was getting from Griffin as he started saying that Bush might not join:

> **LaMar:** Your time is still—I'm going to tell you what me and Mike talked about yesterday when he picked me up from the airport. And this is what Mike said, and you can call Mike and ask him. Mike said, "Look, I don't know if we're going to get Reggie or not, but we've done signed so many other guys already." He said that, "No, we might not get the big money, and that's a loss, a cut that you take." See, you talking to you, and talking to him is different. Mike is a businessman.
>
> **Lloyd:** Mike ain't a businessman. Not saying that, because right now this business, this business is going to fall apart.
>
> **LaMar:** Why?
>
> **Lloyd:** Who's going to pay Dave [Caravantes] that money every month?
>
> **LaMar:** What are you talking about? You're making money off the clients that you have.
>
> **Lloyd:** When did the clients come in? When do we get paid off of them?
>
> **LaMar:** They come at the end of the year when they get contracts.
>
> **Lloyd:** OK, you know how much we got to give them and pay them to train and everything?
>
> **LaMar:** Well, then pay them. What are you talking about? Mike says, and you told me and Mike told me, "If Sycuan don't come into the business, we'll be OK."

At another point in the conversations, Griffin tried to distance himself:

LaMar: I can't be on the same team, I've got to be in the middle of it. I can't go against him, and I can't go against you. But that's my son.

Lake: I understand that and I respect that, but all I'm saying is listen. Let's listen to logic one time, OK?

LaMar: What?

Lloyd: OK, let's say this. You know Sycuan's coming in and it's going to be me and you because I think they got to get Mike out of the business. Me and you and Sycuan. They are giving us $3 million. Reggie's coming in with $3 million behind us to push the company with his name.

LaMar: OK, now stop right there. I know what you're saying, Lake.

Lloyd: Hold on, I didn't get to finish $3 million to get his name. We got [agent] Dave [Caravantes] and we got [agent] Bus [Cook]. Bus is one of the best agents, period.

LaMar: I know, I've talked to Bus. Go ahead and finish.

Lloyd: So you know for sure Reggie's contract is getting done right, right? So you are not going to lose any money. We've got the group of Penske and NASCAR to do our marketing with us, fifty-fifty, right? So you tell me why would Reggie want to go with someone else that's not going to give him any ownership in anything?

LaMar: Now see, now stop right there. You're talking to dead—now that same thing you gotta bring to the thing and say, "Reggie, this is what we've got."

Lloyd: And you know what? I want you to talk to Reggie, too, because I found out through a partner that damn [actor] Faizon [Love] told Reggie some shit about me as far as like a record or something that I've been in trouble.

LaMar: Now you're name's going around like somebody's bread, bro. I'm going to tell you something, Lake. If you keep telling me that—I don't come to you about stuff like that. I heard something about you in New York. I heard something about you when I went down to L.A. Man, you are the talk of the town about you.

Even though the business was beginning to teeter through the middle of December 2005, Caravantes was sending emails to Michaels about booking airline tickets for potential clients, such as Eastern Washington running back Joe Rubin. Rubin was supposed to make a recruiting visit to San Diego. In late December and early January, Caravantes received emails at his New Era Sports & Entertainment email address detailing travel itineraries for San Diego State offensive lineman Jasper Harvey to attend the East-West Shrine Game in San Antonio and for Rubin, defensive back Marques Binns of Oregon, linebacker Naivote Taulawakeiaho of San Diego State and Roderkus Wright, a defensive end who had once attended Oregon, to attend All-American Classic.

Both the Shrine Game and All-American Classic were postseason all-star games where players who had recently used up their college eligibility would play to show off their talent for NFL scouts and coaches.

As that was going on, Lake and Michaels were trying to save the business. Around New Year's Eve, days before Bush played against Texas, Lake put him on the phone with Caravantes, according to two sources. A few days after that, Lake put Caravantes on the phone with infamous rap producer Suge Knight, telling Caravantes that Knight might help fund New Era Sports & Entertainment if Sycuan dropped out.

Still, the bottom line is that from all this activity it was clear that New Era Sports & Entertainment was working toward becoming a legitimate business entity, not simply a pipe dream or even a sophisticated scheme hatched by Lake, Michaels, Bush, and Griffin.

Caravantes and Michaels continued to exchange emails, about players and the progress of the business, even after Bush started to bail on the company.

On January 15, 2006, Caravantes wrote to Michaels in an email: "I feel confident with you in charge and can handle everything with Sycuan. Please let me know when you can help Matt [Cohen] and me. I do need to get out to Texas tomorrow to sign Frostee."

Michaels replied the next day: "Nice list. I hadn't even thought of what the success of it could be without Reggie. I think there's something there. I'm gonna talk with my attorney tomorrow and get this thing funded."

On January 18, 2006, Caravantes followed up with another email to Michaels: "Hey what's going on. I need to know if we are a go and going

forward. We have our QB Justin Holland coming back Thursday and will need to room and Matt is getting kick out of his place because he has not been paid correctly. I need some assurance we are moving forward with Sycuan and need financial help now. Sorry to be so blunt. Please get back to me A.S.A.P. I have tried calling you for two days now."

Michaels replied on January 19, 2006: "I've had court testimony for the last two days and it's been tough. I have talked to our attorney and we're going to set things up to take over New Era 100%. You will need to submit up to date numbers for salaries and operating budget. ALL THE NUMBERS for operations and capital expenditures. Thanks for list of clients. I am confident that this will be successful."

On January 20, 2006, Michaels followed up with another email to Caravantes, attorney Brian Watkins, and Scott Matthews, a friend of Michaels. Wrote Michaels: "I want to introduce you three. Brian [my attorney] meet Dave [sports agent, New Era] and Scott [Hollywood consultant]. Scott, meet Dave and Brian. Dave, meet Brian and Scott. I've been tied up by with this US Grant litigation. We should win the case though. $5,000,000 on the line. I need your coordinated, professional assistant with this RB thing. Brian, can you take the lead and talk to Dave and Scott. They're trust worthy and may assist you with things we need. Dave . . . Call the Resort, tell them what you need. Email me what you tell them and I'll call them to confirm later. It'll be done. Scott . . . I'm working on all the paperwork moving us forward. Thanks for patience and understanding. Crazy, I know?? Thanks Guys . . . this will soon be a thing of the past."

However, by the end of the month, New Era Sports & Entertainment appeared to be close to the end. On January 30, 2006, Caravantes emailed Michaels again, requesting money: "How are Matt & I supposed to keep this thing going without being paid for the last two months now and no money to live on. I am at my breaking point. We need help until it goes over to Sycuan."

Michaels replied at 2:05 A.M. on January 31, 2006, with a telling email: "I understand totally. Lloyd is a friend, however, his business practices have compromised some good situations. I'm out over $200K CASH with these damn guys! I trusted him and I trusted Reggie. Now they're both acting like idiots. I wish them luck. It's unfortunate that we are at

this point. And I am doing what I can do. I know you're stressed. But you have no right to threaten suit against me and at the same time ask for a loan or something. You must be that far gone. I was willing to personally loan you and Matt money, but you guys added too much insult to my injuries. I'm very well known for being straight up, generous and a man of his word. However, I REFUSE to be disrespected and/or walked on. I know none of this makes sense to you right now because your only goal is to get some money, in which you are rightfully entitled to (and then some). You need to show that you know who it is you are mad at and not release those frustrations in the wrong direction. We should be able to meet with Danny or Glenn sometime after 10 am tomorrow [Tuesday the thirty-first]. Explain to them the good and the bad of New Era. Where it stands and its potential, and your and Matt's financial situation. I'll try to get Kam Li or Fred Taylor on the line. They're our attorneys working to create the entity under Sycuan umbrella. Tomorrow, I think Sycuan will cut you and Matt a check. Bring those operating budgets that you had regarding the payroll."

"Danny" from that message was Daniel Tucker, the chairman of the Sycuan Tribal Council. "Glenn" was Glenn Quiroga, the president of Sycuan Ringside, the tribe's boxing promotion company.

At this point, New Era Sports & Entertainment was basically on life support. The tribe never ended up funding the company.

All that was left was for the story to blow up.

NINE

A Second Lover:

Michael Ornstein

In the summer before the 2005 season, the University of Southern California approved a summer internship for star running back Reggie Bush to work for marketing agent Mike Ornstein.

Bush and Ornstein filled out all the paperwork for USC, which in turn submitted everything to the NCAA. As the paperwork was rubber stamped, it was the official beginning of a relationship that ultimately may have bounced back against USC. Strangely, USC ignored Ornstein's sometimes criminal and always controversial past in allowing Bush to work for him.

But for Bush, who was already taking money from one suitor, the alignment with Ornstein was more of what he was after: a way to cash in while in school and be ready to cash in after he turned pro. Ultimately, Ornstein used his guile to steal Bush away from New Era Sports & Entertainment, the fledgling sports marketing company Bush had agreed to start during the 2004 season.

As Bush was working for Ornstein, he made no secret of it to Lake and Michaels. Bush even told Lake he was taking money from Ornstein.

"He told me about Ornstein," said Lake. "That's the only person he

ever told me about. It was like he was using Ornstein. . . . That's how he played it to me. Basically, 'I'm taking money from him, but we're still doing what we're doing. I'm working for him and I'm using him.'

"I knew he was taking money elsewhere. I know a lot of people in L.A. and a lot of people in different circles."

Still, Lake said he wasn't worried because Bush had given his word and because Lake and Michaels were so heavily invested in the project.

"[That's] part of the business. I couldn't react because of the simple fact you know that's going on and I can't tell him don't take money because somebody said, 'OK, here goes $500.' It's not like, 'Here goes $500, you're coming with us.' There's giving it to you just because they want you to think about them. They just want to leave something on your mind.

"This is at the beginning, but I know that's going to be. Everybody's getting money, but we just gave a substantial amount of money and we had an agreement. . . . We had a verbal agreement. It wasn't like there goes $500 just so you can think about it, just giving it to you to give because we want a chance to get you. All of this is supposed to be done. So that's the difference. So I'm not concerned."

That changed by December 2005, when Lake not only heard that Ornstein attended the Heisman Trophy ceremony with Bush's family, but was told in a taped conversation with LaMar Griffin that Ornstein had helped line up prospective contract agents for Bush to interview. Griffin also implied in the conversation that Ornstein had threatened to sue Bush and his family at one point:

LaMar: I've never said, and I told Reggie, I've never said I would not support the company because I'm part of the company.

Lloyd: But you're not supporting them with Reggie, so that would be not supporting.

LaMar: But see, but Reggie, you don't know how many times I've talked to Reggie about this. I've talked to Reggie almost all the time about this. I mentioned it to [Michaels], I even talked to [Michaels] about doing marketing because you might not pick him, but we can do marketing with [Michaels], and he said, "Yeah, we'll do

that, but we have to see what marketing that he has." So I have been talking to him but still, Reggie you know he has his own mind, and he's going to pick who he wants. I'm not trying to make [Michaels]—I told [Michaels] when we went and ate together—I said, "I'm not trying to put you out or put you down or anything else like that," and see [Michaels] is the one who said, "I know that you're family, and if this was my son, I know how you feel." That's what [Michaels] said. What he tells you, I don't know. But [Michaels] told me, he said. "I know how you feel, and it's up to Reggie." He said, "Some business opportunities don't come out the way they are, but we can still make this thing work." That's what [Michaels] said. Maybe Reggie might not like the guy that he picked if he don't pick y'all and come on board, because he can fire an agent any time he feel like it. But what I'm saying is that if that doesn't work, we still got guys we can work with that can work, but it might not be Reggie Bush. Any business opportunity you gotta look at, just like [Michaels] said, you gotta look at the pros and the cons. You might not get what you want, but then again, you might just gain something somewhere else. People gotta take a loss sometimes to get what you want. And that's the only thing I would say, and I never told [Michaels] I wasn't going to be—because he asked me, "Are you going to help out, will Reggie help get other guys?" I said, "I know a bunch of kids that trust what I say, but I know Reggie is a big-time player." And everybody wants Reggie. That's what you gotta understand, Lake, everybody is talking in Reggie's ear, everybody.

Lloyd: And that damn Mike Ornstein, he's a major influence.

LaMar: Everybody's talking. But I'm going to tell you something about Mike [Ornstein], he's not telling Reggie what to do neither. Reggie said, "Pick out some agents, set him up, talk to JC [Pearson], get his agents to set them up, and then we'll interview them." [Ornstein] calls me every day and tells me everything that's going on with Reggie, everything. If it's from marketing, who wants to talk to him, when me and my wife need to come down there, he tell me. As a matter of fact, he called me this morning, he tells me everything. I told him, "If you don't tell me everything, I'm going

to kick your ass, lawsuit or not, because I want to know." [Ornstein] has not said, "Reggie, don't go with that company in San Diego." He's just saying, "You pick the ones, we'll interview them." So we picked the ones we want to interview—

Lloyd: [Ornstein is] going to be in on the interview, too?

LaMar: "No. It's just going to be me and my wife, JC, and Javon."

As the conversation progressed, Lake became increasingly critical of how Bush and his family allowed Ornstein to become involved:

LaMar: That's only fair to look and see what else is out there. I wouldn't commit myself to one agency and not knowing nothing and not seeing anything. You said that yourself last time.

Lloyd: I wouldn't either, but at the same time, I wouldn't—see, he let the Mike [Ornstein] dude get in his ear and set it up. Hey, I'm not a dummy.

LaMar: Hey, you know what? You are a dummy because you're listening to stuff.

Lloyd: I'm not listening to no one. I know having him in [Ornstein's] office, [Ornstein's] going to bug that damn office.

LaMar: No, he's not bugging no office.

Lloyd: Shit. OK, you keep thinking that. You guys, you're the same motherfuckers that got us enslaved, man, with the mentalities that you guys got. The same goddamn Europeans—the Europeans came as guests.

LaMar: It's time for me to go, man.

Lloyd: That's the mentality. "Oh, he's not going to do this, he's not going to do that." That's your mentality. When the Europeans went to Africa, they came as guests.

LaMar: OK, now tell me something, and I'm going to say something to you. Why should I trust you any more than I trust [Ornstein]? Why? Because you gave me some money? Because you helped my family out? I don't trust you no more than I trust Mike Ornstein, than I trust J. C. Pearson. The only person I trust in is God.

Griffin's explanation that Ornstein wouldn't take part in the interviews of prospective agents ended up being inaccurate. Bush had Ornstein take part in the interviews while his mother and brother did not.

The overriding point is that Lake badly underestimated Ornstein, an extremely well-connected former NFL team and league executive who got his start with the Oakland Raiders in 1975. Lake also underestimated the lengths to which Ornstein—who counts the likes of Marcus Allen, Tim Brown, and Warren Moon as close friends—would go to get Bush.

Like Lake, Ornstein was a convicted felon. In the early 1990s, Ornstein became a key figure in NFL Properties, a marketing entity with the league that was competing with the NFL Players Association for a deal.

Eventually, Ornstein was one of three men convicted, Ornstein pleading guilty to one count of mail fraud. Ornstein was sentenced to five years' probation and four months of home confinement and was ordered to pay $160,000 in restitution plus fines by a federal judge. Privately, the NFL banned him from ever setting foot in the league offices again. Shortly after he was sentenced, NFL owners held a special meeting with former commissioner Paul Tagliabue to discuss the punishment Ornstein received.

"I was kind of caught up in something that somebody else did and I kind of took a fall for it," Ornstein told *Yahoo! Sports* in August 2006. "Anybody who knows the true story knows I was more of a victim than the cause. But to be a good soldier, I took a bullet for the NFL and didn't make a big issue of it. Just faded away from it. I think the fact that it happened to me shows the kind of person that I am."

In Ornstein's defense, he did a good job of getting Reggie Bush numerous endorsements, before the 2006 draft, when Bush unexpectedly went number two overall to New Orleans rather than going number one to Houston. Bush has gotten deals with companies such as Pepsi, Adidas, Subway, and EA Sports. He has also been used prominently by the NFL in commercials to promote the league and by ESPN. In only his second season, Bush ranked with the likes of Peyton Manning and Tom Brady among the most visible players in the league.

In 2006, Bush also helped extensively with charity work in New Orleans in the aftermath of Hurricane Katrina. Bush donated more than $50,000 to Holy Rosary Academy to help keep the special-needs school operational. He paid $86,000 for a new playing surface at a football sta-

dium used by numerous New Orleans high schools. His charitable efforts also have included partnering with the international hunger relief organization Feed The Children, the NFL Players Association, and Urban Impact Ministries to help deliver food and toiletries to needy families in New Orleans.

Almost all of that was arranged by Ornstein.

"Ornstein has done a heck of a job marketing [Bush]," long-time agent Leigh Steinberg said. "There's the irony. Mike Ornstein has done an amazing job and you can't get around that. You had Matt Leinart, Vince Young, and Reggie Bush in the same draft. If you were handicapping that, there's no way Reggie Bush ends up being the endorsement king of that draft.

"I've never seen anything like it. I thought those three were the three greatest marketing athletes to come out of college in the same year. You have the Hollywood quarterback from USC, from the second-largest TV market in America. You have the quarterback of the national champion Texas Longhorns, who have among the greatest and most rabid followings of all college teams. And you have the human highlight reel Heisman-winning running back. [There have] never been three players like that before. Ornstein has blown those other two players off the screen."

Some have contended that anyone could have marketed Bush effectively. Steinberg disagreed. "Not true. History is replete with players that haven't gotten what some might say they deserve. Reggie will never be on that list. He's a part-time player playing in a marginal market. He took it one step further. He did a PSA [public service announcement] for Darfur relief. I called Ornstein and told him I have waited thirty years to see an athlete do something like that. Michael Jordan wouldn't do it. Tiger Woods wouldn't do it. I told Mike I was proud of Reggie. That's the complexity of human life. The same person who can do things that don't make sense can be the person who leaves an incredible legacy," Steinberg said.

But others in NFL circles do not paint as favorable a portrait of Ornstein, who also was subpoenaed by a U.S. grand jury in northeastern Ohio in September 2006 as part of an investigation into ticket scalping and tax evasion revolving around a consulting job Ornstein had with the Cleveland Browns from approximately 2002 to 2004.

"Why does anybody plead guilty to a felony?" one NFL team executive pointed out. "It's because they're afraid they're going to be convicted of other felonies . . . the NFL had the goods on Ornstein and I don't understand why he's still around the league in any capacity."

The other question may be why USC allowed a convicted felon to work with one of the highest-profile athletes in the country and in school history. USC athletic director Mike Garrett and football coach Pete Carroll both declined to be interviewed for this book.

According to Ornstein's former business partner, Lee Pfeifer, the relationship between Ornstein and Bush started before the summer of 2005. Pfeifer and Ornstein were partners in CWC Sports until April 2005. Pfeifer remembered seeing Bush in the company offices at one point with Ornstein.

"Before we split in 2005, I saw him in the office a lot. I didn't think anything of it because Mike had athletes come in all the time. I don't think he was an intern . . . we split in April of 2005, so I think he was an [intern] in May or June," said Pfeifer, who was one of the first witnesses to speak with the NCAA in the organization's investigations of Bush. "He was recruiting him in his own way. I didn't know what was going on behind the scenes . . . while [Ornstein] was working for me. He obviously had some kind of relationship with Reggie he was building.

"You think Reggie Bush is a great guy? He's a kid. Not a very articulate kid, not a smart kid. He's a street kid. And Mike just sucks up to him. He gave him some good deals. He made him some money. Mike does know football. He has a lot of contacts. He did have some use. I am not saying he didn't perform. The way he did things was just not the way I wanted to do business."

An NFL source with extensive knowledge of Ornstein said the techniques Ornstein employed were similar to those used in counterespionage.

"It's the classic way CIA operatives used to turn Russian spies," the source said. "Mike starts with little gifts, small things that ingratiate him. Then the gifts get bigger and bigger until it's like there's a bond, a sense of loyalty."

What impressed Bush was that Ornstein had plenty of relationships with other people, particularly in and around the NFL. Ornstein was a consultant for Reebok. In 1997 and 2001, he had worked as a consultant

with Green Bay and Baltimore, respectively, when each made it to the Super Bowl. He had been brought on as a partner with *MOVES* magazine, a lifestyle magazine targeted for athletes and sports executives, but otherwise not available to the general public.

Bush was on the cover of the 2005 winter edition of the magazine. *MOVES'* CEO and publisher Scott Miller told *Yahoo! Sports* in 2006 that he had known Ornstein for almost ten years.

"[Ornstein is] probably as well-connected, certainly in the NFL, as almost anybody I've ever met," Miller told *Yahoo! Sports.* "I'm constantly amazed. There's virtually no one I call in any sport that doesn't know him."

Those connections go all the way to the top of the NFL's food chain to commissioner Roger Goodell and former commissioner Paul Tagliabue.

"I have seen him talking with Tagliabue," Miller said. "I'm not going to tell you what was said in the conversation. But, yes, I have certainly seen him talk to Paul Tagliabue. . . . I've seen him talk to the commissioner many times . . . Paul Tagliabue. Mike Shanahan. Bill Parcells. They all know him. They all call him Orny."

However, Miller suggested another nickname was more appropriate.

"Call him the Godfather," Miller said.

In an interview with *Yahoo! Sports*, Ornstein said, "The Godfather, I don't know about that. But I've been doing it for thirty years. If you don't know everybody after thirty years, you must be doing something wrong. Whether it's the equipment managers, the trainers, the coaches, the players, the general managers, they know me. And most of them I have a pretty good relationship with. They know me as a guy that can get something done."

What Ornstein got done for Bush and his parents was more of what they were already getting from Michaels and Lake: cash and other benefits.

According to a *Yahoo! Sports* report in September 2006, the first direct alleged violation occurred in November 2005 when Ornstein paid for Bush's family to travel from San Diego to Oakland to watch Bush play against the University of California. LaMar, Denise, and son Jovan Griffin flew to Oakland on Southwest Airlines, leaving on flight 558 at 6:35 P.M. on Friday, November 11. From the airport, the three took a limousine to the Ritz Carlton Hotel in San Francisco where they stayed for the week-

end. They returned on flight 700, departing Oakland on Sunday, November 13, at 9:05 A.M.

The airline tickets, which came to a combined total of $595.20, were paid for with an American Express card ending in 4007 on October 26, 2005. The American Express card belonged to Jamie Fritz, an Ornstein employee who also worked for Pfeifer before Ornstein and Pfeifer split. Fritz's card was later used to purchase a Southwest Airlines ticket for Ornstein when he went from Los Angeles to Nashville on August 11, 2006, to attend Bush's exhibition game against Tennessee the next day.

The records were uncovered by Pfeifer.

"Since everything was under CWC when they booked those reservations, I was checking my own thing and I saw this. My ex–travel agent was under CWC so they made the reservation under CWC . . . I saw those records and said I wanted all my records.

"When I saw the record I said, 'What's this?' " Pfeifer recalled.

Ornstein denied giving Bush or his family benefits and called the accusation a lie. Ornstein said the purchase of airline tickets was merely a loan through Fritz and was repaid by Bush's family.

"Reggie Bush never received an extra benefit from Mike Ornstein other than what he was allowed to get from the NCAA when he worked with us," Ornstein told *Yahoo! Sports*, referring to pay Bush received as an intern. "I feel pretty damn good about that."

When asked about why Fritz paid for the airline tickets and limo ride, Ornstein said there was a reason.

"Jamie may have paid or put it on his credit card," Ornstein said. "I don't think [Reggie's] parents have a credit card, but his parents paid for everything."

Fritz declined comment when reached by *Yahoo! Sports.*

According to Pfeifer and another source, Fritz booked the trips on his American Express card to get benefit points to help pay for travel expenses. At the time, Fritz was working in Ornstein's Santa Monica office, but his wife was living in New York.

The card establishes a direct link between Bush's family and Ornstein's office while Bush was still at USC, but Ornstein insisted it was merely a matter of helping the family.

"If the dad asked, then maybe [Jamie helped]," he said. "The [family]

went on other trips. I'm sure the father—if it was anything that needed a credit card to guarantee the hotel and everything—then I'm sure Jamie will have documentation and cash receipts from the father. I guarantee it."

As early as December 2005, word had gotten back to Lloyd Lake that Ornstein was paying for plane tickets. During one of the taped conversations from that month, Lake and LaMar Griffin discussed the plane tickets. Griffin double-talked his way through the discussion, first seeming to claim that he paid for the tickets and then saying that it didn't matter if Ornstein had purchased the tickets because it wouldn't be considered a violation. However, under NCAA rules, such a purchase would be.

Lloyd: [I heard] that [Ornstein] has been buying you guys' plane tickets and stuff like that on his credit card and he's going to try to bribe with that.

LaMar: Ain't nobody going to bring that, I figured y'all got them.

Lloyd: OK, well, that's the rumor then.

LaMar: No, the last couple of times we went out of town, y'all paid for that.

Lloyd: No.

LaMar: When we went to Frisco? No, no, no. We'd used his travel agent, he didn't pay for it. We used it because she got the best deal for us.

Lloyd: Well, that's against the rumor, that's what I heard.

LaMar: Well, we paid for that stuff. And if he did buy us plane tickets, it doesn't matter. It's not going to screw up Reggie if somebody bought plane tickets. He's not an agent. It ain't going to screw nothing up if he did it. He could have bought a ticket to damn Tokyo.

Lloyd: If he wanted to, huh.

LaMar: It doesn't matter, as long as he ain't no agent.

Ornstein was asked if he knew that such loans could constitute an NCAA violation.

"I have no idea," he said.

According to NCAA bylaw 12.3.1.2: An athlete shall be deemed ineligible if he or she accepts benefits from agents or marketing representatives. Furthermore, the rule states that student-athletes, their family, or friends cannot receive benefits or loans from agents and marketing representatives. Under NCAA bylaw 12.1.2.1.6, athletes also cannot receive preferential treatment, benefits, or services because of the individual's athletics reputation or skill or payback potential as a professional athlete, unless such treatment, benefits, or services are specifically permitted under NCAA legislation.

Yahoo! Sports continued to investigate other elements of the trip, such as the stay at the Ritz Carlton Hotel. On October 3, 2006, after *Yahoo! Sports* made several calls to the management of the Ritz Carlton, attorney David Cornwell sent an email to *Yahoo! Sports* reporter Jason Cole and approximately a dozen other reporters at various news outlets around the country, including Mark Maske of the *Washington Post*, Michael Wilbon of the *Washington Post*, and Sam Farmer of the *Los Angeles Times.*

> "The Ritz Carlton asked me to intercede on its behalf to request that you stop harassing its employees with your repeated telephone calls. You should have concluded by now that your calls will not be returned. Now, you know for sure. We expect that your harassment will cease. Immediately."

Bob DeMartino, a memorabilia dealer who tried to negotiate a contract with Ornstein for Bush, said he witnessed an "allowance" payment Ornstein made to Bush's family during the weekend of the Heisman Trophy ceremony in December 2005.

According to an April 2006 report by the *Miami Herald* and a September 2006 report by *Yahoo! Sports*, Ornstein borrowed $500 from him to help make an "allowance" payment to Bush's family. DeMartino, who has known Ornstein for about twenty years, said he was at the family's hotel

in New York to meet with them about a memorabilia proposal that he had submitted to Ornstein in November.

"We were standing around waiting for the family to show up," DeMartino said, recalling the December 9 meeting. "Mike says to me, '[expletive], it's pay day.' He looked in his wallet, said he was a little short and asked me if he could borrow some money till the next day so he could give the family their money."

DeMartino said Ornstein explained to him that Bush's stepfather received a weekly payment of $1,000. Bush's mother received $500, and Bush's younger brother also received money.

"I'm not going to lie for the guy [Ornstein]. You asked me a question, I'm going to tell you the truth," said DeMartino, who received payment after settling a financial dispute with Ornstein. The day after settling, DeMartino told *Yahoo! Sports* that he stood by his statements regarding his interaction with Ornstein in New York.

"That is a 100 percent lie," Ornstein told *Yahoo! Sports.* "That never happened. I swear on my son, I swear on my mother, I swear on my brother. . . . I swear on my whole family. Let them all die tomorrow if I'm telling a lie."

DeMartino said Ornstein introduced him to Bush's family as "Reggie's memorabilia dealer" during that weekend. The deal eventually fell through after a series of email negotiations between the two failed to produce.

But the problem with that is that Ornstein was operating as Bush's marketing agent *before* Bush had even declared that he was going pro, let alone finished his season with the Trojans on January 4, 2006.

On December 14, 2005, DeMartino sent an email to Ornstein regarding the deal, which originally was supposed to include USC quarterback Matt Leinart. Leinart's representatives expressed only moderate interest in the deal before backing out, DeMartino said.

Mike,

Keep this confidential. The numbers remain the same as you have now . . . but . . . if we can do both Reggie and Matt, we can get up to the numbers attached . . . realize that we can for 3 years command a premium by being the only place any one can get both sigs on the

same item . . . that would bring Reggie's number over 4 million and Matt's over 6 million.

Also, as we discussed, Mark is willing to give both Matt and Reggie 1% of the company, Athlete Shares, meaning they would earn on every player that comes on board for the life of the company and earn should the company ever go public, beyond just their deals. Further, we have a point (1%) of the business that we can give to you or split ½%–½% for you and whoever it needs to go to for Leinart. Again, that represents an interest in every player that we contract for.

Call me with any questions.

Separately we need to know, if we can find the 500K, will that be paid back from the first money on ANY marketing money that comes in . . . for example; should Reebok pay him $1,000,000 on January 20th, can that 500K be paid back from that . . . basically a bridge loan.

Also, I need to reach out on a $2,000,000+ Bret Favre LLC we want to do. Let me know what the scoop is with Leinart . . . also, we really should meet with the family (Bush's also) to make sure this is presented properly. That way if any questions arise your off the hook also because we presented it.

Bob DeMartino

On December 29, Ornstein sent an email to DeMartino about the deal.

Bob, I am in the office today, At this time I am going to have to start looking at other deals for Reggie, I believe in this program, but like a NFL team that will be giving Reggie a 30 million bonus up front, because they believe in his future, you guys are not willing to take that chance. If you believe in your program and the ability to get it done, you need to take a little risk. That risk is 500,000. Let me know. Orny.

DeMartino replied to Ornstein on the same day.

Mike,

Attached is a document explaining exactly how we can proceed with the Athlete Shares Memorabilia Program presented to you, Gary Wachard and Chuck Price as it relates specifically to Reggie Bush and/or Matt Leinart and the financial request/requirement that was presented to Athlete Shares.

Mark and I fully understand that you (collectively or individually) requested a $500,000 payment for both Bush and Leinart from Athlete Shares that would assure the Athlete Shares Memorabilia Program could begin implementation as soon as Bush and Leinart's NCAA eligibility was completed.

Your team explained the reasons for the required payment and Mark addressed the realities, requirements and regulations that the Athlete Shares Memorabilia Program faces with regard to regulatory agency requirements and documentation when dealing with investors. That notwithstanding, we have been able to address those issues and have laid out what really is the only viable option (herewith attached) to meet the financial requirement you proposed. The attached is self-explanatory and accomplishes what everyone needs. That being said, it is NOT the unsecured, non refundable, unconditional payment you requested. Frankly, we will not pay a fee of that nature simply for the right to implement the Athlete Shares Memorabilia Program, a program that I know you will agree will not come close to being matched by any party in the memorabilia industry.

That being said, take a look at the attached, and give Mark or me a call with your thoughts.

Separately, Athlete Shares has other programs being implemented with current professional athletes as we speak and we are in the process of kicking off these other Athlete Shares Memorabilia Programs. Additionally, we discussed the opportunity at the Sundance Film Festival, whereby we are preparing to promote the Athlete Shares programs and athletes to those in the entertainment industry, something I think both Bush and Leinart would benefit from. Also, Mark put some equity on the table should these Athlete Shares Programs come to fruition so I hope that the attached in manageable and can be implemented.

Bob DeMartino

On January 2, 2006, DeMartino sent another email to Ornstein.

Mike,

Give me a call.

Just so you know, we worked out that last piece of the Bush puzzle in respect of an advance against revenues, and we're prepared to present it to Reggie and his family.

Bob DeMartino

On January 9, 2006, DeMartino sent yet another email to Ornstein about the deal.

Mike,

We're having a problem with the investor who agreed to put up the $500,000 advances for Bush/Leinart. The investor has insisted on being in the loop this whole time, and, quite frankly, has gotten skittish about (a) the delay in getting a signed commitment agreement, (b) discussions about taking cards out of the deal (which would have increased his risk), and (c) the back and forth between you and Athletes First. Quite honestly, this has taken too long, has stretched out too far, and should have been completed last Friday.

Unfortunately, the investor has just informed us that, since we don't have a signed deal, he is pulling out. We are still working with him, but at this point, we can no longer offer the $500,000 advance as part of the deal pending our resolution of the issue with the investor.

What we can offer, however, is that the athlete gets distributions of the first $500,000 in proceeds from all sales pending the sale of the deal. Accordingly, these guys won't get a lump sum on day 1, but they will get a large amount of money and still will not miss out on any deals.

In the end, this deal is STILL far and away the best deal for the athletes—especially in consideration of what fragile careers can be (ie: Carson Palmer yesterday). They will begin receiving revenues from the LLC immediately, and they will get a lump sum payout upon the sale of the shares (which will occur as quickly as possible).

It should be noted that the $500,000 advance was never intended to be part of this deal. You made this promise to the athletes, and we did everything that we could to make it happen. In the end, the investor got cold feet and, despite our best efforts, we could not accommodate this request, at no fault of our own. All we can do is offer the two largest memorabilia deals in the history of the NFL to the athletes.

I have to tell you, I am pissed at all the time and effort we put into this, and still today we have nothing ready to go. The numbers are there, these two deals are still ready to be implemented, but the bullshit has got to stop. . . . I can't believe these two kids are potentially going to lose multimillion-dollar memorabilia deals, the like of which blow away many actual player contracts in value because we can get the right information on who is handling this and is responsible for it.

Please advise, and alternative suggestions are welcome.

Thanks,
Bob DeMartino

Finally, on January 28, 2006, after Ornstein had Bush signed with a different memorabilia company run by Gary Takahashi of Hawaii, DeMartino sent the following message:

Mike,

For months I have lost sleep over your dealings with Reggie and then the hoops we've jumped through to get the best possible memorabilia deal on the table for not only Reggie but Leinart as well. Then we complete by your own admission the best package for Reggie and Thursday night you tell me to get paperwork to you, based on the numbers its a done deal and like when we were told by you and Chuck Price that the Leinart deal was a go . . . you bailed out and we get screwed here.

But worse yet, now I see all over the Internet, signingshotline.com, Triumph Sports, etc, that you gave Bush to Gary Takahashi and GTSM. Further, you tell me its because you need the $450,000 that GTSM is willing to pay on signing with another $450,000 in a week

and that it is a 3 year deal GUARANTEED at $900,000 per year. Well you didn't share the terms nor who it was (at least one would have hoped you'd have gone with Upper Deck, pretty much securing that years 2 and 3 would be realized) and frankly, I will tell you right now and as you agreed the other night, you are taking a deal that is not the best that is on the table and I don't think the short sighted opinion of taking $450,000 immediately and the additional $450,000 next week is in the best interest of your client when in fact you could receive a total in excess of $1,000,000 in the next 90 days or so with an additional $1,000,000 plus put in escrow and guaranteed to your client, and, that is before you consider the potential $3,000,0000 plus in upside revenue we laid out over the term.

This deal, as you stated, is being taken purely because of the immediate cash, you are failing to realize what you did realize when I put the $500,000 deal together for your client Tim Brown, specifically that our intent in both cases is to BUILD the athletes brand and value. Our interest is building the athletes business and value for the future, while securing it today. Just one example is: after our deal would close, Reggie would have $1,000,000 and another in escrow payable as long as he does his signings and appearances. Should Reggie slip and fall on the street and never play a down in the NFL, he still has $2,000,000 plus guaranteed, should Reggie get hurt as did Carson Palmer early in a game next season, Reggie still has his $2,000,000 guaranteed etc etc etc. How is the GTSM deal secured????

I don't know what else to say beyond our recent conversation.

Bob DeMartino

As with the "allowance" payments and the purchase of the airline tickets and a limo ride for Bush's family, the negotiations by Ornstein could constitute an NCAA violation. According to NCAA bylaw 12.3.1: An individual shall be ineligible for participation in an intercollegiate sport if he or she ever has agreed (orally or in writing) to be represented by an agent for the purpose of marketing his or her athletics ability or reputation in that sport. Further, an agency contract not specifically limited in writing to a sport or particular sports shall be deemed applicable to all sports, and the individual shall be ineligible to participate in any sport.

"All of that was based on only if I got him as a client," Ornstein told the *Miami Herald* in April 2006. "It was only going to be if and when I signed him. No deal was ever consummated until Reggie signed with me after the season.

"That's pretty standard practice in the agent business. Basically, you have to be able to show a prospective client like Reggie Bush, 'Hey, if you sign with me, this is what I can bring to the table for you.' I can show you a spreadsheet back at my office where I did this with seven or eight companies."

Finally, during the weekend of the Heisman ceremony, according to *Yahoo! Sports*, Ornstein also paid for Denise Griffin to get a makeover and paid for some of Bush's friends to come to New York for the weekend. The entourage went out on the town to celebrate, Ornstein picking up the check as well.

DeMartino was interviewed by the NCAA in January 2007. He said he left a message for both athletic director Mike Garrett and head coach Pete Carroll in November or December 2005 to warn them of the problems they might have with Ornstein and his relationship with Bush. DeMartino also handed the email messages over to the NCAA.

Finally, Ornstein also paid for Denise Griffin's sister Valerie Packard to stay at the Sir Francis Drake Hotel in San Francisco at the end of December 2005 for New Year's Eve. As when Bush stayed with the Venetian Hotel in Las Vegas on Michael Michaels's credit card, Ornstein filled out a form with his credit card so that Packard could charge the room to him.

If it all sounds very desperate on Ornstein's part, that's in keeping with his character. Ornstein got his first job in the NFL working for the Raiders. He was straight out of Indiana State University after having grown up on the East Coast.

In the wee hours of the morning, Ornstein would come in and scrub toilets before going to work as an administrative assistant to coach John Madden. For eighteen months, Ornstein scraped by with no salary. He would head to local hotels on alternating days to munch on free hors d'oeuvres during Happy Hour.

"I can't even look at a little meatball or a little hot dog anymore," Ornstein told *Yahoo! Sports* in 2006. "Still to this day I gag when I see those things."

Ornstein parlayed his work ethic into a move up the team's job ladder, even though he created controversy along the way. According to a *Los Angeles Times* article, Ornstein "won undying fame before the 1984 Super Bowl victory in Tampa by ordering Irv Cross of CBS off the sideline—while Cross was on the air."

In 1986, Ornstein got into a fight with fellow senior administrator John Herrera. The squabble reportedly was over who had used a movie projector last. Ornstein punched Herrera. Herrera pressed charges and Ornstein pleaded no contest to misdemeanor battery.

"When you work for Al [Davis], you kind of think you can do whatever you want," Ornstein told *Yahoo! Sports*. "As a young guy, I was a feisty guy. . . . I did a lot of stupid things. I try not to do too many stupid things anymore.

"I haven't punched anybody out in twenty-five years."

Ornstein had a rocky relationship with Raiders owner Al Davis, who Ornstein said fired him "three or four times." The final time was for good in 1989, when Davis found out that Ornstein had interviewed for a job with the Los Angeles Rams.

After he was fired Ornstein's grudge reached odd heights. He supposedly consulted a voodoo expert who told him that if he wanted to bring bad luck upon the Raiders he could keep a Raiders helmet in a refrigerator. Ornstein did it, according to Pfeifer.

"He hated the Raiders so much, Al Davis, he put things in the freezer so they wouldn't win. Raiders stuff, almost like voodoo shit," Pfeifer said. Moreover, Pfeifer's experience with Ornstein was what he described as "difficult."

"We really didn't get along. He rants, he raves. He's just a very difficult guy to get along with. After we sold the yearbook business, we stayed together for a little while but he was impossible to work with. He's just a very difficult human being. He's abusive, loud. Screams and yells. Doesn't know how to handle his own emotions, can't do anything rationally, just a really arrogant type of guy," Pfeifer said.

"When I met him he had a bracelet around his ankle. Everybody else went to jail but him so I don't know what that means, draw your own conclusions. . . . He grew up in the era with Al Davis. Al Davis was a screamer, yeller, an abusive guy. Mike Ornstein was probably abused as a

kid. He's a very insecure guy who probably got beat up as a child, that type of guy. And he abuses other people. He screams, he yells, he thinks he's Al Davis. He thinks he's a tough guy. He's not. He's a wussy. He's a big blowhard. That's him in a nutshell. And because he hung out with athletes, who were probably physically tough guys, he thought he was a tough guy himself. But he's not. He threatens people. This is his mentality, so he takes it to the business and he becomes abusive. But he can also . . . on the flip side he can be very endearing because he's funny . . . he has guys he takes care of and he's friendly with them. He's like a jock sniffer."

TEN

Mom and Dad Make Their Way to the Trough

By April 2005, LaMar and Denise Griffin were out from underneath $28,000 in credit-card debt. They were living in a brand-new home on a hillside in the San Diego suburb of Spring Valley. For a pair of working-class people who had been living in an apartment only a month before, life was good. Very good.

But not quite good enough. With Lloyd Lake and Michael Michaels serving as the cash cows, Reggie Bush and his parents were ready to spend and spend. From furniture to travel to spending cash to expensive dinners to helicopter rides, Bush's family was living large.

The first stop was a shopping spree to furnish the new home in May 2005.

"I went with them to pick the furniture out," Barbara Gunner said. "It was a consignment store. It's got really nice things at the consignment store, some with the tags still on it, and some that these rich people change furniture every two or three years and there's not a mark on it. She just had a ball in there. She must have spent $9,000 or $10,000 . . . I didn't know [at the time that] Michael had given them the money to buy it."

According to documents furnished by Lake's attorneys, the Griffins demanded $7,000 for furniture in May and eventually spent $12,000 for furniture overall.

Then came the washer and dryer.

"I bought them a washer and dryer. They needed money because when they moved they didn't have that. [My attorney] got all my receipts and everything and they admitted it. I think they told our attorneys that they did receive it," said Gunner, who spent exactly $1,064.98 on the appliance set, according to the documents.

When the family was finally evicted from the home in April 2006 after a year of not paying rent, they took every stick of the furniture with them, according to reports by *Yahoo! Sports*, which were confirmed by Lake and Michaels's attorneys. The next step for the Griffins was to bring Lake, Michaels, and other family members to the church the Griffins attended.

The Life Changing International Church Ministries building located at 5085 Logan Avenue in San Diego can best be described as ramshackle. The church sat in a rundown strip mall, beat up from years of neglect and lacking any real businesses aside from a market at one end and a convenience store at the other. During the middle of the day, there would be a few cars in the parking lot. Most of the former stores were turned into various churches. Many of those churches sublet to other organizations, depending upon the day.

A banner in front of the church—where Bush's family worshipped—was a picture of Bishop Katie Woods. After Bush had turned pro, there also would be a collection of high-end cars by Mercedes, Lexus, and Hummer sitting in front on Sunday morning.

Even before Bush made his run to the NFL, there were new donations coming in. Michaels told *Yahoo! Sports* that he made donations totaling several thousand dollars. Gunner said she gave hundreds. Lloyd Lake said the church was part of how the Griffins set him up. His sister Lisa Lake said she couldn't stand the church after attending a few times.

Watching LaMar Griffin give the sermon repulsed her.

"After I went there the day that he preached—that was probably my third visit—I said I wouldn't go back because it was really a mockery," said Lisa Lake, who spent ten dollars to buy a copy of Griffin's sermon, in

part out of amusement. "He had no business trying to preach, really. I take that stuff serious because I try to go to church every Sunday. But I said I wouldn't go back. I liked the bishop [Katie Woods], she was very nice. I did get something out of that when I went."

To Lloyd Lake, however, it was all part of the plan by Bush and the Griffins to convince him the business was legit.

"They say the best con men use religion as a way to pull off their con because it makes a person relax, thinking, 'OK, he's into God, he wouldn't do anything wrong.' And they got me in that mode," Lake said.

"They put me in that religion mode, thinking, 'OK, these people are honest people.' But they're really crooks deep down. They can label me. But they're the real crooks. They don't even have any honor amongst themselves. To sit there and lie, that's what really got me."

The problem, according to Lake, was that he didn't see through it fast enough. He said he noticed the lying by LaMar Griffin right away. He and Griffin got close over the months after they started the business, and Griffin eventually confided in Lake about his personal life.

Lake said the image of Griffin as a preacher is also shattered by the contents of the tapes Lake made as the deal was falling apart.

"You listen on those tapes, you hear him cussing like a sailor a lot of times. He exposed a lot of himself when he is on these tapes. He goes into church and put on a show where you'd never think he'd be using this kind of language."

According to a report by *Yahoo! Sports,* on more than one occasion, Michaels paid for Griffin, his wife, Denise, and their younger son, Javon, to attend Lakers games. Michaels got them courtside seats. The family liked the limelight of the game, making it obvious to anyone that they were related to Reggie Bush. They ate, drank, and bought souvenirs on Michaels's dime. They even traveled to the game in a limo provided by Michaels.

Before one of the games the family attended, Griffin even asked to meet with players and told them about the marketing company. He went so far as to seek out Lakers superstar Kobe Bryant, even trying to recruit him.

Despite the red flags, Lake and Michaels kept supplying the money. From June through August 2005, the Griffins demanded another $10,000

in advances on the company's earnings, according to documents. The money was advanced by Michaels directly.

The week before USC opened the 2005 season at Hawaii on September 3, Barbara Gunner received an urgent call from LaMar Griffin. The family was going to the opener, their first trip to the islands. They were excited to travel and to see Reggie begin what would be his last season at USC.

The only problem was that they didn't have any spending money for the weekend away. Michaels had promised to give them $5,000 for the trip, but he was out of town and the family was about to leave. Gunner got the money out of her account, as her daughter Lisa recalled.

"The time when she was expressing the concern about the $5,000, I think they were going to . . . Hawaii. It was [USC's] first game in Hawaii and I guess Michael was going to get them money. Michael wasn't in town at the time, but he was paying for their house, his house. She told them that she would get the money and basically before I could hang up the phone, LaMar was at the front door to get the $5,000," Lisa Lake said.

Gunner confirmed that she gave LaMar Griffin $5,000 for the trip to Hawaii. It was part of what she estimated was $70,000 to $80,000 she loaned her son or contributed directly to help start the business. Lisa Lake estimated that she gave between $25,000 and $30,000 to support her brother in this project.

Lisa Lake said the attitude shown by Bush's family and LaMar Griffin, specifically, was consistently materialistic.

"Then in the summer [before the 2005 season], my boyfriend fixes up trucks and does all this stuff," she said. "So we have this Avalanche with the twenty-four-inch rims, all sparkly and shiny. I remember [LaMar Griffin] saying when he first saw it—because we don't drive it that often—he saw me and [said] . . . 'Oh, when are you going to let me hold on to that truck, Lisa?' I just remember thinking, 'Why would you want to do that?' He wanted to borrow that black Mercedes [that Lloyd owned]. It was always about the cars and the material things. That just always raised red flags.

"They always wanted to borrow [Lloyd's] Mercedes and go to L.A., it was just all about things . . . I went over to the house [in Spring Valley] one time when they had been in Michael's house [in Spring Valley] and

the furniture, all this nice stuff. And then the night we went out, I was like, how are they doing all that? Did Michael buy the furniture? The night we went on the helicopter ride, Denise had one of those new digital cameras. I was thinking to myself, 'Where is this stuff coming from?' "

The night out and the helicopter ride were part of a celebration of Denise Griffin's birthday and the birthday of Michael Michaels's sister. The group, including Michaels, his sister, her husband, the Griffins, Lloyd Lake, and Lisa Lake, rented two helicopters to tour San Diego, Michaels picking up the tab for that. The group then went to a fancy restaurant in San Diego called Peohe.

The night provided for a comical story of LaMar Griffin's unmitigated gall.

"This was later in the year and there were two things I remember that night that hit me right away when we were sitting at dinner," Lisa Lake said. "We went to the helicopter ride and then we went to Peohe's. It was Michael's sister's birthday as well, so his sister and her husband joined us. It was Denise and LaMar and their son Javon. It was Lloyd and his girlfriend at the time, Maiesha [Jones]. I was there, Michael Michaels was there. It was a pretty big party.

"We all had dinner, they are ordering everything on the menu. During the dinner I was sitting and Denise was to my right and I remember Denise saying, 'Yep, all these people [other agents] are talking to us, but nope, we've already told them what we're doing, we've already told them.' It was just the way she was saying it, I just wanted to say no because she was just very monotone. It just raised a red flag for me. Then when the dinner was over, Michael paid for the whole tab and LaMar was like, 'No, I'll get the tip.' And then he said, 'How much you think I should leave, five dollars, ten dollars?' At the time I said, 'You know what, the bill is probably $800 or $900. You really need to tip based on that, and it's a large party, so really your tip should be about $90 or $100, conservatively.'

"He said, 'For what?' I said, 'Because that's how you tip, based on your bill and the number in your party.' He was going to leave them ten dollars. First of all, I think it was already automatically done and [then we] come to find out the bill was $1,500. I just could not believe it, and, to top it off, all of a sudden he said, 'What you all going to give Denise for her birthday?' "

Lloyd Lake recalled LaMar Griffin also saying, "Aren't you going to take her to the mall and let her go buy some stuff?"

Perhaps the level of gall shouldn't be so surprising. While the Griffins were taking money from Lake and Michaels, they evidently were also receiving money and benefits from Ornstein by the time the 2005 season started.

To Lloyd Lake, it was obvious that everyone in Bush's immediate family was treating Reggie Bush like a meal ticket. Lake said he had no direct interaction with Bush's biological father, Reggie Bush, Sr., a man who was unable to work and was close to destitute while living in Los Angeles while Bush was playing at USC.

However, Lake said he observed Bush's real father and LaMar Griffin argue on at least one occasion.

"No, I've never talked to him [Bush's real father] one time. It was all LaMar," Lloyd said. "I remember they got into it one time where LaMar wanted to go up there with him with a whole bunch of people. I'm not going to go get involved with nothing like that with the real dad. They almost got in a fight up there. LaMar wore the dad [jersey] and then Reggie [Bush Sr.] wore the real dad jersey. [It got] competitive like [Bush] was a piece of meat or something, a piece of gold and who owned it.

"They had security out to escort the real dad out and not let the real dad into the stadium anymore. They almost got in a fight on the field after the game. Security had to break it up."

However, by the beginning of the holidays, it was apparent that the situation was coming apart.

"I had to prepare this large Thanksgiving dinner because they [the Griffins] were all coming over for Thanksgiving. They didn't show up and I called and said, 'What happened? We have been waiting and I've got all this food,' " Barbara Gunner said. "[Denise Griffin] said, 'My [relative] came down from Los Angeles and we just decided to eat at home.' I said, 'It would have been nice if you had told me, I made all this food.' She said, 'Oh, I'm sorry, I should have called you.' After that, I could hear Michael saying, 'That's not right.' "

Shortly after that, Gunner advised Lloyd Lake to record conversations with Bush and his family. Lake purchased a small digital recorder that

was easy to conceal. In one of the conversations, LaMar Griffin advanced the notion that there was a problem between the sides, saying it revolved around agent Dave Caravantes and his lack of experience with high-profile players.

Lloyd: You know with [agent] Dave [Caravantes], he's getting a bum rap.

LaMar: But see, you need to talk to him, I don't know what Mike's going to do about that.

Lloyd: We need to all sit down with Dave, me, you, and Mike. And you need to drill him and let him show his evidence, and if it's not right then we'll get rid of him.

LaMar: But see what I'm trying to tell you is that if getting somebody else is going to get Reggie, it might not do that. You might not get Reggie because of it's a new agency, and a lot of players that are big time like Reggie, they like going with the big agents. Even though the money might be good on one end, this kid—I've done told Reggie many times that sometimes big agents are not good. But he's still going to make his decision. I'm not trying to railroad nobody, or use nobody or put nobody on the back burner, but I also got to say, "Hey, when he comes and you set up in the there and what [Caravantes] says beats David Dunn and Spiegel Regal [Joel Segal, Bush's eventual agent], whatever his name is, and all these guys, when they come up to him"—see, we can put our two cents in.

Furthermore, Griffin expressed regret over starting the business in the first place:

LaMar: I'm going to change the subject real quick. I ain't got nothing against you, I love you and the family. But this situation right now, which I wish I never would have started.

Lloyd: Me, too, I say that, too.

LaMar: I wish I never would have started it. My wife say that, "You know what? We never should have got involved." Because I knew Reggie was going to change his mind. I told him, I said, "Son, I

don't know what you said to them, but you got opportunities to look at all avenues of this thing. Don't tell nobody you're going to come with them and then turn around and do whatever you're doing with them." I said, "You're kind of telling them you're going to do it, but you're not going to do it, or you're thinking about going somewhere else." I told him that myself.

Lloyd: Right, and what did he say to that?

LaMar: He said, "OK, Dad, I'll take care of it." So I guess he's supposed to talk to you, Mike, and everybody else. He called me last night.

Lloyd: And what did he say?

LaMar: He just said that you told him I said he was coming. I said, "I didn't say nothing like that. From what I understand you said that." I said, "Son, it's me and you in this. I can't worry about Lloyd Lake and Mike and them. I got to worry about my family. So whatever you said, I don't know what you said or not. You said it's on me, but I didn't say it. They said you told them that." And then we started talking about some other stuff. So but I told him, like he told the news reporters and stuff, the decision is his.

Lloyd: I understand that, you told me that, too. But what I'm saying is that I need your support still.

LaMar: Like I said before, I haven't backed off of y'all.

Clearly, the investment Michaels and Lake had made in Bush and his family was no longer meaningful. During the taped conversations between Lake and LaMar Griffin after the Heisman ceremony, Griffin essentially admitted that, much to Lake's dismay:

LaMar: But you ain't given it a chance yet, you ain't gone down and presented the agency. Last week when we talked you said, "Look, I gotta present the agency to Reggie." You know what I'm saying? You present it, you know. Everybody's on equal ground.

Lloyd: It shouldn't be everybody on equal ground.

LaMar: It should be because he has the right to see what else is out there besides just this agency.

Lloyd: I understand that, but it shouldn't be on equal ground because everybody has not been taking care of you guys for the last eighteen months and him.

LaMar: That's doesn't matter.

Lloyd: It does matter. How do you say it doesn't matter?

LaMar: You make a choice, Lake. You say, "I'm going to do this for the family," you was after my son.

Lloyd: Right, and your son agreed to it, and you agreed to it.

LaMar: I didn't say—I tried to get him to the business. I said the decision is left up to him, that's what I told you.

Lloyd: At the end you said that. At the beginning you said I'll get my son.

LaMar: Because that's what he told me. And Mike said, you know what, if that was my son I'd have said the same thing because the last thing that has to be said, I can't go tell Reggie, "You're going to this business." I can't do that.

The situation continued to deteriorate, Lisa Lake said. At one point, she was talking to LaMar Griffin by phone.

"I just remember when it started getting to the end and it was really apparent that this was not going to go down . . . I was trying to salvage this. I said, 'You guys have worked on this for a while now. Isn't there something you guys can do to sit down to work this out?' [LaMar Griffin] was like, 'No, no, no. You're going to get your money.' This was January 2006. It was before he officially signed with all of them. It was before that. It might have even been late December when we went to Palm Springs."

Strangely, even after it was clear that the deal had fallen through after January 2006 and that the sides were headed to dispute, the Griffins continued to live in the house in Spring Valley. The corner home had a reverse plan, with the kitchen, living room, dining room, and master bedroom on the second floor. The bottom floor featured a television room and two bedrooms, one of which was Reggie's when he stayed there, according to Lloyd Lake. Better yet, Reggie's Heisman Trophy was strate-

gically placed on a horizontal mantel under a skylight window, seemingly close enough to touch when you walked upstairs.

Even after writing THE GRIFFINS "05" in the driveway concrete, they had no shame about the fact that they were living there rent-free using the house of someone they had jilted. The Griffins easily could have gotten money from the marketing deals Bush signed before the April 2006 NFL Draft and paid for the house. They didn't. They were served with an eviction notice on April 3, 2006. On April 12, attorney David Cornwell told Michaels that the family would vacate the home by April 21.

By that time, the family had built up a bill of $50,807.50 in unpaid rent, according to documents.

The worst part is that the day before the family vacated the house, reporters from *Yahoo! Sports* and the *Miami Herald* showed up and started asking questions about what was going on.

It was all part of an ending that has Lloyd Lake shaking his head to this day.

"What's even more amazing to me when you just ask someone and they're trying to give you your money back," Lake said. At that point, Bush's family seemed to forget how much they had borrowed and spent.

According to Lake, LaMar and Bush said to him, " 'Look, man, I am just going to give you your money back. OK, OK, I owe you about $35,000.' They forget what you've really given them. Then, you know how offended you are with that?" Lake said. "You don't want to give me any interest on my money and my time, and you want to short me? It's like you can't believe the audacity of some people. Like, are you serious? I couldn't believe that comment even came out of his mouth. [Bush] told me he was going to give me back [$40,000]. 'I'll have your money this week.' I told him he could keep it."

ELEVEN

The Unraveling

After Bush's family did not come to Barbara Gunner's house for Thanksgiving 2005, it had become apparent to Gunner—and her son Lloyd Lake—that something was amiss with the relationship. After months of giving money to Bush and his family, donating money to the Bush family's church, helping them with a place to live, furnishing the home, and giving Reggie Bush money to buy a car, there was simply no bond.

Lake was in trouble with the law again and he claimed that the pressure of trying to keep the business going led to his problems. In November, he violated his parole by getting into a fight with his girlfriend, Maiesha Jones, who was left with a broken arm. *Yahoo! Sports* reported that during court testimony on November 25, 2005, a week before USC finished the regular season against UCLA, Lake said the stress of dealing with Bush and the company prompted the fight. Lake also said that Bush and USC offensive tackle Winston Justice were supposed to join the company.

Lake testified that both Justice and Bush were supposed to spend the night out with him. In his testimony, Lake explained that Jones had gotten upset with him for planning to go out with Bush, Justice, and some of Bush's friends.

"Well, I had a sports agency we had formed, and we had a guy in, Winston Justice, from USC," Lake testified. "And [my girlfriend] had planned to go out with us that night, but Reggie Bush came into town. And at that time, he was going to go out with us, so I told her all his friends were coming and that it wasn't a good night for us to go out, and that kind of got her upset."

Lake said the group took a limousine to a club. Eventually, Justice was dropped at the Hotel Solamar, an upscale, $300-a-night resort hotel in San Diego's Gaslamp District. Jones didn't press charges in the matter against Lloyd, but Lake eventually went back to federal prison in Victorville, California, in February 2006 because the incident was considered a parole violation.

Before returning to prison, Lake recorded two conversations he had with Griffin in person in December 2005, one before the Heisman Trophy ceremony in New York on December 5, and another after Griffin returned from the ceremony. Later in the month, Lake recorded Reggie Bush during two telephone conversations.

What's detailed in the conversations is that by this time it was clear that the plan for New Era Sports & Entertainment was little more than a fleeting thought for Griffin and Bush. Unlike the situation when Griffin showed up for meetings with the Sycuan Tribal Council or when Bush met with Michaels and Lake to discuss the idea and solicit funds for Bush and his family, Griffin and Bush were distancing themselves from the company.

Griffin started off by saying that agent Dave Caravantes, who had been hired by Lake and Michaels to be the contract negotiator, wasn't qualified to represent Bush. Later, both Griffin and Bush criticized the group for being too inexperienced for Bush's needs.

Several times in the conversations, Lake asked to meet with Bush personally, but Griffin put Lake off by saying Bush was too busy preparing for the National Championship game. Meanwhile, Bush was preparing interviews with other contract agents. Griffin even said during the conversation that Bush told marketing agent Mike Ornstein, who ran the same kind of business Lake and Michaels were proposing, to line up prospective contract agents for interviews.

Griffin also said Lake needed to present the agency proposal to Bush personally, while also telling Lake not to approach Bush about a settle-

ment over the money advanced to Bush and his family. In the end, after sometimes terse and threatening conversations, both Griffin and Bush promised to pay back the money they had taken, Lake said.

However, when settlement talks fell through, the story slowly leaked out to reporters.

In the first taped dialogue between Lake and Griffin, on December 5, 2005, in the parking lot at Morse High School, where Griffin is still a security guard, Lake admits to being stressed, as it appeared that the business was in trouble:

Lloyd: Hey, I'm out in front. Big Dog, nothing, what you doing?

LaMar: Going crazy like usual, just chilling. What's going on?

Lloyd: Man, I'm under so much pressure, look at me. I'm a mess.

LaMar: Why are you letting stuff get to you like that?

Lloyd: Because it's like Mike's down. I ain't talked to Mike, he's mad at me because of the situation.

LaMar: What's Mike mad at you about?

Lloyd: His credibility with the tribe and everything.

LaMar: Oh.

Lloyd: That's why I'm trying to figure out, it's like this: You think back when we first got involved, right? Remember when we first met and we talked and I laid it out to Reggie and you, and then Mike gave twenty-six [$26,000], that's why he thinks we're partners the whole time, which we are, but, it's like Reggie kind of like promised he was coming he did. Last night when I talked to him I said, "Reg, you gotta understand, your word means a lot." You see what I'm saying? Me tell somebody something, they're going to move off of that. He understood that a little bit.

LaMar: But did he say that?

Lloyd: He did. He said, "Well, you know you guys still got the best chance." I explained to him that his word means a lot. You see what I'm saying? I wouldn't be in this right now with my relationship with Michael and the tribe in jeopardy. I could have found another venture to come to them with. This is a golden opportunity for us. And it's kinda like remember when you first told him, "Reggie's

coming," and when we first gave the money. Remember what you said? I said, "Big Dog, what's the thing?" "Reggie's going to come to the company." So I'm trying to see what do we need to still pull that off without jeopardizing [Michaels's] little career up there with the tribe? He's depressed and I'm depressed because I got him in the situation.

LaMar: I don't know, because see that's when a couple of months ago I told you, I said, "It's going to be his decision." And no matter what his word said, you're talking to a twenty-two-year-old kid that's looking at the opportunity of a lifetime. He's the best player in college football. And I got to tell you, he's got to look at all avenues. And I talked to Michael about this. And Mike said, "All business transactions don't always happen the way they are." If you going the same thing to me to my wife, she's going to be upset. As long as Reggie said that, then that's fine, but it's still up to Reggie.

Lloyd: I understand that, I'm not arguing with that. But what I want Reggie to understand is how much his words mean. You see what I'm saying? I'll give you an example. [Lloyd discusses compromising personal secrets told to him by LaMar.] What if I say, "Oh LaMar, things change," would you be mad at me and still say we're friends?

LaMar: Yeah, I would say that.

Lloyd: No, you wouldn't.

LaMar: You can't dictate somebody's life.

Lloyd: Would you be mad at me?

LaMar: That's a different ballgame. I'd be mad at you.

Lloyd: That's what I'm saying, it's words.

LaMar: You can be mad at Reggie all you want, but he don't care. He don't care if you're mad at him. You gotta understand, man, this is his future, his decision. It's up to him.

Lloyd: But I need your support. I want to sit down, me, you, and Dave [Caravantes].

LaMar: I found out something about Dave. Dave ain't never done a contract. I am not putting Dave in front of my son. I'm not doing

it. Dave ain't doing it. That's all I'm saying. You're not going to change my mind. I am not going to put him to do something like that to somebody that never negotiated a first-round contract.

Lloyd: He has, that's what I want to show you.

LaMar: He has not, man.

Lloyd: I got the proof of it.

LaMar: I asked the dude, the other dude he worked for for five years. He talked to me personally on the phone. He said, "He has never negotiated a contract first round ever." He said for five years, he's done all of them.

Lloyd: He's lying, I got proof of that.

LaMar: I don't like Dave.

Lloyd: You gotta understand though. I understand that. But look, this is what I'm saying, there's ways around it. We gotta go find someone else.

LaMar: You might need to find someone else completely that had no part with him or Lemon [Campbell] or nobody. It's going to have to be somebody plain out a good agent that's going to represent this boy. Before I even finish, I know the whole story about words and this and that, but I didn't say the words. I told you before, Reggie told me to tell y'all it's his decision. Now y'all can come down and state your case if that's what he said. I'm not even picking the agent that he's interviewing.

Lloyd: I know.

LaMar: He's doing all that. I'm just coming down, I'm getting the name and looking over the brochures at the house, that's all I'm doing. He's seeing everything, and he's doing everything.

Lloyd: I understand.

LaMar: I even got in trouble for saying about him—he got mad at me about saying about going to the next level in the papers, all over the paper that I said that. So there is nothing really, you know what I'm saying?

Lloyd: But what is Denise mad at me for?

LaMar: Because Reggie called and said that you said that I said he was coming to the agency.

Lloyd: This is exactly what I said, "Reg, there's a lot right now." Because [Michaels is] mad and everything up there with the tribe. Before I brought you up, I brought what he said up first. What he said and he admitted he said it. And I said, "Your dad said a while back that you were coming to the agency." I don't want an ugly situation to get ugly, you see what I'm saying?

LaMar: It shouldn't get ugly because whatever happens to this relationship, it shouldn't get ugly, period. It's this kid's life.

Lloyd: I understand that, but he knew it was his life before he got everyone involved. Reggie's not dumb, he knew what he was doing.

LaMar: But see, you can't hold him accountable for that, man, that's wrong.

Lloyd: How come you can't?

LaMar: I'm going to tell you something, I'm going to tell you right now and I'm going to tell you from the bottom of my heart, if this comes out to anybody try to destroy my son's life, I'm going to destroy some other people's lives.

Lloyd: I would expect it, that's the art of war. That's what you are supposed to do.

Lake and Griffin continue to discuss Caravantes as an agent, with Griffin essentially saying that he will not allow Caravantes to represent his son.

Lloyd: And then for you guys to have stuff on Dave that's not true, I mean I got proof Dave done those contracts.

LaMar: I don't know why these guys he worked for for five years would lie on him.

Lloyd: Because you know how they fell out? You know how he and [agent Joel] Segal fell out? Dave was having the son, and Segal had

put his name on that one contract, and Dave was hot with him because Dave helped with it.

LaMar: Well, Dave needs to change his attitude.

Lloyd: That's why I'm saying you need to sit down and you need to check him. Both of you guys, you own the company.

LaMar: But see, if Dave gets up in front of Reggie, Reggie's not going to pick the agency. Dave is not good enough to represent Reggie in no contract. I'm telling you that right now. He's not good, and Reggie's not going to, and JC's not. You got to remember, JC's on that side of the table, I'm on that side of the table, my wife is and Javon. This cat's screwed up because of the sour note he left when we left that meeting. The meeting should have never took place.

Lloyd: It shouldn't have.

Lake and Griffin continue to talk about the company, Griffin even saying he's still part of the operation. They continue to argue about Caravantes, with Lake offering to solve the problem by hiring another agent. At the end, Griffin gives a tacit admission that Bush was taking cash, arguing that it shouldn't matter to Lake if Bush was on the take.

Lloyd: Everybody keeps missing the principle. I just want you to be with the company and help us go in the direction we want.

LaMar: I didn't say I never would.

Lloyd: I know, but you're not telling me what we need to do now.

LaMar: I don't know what you need to do now, that's Reggie's decision.

Lloyd: No, I'm saying with the agency. You don't like Dave, you say you don't like Dave.

LaMar: No, I don't like Dave.

Lloyd: Well, what's the remedy for that?

LaMar: Mike don't like Dave.

Lloyd: OK.

LaMar: That's what Mike told Dave. He said he don't like his attitude, his attitude is nasty. That's what Mike told me.

Lloyd: OK, so what's the remedy now? Do we go hire another agent? That's what I'm asking you as a partner.

LaMar: But you hired another agent to try to get Reggie. That's what you're doing. But see, what you need to do is—you've got players. You done signed seven or eight players already.

Lloyd: Seven or eight players, but none of them will do for the agency what Reggie will do, and that's why I'm in this. I didn't come in this to sign them seven or eight other players.

LaMar: But see, that's like Mike told me. He said, "Sometimes that's how the ball goes." That's what we were saying, if Reggie don't come to the agency, will the marketing work? And everybody said yeah, yeah, at the table. Now it's everybody's depressed and mad at Reggie.

Lloyd: I'm not mad at Reggie and I'm not mad at you. I don't want you to take me talking with you as being mad, but Reggie has been taking money from people, I know he has. He can say what he wants.

LaMar: Every player out there taking money, not just Reggie.

Eventually, Griffin backed off the point about Caravantes, agreeing to a meeting:

Lloyd: That's all I'm asking for is your two cents.

LaMar: At the end of the day, he's going to pick who he wants. Whoever got to go home, gotta go home. That's not up to me, it's up to him. I never said that I was going to stop dealing with the company.

Lloyd: Because if I ask someone about LaMar that he got a falling-out with, of course I'm going to get a bad opinion for LaMar.

LaMar: Me and Dave can sit down and talk, but I'm not going to sit there without Mike being there.

However, at another point in the conversations, Griffin accuses Lake of creating problems within his family. Griffin talks dismissively about New Era Sports & Entertainment and tries to keep Lake from speaking with Reggie. Griffin also expresses regret for having gotten involved in the business.

Lloyd: But I'm a man of principle. If I say something . . .

LaMar: But see, you're pulling a family apart.

Lloyd: How?

LaMar: You're coming between this with this little bullshit ass agency, you know what I'm saying? You pull in between and pull my son out like that and put him on a burner. You shouldn't have called him anyway and talked about this shit right now because he's trying to finish a goddamn schedule on a career that he's trying to do. You call him and discuss this bullshit.

Lloyd: I didn't call him and discuss that.

LaMar: But see, it should have never got to that. He's trying to finish this schooling. He should have said, "Look, Lake, I don't want to talk about this right now."

Lloyd: I told him that, I said we'll sit down. But he needs to understand.

LaMar: But not now, Lake.

Lloyd: I understand, Big Dog, I didn't talk to him now. It came to that. I said, "Reg, I need to talk to you." He's the one that started to talk over the phone. My issue was right there. I don't want it to get ugly though.

LaMar: I don't like this whole thing. I should have never got involved with it.

Lloyd: I wish you wouldn't have. If I had known it was going to be like this, I would have never gotten involved.

LaMar: Never would have gotten involved because you see now, now you're pushing, everybody's pushing, everybody's worried about their credibility.

Lloyd: Yeah, just like you're worried about Reggie's credibility.

LaMar: But see, his credibility, it doesn't matter about his credibility. Y'all been an agency, if you got one kid don't come, you've got [this guy], you've got [this guy].

Lloyd: But that ain't why we built the agency.

LaMar: But that's not Reggie's . . .

Lloyd: I wouldn't be in there if it weren't for Reggie. If it wasn't for me talking with you and Reggie, I wouldn't be in this.

The tension between Lake and Griffin grows as the conversation progresses. Lake insinuates that the entire affair could get "ugly." Griffin also states that Bush should be afforded privileges with Lake because of his status as the best college player in the country. At the end, Griffin challenges Lake to file a lawsuit against them:

Lloyd: I understand that, but you're not being fair to the business.

LaMar: I can't be fair to the business when it comes to my—I'm not going to let you, Mike, Dave, the family, nobody come in between me and my son. You can take us to court, whatever you want to do, but I cannot let me, as being a dad . . . now if Reggie decides to go with the agency . . .

Lloyd: I'm just saying I don't want it to get ugly.

LaMar: It shouldn't get ugly, it shouldn't get ugly. You should respect the boy's wishes. He's the best college football player in the country.

Lloyd: I understand that.

LaMar: And he has to have every opportunity to look at the other avenues.

Lloyd: I didn't tell him not to.

LaMar: But if he don't pick you, then it's going to get ugly. That's bull, that's bull crap.

Lloyd: Big Dog, listen to what I'm saying, you're taking it there. I'm saying it could.

LaMar: It shouldn't be a could.

Lloyd: It's business though.

LaMar: No, no, some business take their losses and get moving.

Lloyd: Sometimes they file lawsuits because it's part of business.

LaMar: Well, then file a lawsuit then.

The conversation calmed for a while as Lake expressed regret, saying he wished Bush had simply asked for a loan instead of making Lake and Michaels believe he would join the company they were forming:

Lloyd: I just wish Reggie would have just said, "Lend me some money, no agency, I'll give you some interest on it and whatever," and that's it. I just wish he wouldn't have me out here paying Dave out of my pocket, because if it's not for Reg, I'm not doing this. See what I'm saying? I'm not going up there with Sycuan and getting my name on the line.

LaMar: But you don't understand something, it's a different ballgame now because . . . I told Reggie to tell me everything that's going on with you. He said, "Dad, I'm going to tell you everything." Now see, there's some stuff that came out about some money that I knew nothing about. You see what I'm saying? I'm not going to say nothing to Reggie, but I'm just saying.

Lloyd: A whole bunch of times.

LaMar: He put hisself out there. I love my son, but he put hisself out there. I'm assuming, don't saying nothing, I'm assuming that, "If you do this for me, if you help me out, get my car done and this and that, I'll come to the agency." I'm assuming that's what was said.

Lloyd: Yeah, it was like this, "Everything you're doing for my family and everyone, we're going to build this agency." Thank you and, "If you need anything call." And so he'd call me every time he needed something. Any time he needed anything.

LaMar: He can't do that then.

Lloyd: That's what I've been telling you.

LaMar: But see, what I'm saying is that, I didn't know this, so I'm kinda like out of the picture because it's between you and him, because I didn't know.

Lloyd: I'm telling you, that's why I'm like, "Reg, you can't do that." If you say certain things and have people doing this, I'm taking trips up to L.A. in the middle of the night, taking money.

LaMar: See, I didn't know that, you see what I'm saying? That's something that—now if he'd have told me this straight out, then I'd been like, "Well, son, you gotta stand by what you said."

Lloyd: That's why I said words mean a lot. Remember when I was telling you? If I say anything, that's why I kept saying words mean a lot. If I say, "LaMar, I'm giving money for the bishop [of the Bushes' family church]," you expect that from me, right? Regardless of the situation because you said it.

Eventually, the conversation turned to Mike Ornstein. This conversation was held after the Heisman ceremony, when Ornstein flew to New York with the family. Ornstein stayed with the family throughout the weekend, during which time Ornstein introduced them to memorabilia dealer Bob DeMartino.

At this point, it was becoming clear to Lake that Ornstein had trumped him, despite denials by Griffin. Beyond that, Griffin makes two further admissions about money he received from Michaels and about how he and his family were going to get a stake in New Era Sports & Entertainment. By the end of the conversation, Lake is extremely agitated:

Lloyd: Look, Big Dog, what I'm saying is—and you tell me if I'm right or if I'm wrong—if you were in my shoes, would you be pissed that you did all this looking out and then some white dude [Mike Ornstein] come in out of the mist out of nowhere and run around every paper [saying], "I'm doing Reggie's marketing and flying to New York and doing everything."

LaMar: That's bullshit. Because one, you're being stupid because nobody has hired no marketing guy.

Lloyd: I didn't say hire, but if he's running around . . .

LaMar: He can run around—I got so many people running around doing stuff for the Griffin family if they wanted to. I admit, just like I told you, anyone can do anything because they're trying to get Reggie. You may say about the money that you gave me, I say I didn't give you no money, that's bull. I had guys offering me $20,000 when I was up in New York City. They had it in their hand and was going to give it to me.

Lloyd: What is that? What is that compared to what we gave already? That is nothing, $20,000 is nothing. [Michaels] gave you $26,000 the first time he met you, and that was a year and a half ago.

LaMar: Me and Mike talked about that.

Lloyd: But I'm saying that was a year and a half ago.

LaMar: But you're listening to bull crap. Do you know how much stuff I hear about my son, about you, about [Michaels], about [Caravantes], about the other guy? Do you know how much stuff I hear? Do know the stuff I heard in New York about you guys? Y'all ain't shit, that's what I heard, from you on down.

Lloyd: Who said that?

LaMar: I'm not going to tell you who said that.

Lloyd: No, they might say that.

LaMar: That's bullshit. Somebody out here saying, "I heard about a white man [Ornstein] doing the marketing." Reggie can't hire no marketing until he . . .

Lloyd: But I'm saying he's already—if the white dude [Ornstein] is saying and running with him, he already feels comfortable for what's going on.

LaMar: And the same thing you did. He is in the same shoes that you was in when you came in the business. We got together, you said, "If I do this, do this, this will happen." He's doing the same thing y'all did from the beginning, it's the same thing. Everybody's after Reggie Bush.

Lloyd: Right, but did he offer Reggie or your guys any part of the company?

LaMar: It doesn't matter the part of the company. You know what? Right here and now, I don't care about your company, I don't care about his company, I don't care about IMG, I don't care about David Dunn, all these guys. I told them when I walked into the Jets game, every agent was sitting in the room. I said, "I'm not talking about nothing or nobody with nobody. I'm here to enjoy my son's Heisman Trophy win and that's it." I had eight financial guys sitting in there. I had seven agents sitting in there when I walked in that door. That dude told me nobody was going to be there. I told everybody in the room. I said: "I'm not talking about shit today. Call me when I get back home." The dude set me and my wife up.

Lloyd: They got you to the game?

LaMar: Yeah, we went to the game, we walked in there and boom. First one jumped in my face, guess who? IMG. "How you doing, how you doing?" I'm like, "Wait a minute, who is this?" "I'm LT's agent." "Oh really?" The other dude, David Dunn, sitting right there, had them all in there. [Segal] sitting right there. I'm like, me and my wife was like, "What the hell is going on?" Business guy I talk to in L.A. been calling me for like three weeks. Guess who is sitting there? He is.

Lloyd: The financial dude?

LaMar: Yeah, he's sitting there. Then when I leave, because I left the game at halftime, everybody else left with me. The whole damn room was empty. Me and my wife was like, "OK, now I see." The dude they come to the Jets game, they come check it out. You know what I'm saying? I got a room full of agents in there and financial advisers.

Lloyd: But see, the difference is with that, we had an agreement before we got started.

LaMar: But still, you haven't went down and presented the agency to Reggie.

Lloyd: I just feel like it's going like this. Hold on. I just feel like we're being counted out from the beginning.

LaMar: If you've been counted out, Reggie would have told you right off the bat, "Don't even come down here." Reggie's not scared

to say that because when Reggie declare on the fifth, he's going to have more money in there. He could say, "Here's all your money, here's all your time, I'm done." He could say that right now. But he says "No, Lake, come down and bring your agency down and present it to me." And that's all you can do.

Lloyd: You know what? Me and you need to sit down in there and ride up and talk with Reggie.

LaMar: I'm not talking to Reggie about anything right now, nothing. And you shouldn't talk to him about nothing because it's not important. That championship game is important, not going and talking about some stupid ass agency because he's not going to talk to you, Lake. He's not going to talk to you because he has a right not to do that.

Lloyd: I'm to the point where I don't care about none of this shit here. I gotta do like everybody else and go for self because that's what everybody's doing when the money come off the fucking table. Everybody's saying, you know, everybody's scattering from their promises. Everybody is. I'm like fuck it, fuck it. Everybody is not doing nothing they said they were going to do.

At another point, Griffin confirms that Ornstein is playing a role in Bush's selection of a contract agent. Ornstein did this at Reggie's request, according to Griffin. However, Ornstein also wanted to make sure that whoever was hired as the contract agent would not want to do any marketing for Bush:

Lloyd: But how do you let the white man [Ornstein] come in like that and dictate the whole show?

LaMar: He's not dictating anything.

Lloyd: He picked the agents.

LaMar: No, he didn't. JC [Pearson] picked the agents.

Lloyd: JC said when he was in there that Mike picked the agents.

LaMar: JC picked the agents. They both got together. He picked some agents, and Mike picked some agents. We got a total of ten

agents that we are going to interview. He picked five and Mike picked five, and they came to the point to talk together, who's this, who's that. They had about eighteen agents. They eliminated eight of them. See, you're listening to all this bull crap that people are telling you. I know what's going on. I talk to JC and Mike [Ornstein] every day. And they say you're listening to so and so, oh, the white guy this, the white guy that.

Lloyd: But I don't even know how you would let him come into that position.

LaMar: Because Reggie developed a relationship with him because he used to work for him. And you know the guy looks awesome as an agent, I'm not going to lie to you. They are some good agents. Reggie said, "JC, Mike, pick the top agents that you know and give them to my mom and my dad." And that's what they did. We got to hire IMG because JC said you've got to talk to him. But he don't like IMG because they done him wrong but they still got to talk to him. You see what I'm saying, because they are a big-time agency. They got big-time players and they got big-time money. So you got to talk to them. David Dunn, you gotta talk to him, he's big-time.

Lloyd: [Leigh] Steinberg.

LaMar: Now see, Steinberg, we might not talk to. The dude that's controlling Michael Vick, we're not talking to him.

Lloyd: [Joel] Segal?

LaMar: Segal, yeah.

Lloyd: He's the one that lied on Dave [Caravantes].

LaMar: Yeah, he's been calling me—he called me in New York twice and then turned around and called someone else because they called me. So all this stuff, that all this stuff you're hearing, man—you better stop believing this and listening to this stuff. I know what's going on. Reggie told [Ornstein] and JC, "Let my dad know everything that's going on." I know everything. I know everything. So you see you sitting up there and reading these books, and listening to this and listening to these people talk . . .

The conversation then turned to Bush's paying back Lake and Michaels, but Lake was impatient about the timetable. Again, Griffin confirmed that Lake had put in time and money to get the agreement going:

LaMar: OK, so when he get the money, he will say, "OK, Lake, well I need to sit down and talk to you about how much money I owe you," if that even goes that way.

Lloyd: No, you need to do that before you get the money.

LaMar: Not now, it's not going to happen now. And I'm going to tell him not to talk to you right now because he's got a championship game to play. His mind is on that. You don't do that, Lake. You don't do that. And if that was your son, I wouldn't do it to your son. I wouldn't say, "Hey, I need to talk to you about what you told me and you got a big game coming up in two weeks."

Lloyd: Three weeks, and it ain't nothing about the business, it's just about—why would you not?

LaMar: I wouldn't do it because I'm thinking about your son worrying about—and you know what? I don't think you consider him—all this stuff that's going on with this kid, he didn't get to sit down and rest not five minutes when he was up in New York City, not five minutes. And now he's come back to California and now here you come with some stuff about, "What can you do when you don't come, how much are you going to pay me back when you don't come through?" That is not fair for Reggie. And I'm not going to allow it, Lake. I'm not going to allow it.

Lloyd: You always look at what's not fair for Reggie, but you don't look at the other person. You always look at . . .

LaMar: You can't do that. You cannot do that. It is not fair for you or for him. See [Michaels] in there . . .

Lloyd: I don't give a fuck about what [Michaels is] doing. Mike's situation is different than mine. I put a lot of time in, Mike don't do nothing. I put all the time and effort in and my money.

LaMar: That's true.

Then the conversation again became terse and threatening:

Lloyd: Everybody's going—Reggie's going for self right now, you're going for self.

LaMar: He's not going for his self.

Lloyd: He is, Big Dog, no matter how you want to put it. He's doing what's best for him.

LaMar: And that's supposed to be the main thing.

Lloyd: So I'm supposed to do what's best for me then right now, right?

LaMar: What are you going to do, sue him? So sue him.

Lloyd: I'm going to do more than sue him if I wanted to. If I was going to go that route, I'm going to go talk to the attorney and see the best thing. I got so many different options right now that I can go get me some bread. If nigger say, "OK, fuck it, let's go for self." I don't get caught up. I'm not a groupie-do. I don't care about all that. I talk to Suge [Knight] like this is what you should do.

LaMar: You do.

Lloyd: And he told me. OK.

LaMar: That's all I can say.

Lloyd: Big Dog, I don't want to go that route, I'm just giving you an example of how everyone is going for himself.

Finally, Lake laid out his plan for what he might do. Not included in that plan was what he did do later in a telephone call to Denise Griffin.

Lake said that the conversation with Denise Griffin turned emotional and argumentative after he, wanting to stress the importance of honesty in any relationship, repeated compromising personal secrets told to him by LaMar. Lloyd said the call was prompted when LaMar alerted him to avoid Denise because she was upset: word was spreading that Lloyd was telling people around Los Angeles and San Diego that Reggie Bush owed him money.

"I wasn't going around telling anyone that and I wanted to her to know that, so I called her," Lake said.

The conversation quickly escalated, further damaging an already fragile relationship that was now both bitter and personal.

Lloyd: Right now if I was one of them scandalous dudes, what I could do. Listen to what I'm saying. Now listen, and I'm just showing you for self. Do you know right now, you know how easy I can get you in the media, right now? But listen to what I'm telling you.

LaMar: But I'm telling you what, your mom and your sister will hate you for life if you done that.

Lloyd: They wouldn't hate me for life.

LaMar: Yes, they would.

Lloyd: No, they wouldn't.

LaMar: Your momma would be like, your momma would ask you, "Why are you doing this?"

Lloyd: "You know, Mom, why I'm doing it? Because people weren't honest to me, and they went for self and so I'm going for self to look out for my family and get this money."

LaMar: I'm looking forward to an attorney calling me.

Lloyd: I'm not going to no attorney, if I did anything the first thing I would do . . .

LaMar: I'm looking forward to it.

Lloyd: Why would I have an attorney call you?

LaMar: Whoever, if somebody's going to call, if you're going to try to take us to court, so do what you gotta do, Lake.

Lloyd: Big Dog, you see, you think you guys so smart. You think that's how it works? I'm going to call an attorney and take you to court? First thing I'm going to do, I'm going to . . . [Lloyd discusses personal secrets told to him by LaMar] then I go do this book deal from the people from the media that want to get this book, I'll get me a million up front from everything I know, from all the knowledge from the last eighteen months, and I get me a couple of

million, and it's all over with. And Reggie loses probably $10 million in endorsement money behind the bullshit that he was doing. If I wanted to be scandalous like the white people would do, that's what I would do. They would tell you right now, either you sign or this is what I'm doing. And it's nothing wrong with this, and it's nothing illegal about it. I'm not saying I will, but that's what they would do to you. I already passed up that half a million one time. I told you about it.

Later in December, Lake and Bush held two conversations that lasted more than twenty minutes. During one portion, Lake tries to save the plan for the business:

Lloyd: But see that's what I'm trying to tell you. We're trying to talk like businessmen right now, and I'm letting you know.

Reggie: That's not business, what are you talking about? That's some bullshit you got going on behind my back.

Lloyd: Well, you're putting it on me because your dad is doing that.

Reggie: You're calling me, I'm not putting it on you.

Lloyd: I'm saying you're saying this is some bullshit going on behind your back. Your dad is telling us you knew what was going on.

Reggie: Fuck no.

Lloyd: But see, I don't know that.

Reggie: If I knew what was going on, man, don't you think I would have told you a long time ago that I wasn't coming with you all's company. If I knew what was going on I would have told you myself that I was coming.

Lloyd: Reg, I understand that. How would I know that? How would I know that?

Reggie: Unless I told you, right.

Lloyd: Reg, only thing I know is you said, "Do this and do that."

Reggie: And didn't I say get it up and running, I am not going to go with a company that has nothing to show for it. At least have something.

Lloyd: I mean we got it all up and running and going like we going like you said. With Sycuan behind us.

Reggie: You got to stand up and show me what are you talking about.

Lloyd: I know, I'm going to show you. But see what I'm saying, Reg, is I'm going to put everything on the table and show you exactly what's going on and you're going to be impressed. With Sycuan behind you, $3 million.

Reggie: I understand that. That's not going to make me say yeah. You know what I am saying?

At a later point, it's increasingly clear that Bush is backing away from the company:

Lloyd: I understand that, Reg, I just want you to know that everything you've ever asked, we're going to get. We work for you. You're the signature player. Whatever Reggie want, he's going to get. You're pushing the line with the company you came with. We got Team Bush, everything Reggie wants, he's going to get. I said everything you ever want like as far as anything you want to do, you know right now I got it hooked up for you to get free.

Reggie: You keep saying that. I understand all the shit you're saying right now. But the way you're going about it, it's making me like, every time you bring some shit to me, or you talk to me, it's like . . .

Lloyd: I want you to tell me how you feel.

Reggie: More and more less interested.

Lloyd: Talk to me about it.

Reggie: You're making me more and more less interested the more you talking about it.

From that point, the deal was essentially over. Bush declared for the draft on January 12, 2006, eight days after USC lost in the National Championship game against Texas. He picked Joel Segal to be his contract agent while Ornstein, who made sure Segal would have nothing to do with the marketing deals for Bush, was Bush's marketing agent.

Also that month, Bush retained lawyer David Cornwell to represent him in dealings with Michael Michaels and Lloyd Lake. Cornwell was hired on the advice of Ornstein, who had known Cornwell for years. Cornwell got his start in the NFL as an assistant general counsel for the league. After that, he eventually left and worked in the office of agent Leigh Steinberg before branching off on his own.

Cornwell had begun to develop his practice with a specialty in athletes, particularly NFL players. His primary expertise was in the NFL's substance abuse policies, which he helped write when he was in the league office. At that point, former Miami and New Orleans running back Ricky Williams had been Cornwell's most prominent client. Cornwell had also helped represent agent Leigh Steinberg against fellow agent David Dunn after Dunn had left Steinberg's firm and taken numerous clients with him. Steinberg initially won the suit, but it included embarrassing testimony about his private life that Cornwell did little to stop.

Along those lines, Cornwell had also developed a reputation for public grandstanding and taking a very aggressive approach. The aggressive portion of his character played out in negotiations with Michaels and Lake that month.

Cornwell arranged for a meeting between Michaels, attorney Brian Watkins, who was representing Michaels and Lake at that point, and Bush's side. Denise Griffin and Cornwell also were there. The meeting was held at Ornstein's office in Santa Monica. LaMar Griffin was noticeably absent.

It was contentious from the beginning. Cornwell had former FBI agents present to search Michaels and Watkins for recording devices, Watkins told *Yahoo! Sports,* the *Los Angeles Times,* and the *San Diego Union-Tribune*. When the two sides sat down, Cornwell quickly offered $100,000 to settle the whole matter.

At that point, Michaels looked at Bush and said, essentially, "Reggie, I thought we had worked out a number and that's not even close." Before

that meeting, Michaels and Bush had held brief talks, and Michaels believed that Bush would settle for a figure of just over $300,000. Cornwell then essentially stopped the meeting.

"I'm speaking for Reggie and his mother, you need to talk to me," Cornwell said, according to a source. Cornwell had both Bush and his mother leave the room. Cornwell then proceeded to berate Michaels and Watkins, a source said, and told them he wasn't offering more than $100,000. Michaels declined the offer and he and Watkins left.

"It wasn't a negotiation, it was a take-it-or-leave-it offer," a source said.

Cornwell later asked Watkins to draft a letter seeking a settlement. The letter, which was dated February 13, 2006, was first reported by *Yahoo! Sports,* the *San Diego Union-Tribune*, and the *Los Angeles Times* in April 2006. In the letter, Watkins asked for $3.2 million to settle the case, saying he would seek that in actual and punitive damages if the case went to trial.

In addition, Watkins wrote: "Please advise if it is your intention to involve the University [of Southern California] in these settlement negotiations. We would not object to their participation as we understand their wanting to be involved due to the fact this matter was ongoing during their Championship season of 2004 as well as the entire season of 2005, and any lawsuit filed might have an adverse effect on them."

While Cornwell and Watkins haggled, word started to leak through the agent community about Reggie Bush having problems with an Indian tribe in California. Caravantes, worried about what was happening to New Era Sports & Entertainment, told other agents and other league sources.

From there, the story slowly spread to reporters Jason Cole, then of the *Miami Herald,* and Charles Robinson of *Yahoo! Sports,* who found out in late January and February, respectively.

By April, the story started to percolate. Cole found property records that showed Bush's family lived in a home they didn't own, which appeared to be beyond their financial means. Likewise, Robinson had heard from other NFL personnel people that Bush was having issues and eventually uncovered Michaels's name.

Both reporters contacted Sycuan tribal spokesman Adam Day approxi-

mately two weeks before the NFL Draft. Day informed the reporters of the dual interest in the story. At that point, the race was on between the two news organizations.

Cole and Robinson ended up in San Diego on April 20, 2006. Day agreed to talk to them only if they were together. The two reporters ended up staking out the home where Bush's family lived. When Denise Griffin returned from work that evening, the reporters approached her.

"I don't want to talk," Griffin said. According to the *Miami Herald* report, when asked who owned the home, she closed her eyes, sighed, and again declined to discuss the matter.

"I'm tired, and I want to get something to eat. I just got back from work," she told the *Herald.*

"I have absolutely nothing to say," she told *Yahoo! Sports*. The next day, moving vans showed up at the home as the family moved out. Coincidentally, the family had been served the eviction notice earlier that month.

On April 23, *Yahoo! Sports* broke the story in the afternoon on its Internet site. Shortly thereafter on its website, the *Miami Herald* printed its story detailing the possible improprieties. The *San Diego Union-Tribune* and *Los Angeles Times* quickly reacted. The *Union-Tribune* reported that LaMar Griffin had showed a copy of the brochure for New Era Sports & Entertainment to one of its reporters on December 2, 2005. Griffin described it as "a new company opening. They sent me a brochure. They're here in San Diego."

The *Union-Tribune* also was the first to extensively quote Michaels and Watkins on the matter. Watkins detailed the relationship between Michaels and Bush.

In its April 27, 2006, edition, the *Union-Tribune* talked to Michaels about the house and other financial arrangements.

"I never agreed to let them live rent-free," Michaels told the *Union-Tribune*.

Meanwhile, Cornwell was fighting the deluge of bad press for Bush. At 2:40 A.M. on April 24, 2006, after multiple news sources had weighed in on the story, Cornwell issued a statement indicating Bush had no knowledge of his parents' living arrangements.

"Mr. and Mrs. LaMar Griffin previously leased a house in the San Diego area from a San Diego businessman, Michael Michaels. They are no lon-

ger living in the house," Cornwell wrote. "Reggie Bush was a full-time student at the University of Southern California and never lived in the house. As is the case with most twenty-year-old college students, Reggie was not aware of personal or financial arrangements relating to his parents or their house. Mr. and Mrs. Griffin now realize that, given Reggie's public profile, their personal decisions can reflect on their son."

On April 26, 2006, Bush said he was sure his family would be cleared of any wrongdoing.

"I'm confident and I know what the truth is," Bush said at a pre–NFL Draft appearance in New York. "I know for a fact that everything is fine and this is all blown out of proportion and there's more to the story than is being told right now."

On April 27, 2006, Bush put off more questions about the situation.

"I would love to talk about it, but now is not the time," he said in an article in the *Union-Tribune.* "There's a time and a place for everything and this isn't one of them."

When asked for a timetable on when he might be able to clear the smoke, Bush said he couldn't say.

"Are we talking weeks, months?" a reporter persisted.

"Oh, no, not months," Bush said. "I have to play football, you know what I mean?"

Late in the week, however, Cornwell went on a strong offensive. In a report by the *Los Angeles Times* that was published on April 29, 2006, Cornwell asserted that Michaels and Lake were trying to extort millions from Bush.

"We identified their scheme months ago and collected written evidence over the course of the months," Cornwell said in the *Times* story. "And we provided that evidence to the NFL Players Association and NFL security."

Cornwell further said the league has subsequently notified a number of teams that Bush was the "target of improper threats."

In a brief statement released April 28, 2006, the NFL said only that it has advised Cornwell to "consider referring these matters to law enforcement authorities" and would continue to monitor the situation.

Watkins responded in kind with a press release that was issued on April 28, saying that Bush's parents, "defrauded our clients out of large

sums of money by holding the carrot of Bush's future football career in order to entice our clients to invest in their sports and entertainment company."

According to the *Los Angeles Times* report, Watkins further explained that "as Mr. Griffin, Mr. Lake, and Mr. Michaels began working on the technicalities of the company, ongoing meetings with Mr. Griffin began to reveal that Reggie's continued participation came with conditions. Mr. Griffin suggested that in order to 'keep them happy,' Michaels and Lake would have to help them with some of their personal problems."

But while Michaels and Lake provided the money, it was all too clear by the end that nobody was happy.

TWELVE

The Suge Factor

Lloyd Lake—who lived in the hip-hop world—thought he could reach out to Reggie Bush, who loved the hip-hop world, through Suge Knight. In his industry, Suge is known as a no-holds-barred character, the man who created Death Row Records and was called the John Gotti of hip-hop. A telephone call from Suge is one of those rare moments that brings everyone to attention.

And Lake needed Bush's full attention as they tried to work through their business dispute in late November 2005. In addition to Suge, Lake also secured actor and comedian Faizon Love, whom he had known from his San Diego youth, to help settle his issues with Bush.

"I was just trying at this point to find somebody he [Bush] knew and maybe he was comfortable with and that he respected in the business they've been through in the past, and giving their advice," Lake said. "I was looking for somebody that can help mediate the situation without it getting out of hand. I thought those were good people that had been through a lot and could tell and help the situation get resolved."

In many disputes, people reach out to professional mediators, many of whom hold a law degree. Not many people reach out to an ex-convict

who helped mastermind the careers of Dr Dre, Snoop Dogg, Tupac Shakur, and a veteran actor whose profile grew even higher with appearances in the movies *Blue Crush, Elf*, and *Who's Your Caddy?* to do so.

Of course, this wasn't your normal mediation.

"I told [Suge] about the situation and he was like, 'Let me try to resolve it because you know he doesn't need it and you don't need it. Get it resolved and go about your way. Go on your separate ways,' " Lake said. "That's what we were trying to do."

In a late-night telephone conversation probably better suited for the television show *Access Hollywood,* Lake, Bush, Suge, and Faizon all had the opportunity to either say their piece or make peace.

In that conversation—Suge Knight recalled in a November 2007 telephone interview with the authors of this book—Knight said that Reggie Bush deserves the Heisman Trophy, he deserves to have gained all those yards at USC, and now with the New Orleans Saints, and he deserves to be a successful businessman off the field. Yet Knight also believes that Reggie's decision not to reimburse Lloyd Lake was a mistake and USC doesn't deserve the possible ramifications from it.

If Bush is found to have violated NCAA rules, the USC program could face sanctions. Bush's 2005 Heisman Trophy could also be in jeopardy.

"I've known each of those guys for years, and I believe if guys have friendship, then don't let business or money get in the way of that friendship," Knight stated.

"Even if you disagree, settle it so you can still be men and still be friends. When it came down to Lloyd and Reggie, whatever you got going on personally, you shouldn't let it get out of hand where it affects your school and the players; it's not fair to the other guys who put their time and hard work in because some other guys out there are being hardheaded because of jealousy or stupidity, and they are throwing everyone else under the bus."

Knight confirmed the four-way telephone call at the request of Lloyd more than two years ago. Knight stressed he did not take sides between Lloyd and Reggie in the dispute, instead encouraging both to resolve their differences before things went too far.

"I think it should have been worked out; they should have got it resolved," Knight said. "They are both grown men. If Lloyd wanted to get

it worked out, if Reggie wanted to get it worked out, they should have got it done. It doesn't make any sense to me. If Reggie owed Lloyd a dollar, Reggie needed to pay the dollar, and move on with your life. Don't let it affect innocent people.

"I think Reggie is a good person and Lloyd is a great friend. Whoever does the right thing, that's a man. Whoever doesn't do the right thing, that's a coward. Nobody knows the truth but those two guys."

Lloyd: I told you at the beginning, you told me don't tell Reggie. Remember I was going to tell him [and you were], "No, don't tell him."

LaMar: But see you was going to be put out there anyway because you told me Suge . . . Reggie knows that. Suge ain't nothing but a crook. They think you are a hustler, that's one thing, everybody thinks that about you. You see what I'm saying? I'm not going to come to you and say, "I'm not dealing with you, man." I'd say we were friends but right now I don't deal with common guys like you anymore. I used to do that, but I don't do that. The only reason I talk to you is because I met your dad. If I hadn't met your dad, I wouldn't be standing here talking to you right now if I didn't meet your dad. Your dad is the one who told me about you. He's the one that came into my house when . . . no, I seen him at the [Helix] football [games]. He saying, "I got a son there, he's got a little this and that, but he's a cool guy." I know about this before you even came to the house because your dad told me. So I'm not listening to this here, I've got Reggie acting a fucking fool right now.

Lloyd Lake first met Marion "Suge" Knight around 1995 when Lake was working in the rap music recording industry. Lake had operated a struggling recording company called Breakbread Records in San Diego before it went out of business. "We just ended up clicking," said Lake, who in late 2007 continued to drive from his San Diego home to Los Angeles to meet with Suge.

While Lake was a tiny player in rap music, Suge—that's his trademark nickname for "Sugar"—was larger than life.

Suge's company, Death Row Records, based in Los Angeles, once boasted annual sales of $200 million and the moniker "Motown of the Nineties." It played a major role in exposing West Coast rap to an international audience with artists like Tupac Shakur, Dr Dre, Snoop Dogg, and Tha Dogg Pound (Kurput and Daz Dillinger).

Death Row, however, was blasted by several activist groups and public figures in the media for its glorification of the violence associated with the gangsta rap image that most of its artists promoted. And the company imploded almost instantly because of that violence, when Tupac was killed in Las Vegas in September 1996 while riding on the passenger side in a car driven by Knight. Soon after, Knight was sentenced to nine years in prison for a parole violation relating to a fight that both he and Tupac were involved in on the night of Tupac's death.

Even behind bars, trouble followed Suge. He became a subject in the investigation of the March 1997 murder of rapper Christopher Wallace [Notorious B.I.G.] when a getaway car linked to the murder was found at one of Knight's houses. While the investigation was later dropped for a lack of evidence, he's still facing a civil trial in which the family of B.I.G. claim that he was gunned down by hit men hired by Death Row as part of an East Coast–West Coast rap feud.

Knight was released from prison in 2001 and tried to restart Death Row. But an arrest in 2002 for associating with gang members and a second arrest in 2003 for allegedly punching a parking-lot attendant hindered his efforts. In April 2006, due to a civil suit filed against him by Lydia Harris, who claimed she was denied her 50 percent stake in Death Row Records, Knight filed for Chapter 1 bankruptcy. It has been reported that in his personal bankruptcy case Death Row is listed as a creditor to which Knight owes roughly $150 million.

Knight reportedly claims to have experienced a spiritual rebirth in 2007. He wants to form a record label dedicated to a more positive spin and is the subject of an upcoming reality show called "Suge Knight's Unfinished Business."

Suge was an accomplished football player who played at the collegiate and professional levels.

Born on April 19, 1965, in the Compton area of Los Angeles, Suge developed into a good student and strong athlete. Eventually, he

managed to escape his hometown and surrounding trouble—he was allegedly a member of the Piru Bloods street gang—with a football scholarship to the University of Nevada at Las Vegas, where he also made the dean's list. Suge, a barrel-chested defensive lineman, played professionally for the Los Angeles Rams for a short time. He found steady work as a concert promoter and bodyguard for celebrities, including Bobby Brown.

After facing legal problems in 1987 for auto theft, concealed weapon, and attempted murder charges—Suge ultimately received probation—he formed his own music-publishing company. Suge allegedly made his first big fortune in the music business by coercing rapper Vanilla Ice into signing over royalties from his hit "Ice Ice Baby," owing to material that he supposedly sampled from one of Suge's company associates. As the story goes—it was featured on the music television station VH1—Knight held Ice by his ankles off a twentieth-floor hotel balcony to help persuade him to sign over his royalties.

Suge had no intention of hanging Reggie Bush by his ankles over a hotel balcony.

He just wanted to talk to Bush.

Finally, all four parties were connected by telephone—Lake, Reggie, Suge, and Faizon. The conversation lasted thirty minutes or so and Lake said everyone had an opportunity to speak. Lake said both Suge and Faizon agreed and told Reggie he needed to compensate Lake.

"It was them [Suge and Faison] basically just hearing both sides of the story," Lake said. "Suge was trying to let him know that you are wrong and you guys need to as men figure how to get it right and go on so it doesn't get out in the media. Suge was basically trying to get him to understand, you should do what's right, it's wrong and it's going to get ugly for you. He [Suge] wasn't on either side. He basically was telling him [Reggie] that when you're wrong, you're wrong. When you're right, you're right. Get it taken care of."

Like Knight, Faizon—who grew up in Newark, New Jersey, and San Diego, and started as a stand-up comedian at the age of fifteen—confirmed Lake's account of the conversation.

"I just told Reggie that if it's true what Lloyd is saying—and I've known Lloyd a long time—if it's true, he has to go ahead and take care of Lloyd," Faizon said in a November 2007 telephone interview with the authors of this book. When asked if he believed Lloyd made payments to Bush, Love said, "I know it happened, I know it happened, I know it happened. He [Lloyd] is a knucklehead, but he's honest with it.

"When I first saw Reggie, I told him not to do any business with [Lloyd]; because he's for real about it. When Reggie called me and told me, 'Hey, he [Lloyd] is on my back,' I am like, 'Oh, man, what the fuck? What did you think? That's my homeboy, my neighborhood. He's trying to make a legitimate [deal].'

"I would have done the same thing [as Lloyd]. He had all his ducks in a row. Reggie, I guess, was [thinking] the gang-bang thing, thinking he [Lloyd] couldn't do it, that he really put it together. Somebody must have got in Reggie's ear not to do the thing [agency]."

Lake said he lost his temper at one point during the call when he said Bush called him a liar. "I told him I am going to slap the shit out of you when I see you for calling me a liar because I didn't appreciate that," Lake said. "Reggie said, 'See, Suge, what I am saying?' That's the wrong guy for mercy if that's what you are looking for. I was real angry because he was trying to make me out to be a bad guy, like I am lying about everything. . . . They [Suge and Faizon] just so happen that they know me enough to know that I wouldn't do anything like that and it didn't make sense."

Lake had hoped the conference call would settle his differences with Bush.

"Reggie didn't understand business at the time, he might now," Lake said. "You make an agreement, honorable or not, and you renege on it, whatever, you have to compensate the people you have running around. That was my thing. You took money, a whole bunch of it, let's figure out how we can make it right and go on our separate way and we still could have still been friends. We don't have to be friends, we don't want to have bad feelings, this wouldn't be happening. That's all I wanted from him. I thought those were good people that had been through a lot and could tell and help the situation get resolved. They both told him [Reggie] he was wrong. That was that."

Knight believes New Era would have succeeded if Bush and Lake had partnered together as initially planned.

"I think the idea was great," Knight said. "I think it was a great situation for our community, for our inner city, to get together and network and do something great."

Though there are no direct links between Suge and Bush or USC, there are some indirect connections. For starters, Suge is a big fan of the Trojans. "I think it's a great program with great coaches," he said. "I have a lot of respect for that school." Three former artists for Knight's Death Row Records—Snoop Dogg, Dr Dre, and Warren G.—spent significant time on the USC sidelines during the Trojans' 2005–6 season. Snoop Dogg was such a regular that he often took passes from Matt Leinart during practice

When Bush was asked by the media if Snoop Dogg gave him on-the-field advice, Bush laughed. "Nah, Snoop is a rapper—he doesn't know anything about football! No offense to Snoop, I'm just joking around. But he didn't try to give us too much advice. He's a huge fan of USC and it was great to have him out there to be a part of that—not only for us, but for him as well. He had a great time and we liked having him there."

The celebrity presence on USC's sideline eventually became an issue for the NCAA. For the 2006 Rose Bowl, Championship Series administrators "issued a directive to officials of the four BCS games to substantially limit sideline access." They requested teams limit themselves to five "wild-card" sideline passes to be issued to former players only. The NCAA postseason handbook states, Sideline credentials should be limited to "individuals who have responsibilities that require their presence on the field."

Snoop Dogg managed to qualify for a sideline pass for the Rose Bowl because he took on the responsibility of wearing a microphone and recording "sound bites and color" for *ESPN Hollywood.*

THIRTEEN

Leaving for the NFL

Reggie Bush looked around and realized his professional stock was never going to be any higher. Although he hinted there was a slight chance he might return to USC for his senior season and the opportunity to join Ohio State's Archie Griffin (1974–75) as college football's only two-time Heisman Trophy winner, nobody really believed him.

In fact, NFL scout Chris Landry had watched plenty of videotapes of Bush, and he was convinced Bush was the most talented player in the 2006 NFL Draft. Landry described Bush in media interviews as a "transcendent-type player in the Marshall Faulk mold" who could line up at receiver, in the slot, or in the backfield and return kicks as well. "There's not anything he can't do," Landry said.

Except possibly run and hide.

Bush probably realized that, at some stage, somebody would find his way to the money trail he and his family had left behind in their dealings with New Era. Naturally, those actions could jeopardize Bush's amateur status if uncovered while he was still at USC, not to mention cause an embarrassing situation for California's oldest private research university.

In reality, however, if Bush thought seriously of rejoining his Trojan

teammates in 2006, it was probably for a fleeting moment that only lasted as long as it took him to buckle his chinstrap. Bush was entering a new era in his football career, and there were millions of dollars—legitimate dollars—on the table for Bush, since he was considered a top selection.

While the NFL makes no secret about its position on underclassmen entering the draft—the league sends a pamphlet to underclassmen considering the draft titled "Stay in School"—Bush was talented enough and eligible, under NFL rules, to turn professional after his junior season.

On January 12, 2006, in an announcement that didn't come as a surprise, Bush said he would forgo his senior season at USC to enter the NFL Draft. The decision had been speculated about since December 2005, when Bush won the Heisman Trophy by a landslide after leading the nation in all-purpose yards with 222.3 yards per game, rushing for 1,740 yards.

"I'm excited about going to the next level," Bush told reporters. "I felt this was the right time. I don't have a problem playing with Houston if they were to pick me. Just the chance to play for an NFL team would be great. I'm going to have to position myself so I am able to make an impact immediately. It's going to take a lot of work, and it's not going to come easy."

Just as quickly as Bush made his announcement, another question arose: Would Bush stay as the projected number-one pick, which belonged to the Houston Texans, or would he be available at number two for the New Orleans Saints? Bush had three and a half months until the draft on April 29 to show Houston—and the nation—that he was worthy of the top pick.

Lloyd: But we're not going to talk like the formal meeting, I just want to show him the [Roger] Penske [of Penske racing] dude, the Super Bowl, and let him know the dude wants to open the cards up. Figure we don't even have to talk about money. I'm saying that support from you.

LaMar: I understand that, but see, I'm not going to go against him if he's not going to . . . I'm not going to go up there and waste time and say, "Reggie, we need to talk." And he says, "Dad, I told you I

don't want to talk to nobody right now about anything. Tell Lake I'll talk to him." You know what I'm saying? But man, the boy is so dang busy, he don't have five minutes for himself. We got off the plane and we were in the airport at quarter to five in the morning. There were people in the airport wanting to get autographs. We couldn't even get in the goddang limousine. Last night we had to walk him out the back door to get out of the damn building. So right now he don't even have any time to talk. He can't even talk to [coach] Pete Carroll because he just don't have any time. I talked to him last night, he is so worn out that it is unreal. When we were in New York City [for the Heisman], Lake, this kid was in and out of his room every time. We gotta go to *Letterman*, we gotta do *NFL Today*. You gotta go do this. Man, I called him one time and he said, "Dad, I haven't slept for three days." He's trying to get rest now, but see, he's not resting because now he's got midterms and tests now. He's in a room right now taking a test after all this other stuff, then later on tonight he gotta go interview with somebody else. Practice is Friday and then he's got midterms all week. That's why he came back early, because of midterms. And nobody's trying to say, "Oh, we don't want to sit down and talk to you," but the boy just ain't got no time. That's the only thing I'm saying. We've seen Reggie at the Heisman ceremony, this boy walked right by me in the hotel room and said, "Dad," and just kept right on going. I talked to him three times out of six days.

Lloyd: He's busy, I understand that. I'm not arguing with that. All I'm saying is, "Reg, give us a chance to sit down without everybody else, just me, you, and your dad, so I can just show you what's going on." I'm not a dummy. How do you think I got us hooked up right now with somebody who's worth $2 billion that's ready to open up car dealerships for Reggie right now?

LaMar: Okay, hold on. Now, let me tell you something. Don't you know that there is eighteen thousand guys saying the same thing you are saying? "I got the deal, man, I got the deal for these, bro." You know every marketing, everybody has called Reggie, has called me. I have turned down so much stuff, Lake, that you can't even imagine.

Lloyd: Yeah, but it won't get any sweeter than that. You know, car dealerships, do you know how much money that makes?

LaMar: There's a guy right now that's trying to get a car dealership, that already got a dealership with him. An attorney or some other guy called me the other day and said, "Man, I got this thing on the table right now." I got LT's [LaDainian Tomlinson of the San Diego Chargers] marketing guys telling me he's got stuff for Reggie.

Lloyd: LT's marketing guy is bullshit, look what it did for him.

LaMar: What you think I don't know that? He called me three times in New York City. You know what he was going to do? Give me a limo to take me to the airport, and bring me back home from the airport in a limousine. I said, "No, bro, I got my buddy coming to get me."

Lloyd: I know, Big Dog, I understand.

LaMar: That's why I'm saying it's not a good time because everybody—but when you coming up saying the same thing, he's going to be like, "Okay, I understand he's got a big deal." Everybody got a big deal. He gets text messages, "Hey, Reggie, I got this." I was reading one yesterday, "I got this big deal from . . ." I can't remember the car dealership. "Man, we can make two or three bills off of this if you just come down and be a spokesman for us."

Lloyd: That is nothing compared to what I've got for him. Penske will fuck up everybody that he got on the table right now.

LaMar: See what I'm trying to tell you, Mike [Michaels] told me the same thing about this when we were driving down the street, he told me the same thing. But see, what I'm trying to say is that, if you try to talk to him now, he's going to say "Okay," and you're not going to have his full attention and everybody else is talking to him. He's in L.A., and everybody got a pipe dream that they just flip—I had a woman call me yesterday, call my wife. She went shopping with her one time. Now she's Denise's best friend. Some girl named Jackie. Who the hell is Jackie? She said, "Well, you remember I went shopping with you, and you and . . . and I've been looking for your number for about four months." You're a damn liar. You seen Reggie on TV and now you want to call and give you a little stuff.

> What you got, Lake, I'm not trying to say you ain't got a good deal for Reggie. But what I'm trying to say is that, if you go down there and try to present this thing to him and tell him what you got, he's going to look at you like everybody else. Because everybody else has got something that sounds so good. If I was you, I would want you to come home for Christmas, that's what I would do. Wait until he comes down here.

It's obvious that competition for a spot atop the professional football pyramid is intense. Bush, of course, had scaled his way toward the summit and was nearly close enough to touch it. The 2006 crop of NFL draftees was expected to sign contracts valued at more than $300 million, and the disposition of that cash would be heavily tilted toward top-round draftees such as Bush.

Bush and other potential top-ten selections such as defensive end Mario Williams of North Carolina State, quarterback Vince Young of Texas, and Bush's teammate at USC, quarterback Matt Leinart, had beaten the odds and were poised to enjoy riches and fame beyond their wildest dreams.

Each year about one million high-school football players graduate. About sixty thousand of those athletes play collegiate football, according to the NFL Players Association, and just six thousand draw interest from an NFL scout. Only about three hundred find a home on an NFL roster.

The math and odds aren't any better for player agents. About one thousand agents are registered with the NFL Players Association. But about seventy agents, each representing eleven or more clients, account for roughly half of the league's active players. When agents who represent between six and ten players are included, 10 percent of the agents represent 75 percent of all players.

It's a high-stakes game that New Era desperately wanted to join, and company representatives such as Lloyd Lake figured Reggie Bush, as their signature client, would help give them instant credibility. Of course, Bush, known for his shifty moves on the field, was just as shifty off. Bush cut back in the open field and selected agent Joel Segal and marketing representative Mike Ornstein in January 2006, effectively ruining Lake's dream of opening a sports marketing agency in his hometown.

"I was really excited," said Lake, who spent a year in federal prison

starting in February 2006 for a parole violation. "It was like a chance when you don't have to even take any chances of ever going back to prison, being legit. It was something I liked. I liked sports, and it would have been good. A lot of good athletes come out of San Diego, especially football. So it would have been a good spot to have a good agency base."

Everyone was off-base in this business venture, starting with Bush.

Lloyd Lake had a feeling that New Era was losing ground in the race to secure Bush as a client. Bush was dodging Lake's repeated telephone calls and, when Lake was able to get Bush on the line, Bush was vague in his responses. Plus, word began to spread in late November 2005 that Bush and his family planned to hold interviews the following month in Mike Ornstein's office in Santa Monica with seven or eight potential agents.

The posturing to represent Bush was likely the most intense ever over the representation of any potential NFL star. The agent derby for Bush was originally conducted by Michael Ornstein. However, USC football coach Pete Carroll also involved himself in the process as permitted by NCAA rules. Carroll actually had two former National Football League executives—Joe Mendes of the Washington Redskins and Pat Kirwan of the New York Jets—speak to the Trojans following their December 20, 2005, practice in preparation for the January 4 Rose Bowl against Texas. "You guys are your own little business," Mendes said to the team, according to a *Los Angeles Times* story. "You have to figure out the best way to optimize your value."

Reggie Bush, of course, was well on his way to figuring out his optimum value. Media speculation during that time was correct: Bush's camp had narrowed his possible representatives to three: Joel Segal of Worldwide Football, Inc., based in New York City; Leigh Steinberg of Newport Beach, California; and Todd France of Atlanta.

Segal, who was decertified for a year by the NFL Players Association in the early 1990s, had landed Atlanta Falcons quarterback Michael Vick after Vick fired Octagon in 2004; Steinberg has represented the number-one pick overall in the NFL Draft a record eight times, a milestone unrivaled within the sports industry; and France has represented high-profile players such as Nate Clements, Ronnie Brown, and Takeo Spikes but has never had a first-round pick.

Reggie "loved Warren Moon," Steinberg said in an interview for this book. "We walked away from that thinking we're going to get Reggie Bush. We were against two other people who had never done the first pick in the draft. After the presentation, Ornstein told us he would set up dinner for us to go out with Reggie. That never happened. After those interviews, Pete Carroll set up a new process and took control of it. We didn't get included in that. I think Pete did that after a story that came out about Mike [Ornstein] being involved and Pete wanted to take control. The story linked Mike with something negative. At that point Carroll freaked and took control. The irony is that after all that, Reggie picks someone who had been decertified."

ESPN also reported that three other agents who made final pitches to Bush in December 2005 included David Dunn of Athletes First and Ben Dogra of SFX Sports. Dunn's client list had included players such as quarterbacks Matt Hasselbeck and Drew Bledsoe; Dogra is considered one of the top recruiters in the country and landed contracts for fullback Mike Alstott of Tampa Bay and receiver Roy Williams of Detroit. While it was not clear who would be handling Bush's marketing, Athletes First, which represented former USC quarterbacks Carson Palmer and Matt Cassel, was believed to be in the running with Ornstein for the job. Of course, Ornstein was already heavily involved with Bush and his family at this point.

Picking an agent was anything but an easy process for Bush, but he believed he had the right man for the job when he announced he had selected Segal to represent him in contract negotiations. Bush made the announcement during the same news conference at which he announced he would turn pro and not return to USC for his senior season. Bush said at a news conference that Segal was "a strong agent who will do a great job in representing me." Bush also said he was still considering candidates to negotiate his marketing deals.

Sports marketers predicted Bush would attract a healthy portfolio of companies early in his NFL career. "Reggie has done a really good job this year in proving that he can shine in the limelight," David Carter, executive director of the Sports Business Institute at USC, told ESPN. "Being that he was in Los Angeles and he learned by watching and doing what Matt Leinart did, he already has gone through the sports marketing equivalent of his rookie year."

Leinart, meanwhile, had signed with Creative Artists Agency to represent him in his marketing and licensing deals. The quarterback eventually signed Steinberg to do his contract work. "I don't think there has been a draft that I can remember that has three more dazzling prepackaged stars coming out of the top of the draft," Steinberg said in December 2005. "The competition is so fierce, it's like *Star Wars*. Reggie is a human highlight show, Leinart is a movie star, and Vince Young is dazzling."

Bush—the human highlight show—still had plenty of moves in him.

One of the few questions concerning Reggie Bush was whether he was durable enough to handle eighteen or nineteen carries a game in the NFL and be an effective runner if teams turned him inside between the tackles. Plus, Bush was actually a part-time player for the Trojans, sharing the load with the counterpunching LenDale White. USC coach Pate Carroll, a former NFL coach, believed Bush was going to be an impact player, regardless of numbers and how teams attempted to defense him.

"He's a game-changer, with speed, instincts, and competitiveness," Carroll said in a 2006 statement released by the school. "He'll take that talent to the NFL and wow them there as a runner, receiver, and as a returner, and I can't wait to watch him."

As the 2006 NFL Draft approached, the pundits had plenty to discuss. Should Houston stick with struggling David Carr at quarterback and choose Bush, who was being compared with Gale Sayers and Marshall Faulk? Or should the Texans draft Young, who was considered the best quarterback at the game's most important position? (Quarterbacks had been selected number one in seven of the eight years leading into the 2006 draft.)

"I will be really interested to see where these guys end up, because Reggie is so rare and so different, but at the end of the day, it's still a quarterback's league," NFL.com analyst and former NFL team executive Pat Kirwan said before the 2006 draft. "At this time last year, nobody thought Alex Smith would be the number-one pick in the last draft."

Phil Savage, general manager of the Cleveland Browns, felt Bush's size could play a role in how teams planned to use him. Bush carried 437 times in his three-year career with the Trojans. Twenty carries per game

over an NFL season is 320 carries; an average of twenty-five is 400 carries.

"In my opinion, with Reggie Bush, more may be less and less could be more," Savage said at the 2006 NFL Combine in Indianapolis. "I think when you get in a situation at his size, when you're carrying it twenty or twenty-five times a game for sixteen games, that's almost an impossibility for somebody to do that the way the game is played right now. . . . Whichever team takes Reggie at the top of the draft, if they utilize him in the right way, he can still be a Heisman Trophy winner at the pro level, even if he's touching the ball ten or fifteen times a game."

As odd as it might sound, a running back has been the number-one pick in the draft only six times since 1970. The first was Ricky Bell by the Buccaneers in 1977. The last was Ki-Jana Carter by the Bengals in 1995. The other four—Earl Campbell (1978), Billy Sims (1980), George Rogers (1981), and Bo Jackson (1986)—proved productive despite injury-shortened careers.

Reggie said all the right things to the media when he described his style. Draft pundits felt Bush easily topped the incoming class of running backs. Four of the top five running backs were juniors, including Bush's USC teammate LenDale White, Minnesota's Laurence Maroney, and UCLA's Maurice Jones-Drew. Memphis's DeAngelo Williams was the lone senior of the quintet. A glimpse into Bush's mindset at the time came during the NFL Combine in Indianapolis when he was asked by the media what he liked most about Houston with the number-one selection. "No state taxes," Bush said, referring to the fact that Texas has no income tax.

The fans wanted to know about Bush the football player, not Bush the accountant.

"Well, I like to think of myself as an every-down back," Bush said. "That's something that I feel like I want to, I guess, emphasize, to the teams. Even though I am not the biggest guy—I'm not 220 pounds—that I can still carry the load and be in there when the game is on the line. Obviously, I'm going to want the ball in my hands. I'm a playmaker . . . I just feel like I can do it. I don't know what happened to the other past running backs and why they weren't successful and what they did, but I know that I'm going to be successful and I won't fail."

However, Bush failed miserably when it came to returning a telephone call to Houston general manager Charley Casserly.

Charley Casserly—now in his second season as an analyst and general manager for the CBS Television Network's NFL pregame show—was considered one of the most respected general managers in the NFL throughout a career that spanned twenty-four years. He served as senior vice president and general manager of football operations for the expansion franchise Houston Texans from 2000 to 2006.

According to media reports before the 2006 NFL Draft, Casserly liked the way the top of the draft had shaped up. In addition to Bush, junior quarterback Vince Young of Texas also declared his intention to forgo his senior season and enter the draft. "All we can say is what has happened here with Reggie Bush and Vince Young declaring, with the addition of Matt Leinart among other players, is that you have a real strong top of the draft," Casserly said. "I think it's much stronger than it was a year ago. So what's that mean? It means we're going to get a real good player if we keep the pick, and if we trade the pick, we've got certainly a very valuable commodity to trade."

The Texans, however, did not plan to trade the top pick. In a flurry of behind-the-scenes maneuvering, Casserly and Houston's brass postured and pulled a draft-eve move that sent shock waves around the NFL. That's when the Texans opted to sign North Carolina State defensive end Mario Williams instead of virtually every expert's can't-miss choice, all-purpose back Bush. Ironically, Williams was represented by Dogra, who was part of the agent audition process held by Bush and his family in late December 2005.

"It came down between Reggie and Mario Williams," Casserly said in an exclusive interview for this book as he explained Houston's draft strategy.

"We weren't going to tell the press what we were doing. In Houston, there was a lot of pressure to take Vince Young. The press obviously assumed when we exercised the option on [quarterback David] Carr that we were going to take Reggie Bush. We bring Mario Williams in and the press just reported that it was simply leverage on Bush. The whole time

internally, we know it's between those two players. Then the decision was made to negotiate with both players. If we can only sign one, that's who we were taking. If we can sign both, we have to make a decision."

Casserly—who helped lead the Washington Redskins to four Super Bowls, winning three—said the discussion with Houston coach Gary Kubiak and the Texans brass concerning Bush was the same one conducted by the media and fans.

"The discussion on Bush from day one was, 'Could he be the complete back? Could he run inside, outside? Could he be the guy?' " Casserly said. "Kubiak felt that he could. In the Denver offense—which Kubiak coached before joining Houston—where it's one cut and go, they had played with some guys that hadn't been the biggest backs and been successful. I asked the question whether he was just a 'situation guy' where you had to game plan him into the game, and therefore people would know what you were going to do and not do when he comes into the game. The coaches didn't feel that way. They felt that they could use him in enough ways that people wouldn't get a bead on the guy. There was still some question in my mind about that."

Casserly also had other questions for Bush, and those questions dealt with the rumors that suddenly swirled around Bush and his family and their dealings with New Era representatives Lloyd Lake and Michael Michaels. Word began to spread that Bush's parents had lived in a spacious home, rent-free. Bush denied the accusations. Texans owner Bob McNair was quoted in the *Houston Chronicle* as saying, "If that's all there is, if it's still a minor thing, then I doubt it would have any effect on what we do." Casserly had a difficult time reaching Bush, an unfathomable scenario with the draft only a few days away.

"Sometime over the weekend before the draft it started coming out about his parents being in a house and where was the money coming from and these two men who had claimed they'd given Reggie money to go into business with them," Casserly remembered. "Reggie had backed out. Reggie had kept the money. Both of these guys had criminal backgrounds. You had a lot of stuff swirling.

"At this time, we're talking to Bush's representative Joel Segal about the contract. So on Monday, I told Segal I wanted to talk to Reggie. I've got some questions to ask him, obviously. Reggie, it seemed that Mon-

day, did every talk show in America. I say that tongue in cheek, but he did a lot of interviews. The one interview he didn't do was with me! He didn't call me back until Tuesday evening after numerous calls to Joel Segal and even a few calls from me to his cell phone where I left messages. No return call. Segal's in the middle. He's telling Reggie to call me. Finally on Tuesday evening he calls and says he's on a plane and is flying to New York and he'll call me when he lands. No call comes. I'm not happy, to say the least. He was told to call, and he didn't call. That's wrong. There's no getting around that. You call.

"That call needs to be the most important thing in front of him at that point in time. In the meantime, I talk to his mom. I tell her I'd like to ask about the payment for this house. The mom's comment was, 'The lawyers have told me not to talk to anybody.' I didn't try to find the stepfather. I'm just waiting to hear from him [Bush].

"On Wednesday, we finally talk. I ask him something to the effect of, 'Reggie, are your parents paying for the house?' He said, 'I don't know who is paying for the house.' I said, 'Reggie, have you ever accepted any gifts, money, anything? Have you done anything that violates any NCAA rule?' The answer was no. I asked, 'Did you make a deal with these two guys [Michael Michaels and Lloyd Lake] for a marketing firm which would violate NCAA rules as I understand it?' His answer was no. He didn't elaborate. I asked one more time, 'Did you accept any money from these people?' His answer was no. My last question was, 'Did you know these two guys had criminal backgrounds?' Again, his answer was no.

"I am told that he absolutely knew that they had criminal backgrounds. It is illogical to me that he does not know who is paying the rent on his parents' house. That's just illogical. On the other point, I had people telling me he and his stepdad had accepted money to start this marketing business and never repaid the money when Reggie nixed the deal with them. He agreed and backed out. Bottom line, I asked him the questions and those were the answers. NFL security gives us a report after interviewing Reggie that they can't find anything illegal. They asked the questions and that was their report.

"We're making the football decision to draft Williams at the same time I'm talking to Reggie, but we don't have a contract signed yet. He could have still been our guy. The owner asked me what I thought. I said,

'I think his story doesn't make sense, however right now we have no proof there's any criminal activity. Could there be some tax evasion problems here? Some people are telling me yeah, he might have issues there if some of this is true. There could be some NCAA issues there with USC, which could be some publicity issues but wouldn't violate any NFL rules. We can't sit here and say there's a criminal reason out there not to take the player, but I don't think he was telling me the truth. I don't like the fact he didn't call back. I don't necessarily believe everything he's telling me. But we've found nothing criminal.'

"There's some questions here: You're going to pay this guy $9 million a year and is this someone you can trust? But when we made the decision to go with Mario and he agreed to our contract, it ended up not mattering. Did I like what I was hearing? No, I didn't like what I was hearing. But I couldn't pin down enough things to tell the owner in a very open discussion that we should forget this guy totally. There were too many moving parts. Did I believe everything he was telling me? No, I didn't necessarily believe it. Did it make us more comfortable that we knew Mario had none of these issues? No question. Between the two of them, Mario had none of these issues and no distractions. Reggie was already a conglomerate."

Casserly also telephoned Lisa Lake in the days before the draft to inquire about Bush and his relationship with New Era. "Casserly said, 'I just spoke to someone that I really trust in San Diego and he told me to give you a call,'" Lisa Lake recalls. "They said if I want the truth about what's going on, to call you, so that's why I'm calling you. He said, 'I've been talking to Reggie, and he's been in my office.' Something about when you talk to a man and you can look in his eyes and tell us what went down and that way I can help you, and he looks at me and tells me, 'I did nothing wrong.' I just had heard too many other stories."

Leigh Steinberg was dumbfounded when told that Bush was tardy on his return telephone call to Casserly. "If he wants to be number one—and there has to be a great reason why you wouldn't—that call is the most important thing he should do. The next fifteen years of his life is dependent on making that call. Every single minute of everything you've done from the first day of Pop Warner to that moment has led toward making that phone call. If after everything, you're down to that moment and a

general manager says, 'One last thing. I need to talk to the player.' We move heaven and hell to make sure that connection is made. I don't mean to dump on the agent, but it is impossible that a player not understand the importance of that call."

On the Monday before the draft, Casserly, Kubiak, and the Texans staff met to discuss the group's thoughts on the top selection. Would it be Bush or would it be Williams?

"Everyone got to say what they wanted to say," Casserly said. "Then myself and Gary Kubiak met. We both were in favor of Mario Williams. We went to the owner, who was basically going to take our recommendation. We told him the reason was we thought Mario Williams was a complete player. We were going from a 3-4 to a 4-3. We did not have any defensive linemen like him, so we felt this was a guy we could build our defense around and we thought he was a hell of a prospect. We said if Bush wasn't in the draft, there wouldn't be any discussion that this guy is number one or not.

"The other point was that we had Dominic Davis; even though he had a knee injury we were expecting him to come back. The feeling was that maybe we couldn't get a back like Bush, but Kubiak felt there were more opportunities to get running backs than there were top defensive linemen. We did try to trade for Laurence Maroney and DeAngelo Williams, and it didn't work out. The draft was deep in running backs.

"But back to the real point. If Mario Williams refused to negotiate with us and Bush did, we were going to take Bush. We negotiated with both parties. We started before the first week though Mario Williams didn't believe us at first. His representative, Ben Dogra, let me know they didn't want to be used. I told him we were dead serious. As we go through this, the Tuesday before the draft we had reached an agreement on the total package, which was $54 million. Same number for both players. Neither had agreed on a signing bonus at that point in time. Danny Ferens was our contract negotiator. There was no question on that day that we could complete a contract with both people.

"Now the thing was you can't keep negotiating with both guys forever. There's still work to be done here and you have to make a decision and go

with it. On Thursday before the draft, we make a decision that it's Mario Williams and we're going ahead. We decided that Mario was going to be on the field for sixty plays and make a difference. I didn't see Reggie Bush on the field for sixty plays and I'm not sure you pay a guy $9 million that is not going to play sixty plays. We wanted it done before the draft on Saturday. The owner was in New York and we had a conference call where we all agreed this is what we're doing. Danny went to work on negotiations, we completed it on Friday, and announced it Friday night."

The Texans, of course, announced that they had signed the North Carolina State standout to a six-year, $54 million contract—$26.5 million in guarantees—ending speculation the team would take Bush or hometown product Vince Young. While Casserly stated that he thought both Bush and Young would be excellent professionals, he said the Texans chose to improve defensively. On Saturday, April 29, 2006, Williams was selected as the number-one overall draft pick for the Houston Texans. As Williams approached the podium against the gilded backdrop of Radio City Music Hall, fans began to boo and chant, "Overrated!"

Many commentators immediately criticized the decision to select Williams ahead of Bush. ESPN analyst Len Pasquarelli claimed that the administration of the Houston Texans was "suffering from astigmatism"—when vertical and horizontal lines are in sharp focus at two different distances—while ESPN columnist Bill Simmons suggested that all professional sports teams should hire a vice president of common sense.

The Saints, meanwhile, could barely contain their enthusiasm when it was their turn to select at number two. If ever a city deserved a break, New Orleans did.

While the Texans took Williams over Bush because they decided the six-foot-six-and-a-half, 292 pounder was the kind of defensive impact player who can take a team to a Super Bowl, the city of New Orleans couldn't care less. Saints fans were simply giddy over the selection of Bush despite the fact that members of the Bush camp had reportedly hinted that Bush would prefer not to play for the Saints if the Texans passed on him. The Tennessee Titans selected Texas quarterback Vince Young with the third overall selection.

Eight months earlier, New Orleans and the Gulf Coast had been flattened by Hurricane Katrina. New Orleans flooded as its levee system catastrophically failed. When Reggie Bush visited the city for the first time only weeks after his draft selection, he strolled into a welcome that rivaled that accorded rock stars. As ESPN reported, "A city struggling to get back on its feet has a superstar capable of bringing fans out of their seats on Sunday afternoons."

"To tell you the truth, it was a little overwhelming, and I really didn't expect it," Bush told the media. "But after seeing some of the devastation here, so much worse than you can imagine even after watching it on TV, you gain some appreciation for what these people have been through and what they're still facing. Hey, I'm no savior, and I can't make everything better. But I want to do my part. I know now that I'm coming here to be more than just a football player. The people immediately made me a part of the community and I'm going to do my share. This really was an eye-opener for me. But it was very uplifting in a way."

As much as New Orleans needed Bush, he needed New Orleans, too, after the events of the past week. Or, as the city's news reports said, he needed the unrelenting lovefest it showered on him. "I think," said Saints general manager Mickey Loomis, "it got him past the emotions of what had gone on. There's no doubt that, when we spoke to him on Friday night, he was pretty down. Who wouldn't be? I mean, he had prepared to be the first guy chosen, and all of a sudden, he wasn't. By the time he left here, though, I think he was feeling pretty good about himself and about his situation."

When Bush visited Emeril's—one of the several upscale restaurants that TV star chef Emeril Lagasse owns in New Orleans—the patrons erupted. "In all my years of doing this," Joel Segal said, "I've never seen anything like it. A standing ovation. People trying to get close to him. People chanting, 'Reggie! Reggie!' It was like we were at Yankee Stadium maybe twenty-five years ago. Man, wait until he actually gets on the field."

Back in California—far away from New Orleans—Lloyd Lake sat in federal prison wondering what his future held and how he could get Bush to

return the money Lake and his family had given him and his parents. The solution was simple, according to Leigh Steinberg, who said that this would have been his advice if he had been Bush's agent: "Pay it back."

"[Bush] needs to understand that he's about to be the first pick in the draft and he needs to get rid of any issues," Steinberg said. "People can forgive just about anything as long as you're honest about it. Let's figure out how to be honest and get past it. If we stonewall and are untruthful, it will come back to haunt us. We're better off dealing with it early than letting it hang. Come up with the money. Pay it back. For better or worse, what happened happened. You may argue that the relevant body here [the NCAA] doesn't have subpoena power, that you can stonewall this out. But we're living in an era of two hundred competitive television stations, nonstop talk radio, nonstop Internet, and nonstop investigative reporting, and if you want to live always looking over your shoulder, I'm probably not the right agent for you."

New Era was obviously not the right agency for Bush.

LaMar: That's what I'm talking about, Lake. He's not doing nothing. If Reggie thinks you're an agent, Reggie walks away. Reggie don't even shake his hand, because if you shake your hand it's like, "Oh, okay, I got a chance." This fucking dude, what's his name? Light skinned cat.

Lloyd: Mitch Frankel?

LaMar: That's him. He's been in every fucking town I've been in. Lake, I went to the bathroom, this dude is behind me. I'm going to the bathroom, I come out, he's standing right there. My wife, "Oh, you look so beautiful today, Ms. Griffin." He said that about eight times to her. This guy, "Oh are we going to talk?" We ain't talking to him. You see what I'm saying?

Lloyd: Right.

FOURTEEN

Why Not Return the Money?

Reggie's decision was made. He was headed to the New Orleans Saints and the National Football League, where riches awaited him both on the field and off. The only thing that could damage him was the discovery that he was a cheater while in college. That could happen if documents, financial records, and other evidence were to be released showing that he had indeed turned his final year at the University of Southern California into a $300,000 job.

In January 2006, Bush engaged Atlanta-based attorney David Cornwell, whose job it was to keep this from becoming public, to negotiate settlements. In one email to Lloyd Lake's sister, Lisa Lake, Cornwell even says that it would be better if these discussions were kept quiet. The attorney decided to negotiate separately with Lloyd Lake and Michael Michaels, who were coming at this from two different angles.

Michaels is a businessman who would be okay with or without the money. But Lloyd Lake—by his own admission—saw this as the opportunity to help him change his life. He used his family's money to make it possible. Lloyd didn't just have money on the line, he had credibility issues that made him a much more difficult person to negotiate with. Lloyd

didn't just want his money back, he wanted money back for his time and his effort. At a certain point, Cornwell said they weren't going to deal.

Lloyd Lake may have been a gambler, but Reggie showed Lloyd he could gamble, too. Cornwell dismissed Lloyd and his family, and challenged them to file a lawsuit.

Anyone following this story has probably asked a very simple question: Why didn't Bush just immediately pay back Michaels and Lake the money he had taken once he had decided to sign with agent Joel Segal and marketer Mike Ornstein? Why did Bush risk this story ever getting out?

"That's the million-dollar question," says Lisa Lake.

"Because he's a little hustler," offers Barber Gunner, who estimates she gave upward of $80,000 to the failed venture. "He's a street punk, and he thought somehow that you can just take people's money.

"Lloyd told me, 'I am glad I have changed my life because it would be on. I wouldn't let anyone take my money. And it's not all my money. It's my momma's money and my sister's money.'

"Everybody had good intentions when it started. It started as a good business deal for everybody. Their thing was that they never had good intentions. They never intended to do this from the very beginning. Maybe a few months after, they knew that they weren't going to do it, and they should have cut it off then, and just said, 'It's not going to work, I'll reimburse you your money.' How can you be so cruel and cold-hearted after you get your bonus not to say, 'Listen, it didn't go well, and I'm not going to go through with it, here's your money back.' That's all we asked for; just give us our money back."

While Bush eventually did settle with Michaels—paying between $200,000 and $300,000, according to sources—after private mediation in what was supposed to be a closed matter, the process wasn't pretty. The settlement with Michaels took more than a year to accomplish and was signed in April 2007. With Lake, the sides talked about settling but were never able to reach an agreement. The reason is that there has been a significant clash of egos along the way. Initially, when Bush sought to settle the matter with Lake, Bush offered Lake only $40,000. Lake's reaction

was amazement, even if he tried to make excuses for Bush. While Lake was guilty himself of making improper payments to Bush under NCAA rules, he also thought of the consequences of Bush's decision not to pay him back and how it might affect USC. Questions have also arisen about whether Lake violated state law by acting as Bush's agent.

"I'm fair, no matter what business it is, I want everybody to be happy and be fair," Lake said. "Now, let's sit down and put something together that's fair. He offered me $40,000 at one time, and I think it got up to $100,000. This was after the media and everything, but early on when nobody knew anything, he said, 'I'll give you back your $40,000.' What kind of math are you doing? That's what I'm thinking. I know Reggie was taking so much money from so many people, he lost track. He was losing track, everything was moving so fast. I understand he was in a vortex, something he couldn't get out of, spinning, and everything is moving fast, no time to sleep. There might have been a little delirium at the time. He was under a lot of stress, a young kid. I'll give him all the benefit.

"That shows you the character the guy has, his character, because I would have settled just because what I could do to my school. Fuck me right now. The school, you have to look at the consequences of your actions and what it could do to other people. You are in the league. What about the other kids coming up that might need scholarships and now they might not be able to give out any scholarships because of your action and you don't want to settle to make it go away? That was selfish to me. You never settled and now we are here now and I am going to end up making way more money from him not settling. I wasn't trying to hurt him. I didn't want to talk about him. Sometimes you force a person's hand, and that's what he did right now."

"One night he [Lloyd] came in my room and he knocked on my door, and he said, 'Mom, LaMar's attorney just called me.' It was nine o'clock at night," Barbara Gunner said. "I said, 'No attorney is calling anybody at night.' Lloyd said he threatened me and he told me, 'I know everybody and if you don't back off, I am going to make life really hard for you.' I said, 'No attorney would call you at nine o'clock at night. They would have written you a letter. Nobody would have talked to you like that. He said, 'Mom, it was his attorney.' I am going, 'No.' If the guy did it, he's a nut."

Although extortion claims from the Bush camp against Lake and Michaels were first reported by multiple media outlets in April 2006 before the NFL Draft, Cornwell used the word "extortion" much earlier in a lengthy email he sent to Lisa Lake at her personal and business email addresses. It was dated Friday, January 20, 2006, at 7:38 A.M. Lisa also said that Cornwell had telephoned her the night before and then on the morning of January 20, 2006, to alert her of his email.

"He called me on a Thursday night around seven o'clock and he said, 'I'd like to talk to you.' I said, 'Well, I really can't talk to you right now, and I don't think I'm going to be talking to you, but let me get an attorney and I'll have them talk to you,' " Lake said. "I was taking my kid to a dance and I told him, 'I really can't talk right now, but I'll find someone.'

"Friday morning, and I'm not kidding you, the [email] came in at [7:38 A.M.]. He first called me at seven in the morning and said, 'I thought you said you were going to have an attorney.' I said, 'Number one, it's seven in the morning here and I haven't even had a chance to call an attorney. I don't know if you've realized that.' He said, 'Well, have you checked your email?' I said, 'No, I haven't checked my email.' He said, 'I think you'd better check your email.' He was just really combative, argumentative. I said, 'You haven't given me a chance to call an attorney, it's seven in the morning.' He said, 'Well, you better read your email.' So I looked on my email. He sent an email to me at my job. It said, 'We have reason to believe that you're involved in a conspiracy to extort money from my client,' and it just went on and on."

Here is that email:

Ms. Lake:

I have some thought to our brief telephone conversation yesterday. I thought it prudent to share with you my issues that you can share them with the individuals involved on your side.

At the outset, I want to make clear that I am attempting to balance the need for absolute clarity regarding extremely serious issues with my objective to have a productive rather than threatening communications.

I am confused by the status of the parties. When I spoke to Brian

Watkins, Esq. yesterday, I asked him whether he represented you and your mother. He told me that he did not. He also told me that in dealing with him and his clients, i.e., your brother and Mr. Michaels, I would be addressing all proper and necessary parties. Obviously, our discussion yesterday suggest otherwise. Please let me know when you have retained counsel and I will confine my communications to your lawyer.

Regardless of the status of discussions among the parties on your side, I am compelled to protect my clients' interests. I have spoken via cell phone to your brother 5 times. I have reviewed other communications that he has had with my clients (including text messages) and I have received reports about still more communications between him and my clients. With the exception of the last 2 conversations that he and I had on Sunday evening (there were 3), in each communication your brother made extortionist threats against my clients. Among other things, he has threatened to disrupt a marriage and a professional career before it gets started. He has also admitted to violating California Penal Code's prohibition on surreptitiously recording confidential communications. Given your brother's criminal record, I take his threats and his admitted criminal conduct seriously—especially since your brother seemed to take pride in declaring to me that he had no problem returning to jail if that was the outcome of implementing his extortion plan.

Based upon the communications that you and Mr. Michaels have had and have sought to have with my clients, I conclude that you, your brother, your mother and Mr. Michaels have common interests and that all of you have acted in concert with each other. I believe these common interests and concerted conduct is evidence of an agreement—the essential element of a conspiracy. My understanding of the law in respect of criminal conspiracies is that once an agreement to conspire is formed, each co-conspirator is liable for the acts of one co-conspirator—regardless of whether there is a subsequent agreement sanctioning that individual co-conspirator's subsequent actions. Accordingly, I believe that there is a sound legal basis to hold you, your mother and Mr. Michaels liable for your brother's attempts to extort my clients.

In this regard, the parties on your side should be advised that before I called your brother on Sunday, I met and discussed this matter with an FBI agent here in Atlanta. I have also discussed this matter with other public law enforcement personnel and individuals with private security interests. While I have been tempted to do so, I have not yet contacted Constantine Wilson, who I understand to be your brother's probation officer in Chula Vista, CA, or the San Diego Chargers to discern the existence and nature of any professional association that Mr. Michaels may have with the club or the NFL.

I am prepared—actually anxious—to meet with whoever is appropriate to get a handle on this matter and resolve it. So, subject to schedules, I am committed to making myself available. I believe that notwithstanding the competing interests of the parties (those on your side and my clients) the law and common sense provides fertile ground for a private resolution. We should work on achieving that result sooner rather than later.

If it becomes necessary to postpone our meeting on Sunday (I sincerely hope that everyone can make themselves available on Sunday @ 3:30 in Long Beach, California), I expect neither your brother nor you, your mother or Mr. Michaels will make any further attempts to communicate with my clients. I have authority to speak on their behalf. If there are any efforts at such communications, I will conclude that the conspiracy to extort is still active and that the delay in meeting is merely a smokescreen designed to give cover for continued efforts to implement the extortion plan. Given the evidence and the law as I understand both, I will take all appropriate actions to protect my clients' interests.

If you have any comments or questions regarding the foregoing, I am available to discuss them at your convenience. In any event, I look forward to hearing from you soon.

dc

A volley of letters and emails followed over the next two months, specifically between Brian Watkins and David Cornwell. Meanwhile, Lloyd Lake surrendered to authorities on January 18, 2006, after a warrant was issued for his arrest December 21, 2005, stemming from a domestic

violence incident with his girlfriend a month earlier. Lake was incarcerated for nearly a year in federal prison in Victorville for violating conditions of his parole.

Watkins sent Cornwell a letter dated February 13, 2006, in an effort to resolve this issue with Bush for $3.2 million—the amount included $3 million in lost capital. Watkins told the *San Diego Union-Tribune* on April 27, 2006, "It was basically [left that] we can't come to a meeting of the minds on a number, so do what you're going to do and I am going to do what I'm going to do, is basically what [Cornwell] said. He starts going to the press and throwing out words [like] 'extortion' and I never even wanted to go there. We were just preparing a lawsuit." Asked about the letter by *Yahoo! Sports* in April 2006, Watkins said it was a standard document that he would typically send when settling financial disputes out of court. "That letter is a professional lawyer letter that we do all day every day," he told *Yahoo! Sports.* "If you grab any lawyer's file and look inside, it looks and sounds like this. This is not [extortion]. That word is such a strong word. You know what is key about that letter? [It states] I want to mend our relationship. Does that sound like 'I'm going to tell personal business of yours if you don't pay me $3.2 million'?"

Here is Watkins's letter to Cornwell:

> Dear David,
>
> I apologize for the delay in following up to our previous meeting. Our position has changed in that we now wish to mend our relationship with Mr. Bush and seek to develop a new business relationship with him. We still hope that we can maintain a relationship with him and have a future business relationship with him. Please discuss this with your client and advise if he desires the same.
>
> If this is also desirable to him, we will in a good faith effort to resolve prior business dealings agree to settle the matter for 3.2 million. This amount does include 3 million in lost capital but does not include over 100,000.00 in cash disbursements to your client. We would also be amendable to entering into a confidentiality agreement at your request.
>
> Please advise if it is your intention to involve the University in these settlement negotiations. We would not object to their participation as we understand their wanting to be involved due to the fact

that this matter was ongoing during their Championship season of 2004 as well as the entire season of 2005, and any lawsuit filed might have an adverse affect on them.

Your prompt attention to this matter is appreciated, because if a civil filing is necessary we do not wish to needlessly delay it.

Sincerely,
Brian E. Watkins and Associates

The correspondence continued. In an email from Cornwell to Watkins, copied to Lisa Lake, on March 2, 2006, Cornwell wrote:

> We have reason to believe that Lisa Lake either never retained you as her counsel or terminated your representation of her. To ensure that we identify all co-conspirators to be held liable for your recent $3.2 million demand, please advise if our information is incorrect. In respect of Mr. Lloyd Lake, has he disclosed his alleged claim for "damages" as among his assets in any declaration to Federal Prosecutors, Constantine Wilson, or Federal Prison officials? It does not appear that Mr. Lake disclosed his employment by "New Era Sports Management Co." in connection with his recent arrest and or his current incarceration. Did you intend to include either Ms. Lake or Mr. Lake in the group of "employees" of "New Era Sports Management Co." that you claim to represent.

Despite her financial participation in New Era to an amount of around $30,000, Lisa Lake managed to remain out of the news concerning the company's connection with Bush. When stories about her brother and other participants in the venture were reported on-air, Lake said a coanchor handled that particular segment. Lake said her involvement in New Era was legitimate and aboveboard.

"Lloyd asked me to be a part of the company in PR and consulting, and also to help with Reggie preparing for interviews and because of the media thing," said Lisa Lake. "But it never got there. That was going to be my function in the company. He said, 'You know, you can still keep your job and you could have extra income.' He wanted to have a company where all of the family members could have some part of it, and be a part of it, and so that was what I agreed to. But it never got to that. As far as

the extortion and all those kind of things being mentioned [on-air], I think they probably just made it a professional courtesy. They know that I'm solid."

The FBI also wanted to make sure New Era participants were solid, as it decided to investigate claims of extortion from Cornwell.

Barbara Gunner first heard from the FBI in late September 2006 but declined to talk to aggressive investigators. "They were camped outside of my house, coming to my job, calling and threatening me as to what they were going to do. 'If we don't talk to you by a certain time, we're going to subpoena you,' " Gunner said.

Lake's mother wanted to be subpoenaed, to appear in front of a grand jury, and her wish was granted. She received a subpoena to appear at the Federal Office Building in San Diego on October, 13, 2006, in the grand jury room on the fifth floor. Lloyd Lake's former girlfriend, Maiesha Jones, was also subpoenaed. They were also commanded to bring the following documents or object(s): "Any recordings in your possession of conversations between Lloyd Lake and Reggie Bush, Denise Griffin or LaMar Griffin."

"I told the [FBI], I'm not talking to you, I'll tell my [story] to the grand jury because I want them to get it straight," Gunner said. "It's going to be recorded right there, and I'm not talking to you. I will talk to the grand jury. So I went before the grand jury, and Maiesha, too, and we told you the same thing we're telling you here. They were after my son to send him to prison for extortion. They [FBI] said, 'This was extortion, you were part of extortion.' I said, 'It's all how you look at things, but what I think is you just heard one story and that's what you believe, you haven't heard the other side.' "

The public first heard a different side of the story on January 24, 2007, when *Yahoo! Sports* reported that a federal investigation into extortion claims by Bush and his family has revealed the existence of recorded conversations that could confirm Bush took cash and gifts while he was playing football for the USC. *Yahoo! Sports* also reported that it learned that LaMar Griffin spoke with federal investigators in spring 2006 and acknowledged the existence of the recordings. In an appearance before a grand jury on January 12, 2007, Barbara Gunner testified that she had

heard portions of tapes made by her son, in which LaMar Griffin states that Reggie Bush intended to repay New Era Sports financiers "their money," as well as for a car that was purchased for the former USC running back. After sending many emails that expressed his concern over Lloyd Lake's extortion plan nearly ten months earlier, Cornwell offered a short statement to *Yahoo! Sports.* "I respectfully decline to comment on the media frenzy regarding Reggie Bush, his family, and his college career," he said.

Meanwhile, FBI agents showed up at Lisa Lake's television station in September 2006 to discuss the extortion claims. Lake agreed to talk with the agents but also made a taped recording of the meeting. "I didn't have any more money, I can't pay $5,000 to a lawyer to just say, 'She's not talking,' or to accompany me to a grand jury.

"I didn't have anything to hide, so if they wanted to talk, I sat down and talked, but I made my own recording. You guys take your notes but then later on it's your word, so I'll sit down and talk to you but I have to record the conversation. So they said, 'Okay, you can record it.' So then later on, I was glad I did it. The truth is what it is. I can tell you what I know, what I don't know, I can't tell you. That's what I did, pretty much everything I've told you here is exactly the same, so I made the recording. When they finished the interview, they called back and said, 'Can you give me a copy?' That's when they said, 'You can just bring it up here and we'll just make a quick copy of it.' I said, 'No, I did this for me.' "

On October 9, 2007, *Yahoo! Sports* reported that the FBI briefly investigated claims of extortion from Bush's attorney, including interviewing several of Lake's family members and acquaintances before a federal grand jury. After the depositions, a federal source told the Internet service that the FBI would not be pursuing the extortion claims.

As New Era imploded around them, Lloyd and his family attempted to reach out to Bush and his family in last-ditch efforts to make their agreement work. But their pleas fell on deaf ears. While many believe Bush opted to distance himself from New Era and Lake for reasons that ranged from professional to personal, Lake figures he knows why. "I think he didn't pay because I think he's competitive and he thinks that somebody is supposed to because he's Reggie Bush, treat him like . . . I don't care

about him, I never even asked to ever take a picture with him, ever have him sign an autograph. I didn't care about that.

"I've been around people like that, money, it's not like I am a groupie . . . never was going to kiss his ass because he played football. That was not my character so I guess he thought certain things. I was supposed to talk to him a certain way, I talked to him like I am talking with you. But I think it was more of a way that we kind of got in a little arguing, bickering back and forth, and I said certain things and spoke my mind and that made his family mad. So I think they are like, 'We are not going to give him anything.' Sometimes you have to chop up your losses and go even with pride on the line and go your separate ways. There have been plenty of people that settle with people that they didn't want to or settle with people they didn't like. But they knew it was in their best interest, regardless of I don't like them or not, this is better for me to just make this go away. But he doesn't think like that. It was more like pride. I am mad at what he did and what he said so I am not giving him nothing. That's it. That's the bottom line."

Barbara Gunner said she last saw Denise Griffin a few weeks after the family arrived home in San Diego from the Heisman Trophy presentation on December 10, 2005. Barbara said Denise telephoned her to say she wanted to talk about Lloyd, and the two agreed to meet at a Black Angus restaurant.

"Denise said she wanted to talk to me about Lloyd, that this wasn't going to work out," Barbara recalls. "She said that Reggie had changed his mind and he has a right to change his mind if he wants to. I said, 'That's right.' She also said, 'If I had known that Lloyd had been in problems with the law before, I would have never gotten involved with him because I'm with the Sheriff's Department.' I said, 'I'm with the Corrections Department.' She said, 'Lloyd is going to end up back in jail.' I said, 'Yeah, and if your son keeps reneging on things, and you, too, he might not be the only one in jail and in trouble, so let's not go there.' She said she was going to get back to me. 'I can't make Reggie do this.' I said, 'We don't want to make Reggie do anything, I understand that.' So I never heard from her after that night. It was like she felt that I was going to say, 'Well, we're just going to drop it.' That's my son. You're telling me what a great guy your son is, and I'm telling you your son has been taking money from my son and from me, and you have, too."

Lisa Lake said she last talked to Reggie Bush during the holidays, either in late December 2005 or early January 2006, on her way home to San Diego from Palm Springs following a quick vacation. Lisa offered to meet with Bush to see if she could help mend fences between the feuding parties. She said Bush reiterated that he planned to pay the money back.

"I just remember when it started getting to the end, and it was really apparent that this was not going to go down," Lake said. "I told him, 'You guys have worked on this for a while now. Isn't there something you guys can do to sit down to work this out?' He was like, 'No, no, no. You're going to get your money.' I was like, 'Let me drop [my] kids off in San Diego, and I'm willing to come up there and sit down and talk to see if we can work this out. I lent my brother a lot of money, and I worked very hard and it took me a long time to save it.' Reggie kept telling me, 'You're going to get your money back.' I tried to call him that day about two more times, left a message, but he never called back. Then LaMar called and he just kept saying, 'You're going to get your money back.' I guess he was upset that they had been going back and forth. Denise was upset. And that was the last time I really heard from them."

Louis Lake, Lloyd's father, reached out to LaMar Griffin to see if he could help. The pair met at Jimmy's restaurant in Spring Valley late one night in February 2006. Lake also believed that Zen Sports Balm could open financial doors for Bush, who first used the product as a sophomore at Helix High School. Lake remembers Griffin didn't believe that Lloyd Lake had the necessary experience to help Bush succeed in the marketing and business ventures associated with professional football. Louis understood, but he also hinted to Griffin that his son had protected himself in case LaMar, Denise, and Reggie decided not to pay back the money. Business was business.

" 'If Lloyd gets riled up,' I said, 'Lloyd's going to get his money, I am going to tell you that. I don't know if you know that or not, but I know that he's protecting himself.' And he [LaMar] said, 'He can't prove it, he can't prove it.' "

Lloyd Lake said he last talked to Reggie in person before the Heisman Trophy presentation in December 2005. The two had been bickering and the conversation was much like the others and left far too many open-ended questions, as far as Lloyd was concerned. Lloyd saw LaMar Griffin at a Lincoln-Morse High School football game in October 2007 in San

Diego. Lloyd said the two didn't speak, but Lloyd commented on their recorded conversations as he walked by Griffin.

"I just walked by and gave him a comment on the tapes and wanted to just shake him up a little bit," Lake said. "I played with him a little bit. Let him see if he remembered that. When he said Reggie said he's going to give you back all the money he gave you. I want him to think, 'Damn.' They played with my head a little bit, now I played a little bit with him. I walked by him and said, 'Reggie said he's going to give you [Lloyd] back all the money, so why won't you believe what Reggie is going to tell you.' "

Larry Pierce, who played football with Bush at Helix High and has remained in contact with Bush over the years, says he's not surprised that Reggie elected not to reimburse Lloyd for his money and effort. Pierce—also a friend of Lloyd's after the two were introduced by Bush during USC's 2005 football season—believes Bush received bad advice from his family and advisers. He also thinks Lake's criminal record played a role in their decision to ignore Lloyd's requests for payment.

"I kind of feel the people in his corner, they are kind of like telling him everything is going to be all right, you don't have to worry about anything," Pierce said. "When it came time to pay him back, instead of Reggie doing the logical thing like, 'Okay, this is how much money they gave me and let me just go ahead and give you that plus this and call it a day,' I think those people kind of got in his ear like, 'No, you don't need to do that. Everything is going to be all right. He's not going to be able to get that money out of you, just don't even worry about him anymore. If he wants to take us to court, he can take us to court.' I think it's kind of like those people put that in his head that, 'You are going to win in this situation, don't even worry about it.' He [Lake] has been to jail, you don't have to worry about him. It's all going to blow over. Once this hits the media, they won't . . . they will take him lightly."

As Barbara Gunner and Lisa Lake sat next to each other in the living room of Barbara's home in Southeast San Diego in September 2007, they were asked if Reggie contacted them right at that moment and wanted to make it right financially, would it be too late? Here is the dialogue between the pair:

Lisa: Not to me [too late].

Barbara: It is to me.

Lisa: Because I just believe if people come to you and ask for forgiveness that you should forgive them. And if you can make it right, then you should make it right.

Barbara: I have forgiven him now, it's just too late to forgive. They messed with my mind, my son's mind, they have caused sleepless nights.

Lisa: Exactly. It causes you sleepless nights. I bet you they haven't skipped a beat.

Barbara: That's what I want them to do now, is skip some beats.

Lisa: But they probably will.

Barbara: They will. Trust me, they will. You can't give that right now.

Lisa: You can't because if he agreed to apologize publicly and pay back the money and say, "I screwed up."

Barbara: But how can you pay back the money and the time? Do you know my son ran up and down the freeway for a whole year talking to those guys? How do you feel about not just the money? What about his time?

Lisa: And it was a lost opportunity. Well, you just have to let it go.

Barbara: I've let it go. I am letting it go right here. I let it go when I went to the grand jury and I told them everything.

Lisa: You said at this point you can keep the money, but we are telling the story. People should know.

Barbara: But they are thinking my son is a thug.

FIFTEEN

The Denials

LaMar Griffin, arms outstretched and a set of keys in his left hand, leaned back on a bench near the Twain Center on the campus of Morse High School. Griffin, a security officer at the school, was dressed casually in athletic shoes, gray slacks, and a gray, striped polo shirt. The adjoining patio area was empty this particular Thursday morning as classes were in session for the nearly three thousand students in grades nine through twelve.

Griffin was polite and cordial when approached by this book's authors on the morning of October 18, 2007. Following a quick introduction, Griffin extended his left hand as a courtesy handshake and inquired about the visit. When informed of the existence of this book and asked of his involvement in New Era and whether he and his family, including Reggie, accepted gifts and money from Lloyd Lake and Michael Michaels, Griffin gently shook his head side to side and offered these comments during the first few minutes of the conversation:

"Enough has been said.

"I can't talk about it.

"It's all lies.

"I love my son dearly."

Griffin added that his attorney, David Cornwell, had instructed him not to discuss the raging controversy that has engulfed his family. Griffin also indicated that he wanted to address the situation and offered to telephone his visitor after he talked with Cornwell over the weekend. Griffin and his visitor casually talked football and recruiting before the school bell signaled the change of class.

The call never came.

Reggie Bush took care of Michael Michaels in April 2007. He settled out of court for a sum that sources placed between $200,000 and $300,000. That settlement included a confidentiality agreement that barred Michaels and his attorney from commenting.

While the settlement was a sign that Bush was taking care of a delicate situation, it appeared Bush acted far more carelessly with Lloyd Lake. Lake, released from prison months earlier, sat in a Santa Monica, California, courtroom in June 2007 in an effort to settle his dispute with Bush through a mediator. While Bush did not attend the mediation, David Cornwell and Mike Ornstein—Bush's marketing agent—represented the running back. Lloyd Lake was joined by his attorneys, Brian Watkins and Paul Wong.

Although the presiding judge ruled that the mediation was confidential, he also probably needed to hand out boxing gloves and spit buckets. For starters, Lloyd was upset with his attorney's position that $150,000 would make Lake whole. The thought was, that amount would allow Lloyd and his family to recoup their investment, pay attorney fees, and leave enough money left over to pocket. Lloyd had a much larger figure, undoubtedly at least two times that amount, in his mind.

It was even more acrimonious on the other side of the table, where an arrogant Cornwell attempted to dictate the terms of the mediation hearing with the judge. The judge firmly reminded Cornwell that he had the guidelines backward. At one point, Cornwell started yelling, packed his briefcase, and stormed out of the hearing, not to return. Ornstein stayed, while Wong, Watkins, and Lake sat in their chairs and looked helplessly at each other. They were absolutely flabbergasted. Did that just happen? Did that just *really* happen? No way.

It did.

It's no secret that the tone between the Bush camp and New Era financiers—specifically Lake and Michael Michaels—turned heated and emotional as the dispute over payments made by Lake and Michaels to Bush and his family magnified. There also came a point when Bush's public denials pressed on an exposed nerve with Lake and his family.

Bush angered Lake and Michaels when he accused them of extortion in an interview aired September 13, 2007, on ESPN's *Outside the Lines.* In that interview with reporter Shelly Smith, Bush said of the NCAA investigation and his family's alleged impropriety: "For me, I look at it as—and my family looks at it as—extortion. Because these were guys we'd known our whole lives—when I was a freshman in high school, they weren't asking for money. When I was getting older, and then all of the sudden my year with the possibility of me coming out all this stuff comes out." Bush also claimed his parents simply "got behind" on rent when they lived in their brand-new home in Spring Valley.

"It was basically, you know, just my parents, you know, renting a house from a friend of ours, and they got behind on some rent, you know, a couple of months on some rent," Bush said on the ESPN segment. "And all of the sudden it's like the media blew up this whole thing—'Oh, they were living in this house rent-free'—which wasn't the case. We rented a house and just like any other family, you know, you get behind on bills. You don't have money; my family isn't rich. We didn't have a lot of money.

"So my parents struggled to pay bills here and there, one of those things being rent. I think just like any normal average family, you struggle to pay bills sometimes, and that's all it was. And the media kind of blew it out to kind of make it seem like we were living in this nice gorgeous house—which I never lived there—living in this nice, gorgeous house rent-free, and it wasn't anything like that."

Lloyd Lake says he felt good about his decision to secretly record his discussions with Reggie Bush and LaMar Griffin when he heard comments Bush made on ESPN.

"My decision to tape was to protect my interest," Lake said. "Look now. Look at Reggie and them on ESPN right now. Imagine if I didn't have those tapes. Who would they believe?" That's why I did it, because

I knew what was going on. And my mom was like, you better figure out, because these people look like they don't have good character about themselves, so you better decide how you are going to get proof that you gave these people some money. So I decided to go with the tapes as my evidence. Right now, on ESPN, you heard it yourself. 'My parents just fell behind in the rent. I went to the NFL, that's when they came with this extortion.' Now, if I didn't have those tapes, I would be in trouble right now. Who would you believe?"

Barbara Gunner said, "I guess we should have been recording it the whole time, all the different times when it was going really good. With all the street sense and things Lloyd's got, he's loyal and he's trusting, so he trusted them. I have no problem with that because we did also. And even the parents, their thing was that they were hustling each other. They didn't know that Reggie was getting the money from Lloyd. Reggie didn't know, so they said that the parents were getting all the money."

Lisa Lake complimented Bush's confident, easy on-air presence. "He looks at that camera and lies, and the he does it so well." Lake's former husband, Lemuel Campbell, who had agreed in April 2005 to serve as a licensed sports agent for New Era, echoed those sentiments. "I want to say he's a psychopath," Campbell opined. "If I didn't know Reggie, I would believe him. He was so good he had me convinced—and I knew what was going on. It just kills me that he can stand up and lie about it. All the money he has gotten, all the money his parents have gotten, just everything that has happened."

And plenty has happened.

"He brought it on himself because you stop feeling sorry for a person when they tell lies, when they just boldly say, 'I've done nothing wrong, I've done nothing wrong,' " Lisa Lake said. "And if you didn't have the money and say, 'Well, I don't have it. Whenever I get it, I'll give it back.' But to have the money and don't—that little bit of money, that was nothing. He has paid that attorney twenty times more."

Denials and conflicting views have been a key part to this sordid story. They've come from all corners, in all forms, from all types. Here's a sampling:

Denials and Comments from David Cornwell (Reggie Bush's attorney)

April 25, 2006

"Pac-10 Probing Bush's Living Arrangement."

Associated Press Online. April 25, 2006.

Bush did not answer a question about his relationship with Michaels.

"There will be a later time for details," he said. "As of right now, it's still early and we don't want to get into all that."

April 29, 2006

"Bad News for Bush."

Los Angeles Times. April 29, 2006, home ed.: D1.

Meanwhile, Bush's representatives—who have declined to comment on the purported business relationship—continued to assert that New Era is trying to extort millions from the athlete.

"We identified their scheme months ago and collected written evidence over the course of the months," said David Cornwell, the family's attorney. "And we provided that evidence to the NFL Players Assn. and NFL security."

Cornwell said the league has subsequently notified a number of teams that Bush was the "target of improper threats."

June 1, 2006

Schrotenboer, Brent. "Lawyer: FBI Probes Firm That Tried to Sign Bush."

San Diego Union-Tribune. June 1, 2006. D4.

The attorney for Reggie Bush and his parents said the FBI has contacted him to request interviews with his clients as part of a federal investigation into New Era Sports and Entertainment, the fledgling San Diego sports marketing agency that once sought to represent Bush before he chose other representation.

David Cornwell, the Bush family attorney, said the FBI didn't specify which potential crimes it was investigating but said yesterday the thrust of the inquiry was "certainly the activities regarding [Brian] Watkins' clients' threats against my client and his family."

. . . Cornwell has categorized Watkins' settlement demands as extor-

tion. Watkins has vigorously denied that, saying his clients are just trying to get their money back.

Cornwell previously made the extortion claim to the NFL, which recommended he turn to law enforcement. Asked yesterday who triggered the investigation, Cornwell said the FBI "contacted me. I'm not certain how they learned of it, but I imagine at least in part from public reports."

June 1, 2006

Farmer, Sam, and Greg Krikorian. "FBI Looks at Firm That Courted Bush."

Los Angeles Times. June 1, 2006, home ed.: D3

The FBI has opened an investigation into a fledgling sports marketing firm that tried to recruit New Orleans Saints rookie Reggie Bush as a client.

A federal law enforcement source said Wednesday that the inquiry was "in its infancy" and that it was "way too early to say where this [case] is headed."

The attorney for Bush's family said that he had a "lengthy" phone call with an FBI agent last week, but he would not identify who he spoke with or which FBI field office was involved.

"They're definitely investigating federal crimes, but they didn't identify which crimes or which federal statutes are involved," attorney David Cornwell said, adding that he planned to help the FBI arrange interviews with Bush and his parents, LaMar and Denise Griffin.

The firm's website lists president Linas Danilevicius as a former FBI agent. A phone message left at the security firm's Laguna Hills–based office was returned by Cornwell, who said Watkins' characterization of the FBI's involvement was "all part of the fallacy and fantasy that Watkins is living."

Cornwell added: "When he does the perp walk, he'll know he was wrong."

January 25, 2007

"Report Tape May Implicate Reggie Bush."

Associated Press Online. January 25, 2007.

"I respectfully decline to comment on the media frenzy regarding Reggie Bush, his family and his college career," David Cornwell, Bush's attorney, told Yahoo on Wednesday.

MICHAEL ORNSTEIN
(REGGIE BUSH'S MARKETING REPRESENTATIVE)

April 24, 2006

"Inquiry Set in Bush Family Residence; USC Asks Pacific 10 to Investigate Whether the Reported Arrangements Over Spacious Residence Violated NCAA Rules."

Los Angeles Times. April 24, 2006, home ed.: D5.

Bush, who is regarded as potentially the top pick in Saturday's NFL draft and is expected later this week to announce that he has signed a major shoe deal, could not be reached for comment Sunday. His mother, Denise Griffin, and stepfather, LaMar Griffin, also could not be reached.

"I don't know where that story is coming from," Ornstein said. "I talked to Reggie and he has no idea where that's coming from, what his parents are paying for a house or anything."

April 24, 2006

Schrotenboer, Brent. **"Parents of Bush Face Questions About Home; USC Wants Pac-10 to Review Arrangement."**

San Diego Union-Tribune. April 24, 2006. A1.

Ornstein, his marketing representative, said Friday he has no knowledge of anything that might have taken place between Bush and New Era, and that Bush was probably not going to talk about it.

"This time of year, falsely or unfalsely, this is the stuff that comes up," he said, referring to the days before the draft. "It's a bunch of BS."

April 26, 2006

McCarthy, Michael. **"Investigation Doesn't Curb Endorsement Deals for Bush."**

USA Today. April 26, 2006, home ed.: 3C.

"This has been blown up into a big story because it's the week of the draft," says Ornstein, who also works as a consultant for Reebok, which was acquired by Adidas. "Reggie Bush didn't know anything about this. He never lived in the house."

September 15, 2006

"Bush Responds to Report He and Family Accepted More Than $100,000 From Marketing Agents."

The *Associated Press*. September 15, 2006.

"Reggie Bush never received an extra benefit from Mike Ornstein other than what he was allowed to get from the NCAA when he worked with us," Ornstein told Yahoo. He added Bush was an intern at his marketing company in the summer of 2005. "I feel pretty damn good about that."

PETE CARROLL (USC FOOTBALL COACH)

April 24, 2006

"Reggie Bush Inquiry Report; Probe Could Lead to USC Sanctions."

Daily News of Los Angeles. April 24, 2006. N1.

Among the questions the investigation is likely to ask, if there is evidence that the alleged arrangement violated NCAA rules, is whether Michaels was a representative of USC's athletic interest. If USC was eventually forced to forfeit any games from last season, it would not have to return its share of receipts of the Rose Bowl payout. While schools can be forced to return revenues from the NCAA basketball tournament, the NCAA isn't the sanctioning body for bowl games.

"We don't know anything right now," USC coach Pete Carroll said.

April 26, 2006

"Bush Proves to Be More Elusive Than Ever."

Los Angeles Times. April 26, 2006. D1.

"Mad at Reggie Bush?" Pete Carroll asked me Tuesday during a phone interview. "Why would I be mad at Reggie Bush?"

". . . I'm on my kids at every turn, every day, doing whatever I can to keep outside influences from clouding their thought processes," Carroll acknowledged.

". . . Some say there is no way a college kid could know the finances of his parents' living arrangements.

"Think back to when you were in school, did you know how your parents paid the mortgage?" Carroll asked.

". . . We talk all the time about people who come after our players,

people without the best of intentions, people just trying to get what they can," Carroll said.

April 30, 2006

Plaschke, Bill. "Falling Stars; Tough Week Gets Tougher for Trojans."

Los Angeles Times. April 30, 2006, home ed.: D1.

It's been quite a week for the Trojan football program, whose perception has suffered the same fate as its four highest-profile players on Saturday's draft day.

. . . Reggie Bush, surrounded by questionable advisors, fell out of the top spot into No. 2, a $6-million plunge.

Matt Leinart, plagued by a questionable arm and Hollywood focus, fell from last year's probable top spot to No. 10, a plunge worth double-digit millions.

LenDale White, reported to have some character issues, fell from projected top 10 to 45th, a drop as large as Coach Pete Carroll's infamous high dive.

Winston Justice, who also faced questions about his past, fell into the second round in a league desperate for offensive linemen.

It was a statement of disillusionment not only about the players, but their program.

". . . The worst week since I've been here, yeah," Carroll said in a phone interview Saturday night. "It's been very, very difficult.

". . . This week we learned some things the hard way," Carroll said.

After five years here, is it time for Carroll to tighten his grip?

"We needed to see this coming, and we didn't," Carroll admitted. "It's gone beyond all the heads up, all the alerts, all the education we give these kids. We need to do more."

Carroll said the program needs to focus more on educating the players about outsiders.

"Our guys are marked guys, they have had success and there's people trying to get in on that, and we need to do a better job of making them understand the problems there," he said.

Carroll said he was not going to change the embraceable style that has made him possibly college football's best coach. But he vowed to be tougher on those who would stand between him and his players.

"We have moved into very different territory now, all the hype, all the distractions, all the people who want to influence us, and we will be more aware of that," he said. "We will work harder to control that."

FROM REGGIE BUSH'S TEAMMATES (USC AND PRO) AND TEAMS CONSIDERING HIM FOR DRAFT

April 26, 2006

"New Link in Bush Case."

Los Angeles Times. April 26, 2006, home ed.: D1.

Meanwhile, it remained to be seen if the controversy would affect Bush's draft status. The Houston Texans have the first pick Saturday and had not revealed their intentions.

"At this point in time, we're not aware of anything that Reggie might have done that was improper," team owner Bob McNair said in a telephone interview. "The allegations concern his parents."

McNair said that while the situation raises questions, "our concern is with the behavior of the player we're drafting. As long as his behavior is satisfactory, we can't expect him to control every member of his family."

September 16, 2006

"Bush Says 'We Did Nothing Wrong.' "

Washington Post. September 16, 2006, final ed.: E03.

Saints wide receiver Joe Horn defended his teammate.

"I don't think Reggie did that, but if he did, I would have done it, too," Horn said. "And guess what? Eighty percent of the college athletes that don't have much when they're in college get money, too. So they should ban all of them. They should go after everybody. Don't just go after Reggie because he's Reggie Bush."

September 18, 2006

"White Goes on Defense for Ex-Teammate Bush."

Los Angeles Times. September 18, 2006. D11.

LenDale White . . . an NFL running back. . . .

Defending the reputation of former USC teammate Reggie Bush in the locker room. . . .

"I don't follow it because I don't believe none of it," White said of a

report that Bush and his family accepted benefits of more than $100,000 from agents while the tailback was playing college football.

"Honestly, I don't know nothing about what they're talking about. I went to school with the man for three years. If he had money like that, I need to borrow some."

Bush, now a New Orleans Saints rookie, has denied any wrongdoing.

USC Coach Pete Carroll said Sunday that Bush called him after the Trojans' victory over Nebraska on Saturday night and reiterated that he had done nothing wrong.

"He was very firm about all of that," Carroll said. "He just wanted to make sure and check in. . . . He wanted to make sure I was clear."

"I believe Reggie," White said. "I believe nothing ever happened, ever. And it will be proven at the end of the day.

". . . But Reggie didn't do nothing. I'm with Reggie, that's my teammate. I believe in him."

September 19, 2006

"USC Receiver McFoy Backs Reggie Bush's Stance on Controversy."

Orange County Register. September 19, 2006.

Receiver Chris McFoy said he doesn't believe reports that Reggie Bush accepted improper gifts from a sports marketing firm where both players worked in the summer of 2005.

"I don't know exactly what went on, but I know that stuff didn't happen," McFoy said. "That's just people trying to get Reggie in trouble."

McFoy had a summer internship with Mike Ornstein's SportsLink agency. He was joined by Bush, who later settled on Ornstein as his agent.

McFoy said he was guided to the agency by a USC counselor after he said he was interested in sports marketing. He emailed a resume to Ornstein's assistant, Jamie Fritz, and got the job. NCAA rules allow athletes to work for agents as long as their pay is similar to the going rate.

September 22, 2006

"Players Land on Side of Bush."

San Francisco Chronicle. September 22, 2006, final ed.: D9.

The ongoing revelations about Saints running back Reggie Bush and his alleged receipt of thousands of dollars in cash and gifts from over-

eager marketing types have produced an interesting reaction from fellow NFL players.

For the most part, these players understand exactly why Bush (allegedly) took what he took. And they don't have a problem with it.

"I don't care what anyone says about what Reggie Bush's family got while he was at USC, none of that matters to anyone here, especially me," Saints wide receiver Joe Horn said during the preseason.

"The man earned millions for that school. That much is undeniable."

May 2, 2006

"Unsteady Times at USC; Trojans' Dynasty Takes a Hit Amid Several Allegations; Carroll Not Yet Worried About Forfeiting Games, Titles."

USA Today. May 2, 2006, final ed.: 1C.

But when asked if it didn't look like a classic case of extra benefits, Carroll said, "It looks to me like a classic case of people trying to create some kind of opportunity based on another person's good fortune. To me, it looks like somebody was out to get Reggie's money. I don't see it any other way."

SIXTEEN

The NCAA:

On Reggie's Trail and What It Could Mean

Far away from the sun and glitz of USC and Southern California, sitting on the banks of a little river in Indianapolis, Indiana, are the offices of the NCAA. The low-rise building that houses the largest collegiate athletic organization in the world has four floors and sits within shouting distance of the RCA Dome (home to the Indianapolis Colts) and Victory Field (home to the Triple-A minor-league baseball Indianapolis Indians).

Often pronounced "N-C-Double-A" or "N-C-Two-A," the NCAA is a voluntary association of about twelve hundred institutions, conferences, and individuals that organize the athletic programs of many colleges and universities across the country. And these member schools solemnly pledge to uphold and follow the rules voted on by their members.

Naturally, those schools that don't follow these rules can open themselves up to big trouble. The NCAA's investigative staff can review and determine if an official inquiry of the school is warranted. At least sixteen Division I schools were on probation in 2007 for sanctions that resulted from official inquiries.

Fresh off suspending Oklahoma for a case involving extra benefits

received by two football players, suddenly word started buzzing through the enforcement department that the highest-profile athlete in college football, Reggie Bush, was allegedly on the take while at USC. Furthermore, the rumor persisted that USC knew about it, and that USC coach Pete Carroll had been sent an anonymous email as early as March 2005 alerting him that Reggie Bush's family had moved from a small apartment into a new spacious house paid for by agents.

Assigned to the case were Rich Johanningmeier, associate director of enforcement, and Angie Cretors, assistant director of agents, gambling, and amateurism. The two had worked often together and were considered a formidable team. But that's not to say the NCAA doesn't have a sense of humor—Johanningmeier arrived at his office one morning to discover that a coworker had hung a USC banner on his wall.

The case also has been of special interest to Pacific-10 Conference authorities, who, in turn, launched their own separate investigation.

As the relationships unraveled and stories began to leak, the NCAA realized this might be one of the more significant college football scandals in recent history. An Oklahoma quarterback who was paid $10,000 for a no-show job had recently been penalized, and now the possibility that a Heisman Trophy winner and his family has taken nearly $300,000 in benefits and that USC might have been warned about it had become the scandal that college sports websites were buzzing about.

The challenge is that the NCAA is without subpoena power. All the players involved, including agents and others not linked to USC, were out of the reach of the NCAA, rendering NCAA investigative strategies largely toothless.

On October 30, 2007 Lloyd Lake filed a civil lawsuit in San Diego County Court against Reggie Bush for failing to repay a wide array of benefits that Bush and his family received from Lake while he played for the Trojans. After avoiding the NCAA, Paul Wong—one of Lake's attorneys—said that in addition to filing the suit, Lake agreed to meet with NCAA investigators to discuss Bush's involvement with New Era Sports. That decision gave the NCAA a chance in an investigation that had, up until that point, struggled to secure interviews with the key witnesses.

Paul Wong, a member of the law firm of Milam & Larsen, LLP, has a nice view of the city of Pasadena from his downtown law office. The Rose Bowl Parade, held annually on New Year's Day, passes by his office. Wong had hoped the interview with the NCAA would help sort things out—and establish Lloyd's story as credible.

After nineteen months of telephone calls, posturing, and mixed signals, Lloyd Lake, with his attorneys Wong and Brian Watkins, sat down for the first time face to face with NCAA officials Rich Johanningmeier and Angie Cretors on Tuesday, November 6, 2007.

The five sat across from each other in a small conference room in Wong's law office.

The eight-chair conference table was flanked by floor-to-ceiling bookshelves filled with manuals of California appellate reports and annotated California codes. A small fan was in the corner. A waist-high cabinet stretched across the back of the room. Above it were two windows with an obstructed view of the corner below.

Wong, who admittedly dresses casually for work, was in a black suit to meet with the NCAA. Brian Watkins, handsomely attired in a blue suit, showed an hour before the conference after appearing in court in San Diego earlier in the morning. The polite yet focused Watkins, thirty-eight, a former linebacker at the University of California (1987–92), immediately huddled with Wong in his office.

Johanningmeier and Cretors arrived a short time later and, after formal and friendly introductions with Wong and Watkins, huddled in the conference room. A few minutes later, Lloyd Lake confidently strolled in and was introduced to the NCAA investigators. Lake, in a long-sleeved dress shirt and designer jeans and sporting a fresh haircut, appeared calm. Lake had driven the 114 miles from San Diego on Monday and spent the night at a hotel in Manhattan Beach.

"I wasn't nervous at all," said Lake, who added he could not discuss specifics due to a confidentially agreement he signed with the NCAA after the six-hour session. "I've been over this one hundred times—I just told the story of how it went. I wasn't nervous, but I didn't want to do it. I'll be honest, I didn't want to do it because I don't like to . . . I just wish it could have been avoided. I don't want to see anybody get sanctioned, him [Bush] lose his [Heisman] trophy.

"I am pretty sure they are going to find some violations."

Lake submitted to a wide range of questions from Johanningmeier and Cretors, in addition to turning over documents and listening to excerpts of the recorded conversations between himself, Reggie Bush, and LaMar Griffin.

Watkins believed his client handled the NCAA scrutiny well. "He was very straightforward," Watkins said. "Of course, he would [be] a little upset as he relived the fraud and betrayal that he had to experience. He got a little emotional but other than that he was very straightforward. It is just a matter of fact; these are the facts. Angie Cretors told me nineteen months she had been waiting for this. She waited patiently. I told her that I didn't see a problem with it after we filed our lawsuit. And we kept our word."

The NCAA, for the first time, had the key witness in its investigation into whether Reggie Bush had violated eligibility rules.

Lloyd, Wong, and Watkins were pleased with what had just transpired. However, the entire afternoon could have been avoided if Lake and Bush had settled their differences nearly two years ago. Wong described the principals' ordeal as being like that of skydivers who leaped from a plane without their parachutes.

Wong said, "I never thought I would be meeting with the NCAA. I would have never thought this wouldn't have been resolved in a professional and respectful manner."

USC, meanwhile, was not invited to attend the session. "We have repeatedly requested to be included in all interviews and all aspects of the investigation," Todd Dickey, USC senior vice president and general counsel, told the *Los Angeles Times*. "We were not given the opportunity to participate."

While Reggie Bush's attorney David Cornwell vowed to fight Lloyd Lake's civil suit "vigorously," arguing that Lake is a convicted felon without credibility, there are others who have alleged that Lake violated state law by improperly acting as Bush's agent. There are also questions about whether Lake broke the law by recording LaMar Griffin and Bush without their knowledge.

Watkins explained both issues: "The California agent law is for un-

scrupulous agents who go around preying on student-athletes. That's not the case here. We have it basically the other way around. We have a family and an athlete who was headed to the big time for all intent and purposes. Actually when Lloyd really got involved with him he wasn't that profile of a player but he really developed into one. And they basically preyed on people because they knew that, hey, people will be coming after me, I am going to be a commodity and I can cash in on it early. And that's what they did. They basically took advantage of my client at that point and basically sucked a lot of money from him and jumped ship and said, 'Well, there's not much you could do about it, it's all cash.' He agreed to pay him back some of his money, a very small portion of his money, and figured that he should just go away. Let alone the year and a half of his time that he spent dedicating his life in trying to get this business up and running. They felt that was worth nothing. It's unfortunate.

"The law in general says you have to have a person's consent to tape them. However, it carves out some exceptions mainly to prevent a crime, someone is calling you threatening to kill you, you can record them and show the cops—that's a criminal-threat violation of penal code section 422. Same as when you are going to protect yourself against fraud. In this case, they are saying you gave us cash, you can't prove cash. All I have to do is deny it, and you are being told this after you're out hundreds of thousands of dollars. You are about to be defrauded and they're basically throwing it in your face. You can do that to protect yourself against a felony fraud like that. But then of course there's also when you're recording that there's impeachment value, which means if someone were to get up there and lie. They can't suppress that evidence and then get up and lie about it. Say, well, I know you have me on tape saying this but if I get that excluded then I am going to go ahead and deny it. The law doesn't allow you to do that."

Watkins is also confident that his client will prevail in his suit against Bush, saying, "I think any jury will see, look right through people and [see] it's a fraud. People want to say, 'Oh, student-athletes, they didn't know any better.' Those are grown men. You are over eighteen, you are living on your own. And to say this kid doesn't know anything about money is just ludicrous all right. Kids know about money. They are not kids when you are in college. You know about money, you are paying

your own bills. To say that he didn't want to cash in early? He did. He wanted the expensive car, he wanted the expensive rims, he wanted all that expensive stuff. It's a valid want. Every kid wants it. Most kids don't have the means to get it. He did. And that's the way he chose to get it—he cashed in early. He couldn't wait. He couldn't wait to open his Christmas present and that's what happened here."

In the final days of writing this book, the authors were granted a rare interview with David Price, executive director of the NCAA's enforcement staff. Although Price refused to answer specific questions about the organization's continuing investigation of Reggie Bush and USC, he did address the issues that create the backdrop for this investigation.

Authors: What are the NCAA's challenges when, as is the situation with the USC case, key witnesses have no connection to the university?

Price: It's not rare but it's unusual when we have situations that involve both lawsuits and individuals outside of our jurisdiction as we do here. Both of those examples tend to have an inhibiting effect on getting people to talk to us.

Authors: In this particular case, it does appear that at least the two gentlemen who have claimed to be involved with providing extra benefits to a student-athlete have no relationship to the university. Is that a reasonable rarity?

Price: No, it's not. What you're dealing with in a general sense—I'm not saying you are, but we often get issues where we're dealing with agents or runners who do not have relationships with the institutions; therefore, under our rules, cannot be representatives of the institutions' interests. What we have to have in a general way is that we have to have some knowledge that the institution either knew or should have known that this was occurring. In the past by in large when you have someone completely operating outside the system, we have not had that tie-in. I'm not saying we have it here either, but if I can give you an example: Charles Woodson at University of

Michigan received benefits from an agent. That all became known publicly sometime after he had left the institution. We had no information that there was any institutional knowledge; therefore, we did not take any action against the institution or even bring charges. There's a little bit of a side note to that and that is if they compete in NCAA championships, we will take action regardless and that's in part because we attempt to protect the integrity of the championships.

Authors: Because football is not an NCAA championship sport?

Price: Football does not have an NCAA championship in what's popularly known as Division IA. It would be the BCS, which is outside the NCAA's realm.

Authors: Do all universities require student-athletes to register their vehicles and where they live?

Price: I think that's common at the Division IA level.

Authors: Common, but not required.

Price: It's not required under NCAA rule.

Authors: But does doing so show an effort by the university to prove that it has some level of control?

Price: Well, that and to keep an eye out—a preventive eye itself. I should suppose that you tie in. The answer to your question in short is yes.

Authors: So how does the infractions committee and the NCAA look at an institution if it is not monitoring well in that area? Because it's not required is it a black mark?

Price: It's going to depend on the individual circumstances of the case and normally it's going to be the responsibility of the enforcement staff to bring an allegation. That allegation would be either a lack of institutional control or a failure to monitor. That gets the issue on the table in front of the committee on infractions and then the committee on infractions would question the institution extensively at hearing as to how much it monitored and why it did not monitor more.

Authors: Can you, can you describe failure to monitor? What does that mean?

Price: An institution has a responsibility to monitor its program to attempt to ensure that violations have not occurred and that it is competing with student-athletes who are eligible. I think there's kind of generally an institutional standard that the committee on infractions expects most institutions to meet. Maybe I should have said, an industry standard, and they will be asked questions. It can run in a variety of areas. For example, the one that has come up more frequently recently has been when transfer students are brought to campus before school starts—usually during the summer and they are living in the area. If there are a large number of them, the committee on infractions expects the institution to know what's going on and to monitor their status so that they are not violating NCAA rules and that they are indeed eligible when they enroll in school the following fall.

Authors: The NCAA governs everything from water polo to Division I football and basketball—the high-level-revenue sports. In your mind, is there a special responsibility that a university must show to its higher-profile revenue-producing athletes? Do they need to be a little more careful when you've got an athlete who a lot of people could be looking to earn money by representing them?

Price: I think that's just a practical reality. History will tell you you'll have more problems with a highly visible athlete in a highly visible sport. So, yes.

Authors: The NCAA did involve itself with USC in the Dwayne Jarrett situation—he was staying in a condo that was being paid for largely by Matt Leinart's father—that was self-reported, right?

Price: I'm aware of that, yes.

Authors: Okay, if you have a situation where that occurred and about the same time that all this Reggie Bush stuff was alleged to have occurred, would you say that USC should have been on a heightened alert? They're in the middle of this amazing run. They have all these athletes that are the biggest stars in Los Angeles . . .

Price: You're getting on back to a specific case and a specific institution which is under investigation. I can't answer that question.

Authors: Okay. You're a former student-athlete, but your actions while you were a student-athlete have come under investigation. It is alleged that there's a private citizen who was giving you money and you enter into a settlement agreement with that person and part of that agreement is that they cannot meet with the NCAA. Is there anything the NCAA can do about that?

Price: Well, a former student-athlete would be outside our jurisdiction at that time. The one avenue that we might have would be to go to the institution and ask the institution to seek the cooperation of the individual and if the individual refused to cooperate ask the institution to take action against the individual, which would be a disassociation type thing. Other than that I think the NCAA's hands are tied.

Authors: Do you often encounter that?

Price: No, it would be a rare instance.

Authors: In this particular case we have been told that Reggie's settlement with Michael Michaels does not allow him to speak to you.

Price: I can't answer that for you on the record.

Authors: In that situation, do you have a fear as an enforcement director—someone whose responsibility it is to enforce these rules—that the message that's being sent out is, "Here's your answer." Here's how you keep the NCAA from doing something. If, in fact, to keep Michael Michaels from meeting with the NCAA, Reggie Bush settled with him and inserted a clause in that settlement that says you cannot talk to the NCAA, and if he lives by that clause to avoid violation of his settlement agreement, which keeps you from being able to interview him, it could become known that this is the way to get around participating in your investigation. Are you worried that might send the word out to other people in the future. Hey—if you're trying to avoid participating in an NCAA investigation, build that clause into your settlement?

Price: That would be worrisome unquestionably and we would have to look in conjunction with other information that we have to determine if we could take some kind of action. I'm being vague here, but I think you can read between the lines. It has dangerous implications, no question about it.

Authors: I've read a couple articles quoting the University of Oklahoma president specifically relating to the investigation, expressing frustration that the NCAA hasn't been able to get more done in the USC case. I assume you've read some of these same articles.

Price: I don't recall seeing the Oklahoma president make that remark. I've seen media members make that remark.

Authors: Do those kind of comments—obviously if it's from the media you might not care, but if it's from your members you might—do those kind of comments increase the pressure in any way on the NCAA to move more aggressively on a particular case?

Price: For the most part I don't think so. In the end we've got to do our job and call shots as we see them and whether we like it or not we generally have to have tough hides in this business. It adds to the frustration and it can add to morale issues within the staff at the frustration of not being able to get to certain things, but we talk to our staff about those things constantly and our job is to get the facts, get the evidence the best we can and proceed. We recognize that we are operating under certain handicaps when we do that, but given that we still proceed in the best way we can.

Authors: Is there anything you can do to force a former student-athlete, someone who's now in professional football, to talk to you? Is there anything you guys can do at all?

Price: The only things I believe we can do is through the institution. We do not have any direct authority or jurisdiction over the former student-athlete.

Authors: What would it take for you to ask an institution to do that? I assume this is not something you would do early in an investigation—you wouldn't say do us this favor. You would to have some level of confidence that a violation occurred.

Price: Well we would have to consider it to be a very serious issue and we would have to consider the noncooperation by the former student-athlete to be significant. It would be perhaps a little analogous to our alleging an unethical conduct charge against a coach; we don't do that just as a matter of course. We have to have good reason to bring that charge and they have to be serious because the consequences can be very significant—when you're dealing with a coach or an enrolled student-athlete you could be dealing with a career-ending decision or perhaps a competition-concluding decision. So we realize the analogy only goes so far, but if we're going to do that with a former student-athlete, it's going to have to be a very, very serious case.

Authors: And how often in your career at the NCAA have you actually asked an institution to make a conversation like that happen?

Price: I don't believe that we've ever gone to the point either threatening or alleging conditions and obligations of membership for refusing to cooperate which essentially is what you'd be dealing with with the institution. We have certainly gone to institutions many times and asked them for their cooperation in trying to get their former student-athletes to talk to us. Sometimes we're successful and sometimes we're not.

Authors: Would you, I mean I hate to ask such a general question, but is it a fifty-fifty thing?

Price: I wouldn't want to put a percentage on it. It's not usual because we probably are dealing more with recruiting and extra-benefits type things than we are with former student-athletes in a general way in our enforcement program. If you want to size something, look at the Michigan case, those individuals who were named in the Fab Five were disassociated from the university and continue to be till this day.

Authors: Okay, that's a good example, and the reason they are disassociated from the university is because they wouldn't cooperate with the NCAA even after a request from the university.

Price: In part—in large part.

What happens if the NCAA believes that Reggie Bush accepted improper benefits from a prospective sports agent?

Bush could be deemed retroactively ineligible, and USC could be forced to forfeit games. In his three seasons at USC, the Trojans went 37-2, won one national title, and shared another. Bush might also be asked to return the Heisman Trophy he won in 2005 before he left school for the NFL with one season of eligibility remaining.

USC could also face further sanctions if it were proved that coaches and administrators knew or should have known about the alleged benefits. Remember, word began to spread that Pete Carroll had been sent an anonymous email as early as May 2005 alerting him that Reggie Bush's family had moved from a small apartment into a new, spacious house. In interviews for this book, Lake says he was in the television room of LaMar Griffin's home with Griffin when Carroll returned a telephone call to Griffin and discussed the family's housing arrangements. New Era representative Lem Campbell said LaMar told him that Carroll's telephone call focused on the lease agreement involving the Griffins' residence. "LaMar called and said he [Carroll] was inquiring about the house and this was the first time I realized the house was actually in Michael's [Michaels] name," said Campbell, a graduate of Morehouse College and the University of San Diego Law School. "I couldn't believe they had done that." Over the next few weeks, Campbell said he met with LaMar Griffin and Michael Michaels to discuss "how they needed to work the lease to make it really look legit." Campbell said the final draft of the lease was completed by Michaels's personal attorneys.

Carroll declined interview requests for this book.

Lake said that he and New Era partner Michael Michaels didn't just attend USC home games but also went into the Trojan locker room after games. A team's locker room is considered its sanctuary, and most schools severely limit access to it. Lake also said that USC assistant coach Todd McNair knew of Bush's relationship with both himself and Michaels. Lake says McNair spent a night out in San Diego with Bush, Michaels, and Lake and knew Bush was spending the night in a suite at the city's Manchester Hyatt. While there is no evidence that McNair knew about the payment, the authors of this book obtained a receipt for the stay that was paid with Michaels's credit card.

Other items of interest to the NCAA would include phone records, emails, and internal correspondence of all USC athletic department staffers. They would also include all compliance department files on Bush plus the Trojans complimentary ticket lists, gate passes, and locker room and sideline access lists. USC officials have refused to release those items to media outlets, citing its status as a private school. USC officials also declined to be interviewed for this book, citing the continuing investigation by the NCAA and Pac-10.

However, even if the NCAA finds that Bush accepted improper benefits, that doesn't necessarily mean that USC will face penalties. The most important factor will be how much school officials knew about such contact and when they knew about it. The *Los Angeles Times* reported that, in January 2006, Lake's attorney Brian Watkins said USC running backs coach Todd McNair socialized with his client on one or more occasions but might not have known about any business arrangements. Michaels's attorney, Jordan Cohen, said that in researching the case he found "no information or indication that USC had actual knowledge of any of this."

Under an amended policy, the NCAA also eased the burden on schools whose athletes are targeted by unscrupulous sports agents.

Steve Morgan, a former NCAA enforcement chief who oversaw the NCAA's enforcement division from 1985 to 1996 and now works for a law firm in Kansas that represents schools in NCAA matters, told *Yahoo! Sports*: "It's extremely difficult for an institution to police that. So sometimes a benefit can be conferred by an agent, but there never would really be any institutional responsibility about that." Morgan, however, added that schools must take appropriate action if they become aware of an apparent rule violation involving an athlete accepting improper benefits. Morgan said that NCAA investigators looking into such a matter will scrutinize how a school responded when it learned about possible rule violations.

A *Los Angeles Times* story documented the presence of agents at USC during the 2005 season. In January, according to the *Times*, USC offensive line coach Pat Ruel surveyed the lobby outside the football offices and saw more than a dozen unfamiliar faces. "I know what cockroaches look like," Ruel told the *Times*. "And I know what agents look like."

The *Times* also reported that Coach Pete Carroll, in April 2006, took steps to regain control of the situation. According to the *Times*' story, Car-

roll sternly warned agents not to contact any high-school prospects who attended the school's pro day—where USC's NFL prospects worked out for scouts. In another apparent effort to head off rule violations, USC players and their parents were required this fall to provide more detailed information about where they reside. Morgan told *Yahoo! Sports* that the actions USC took in response to alleged infractions could prove pivotal if the case goes before the NCAA's Committee on Infractions.

At one time, the NCAA stated that if a student-athlete knowingly accepted money or anything of value from a prospective agent, the school suffered sanctions. Massachusetts and Connecticut were forced to return money from the 1996 NCAA basketball tournament and forfeit games even though the NCAA acknowledged neither school knew its players had accepted extra benefits from sports agents. "There was a strict responsibility," Morgan said.

Bill Saum, who oversees agent and gambling issues for the NCAA, acknowledged in 2002 that agent-related problems were widespread in college athletics. Saum told the *Fresno Bee*: "We're not naïve to the problem. We've been quoted for many years that our first-round draft picks probably have either been offered or accepted inducements [in their playing days]."

In addition to facing possible NCAA sanctions, the Trojans might suffer penalties from the Pac-10 and the Bowl Championship Series, which governs the national championship game. BCS officials told *Yahoo! Sports* that if Bush is ruled ineligible by either the Pacific-10 Conference or the NCAA for even one game during the 2004 season, the BCS will discuss amending its rules to allow it to force the Trojans to vacate the National Championship. While the NCAA could strip the Trojans of all their victories in 2004, it could not force USC to vacate its title, because the BCS championship is administered outside NCAA jurisdiction.

In 2004, President George W. Bush signed into law a bill targeting unscrupulous sports agents. The bill, pushed for legislation by Tennessee congressman Bart Gordon and former Nebraska coach and current interim athletic director Tom Osborne, was designed to protect student-athletes from predatory agents who make false or misleading claims to lure student-athletes into turning pro. This law allows universities and state attorneys general to take legal action against an agent if the agent has violated the provisions of the law.

In late April 2006, the Trojans were alerted by the *Los Angeles Times* of a possible NCAA violation concerning the living arrangements of their All-American receiver Dwayne Jarrett. The previous year Jarrett had shared an apartment with quarterback Matt Leinart. The rent on the apartment was $3,866 a month—Matt paid $650 a month, Jarrett paid $650, and Bob Leinart paid the difference.

School compliance officials started an investigation because Jarrett paid less than half of the lease. The *Los Angeles Times* reported on April 30, 2006, that Bob Leinart had been alerted that Jarrett might have to repay him $10,000. Bob Leinart said during the 2006 NFL Draft that "they leased the apartment in a secured building last June because fans started showing up at Matt's previous residence near campus." Bob Leinart put his son and Jarrett on the lease at the Medici complex, charging both students $650 a month.

In early May 2006, Pac-10 commissioner Tom Hansen said the arrangement constituted a violation. The living arrangement was determined to be an "extra-benefits" violation, and in June 2006 it was reported that Jarrett would have to apply for eligibility reinstatement.

In the end, the NCAA reinstated Jarrett on August 10, 2006, before the start of the regular season. The NCAA also ruled that, instead of having to repay Bob Leinart, Jarrett had to give the $5,352 in difference for rent to a charity of his choice. NCAA director of membership services and student-athlete reinstatement Jennifer Strawley said, "Mr. Jarrett made a mistake, and we believe that had he known he was required to pay his full share of the rent for the apartment, he would not have chosen to live there."

As a result of the Jarrett situation, USC compliance officials now require players and parents to provide more detailed information about their residence. Carroll told the *Los Angeles Times,* "We're just trying to find a little more out, trying to just be more aware of what's going on for obvious reasons."

By that time, the Griffin family already had been served eviction papers by lawyers for Michael Michaels. In a year of living in Michaels's home, according to the lawyers, they had paid not a dime of rent.

SEVENTEEN

The Fallout

Of all the costs that Reggie Bush may be required to pay for his poor business decisions, the most expensive may involve nothing more than shipping.

In the early 1980s, the Downtown Athletic Club board of directors, keepers of the Heisman Trophy, agreed to a provision that allowed for the trophy to be recalled if a player was penalized by the NCAA if the winner committed a serious violation during his Heisman season. No one is quite sure what prompted the rule change, but everyone is sure that there has never been a serious possibility that clause could come into play.

Until now.

A dozen Heisman voters, interviewed for this book, were unanimous: If it is true that Reggie Bush took hundreds of thousands of dollars from Lloyd Lake and Michael Michaels and the NCAA sanctions Bush, "It would make a great statement if we the Heisman voters said enough is enough," said the *Orlando Sentinel*'s Mike Bianchi.

"If all this proved to be true, I'd feel gypped as a guy who voted for him," said Tom Dienhart of *Sporting News.* "He seemingly was operating outside the NCAA rules and knew what he was doing. If there is a way

that we could go back and have that award vacated, I'd vote for him being stripped of the trophy. I'd expect the Heisman Trust to force it to happen. Maybe in the future this would make someone think twice about doing something like Reggie did. Probably not, as I hear myself say that. But it's a nice thought. No one ever believes they'll get caught. It would add credibility to the Heisman as an award if they stripped someone for violating the rules. If they protect their integrity, that would send a strong message."

Bryan Burwell, a columnist for the *St. Louis Post-Dispatch*, said the fact that information about Bush's misdeeds is coming from people who were equally culpable originally caused him to pause before deciding what to think. "Then I realized Reggie was as much a part of the deal as they were," Burwell said. "I'm not naïve enough to believe Reggie would be the first Heisman winner to take money . . . but he clearly would be the first to get seriously caught. That is a pretty interesting point: that no one has ever been caught in this situation before. I guess Reggie must be the first one to renege on the deal. Most guys who are taking cash, in my experience, know to keep it low key and not roll onto campus with a hot car.

"I have to hold myself to the same standard that I have in the steroid situation: Do you believe me or your lying eyes?" Burwell said. "I've got to believe my lying eyes that something happened, because it sure looks that way. In this case, Reggie being a willing participant in this thing would cause me to pause to reconsider my vote.

"Reggie's greatest mistake here appears to be not understanding the law of the street. There's a code, and he broke the code. Some of the money invested in this company didn't just come from the guys but from their moms and their sisters. If this was just a thug taking ill-gotten gains and investing it in a player, that's one thing. If it goes south, that's life on the street. But when your mom invested money, that's a whole different level. If Reggie had just done what every other smart athlete had done—shown honor among thieves—this wouldn't be coming up. This decision has put Reggie's business out in the street."

"I think it would be disappointing if the guy who was the most dominant winner in Heisman history was found to be ineligible," said Jenni Carlson of the *Daily Oklahoman.* "What a sad commentary. With the

provision in the ballot that says the winner has to be eligible, I'd say we have to vote to take that trophy away. When you look at the numbers that are being discussed—hundreds of thousands of dollars—being stripped of the Heisman is definitely not out of bounds. I hate to see an entire team take the fall for the actions of one athlete, but in this case this is an individual award and taking away the Heisman seems a reasonable punishment."

Ever the quipster, Brett McMurphy of the *Tampa Tribune* suggested, "Maybe we should just go ahead and declare him the winner of the first-ever *Heistman* trophy.

"I have to tell you I'm not surprised by much any more," McMurphy said. "But hearing what I'm hearing, you have to ask if this isn't the year for us to take that trophy back and give it to Vince Young. The irony is that if the balloting had occurred after the Rose Bowl, Vince would have won it anyway. Maybe what we do is put an asterisk by his name. It would be tough to physically get the trophy back from him, especially if he decides to put it up on eBay to help pay his legal bills. The magnitude of it is what gets me. I don't think I've heard of an individual player and his family involved with numbers like that."

The Heisman Trust—which replaced the Downtown Athletic Club as protector of the trophy—has no statement planned. "I know the trust intends to refrain from making any comment unless this reached a boiling point, so to speak," said Jim Corcoran, one of the nine trustees and a former four-sport star at Georgetown. "If the NCAA makes the bold move of disciplining USC, we'd have to evaluate what to do next. Let's assume this happened and the NCAA puts USC on probation, awards won by those players would have to be considered. Where do you draw the line? In the history of the award, this is a line that hasn't had to be drawn before. There's never been a situation like this for us to face before. It is certainly not anything we'd ever like to face."

New York Times sportswriter Bill Pennington is revered as an unofficial Heisman historian. His 2004 book, *The Heisman: Great American Stories of The Men Who Won*, is required reading for those who want to understand the trophy's significance.

"To call the Heisman iconic is an understatement," Pennington said. "In terms of a recognizable trophy, there's nothing like it. Close your eyes and envision what the American League Most Valuable [Player] trophy looks like. Now close them and see the Heisman. That's the point.

"Winning the Heisman comes with a lifetime of benefits, ones you don't get for finishing second," Pennington said. "There's a host of people who finished second that kind of walked through life differently. You talk to any Heisman winner and they'll tell you their life was never the same from the moment they won it. Guys like [Jim] Plunkett and [Pete] Dawkins told me stories about how every time a FedEx was delivered to their house the driver wants to come in and see the trophy. And not just FedEx, but UPS and DHL, too. Gary Beban talked about going for walks in his neighborhood and seeing people taking pictures of his house. He couldn't figure out why and he went over and talked to one of these guys and asked. The guy told him, 'This is Gary Beban's house and he won the Heisman. If you take the shot from this angle, you can see through the den and see the trophy!' That is not unusual."

What is unusual, he said, is the possibility that Bush might actually become the first winner to suffer the high-profile fate of being asked to return his award.

"It's never happened, so I don't know that there's actually a process in place on how it would be done," Pennington said. "They are very protective of the Heisman and feel very strongly about what it represents. If it ever got to the point that the NCAA stripped USC of a bunch of victories because Reggie Bush was ineligible, I can't imagine that they wouldn't say, 'Wait a minute, this taints the whole Hesiman vote, as well.' They're too protective. I think they would act.

"This award changes lives. To give it up would have to be a real blow to your reputation and image. I don't think there's any question.

"If he were to lose the trophy, he would become the Richard Nixon of college football," Pennington said. "He would be like Nixon among Heisman winners in that he would be the only one to ever be stripped of his trophy. Nixon committed crimes against the nation and it doesn't sound like Reggie did anything criminal so its not a totally apt analogy. But you get the point. It would be highly damaging. Who wants to win

the most famous sports trophy in America . . . and have it taken away because you didn't play by the rules?"

The question hung there as the interview ended. No answer was necessary. As several voters said, the case of Reggie Bush may set in motion events no one ever saw coming.

Least of all Reggie.

Cast of Characters

Reggie Bush

The six-foot, 203-pound running back was the New Orleans Saints' first pick in the 2006 NFL Draft, making him second overall. Bush agreed to a six-year contract that could pay him up to $62 million—with a little more than $26.3 million guaranteed. Bush starred at the University of Southern California (2003–2005), where he led the Trojans to a national championship over Oklahoma in 2004, and won the Heisman Trophy as a junior in 2005. Bush stands at the center of a controversy over whether he and his parents received improper benefits from a prospective sports marketing agency, New Era Sports & Entertainment, during Bush's career at USC.

New Era Sports & Entertainment

A fledging sports marketing agency firm in San Diego, California, that was formed by LaMar Griffin, Lloyd Lake, and Michael Michaels in late 2004. The group intended to build the company around Griffin's stepson, Reggie Bush, with the hope that Bush's presence would attract other professional athletes. The firm ultimately failed when Bush signed with other representation in January 2006 after Bush announced he would forgo his senior season at USC and enter the NFL Draft. According to Lake and Michaels, Bush and his family accepted about $300,000 in cash advances and gifts from New Era representatives while Bush was a student-athlete at USC.

MICHAEL MICHAELS

A financial backer for New Era Sports & Entertainment. Michaels was approached by LaMar Griffin and Lloyd Lake in October 2004 at a San Diego Chargers football game. It was suggested to Michaels, a real estate investor and an officer for the Sycuan Indian Tribe's development corporation, that he, Lake, and Griffin could be partners in a sports and marketing agency that would feature Reggie Bush as its anchor client. Michaels, Lake, and Griffin also attempted to partner their business venture with the Sycuan Indian Tribe. Ultimately, the Sycuans chose not to be involved. Michaels settled a lawsuit with Bush and his parents in April 2007 for reportedly $200,000 to $300,000.

LLOYD LAKE

Co-founder of New Era Sports & Entertainment. A family friend of Reggie Bush and LaMar Griffin, Lake introduced Griffin to eventual backer Michael Michaels. Lake also did much of the legwork in helping establish New Era as a corporate entity. Lake filed a civil lawsuit in October 2007 alleging the he and Michaels gave around $300,000 in payments, lodging, and other accommodations to Bush and his family from November 2004 to January 2006. Lake also met with NCAA investigators in November 2007 to discuss allegations that he supplied Bush with cash and gifts while Bush was still at USC.

LAMAR AND DENISE GRIFFIN

The stepfather and mother of Reggie Bush. LaMar Griffin and Lake met with Michaels in late 2004 to discuss the idea of forming a sports agency that would feature Griffin's stepson, Reggie Bush, as it signature client. Attorneys for Lake and Michaels allege that Griffin used Bush's future as a potential New Era client to collect around $300,000 in cash and benefits form Lake and Michaels before Bush eventually signed with other representation in January 2006.

MIKE ORNSTEIN

Was hired in January 2006 by Reggie Bush to serve as his marketing agent. However, Bush fired Ornstein, who is based in Los Angeles, for at least the second time in November 2007. Bush's assortment of endorse-

ments includes deals with Subway, Hummer, PepsiCo, Adidas, Visa, EA Sports, GTSM Memorabilia, and Halcyon Jets. Ornstein is also alleged to have given thousands of dollars in gifts and cash to Bush and his family during Bush's final season at USC. Bush's ties to Ornstein began when he took an internship in Ornstein's office in the summer of 2005.

DAVID CARAVANTES

San Diego–area agent solicited by New Era Sports to negotiate Bush's NFL contract. Caravantes's involvement with New Era was contingent on Bush's involvement with the agency. That never occurred, and Caravantes disassociated himself from the company.

BRIAN WATKINS

San Diego–based attorney for Michael Michaels and Lloyd Lake. In April 2006, Watkins outlined intentions to file a $3.2 million lawsuit claiming that Michael Michaels was defrauded out of "large sums of money" by Bush and his parents, Denise and LaMar Griffin, during a business relationship. Watkins negotiated a settlement with Bush in the spring of 2007 reportedly for between $200,000 and $300,000. Watkins, fellow attorney Paul Wong, and Lake filed a civil lawsuit in October 2007 against Bush and his family to recoup nearly $300,000 in cash and gifts they allegedly accepted from Lake and New Era representatives during Bush's sophomore and junior seasons at USC.

PAUL WONG

Los Angeles–based attorney for Lloyd Lake. Attempted to reach a financial agreement with Reggie Bush through mediation during summer of 2007 but was unsuccessful. With fellow attorney Brian Watkins, Wong and Lake filed a civil lawsuit in October 2007 against Bush and his family to recoup nearly $300,000 in cash and gifts they allegedly accepted from Lake and New Era representatives during Bush's sophomore and junior seasons at USC.

DAVID CORNWELL

Atlanta-based attorney for Reggie Bush and his parents, stepfather LaMar Griffin and mother Denise Griffin. Cornwell has been at the forefront of

deflecting allegations made against the Bush family. In spring 2007, Cornwell and Bush reached a private settlement with Michael Michaels, reportedly for between $200,000 and $300,000. Cornwell has vowed to fight Lake's suit, filed in October 2007, "vigorously." Cornwell has argued that Lake, a convicted felon who has been in and out of prison, has no credibility.

LEE PFEIFER
Head of CWC Sports.

Pfeifer filed a lawsuit against Mike Ornstein for breach of their partnership in CWC Sports.

Timeline of Events

September–October 2004

LaMar Griffin, on the behalf of his stepson, Reginald Bush, discusses with family friend Lloyd Lake the formation of a sports agency and marketing company. A meeting is held at LaMar and Denise Griffin's home. At this meeting, Griffin confirms that Reggie will join "any sports venture" formed by his parents. Also, it's asserted that Bush wants ownership interest.

Lloyd Lake, LaMar Griffin, Denise Griffin, and Reggie Bush agree to form a partnership for the purpose of acting as a sports agent for Bush and other potential sports figures. Shortly after this meeting, Lake claims he communicates with Bush and gets confirmation of his willingness to join the venture.

October 2004

Upon confirmation from Bush, Lake suggests to Griffin that the company seek funding from his business acquaintance, Michael Michaels, a development officer for the Sycuan Indians. Later in the month, Lake introduces the Griffins to Michaels in his luxury suite in Qualcomm Stadium after a San Diego Chargers football game. They discuss the sports company and possible partnership with the Sycuan tribe and agree to meet again.

November 2004

The Griffins meet with Lake and Michaels to discuss the sports company. Again, the Griffins confirm that Bush will be the first athlete to join the

company. The parties agree to form a partnership, which will become New Era Sports & Entertainment with Bush as the anchor client.

Michaels demands a meeting with Bush to confirm his commitment. Later in the month, Bush meets with Lake and Michaels at a Friday's restaurant in Mission Valley, San Diego. At this meeting, Bush confirms his commitment. Michaels becomes the primary financial backer of the company. Also, in or around November 2004, Bush travels with Lake and Michaels to the Bonita Plaza Shopping Mall and later to Lisa Lake's home to solicit her participation in the sports company.

It is during the month of November that Bush allegely asks payment for living and entertainment expenses while he is a student-athlete at the University of Southern California. He wants $3,000 a month as an advance on his future income and for participation in New Era Sports.

This series of events leads Lake and Michaels to fund New Era Sports. In addition, they agree to pay $3,000 a month to Bush because the Griffins lack the resources to support the business venture and the lifestyle expenses of their son.

November–December 2004

The Griffins allegedly demand $28,000 from Michaels to pay off their debts so they can focus on the formation of the sports company. New Era Sports claims the Griffins held Bush's commitment as leverage to get the money.

January 4, 2005

USC defeats Oklahoma 55–19 to win the national championship.

February 2005

Bush is paid $13,000 in cash for the purchase of a 1996 Chevrolet Impala SS. Bush instructs Lake to give the payment to LaMar Griffin. Shortly after the purchase of the vehicle, Bush asks for $4,000 for aftermarket tires and rims.

March 2005

March 4

Bush attends a birthday party for St. Louis Ram Marshall Faulk. He stays at the Manchester Grand Hyatt for two days. Michaels pays for the stay with his credit card, total cost $1,574.86.

March 11

Bush visits Las Vegas for a two-day stay at the Venetian Resort and Casino. Michaels pays for Bush's room with his credit card, total cost $623.63.

Late March

LaMar and Denise Griffin ask Lake and Michaels—on behalf of New Era Sports & Entertainment—to acquire for them a new residence. The Griffins promise to repay the incurred housing expenses out of the sports agency's future income.

Michaels, on the behalf of New Era Sports and Reggie Bush, drives the family around the San Diego area shopping for a residence. The Griffins and Bush select a home. The Griffins agree to lease the property from New Era Sports and Michaels.

On March 29, 2005, Michaels purchases the 3,002-square-foot home for $757,500 with a down payment of $36,000.

April 14, 2005

Lake and Michaels purchase a washer and dryer for the Griffins, total cost $1,064.98.

May 2005

The Griffins ask for $12,000 toward furniture and other incidentals that would be used at the residence.

Summer 2005

Bush starts internship with Mike Ornstein, a consultant for Reebok.

June 2005

The Griffins enter into a written agreement to lease the home on 9715 Apple Street in San Diego. The lease commences on June 1, 2005, and terminates on June 1, 2006.

The Griffins allegedly fail to pay the first several months of rent. Yet they tell Michaels they plan to purchase the home once Bush declares for the draft and signs with New Era Sports.

It is later reported that from June 1, 2005, to April 21, 2006, the Griffins failed to pay any rent or expenses related to the Apple Street lease.

July 9, 2005

Lake, Michaels, and Barbara Gunner meet with the Griffins, Bush, and attorney Phillip Smith to incorporate a business entity.

September 2005

Lake and Michaels allegedly visit Bush in the USC locker room following a game. The Griffins ask for $6,000 for travel expenses for a football game in Hawaii.

October 2005

Early October

Lake approaches sports agent David Caravantes about negotiating Bush's NFL contract. Caravantes agrees to join New Era if the firm lands Bush.

Mid-October

Lake, Michaels, and Griffin attempt to start a partnership between the Sycuan band of Kumeyaay Indians and New Era Sports for the purpose of securing additional investments and funding. Allegedly, at this meeting, Griffin says that Bush had agreed to join the company and that his participation would bring other professional athletes on board. The Sycuan tribe passes on the partnership.

November 2005

Again, Michaels and Griffin meet with the Sycuan Tribal Council, to no avail.

Ornstein, who Bush had interned for the previous summer, becomes an adviser for the Bush family and their search for prospective agents.

November 23

Papers are filed to form New Era Sports & Entertainment.

December 2005

December 2

Griffin shows a *San Diego Union-Tribune* reporter a brochure for New Era Sports & Entertainment. According to *Yahoo! Sports*, he describes it as ". . . a new company . . . they sent me a brochure, they're here in San Diego."

December 10

The day before the Heisman Trophy ceremony Ornstein allegedly borrows $500 in cash from New Jersey sports memorabilia dealer Bob DeMartino to make a payment of more than $1,500 to Bush's family. DeMartino alleges that the money paid for a makeover for Denise Griffin, the suits LaMar Griffin and Bush's younger brother wore to the Heisman ceremony, and a limousine to escort the family around New York City.

December 11

Bush wins the Heisman Trophy.

December 29

Ornstein emails DeMartino asking for a $500,000 advance on a memorabilia contract DeMartino had proposed for Bush.

January 2006

The Griffins and Bush retain David Cornwell in connection with the dispute over New Era Sports.

January 4

USC loses the national championship to Texas, 41–38.

January 12

Bush declares for the NFL Draft.

Mid-January

Bush hires Ornstein to be his marketing representative and Joel Segal to represent him as a professional athlete.

January 30–February 6, 2006

Lake—sentenced to federal prison for beating his girlfriend while on probation for a drug-related charge—has his attorney, Marc Carlos, testify on his behalf at his parole violation hearing. At this hearing, it's revealed that Lake had been trying to form a sports agency with Bush and that a falling-out had occurred.

February 2006

Allegedly, Bush and Denise Griffin engage in settlement talks with Michaels and his attorney, Brian Watkins. Bush's attorney, David Cornwell, also attends the meeting. They meet at a Santa Monica office belonging to Ornstein. Security guards pat down Michaels and Watkins, looking for recording devices.

Sources tell *Yahoo! Sports* that Michaels attempts to speak to Bush directly. Cornwell asks his client and his mother to leave the room, and according to *Yahoo! Sports* sources, offers $100,000 to settle the dispute. Michaels and Watkins refuse and indicate they plan to file a lawsuit to recover potential earnings lost and the money given to the Griffins and Bush.

February 13

According to *Yahoo! Sports*, Watkins sends a letter to Cornwell "requesting $3.2 million to settle the dispute over 'lost business capital' and monies given to the Bush family while attempting to build a sports agency that he was to join." *Yahoo! Sports* reports that Watkins wants to know if USC will be part of the negotiations since, "as we understand their wanting to be involved due to the fact this matter was ongoing during their championship season of 2004 as well as the entire season of 2005, and any lawsuit filed might have an adverse effect on them."

April 2006

April 3

Lake and Michaels, via their attorneys, serve the Griffins a notice to vacate the Apple Street residence.

April 12

The Griffins, through their attorney David Cornwell, advise they will vacate the home by April 21, 2006.

April 20

Yahoo! Sports attempts to interview Denise Griffin at the Spring Valley residence. She declines to comment about the family's ties to New Era Sports.

April 21

The Griffins vacate the home, allegedly taking $12,000 in household furnishings paid for by New Era Sports.

USC asks the Pacific-10 Conference to investigate the residence and New Era Sports.

April 24

The NCAA joins the investigation.

According to *Yahoo! Sports*, Houston Texans general manager Charley Casserly leaves a telephone message for Bush asking him to explain media reports about his family's living situation.

April 25

Yahoo! Sports reports that Casserly reaches Bush. However, Bush says he's getting on a plane to New York City and will call him back when he lands.

April 26

Bush returns Casserly's call. According to *Yahoo! Sports*, Bush refuses to discuss his parents' living arrangement and says to Casserly, "It will be taken care of in a couple of days."

April 28

ESPN reports that Cornwell turns over evidence of an alleged extortion plot against Bush by New Era Sports representatives to NFL security and the Players Association. The NFL issues a memo in which Bush denies knowledge of his parents' financial ties to New Era Sports.

The same day the Texans, with the number-one draft pick, pass on Bush. *Yahoo! Sports* reports that a source with the team says Bush's reluctance to discuss his parents' living arrangements affected the Texans' decision.

June 2006

The FBI opens an investigation into New Era Sports & Entertainment. The investigation is later dropped.

October 2007

Lloyd Lake promises NCAA investigators financial records and other evidence linking Reggie Bush and his family to close to $300,000 in benefits while he was enrolled at USC. Also, he alleges he has confidential emails from officers of New Era Sports & Entertainment showing the agency soliciting marketing and memorabilia deals on Bush's behalf.

November 2007

Lloyd Lake files suit against Reggie Bush and his parents to recoup nearly $300,000 in cash and gifts. The suit claims that between November 2004 and January 2006 his family received $291,600 in cash, living arrangements, and other benefits.

November 6

Lloyd Lake, accompanied by his attorneys Brian Watkins and Paul Wong, meets NCAA investigators for the first time at Wong's law office.

A New Era of Spending

Obtained through documents and interviews for this book, here's a general review of money alleged to have been paid and advanced to Reggie Bush and his family from December 2004 through April 2006.

December 2004–January 2005: Griffin family received advance payment of $28,000 to pay off their debts.

January–October 2005: Reggie Bush received an average monthly advance of $3,000 for living expenses ($30,000).

February 2005: Reggie received $17,000 for the purchase of a Chevrolet Impala and accessories.

March 2005: Down payment of $36,000 for the purchase of residence for the Griffin family.

April 2005: Lake and Michaels jointly funded $95,000 to New Era, to be operated by the Griffin family.

May 2005: Cash advance of $19,000 to Griffin family for new furniture and incidentals.

June–August 2005: Griffin family received $10,000 for future living expenses, including meals and entertainment.

September 2005: Griffin family received $6,000 related to travel expenses for USC's season opener at Hawaii.

June 2005–April 2006: Lease payments totaling $50,000 for Griffin family.

Estimated funding: $291,000.

Acknowledgments

This book, written on a tight deadline, is the product of a true team effort. From research to writing, this was an all-hands-on-deck project. But before we acknowledge those who helped pull it together, we should take note of those journalists whose work before us in investigating this story gave us a wonderful road map. Jason Cole and Charles Robinson of *Yahoo! Sports* were certainly out in front of nearly every major development in the Bush investigation, and the hundreds of inches they penned on the subject proved invaluable.

In addition to Cole, Robinson, Dave Morgan, and Dan Wetzel at *Yahoo! Sports*, among those whose works we turned to include Austin Murphy at *Sports Illustrated,* and Joe Schad at *ESPN's the Magazine.* At the *Los Angeles Times:* David Wharton, Gary Klein, Jerry Crowe, Sam Farmer, and T. J. Simers; at *The San Diego Union Tribune:* Brent Schrotenboer, Tim Sullivan, Jim Trotter, Anthony Millican and Chet Barfield; at the *Orange County Register:* Mark Saxon, Jeff Miller, and Todd Harmonson; at the *Daily Trojan:* Dan Greenspan and Dan Loeterman; at *The* (Riverside) *Press Enterprise:* Dan Weber and Jeff Eisenberg; at the *Daily News of Los Angeles:* Tom Hoffarth; at the *San Jose Mercury News:* Bud Geracie; at *USA Today:* Jack Carey, Tom Weir, Jill Lieber, and David Leon Moore; at *The Sporting News:* Tom Dienhart; at the *Associated Press:* John Nadel; at the *Chicago Tribune:* Don Pierson; at the *Chicago Sun-Times:* Carol Slezak; at the *New York Times:* Bill Pennington and Pete Thamel; at the (New York) *Daily News:* Gary Myers, Tim Smith, David Hinckley, and Matt Gagne; at *The Washington Post:* Marc Carig, Les Carpenter, and Teresa Wiltz; at the *Washington Times:* Dan Daly; at the *Boston Globe:* Mark Blaudschun; at

Esquire: Chris Jones; at *Newsweek:* Allison Samuels; at the *Orlando Sentinel:* Mike Bianchi and Dave Curtis; at the *Tampa Tribune:* Brett McMurphy; at *The Daily Oklahoman:* Jenni Carlson and George Schroeder; at the *St. Louis Post-Dispatch:* Bryan Burwell and Jeff Gordon; other sources: the Heisman Trust, CBS News, *The Contra Costa Times,* and the Sycuan Band of the Kumeyaay Nation website.

On the writing end, Tiffany Brooks's talents were immeasurable; she once again delivered beautifully and helped us stay on course. Forrest Anderson proved invaluable in research under tight deadlines, and the versatile Jenny Fernandez, who came to work for us last year, also contributed as she balanced other projects. Our office staff, specifically manager Heather Wartenberg and Meghan Kelly also contributed to our immediate organizational needs.

This project was the brainchild of literary agents Ian Kleinert and Jarred Weisfeld, who were able to pry the all-important audio tapes from Lloyd Lake long before we became involved. At Simon & Schuster, editor Margaret Clark, associate publisher Anthony Ziccardi, and attorneys Henry Kaufman and Felice Javit worked like a well-oiled machine while pushing this book through. We hope to never again have a deadline like this . . . but if we do, we'll want you on our side.

While we mentioned in the Author's Note that we were unable to speak with Reggie Bush, he was often interviewed by the media after the allegations detailed in this book first surfaced publicly prior to the 2006 NFL Draft. One of Bush's responses caught our attention and we believed spoke volumes of his mind-set, which surely continues to this day. Bush said, "I just focus on the goal—the ultimate goal—just focus on playing football and not worry about the allegations and what's going on outside of football. At the end of the day, I know what's true. And it will come out and everybody will see that I'm still a good guy; that I'm still the same guy that I was from day one."

At the end of these pages, I think everyone will know what is true.

—Don Yaeger and Jim Henry

T0114793

Nengoma anampita Zengeni ambaye anamkata jicho na kutabasamu. Akiwa hana hili wala lile, Zengeni anafumwa na mkewe akimkata jicho. Nengoma anamuuliza mumewe. "Mbona umeduwaa unanishangaa nini? Jitahidi ukubaliane na ukweli dear."

Zengeni hajibu na Nengoma anaachana na swali lile asijue moyoni Zengeni anajisifu kwa kujua kuchagua. Ukiongezea na utondoti na kikuba ambavyo huwa havibanduki maungoni mwake, si haba. Mashallah!

Nengoma anarudia kuuliza kinachomshangaza Zengeni asijue mwenzie ndiyo hivyo tena!

Zengeni hajibu. Nengoma analiacha swali lake bila jibu na kuingia ndani na kutua ndoo yake huku akihema na kulalamika kuchoka.

"Mume wangu, kama hali ikiendelea kuwa hivi, siyo siri, maisha ya hapa yatatushinda. Hawa wanasiasa waongo walituahidi pepo sasa wanatupa jehanam na jongomeo! Hawana lolote. Ni matapaeli hata kama wana madaraka wanayofuja." Anajisemea baada ya kurudi kuungana na mmewe kiambazani baada ya kutua ndoo ya maji. Inaonekana umbali wa kupata maji na uchafu wa maji vimemchefua roho kiasi fulani.

Zengeni anageuka taratibu kujibu swali la mkewe anayemjongelea akiwa anajifuta jasho. Anaonyesha kuchoka.

Anasema. "Mama we, unataka maisha yatushinde mara ngapi? Tunajikongoja kwa matumaini tukitegemea angalau kesho inaweza kuleta neema lakini mwisho wa yote nadama zinaongezeka. Imefikia mahali jana inakuwa bora kuliko leo!" Anatikisa kichwa kwa masikitiko.

Anajipanga vizuri kigodani na kuendelea "Ila ujue wazi kuwa kukata tamaa au kukubali kushindwa ni kujizika hai. Lazima tupambane kila uchao na inshallah Mwenyezi Mungu anasikia. Tuzidi kupambana mambo yatabadilika hata kama ni baada ya muda mrefu. Mgaagaa na upwa."

Anamkazi macho mkewe aliyekuwa akimsikiliza kwa makini na kuendelea, "Tumshukuru Subhana kwani hapa si haba. Siyo kama kwa mama Mzaramizi aliyetutesa kwa sababu ya banda lake la urithi. Wanasiasa kwa kusema wasichotenda na kutenda wasichosema ni kama wamelaaniwa."

Anakohoa kidogo na kuendelea. "Umesikia kashfa ya kampuni la Richmen Development and Innovations?"

"Bwanawe nchi hii imekuwa donda ndugu la kashfa. Juzi kulikuwa na kashfa ya wizi Benki kuu. Kabla haujafumka huu kulikuwa na wizi wizara ya madini na nishati. Pia kumbuka ule wizi baba lao ambapo Rais mstaafu aligundulika kuwa na biashara za siri na chafu nje ya nchi. Sasa hatujapumua wizi tena mwingine! Je hii Richmen nayo siyo yao hao hao wakubwa? Maana ukichunguza vizuri hakuna wizi ambao hauna mkono wao. Mwe! Jamani hawa watu watakuja kuuza roho zetu hata makaburi ya babu zetu! Mipesa yote hii ya nini au kichaa cha kuona manoti?" Nengoma anaamua kuangusha kilio chake baada ya kupewa taarifa za kuwapo kashfa nyingine."Huoni walivyonenepeana na kunoneana kama nune kwa maghusubu huku tukifanyiwa magube?" Anaongezea Nengoma."Mama wewe kwa kunga na misamiati na kufunga nyama sina hamu kabisa!" Zengeni alimtania Nengoma.

Nengoma anaonekana kuchukia na kustushwa na kashfa hii jahara. Naye anatikisa kichwa chake huku akiamka kuondoka kuelekea ndani kutoa jiko nje lau likolee moto.

Alimrai mumewe. "Unaonaje ukanipa muda kidogo niangalie jiko langu; nirudi tuuguze madonda haya ya kuibiwa na kuzikwa na wale tuliodhani ni wenzetu wakati siyo?"Nengoma anamalizia rai yake huku anatokomea ndani ili aende akatoe jiko lau aliwashie nje lipulizwe na upepo ili mkaa ushike moto mapema atungike maji ya chai haraka.

Zengeni najibu, "Leo maongezi na chai fahuwa." Anasema huku akitikisa kichwa kama ishara ya kukubaliana na pendekezo la mkewe ambaye hasikii alichosema. Mara kitambo kidogo, Nengoma anatoka ndani na jiko la mkaa ambalo tayari keshalilisha. Kama ada, jicho la Zengeni halibanduki maungoni mwake. Zamu hii Nengoma hakuona jinsi alivyokatwa jicho la mahaba. Hata hivyo aliishazoea. Maana hana jinsi ya kulaumu bali kujivuna. Maana ni mumewe tena wa kujichagulia.

"Mtu chake bwana." Alizoea kusema Zengeni alipokuwa akifumwa akiiba maungo aamuapo kujibu kama siyo kupuuzia kama alivyofanya kitambo. Siku moja Nembogha alimtania kuwa angelimfungulia mashitaka kwa kumkonyezea na kumkodolea. Wacha Zengeni acheke.

Alizoea kujitetea kuwa nani angeweza kuiba chake mwenyewe? Na isitoshe hizi ni sheria za kipuuzi toka wataraghani ambazo tumezipwakia toka kwa wakoloni wanaotaka kutuchonganisha ili wazidi kutudhoofisha na kututawala kirahisi."Nengoma alizoea kujibu kwa kulinganisha na watawala wanavyojiibia wenyewe mali za nchi yao.

2
Nyumba

Nyumba yake ni ya kawaida tu. Ni ya kawaida kama nyumba lakini si ya kawaida ilivyojengwa. Ni nyumba ya kwaida kwa watu wa kawaida. Lakini kwa wenye jeuri ya pesa si nyumba saa nyingine banda hata hame.

Nyumba yake ni nyumba ya matofali mchanganyiko ya kuchomwa na yasiyochomwa. Hata bati zake nazo ni rangi mbili; mpya na kuu kuu. Ni nyumba rangi mbili kama dawa ya kaswende iitwayo capsules.

Nyumba ya Zengeni ni nyumba ya msomi kabwela anayehenya sawa na wasiosoma. Ni nyumba ya ajabu kuielezea. Maana si mpya ingawa ilijengwa miaka miwili iliyopita wala si nzee. Maana haijazeeka zaidi ya kuzeeshwa na kipato cha kijungujiko!

Ni kielelezo tosha cha jinsi wasomi walivyopigika huku baadhi ya matapeli wasioelimika wakielea kwenye utajiri wa kutupwa!

Nyumba ya Zengeni siyo nyumba inayopaswa kujengwa na msomi kama yeye kama siyo kuishi kwenye jamii iliyotekwa na kunajisiwa na maovu yote yaandamanayo na wizi katika hazina ya umma na taasisi zake. Hata hivyo, hii nyumba siyo tunda la kazi aliyoisomea ya ualimu bali ni tunda la kazi ya umachinga au uchuuzi aliyoifanya baada ya kulazimika kuuachana na ualimu alioupenda sana.Japo ni nyumba isiyendana na usomi, bado inaitwa nyumba. Maana hata kiota cha nyuni huitwa nyumba ilmradi usingizi unatononolewa. Hata shimo la kenge, mhanga na nungu nungu ni nyumba. Kwani maisha huenda. Lakini hawa ni wanyama. Zengeni si hayawani. Ni binadamu tena msomi.

Hata Zengeni aikane na kutoridhikana na nyumba yake, bado inamilkiwa na msomi hata kama siyo stahiki yake! Ni nyumba jina na kitendawili! Ni tata na tete. Hivyo, ndivyo kila jicho lililobahatika kuiona linavyoweza kuielezea.Pamoja na kuwa hii nyumba ni matokeo ya jasho lake na mkewe, haipendi wala kuridhika nayo. Japo ameijenga baada ya kujaribu kila aina ya pirika halali, bado haridhiki nayo. Japo inampa usingizi, ni donda la mstakabali wake kama msomi na raia wa nchi iliyojaliwa kila neema kuanzia chini ya ardhi hata juu ya ardhi mpaka kwenye tabia na hulka ya wakazi wake wapole na wastaarabu.

Japo wakazi wa Mafuriko -taifa la Zengeni- wanasifika kwa uvumilivu na ustaarabu wao, taratibu, wanaanza kubadilika na kuharibiwa na utawala mchafu na kidhabu. Uvumilivu wao umewalisha mbovu na ustaarabu wao umewaletea ushenzi hasa pale wanapotumika kama mwiko kusonga ugali usile.

Uvumilivu unazidi kuwatupa mkono huku stahamala nayo ikiwapa kisogo. Ndiyo maana Zengeni amejiinamia akitafakari mambo mbali mbali anayoona yanaenda ndiyo siyo huku wafanyayo siyo wakiwaminisha ndivyo!

Zengeni amelazimika kujenga kwenye makazi yasiyo rasmi wala kupimwa. Wamelazimishwa na mfumo mbaya uliofilisika na kuchoka kimipango na kimkakati bila kuongelea sera na mawazo mapya. Roho yake siku zote inamuuma kila anaporejea au kutoka nyumbani akipita kwenye majumba yafananayo na mahekalu ya kifalme yaliyojengwa na mbweha, mibaka na mafisadi waliomkwamisha na raia wenzake wema. Hajawahi kuiita nyumba nyumba yake. Huuita banda tu.

Hawezi kuridhika na maisha na nyumba yake wakati anaona makasri yakioteshwa na watu wasio na taaluma zaidi ya ghilba na unafiki, udokozi na sura za kinyonga. Anaumia kuona mbweha, vyangudoa, fisi, kunguru na kila kinyama cha usiku vikijenga makasri kwa chumo la wizi ilhali yeye kwa pesa halali anashindwa kujenga lau nyumba achia mbali kasri.

Kila uchao kwenye maeneo ya wenye nazo zinaota nyumba kama uyoga karibu kila mtaa nchi nzima. Migari ya bei mbaya ndiyo usiseme!

Nani ataridhika anaona na kujua nchi yake iliyogeuzwa sindano ambayo hushona nguo nyingi lakini ikaishi ikiwa uchi mtupu tena milele?

Haya, bahati mbaya sana, yamekuwa ndiyo majaliwa ya nchi yake! Ni majaliwa ya kutengenezwa na wanadamu wachoyo na wenye roho mbaya ambao ulafu wao ndiyo umegeuka dhamira za matendo yao.

Ataridhikaje na nchi ya mbwa ambaye hulinda mali nyingi lakini akaishi kuwa maskini hadi anatupwa nyikani au shimoni tena bila sala wala matanga? Nani aliwahi kuona au kuhudhuria matanga ya mbwa? Hata kuku ana nafuu maana huombolezwa mezani kwa vicheko na mbwewe!

Nani aweza kuridhika na hali hii iwapo, kwa Zengeni na wengine kama yeye kama siyo kulazimishwa kuacha kazi aliyoipenda ili aishi hata kwa kugeuka machinga asingekuwa na hilo banda lake? Hana jinsi. Isitoshe wapo akina Zengeni wengi japo hawajitokezi wala kujenga chuki juu ya nyumba walizozijenga baada ya mfumo kuwasaliti na kuwachukia.

Mtaka cha uvunguni sharti ainame. Kwani nyumba yake isingekuwapo kama angeendelea kufanya kazi ya ualimu. Maana bila yeye na mkewe kuamua kuachana na ualimu na kukumbatia umachinga, nyumba kwa Zengeni ingekuwa kama ndoto ya mchana. Angeishia kuwa kama mjusi alalaye kwenye za wenzie asiwazie kujenga yake siku moja. Lakini mjusi ni hayawani na Zengeni ni mtu tena msomi na mwalimu. Mjusi ana nafuu. Maana hajawahi kupewa notisi ya kuhama wala kupandishiwa kodi.

Japo anayo nyumba iitwayo yake, hajaridhika nayo wala hali yake kimaisha. Na nchi kadhalika. Ataridhikaje iwapo kila jana inaonekana bora kuliko leo japo si bora? Ataridhikaje katikati ya jamii ya mashaka, hofu, nadama na taabu isiyo na usalama kwa sababu kikundi fulani cha watu kimeamua iwe hivyo? Ajabu! Watawala wake wanawasifia akina Zengeni kwa amani na utulivu wanavyovitumia kuwavuna kama matunda pori kwenye mti usio na mwenyewe!

Amekalia kigoda cha miguu mitatu. Nyumba na maisha yake si ya kimaskini wala ya kitajiri kwa viwango vya kimaskini. Ila kwa viwango vya kitajiri siyo nyumba bali banda hata lisilomstahili hata mbwa wala ng'ombe wa tajiri wa kundi la watawala wa Mafuriko kuishi ndani mwe! Ni gongo la tembo. Mapaa manne haiwezi. Imeezekwa kwa bati chakavu na mpya. Vigae haviwezi. Hawezi kuvigusa hadi siku mwenyewe atakapozikwa akageuka kigae.Amejenga nyumba hii nje ya mji mkuu wa Mafuriko uitwao Neema ingawa hauna neema bali nakama. Hii ni kutokana na kuepuka mbanano na ughali wa majumba na viwanja karibu na katikati ya jiji ambapo kuna usalama na huduma safi. Japo jina la mji huu ni Neema, kwa kada ya akina Zengeni ni Balaa.

Zengeni alilazimika kuamua kujenga nyumba yake kilometa kama 15 toka katikati ya jiji jambo ambalo humlazimisha kunyonywa na wenye mabasi kila uchao aendapo au kurejea toka mjini kwenye mihangaiko yake. Ni kwenye kitongoji kitwacho Uswekeni waishipo watu maskini wa kutupwa. Hakuwa na uwezo wa kukohoa mamilioni ya shilingi apate kiwanja kilichopimwa katikati ya mji ambako karibu majengo yote ya maana ni ya wageni wa watawala wanaoshirikiana nao kuwaumiza akina Zengeni.

Pamoja na kujenga nyumba, wakati mwingine hujutia uamuzi huu.Una tatizo. Tatizo lenyewe ni kujenga kwenye kiwanja kisichopimwa alichouziwa na mzee Sibulele Sibusiso ambaye hakuwa na watoto. Kutokana na mzee huyu kutokuwa na mtoto hata wa kusingiziwa achia mbali wa kuzaa, baada ya kufa kuna watu walimwijia Zengeni wakisema ni ndugu zake na walikuwa wamerithishwa naye. Walimpa karatasi ya urithi ya kughushi. Nusura apate hasara kama siyo wezi hawa wa mchana kuzungukana na mmoja wao songombingo kuwasaliti wenzake ili angalau apate chake. Kiasi fulani umaskini na ujinga ulimsaidia kutoingia hasara.

Alinunua kiwanja chake shilingi laki tano bila kuhesabu pesa ya hongo kwa mamlaka za mtaa kumpatia vibali vya kujenga na kumilki eneo hili lisilopimwa. Baada ya kununua uwanja ule alikwenda kwa mjumbe wakaandikishiana mkataba kila mtu akaondoka na chake. Na hii ni hatua mojawapo iliyomsaidia kuwagawanya wale wezi. Maana baada ya mjumbe aliyekuwa ameishi na marehemu maisha yake yote kuwauliza kwanini hakuwa amewahi kuwaona hata kwenye ugonjwa wa marehemu, walianza kusambaratika kiasi cha sabasi mmoja kumwendea Zengeni usiku na kumpa ukweli wote. Sadfa na hili, heka heka za ujenzi lau zilimpa wakati mugumu kuusaka ukweli kwa kila namna ili asipate hasara.

Mke wake Nengoma, alimshauri awashitaki vidhabu hawa. Lakini Zengeni, kwa kujua kuwa utawala mbovu umewageuza wananchi waovu, aliamua kumuonya mwizi yule na kumsamehe. Alijenga nyumba yake akiwa na imani: baadaye angeweza kupima uwanja wake lakini wapi. Hakuwa na saada katika hili kutokana na kutamalaki wa ufisidi na usasi wa ngawira katika nchi.Alijikusuru na kujaribu kwenda kwenye wizara ya ardhi na makazi zaidi ya mara ishirini bila kufanikiwa kupata afisa wa kuja kupima uwanja wake zaidi ya kuombwa chai utadhani alikuwa yu mpishi!

Pamoja hofu na kibuhuti vya kiwanja chake kutopimwa na nuksani nyingine za mafuriko, angalau kwa kujua ukweli angeweza kupumua. Kwa hatua hii adhimu hasumbuliwi na mwenye nyumba kama ilivyokuwa kabla hajajenga. Maana kwa mama Mzaramo alipokuwa amepanga kabla ya kujenga aghalabu alisemwa na kusimangwa kiasi cha mkewe kutishia kuomba talaka kama wasingehama pale na kujenga walau chumba kimoja kuondokana na kadhia hii. Siku zote humshukuru mke wake kwa kumtia mashamushamu na kila aina ya shime kiasi cha kuhangaika na kupata uwanja iliposimama nyumba kidonda.

Angalau hata majirani zake wanamuita baba mwenye nyumba. Kwa Mmafuriko, hii ni sifa kubwa sana ya kuweza kumfanya mtu anenepe na kutaradadi na mengine kifua mbele. Angebahatika kupata japo gwechu la gari, si haba angeotesha kiriba tumbo ingawa ni ugonjwa. Hata hivyo hakuwa na rushwa, makandokando na marupurupu yatokanayo na kunyonya jasho na damu za wenzie kuweza kuotesha mzigo huu unaoonekana kuwa fahari wakati ni hatari.Akiwa anaendelea na kutafakari hili na lile, mke wake Nengoma anatokeza akiwa anatweta na ndoo yake kichwani. Kwa alivyovalia, pamoja na mavune ya zigo lake kichwani, huwezi kuamini kuwa ni mwalimu wa sekondari na vyuo!

Moto.

Zengeni anawasha ujiti ya kibiriti. Bahati mbaya upepo unaizima. Hakati tamaa. Anageukia upande mwingine na kuchutuma na kuwasha ujiti mwingine. Nayo kama ya kwanza, unazimika. Anausonya upepo utadhani unamuelewa! Anaendelea. Ujiti huu pia unazimwa na upepo. Anausonya tena na kusema. "Leo naona upepo ni mkali si kawaida."

Hakati tamaa. Anageukia upande mwingine akiwa anazidi kujikusanya utadhani anaweza kuukumbatia moto! Anakikirika na jiko hadi moto unawake.

Zengeni akiwa anatikisa kichwa anasema. "Kwanini usiwe mkali iwapo miti yote imefyekwa kiasi cha ardhi kuachwa uchi?" Alisema kwa uchungu.

Aliendelea kama anajijibu. "Lakini wahusika wanajali nini iwapo wanatumia umeme na gesi ilhali makapuku wenye kuwa na umeme wamefungiwa mita za Tumia Umeme Kidogo Uokoe Mazingira (TUKUMA) ili wasitumie bure kama wakubwa?"Ananyoosha mguu wake ambao unaonekana kufa ganzi na kidogo kutokana kukaa muda mrefu. Anaendelea kujisemea. "Serikali imewafumbia macho maafisa wake wala rushwa isijue tatizo la uchafuzi na uharibifu wa mazingira linakua! Wahusika wanajifanya hawaoni wala haiwahusu wasijue dunia ni moja. Ni mtumbwi mmoja. Chizi mmoja akiutoboa tunazama wote."

Anakohoa kidogo na kuendelea, "Hata nchi kubwa ya Marekani pamoja na ubabe wake, imeanza kusalimu amri kwa balaa hili. Maana pamoja na utajiri wao bado wanaihitaji dunia kuliko inavyowahitaji. Isitoshe, makazi yasiyopimwa yanazidi kuwa sehemu ya maisha ya akina yahe." Anajikuna kidevuni na kuendelea "Halafu watu hawa wamelaaniwa!"

Kama aliyekumbuka jambo muhimu anamkazia macho mkewe, na kusema. "Una habari kuwa ile Baa nzuri pale kituo cha Mabasi nasikia ni mali ya mke wa waziri mkubwa? Kiumbe ana tamaa sina hamu. Nina maya naye ajuaye Mungu mwenyewe."

Anamuangalia mkewe kuona amelichukuliaje hilo na kuendelea. "Yaani pamoja na mshahara na marupurupu, rushwa na ofa bado hawajatosheki! Ama kweli, la kuvunda halina ubani. Hivi hawajui wakifa wataondoka watupu kwa machozi na mnuno kama walivyokuja?" Anatikisa kichwa chake kwa ishara ya kutoridhika au kuonyesha dharau kwa waziri mkubwa aliye naye maya.Nengoma amehangaika na kibiriti hatimaye uvumilivu wake umelipa. Maana moto umeshika na mkaa unaendelea kuwaka bila wasi wasi na ukichukulia kuna upepo mkali, hana hata haja ya kuwa na shaka na moto.

Anajongea alipo mumewe tayari kupiga soga huku akingojea moto ukolee ainjike maji ya kifungua kinywa. Hana haja ya kusururika mitaani kusaka vitumbua: mihogo waliyokula na jana ilibakia. Hivyo, watakunywa chai na kiporo. Na isitoshe, Nengoma ni mpenzi wa mihogo.

Akiwa anasogeza makaratasi na uchafu mdogo mdogo ili akae, anakusanya kusanya khanga yake tayari kukaa kwa staha hata kama anakaa mbele ya mumewe. Hawezi kukaa kama mwamamke asiyefundwa.

Baada ya kukaa, anaanza kusema akiungana na hoja za mumewe.

Anasema. "Wewe unashangaa ile B?baa? Na wale ng'ombe pale Kilimamoshi? Hujui hata ile Baa ya pombe ya kienyeji ni ya mkewe waziri mkubwa! Nasikia eti ana danguro Ulaya ambapo wasichana vigoli huvushwa toka hapa na kupelekwa kufanyishwa biashara ya ukahaba. Huyu sawa na nune zizini. Kila uchafu wake! Aonapo mali hupandwa na wahaka iwe yake."

Kabla ya kuendelea, Zengeni anadakia. "Japo sijaamini, kuna uvumi kuwa huwa anafanya biashara ya mihadarati. Unakumbuka kile kisa cha waziri wa mambo ya ughaibuni kunaswa uwanja wa ndege na kuokoka aibu almanusura? Hawa watu si wa kuamini. Kila palipo na pesa, kama inzi na uvundo, nao wapo kadhalika."

Nengoma anajibu, "Kumbe kuna kipindi tunaishi na

vichaa tena waliolaaniwa tusijue wala wao wasijijue! Sasa hayo mabilioni ya pesa wanayokimbizia ughaibuni wanaweza kuyatumia na kuyamaliza?" Zengeni anajibu. "Thubutu! Hata vilembwe na vilembwekezi hawawezi kuzimaliza. Ubaya ni kwamba wafa kwa shilanga ndiyo wanaozalisha chumo lao huku wao wakiisha kwa dhiki!"

"Sasa kama si roho mbaya na kichaa, mapesa yote ya nini? Wanafanya mambo utadhani hawatakufa!" Anauliza Nengoma kwa mshangao.

"Kumbe mke wangu hujui! Wenzio wanazidi kuiba ili watumie pesa hii kutuhonga wakati wa uchaguzi-mbuzi waselelee madarakani wakiiba na kutoa amri. Kwani siri? Nani asiyejua Rais akimaliza muda wake ana mpango mchafu wa kumrithisha waziri wake mkubwa kibaka na fisadi wa kupindukia? Lakini kwa madudu wanayofanya na tamaa ya mtu mwenyewe, sijui hata kama atamaliza hiyo ngwe. Alijinyoosha kidogo na kuendelea. "Basi kama hujui basi jua: wenzako wanajiandalia kututawala wao na vijukuu vyao milele; kama hatutawazuia. Hujamuona yule Dr. Munyui mtoto wa Rais wa zamani au yule Rais wa visiwa vya Jaziba Karumekenge mtoto wa Rais wa zamani? Hapa ni ufalme kwa mlango wa nyuma; taka usitake." Zengeni anamjibu mkewe huku akiwa anatikisha kichwa kwa masikitiko.

Anasogeza gazeti pembeni na kuendelea, "Hawa watu kwa jinsi wanavyohoka kutuibia lazima waselelee madarakani ili wawe salama. Nje ya madaraka wataishia korokoroni."

"Wanajidanganya. Nani ataishi milele hapa duniani? Mbona wapo wengi waliwatangulia kufanya kama wafanyavyo wakaishia kuumbuka baada ya umma kuchoka!" Anajibu Nengoma huku akionyesha kuudhika.

Maongezi yalipokuwa ndiyo yanaanza kunoga, mara upepo uliputa kwa nguvu kiasi cha Nengoma kulazimika kukimbilia sufuria yake iliyokuwa inaanza kushambuliwa na michanga iliyorushwa na upepo. Hivyo, kikao kisicho rasmi ilibidi kife rasmi huku Zengeni akitikisa kichwa chake kwa hasira kutokana na upepo uliokuwa ukisababishwa na uchafuzi wa mazingira kufanya maisha yao yawe mabaya zaidi.

Alijihimu kuyanusuru magazeti yake yaliyokuwa yameanza kusombwa na upepo.

3
Kashfa Kashfa Kashfa

Chimbuchimbu

Baada ya Nengoma kurejea kutoka ndani alikonusuru sufuria lake na kukaa vizuri, Zengeni anampa gazeti la Chimbuchimbu ambalo ameishalipitia na kugundua baadhi ya mambo ya kuudhi. Ni gazeti la kila siku la asubuhi. Ndiyo katoka kulikopa toka kwa muuza magazeti wa pale mtaani kwao, Kapende, ambaye ametokea kuwa rafiki yake tokana na kununua magazeti kwake kila asubuhi. Leo mfuko wake una kipindupindu cha muda. Isitoshe, hana kikwazo kukopa. Maana kila apatapo fulusi ni mlipaji mzuri. Hivyo, anaweza akafika ubaoni kwa Kapende wakati wowote na kuchukua gazeti na kulipa baadaye. Kwake kukopa siyo harusi wala kulipa matanga bali kuwajibika. Isitoshc, anajua machungu wanayopata watu wa kada kama yake hasa wasioona ubao vizuri kama Kapende.

Gazeti hili la Chimbuchimbu ni chimbu chimbu kweli. Kwani linasifika kwa kuichimba chimba na kuichimbua chimbua serikali. Linamilkiwa na kampuni moja ya tajiri aitwaye Mpayukaji Msemahovyo. Huyu muungwana hana mahusiano mazuri na serikali. Zamani alikuwa na mahusiano mazuri na serikali. Lakini serikali ilipoanza kumpangia cha kuandika na kutoandika kwenye magazeti yake, aliamua kuvunja ndoa yake kiasi cha, hata wakati mwingine, serikali kumnyima matangazo kwenye magazeti yake. Aliandika kwenye motto yake, "Heri kanga aishiye mwituni akawa huru kuliko kuku ashibishwaye kwa nafaka ya kuletewa akaibiwa mayai yake na kuishia kuzikwa mezani."

Kwa Msemahovyo, mbwa mwitu ni bora kuliko mbwa hata awe wa kizungu. Kwake mbwa ni mbwa hata alale ghorofani hata hekaluni. Hata alie kwenye sahani ya dhahabu na kulalia busati, bado mbwa ni mbwa. Yeye ni mbwa mwitu kuliko mbwa. Ni kanga si kuku. Hakika, yeye ni huru kwa maana yake. Si mfugo wala nyumba ndogo ya serikali wala kundi la wezi wenye madaraka na ukwasi wa kuiba.

Hivyo, pamoja na Msemahovyo kujua kuwa hatua ya kutoshirikiana na serikali ingemgharimu kwa kukosa matangazo, alimua ashike njia yake huru na kufa lwake kuliko kuweka rumenya na serikali chafu.

Zengeni pamoja na ukata wake, ni nadra kulikosa gazeti asubuhi hata kama akilipata kwa kukopa au kulifukuzia mitaani pale Kapende anapochelewa kulipata. Lazima asome gazeti kila siku kujua dunia inavyokwenda. Na si dunia tu bali nchi yake inayosifika kwa kuvamiwa na watawala mbweha watu wanaoitoboatoboa kama mzoga.

Asubuhi huwa na ratiba ya kusikiliza vituo vyote vya Redio kupata habari. Tabia ya kupenda habari imepanua uwezo wake wa kutafakari na kujadili mambo. Maana, hata waliosoma naye humshangaa anajuaje mambo mengi hivyo!

Japo ana uwezo na nia ya kununua runinga, anashindwa kutokana na nyumba yake kutowekewa umeme. Maana shirika la umeme la Mafuriko National electrical Company (MANESCO) lilimtaka alipe shilingi laki nane na ushei ndiyo awekewe umeme kwenye banda lake.

Hapo bado rushwa na kupigwa tarehe kila siku na bughuda na adha nyingine nyingi. Maana kwa watawala wa Mafuriko umeme ni starehe na ni kwa ajili ya wakwasi wachache. Kwao, nishati hii siyo nyenzo ya maendeleo! Isitoshe ni aghali kwa watu maskini kama Zengeni wanaotegemea mkaa na mafuta ya taa kwa vibaba. Wakubwa na serikali pamoja na kujua adha wanazopata wananchi, bado hutumia umeme vibaya tena bila kulipia anakara zao. Mchezo na tabia yao hii chafu vimeshaligharimu shirika la umeme kwani ni "mkangafu ambao kama ng'ombe aliyekonda, unangojea kupigwa mnada kwenye gulio la wawekezaji toka Ughaibuni."

Kuongeza chumvi kwenye kidonda cha Zengeni, matapeli waitwao vishoka walikuwa wameishamtapeli jirani yake Kinyahende pesa kibao wakidai wangemuunganishia umeme asijue walikuwa wakimuunganishia matatizo! Isitoshe Zengeni ni msomi hawezi kukubali upuuzi huu wa kuliibia taifa ingawa watawala wake wanaliibia kama siyo lao!

Hivyo, kama kawaida ya gazeti la Chimbuchimbu, huchimbua kila kinachotokea bila ya kujali nyuma yake kuna nini au nani awe kikaka. Gazeti hili limetokea kuwa mwiba kwa watawala wa Mafuriko ambao huwa wakilitishia kulifunga kila mara lakini hukosa sababu nususi ya kufanya hivyo.

Chimbuchimbu limetokea kuwa gazeti la wananchi wanaoona kuwa mambo hayaendi barabara. Maana magazeti yenye kuelemea serikali ni kama kasuku. Kazi yake ni kuimba utukufu wa serikali hata inapopaswa kulaumiwa. Hayawezi kuikosoa wala kuiambia ukweli serikali. Maana ni mkono unaoyalisha tena mchafu. Wahariri wa magazeti "Vyangudoa" kama Zengeni ayaitavyo, wameridhika kuwa kuku. Wanatumia na kutumikia matumbo badala ya vichwa vyao. Ajabu madume mazima yaligeuzwa rambuza kisa riziki udohoudoho! Wamejigeuza watumwa wa hiari ili waishi utadhani kuishi ni zawadi ya watawala wakati ni zawadi toka kwa Maulana mwenyewe! Hata mtilili awazidi maana hula awindacho siyo kama wao walao wagawiwacho tena riziki mapepeta utadhani hawana mawege au mapiswa! Ajabu wanafanya hata ria wasijue umma una maya nao!

Kichwa cha habari cha gazeti la siku hiyo ni;

Kampuni ya Richmen ni mali ya wakubwa serikalini

* Ni kampuni ya mfukoni na ya kitapeli inayotumiwa kuliibia taifa.

* Imeishalipwa dola milioni 59 bila kufanya kazi yoyote.

* Imeishauza tenda yake kwa kampuni nyingine yenye utata.

* Imesajiliwa Mafuriko miaka miwili iliyopita!

* Serikali yapanga kuizima kashfa hii kinamna.

Imegundulika kuwa kampuni ya Richmen iliyoletwa toka nchi ya Ahaha kushughulikia kujenga mitambo ya maji ni kampuni ya kutengeneza sumu za kuulia wadudu.

Pia kampuni hiyo ni mali ya wakubwa wachache waliomo serikalini wanaoitumia kuiibia mali na pesa ya umma kwa manufaa binafsi wakiwatumia mawakala wao wanaojionyesha kama wafanyabiashara na waendeshaji wa Richmen ilhali si wafanyabiashara chochote bali matapeli na wala makombo.

Chanzo chetu cha habari toka nchi ya Munamuna kimeeleza na imegundulika kuwa Richmen ni bomu litakaloifilisi nchi yetu. Habari kamili inasomeka kama ifuatavvyo;

Kampuni ya Richmen licha ya kuwa Kampuni ndogo isiyo na ithibati wala historia ya mafanikio; ina kesi Mahakamani kwa kudanganya kuhusu kiwango cha ubora wa bidhaa zake. Ni Kampuni ambayo imekuwa ikibadili majina kila wakati kila ifanyapo utapeli wake.

Chanzo chetu kimeendelea kusema kuwa nyuma ya Richmen (M), kuna watu wazito kwenye Serikali ya sasa hasa Waziri mmoja mkubwa ambaye kwa kutumia ushawishi na mtandao wake na mshirika wake mkuu wa kibiashara ambaye ni Mbunge na mzito kwenye Chama chake, anafanya kila juhudi kuizima kashfa hii. Ameishatoa onyo kwa Wabunge au mtu yeyote atakayeendelea kuipekenyua kashfa hii atakiona cha Mtema kuni. Habari zilizokariri baadhi ya Wabunge zinasema: wabunge wameapa kumuumbua siku ikifika. Kama wabunge, Gazeti hili halitasalimu amri kwa vitisho hivi. Badala yake vitakuwa ndiyo kichocheo cha kuichimbua chimbua zaidi kashfa hii yenye madhara makubwa kwa taifa.

Gazeti halikusua sua japo halikumtaja jina Waziri mkubwa Bwana Edmond Ngoyaegg Mpendamali wa Luwasha, lilichora picha kimaelezo iliyoonekana wazi wazi kuwa aliyekuwa nyuma ya Richmen alikuwa ni yeye tu.

Linaendelea kuripoti;

Chanzo chetu cha habari kimezidi kueleza: Richmen, kimsingi, zipo mbili. Ipo ile iliyoanzishwa miaka miwili iliyopita katika nchi ya Ahaha na Richmen Mafuriko iliyoanzishwa mwezi jana. Anwani ya Richmen Ahaha ni St. Moneybag ML, A1A 2G7 Munamuna.

Anwani ya Richmen (M) ni SLP 333 Wizi street, Kwa Vikaka, Neema, Mafuriko.

Gazeti lililendelea,

Licha ya ukweli huu usio na shaka ambao unapatikana hata kwenye mtandao wa Internet, serikali imeendelea kukaa kimya juu ya sababu za kutoa tenda ya mamilioni ya dola za kimarekani kwa kampuni yenye kutia shaka

Gazeti hili lilijaribu kuwasiliana na waziri mwenye dhamana Lakini msemaji wa wizara ameshikilia kuwa tenda nzima ilifanyika kwa uwazi bila aina yoyote wala harufu ya rushwa.Kuna uvumi kuwa hata mabenki yanayojua utapeli wa kampuni hii huko Munamuna itokoka yamekataa uitolea dhamana wala kuhusishwa na biashara hii hasara linamoingizwa taifa la Mafuriko kutokana na uroho na upofu wa watu wachache waliopewa madaraka.

Gazeti hili lilipombana msemaji wa wizara aeleze ni kwanini serikali ilitoa tenda kwanza bila kufuata utaratibu na pili kwa kampuni isiyo na historia wala utaalamu na ujenzi wa mitambo ya maji, msemaji alisema hilo siyo tatizo. Kwani tatizo ilikuwa ni kama kuna rushwa kwenye tenda.

Gazeti liliendelea.

Kwa hali ilivyo, pesa ya wananchi imeliwa. Kwani licha ya kampuni ya Richmen kushindwa kutimiza kazi yake, imeuza kazi kwa kampuni nyingine yenye kutia mashaka iitwayo Deiwaka Dooms inayomilkiwa na Rostitamu Azoul jamaa mwenye ushawishi kwenye chama tawala na serikali yake akiwa swahiba mkuu wa Rais na Waziri mkubwa.

Katika hali ya kustaajabisha, serikali imeunda tume ya kuchunguza kadhia hii ambayo nakala ya ripoti yake itakayotolewa siku chache zijazo inaeleza kuwa zoezi zima lilikuwa limetosheleza vigezo vyote vya utoaji tenda ukiachia mbali zoezi hili kufanywa kwa dharura kulingana na tatizo linaloikabili nchi. Msemaji wa Richmen Mafuriko alipopigiwa simu alikuwa amefunga simu yake.

Gazeti linaendelea.

Chimbuchimbu ilipomtaka kutamka ni lini mradi husika ungetegemewa kuwa umekamilika. Msemaji huyo wa shirika alisema yeye siyo mjenzi. Ila alisisitiza kuwa vyombo vya habari viache uvivu wa kufikiri angalau viisifie serikali kwa kununua tanki linalohudumia jiji la Neema ingawa si wote wanaopata maji. Lakini angalau wakubwa walikuwa wakipata maji na hivyo kutokabiliwa na kupoteza muda na mawazo kufanya shughuli za umma. Wanaoga na kunywa na hawaendi maofisini wakiwa na uchafu. Hata si haba bustani zao za kuwaliwaza zinapata maji.Isitoshe bomba linalopigiwa upatu limenunuliwa kwa bei ya kuruka kutokana na serikali kutofanya utafiti. Maana inasemekana lile tanki kule ughaibuni huuzwa kwa dola laki tano ambapo serikali imeuziwa dola milioni moja na laki saba!

Baada ya kusoma maneno hayo hapo juu, Nengoma alitikisa kichwa na kuacha kusoma gazeti.Nengoma alisema, "Mume wangu, kama mambo ni haya, nchi hii imeingiliwa na mdudu mbaya ambaye ataiacha ikiwa imeoza. Kama wakubwa wamejiingiza kwenye uchafu wa aina hii basi elewa tuendako nchi hii haitakalika maana watasababisha shida na umaskini kuongezeka kiasi cha jinai nayo kuongezeka."

Zengeni huku akitikisa kichwa anakubaliana na mkewe anasema. "Jinai iongezeke mara ngapi iwapo wizi wa kutumia bunduki umekuwa jambo la kawaida. Mardudi ya jinai ndiyo usiseme. Hukumbuki mwezi jana majambazi walivyovunja kiduka cha Shemtwashua na kumjeruhi yeye na familia yake? Ajabu baada ya wezi kukamatwa na kutoa gathogo habari zisizothibitishwa zinasema waliachia na wanaendelea na kazi kama kawaida!" Alisogeza talawanda zake pembeni na kuendelea, "Watu wetu wamekuwa vipofu na mataahira. Badala ya kupambana na gendaeka na maharashi wanaoiba mamilioni kama haya, wanajiingiza kwenye jinai ya kuibiana wao kwa wao wakati kimsingi wote ni maskini wa kutupwa."

4
Vibaka, mibaka na wauaji

Wakati wanaongea mara wanasikia kelele za mwizi. Kelele zilihanikiza. "Mwizi! Mwizi! Wezi hao! Wezi hao!"

Eneo la jirani mtaani mama mmoja alikuwa amenyang'anywa mkoba wake na kuvuliwa hereni na kuchukuliwa simu ya mkononi. Haya yalikuwa yamefanywa na vijana wa mtaa ule. Mama huyo inasemekana alifuatwa kuanzia nyumbani kwake. Haya ndiyo yalikuwa maisha ya kawaida kwa watu maskini wa Mafuriko wa madongo poromoka. Kwani hazikupita siku bila mtu kuchomwa moto au nyumba yake kuingiliwa na majambazi. Ilifikia mahali wakawa wanahoji uwepo wa polisi waliokuwa wakilipwa mishahara chekwa toka kwenye kodi zao bila kuwalinda wananchi.

Mtu mwenyewe aliyibiwa kumbe ni jirani yao Dzani maarufu kama mama Ntetela! Alipofika kwenye ule uchochoro uendao kwenye kiwanda cha nguo cha tajiri mmoja toka bara Bwindi mwenye kutia mashaka cha KABARI, alistukia akionyeshwa jisu kubwa na kuamriwa asipige kelele bali kutoa zawadi ya wazee ambayo ilimaanisha kila alichokuwa nacho. Hakuwa na la kufanya zaidi ya kukefya huku akijipapura kila alichokuwa nacho kunusuru maishaye. Baada ya wale wezi kuchukua chao, ndipo mama Ntetela alianza kupiga kelele za kutaka msaada. Wakiwa hata hawajamaliza kutafakari habari za gazetini na za mwanamke kunyang'anywa mali zake, mara wanaona kundi la watu likitimka kuelekea kiwanda cha KABARI. Filimbi za walinzi wa kiwanda zinahanikiza. Makele ya mwizi! Mwizi! Ndiyo usiseme.

Zengeni naye hawezi kujibari. Anajihimu kuelekea kunako ndumo. Anaamka na kuelekea huko. Maana aliyeibiwa ni jirani yao. Hivyo, anapaswa kutoa msaada kama ada. Hawezi kujua leo kwa yule jirani kesho itakuwa kwa nani. Maana wahenga walinena: leo kwangu kesho kwako. Hawezi kujua.

Anavuta talawanda zake na kuondoka kuelekea kwenye kiwanda. Anamwambia mkewe, "Hebu nipe kofia yangu niwahi kutoa msaada maana hujui aliyeibiwa ni nani."

Wakati anaanza kuondoka Nengoma anamtahadharisha. "Uangalie hawa majambazi huwa wanaua na isitoshe wana majambia na bisibisi." Hii ni baada ya Nengoma kuingia ndani na kumletea Zengeni kofia yake na Zengeni mbayo anaivaa haraka haraka tayari kwenda kwenye tukio.

"Umesikia mume wangu." Nengoma anamkumbusha mumewe kwa msisitizo kuchukua tahadhari.Hajibu anahamanika na kukaza mwendo kenyekenye. Huyo katimka joshi kuelekea kwenye tukio! Maana pamoja na watu wa Mafuriko kuharibiwa na utawala mbovu wa watawala kengewa, bado wana moyo wa kusaidiana katika matatizo kama hili. Wanajuburishwa na hali halisi.

Baada ya Zengeni kuondoka, pamoja na mambo mengine, Nengoma aliendelea na maandalizi yake ya kifungua kinywa. Jicho lake lilitua kwenye habari nyingine kwenye gazeti la Chimbuchimbu. Nayo ilikuwa ni juu ya serikali kujisafisha kuhusiana na kashfa ya Richmen.

Alijisemea kwa uchungu na kukata tamaa. "Nyinyi safishaneni. Lakini hamtatakata. Arobaini yenu ikifika yote yanayofanyika nyuma ya pazia yakawekwa uchi mbele ya hadhira, mtatamani ardhi ifumke muingie isifumke." Alimalizia kwa kutikisa kichwa kwa hasira.

Kwa ufupi habari yenyewe iliyoongelea yafuatayo

haikumvutia sana kwani waliishazoea kuona mauzauza kama haya yakifanywa na wasanii wa kisiasa.

Baada ya kashfa ya Richmen kuwa mwiba na wimbo kwenye vyombo vya habari, serikali kwa upande wake iliunda tume ya kuchunguza. Tume hiyo iliundwa na maafisa wa polisi na waliokuwa wamewekwa rumenya na serikali na wale wa ofisi za Rais na waziri mkubwa.

Tume yenyewe haikuchukua muda mrefu. Ilitumia wiki mbili kuja na mazingaombwe yake ambayo japo serikali ilijiaminisha kama kulastra kuwa ilikuwa imejisafisha, umma haukuiamini ripoti ya tume. Yalisikika makelele kuizodoa taarifa ya tume yaliyoiita mazingaombwe na usanii wa kisiasa. Hivyo, serikali ililazimisha ripoti hiyo na kuiua kashfa kinamna namna kwa aibu ya hali ya juu. Hadi leo wananchi wa Mafuriko wanajua nani alitoa nini na nani alipokea nini. Wanajua hata baadhi ya pesa zilikofichwa. Lakini wangefanya nini iwapo mwenye nacho siyo mwenzako na mwenye nguvu mpite? Na isitoshe serikali yao ilikuwa inajulikana kwa ujambazi wake.

Baada ya Zengeni kuondoka, Nengoma aliendelea na shughuli zake za kuandaa kifungua kinywa huku masikio yakiwa nje kama lolote lingetokea alikokwenda mumewe. Hakuwa na wasi wasi sana. Kwa vile hali ile ilikuwa imezoeleka kwenye mitaa yao. Pamoja na hali kuwa mbaya kiasi hiki, bado watawala wa Mafuriko, bila hata chembe ya aibu, walizoea kujisifu kuwa walikuwa wamedumisha amani; wakati ukweli ni kwamba kilichokuwapo si amani bali kutokuwapo vita ya kuonyeshana bunduki na kudai haki. Amani kama amani haikuwapo. Ingekuwapo vipi wakati hapakuwa na haki? Ingekuwapo vipi iwapo genge la watu wachache lilikuwa likiwatumia walio wengi kujineemesha huku wao wakiangamia? Amani ingekuwa wapi iwapo vibaka walikuwa wakihukumiwa kwa kuchomwa moto ilhali "mibaka" ikizidi kunenepeana kama paka wa dukani kwa mwarabu? Zengeni hakuchukua muda njiani. Kwani kiwanda cha KABARI kiko karibu tu ukiachia mbali na kujihimu. Ni kama umbali wa mita mia sabiini toka nyumbani kwake. Njiani, aliandamana na majirani zake wengine waliokuwa wanakimbilia kwenye eneo la tukio. Walikuwamo wakubwa na wadogo. Walikuwa na malengo tofauti japo walikuwa kwenye msafara mmoja kwenda eneo moja. Na hii ni kawaida katika matukio kama hili kwa kaumu ya watu wa mjini isiyo na kazi.

Vijana walitimka mbio huku wanawake wanene wakitembea kwa nyonde nyonde zao lau washuhudie kipopo ambacho wangekipata wale vindengereka.

Wapo akina Zengeni waliokuwa wanakwenda kutoa msaada na wengine waliokuwa wanataka kutumia tukio hilo kujipatia chochote. Wapo pia waliofuata mkumbo lau wapoteze muda kutokana na kutokuwa na la ufanya. Wapo hata ambao hawakujua walikuwa wanakimbilia kule kufanya nini! Hawa waliendeshwa na matukio badala ya kuwa wenye kuyaendesha matukio. Watu wa Mafuriko hupenda sana mikusanyiko na vikoa hata wakati mwingine vigwena. Kuna kipindi tena katikati ya mji watu walikusanyika kushuhudia mabeberu mawili yakigombea jike! Wakati mwingine hasa akina mama walizoea kufuata ngoma ya mdumange ilipokuwa ikipita mitaani kwao. Kuna mama aliachika kutokana na kuufukuzia mdumange na kusahau mapishi kiasi cha kuunguza chakula na nyumba yake kuingiliwa na kuibiwa baadhi ya vitu.

Huko kiwandani kumbe walinzi wa kiwanda walikuwa wamefanikiwa kuwakamata vibaka watatu waliokuwa wameingia kwenye uchochoro ulioko nyuma ya kiwanda. Nia yao ilikuwa ni kuelekea kwenye bonde la Nsanje ili wavuke kwenda ng'ambo ya pili mitaa ya Mzuzu na Kalonga.Vibaka hawa hawakujua kuwa ile njia ilikuwa imeishazibwa ili kuepuka tishio la majambazi kuja kuitumia tena usiku kupora kiwandani kama ilivyokuwa imetokea mwaka uliokuwa umepita. Na kama wasingepuuzia onyo la walinzi kuwa hapakuwa na njia, hata wasingekamatwa. Walipoambiwa njia ilikuwa imezibwa hawkusikiliza. Wao waliamua kupuuzia wasijue kilikuwa chao kiama! Maana hawakuwa na njia ya kurudi nyuma ambako mbiu ilishapigwa wakamatwe na kuishia kuwa kuni ingawa ilikuwa ni suala la muda. Laiti wasingepuuzia ile nyungwanani ya walinzi, yote yasingewakuta!

Huko nyuma kelele za mwizi zilizokuwa zimehanikiza ziliwastua walinzi na kuwaweka wale vijana chini ya ulinzi pindipo walipoingia kwenye lindo lao.

Wakati walinzi wa kiwanda wakiwahoji wale vijana, kundi la watu waliokuwa wameitikia mwito wa mama Ntetela alikuwa kaibiwa vitu vyake lilifika na kuwataka walinzi wawape watu wao! Mtu mmoja alisikika akisema, "Mabwana, mnajua kinachofuata baada ya watu kama hawa kuingia kwenye anga zetu."Mlinzi mmoja alijibu, "Unamaanisha nini?" Yule mwananchi alijibu, "Bwana we, unakuwa kama mgeni jiji hili! Hawa lazima leo waingie motoni wakakutane na shetani aliyewashauri wapore. Wamezidi hawa. Hapa wanakwenda kukutana na shetani leo leo akawasalishe huko motoni."Mlinzi mwingine alipinga wazo hili kwa kusema, "Lakini hamuoni kuwa ni unyama kuwaua mahuluku hawa kwa udokozi wakati wezi wakubwa tunawapigia saluti?"Jamaa hakutosheka alijibu. "Kaka siasa baada ya shughuli. Hawa huu mwisho wa ghururi na siku zao. Maana kwa kuwachoma moto wadudu hawa huenda serikali itastuka itupe ulinzi na kutenda haki tunapowafikisha vituo vya polisi. Isitoshe, wakikupata vizuri kwenye anga zao ama wakuachie ngeu au wakunyotoe roho. Isitoshe wanatuibia sie walalia mkabilishamsi na ujaka badala ya kwenda kwa wezi wakubwa wenye kila uhuru wa kuiba bila kufungwa."

Wakati mlinzi mmoja akiongea na huyu mjumbe wa kifo, walinzi wenzake waliwauliza wale vijana kama kweli wale vijana walikuwa wameiba. Vijana walikanusha huku wakitarakanya wasijue la kunena. Lakini walipowauliza ni kwanini walikuwa wanataka kupita sehemu isiyoruhusiwa tena wakitimua mbio na kupuuzia nyungwanani, vijana wale hawakuwa na la kusema. Waligwaya utadhani panya aliyeangukia kwenye maji mengi! Mmoja alijaribu kufanya kibedi kwa kukimbia lakini walinzi walimzidi ujanja wakamkamata jambo lililofungulia kipigo cha mbwa mwizi.

Wakati sakata lile likiendelea, bosi mmoja wa kibwindi alisikia makelele na kutoka nje ya ofisi yake. Akiwa amefura kwa hasira kukuta kundi la watu. Alikuwa amefura si mchezo. Maana kelele zile zilimfanya akatishe maongezi na ndugu yake wa Bombay aliyekuwa akiongea naye kwa simu mipango ya kuwatafutia vibali ndugu zake waje kufanya kazi ambazo wamafuriko wangeweza kuzifanya kiwandani kwake. Isitoshe alikuwa hawaamini wamafuriko.

Alisema."Hapa iko nini vatu napiga kelele nasumbua employees yangu?"

Mlinzi mmoja kwa unyenyekevu alijibu. "Bosi kuna hawa vibaka wamemwibia huyu mama." Alinyoosha mkono kumuonyesha mama Ntetela ambaye naye alitikisa kichwa kukubaliana na maneno ya mlinzi wa kiwanda aliyekuwa anaongea kwa unyenyekevu utadhani alikuwa akiongea na mkwewe! Kwa tafsiri rahisi ya Kiswahili, Mbwindi alijibu kwa dharau na hasira huku akibeua midomo na kurusha mikono hewani, "Mimi haikotaka kesi. Toa Jana hiyo kwa vatu imalize yeye maana nazidi kuiba mali ya vatu sikii." Aliwageukia wale vijana na kusema, "Nyinyi bado iko changa sana. Kwanini naiba vitu dogo dogo kama kuku?" Umati wa watu ulicheka kwa jinsi alivyokuwa akiharibu lugha yao. Wapo waliosema kuwa wahindi hujifanya kutojua kimafuriko. Lakini ukweli ni kwamba walikuwa wakikijua kuliko hata wamafuriko wenyewe.Mbwindi aliugeukia ule umati wa watu na kusema. "Chukua yeye polisi station ipatiwe dawa yake. Kule jusi taonja joto ya jiwe."

Mkota mmoja toka kwenye ule umati wa watu alisema. "Kanji umenena. Hakuna anayetaka kesi. Tutawapeleka kuzimu ili liwe somo kwa wengine. Maana ukiwapeleka polisi wanatoa kitu kidogo na kuachiwa. Tena wana simu na gold! Polisi wanatuchezea mahepe wakitugeuza mabunga. Watawachojoa na kuwaachia. Si unajiua Mafuriko bosi wangu?"Mbwindi hakusikia vizuri yaliyosemwa isitoshe hakuhitaji utondoti wowote. Maana hayakuwa yakimshughulisha mambo ya watu maskini zaidi ya jasho na pesa yao wanunuapo bidhaa zake. Hivyo, aliamuru walinzi wawakabidhi wale vijana kwa umati wa watu ili shughuli zake pale kiwandani zisikwamishwe na suala ambalo halimhusu.

Mbwindi alipiga hatua kidogo halafu akarudi na kuuambia umati. "Peleka hii jana polisi station. Kama nahukumu yeye, toka kiwandani yangu sikia?"

Aliwageukia walinzi wake na kusema. "Guards, fanya bidii toa vatu yote kiwandani yangu." Walinzi waliitikia kwa pamoja huku wakiinamisha vichwa vyao kuonyesha utii.

"Ndiyo Bwana mkubwa." Walinzi waliitikia.

Walinzi, japo walijua kuwa kitendo walichofanya ni sawa na kumwacha mtu majilini, hawakuwa na jinsi bali kutii amri ya bosi wao. Hivyo, kwa sononeko na nyongea, waliwakabidhi wale vijana kwa umati wa wananchi waliokuwa wana hamu ya kuona nyama ya binadamu inavyoungua wasijue walikuwa wakiwaumiza ndugu zao bure! Walinzi walikosa nyemi kwa kushindwa kuwaauni wale vijana.

Baada ya umati kuondoka, mlinzi mmoja alimwambia mwenzake. "Yaani tumeruhusu watu watatu wachomwe moto!"Mwenzake alimjibu. "Kama wamepora walitegemea nini kwenye nchi hii ambapo umati wa watu wenye hasira umekuwa ukiua watu bila kuchukuliwa hatua? Wengi wape bwana. Isitoshe hatukuajiriwa hapa kuwakoa vibaka bali kutafuta mkate wa wanetu. Hata kama inauma utafanyaje iwapo polisi na wahusika wengine wenyewe wameendekeza njaa kiasi cha umma kukosa imani nao?"

Lakini huoni kuwa na sisi tumechangia kwa kuruhusu watuhumiwa wachukuliwe tukijua kitakachowatokea?' Alilalamika yule mlinzi kwa masikitiko.

Mlinzi wa pili alijibu. "Najua kila kitu. Maana mimi si mgeni mji huu. Lakini bosi aliyetuajiri kwa matulubu yake kulinda kiwanda chake kaamua wewe ungefanya nini. Nambie ungetumia busara gani kunusuru vibaka wasipelekwe kaburi sadfa na kazi? Kwanza, mbwindi anajali nini iwapo mmafuriko akiuawa? Kwake ni heri maana hawezi kutofautisha na wale waliovunja kiwanda chake au waliowaua wabwindi wenzake kwenye duka la kubadilishia pesa pale kwenye mtaa wa Ubayani na hawa wanaoitwa vibaka."

Kwa vile walinzi walikuwa hawana la kuweza kufanya kuwaokoa wale vijana, waliachana na suala la hatima yao na kuendelea na kazi zao za kawaida ingawa walijua fika wale vijana ile ilikuwa siku yao mwisho ya kuishi duniani.

Roho ziliwauma. Lakini kama mhindi ambaye alikuwa kama ndiye mgawa riziki mwenye kiwanda chake kaamua, wao walikuwa nani kuingilia kuwanusuru wale vijana maskini ambao tamaa na ujinga viliwaponza?

Mmoja wa walinzi alisema, "Tutauana wenyewe kwa wenyewe nyutinyuti wakati wezi wetu wanatukoga kwa maneno ya uongo kuwa nchi ina amani na inaendelea hadi lini yarabi?" Alitikisa kichwa na kujiinamia kuwazia hali hii ambayo ilikuwa inatia kinyaa kwa nchi huru kuwa kama vile ni kambi ya wanyama hasa fisi.Alizidi kutikisa kichwa na kusema, "Ewe Mwenyezi Mungu waepushe wanangu kuingia kundi hili. Yaani nilaliavyo tafi, dagaa na ujaka wake ili lau wasome, itakuwa hasara kiasi gani Yarabi? Maana nawatakia ghanima si kingine ya Maulana."

Mwenzake alijibu, "Mimi hata kama mwanangu ataamua kuchagua kuwa kibaka akitiwa nari sitahuzunika maana kachagua mwenyewe kwa hiari yake na upumbavu wake."

"Usimtukane mamba kabla hujavuka mto ndugu yangu. Huwezi kujua Mwenyezi Mungu kakujalia lipi. Omba Mungu wanao wasiwe viparuzi lakini siyo kukamia hivyo" Alionya mwenzake."Mie n'shasema. Mwanangu akichagua kuwa kibaka akachomwa moto au binti akichagua kuwa changu akagongwa na miwaya sitajali" Mlinzi alizidi kusisitizia msimamo wake."Omba yasikukute ndugu yangu. Hujafa hujaumbika. Isitoshe mtu mwenyewe pangu pakavu tia mchuzi." Mlinzi mwingine alionya.

Wakati gumzo la mstakabali wa watoto wa walinzi likiendelea, gari la bosi mwingine wa kihindi lilitia breki langoni. Hivyo, walitawanyika na ghamu yao na kuachia habari za watoto wao pale. Waliendeleaje? Nani anajua?

5
Ubaya ubaya tu

Baada ya wananchi wenye hasira, kama walivyokuwa wakijulikana kwenye mji wa Neema, kutoka kwenye uzio wa kiwanda, walitoa kile walichokiita salamu za mwisho. Walianza kuwatembezea kipigo kikali wale watuhumiwa hata bila kuhangaika kutafuta ushahidi wa tuhuma zilizokuwa zikiwakabili! Kwao tuhuma zilitosha kuwa sababu ya kutoa hukumu ya kikatili na ya kinyama bila kujihangaisha na kudadisi wala kupima mambo. Hao ndiyo wananchi wa Mafuriko nchi ya amani! Je kwa hali hii bado Mafuriko ni nchi ya amani?

Wananchi hawakufanya ajizi. Waliwasachi wale vijana na kuwakuta na kila kitu alichokuwa amedai mama Ntetela. Hii ni baada ya kipigo kutembezwa kiroho mbaya. Tofauti ni kete za mihadarati walizozikuta mifukoni mwa mmoja wa wale vijana watatu.

Baada ya wananchi kuridhika kuwa wale vijana walikuwa vibaka sawa na mibaka ya Richmen, ndiposa vipigo zaidi na zaidi viliendelea. Mwenye tofali alipiga kwalo. Mwenye kupiga ngumi au teke alijihudumia; ilmradi kila mtu alimaliza hasira zake alivyotaka! Kwa ufupi kila mtu alimaliza mafutu yake kulhali.

Wakati watu wakiendelea kuwapiga wale vibaka, wengine walienda nyumba jirani kuomba mafuta ya taa na wengine kukusanya takataka za kuwachomea wale vijana.

Zengeni aliingilia kati kutaka wale vijana wasiuawe bali wapelekwe polisi kama walivyokuwa wameshauriwa na mhindi. Lakini umma ukishaamua, hakuna wa kuuzia. Kwani watu waliokuwa wamechoshwa na vibaka walishikilia kuwa wale vijana wachomwe moto! Mtafaruko na ubishi juu ya nini kifanyike haukuwa kidogo! Kila mtu alishikilia alilolitaka hasa wengi wakipendekeza wale vijana waadhibiwe kwa kuchomwa moto kama ilivyokuwa imezoeleka bila kujali wale walikuwa wanadamu kama wao!

Zengeni alijikaza na kuzidi kurongaronga akishauri wale vijana wapelekwe polisi. Umati wa watu ulishikilia lengo leka kidinindi kwa kumwambia achague moja; kunyamaa au kuchomwa nao kama alikuwa anajiona yeye ni nabii. Kejeli hii ilimtosha akaamua kunyamaza na kibuhuti chake huku akimbwaga manyanga.

Mmoja kwenye umati ule alisema. "Zengeni tunakufahamu. Usitake tugeukane sisi kwa sisi na kuuawana bure wakati wenye shughuli wapo hapa; na wametaka watakachokipata. Tukiwapeleka polisi watahonga na kesho utawaona wakipeta na kutishia tena."

Kabla ya kumaliza mwingine aliingilia. "Tumewaonya wazazi wao tukaambulia kuambiwa ni wambea na tunawaone wivu watoto wao. Hapa lazima tuwachome moto ili wazazi wao wapate salamu kuwa asiyefunzwa na mamaye hufunzwa na dunia; na hufunza kikatili hivi."

Mwingine alisema. "Huyu Mabutu namfahamu ni mtoto wa mjumbe. Juzi juzi kaleta bonge la TV; na baba yake akawa anatukoga kuwa hatuna TV. Sasa wacha aone matokeo ya mali za kuibuka kama uyoga bila kuuliza zilipopatikana."

Mama mmoja jirani wa Zengeni aliyeitwa Coltide alisema. "Mimi nilipomtonya mama yake kuwa ile TV ilikuwa ya wizi tena toka bandarini, aliniuliza nilijuaje kama si umbea na ngoa? Alisema ni maneno tu isitoshe siku hizi ujanja kupata. Sasa wacha aone mwisho wa ujanja kupata bila kujali kupata kunakujaje na kukoje. Halo! Halo! Wavishe mikufu (magudumu) ili wawahi walikokutafuta mwaya." Alimalizia akiangua kicheko utadhani alichokuwa akishabikia kilikuwa kitu cha maana na cha kawaida!

Zengeni alitikisa kichwa kwa huzuni asiwe wala kujua na la kufanya. Wakati Zengeni akiwa anajiuliza chanzo cha unyama huu wa kutoa uhai wa mtu kwa ajili ya vitu vidogo, waliokuwa wameendea mafuta walikuwa ndiyo wameisharejea. Haraka haraka, moto ulikokwa na wale vijana waliokuwa wakichuruzika damu walivisha matairi na kuanza kulalamika na kuomba wasiuawe kwani wasingerudia tena. Hakuna mtu hata mmoja zaidi ya Zengeni aliyewasikiliza vijana wale maskini! Kumbe binadamu anaweza kuwa mnyama bila ya yeye kujua hivyo!

Zoezi la kutia moto mara lilianza kama mzaha kwa Zengeni asijue wengi walikuwa wameishapoteza maisha namna hii!

Bokasa, mmoja wa wale vijana alisema. "Jamani wanamafuriko mmeamua kutuua kinyama hivi na kusahau kuwa mnatujua. Jamani msifanye hivi ni shetani alituingilia."

Mtu mmoja alisema kwa vicheko. "Ndiyo tunawajua ndiyo maana tunawachoma moto ili nanyi mjue tunavyowachukia. Basi tutawachoma ili mwende mmwambie shetani aache kuwaingilia nanyi pia muache kumsikiliza." Zengeni alidhani watu wangeingiwa na huruma na kuwapeleka wale vijana kituo kidogo cha polisi cha Amatikonda lakini wapi. Walikuwa wameshikilia msimamo wao wa kuwaangamiza wale vijana maskini!

Zengeni alitikisa kichwa tena na kuamua kunyamaza akiwa amechanganyikiwa na kujaa huruma juu ya unyama aliokuwa akiushuhudia. Alijilaumu hata kwanini alikuwa amekwenda kushuhudia unyama ambao alikuwa akiusikia na kuusoma magazeti. Kwa upande mwingine alifarijika kuwa ameona kiasi cha kuweza kufikiria jinsi ya kutafuta jibu ambalo kwake ilikuwa ni kupambana na ufisadi wa watawala mafisadi. Alijistukia akijisemea. "Kama tufanya jicho kwa jicho na mdomo kwa mdomo tutakuwa na jamii ya vyongo na wajihi watupu! Hakika, huku ni kushindwa vibaya kwa serikali inayojiita yetu." Baada ya kujihakikishia kuwa hakukuwa na jinsi ya kuwasaidia wale vijana, Zengeni aliamua kuondoka kwa majonzi akizongwa na maswali hasa moja kuu: ni kwanini watu wamegeuka wanyama kiasi hicho kuwaua watu kwa ajili ya vitu vinavyoweza kutafutwa na kupatikana? Mama Ntetela hakuficha hisia zake. Alisema. "Namshukuru Mungu binti Mtendeweka mie. Maana vifaa vyangu vimepatikana. Sijui kwenye harusi ya mtoto wa kaka ningeeleza nini kwenda bila dhahabu na mtandao. Isitoshe mume wangu angepandwa na presha bure tokana na roho ya mbwa ya vidokozi hawa. Nendeni mkalipie huko motoni habithi nyie. Halo! Halo!" alimazia kwa kicheko cha kebehi iliyochanganyikana na furaha ya ushindi.Yeye kwake vifaa vyake na rununu au rukono, vilikuwa na thamani kuliko utu na uhai! Ajabu mama Ntetela huwa ni mtu anayeonekana mwenye huruma. Lakini kweli jinai hailipi. Maana ghafla utu na huruma yake viliingiwa nyongo vikatibuka na kugeuka unyama tena katili!

Mmoja wa wale vijana waliokuwa wakiungua moto aliyeitwa Bokasa, kwa machungu makubwa, alisema kwa huzuni sana, "Jamani nisameheni nikitoka hapa nitaokoka niwe mchungaji badala ya kibaka."

Mmoja wa ule umati alijibu kwa kejeli, "Utaokokea mbele ya safari. Nenda ukawahubiri vibaka wenzio waliokutangulia hapa hapakufai tena. Tazama hatma yako sasa ni kifo cha kuchomwa moto."

"Ai we! Yaani mmeamua kutuua kinyama hivi! Hatukupenda tuwe vibaka ni maisha." Alizidi kulalamika yule kibaka aliyekuwa akiwaka moto.

Mtu mmoja alisema, "Jamani maisha haya tusipoangalia na kufikiria tutawamaliza vijana wetu bure huku wakubwa wakitumbua na kufurahia tunavyomalizana wenyewe. Mbona mitaa ya wakubwa haina unyama kama huu Yarabi toba!" Mama mmoja aliyekuwa kakunja midomo kutokana na kinyaa cha jinsi ile miili ya wale vijana ilivyokuwa ikiteketea alisema. "Unayosema ni kweli. Wakubwa wameamua kututengenezea umaskini ili tusijue wanavyofaidi jasho letu. Wao wana hasara gani iwapo watoto wao wanasoma shule nzuri Ulaya?" Alifunga kanga yake vizuri na kuendelea. "Wametutengenezea mazingira ya kuchukiana na kumalizana, kupatilizana sisi kwa sisi huku wao wakituhadaa kuwa wanatutakia mema wakati mema kwao ni sisi kukubali kunyonywa nao!" Alitema mate pembeni kutokana na kinyaa kilichokuwa kimemjaa kutokana na kuungua kwa wale vijana aliokuwa, kama Zengeni, akiwahurumia.

Maongezi yaliishia hapo baada ya kuona kila mmoja anajiwahi kuondoka kwenye eneo la tukio baada ya kufanikisha yale mauaji ya kinyama ya vibaka.

Zoezi la kuwachoma wale vibaka lilienda kama lilivyokuwa limepangwa. Kwa mtu ambaye hajawahi kushiriki unyama huu, asingeamini. Angedhani yumo ndotoni au anaangalia mchezo wa kuigiza! La kusikitisha na kufedhehesha ni ile hali ya binadamu kufanya unyama kama huu huku akicheka na kutohofia uhai wa binadamu mwenzie! Baada ya kichwa cha mmoja wao kulipuka ntuuuuuuu! Sanjari na kupasuka kwa bufuru yalisikika makelele ya kushangilia toka kwenye umati wa wauaji wenye hasira! "Yaaa."Baada ya kujiridhisha kuwa yale yalikuwa ndiyo stahiki ya wale vijana, watu wote walitawanyika haraka haraka na kuwaacha wale vijana wakiungua kama magogo. Ajabu wengi wa watu walitawanyika wakiwa na furaha nyusoni kana kwamba walikuwa wamewachoma moto nyoka! Ni unyama kiasi gani hata kama hawakuwa wakiuhisi.

6
Kafara ya ukondoo

Zengeni aliondoka kwenye eneo la tukio akiwa amejawa na gegezi kutokana na kushuhudia wale marehemu walivyokuwa wakichomeka. Punde alipofika nyumbani kwake alimsimulia Nengoma yaliyojiri. Nengoma alionekana kufurahia kitendo kile. Hakika jambo hili lilimuudhi, kumfedhehesha na kumchukiza Zengeni. Maana alidhani mke wake angekuwa na huruma kama yeye kumbe siyo!Alimuuliza ni vipi angekuwa na ubavu wa kufurahia jinai kama ile. Alisema. "Yaani mke wangu umekuwa mnyama kiasi cha kushangilia na kufurahia vifo vya vijana walioharibiwa na jamii ambayo imewageuka na kuwaua tena kwa kifo kibaya hivyo! Tena msomi kama wewe mke wangu!"

Nengoma alijibu akiwa na wahaka wa kueleweka vibaya. Utadhani alikuwa amejiandalia swali lile. Alisema. "Mume wangu siyo unyama wala kutosoma. Ni mafutu kwa vitendo vyao. Nikikumbuka majambazi walivyombaka yule mwanamke jirani sina hamu na vibaka wala majambazi. Umesahau ule mkasa uliousoma gazetini mwaka juzi ambapo mwanamke mmoja aliharibiwa urembo wake kwa kung'olewa sikio kisa vibaka walitaka dhahabu zake utadhani wanajua aliyemnunulia! Katika uchafu huu, hujui, kuwa watu wasio na hatia ama wamekufa, kutiwa vilema na wengine kuambukizwa ukimwi! Fikria yule aliyebakwa au kung'olewa sikio angekuwa mimi." Alimkazia macho mumewe.

Zengeni hakuwa na la kujibu bali kusonya na kutikisa kichwa. Kwani kwa jinsi mke wake alivyomjibu asingeweza kupata jibu. Alikuwa kamshika pabaya kwa kutolea mfano kwake mwenyewe.Alinyamaza kidogo na kusema. "Lakini mke wangu tukubaliane kuwa wanavyofanya wananchi wenye hasira ni vibaya tu hata kama serikali imeamua kufumbia macho ubaya huu. Hakuna utetezi wala namna ya kuweza kuunga mkono unyama huu. Baya haliondolewi kwa baya tena baya zaidi. Lakini je hilo ni jibu? Kama tutasema jicho kwa jicho na mkono kwa mkono kwa jamii yetu ilivyoharibika huoni kuwa tutaambulia kuwa na chongo kila nyumba? Mkono kwa mkono jicho kwa jicho ni mambo ya kizamani wakati ambapo uwezo wa binadamu kutatua matatizo ulikuwa mdogo."

Anakohoa na kuendelea, "Sisi kama wasomi inabidi tuanzishe na kuongoza mapambano dhidi ya mafisadi wetu wanaopoteza muda kujinufaisha binafsi wao huku umma ukiteketea. Hawa ni wachuuzi wa miili na roho zetu hata mstakabali wetu na vizazi vyetu." Alimalizia Zengeni aliyeonyesha kukirihika wazi wazi.Nengoma naye hakuridhika na mawazo ya mumewe. Alijibu. "Tatizo ndiyo lipo tena kubwa tu. Lakini wahusika ambao ni serikali hawataki kulikubali na kulikabili. Kutofanya hivyo kunafanya wananchi wajitafutie njia mbadala hata kama ni za hovyo na kikatili kiasi cha kugingiza kama mauaji ya halaiki. Ndiyo huu ni unyama. Ni kutapatapa na kuharibikiwa kwa jamii. Maana badala ya kuwalinda vijana wake sasa imewageukia na kuwamaliza yenyewe huku maadui wa kweli wakiendelea kuzaa na kulelea Ulaya. Lakini kila mtu anaipenda nafsi yake na mali yake isitoshe kwenye lindi hili la umaskini."

Zengeni alitikisa kichwa kukubaliana na mkewe Nengoma. Aliendelea. "Hivi unadhani polisi wangekuwa wanawafikisha wahusika mbele ya sheria na haki inatendeka wananchi wangejichukulia sheria mkononi?"

Nengoma alijijibu na kusema, "Wananchi siyo wapuuzi

wala wanyama kiasi unachoweza kufikiria kutokana na ukatili ulioshuhudia. Wanalazimika kufanya unyama huu. Hii ndiyo ikirari yangu. Maana hawana jibu zaidi wala pa kukimbilia. Na isitoshe, watu wengi wa kawaida hawana muda wa kuumiza vichwa vyao wakati kuna njia ya mkato hata kama ni ya hovyo. Yeyote akipiga mbiu, wao wanamshughulikia mtu hata bila kutafuta ikirari."

Zengeni alijibu, "Pamoja na kwamba tatizo ni polisi na serikali kwa ujumla wake, mzizi wa tatizo hili ni ubadhirifu na umaskini na jamii kwa inayoridhia kuishi kwa matumaini. Maana vijana, licha ya kutokuwa na elimu wala ujuzi, hawana hata hivyo vibarua. Isitoshe nao ni wanadamu. Wanataka kuishi kama watu. Sema tatizo lao ni kutumia njia haramu kutatua matatizo yao. Ni hawa hawa ambao hawashiriki kwenye uchaguzi ambao wangeutumia kuingiza serikali inayowajali badala ya hawa wachumia tumbo."

Nengoma. "Hapo mume wangu nakubaliana nawe mia kwa mia. Lakini zaidi ya serikali ni nani anasababisha tatizo hili? Wakati vijana wakiteketea kwa moto na jamii inateketea, tukukumbuke. Maana wataendelea kuawa na kupotea huku nguvu kazi ikizidi kupotea. Na isitoshe, nao hawatakubali kufa hivi hivi. Watakayempata ataumia."

Alikohoa kidogo na kuendelea. "Hapa ndipo jamii isiyokuwa salama inavyojengeka. Maana wakiibuka wanashambulia kama koyokoyo wakijua fika ukiwapata wanaangamia. Hivyo, hapa ni ama zangu ama zako. Hii siyo jamii tuliyotarajia tulipopata uhuru unaogeuka kuwa udhuru."

Zengeni."Ni kweli mke wangu. Japo tunaambiwa kuna amani na mambo kama haya, hii ni amani ya watu wachache wenye madaraka na nguvu mifukoni. Hata nao wanajihadaa tu. Maana siku wanapopatikana ndiyo haya mambo ya kubakana na kuuana. Wamekuwa wakituhadaa wakidhani hatutakengeuka. Wanapodai kuna maendeleo jua ni maendeleo ya matumbo yao siyo taifa. Lakini wanajidanganya."

Zengeni aliinama kuchukua gazeti lililokuwa linapeperushwa na upepo na kuendelea, "Lakini mke wangu ukumbuke kuwa maeneo ya wakubwa yana polisi tena wa kumwaga. Wao wanaishi kwenye pepo ya maraha na utajiri katikati ya jehanam ya umaskini unaonuka. Huoni nilivyofuatilia umeme hadi nikasalimu amri? Hukumbuki wizarani walivyonipiga tarehe hadi wasomi wazima tukakulazimika kujenga na kuishi kwenye kiwanja kisichopimwa utadhani hatujui madhara yake!"

Nengoma alijibu, "Ni kweli hapa ni ama zangu ama zako. Haya siyo maisha. Maana wadogo tumegeuzwa asusa ya wakubwa. Tunaishi kwenye ulimwengu wa kutaataa kama nyoka tuliokuwa tukifundishwa kwenye somo la bailojia na mwalimu wetu tuliyezoea kumuita Palenkaima kutokana na kupenda kulirudia rudia neno hili."

Anatabasamu na kuendelea, "Si shimali wala matlai kote wamehanikiza kwa vilio vya ugumu wa maisha na kutamalaki jinai!"

Anaendelea baada ya kustuka utadhani kakumbuka kitu muhimu. "Ahaa! Kumbe ndiyo maana tulipokuwa tukifundisha wanafunzi walipotuita mama Vitafunwa na Mwalimu Machinga hukujali! Ulikuwa unalipwa kwa kupewa majina bandia kama ulivyokuwa ukiwaita walimu wako!"

"Sasa kumbe. Mara hii umesahau utoto na maisha ya shule?" Alijibu Nengoma akiwa anacheka.

Zengeni alisema, "Lakini mke wangu tukubaliane: kifo kinatisha. Maana ukiona wale vibaka walivyokufa kwa mateso huangalii mara mbili. Hakuna kitu kimenihuzunisha na kunitisha kama kichwa cha mtu kulipuka ntuuuuuu huku umati ukishangilia utadhani limefungwa goli! Huo ndiyo ulikuwa mwisho wa chachawizo zao za kuomba wanusuriwe maskini!" Alifumba macho na kunyama za kidogo na kuendelea. "Kumbe binadamu si chochote si lolote. Maana ukiangalia hiyo nyama huangalii mara mbili. Binadamu hovyo kabisa hata tujidai tumesoma, tuna mali, tuna madaraka na kila aina ushufaa na ushaufu. Bure kabisa. Bahati mbaya wanachomwa vidokozi wanaheshimwa majambazi na magawadi wetu."

Nengoma hakusikia vizuri haya maneno. Pia alitaka kupoozesha hasira za mumewe juu ya msimamo wake juu ya mauaji ya vibaka. Kwani alikuwa akijifanya kuendelea kuchekelea ule utani wake wa majina yao waliyokuwa wamepewa na wanafunzi. Aliendelea kucheka na kujizoazoa kuelekea jikoni kuangalia mapishi yake. Kwani kitambo kilikuwa kimepita bila kukagua jiko lake. Hivyo, ilibidi akatize maongezi na kwenda kuangalia kama kifungua kinywa kilikuwa tayari.

Ananyanyuka kwenda jikoni kuangalia chai kama imeishachemka. Anasema. "Tumeingia mambo ya vibaka na makurubundi na masahibu yao hadi nimesahau kuwa chai iko mekoni! Acha basi nikatenge chai ili kila mtu angalau aende zake kuhangaika na maisha haya ya aibu!" Anatokomea jikoni.

7
Waja wageuka wanyama!

Baada ya wale vibaka kuchomwa moto na kila mtu kutawanyika, huko nyuma polisi wa kituo kidogo cha Uswekeni walipata taarifa kuwa kulikuwa na watu watatu waliokuwa wameuawa kwa kuchomwa moto. Habari hii waliipata toka kwa mwandishi wa habari wa gazeti la mchana aitwaye Nkwae wa Mdwadwage anayeishi kwenye eneo hili la Uswekeni.

Kwanza, walimtaka awaeleze alipopata hii habari hasa wauaji. Naye alikuwa ni mtu na maadili ya kazi yake aliwajibu kwa mkato kuwa maadili ya kazi yake hayamlazimishi kuwaeleza chanzo chake cha habari zaidi ya kutoa taarifa kama wajibu wa raia yeyote mwema mwenye kuheshimu na kufuata sheria. Hakuwa tayari kuingia kwenye undani wa suala hili. Alisema kwa ung'eng'e "My duty totally and fully exonerates me from the onus of proving anything further than reporting." yaani maadili ya kazi yangu hayanitwishi wajibu wa kufanya lilote zaidi ya kutoa taarifa.

Polisi kuona kuwa hawana uwezo kisheria kumlazimisha mwandishi wa habari kufichua chanzo chake cha habari na isitoshe haya hayakuwa mauaji ya binafsi, ukichanganya na kimbombo alichomwaga, walijiuta wakifyata mkia. Hivyo, waliamua kwenda pale kwenye tukio kujaribu kukusanya ushahidi wakiwa wameudhika kutokana na maudhi Mdwadwage. PC Fadhili maarufu kama Tumbo kubwa na PC Chepe maarufu kama Mkomamanga walihamanika kwenda kwenye eneo la tukio. Ajabu hawakukuta mtu hata ili angalau wamuulize au waanze pa kukusanyia ushahidi na taarifa za tukio.

Haraka haraka, waliamua kwenda kiwandani kuuliza kwa walinzi kulikoni. Bahati nzuri, afande Tumbokubwa alikuwa ukuruba na mmoja wa walinzi wa kiwanda na nwenye kiwanda cha Kabari.

Tangu wizi ufanyike kiwandani pale, kulijengeka usuhuba na mwenye kiwanda kiasi cha, mara moja moja, alipokuwa kawamba kupita na kupata chochote kitu.

Binadamu atakunyima tonge lakini si habari. Hivyo, walitegemea kupata angalau fununu. Na isitoshe wale walikuwa ni walinzi ambao nao ni kama askari. Hivyo, ilikuwa rahisi kupata mkanda mzima wa yaliyokuwa yametokea. Katika kuelezea jinsi tukio lilivyoanzia kiwandani na mwenye kiwanda alivyoshauri wahalifu wapelekwe polisi, songombwingo Tumbo kubwa alinusa harufu ya ulaji. Kama mnandi kwenye mawindo yake, mara moja aliomba aonane na mwenye kiwanda. Haraka haraka, simu ilipigwa kwa bosi wa kiwanda.

Naye hakufanya ajizi. Alikuja joshi kusikiliza polisi walichokuwa wakitaka. Maana aliishajua kuwa ujio wao ilikuwa ni katika kuchunguza yale mauaji japo nyumaye chochote kingemtoka bila kufanya geresha yoyote. Maana, hii ndiyo Mafuriko lazima mkwiji wa polisi usiondoke patupu. Katika nchi ya Mafuriko wabwindi walikuwa na hofu na polisi. Hivyo alijua, hata bila kuambiwa, pesa ingemtoka ili wasimpotezee muda wa kwenda kuandika maelezo kituoni au hata kumwita kama shahidi mahakamani kama kungekuwapo na kesi ya kujibu baada ya kumpata angalau mhusika mmoja wa mauaji haya ya kinyama ingawa huwa ni nadra katika hali kama hii. Hata akipatikana wakati mwingine huishia kutoa chochote kitu na kuachiwa.

Mbwindi yule aliyejulikana kama Kanji alikuja akiwa anatabasamu na kusalimia. "Karibu afendi. Leo iko nakuja ona sisi?" Alisema kwa tabasamu la uongo kana kwamba alikuwa hakujua kulikoni!Afande Tumbokubwa alimtaka waingie ndani. Tatizo lilokuwa limewaleta halikuwa dogo. Mwenye kiwanda hakupinga pendekezo hilo. Moyoni alianza kupiga mahesabu ya kiasi cha pesa kidogo ya kuwaondoa askari huyu mpenda pesa asimpotezee muda.

Waliingia ndani na kukaa kama dakika thelathini hivi. Baada ya maongezi yao, Kanji aliwasindikiza wale polisi huku wakiongea kwa uchangamfu.

"Ukiona hivyo kipanga keshamzoa mkundaji. Zake ni hoihoi na vifijo akielekea zake kiotani akahomoe na wanae. Lazima uwe mkimwa; vinginevyo mambo hayaendi." Mlinzi mmoja alimwambia mwenzie kuonyesha shuku yake ya uwepo wa chauchau na bakhshishi.Wale mapolisi waliwaanga wale walinzi na kuondoka kuelekea kwenye eneo la tukio. Kwao, safari ya kiwandani ilikuwa bora kuliko kutimiza wajibu wao wa kuwasaka wahalifu!

Wakati polisi wamekwenda kiwandani, Mdwadwage alijaribu kutafuta habari kamili jinsi ya tukio. Baada ya kuwahoji majirani wawili watatu ambao wote walikana kushuhudia mauaji yale, aliona ni bora awangoje wale polisi ajue kama taarifa zingetumwa kwa kamanda wa polisi wa mkoa ili baadaye aende kule kuthibitisha habari hii na baadaye kuiripoti kwenye safu ya matukio ya jiji.

Polisi walipofika walimwambia Mdwadwage kuwa wangefanya upelelezi kwanza na taarifa hizo zingetumwa baadaye. Alipowaulilza kama walipata fununu yoyote pale kiwandani, polisi walimjibu kuwa si rahisi kuelezea jinsi wanavyokusanya taarifa zao. Hivyo, hiyo haikuwa kazi ya mwandishi kujua ni wapi wanapata habari.

Afande Mkomamanga alimwambia mwandishi. "Mwandishi kama maadili ya kazi yako yasivyokuruhusu kuieleza polisi ulipopata habari, kadhalika na sisi maadili ya kazi hayatulazimishi kumwambia mwandishi wa habari nini tumepata; na nini tumekosa. Okey!"

Mwandishi ilibidi akubaliane nao japo moyoni alijua kilichowapeleka kiwandani ilikuwa ni kujitafutia chochote cha kutia mfukoni na si ushahidi. Maana polisi wa Mafuriko kwa mafamba na rushwa ndogo ndogo za mbango na zawadi zisizo na sababu walikuwa wamekubuhu.Hivyo, Mdwadwage alifunga safari na kuelekea zake ofisini kutimiza majukumu mengine ya siku ile.Baada ya polisi kuona hawana la kufanya, walikwenda nyumba za jirani na kuwaamrisha wananchi waende kituoni kuandika maelezo ya wanachojua kuhusiana na tukio hilo. Baadaye walibadili mawazo na kwenda kwa mjumbe wa eneo hilo.Yote hii ilikuwa ni kuwapotezea wananchi muda. Hata hivyo, polisi walikuwa wenye furaha. Maana kufa kufaana. Wale vibaka wasingechomwa moto polisi wasingepata kisingizio cha kumtoa upepo Kanji.

Kwa bahati mbaya, mmoja wa vibaka waliokuwa wamechomwa moto alikuwa ni mwanae mjumbe walikokwenda walkenda kumuona. Naye kwa hasira za kupoteza mtoto wake, alitaka angalau wahusika wapatikane. Tatizo ilikuwa ni wapi pa kuanzia.

Haraka haraka, polisi walirejea kwenye tukio ambapo wale vibaka walikuwa wakiadhirika utadhani mizoga ya nyuni! Hata mizoga ya nyuni huwa na kunguru na vimburu wa kuisitiri.

Polisi walipiga simu zao makao ya wilaya na gari la polisi lilikuja kuchukua zile maiti zilizokuwa zimeungua vibaya. Mabutu alikuwa amekufa akiwa amepanua mdomo kutokana na maumivu wakati Moi alikuwa amejikunyaka kama mtu aliyekuwa anakwepa kitu fulani. Bokassa alikuwa hata hatambuliki ukiachia mbali kutambulika kutokana na wenzie kutambulika. Kifo kikifika wakati mwingine ujio wake si mchezo. Japo wende kwa nyonde au matiti ipo siku utazimika kama mshumaa iwe kwa shari au heri. Hii ndiyo jaala ya mahuluku wote kwa sawa bila kujali mbari kipato wala elimu. Walihusia wahenga.

Mara gari la polisi lilikuja kuchukua yale maiti. Dereva na wale mapolisi waliochukua maiti zile wana mioyo ya mawe. Maana walivyozizoa zoa zile maiti hawakuwa na woga wala mpwito mpwito. Kwani, hata walipotimba mafuta mafuta yaliyowatoka marehemu hawakuonekana kujali. Waliwazoa kama vile walikuwa wakizoa magunia ya nazi, kuyu hata magogo! Walikuwa wakiendelea na maongezi yao kwa udamisi huku wakizibeba zile maiti kuzipakia kwenye karandinga lao. Baada ya kuzipakia, polisi mmoja aliwasha sigara yake na kuanza kuvuta utadhani hakuwa amebeba maiti! Hata nyuso zao mapolisi hazikuonyesha chembe ya woga wala simanzi!

Kweli binadamu ni viumbe wa ajabu! Mauja ni kwa watu walioshudia zoezi hili la uzoaji walijawa na kunyanzi na majonzi utadhani baadhi yao hawakushiriki mauaji yale!

Baada ya maiti zile kupelekwa, polisi walianza zoezi la kuzitumbua. Kwa bahati nzuri tukio hilo halikuwa gumu kwani marehemu wote walikuwa ni watoto wa mtaa ule. Na isitoshe, baadae iligundulika kuwa kumbe walikuwa kwenye vitabu vya polisi kwa tuhuma za kutenda makosa mbali mbali mtaani pale na kwingineko.

Hata polisi waliwajua kama vibaka wazoefu lakini wenye kukata mshiko mzuri. Hivyo, walikuwa wakiwaachia mara kwa mara. Kuna kipindi mmoja wa vibaka wale alimkwapua mzungu mkoba uliokuwa umejaa maelfu ya madola. Polisi walipopata habari walimkamata na akawakatia chao naye akabaki na chake mchezo ukaishia pale mzungu akawa amenoa. Mzungu alipokwenda kituoni na kutoa taarifa alipigwa tarehe hadi visa yake ikaisha. Kilichomsaidia mzungu yule kurudi kwao ni ubalozi wake kumkatia tiketi ya kurudia kwao. Wazungu si kama Wamafuriko, hawatupani hata kidogo. Maana kuna taarifa zilikuwa zikipokelewa kwa vijana wengi wa Mafuriko walifariki ughaibuni na kuchangiwa na watu baki huku mabalozi wa Mafuriko wakijifanya kama hawahusiki! Haijulikani yule mzungu alipofika kwao alipakaza vipi?

Hivyo, polisi hawakupoteza muda sana kwenye utambulisho. Kwa vile walishavuta kitu kwa mbwindi, hawakuwa na haja ya kupoteza muda wao kwa watu walioonekana kama walikuwa wamejitakia kifo. Isitoshe, hii haikuwa mara yao ya kwanza wala ya mwisho kuitwa kwenye matukio kama haya.

8
Uhuru au udhuru?

Huko nyuma kwa Zengeni, Nengoma alitenga chai kwenye sinia lililotonwa maua maua ambalo linaanza kuchakaa na kumkaribisha mumewe tayari kuishambulia ile chai na mihogo. Ni chai ya rangi. Kwa watu kama Zengeni, maziwa ni kitu cha starehe hata kusikia mpaka iwe ni sikukuu au mtu aumwe. Lakini wameishaizoea maisha yao ya kijungujiko. Kwani chai hii na wanaikubali hivyo hivyo watafanya nini?Maongezi yao wakati wakinywa chai yalirudi kwenye gazeti na tukio zima la kuchomwa vibaka.

Alianza Zengeni. "Mke wangu unaona mambo yanavyoshabihiana hata kutangamana? Tulikuwa tukisoma tukio la wakubwa serikalini kuleta kampuni nuhusi ya kutengeneza sumu za kuulia wadudu kujenga mitambo ya maji. Bahati mbaya hata kabla ya kutafakari wizi huu, tukio la kukwapuliwa simu na dhahabu mama Ntetela na hatimaye kuchomwa moto kwa vibaka lilitukia."

Aliendelea "Kwangu naona hawa vibaka japo walikosa, chanzo cha masahibu yao ni wakubwa wachache serikalini na washirika wao kuiibia nchi na kusababisha umaskini na ukosefu wa ajira kiasi cha vijana kujiingiza kwenye jinai. Ajabu, majambazi hawa wa kisiasa wanajinata na kujinaki wameleta maendeleo wakati wameleta maangamio!"

Anakunywa chai na kukatua kipande cha mhogo na kuendelea, "Je kama wakubwa wataendelea na kasi hii katika kuiteketeza jamii kweli kuna haja ya kuzaa?"

Nengoma alijibu. "Ni kweli kabisa mume wangu. Lakini wenzio pamoja na kwamba wizi wao ni mkubwa na wenye madhara makubwa wana ulinzi. Hata sheria yenyewe inatoa adhabu kidogo kwa makosa ya wakubwa huku ikitoa adhabu kali kwa vibaka na wezi wengine wadogo."

Naye anakatua kipande chake cha mhogo na kunywa chai na kuendelea, "Kuzaa hakuna mjadala hapa. Maana hata wakati wazazi wetu wakituzaa sisi kulikuwa na mashinikizo mengine makubwa kwa madogo wakati ule. Lakini walipiga moyo konde na kutuzaa. Wazazi wetu walikuwa wakiogopa kuzidi kuingia kwa mambo ya Kiulaya kama umalaya, mavazi yasiyo ya staha, madawa ya kulevya na mambo mengine lukuki kama hayo. Lakini bado walijitahidi wakatuzaa na hatujaharibika. Hivyo..."

Zengeni hangoji amalizie hoja yake. anasema. "Jamani sasa tunakwenda wapi kama watu wanaweza kupata ithibati ya kuwachoma watu tena watatu mchana kweupe lakini watu hawa hawa wakawaogopa watu wachache wanaosababisha madhara kwa jamii nzima?"

Alichukua kipande cha mhogo na kukitafuna na kuendelea. "Lakini pia sisi wananchi tunastahili lawama. Kwani kila tunaposoma habari za uchafu kama huu ni wachache wanaokaa hata kujadili zaidi ya kuchana gazeti na kuwashia moto au hata kufungia vitumbua na mambo yanaishia hapo."Alishikwa na chafya. Alipiga chafya mara mbili na kumuomba msamaha mkewe kwa kupiga chafya na kuendelea."Yote hii inasababishwa na vumbi kujaa hewani. Isitoshe hiki kiwanda cha KABARI kinachafua mazingira na kutishia uhai wetu. Kweli kimetukaba kabari si haba. Lakini mwenye nazo si mwenzio. Nashangaa hata tume ya mazingira kila siku inapelekewa habari juu ya athari tunazozipata lakini ikipewa chake mambo yanaishia hapa sisi tunaendelea kuumia!"

Nengoma alijibu, "Mume wangu dunia hii sasa imegeuka ya samaki ambapo samaki mkubwa humla mdogo na mdogo humla mdogo zaidi. Sijui chaza anamla tafi au mkunga anamla changu. Hata sijui! Isitoshe tangu uje huu uchukuaji uitwao uwekezaji ndiyo usiseme. Una habari wabwindi sasa wameishainunua Mafuriko kiasi cha kufanya watakavyo?" Wakubwa wameamua kutuchuuza sisi na mali zetu na roho zetu kwa faida zao." Utadhani ugonjwa! Na Nengoma naye anapiga chafya mara tatu na kutikisa kichwa na kuendelea. "Watu wetu huwezi kuwalaumu. Njaa mume wangu. Adui yako muombee njaa. Baya zaidi, watu wetu wana njaa ya kifikra, busara na ya tumboni. Hii ni hali ya hatari kwa jamii. Ni kama bomu linalotika likingoja wakati muafaka wa kulipuka."

"Lakini hata kuchukia kama wanashindwa kuchukua hatua wameshindwa? Je hawaoni kuwa vitendo vya kujichukulia sheria mkononi vitazidi kuongezeka?" Anauliza tena Zengeni huku akimkingia kikombe mkewe amuongezee chai.

Baada ya kummiminia chai mumewe, Nengoma aliendelea kujadili tatizo la watu kujichukulia sheria mkononi na wakubwa kujifanya kama hawalioni. Alisema. "Viongezeke visiongezeke, wakubwa vinawahusu nini iwapo watoto wao wanasoma hata kuishi ughaibuni? Wakirudi nchini wanafanya kazi kwenye makampuni ya baba zao au marafiki zao na taasisi kubwa kubwa zenye mishahara minono na mikururo ya marupurupu zinazoitwa za wananchi huku watoto wa makabwela wakiangamia kwa moto na ukimwi. Hujaona wanavyoshindana kuritishana nyadhifa chamani na serikalini? Hakika ufalme wa Nabkadnezza unarudi."Alichukua kikombe chake na kupiga tama kama mbili na kuendelea. "Isitoshe wakubwa hawaishi kwenye makazi mbanano na maskini kama yetu. Wao ni naizi. Wanaishi kwenye mitaa iliyopimwa yenye kila huduma na walinzi huku na polisi nao wakipiga doria kwenye maeneo haya usiku na mchana adha hii tunayoipata wataipata lini? Kitanda usicholalia hujui kunguni wake. Umesahau ile filamu ya bonde la Shangri- La!"

Anasogeza upande wake wa khanga vizuri huku akimkata jicho mumewe kuona kama naye anamkata jicho kama kawaida yake na kuendelea "Hebu soma magazeti yote ya wiki hii uone kama kuna kisa hata kimoja cha namna hii kimetokea mitaa ya wakubwa. Thubutu!"

Anapiga chafya tena na kusema, "Mume wangu akipatikana mtu wa kununua banda letu tuliuze na kutafuta kiwanja sehemu nyingine mbali na jiji vinginevyo tutakufa tunajiona."Anapiga chafya tena na kuendelea, "Maana kama ni zilzali la maisha ya utepetevu na ufukara hili linatosha mume wangu."Alipiga chafya tena. "Mpfya mpfya!" Huku mkewe akimwambia: "Bless you." Na kuendelea. "Angalia tunavyokesha tukiwinda maji utadhani tunaishi nyakati za akina Adam na Eva? Nani anajali iwapo mitaa yao kila nyumba ina maji kila chumba? Hata huu ukame wanaousingizia kusababisha ukosefu wa maji hauwahusu. Kila siku matanki yanawapelekea maji majumbani mwao juu ya kuanzisha miradi ya kuzidi kutuibia kama huu wa Richmen."

Zengeni alisema. "Lakini ukubwa unawadanganya na kuwapofusha tu. Maana hata kama hawaishi madongo poromoka huku, kuna ndugu zao. Hawawezi kuhamisha ndugu zao wakaenda kuishi nao ukubwani. Ukubwa nini? Hata tembo akifa huliwa na nune."Nengoma naye anaongeza chai kwenye kikombe chake na kusema, "Lakini si mpaka afe na akisha kufa kila kitu si basi ? Wakubwa wetu ndugu yao ni pesa na maslahi yao. Wangekuwa wanajali udugu wasingewauza wananchi wenzao kwa zawadi ya vigari na vijumba vya hovyo na upuuzi mwingine. Isitoshe mchoyo hana ndugu wala rafiki. Na maskini hana ndugu siku hizi Pia ujue...."

Zengeni aliamua kuingilia. "Mie naona ni upofu tu unaowasumbua. Huu ni utapiamlo wa mawazo. Umesahau jinsi wezi walivyoteka gari la waziri wa fedha kwenye msitu wa Ubiri na kumkata kata mapanga na kumuibia kila kitu? Sema nao wanajua jinsi wanavyosababisha madhara kwa taifa lakini uroho na roho mbaya vinawazuzua."

Huku akitikisa kichwa kukubaliana na mumewe, Nengoma alisema, "Je baada ya kuibiwa waziri unakumbuka watu wengi walivyokamatwa hovyo hovyo na polisi na kubambikiziwa kesi mbali mbali ili kumridhisha huyu mheshimiwa? Umesahau kaka Chikwakwa alivyosota ndani mwezi mzima hadi tulipotoa hongo ya laki mbili kumtoa wakati kesi yenyewe ilikuwa ni raia mwema aliyejikuta mahali pasipofaa wakati usiofaa na kushia kubambikiwa na polisi ili kuwaridhisha wakubwa kuwa wapo kuwalinda na tukio lile ni bahati mbaya?"

Zengeni akiwa anajiweka vizuri kwenye msala alijibu, 'Lakini bado hii siyo suluhu bali ni kulea tatizo ukiachia mbali kuzalisha mengine tena lukuki. Maana nijuavyo, bila kukomesha rushwa na ufisadi hata wangekamata wilaya nzima haya matukio hayatakwisha. Tofauti ni kwamba mawaziri na wakubwa wengine hayawapati haya mara kwa mara. Nadhani kuna haja ya wananchi kuamka tukakataa kuridhika kuishi kwenye maisha ya wasiwasi na utumwa ndani ya nchi yetu wenyewe. Kwanini uhuru wetu ugeuke kuwa udhuru wetu nasi tusichukue hatua?"

Kabla ya kuendelea Nengoma naye alimkosoa, "Mume wangu, nchi hii siyo uhuru. Uhuru uko wapi kama wananchi wanaishi kama hinziri?"Alisogeza vizuri Khanga huku akijisogeza vizuri na kuendelea. "Kama upo, basi wanaoufaidi na kuutumia ni wakubwa wanaoiba kwa uhuru bila wananchi kugutuka wala kuchukua hatua. Hawa ndiyo wenye nchi wala nchi na ndiyo wako huru na siyo sisi. Sisi ni waso nchi tuitwao umma wanaouuma tena kwa uma."

"Lakini kumbuka: ndivyo wanavyotwambia; kuwa nchi hii ni huru na watawala wapo kulinda uhuru huu usichezewe na maadui wakati maadui ni wao wenyewe na wageni wao!" Alikumbushia Zengeni huku akinyoosha mkono wake wa kushoto kama anayepiga ngumi.

Nengoma hakuridhika na maelezo ya mumewe. Alibeua midomo na kusema, "Huu siyo uhuru ni udhuru tuna uchuro. Umesahau wanasiasa wetu wasivyotofauti na wana mazingaombwe! Wanaweza kuropoka lolote. Ila ipo siku: mawe yatasema na kuamka na kutembea wakiendelea kutufanya sie majuha. Kama siyo sisi basi wajukuu kama siyo wao, basi vilembwe au vilembweka hata vilembwekezi watakuja kuchukua hatua sahihi amini nakwambia."

"Mama mla kala leo kesho kalani? Hatuna haja ya kuwaachia hata watoto wetu miiba shambani. Umma naamini utazinduka siku si nyingi. Matatizo yamezidi na ni mwalimu mzuri tu." Alijibu Zengeni huku akikuna kichwa kama kukumbuka jambo fulani.

Wakati gumzo hili la kuichambua nchi yao linaendelea, Zengeni alikumbuka kuwa alikuwa na ahadi ya kukutana na rafiki yake mjini ili kujadili taarifa alizokuwa ameomba amkusanyie mikoani kuhusu ununuaji wa vyakula na kuleta kuuza mjini. Aliangalia saa ya ukutani na kukuta kumbe ilikuwa imetimu saa tano.

Hivyo, ilibidi maongezi yafe na awahi zake bafuni tayari kwenda kituo cha mabasi kupambana na miminyo ya usafiri kwenda mjini.

9
Heka heka nyuma ya pazia

Katika ofisi ya waziri mkubwa, Edmond Ngonyaegg Mpendamali mwa Luwasha, kuna kikao. Si kikao bali kigwena. Ni cha waziri mkubwa mwenyewe, waziri wa ushirikiano wa kanda Ibnhim M7ha Bangusilo, katibu wa hazina na mifuko ya pesa ya taifa, Gray Tamaa Mgonjwa na waziri wa maji na mvua na upepo, Niziro Mulangila Kadamage na Katibu wake Amon Mwakipungiro. Kadamage ni waziri wa wizara iliyokuwa ya waziri mkubwa mwa Luwasha wakati wa serikali ya zamani ya Rais Benny Dangerman Makapi. Pia ni mfanyabiashara mwenye kutia mashaka ambaye aliingia serikalini kutokana na kuchangisha fedha na kuufadhili mtandao wa Rais uliomuingiza madarakani kwa kutoa rushwa maarufu wakati ule kama Kirimia.

Huyu, Kadamage na mshirika mwingine wa waziri mkubwa, Rostitamu Ajizi Azoul, ndiyo wanaoendesha mtandao wa ujambazi uliowezesha kampuni ya Richmen kupata tenda ya kitaifa wakati, kimsingi, si kampuni chochote bali kijikampuni cha mitaani tu. Kikao hiki ni cha ghafla sana. Maana mheshimiwa mtukufu waziri mkubwa amerudi jijini Neema kutoka katika mji wa Ukame kwenye kikao kinachoendelea cha bunge. Hivyo, mapumziko yake ya muda wa wiki moja yanavurugwa na habari hii ya gazeti la Chimbichimbu ambayo hakuipenda japo hana jinsi bali kuifanyia kazi.

Mkutano huu ni wa aina yake. Kwani hata mwandishi wa waziri mkubwa, Sudi Mkudajuha hakuruhusiwa kuhudhuria. Bosi wake na wenzake wana jambo nyeti kwa usalama wa nchi yao ya nyuma ya pazia. Hivyo, si vizuri mwandishi kuhudhuria kigwena hiki. Hawataki ajue mambo yao.Waziri mkubwa ni mtu wa makamo kama miaka hamsini na ushei. Jamaa mmoja mwenye sura ya pesa. Ana kiriba tumbo kisicho kikubwa wala kidogo. Nywele zake bado ni nyeusi tii utadhani kijana wa miaka thelathini! Pamoja na nywele kutoonyesha umri wake, uso wake unaanza kuota kunyanzi. Amevalia suti yake ya kichina maarufu kama Chu En Rai. Hii ni suti iliyoanzishwa na waziri mkuu wa zamani wa China aliyesifika kwa msimamo wake kuhusu siasa za ujamaa zilozotetea usawa. Ajabu pamoja na waziri mkubwa huyu kuvaa vazi hili la usawa, amejilimbikizia mali nyingi za wizi na hafanani na watu anaodai kuwaongoza!

Wakati Chu aliwaongoza na kuwakomboa wachina, mwa Luwasha anawaibia tu! Unafiki ulioje! Hana sera wala mpango wa kuwakomboa watu wa Mafuriko. Sera yake ni tumbo na tamaa zake.

Chu alikuwa rafiki na mshauri mkuu wa kiongozi maarufu wa China, Mao Tse Tung, gwiji wa falsafa ya ujamaa na usawa wa binadamu ambao akina Mwaluwasha wanauona kama ujima na kitu killichopitwa na wakati kwa sasa. Wanavaa nguo za Chu kama kejeli kubwa na unafiki vinayolenga kuficha undani wao. Ni ngozi ya kondoo kwenye mwili wa fisi. Ni urembo juu ya mwili uliooza na kunuka kwa ndani. Mafuriko kabla ya kuingia siasa za utando wa wizi, ilikuwa chini ya siasa za kijamaa ambapo kila mtu alikuwa sawa na wenzake. Wakati huu maafisa wa serikali hawakurusiwa kuwa na mishahara ya siri wala utajiri usiokuwa na malezo yanayoeleweka na kukubalika. Nani angetumikia mabwana wawili wakati ule? Kwa sasa anaweza kutumikia hata mia na asiwe kahaba!

Mawaziri walilipenda sana vazi hili. Kwani kwa nje liliheshimika na kuleta imani na matumaini kwa watawaliwa kama alama ya kupenda usawa na kutetea maslahi ya umma ingawa kivitendo haikuwa hivyo. Hii ilitokana na magwiji wengi wa siasa za ujamaa kulitumia kama sare yao kuonyesha falsafa zao. Baadhi ya watawala wa Mafuriko pamoja na kutokuwa na falsafa na sera vinavyoeleweka, walijivalia tu. Maskini hawakujua walikuwa wakijitukana na kujisuta! Kweli usilolijua ni sawa na usiku wa giza tena totoro!

Pamoja na waziri mkubwa kutaka aonekane kama kiongozi wa watu, alishutumiwa kwa kujilimbikizia mali ambazo asingeweza kuzitolea maelezo. Wenzake wamevalia suti zao za bei mbaya. Katibu wa hazina na mifuko ya taifa ni mtu wa miaka kama sitini hivi. Naye, kama waziri wake mkubwa, ni mtu mwenye sura ya pesa. Na kweli, anazo tena za kumwaga. Suti yake iliyoshonwa Paris na magwiji wa fasheni ni ya bei mbaya ukiachia saa yake na pete za mkononi ni vya dhahabu na almasi. Hata vishikizo vya shati lake ni vya dhahabu! Ni mtu na pesa yake. Ni mtu anayejisikia na kujiona kama si wa kawaida sawa na walipa kodi waliomfikisha kwenye kilele hiki cha mafanikio yatokanayo na ujambazi kwenye ofisi za umma.

Waziri wa maji mvua na upepo naye si haba. Amevalia suti yake ya rangi ya kahawia yenye lebel ya Mfiliseni ambaye ni mwana mitindo wa kimataifa anayeshimika san. Ametilia saa ya bei mbaya mkononi. Ni aina yaMadiba ambayo ni aghali kuliko zote duniani na si chini ya dola kama elfu hamsini au shilingi milioni mia saba za Mafuriko. Naye ni mtu anayeonyesha uso wa kuridhika na kujisikia kama ilivyo tabia ya wale waliotembelewa na pesa ya ghafla tena bila ya kuitolea jasho.

Wote wamevaa mipete mikubwa ya dhahabu utadhani wanamuziki limbukeni wa Zaire ya zamani! Ni washamba wa vitu kiasi cha kutojua hata kuvitumia!

Ofisi ya waziri mkubwa ni kubwa kweli yenye hadhi sawa na cheo chake. Ni kubwa na inaficha makubwa! Kuna meza kubwa pembeni ya kuweza kuhudumia watu kama ishirini ingawa mara nyingi huudumia vumbi. Pembeni kuna maua ya bei mbaya. Ilisemekana kuwa Mafuriko ilikuwa ikipoteza siyo chini ya shilingi milioni kama hamsini na moja kwa siku kununua maua ya kupamba ofisi za wakubwa kila siku. Hii haikuhusisha pesa ya kununulia magazeti ambayo nayo mara nyingi wakubwa wenyewe hawakuyasoma. Ikiongezewa ya simu zilizokuwa zikitumika vibaya hasa kwa wafanyakazi wengi kuzitumia kwenye mambo ya binafsi, hakika Mafuriko ilibarikiwa utajiri na pale pale ikapata nakama ya kulaaniwa kwa kuwa na wafujaji kwenye ofisi za umma.

Kwa vile mkutano ni wa watu watatu tu, wanakaa kwenye seti moja ya sofa la bei mbaya yenye ngozi ya chui. Maskini pamoja na kutangaza kulinda mazingira na wanyama walio kwenye hatari ya kutoweka, waziri mkubwa hakujua kuwa chui ni wanyama wanaotishiwa kutoweka kutokana na ngozi yao kutumiwa na watu wajinga kama yeye!Kigwena zaidi ya wajumbe binadamu kinashuhudiwa na masanamu mawili ya ng'ombe dume na jike vikiwakilisha waziri mkubwa na mke wake. Maana kwenye mila yao ng'ombe huabudiwa. Maskini hakujua kuwa tafsiri nyingine ilikuwa ni kwamba alikuwa na akili za hovyo kama ng'ombe!

Chini kuna bonge na busati la kutengenezwa kwa mikono. Hili liliagizwa Uajemi. Inasemekana waziri alipoteuliwa alikuta fanicha kama hii na ya bei mbaya kweli. Lakini kwa vile ile ilikuwa siyo chaguo lake, pamoja na upya wake na gharama yake, aliamua kuihamishia kwenye nyumba yake binafsi na kuamuru hazina kumpa fedha ya kununulia fanicha mpya. Na kama siyo uroho, hakuhitaji hata hizo fanicha maana fanicha za nyumbani kwake zilitolewa zawadi na mkurungenzi wa

Richmen Mafuriko. Hapa ilikuwa imetoka. Kwani busati hili hakulilipia senti hata moja. Hivi ndivyo wakubwa wa Mafuriko wanavyojifurisha na utajiri! Kwao mali ya umma ni ya kuuma haiumi, we umma tu tena kwa uma.

Inasemekana fanicha hizi zilitoka nchi tofauti. Sofa iliagizwa toka China busati Uajemi.Pia kulikuwa na vyungu vya shaba vya maua ambavyo navyo viliagizwa nchini Taiwan na maua yake. Birika la kahawa liliagizwa nchini Misri ingawa waziri alikuwa halitumii kwa sababu siyo mnywaji wa kahawa.Kuna na tufe la mapambo lenye kuzunguka na kubadili rangi kila likizunguka ambalo liliangizwa toka nchini Italia. Pia kuna na shefu ya vitabu ambayo nayo pia iliangizwa nchini Italia. Ajabu vitabu vyenyewe hata huwa mheshimiwa havisomi! Saa ya ukutani iliagizwa kwa magwiji wa kutengeneza saa Uswisi. Imetonwa kwa dhahabu. Viyoyozi ni made in Korea ya kusini huku masanamu ya njiwa wawili jike na dume vikimaanisha yeye na mkewe viliagizwa toka Singapore. Kwa ufupi, hakuna na kitu hata kimoja toka nchini Mafuriko isipokuwa wajumbe wa mkutano! Nani mshamba atumie vitu local?

Kitu kingine pekee toka Mafuriko mbali na wakubwa tu ambao walijulikana kama waheshimiwa kwa mujibu wa sheria za Mafuriko ni kuta zilizotengenezwa kwa zege la ardhi safi ya Mafuriko. Kitu kingine ni ardhi ilipokuwa imejengwa ile ofisi maridadi na aghali ya mtawala huyu anayetawala watu maskini kama akina Zengeni na Nengoma wake na vibaka waliokuwa wamewahi motoni kupata haki yao.Nani angetumia vitu vya Mafuriko ambavyo kwao vilikuwa ni vitu dhaifu kama watu wake?

Nani angenunua fanicha Mafuriko ambapo bei yake ni nzuri na inafahamika kiasi cha kuwa vigumu lakini visivyo na ulaji wa kuongeza cha mbele? Ajabu pamoja na fanicha zile kuangizwa toka nje, hazikuwa madhubuti. Ni mti gani duniani ungeushinda mpingo au mkangagazi na mfune bila kutaja mvule, mlongoma hata mkunguru au mninga?

Lakini wakubwa walizipenda kwa vile zinaharibika haraka. Hivyo huwapa fursa ya kuagiza nyingine huku wakiambulia cha juu ambacho ni mamilioni ya shilingi.

Hii ndiyo sababu pekee iliyowafanya wapende kuagiza vitu nje ukiachia mbali ulimbukeni uliotamalaki kwenye Bara la Mwanga.

Kuna nchi moja jirani na Mafuriko iitwayo Mizengwe, Rais wake alikuwa akiagiza, kondoo toka Argentina, maji ya kunywa toka Ufaransa na karatasi za chooni toka Marekani.Hawa ndiyo watawala wa bara la Mwanga. Watawala waliozaliwa bila hata chembe ya utu, ukwasi wala aibu isipokuwa umahiri wa uchoyo, ulafu na roho mbaya na ngoa kwa watu waliowaamini. Watu wasio na uoni wala mshipa wa fahamu wa kuangalia kwenye lindi la umaskini walikotokea. Watu walioweka roho zao rehani Ili kupata pesa mabaki wapewayo na wezi wa kimataifa!

Mwalimu Mahd Msiyeni alizoea kusema kuwa ni watu waliozaliwa kwenye familia ambazo hadi Mafuriko inapata uhuru walikuwa bado wakilalia ngozi na kula mlo mmoja kama komba huku wakirithi madeni ya mahari ya mama zao. Leo wamegeuka mabilionea ghafla!

Kwa ufupi ofisi ya waziri mkubwa ni ya bei mbaya. Ni kubwa na aghali kama waziri mwenyewe ingawa wananchi waliokuwa wakidanganywa kuwa ni ofisi yao walikuwa hoi bin taabani! Wale wanaoihudumia wakishindwa kuhudumiwa nayo ni maskini wa kutupwa. Wako mkiani kwenye takwimu za utajiri katika bara zima! Hawana tofauti na sindano ambayo hushona nguo nyingi lakini daima ikaishi uchi wala kitanda kilaliwacho chenyewe kisilale.

10
Mkao wa kula

Wakubwa wameishajitenga kwenye viti vyao aghali tayari kuanza kigwena chao. Kila mmoja anaonekana kuwa tayari kusikiliza au kuchangia. Kila kitu kiko tayari. Hivyo, mkutano utaanza wakati wowote.

Ukiondoa huduma ya vinywaji, kila kitu kiko tayari. Wanaanza mkutano wao pindi tu baada ya msichana sena mwenye sura ya kupendeza, mlimbwende vilivyo anayewaka si haba na kuvutia kwa kila hali kuwaletea wakubwa vinywaji na kufunga mlango.

Taratibu kwa mikogo, mineso na matuko vinavyogeuka mazidadi na kivutio kwa waheshimiwa, anatokomea nje ya ukumbi wa mkutano. Kwake inaonekana wameishiwa kiasi cha kila mtu kujenga hoja yake ya siri!

Huyo ananata na kuishia kuelekea mlangoni akiwacha waheshimiwa hoi na nyoyo zao!

Kabla msichana kuondoka, waziri mkubwa anaonekana kumtolea macho hasa pale alipoinama kuwamiminia vinywaji kana kwamba kuna kitu kimeganda mwilini mwake. Hakuna shaka kuwa mke wa waziri mkubwa angekuwapo akaona jicho alilomkata mumewe si haba kingemshuka. Maana ukubwa una mengi tena makubwa kama ukubwa wenyewe na mwanaume ni mwanaume. Ni fisi gani aone nyama tena ya mafuta asitokwe na udenda?

Kwa ujumla wajumbe wote wa mkutano wanakata shingo huku roho zikiwauma na kuwachefuka. Ni mwenye umri kama miaka ishirini na mitano hivi kila mtu kwa tathmini yake na matamanio yake. Huenda aliajiriwa pale kuwapa burudani ya macho wakubwa. Maana ilikuwa ni kama walikuwa wameambiana kumkata jicho kila mtu kwa tathmini na malengo yake binafsi.

Kweli wakubwa wana makubwa. Maana si haba kwa jinsi yule msichana alivyoumbika na kuvaa mavazi ya bei mbaya, mshahara wake nao si wa kawaida. Hata huduma anayoitoa inaonekana siyo ya kawaida!

Baada ya msichana kuondoka mkutano unaanza. Maana angeendelea kuinama chumbani kule si ajabu angegeuka kuwa mkutano mwingine tosha badala ya mkutano kusudiwa! Hata hivyo, kwa kipindi hiki kifupi amekuwa mkutano wa macho na nyoyo bila kujulikana ajenda ni nini. Waziri mkubwa huku akitabasamu na saa nyingine kujisikia fahari kuwa na mhudumu mzuri na mardadi mwenye kuvutia kila jicho hata la matajiri na wenye madaraka, anasema kimoyo moyo "Kitu hiki si kawaida!" Anajitahidi kuwa mchangamfu ili kuficha hofu na hasira za kuvurugwa kwa likizo yake ya muda mfupi ambapo angepanda ndege na kwenda kuwasalimia ng'ombe wake na wazazi wake mkoani kwake.

"Waheshimiwa wajumbe, mnajua kilichotukutanisha hapa." Alikunywa toka kwenye glasi yake ambayo alikuwa akiizungusha zungusha na kuendelea. "Twende moja kwa moja kwenye mada ya kikao chetu. Nilipokuwa Toronto ziarani, niliongea na Mr. Giro ambaye alini-brief juu ya kuwasilisha mzigo." (Alimaanisha chakula cha wakubwa au chau chau kwa maana nyingine). "Nakumbuka uliponipigia kutoka New-York sikuweza kukujibu vizuri kwa kuhofia wenzetu kuingilia maongezi yetu. Si unajua nchi za wenzetu hawana mchezo na yeyote." Anaongea huku akitabasamu akimuangalia Katibu wa hazina na mifuko ya pesa ambaye alikuwa amerejea nchini kutoka nchini Marekani alipokwenda kukutana na mkurugenzi wa kampuni tanzu ya Richmen ya Big guns, ili kumaliza masuala yote yahusiano na "haki" za wakubwa kwenye mradi husika.

Anaendelea. "Kwa taarifa alizonipa mheshimiwa waziri." Alimgeukia waziri wa maji na upepo.

Ni kwamba mzigo wetu umefikishwa salama salimin kwenye visiwa vya Kayman." Anakohoa na kunywa mvinyo wake wa bei mbaya aina ya Monde moderne cognac ambao hupokea toka Ufaransa. Inasemekana kuwa bei ya katoni moja ni dola 1,200 za kimarekani bila ushuru.

Akiwa anatabasamu kwa kuufaidi mvinyo ule aghali na kupata taarifa ya rushwa yao kufikishwa kunakohusika salama, alnaendelea. "Mr. Giro alinielezea ambavyo kampuni yake ilivyo na mpango wa kuchukua tenda na malipo ya awali na kuuza mradi kwa kampuni ya Dooms. Hii ni kutokana na Richmen kutokuwa na muda wa kusimamia miradi mingine mikubwa kwenye nchi nyingine na kushughulikia ujenzi wa mitambo ya maji ambayo tunaihitaji haraka. Na isitoshe, hili nililieleza kwa kina kwenye memo niliyokutumia juzi."

Anatoa leso yake na kujifuta midomo na kuendelea. Kwani alichokuwa anasema kilikuwa ni uongo mtupu tena mchana kweupe.

Anaendelea. "Kutokana na hali hii, inabidi kwenye mkataba wa kutoa tenda hii tuingize na kipengele cha kuiruhusu kampuni kuuza mradi kwa kampuni nyingine bila kutoa maelezo. Hii itasaidia kuepukana na lawama na aibu kwa vile kampuni hii kusema ukweli ni ya kutengeneza dawa za wadudu na siyo kujenga miradi ya maji." Anakohoa kidogo. "Na hapa lazima Dawans waongee vizuri. Nadhani mnanielewa." Anawakazia macho wajumbe. Wanatikisa vichwa kwa pamoja huku wakitabasamu kwa ulaji mwingine wanaoutengeneza kirahisi. Anaendelea. "Tumeipa tenda hii kutokana na kuwa na masharti mazuri. Naamini kila mmoja wenu anajua hili barabara na nchi yetu itaneemeka kwa kuepusha matumizi makubwa ya pesa ya umma."Anagida kidogo tena bilauri yake ya mvinyo huu wenye rangi nyekundu Kama damu ya mzee na kuendelea."Hili halina utata; maana mheshimiwa Rais ameridhia mradi huu; na kama litatokea lolote, atatukingia kifua."Anatabasamu na kuangalia mwitikio wa wajumbe na kuendelea. "Kwanza kabla sijasahau, inabidi Katibu wa hazina na mifuko ya pesa arudi visiwani Kayman kuweka mambo vizuri."

Hapa anamaanisha kuweka mgao wa mzee kwenye akaunti za wana kikoa hiki hatari. Maana, sisi ni binadamu, lolote laweza kutokea, na mabenki ya wenzetu mnavyoyajua; wanaweza kutumia udhuru wowote hata kisingizio kuzuia zile pesa hata kutoboa siri ili ziishie kwenye mifuko yao." Wajumbe wanatikisa vichwa kwa pamoja kukubaliana na mawazo ya bosi wao.

Anatabasamu tena na kuendelea "Hamkumbuki yaliyotokea nchi ya jirani ya Zaire; Rais alipoangushwa na waasi; walivyoanika siri zake kiasi cha kuzuia pesa yake? Sisi hili liwe somo kubwa na muhimu kwetu. Mtu asifanye kosa akaingiza zile pesa kwa majina yetu zaidi ya watoto wetu ambayo nayo yatakuwa chini ya kampuni ya familia. Kwa hili sina shaka sana. Kwa kuziingiza zile pesa kama mali ya kampuni zetu, inakuwa vigumu kugundua kinachoendelea. Isitoshe, likitokea lolote ni rahisi kuua au kubadili jina la kampuni na maisha kuendelea." Anazidi kutabasamu huku akiwavinjari wasikilizaji wake mmoja baada ya mwingine. Nao kama yeye wanatabasamu huku njino zikiwa nje kuonyesha kuwa bosi wao amaeongea pointi. Watanunaje wakati mkubwa alikuwa akibariki dhambi zao na kuhalalisha haramu? Anakunywa tena mvinyo wake na kuendelea huku akiizungusha bilauri yake yenye shingo kama ya korongo na kuendelea. "Katibu ulielezewa kwenye simu. Hukuwapo hapa nchini kuona sura ya kampuni mpya ambayo tumeiita Richmen (M) Development. Hii ni kampuni ambayo itaendeshwa na watu wetu. Hivyo, bado tunangoja wajumbe wa upande wako ili waunde Board of Directors haraka sana. Lazima hili lilifanyike haraka maana hali ya nchi yetu mnaiona isivyotabirika kwa sasa. Na baada ya kampuni hii kuwa na members of Board wetu, itabidi uende Uswisi uifungulie akaunti ya kampuni na baadhi ya pesa zitakazolipwa ziwe wired kule mara moja. Pia uhakikishe inasajiliwa kwa registrar of company na documents zinafichwa. Hakikisha nazo unaziweka kwenye benki kule Hong Kong. Sawa sawa?" Katibu anatakisa kichwa sana kukubaliana na ushauri wa busara wa bosi wake.

Kabla ya kuendelea, waziri wa hazina na mifuko ya pesa ananyoosha mkono kama yuko darasani na kusema. "Mheshimiwa, umeona wambea wa gazeti la Chimbuchimbu walivyokwishaanza kuingilia mradi? Samahani kwa kukuingilia ni baada ya kukumbushia kuwa hali ya nchi yetu haitabiriki na ni kweli haitabiriki." Anaongea akicheka cheka kama mtoto mdogo kuonyesha utii wake kwa Rais na waziri mkubwa. Na hii ilikuwa sifa kuu ya mawaziri wa Mafuriko hata wabunge kumfanya Rais au waziri mkubwa kama Mungu mtu wakati rohoni walikuwa wakimponda na kumhujumu. Waziri mkubwa ambaye huwa na tabia ya kutosoma magazeti asubuhi alionekana mwenye kupigwa na butwaa. Anajibu haraka na kwa mshangao, "You can't be serious!" Anajitahidi kuonyesha uchangamfu huku akifurahia utii wa bandia wa walaji wenzake. Kweli mtumikie Kafiri upate mradi, wahenga walisema.

Habari hii ilionekana kumchefua na kumuyumbisha sana ingawa alijitahidi kutoa tabasamu la uongo. Moyoni hana amani. Maana wabunge wa upinzani walimpa wakati mugumu kupinda na kukwepa hoja zao. Isitoshe kuna tetesi kuwa umoja wa wafanyakazi wa Mafuriko ujulikanao kama Mafuriko Workers Institute for Bringing Accountability (MWIBA),una mpango wa kuitisha mgomo na maadamano nchi nzima kutokana na kukithiri kwa vitendo vya ufisadi na ughali wa maisha kwa umma.

Katibu wa hazina na mifuko ya pesa anachomoa gazeti kwenye mkoba wake; anampa gazeti ajionee habari yenyewe. Kwa unyenyekevu anampa gazeti bosi wake huku na wenzake wakihangaika kuchomoa magazeti yao ili kuonyesha kuwa nao huwa hawapitwi na chochote wakati hawakuwa na muda wa kusoma magazeti.Waziri mkubwa haraka haraka anaanza kusoma ile habari huku akijiweka vizuri kwenye kiti chake cha kuzunguka. Mara ghafla furaha yake inatumbukia nyongo! Maana hakuwa ana habari. Isitoshe huwa na kawaida ya kuchelewa ofisini kwake kutokana na kuanza kuwasiliana na maajenti wa biashara zake zilizotapakaa sehemu mbali mbali duniani. Yeye ni mfanyabishara zaidi kuliko mtawala.Anajisemea ghafla, "Sasa hawa wambea wanalitafuta la kulitafuta. Wanataka kuchezea serikali ya wananchi!"Anaanza kusoma gazeti kwa makini.

Gazeti linasomeka ifuatavyo;

Kichwa cha habari cha gazeti la siku hiyo ni;

Kampuni ya Richmen ni mali ya wakubwa serikalini.

Imegundulika kuwa kampuni ya Richmen iliyoletwa toka nchi ya Munamuna kushughulikia kujenga mitambo ya maji ni kampuni ya kutengeneza sumu za kuulia wadudu.

Pia kampuni hiyo ni mali ya wakubwa wachache waliomo serikalini wanaoitumia kuiibia mali na pesa ya umma kwa manufaa yao binafsi.

Chanzo chetu cha habari toka Munamuna kimeeleza. Yagundulika kuwa Richmen ni bomu.

Habari kamili inasomeka kama ifuatavvyo;

Licha ya kuwa kampuni ya Richmen licha kampuni ndogo isiyo na ithibati wala historia ya mafanikio, ina kesi mahakamani kwa kudanganya kuhusu kiwango cha ubora wa bidhaa zake.

Chanzo chetu kimeendelea kusema kuwa nyuma ya Richmen (M), kuna watu wazito kwenye serikali ya sasa hasa waziri wake mkubwa ambaye kwa kutumia ushawishi na mtandao wake anafanya kila juhudi kuizima kashfa hii. Ametoa onyo kwa wabunge au mtu yeyote atakayeendelea kuipekenyua kashfa hii atakiona cha moto.

Alisita kidogo na kusema. "Unaona hawa wambea wanavyoniingiza moja kwa moja kwenye upuuzi huu? Sasa nitawafilisi na gazeti litasahaulika. Maana huku ni kuchafuliana majina." Aliendelea na kusoma gazeti.

Waziri mkubwa anatoa ufyosi kwa kusonya na kuendelea kusoma huku akitikisa kichwa.

Chanzo chetu cha habari kimezidi kueleza kuwa Richmen kimsingi zipo mbili. Ipo ile iliyoanzishwa miaka minne iliyopita katika nchi ya Munamuna na Richmen Mafuriko iliyoanzishwa mwezi jana.

Gazeti linaendelea.

Licha ya ukweli huu usio na shaka ambao unapatikana hata kwenye mtandao wa internet, serikali imeendelea kukaa kimya sababu za kutoa tenda ya mamilioni ya dola za kimarekani kwa kampuni yenye kutia shaka.

Gazeti hili lilijaribu kuwasiliana na waziri mwenye dhamana. Lakini msemaji wa wizara ameshikilia kuwa tenda nzima ilifanyika kwa uwazi bila aina yoyote wala harufu ya rushwa.

Gazeti hili lilipombana msemaji wa wizara aeleze ni kwanini serikali ilitoa tenda kwanza bila kufuata utaratibu na pili kwa kampuni isiyo na historia wala utaalamu na ujenzi wa mitambo ya maji, msemaji alisema hilo siyo tatizo. Kwani tatizo ilikuwa ni kama kuna rushwa kwenye tenda.

Gazeti linaendelea. Kwa hali ilivyo ni kwamba pesa ya wananchi imeliwa. Kwani licha ya kampuni ya Richmen kushindwa kutimiza kazi yake, imeuza kazi kwa kampuni nyingine yenye kutia mashaka iitwayo Dooms. Hii kampuni ya Dooms, chanzo chetu kimesema inamilkiwa na waziri mkubwa na swahiba wake mwanasiasa mfanya mwenye ushawishi chamani na serikalini.

Katika hali ya kustaajabisha, gazeti linaendelea. Serikali imeunda tume ya kuchunguza kadhia hii ambayo nakala ya ripoti yake itakayotolewa siku chache zijazo inaeleza kuwa zoezi zima lilikidhi vigezo vyote vya utoaji tenda ukiachia mbali zoezi hili kufanywa kwa dharura kulingana na tatizo linaloikabili nchi.

Gazeti linaendelea. Gazeti hili lilipomtaka kutamka ni lini mradi husika ungetegemewa kuwa umeisha, msemaji alisema yeye siyo mjenzi. Ila alisisitiza kuwa vyombo vya habari viache uvivu wa kufikiri angalau viisifie serikali kwa kununua tanki linalohudumia jiji la Neema ingawa si wote wanaopata maji. Lakini angalau wakubwa walikuwa wakipata maji na hivyo kutokabiliwa na kupoteza muda na mawazo kufanya shughuli za umma. Wanaoga na kunywa na hawaendi maofisini wakiwa na uchafu. Hata si haba bustani zao za kuwaliwaza zinapata maji.

Gazeti linaendelea, "Majina ya wenye kuhusika na ufisadi huu tunayo. Na mmojawapo ni afisa mwenye madaraka makubwa na ushawishi serikalini na yuko karibu na kiongozi mwingine mkuu. Mkubwa huyu kwa nje hupenda kujionyesha kama mtu safi na mwenye kuwajali wananchi ukiachia mbali kuwa na historia tata tokana na jinsi alivyopata utajiri wake.

Na huyu ndiye aliyeasisi mpango huu mzima. Wengine katika genge hili hatari ni katibu mmoja wa wizara nyeti sana na waziri mmoja anayeshughulika na masuala ya huduma moja muhimu na hali fulani ya kimaumbile."

Gazeti linaendelea. "Genge hili la majambazi limepinda hata kanuni na maagizo ya baraza la mawaziri kwa kushinikiza wizara nyingine kuridhia jinai hii kutokana na nguvu za mamlaka ya afisa huyu mwandamizi serikali anayeshika nafasi fulani karibu na mwisho wa utawala."

Gazeti linaendelea. "Afisa huyu anasifika kwa tamaa yake kubwa ya utajiri. Maana anasemekana kujilimbikizia mali nyingi kinyume cha sheria. Chanzo chetu kinaarifu: ana mpango wa kugombea hata urais baada ya rais aliyepo kumaliza muda wake." Waziri mkubwa anapofikia wasifu wa watu wanaotuhumiwa na gazeti alisita. Anaweka gazeti mezani na kutoa leso yake tena mfukoni na kujifuta jasho huku akiwa ameduwaa kidogo.

Anashusha pumzi na kusema. "These sons of a bitch. Inaonekana kuna mtu anatuchoma. Wamepata wapi haya mambo yote?" Anauliza huku akionyesha kuchoka hata kuzeeka.

Utadhani katibu wa hazina na mifuko alijua kuwa alikuwa ameulizwa yeye. Alijibu. "Mheshimwa profile ya hii kampuni iko kwenye mtandao. Hivyo inaonekana wame-google na kuipata. Kuhusu viongozi waliopo nyuma ya kampuni, mie naona they are just speculating and guessing altogether. Wangekuwa na uhakika nadhani hakuna striking issue kama hili tunaloongelea. Had they caught wind of it obviously wangemwaga mtama hadharani. Si unajua kiherehere cha vijigazeti vyetu na midomo yao mirefu kama samaki aina ya chuchunge?" Waziri aliamua kujiridhisha. Maana kama wange-google wangegundua mambo mengi kama kutokuwa na ithibati wala mtaji kwa kampuni. Pia wangegundua uongo mkubwa uliokuwa umezagazwa kwenye wavuti wa Kampuni ukidai imeishafanikiwa miradi mingi ulimwenguni wakati siyo.

Wajumbe wanaendelea kukaa kimya bila hata kutikisa vichwa. Kila mmoja amezama kivyake kwenye tafakuri nzito. Anajitenga vizuri kitini na kuendelea, "Mie naona wanajaribu kutuingiza kutokana na ushiriki wetu katika zoezi hili unaotokana na nyadhifa zetu. Out of that, nijuavyo watu wa nchi yetu watashabikia habari hizi kwa kitambo kidogo na baadaye watarejea kwenye mihangaiko yao na kusahau na gazeti litakuwa limeuza nakala nyingi. "That is that" Anamalizia katibu wa hazina na mifuko ya pesa huku akitabasamu. Waziri mkubwa anaonekana kukubaliana naye lakini bado ana wasi wasi. Anauliza, "Do you think this is the only solution mheshimiwa? Kumbuka tangu kuingia kwa uhuru, watu wetu, hasa vyombo vya habari vimegeuka kuwa adui namba moja wa serikali. Vimegeuka upinzani usiosajiliwa." Katibu anajibu. "Importantly ni wewe mheshimiwa kumwambia katibu wa ofisi yako kukanusha uvumi huu haraka iwezekanavyo. Katika kufanya hivyo asitumie lugha ya ukali bali laini ambapo anaweza kuwakaribisha waandishi wa gazeti la chimbuchimbu ofisini kwake na kuwapa vizawadi. Si unajua waandishi wanavyolipwa pesa kidogo na waajiri wao ambao nao ni wanafiki. Maana wanawatumia na kuwanyonya?" Anasogeza gazeti pembeni kidogo na kuendelea.

Waziri wa mifuko ya pesa naye aliongeza pendekezo jingine. Alisema. "Mheshimiwa waziri mkubwa mimi naona ungeamuru tume ya kuzuia rushwa ifanye uchunguzi na kuisafisha serikali haraka. Hassy ni mtu wetu afanye hii kazi haraka."

"Najua watashawishika na kutaka tukiwapa pesa

watanywea. Wakiwa wagumu tunaweza kuwatumia vijana wetu wa kitengo cha kuzuia rushwa. Maana what I surely know hawawezi kukataa pesa ambayo ni kubwa kuliko hata mshahara masihara wao mara mia kwa miaka mia. Kwani huwajui watu wetu?" Anatabasamu huku akimuangalia bosi wake na wenzake ambao wanatikisa vichwa kukubaliana na pendekezo lake.

Anaendelea "They cannot stand seeing bundles of banknotes and leaving them behind to live like paupers." Anatoa pendekezo katibu wa hazina na mifuko ya pesa. Bila kungoja hata waziri mkubwa aseme, waziri wa maji na upepo anaingilia kati. "This may recochete kama ilivyowahi kutokea kwa waziri wa maarifa na usomi. Importantly wangetafutwa watu wa kati wa kuwakabili wahusika. Kwanza wapeleleze wajue ni nani mwenye story hii kuepuka kutumia pesa nyingi hata kwa wasiohusika. Tukishamjua inakuwa rahisi kumshughulikia. Ila inabidi kuwapo umakini wa hali ya juu. Maana hali hii ni tete na tata so to speak."

Katibu anatikisa kichwa kama kukubaliana na mawazo ya katibu wa hazina na mifuko na kusema. "Perfect. Mie naona badala ya kufanya witch hunt, kwanini asikabiliwe mhariri kwa kila mbinu ili aweze kuua story hii. Hili linawezekana kama watapatikana watu mahiri wa kumrubuni. I surely know everybody needs money isitoshe katika hali hii ya ugumu wa maisha. Penye udhia..."

Kabla ya kumaliza katibu anajibu, "Penyeze rupia."

Waziri wa maji na upepo anaingilia bila kungoja waziri mkubwa aeleze mawazo yake. Anasema, "Have you forgotten that bastard. Umesahau kuwa mhariri wa Chimbuchimbu na mmiliki ni mahasimu wetu wakuu wanaopata pesa toka kwa baadhi ya nchi fadhili ambazo licha ya kutoridhika na utendaji wetu haziamini kuwa tunaweza kulinda maslahi yao!"

Anaweka vizuri tai yake na kuendelea. "Tukiingia kwenye nyavu zake anaweza kutumaliza. Namjua Nkweo Nkhwazi nimesoma naye. He is a very shrewd guy. This is but a suicidal attempt so to speak. Maana media is more powerful than you can imagine especially this time around."Katibu wa hazina na mifuko ya pesa hangoji amalize. Anatoa ushauri jinsi ya kulishughulikia gazeti. Anasema. "Kwanini tusimbane kwenye biashara zake kama tulivyowafanyia wafanyabiashara wanaoshabikia upinzani hadi njaa ikawarejesha wakihaha na kulamba matapishi yao? Hamkumuona yule daktari wa sheria alivyorudi mkia miguuni? This is the only viable and reliable way of dealing with them."

Baada ya katibu kutoa ushauri wake hatimaye waziri mkubwa amepata la kusema! Anauliza. "So, tufanye lipi ndugu zangu?" Cheo cha waheshimiwa kilimtoka ghafla. Maana alizoea kuwaita mawaziri, "Mheshimiwa waziri" karibu mara zote alipokuwa akiongea nao. Anaonyesha dalili zote za woga na kuchanganyikiwa tena mbele ya wadogo zake kimadaraka."Well, hapa ni kuhakikisha mzee anatupa uhakika kuwa lolote litakalotokea atakuwa upande wetu." Anajibu Katibu wa Mifuko na fedha. Kabla ya kumaliza waziri mkubwa aliingilia, "Ukiniona mimi umemuona mzee na ukimuona mzee umeniona mimi. Hili siyo tatizo. Kinachotakiwa ni kuwa na maelezo ya kumridhisha. Maana mheshimiwa Rais ameingia mambo haya shingo upande. Na kama siyo mama kutupigia debe saa nyingine usingemsikia kwenye mambo haya."

Anakohoa na kuendelea kuwahakikishia wajumbe mzee alivyo mknoni mwake. "Hivyo, kuhusu kifua cha mzee hilo ondoa shaka kabisa. I am confident and at home over one million per cent." Anasema huku akitabasamu tena kwa mzaa utadhani Rais ni mkewe ambaye anaweza kumuamrisha hata kumsemea atakavyo! Ajabu hata wajumbe wa kigwena hiki hawashangai zaidi ya kucheka cheka utadhani mazuri haya!

Sura za katibu na waziri zinaota furaha na matumaini kugundua kuwa kumbe wana na ngao nzito nyuma yao.

Waziri mkubwa amaendelea. "Mimi nilitaka ku-deal na gazeti kuepuka kuweka picha mbaya kwa wananchi wetu. Kwa mtu anayeona mbali we still need presidency hata baada ya mheshimiwa Rais kumaliza muhula wake. Pamoja na kuongoza nchi hii tutaendelea kuwa na uhakika wa future yetu. Hili tulishalijadili na mzee na kukubaliana kuwa kuacha madaraka hivi hivi kwa watu wasio kwenye net work yako ni kujitia kitanzi kama ilivyotokea kwa Rais wa zamani wa Abimza, Chiliba. Unalijua bara letu. Na isitoshe kuna wabaya wetu hata ndani ya chama chetu wenyewe remember." Anatoa leso yake mfukoni na kujifuta jasho na kuendelea. "Kwanini nisilifungie gazeti hili haraka sana iwezekanavyo huku tukitumia magazeti yetu ya The Independent na Mzawa kudiscredit habari hii?"

Katibu wa mifuko ya pesa hakubaliani na pendekezo la bosi wake. Anakunywa mvinyo wake na kuendelea, "Mzee tutakuwa tunafanya kosa ambalo matokeo yake yanaweza kuturudi na kusababisha kishindo kisicho cha kawaida. Kwani Chimbuchimbu wana backing ya Ujerumani na Scandinavian countries ambao wamewahi kulalamikia jinsi tunavyopambana na ufisadi. Pia tukukubaliane kuwa linasomwa sana nchi nzima. My take on this would be kujadili na adui yako kujua anakupangia nini."

Anaweka miwani yake vizuri usoni na kuendelea, "So, this will be their trump card. Mie naona kukanusha bado ndiyo njia sahihi ya kwanza na kutafuta jinsi ya kuwanyamazisha. Tunaweza kuwanunua baadhi ya wachambuzi wa mambo wenye njaa na tamaa wakapambana nao. Maana hata makala zao wanazochapisha kila siku zinalenga kutupambanisha na wananchi wetu" Anawakazia macho wajumbe akiwamo bosi wake.

Waziri mkubwa anasema, "Hizi nchi tunaweza kuzilainisha kwa kutumia marafiki zetu kama Marekani na Uingereza ambao tumeishafanya biashara nzuri na makampuni yao kama kununua silaha, ndege na mambo mengine." Wakati mkutano ukiendelea simu toka ikulu iliingia ikimhitaji haraka waziri mkubwa akutane na Rais mara moja. Waziri mkubwa anasema. "Mzee ameishapata sumu hii ya press."Aliwageukia wenzake na kusema, "Nakushukuruni sana kwa kuwa wepesi na kuliona hili na kutoa michango yenu adhimu na muhimu. Maana nimeishapata in puts za kumpelekea. Sina wasi wasi. Ananihitaji kujaribu kupanga mikakati ya kupambana na hujuma hii inayoanza kusukwa na watu wa magazeti ya upinzani. Hivyo, naahirisha kikao hadi nitakapopata fursa tena ya kuwaiteni ili tuendelee tulipoishia. Asanteni." Anakunywa tena mvinyo wake. Anamalizia. "Mradi kama tulivyokubaliana, lazima press ishughulikiwe. Na kitu kingine hakikisha jamani siri hazitoki. Nasisitiza. Mnajua ulimwengu tunamoishi." Waziri mkubwa anamalizia huku akimalizia mvinyo wake tayari kuondoka kuelekea ikulu mara moja.

Kabla ya kigwena kuvunjwa katibu wa hazina na mifuko ya umma anasema, "Hivyo mheshimiwa tumekubaliana nguvu isitumike kuwanyamazisha au kuwamaliza wabaya wetu unless otherwise?"

"Ndiyo. Tusianze na njia hii mpaka tutakaoona tumeshindwa na kulazimika kuchuka hatua nyingine hata kama ni kubwa zaidi." Anajibu waziri mkubwa anayeonekana kuchoka ndani ya muda mfupi.

Kigwena kinaisha ghafla na kila mmoja anaanza kuondoka

kuelekea kwenye gari lake tayari kuelekea ofisini kwake kuandaa mikakati ya kupambana na gazeti la Chimbuchimbu. Wakati huu hakuna kisuuza macho chao. Yaani yule nyonda aliyewaletea vinywaji. Isitoshe, joto la jiwe ya kashfa ya Richmen limieshaanza kuzivurujua nyoyo na bongo zao. Hivyo hata angekuwapo wasingekuwa na ithibati ya kumsherehekea kwa macho yao ya ulafu na ukware.

11
Lulu kati ya mawe

Zengeni na mkewe Nengoma walizaliwa kwenye familia za wakulima hasa. Kutokana na mfumo mzuri kisiasa baada ya uhuru wa nchi yao, walifanikiwa kwenda shule hadi kusomea ualimu kwa kugharimiwa na serikali. Hali ingekuwa kama sasa; ambapo serikali imejiingiza kwenye uchuuzi wa roho za watu na mali na miili yao. Huenda wasingesoma kama walivyosoma. Wanalikumbuka sana hili. Hakika limewafundisha uzalendo wa hali ya juu. Hii imekuwa ndiyo kichocheo cha kuikosoa serikali kila wanapoijadili. Maana wanawaona watawala wao kama wezi wa fadhila ambao nao kama wao walisomeshwa na umma wanaounyonya na kuukandamiza. Kwao dhambi hii haina msamaha kwa muungu wowote. Ni usalata unaonuka kama zebaki. Ni kitendo cha unyanyasaji usio na mfano.

Walikutana wakati wakisomea ualimu kwenye chuo cha ualimu cha Maguzoni Teachers Training College, walikosomea stashahada za ualimu katika masomo ya siasa historia lugha na fasihi. Hivyo ni wataalamu wa fasihi kwa viwango vya hali ya juu wanaojadili mambo kwa upeo mkubwa. Ukiwakuta wakivurujua kimaturiko utaona ukweli wa usomi na utaalamu wao wa lugha fasihi na kunga nyingine za kisanaa. Tofauti na watoto wa wakubwa waliosomea nje na kurudi na kila upuuzi wa kizungu, wao huipenda na kuitukuza lugha yao na tamaduni zao. Ni wazalendo wa kupigiwa mfano. Ni sawa na almasi katika udongo wa jangwa wa vijana wa Mafuriko.

Kutokana na kupendana sana waliamua kufunga ndoa walipokuwa wanakaribia kumaliza kozi zao ili kuweza kuajiriwa sehemu moja kama mke na mume bila ya kuhangaishwa na wataka rushwa kama wangeoana baada ya kuanza kazi.

Na kweli walifanikiwa kuajiriwa kwenye shule ya sekondari ya serikali ya Hazina. Mwanzoni waliipenda sana kazi yao hasa somo la fasihi. Kwani liliwapa uwanja mpana wa kuwajenga na kuwapika wanafunzi wao kwa ajili ya kulitumikia vilivyo taifa lao bila kujisahau na kugeuka vikaragosi wa kutumia na wakoloni kuliibia na kulikalia taifa kwa mlango wa nyuma. Zengeni alizoea kuwaambia wanafunzi wao kuwa nchi yao ilikuwa ikitawaliwa na wakoloni kwa kutumia wakolini weusi by proxy hadi wanafunzi wakamuita by proxy. Katika maandalizi ya kazi zao hawakuwa wakipata shida. Maana walikuwa wakifundisha masomo ya aina moja. Walifanikiwa kusoma vitabu vingi sana na kujua mambo mengi. Walifanikiwa kutunga kitabu kiitwacho, "Maskini mama yetu." wakimaanisha Mafuriko iliyokuwa ikiibiwa na kila aina ya vinyamkera na nguchiro tena wa kuzaa yenyewe!

Kitabu hiki hakikuchapishwa kutokana na makali yake na jinsi kilivyoivua nguo serikali. Kila mchapishaji waliyempa mswaada wao aliwaambia ukweli kuwa kitabu chao kilikuwa kizuri. Lakini hakuna mchapishaji aliyekuwa tayari kutangaza vita na watawala kandamizi na nyonyaji wa Mafuriko. Wachapishaji waliogopa jicho kali na mkono mrefu wa serikali ambavyo badala ya kutumika kuwalinda wananchi vilitumika kuwahujumu na kuwaibia! Hivyo hadi leo huwa wanatoa mswaada wao na kuusoma na kuliwazana.

Wameutunza ili watakapopata watoto wao wasome na kufahamu kuwa wazazi wao hawakuwa makondoo ya kufa wanajiona. Walijaribu. Lakini vikwazo vya watawala vikawakwamisha. Wanaamini huenda kuna siku milango ya haki, nuru na uhuru itafunguka na kitabu chao kitachapishwa hata kama kitachapishwa na wajukuu. Maana elimu haiozi na ni dafina ijirudufuyo kila uchao.

Wakati ule elimu ilikuwa na thamani na isitaoshe shule zilikuwa bado zina maadlili kiasi cha kuwa taasisi za kufyatua wanajamii wa baadaye. Huwa wanashangaa vura chafu aliyewavamia wenzao waliokuwa madarakani hadi wakasahau uzalendo na maadili ya jamii!

Zamani elimu ilikuwa ni utu na utumishi wa utu. Ilikuwa ni taa ya kuangazia njia tofauti na ilipogeuzwa kulego la kuzolea utajiri wa umma. Ilikuwa nyenzo siyo mrija na bomba la kunyonyea jasho na damu vya umma. Elimu ilimfanya mtu kuwa mtu zaidi tofauti na sasa ilipomgeuza nyangarika na nunda wa kutisha kiasi cha kumla mwenzie tena bila kujali.

Wakati wakisoma hapakuwa na shule kama miradi ya biashara. Shule zilikuwa ni taasisi za kijamii zilizokuwa zikitegemewa kutoa faida ya watu badala ya pesa. Zilikuwa chemi chemi za maadili siyo makaburi yake. Ulikuwa ni uwekezaji namba moja katika jamii badala ya vitu. Wakati ule hapakuwa na biashara ya tuisheni wala kuiba mitihani. Walimu walichapa kazi kweli kweli na kuonea fahari mchango wao kwa vizazi ambavyo vingefuata baada ya wao kuzeeka na kutoweka. Jamii kwa upande mwingine ilitambua na kuthamini mchango wa walimu kiasi cha kuwa taa yao badala ya aibu na mtihani.

Elimu iliwekeza kwenye mstakabali wa taifa na siyo wa watu binafsi na matumbo yao. Haikuwa nazaa na msiba kama ilivyokuja kugeuka baada ya kuzuka wizi wa mitihani na kughushi vyeti.

Hivyo, mwanzoni Zengeni na mkewe waliishi kwa raha mstarehe kwenye nyumba yao ya kazi waliyokuwa wamepewa na serikali. Isitoshe wangeishije kwa shida wakati maisha wakati ule yalikuwa yana tafsiri inayofahamika kabla ya mambo kuharibika na maisha kugeuka fumbo tata? Kila mtu alikula matunda ya jasho lake. Utu ulikuwa na thamani kuliko pesa hata kama zingekuwa za kigeni. Muda si muda mambo yalianza kubadilika na kuharibika. Pepo wa kusaka utajiri aliikumba jamii ghafla kiasi cha kujikuta ikisambaratishwa na tamaa na laghba kula namna. Zilianzishwa shule za binafsi ambazo kiasi fulani zilikuwa zimelenga kutengeneza pesa badala ya wasomi. Uzuri wa shule hizi kwa upande mmoja zililipa mshahara mnono kuliko wa serikali. Na karo zilizotozwa zilikuwa zinalingana angalau na kipato cha wananchi. Hapakuwa na international academies na makorokoro mengine na makando kando yake vilivyowageuza watoto wayai badala ya wapambanaji wa baadaye.

Kutokana na waliko kuwa wametoka yaani kwenye shule za serikali, iliwachukua muda mrefu kuanza kufikiria kuacha kazi kwenye shule za serikali na kwenda shule za binafsi. Kwao mwanzoni malipo yao ya mshahara hayakuwa na uzito kama kuona wanawafundisha wanafunzi wanafanikiwa katika masomo yao na baadaye maisha yao. Hili hakika liliwapa faraja kama walimu na wazazi wa baadaye na tena wanajamii. Kwao ualimu ulikuwa ni uongozi tena wa kitume. Mwalimu alikuwa ni kichwa siyo makanyagio ya jamii kama ilivyokuja kuwa baadaye. Alikuwa ni kiongozi wa pili baada ya wazazi.Maana waliozoea kuwaambia wanafunzi wao kuwa baada ya wao kuzeeka, wale wanafunzi wao wangekuwa walimu wa watoto wao. Hivyo waliwahimiza wapikwe na kuiva ili watakapochukua nafasi zao wasiwapikie vitu visivyoiva kiasi cha kuliangamiza taifa. Hapakuwa na walimu mfubao wa miezi michache mafunzoni wala ualimu pasina elimu.

Furaha yao iliongezeka zaidi kutokana na wanafunzi kuwaheshimu na kuwapenda wakifanya idili katika masomo yao ya darasani na vitendo. Walizoea kupokea wageni nyumbani mwao. Wageni hawa walikuwa ni wanafunzi waliokuwa wakija kutafuta ushauri mbali mbali. Walianza majukumu ya wazazi hata kabla ya kupata watoto wao wa kuzaa. Kwao wanafunzi wao walikuwa ni watoto na wadogo zao. Walifarijika sana kutimiza wajibu huu adhimu.wazai kwa upande wao licha ya kuwathamini na kuwaamini walishirikiana nao kuwalea watoto wa jamii ili wawarithishe majukumu baadaye. Hizi ni zama za dhahabu ambazo kurejeshwa ni riiya ya mchana kama mambo hayatachukua mkondo mpya wa kukengeuka na kulisaka jibu sahahi haraka.

Majukumu ya walimu hawa vijana waliojivunia kazi yao hayakuishia darasani tu. Kwani Zengeni aliteuliwa kuwa mwalimu mkuu msaidizi huku mkewe akiteuliwa kuwa mwalimu wa nidhamu na malezi pale shuleni.

Majukumu haya mapya pamoja na kuwafariji kuwa mchango wao katika shule ulikuwa unatambulika, yaliwaatia hamasa ya kufanya kazi. Lakini yalikuwa yanakula muda wao mwingi kiasi cha kujikuta wakichoka kila uchao. Kutokana na upya wa kazi na mapenzi kwa kazi yao, hawakufanya haraka kuzaa. Hasa ikizingatiwa kuwa bado walikuwa na mambo mengine katika maandalizi ya familia kama vile kuweka pesa ili baadaye wajenge nyumba yao ukiachia mbali kusaidia familia za pande mbili za wazazi wao. Katika upande wa familia kulikuwa na ndugu waliohitaji msaada kusoma hasa wadogo zao ambao nao wangependa wawe kama wao. Hivyo sehemu kubwa ya mishahara yao ilielekezwa kuwasaidia ndugu kielimu ili baadaye wajitegemee na kuwasaidia wengine. Kulifanikisha jukumu hili kwa jamii kuliwapa faraja kuliko hata kununua gari au kujenga jumba la fahari hata kama wangepata pesa. Zengeni alizoea kuwashauri wenzake kuwa ukiwekeza kwenye watu utavuna utu na ukiwekeza kwenye vitu utatawaliwa na vitu. Kwake kuwekeza kwenye vitu badala ya utu ulikuwa ni mafamba na tendo lisilopaswa kufanywa na mtu au jamii yenye akili timamu zaidi ya ukichaa. Kwake jamii ilikuwa ni kila kitu.

Kutokana na shule za serikali kutokidhi kuchukua wanafunzi wote waliokuwa wakimaliza shule za msingi, umuhimu wa kusomesha kwenye shule za sekondari za binafsi ambazo mwanzoni zilionekana kama miradi ya biashara uliongezeka. Kwa shingo upande, ilibidi wawakubalie ndugu zao waliokosa nafasi kwenye shule za serikali. Maana heri moja pata kuliko kenda rudi.

Taratibu wazazi walianza kuziamini hasa baada ya kuona matunda yake. Shule za binafsi zilianza kubadilika taratibu na kuwa na lengo lile lile la kuzalisha jamii ya wasomi wa baadaye ingawa zilizalisha faida kwa wamilki wake. Na hii ilitokana na serikali kutozipa ruzuku ukiachia mbali misaada midogo midogo kama mihtasari na ushauri kwa kitaaluma, ukaguzi na wakati mwingine miongozo. Hata hivyo baadaye shule hizi zilikuja kugeuka zimwi jingine baada ya kirusi cha utajiri kuishambulia na kuikalia jamii ya Mafuriko.

Kama siyo maafisa wachoyo na fisadi waliokuwa wakizipendelea shule zilizowahonga au kuwa na hisa katika shule hizo, shule za binafsi hazikuwa na ubaya wowote. Baadaye ugonjwa huu wa ulafu ulitamalaki kiasi cha elimu kuwa biashara na stahiki ya wenye nazo. Bahati mbaya waliotunga sheria za kulinda upogo huu ni wale wale waliosomeshwa na serikali kutokana na wazazi wao kuwa makabwela na fukara wa kunuka! Yote hii ilitokana na watu kuanza kufikiri kwa kamasi na matumbo badala ya ubongo kiasi cha kuwa manyang'au na wabinafsi wa kutupwa.

Hivyo, wahitaji wa misaada waliongezeka kutokana na kila mzazi kutaka watoto wake wasome hata kama ni shule za binafsi. Maana kwa wazazi wakati ule hapakuwa na urithi wenye thamani sawa na elimu. Hii ni kabla madawa ya kulevya na wizi wa pesa ya umma kuanza kuwa vitu vya kukubaliwa na jamii.

Hali hii kwa mara ya kwanza ilianza kuilazimisha familia ya changa ya Zengeni kuanza kufikiria jinsi ya kuongeza kipato ili kuweza kuendana na mahitaji ya wakati ule. Maana walijihisi kama ni jukumu lao bila hata ya kinyongo wala malalamiko. Hivyo, kwa mara ya kwanza walianza kufikiria kuhamia kwenye shule za watu binafsi. Hii ndiyo njia pekee ambayo ingewaongezea mshahara ili kuendana na mahitaji yaliyokuwa yakiongezeka huku maisha ya wananchi kwa ujumla yakizidi kuwa magumu kutokana na kuvurugika kwa uchumi. Hii ni baada ya watawala kujiingiza kwenye wizi na ufisadi badala ya kuwajibika na kuchapa kazi. Mwanzoni rafiki yao na mwalimu mwenzao aliyeitwa Mipawa alipohamia kwenye shule ya binafsi walimcheka hata kumuona kama alikuwa amechukua uamuzi wa kibinafsi kwa kujali maslahi yake badala ya jamii. Hawakujua kuwa kungetokea siku nao wangemfuata Mipawa waliyezoea kumuita Pawa. Na alikuwa Pawa kweli. Kwani alikuwa ni kiumbe asiyeficha hisia zake wala kuyumba kwenye msimamo wake hata kama ungezusha utata kama kuamua kuhamia kwenye shule ya binafsi.

Walifundisha kwenye shule za serikali kwa muda wa miaka mitano. Baada ya hapo hali iliwalazimisha kuhamia kwenye shule za binafsi. Shule yao ya kwanza iliitwa Ubiri. Ilikuwa ni shule ya kwanza ya sekondari ya binafsi katika wilaya ya soni mkoani Usambachi. Walifundisha pale kwa miaka saba. Katika miaka ya ualimu wao, walijikuta kila siku wakipambana na changamoto mbali mbali mpya. Kiasi cha kujihisi wamao safarini kutafuta mafanikio kihalali bila kuwaumiza wengine.

Mwanzoni changamoto ilikuwa ni kuhama toka shule za serikali kwenda shule za binafsi ambako walidhani angalau wangepata jawabu la kiu yao ya maslahi ambayo yangewawezesha kukamilisha ndoto za wadogo zao.

Lakini kadri mambo yalivyokuwa yakibadilika haraka, kwa mara ya kwanza na kwa maskitiko ya aina yake, walijikuta wakianza kufikiria kuachana na kazi waliyoipenda tangu utoto wao. Kazi iliyokuwa ni ya heshima kuliko kazi zote. Kazi ya kutumia kichwa badala ya mikono. Kazi ya ualimu. Kazi ya utume. Hata hivyo hawakuwa na jinsi bali kukubaliana na hali na wakati. Baada ya mambo na mifumo mipya tatanishi na popo kuanza kuingia kwenye utawala wa Mafuriko, taratibu kazi ya ualimu ilianza kupoteza mvuto wake na kuwa wito badala ya taaluma.

Kuja kwa tafsiri hii mpya, mbaya na potofu kulisababisha walimu kuanza kupata mishahara yao ikiwa imechelewa ukiachia mbali kutopanda madaraja na mishahara kwa muda mrefu. Ualimu uligeuka ghafla kuwa adhabu na umaskini na kazi ya watu waliofeli mitihani yao!

Walimu walianza hata kuwa kama mayatima na wasio na thamani kwenye jamii huku gulagula wachache serikalini wakiibukia kuwa wakwasi wa kutupwa. Wazazi walianza kuwaonya watoto wao waliokuwa shuleni kutochagua ualimu ambao ulifananishwa na umaskini wa kujitakia. Badala yake uhasibu, sheria na hata uchungaji vilianza kuonekana kazi za heshima na kipato! Lahaula! Zengeni na mkewe na wenye msimamo kama wao ghafla walijikuta wameachwa msambaweni!Hivyo, hali hii ilichangia kuwashawishi Zengeni na Nengoma kubadili welekeo. Maisha ni mapambano ambayo mwisho wake ni kifo. Hivyo Zengeni na mkewe iliwabidi wakiwa Roma waishi kama warumi. Ilibidi wabwage manyanga na kusoma alama za nyakati teana kwa usahihi. Huu ndiyo usomi ambao siku zote ukitumika vizuri; mwenye kuupata hapaswi kubangaiza. Walitaataa wakitafuta mwelekeo usiokwenda kwenye jinai. Kitu wanachojivunia kwenye kazi ya ualimu ni kuweza kuwasaidia ndugu zao bila kubagua wala kubishana. Walijiwekea utaratibu wa kusaidia idadi sawa toka pande zote mbili za mbari zao kwa usawa. Walizidi kufarijika kutokana na pande mbili kukubali hali yao na kila msaada walioweza kuutoa. Kilichowafanya ndugu zao wawaeheshimu na kuwapenda zaidi ni ile hali ya kuwapa misaada bila masharti masimango wala majivuno.

Kwa muda wa ualimu wao walikuwa wamesaidia watu wengi sana. Wengi wa wale waliokuwa wamewasaidia walikuwa na nafasi nzuri kimaisha kuliko hata wao. Na hii iliwazidishia furaha ambalo kwao ndilo likuwa tunu kuliko utajiri. Zengeni alizoea kusema ni heri kulala kwenye banda la makuti kwa amani kuliko hekaluni kwa mashaka.

Wapo walioonyesha shukrani na hata wapo walioiba fadhila hata wakati mwingine kuwasengenya kuwa walikuwa ni familia maskini wasijue wao hao hao ndiyo walikuwa utajiri pekee Nengoma na Zengeni walikuwa nao.

Mara nyingi, watu walipokuja kumshukuru kwa kuwasaidia, Zengeni na mke wake walizoea kuwaambia wale watu nao waende wasaidie wengine kama walivyosaidiwa. Wale waliokuwa wameamua kuiba fadhila walizoea kujiliwaza kwa kusema tenda wema uondoke malipo ni kwa mola.

Alizoea kuwaambia wale waliotambua mchango wao kuwa kuelimika ni sawa na ndege mmoja kulifuma shamba la ulezi. Badala ya kula na kulewa shibe na kusaza, ndege mfuma shamba aliwajibika kwenda kuwaita wenzake ili nao wafaidi alichofaidi. Alizoea kusema kuwa kwake kumjenga mtu ni kujenga umati badala ya kujenga nyumba kwanza wakati ndugu wakiteseka ambapo angeweza kuwabadilishia maisha.

Bahati mbaya wajenga watu walikuwa ni wachache tena wasio na nafasi na wale waliokuwa nazo walijenge vitu kiasi cha kuota kutu kwenye mafamba haya!

12
Mkubwa mwenye moyo mdogo!

Kwa upande wa pili wa maisha, Rais Jack Mfurufu Kitwitwi alikuwa ofisini kwake akimngojea waziri wake mkubwa. Pamoja na urais na madaraka yake, siku hii Rais alikuwa amechukia na kustuka kiasi cha kuwa na woga ni wapi habari hizi nyeti zilikuwa zimepatikana na zingeifikisha wapi serikali yake na maslahi yake binafsi?

Ilifikia mahali akawa kama pelele huku akiongea peke yake kama hamnazo! Hapa ndipo udhaifu wa binadamu ulijitokeza bayana. Maana alikuwa akibatua ofisini kwake toka pembe hadi kona asijue aanzie wapi na kuishia wapi.

Alianza kumlaumu waziri mkubwa kwa kumtia matatani huku ujoho na uamisi wake ukimuishia na kuzama kwenye uchusichusi na mawazo mazito akichelea nafasi na madaraka yake vilivyokuwa vimehatarika si kawaida tangu akalie kiti cha enzi.

Kilichoongeza chumvi kwenye donda ni ile hali ya kashfa kuwa sehemu ya utawala wake tangu alipokuwa ameufuma. Maana bila ya rushwa na wananchi kuichoka serikali ya mtangulizi wake, hakuwa na sifa wala sera za kuiongoza nchi. Hakuwa na bao na hili alilijua ingawa hakulipokea kamani. Alijikuta kizimbani peke yake huku ofisi yake akiiona kama ganjo. Hakujaliwa elimu kubwa wala hekima na maarifa ya kiutawala. Alikuwa ni mtu wa starehe na mwenye kufanya kila jambo kuwa kama mzaha. Ilifikia mahali wachambuzi wakasema huwa anatoa majibu mepesi kwa masuala magumu huku mambo makubwa akiyafanya madogo na madogo akiyafanya makubwa!

Nani angemkengeua iwapo alikuwa amejizungushia wigo

wa wapambe wapumbavu na wasasi ngawira wenye uchu kama fisi wa mali na madaraka wakimtumia kama kijiko kuneemeka?

Lao ilikuwa ni kumsifu hata walipopaswa kumlaumu. Maisha yaligeuka karamu haramu huku umma ulikuwa umefanya kosa kumuamini kwa kumchagua ukiangamia. Hata wale vibaka waliochomwa walikuwa wapiga kura wake.

Uoza na utupu wa kisera ndiyo vitu pekee vilivyomsaidia vikichanganywa na kutoa ahadi nyingi kwa wapiga kura asizitekeleze.

Pesa alikuwa anaitaka ili kufidia ile chama chake na marafiki zake walizotumia kuwahonga wananchi na hatimaye kuchaguliwa kwa kura nyingi. Lakini kuchaguliwa kipindi kingine na kuondoka angalau bila siri zake kufumka alivitaka zaidi ya kila kitu. Huyu ndiye Rais mshaufu na shufaa nyuma ya pazia! Ni mtu kituko aliyepigwa na matendo yake na wenzake asijue hata jinsi ya kujinasua. Kweli ndege mwigo hunaswa na tundu bovu walisema wahenga.

Licha ya kununa na kutikisika, Rais,pamoja na kujua mpango mzima wa uingizaji wa Richmen, alikuwa ameanza kufikiria kukubaliana na baadhi ya ushauri wa washauri wake waliokuwa wamemshauri avunje baraza la mawaziri na kumtimua waziri mkubwa na baadhi ya mawaziri waliokuwa wakiandamwa na kashfa mbali mbali mara kwa mara. Maana ilikuwa imeishaanza kumkera na kula muda na mawazo yake mengi. Kwani kila kulipokucha tuhuma zidi ya mawaziri wake zilikuwa zinaongezeka hasa waziri mkubwa kutokana na historia yake ya kupenda sana pesa na madaraka. Alianza kumhofia na kumuona kama adui wake namba moja. Upande mwingine alipokumbuka jinsi alivyomsaidia kuchangisha pesa ya kuhongea wapiga kura na kuunda mitandao ya ushindi, alijikuta katikati asijue aambue lipi. Hali hii ilimnyima raha sana Rais ingawa waziri mhusika licha ya kumasaidia kwenye kampeni mbinu mbali mbali za kuwashinda wapinzani wake, alikuwa rafiki yake mkubwa. Lakini hali ilivyokuwa, ilikuwa ni lazima Rais ataofautishe majukumu yake kwa umma uliokuwa umemchagua na urafiki na mambo binafsi hata kama rafiki yake alimsaidia kupata urais. Umma haukujua hili na hakutaka ulijue. Hivyo hapa akiwa njia panda, alipaswa kuchagua kati ya waliomchangua na waliomuwezesha kuchaguliwa!

Alipokuwa akikumbuka alivyokuwa akiombekeza wakati wa kuapishwa kuwa angewatumikia wananchi, alichoka kabisa. Maana roho ilimsuta. Hakuwa akiwatumikia wala kuwafaa. Hakufaa hata kwake mwenyewe katika hali hii yenye ombwe na kigegezi. Alijihisi kama bahau kama asingechukua hatua mujarabu.

Licha ya tuhuma dhidi ya mawaziri wake na serikali yake kwa ujumla, kulikuwa pia na malalamiko dhidi ya familia yake. Baadhi ya malalamiko toka kwa wananchi yaliyofanya waanze kumchukia yeye na serikali yake ni kutotekeleza ahadi alizokuwa ametoa kwa wananchi. Pamoja utajiri wa haraka haraka waliokuwa wanaanza kuwa nao ndugu zake ulianza kuwafanya wananchi wamchukie Rais. Hali hii ilifanya watu wamuone kama ameingia madarakani kuchuma siyo kutoa huduma kama alivyokuwa amewaahidi. Tabia yake ya kutoyatolea majibu malalamiko ya wananchi ilizidi kuhatarisha mstabali mzima wa serikali yake.Wakati bomu hili la kuleta kampuni hewa linalipuka Rais alikuwa madarakani kwa miaka miwili bila kutimiza hata ahadi hata moja ukiachia mbali kukabiliwa na shutuma za matumizi makubwa na fisadi ya pesa za umma. Ahadi alizokuwa ametimiza ni zile za siri yaani kuwazawadia vyeo marafiki zao ambao wengi hawakuwa hata na robo ya sifa za vyeo hivyo na kuendelea kuliibia taifa na kulidanganya. Alizidi kuwaudhi wananchi kwa tabia yake ya kupenda ziara Ulaya na nchi za jirani kwa visingizio mbali mbali. Mara kwenda nchi fulani kujitambulisha kana kwamba wananchi wa nchi hizo walikuwa ndiyo wamemwajiri.

Pia kulikuwa na shutuma dhidi ya tabia ya mke na watoto wake kupenda kuandamana naye kwenye ziara zake tena kwenye madaraja ya juu kwenye ndege.Ukiachia mbali familia yake, kulikuwa kumezuka mtindo wa Rais kusafiri mara kwa mara na ujumbe mkubwa ambao ulikuwa mzigo kwa walipa kodi na uchumi wa nchi. Watoto wake nao waligeuka kuwa kama marais wadogo! Walichaguliwa na nani? Usiulize! Watu wa Mafuriko wamempachika jina la Vasco da Gama yule jambazi wa Kireno aliyesifika kuizunguka dunia akipora kama yeye aporavyo maskini wa Mafuriko.Malalamiko hayakuishia hapo. Kulikuwa na madai kuwa taasisi ya mke wake isiyo ya kiserikali ilikuwa ikichukuliwa na wananchi kama uchochoro wa kuibia na kujipatia pesa kiasi cha wananchi kulalamika kuwa ikulu yao ilikuwa ikitumiwa vibaya kwa maslahi binafsi. Hii iliongezwa makali na kufumka kwa kashfa iliyokuwa ikimhusisha Rais wa zamani wa nchi jirani aliyekuwa akifanya biashara na kujipatia mikopo toka kwenye taasisi za umma akiwa madarakani.Wananchi walishangaa ni kwanini mke wa Rais angoje mume wake aingie madarakani ndipo aanzishe taasisi isiyo ya kiserikali wakati inapingana na hali ya mumewe kuwa mwenye serikali!

Sarafu na uchumi wa nchi ya Mafuriko vilikuwa vinaporomoka huku shida kwa wananchi zikiongezeka. Wakati nadama hii ikiikumba Mafuriko benki kuu iliendelea kutoa taarifa za kukua kwa uchumi wakati ukweli ulikuwa kinyume!

Baadhi ya wachambuzi wa masuala ya kijamii walizoea kusema sarafu na uchumi vilikuwa vinaugua ngwengwe na kipindupindu. Ufisadi na wizi navyo havikujivunga. Vilikuwa vinaongezeka kiasi cha kutishia mshikamano wa taifa na mamlaka ya Rais. Maana tofauti ya kipato baina ya maskini walio wengi na watawala wachache ilkuwa kubwa kiasi cha kutisha.Gazeti la Chimbuchimbu kwenye moja ya tahariri zake liliwahi kuandika kuwa Rais alikuwa amewasaliti wananchi na kuwatelekeza kwa kuendekeza urafiki na masuala binafsi tena ya hovyo. Liliuita utawala wake fools' paradise full of parasites!Mhariri wa gazeti hili aliitwa kwenye ofisi za taasisi ya habari iitwayo UFAFANUZI na kupewa karipio. Pamoja na kupewa karipio, gazeti la Chimbuchimbu lilipania kumuumbua Rais kutokana na kusema tofauti na alivyokuwa akitenda. Serikali ilisahau kuwa kulikuwa na mamlaka ambayo haikuwa na uwezo wa kuinyamazisha ya MWIBA. Maana wafanyakazi walijua umuhimu wao kwa uhai wa serikali. Na isitoshe katika nchi jirani kulikuwa kumeishaangusha serikali dhalimu kwa kutumia hoja na nafasi ya wafanyakazi. Kwa hiyo, ukichanganya mambo yote haya, Rais alikuwa anaanza kujikuta kwenye hali mbaya sana kuliko wakati wowote na kinyume na matarajio yake na watu wake. Wapo wasaidizi wake waliokuwa wakiyaona haya yote. Lakini waliamua kufumba macho na kuongeza bidii ya kuiba ili likitokea la kutokea wawe angalau wameishajipatia mapesa mengi.

Rais licha ya kuvurugwa na marafiki zake, hata chama chake kilichomwingiza madarakani kilikuwa na nafasi yake na sehemu yake katika kukuza matatizo na shinikizo kwa Rais. Kwani kadri siku zilivyokuwa zikienda, chama na makada wake walijitokeza kuwa serikali ndani ya serikali bila Rais kugutuka na kuchukua hatua.

Ilifikia mahali chama kikaonekana kama kilikuwa na nguvu kuliko serikali. Na ilikuwa vigumu kuchora mpaka baina ya serikali na chama! Chama nacho pia kutokana na kuwa na utitiri wa walaji, kiliongezea pigo jingine kwenye matatizo na hatari viliyokuwa yanaikabili serikali ya mheshimiwa Rais wa Mafuriko iliyokuwa imefurika dhiki na ufisadi badala ya mafanikio kama Rais alivyokuwa amewaahidi wananchi wakati wa kampeni za uchaguzi uliokuwa umemuingiza madarakani.Huku nyuma maofisa wa ofisi ya waziri mkubwa walimtaarifu katibu wake mkuu wake wa usalama kufunga barabara haraka ili waziri aende kwa Rais kujua kulikoni.

Watawala wa Mafuriko walipenda sana sifa. Isingewezekana Rais au waziri mkubwa kusafiri popote hata kama hapakuwa na umuhimu bila kufunga barabara huku akiandamana na msafara mkubwa bila sababu. Hata kwenye shughuli za misiba na harusi walionekana kama wanafanya shughuli za kiserikali! Walilewa madaraka na madaraka yakawalevya kweli kweli. Ilifikia mahali hata watu wakaanza kulalamika kuwa inakuwaje Rais na maofisa wake wafunge bara bara mara kwa mara kiasi cha kukwamisha shughuli za uzalishaji mali zilizokuwa zikiendesha maisha yao ya dezo tena bila kulipa hata kodi ya serikali. Pamoja na haki ya kufunga barabara kutokuwa kwenye katiba chakavu ya Mafuriko iliyokuwa imefurika viraka vya marekebisho ya kukipendelea chama kilichokuwa kikitawala, watawala waligeuza tabia hii kuwa haki kwa mujibu wa sheria zao za bandia nyuma ya pazia na upenzi wa madaraka na mbwembwe bila kujali kuwa wananchi wa kawaida walikuwa wakiathirika kwa tabia hii mbaya! Kwao raha zao zilikuwa muhimu na lazima kuliko maisha ya wale waliowawezesha kupata madaraka yaani wapiga kura. Zengeni alizoea kuwaita malaya. Kwani alizoea kusema kuwa malaya akishamalizana na mteja wake huwa hata hakumbuki jina lake kadhalika na mteja huwa hakumbuki hata sura ya malaya wake! Pia Zengeni aliwahi kuhoji walichokuwa wakihofia Rais na maofisa wake kwa kufunga barabara. Aliwakumbusha kuwa kabla ya kupata madaraka walikuwa wakisafiri raha mstarehe bila kufunga barabara tena wengine wakienda kwenye harusi na madansi na kurejea makwao salama salimini.Aliuliza kuna nini na nia gani nyuma ya pazia? Maskini hakujua kuwa baada ya Rais kuupata urais kulikuwa na mipango michafu nyuma ya pazia! Alikumbushia kuwa tabia ya kufunga bara bara ilikuwa ya kizamani na yenye hasara kwa taifa. Hivyo alikuwa amependekeza ikomeshwe maana nchi ilikuwa ni mali ya watu wote kwa sawa bila kujali nafasi wala cheo cha mtu.

Pamoja na kushauriwa na kujua madhara ya kufunga barabara na kuandamana na misafara mirefu ya magari, wakubwa wa Mafuriko walikuwa vichwa ngumu. Hawakutaka kuondokana na ukale huu uliokuwa umeanza kuonekana kama ukoloni kwa wananchi waliokuwa wameishakinai serikali yao. Maana baadhi ya wananchi walisema wazi wazi kuwa wakoloni weusi walikuwa hatari kuliko weupe! Mwenye nguvu mpishe. Barabara zilifungwa bila kujali kama kulikuwa na watu wanaoathirika ama kulalamika wawe wagonjwa au waendao kazini! Barabara zilikuwa zinafungwa bila kujali kuwa wafanyakazi wadogo wanapochelewa kazini huadhibiwa hata kufukuzwa kazi wakati wakubwa hawakuwa na wa kuwaadhibu. Maana hawakuwa wakiwajibika kwa wananchi kama ilivyokuwa ikisema katiba. Waliwajibika kwa matumbo yao. Kama kulikuwa na ugonjwa uliowasumbua wakuu wa Mafuriko bila kutibika haukuwa mwingine bali kupenda ukubwa na mambo makubwa. Karibu kila waziri alipenda kuandamana na msururu wa magari. Nani angejali iwapo shibe ya wakubwa ilikuwa ndiyo amani ya nchi hata kama wadogo waliofanya kosa kuwaamini walikuwa wanateketezwa na maradhi ujinga na njaa? Ama kweli walijua kuwatumia watu badala ya kuwatumikia! Walijua kuwachuuza wananchi wao wakidai wanawaongoza! Wakuu wa mikoa hata wilaya nao hawakubaki nyuma. Walikuwa wakiandamana na misururu ya migari ya bei mbaya kwenye vituo vyao vya kazi. Ilikuwa ni kufuru hasa ikizingatiwa kuwa wakati wakifanya utapanyaji huu wa kifedha wananchi wengi walikuwa wakifa kwa magonjwa mbali mbali ambayo yangeweza kuzuilika hata kutibika tena kwa pesa kidogo kuliko waliyokuwa wakiiunguza.

Wakubwa hawa kila walipo kwenda walijizungushia misafara ya wapambe, walinzi na marafiki. Hali ilikuwa inatisha. Kwa mtu mgeni asiyejua hali za wanavijiji wa Mafuriko asingesita kufikia hitimisho kuwa nchi maskini ya Mafuriko ilikuwa tajiri wa kupindukia.

Kuna kipindi wananchi walilalamika kuhusu matumizi mabaya ya kifahari. Waziri wa usafirishaji hakusita kuwapa vipande vyao kuwa walikuwa wakitumia magari ya hadhi zao! Mwingine aliwaambia kuwa nchi haikuwa tayari kutawaliwa na watu wa hadhi ya kawaida!

Nani angejali wakati kwao kuwa serikalini ilikuwa ni kama karamu ya kufarijiana na kufadhiliana kwa kufuata ukoo na urafiki? Nani angejali iwapo wananchi walikuwa hawana tofauti na mateka na wakimbizi ndani ya nchi yao huku wakitekwa na wale waliofanya makosa kuwaamini? Ajabu waziri aliyeropoka hivi alikuwa ametoka kwenye ukoo maskini wa kunuka. Hata jimbo lake la uchaguzi lilikuwa maskini sana ukilinganisha na majimbo mengine nchini Mafuriko. Katika hali hizi zote mbili mtu wa kawaida alikuwa mwenye kudhurika. Kwani mkutano ulikuwa umesababisha barabara kufungwa haukuwa na maslahi kwao bali kuzidi kuwatia matatani. Kama kawaida haukuwa mkutano bali kigwena.

13
Kambale wote wana sharubu

Waziri mkubwa alifika ikulu salama salimini. Alimkuta bosi wake -Bwana Rais- akiwa anamngoja kwa udi na uvumba. Aliongozana na wapambe wa Rais: Waliomsindikiza bila kusita moja kwa moja kuelekea ndani; na kutokomea kwenye jumba la bei mbaya; ambalo ni ofisi na makao ya Rais. Kama kawaida ya itifaki uchwara, waziri mkuu alikuwa na askari wa usalama barabarani maalumu wa kumuongoza mheshimiwa -mwenye nchi yake namba tatu! Vibweka haviishi hapa. Kwani wapambe wa mlangoni walimpa saluti zake na kuwaachia wanaofuata; nao watekeleze wajibu wao.Walinzi walijiwahi kumlaki wengine kwa saluti wengine kwa tabasamu. Yeye hakuhangaika nao. Angehangaika nao vipi wakati ni vibarua wake waliopo kwa ajili yao usiku na mchana; watake wasitake? Wakubwa wa Mafuriko kwa nyodo, nani angewafikia? Pamoja na watumishi hawa kuchangamka huku wengine wakikenua, waziri mkubwa alikuwa akiwapita utadhani walikuwa miti! Hata miti ina unafuu. Maana ukitembelea bustani angalau husimama hapa na pale kunusa au kuangalia maua huku ukiyachuma au kuyagusa. Kwa nchi zilizochelewa kuendelea, hii ndiyo alama ya ukuu hata uwe ukuukuu na ukale.

Wakubwa wa Mafuriko walikuwa wakijulikana kwa unyanyasaji wao wa watumishi wa umma na wananchi kwa ujumla. Kuna waziri mkubwa mmoja hapo zamani alinusurika kukumbwa na kashfa ya unyanyasaji baada ya askari aliyekuwa akilinda nyumba yake kutaka kumpiga mkewe risasi. Hii ilitokea baada ya askari kwenda kwenye bomba la waziri mkubwa na kunywa maji. Alikunywa maji vizuri na akaiweka bilauri aliyokuwa kanywea kwenye vyombo vichafu na kurudi zake lindoni. Ajabu mke wa waziri mkubwa kumbe alikuwa akimuangalia na hakupenda kuchangia vyombo na viumbe wanaoweza kuwalida ingawa walikuwa wakiwaibia. Mama alikuja na kuchukua ile bilauri na kuivunjilia mbali asijue kuwa kumbe na askari naye alikuwa akimuangalia! Kama siyo waziri kubembeleza na kumhoga yule askari, angeumbuka.

Baada ya kuingia ndani waziri mkubwa alikutana na waziri kwenye ofisi ya Rais aliyemlaki kwa tabasamu pana na kumsindikiza hadi mlango wa kuingia kwenye ofisi ya Rais na kuishia hapo. Maana mkutano huu ulikuwa ni watu wawili yaani Rais na waziri wake mkubwa rafiki na msiri wake. Kazi ya waziri wa ofisi ya Rais iliishia hapo. Hivyo alimuaga bosi wake na kutokomea ndani kwenye ofisi yake kuendelea kuchapa kazi. Isitoshe, waziri mkubwa alikuwa karibu sana na Rais kuliko hata makamu wake ambaye hakutaka makuu.Wakati hayo yakiendelea huko nje, ndani mtukufu Rais wa Mafuriko alikuwa amenuna utadhani anga la Mafuriko lingedondoshwa na hasira zake siku hiyo! Alikuwa amenuna na kushtushwa na habari za kwenye gazeti la Chimbuchimbu. Waziri mkuu alikuwa kama kawaida yake. Alikuwa anajiamini hata mahali pasipostahili. Na hii ndiyo ilimuwezesha kutumikia mabwana wawili yaani mali na wananchi, wizi na uongozi na mengine kama hayo. Kama ni kutafuta ubingwa wa unafiki na kujifanya mjamaa, huyu Bwana angenyakua tuzo zote. Maana akiamua kujifanya utadhani kweli ni muungwana wakati alikuwa mwizi wa kawaida aliyejificha kwenye madaraka. Na isitoshe alikuwa ana shahada ya sanaa. Na kama ni usanii aliuweza kweli kweli. Maana kinywa chake kilikuwa sukari wakati roho shubiri. Alijaliwa ulimi hata kuweza kumlaza simba zizini. Alijua kuyapanga maneno na yakapangika japo mwingi ulikuwa urongo na laghba. Silaha yake kubwa ilikuwa uongo na fitina na vitisho nyuma ya pazia. Na bahati mbaya kwa Wamafuriko ni kwamba nao walipenda kuliwazwa kwa maneno matamu kama watoto wadogo. Maana kuna kipindi walikuwa wakiahidiwa au kutendewa vitu ambavyo hata kuku asingweza kukubali. Chukulia mfano jinsi kashfa ya Richamen ilivyozimwa kimasomaso kwa muda tena kwa kuitumia taasisi ya umma na pesa ya umma.

Baada ya waziri kuingia kwenye ofisi ya Rais, walipeana mikono na Rais. Waziri mkubwa alikwenda kukaa kiti mkabala na bosi wake huku akitabasamu tabasamu.

Rais alikohoa kidogo kuliweka vizuri koo lake na kusema. "Nadhani wasaidizi wako wameishakupa taarifa za kuwapo kwa madai ya kashfa kuhusu suala zima la mradi wa maji na ithibati ya kampuni ya Richmen."Wakati akisema hivyo alivuta gazeti la Chimbuchimbu kutoka kwenye mtoto wa meza yake na kuliweka juu ya meza. Kuona hivyo, waziri mkubwa naye hakusita. Naye alivuta mkoba wake mdogo na kuchomoa nakala yake ya gazeti la Chimbuchimbu la siku hiyo huku akimkazia macho bosi wake Kama kumuonyesha kuwa alikuwa anajali, kufuatilia; na kwamba alikuwa amejiandaa kumsikiliza. Hivyo, hapakuwa na sababu ya kujibu swali. Maana lilijibiwa kwa vitendo kwa njia ya kuchomoa nakala ya gazeti la Chimbuchimbu.

Waziri mkubwa baada ya kuchomoa gazeti lake na kuliweka vizuri mezani, alijisogeza vizuri ili kutoa mawazo yake. Alianza huku akitabasamu kama kawaida yake. Alikohoa kadhalika kuweka koo lake sawa tayari kujibu swali la bosi wake aliyekuwa naye kadhalika ameyaweka macho usoni mwa waziri wake mkubwa. Alisema, "Mheshimiwa Rais nimesoma gazeti hili mara kama tano na kukuta kuwa kilichoandikwa ni siasa za kipinzani zilizojaa majungu fitina na uongo wa aina yake."

Aljitenga vizuri kwenye kiti chake na kuendelea, 'heshimiwa Rais, kimsingi, huu ni upuuzi mtupu, what rubbish! Total rubbish so to speak.." Alimazia kwa tabasamu lililochanganyikana na maudhi kidogo.

Alikuwa akijaribu kuhalalisha uongo wa kusema alikuwa amelisoma mara kama tano wakati hata habari yenyewe alikuwa kaisoma punde kidogo tena bila kuimaliza. Ilibidi aongope lau kulinda kitumbua chake.

Baada ya Rais kusikiliza utetezi wa waziri wake ambao kwa namna fulani haukuwa umemuingia akilini alianza kusema. "Rafiki yangu, habari hii hata kama umeichukulia kama ulivyoichukulia, naona itakuwa na madhara kwa serikali yangu ambayo kusema ukweli imeishachafuka vyakutosha. Inaweza kutuangamiza kama sumu yake itafanikiwa kupenya kwenye mawazo ya wananchi ambao kimsingi wameishakata tamaa sana. Kwanza, sijajua jinsi hawa watu walivyopata hii habari! Kuna watu kwenye intelligence wanatuandama nini? Maana siku zote kikulacho kinguoni mwako." Alishusha pumzi na kukohoa kidogo na kuendelea. "Je hii maana yake ni kwamba kuna watu kwenye mtandao wetu wanameasi kiasi cha kuanza kutuchoma? Yaani tumekuwa wa hovyo kiasi cha kuanza kuchomana na kulana wenyewe kama wadudu! Je ni wapi kuna makosa, where did you go wrong Bwana waziri?" Waziri mkubwa hakungoja rafiki yake na bosi wake aendelee kutoa dukuduku lake. Aliingilia kati na kusema. "Mheshimiwa Rais, walichofanya watu hawa ni ku-google na kupata profile ya kampuni. This is it. Kwa hili sina ubishi. Isitoshe najua uchimvi wa magazeti yetu. Pia kutokana na habari za kampuni kuwa kwenye mtandao wa internet, sina sababu ya kufikiria kuwa kuna watu wa ndani wamevujisha habari hii." Alikaa vizuri kwenye kiti chake na kuendelea. "Nimeangalia vizuri mashiko na urari wa uongo wao na kugundua kuwa wamepata profile ya kampuni na kuanza kujenga dhana mbali mbali kiasi cha kuwaingiza maafisa wa serikali kama unavyoona. Hii ni chuki binafsi. Niseme kabisa ni wivu wa kike.Ninavyowajua watu wa magazeti kama wangekuwa na reliable sources and hard evidence, wangelipua bomu zima zima badala ya kuja na this nonsense. Wangefanya hivyo kwa kujiamini kutokana na kuwa na information yote believe me your excellency."Alichomoa leso yake mfukoni na kufuta jasho na kuendelea. "Ukiangalia kwa undani utakuta kuwa sehemu kubwa ya text inaongelea kampuni na kwanini imeaminiwa wakati haina qualifications. Hili liko wazi. Lakini inapokuja kwetu sisi kuwa at stake, wamegusia gusia hisia zao." Alijifuta jasho tena kuendelea, "Nimepitia haraka haraka kwenye google na kukuta karibu kila walichokiandika ni pacha wa profile inayoonekana kwenye wavuti wa kampuni. Pia..."

Kabla ya kuendelea Rais aliingilia na kusema. "Lakini rafiki yangu tukubaliane kuwa habari mbaya za serikali zimezidi kwenye vyombo vya habari. Hili si jambo jema. Hata kama tunakanusha kuna some very irrefutable truths so to speak. Je Richmen siyo kampuni ya kutengeneza sumu? Hapa uongo uko wapi Bwana waziri."

Rais anazidi kumkazia macho waziri mkubwa na kuendelea. "Na isitoshe tangu uliponi-brief nilikuwa na wasi wasi kiasi cha kukubali shingo upande. Maana kila nikiangalia how far we have already fared kuhusiana na ahadi na commitments zetu kwa wananchi wetu, naona kama hatujafanya lolote. Naona kiza to be honest to you Bwana waziri. Generally speaking hatujafanya lolote. Tukubali tumeshindwa. Nchi imetushinda. That is that tusifichane and something has to be done kama tutaka ku-survive haya mawimbi. Huwezi kuleta kampuni ya wadudu kujenga mradi wa maji kusiwe na tatizo. Kwanini hukuniambia ukweli kuanzia mwanzo?"

Anashusha pumzi na kuendelea, "Na baya zaidi pamoja na kutofanya lolote the dark side of the government is dangerously looming and featuring high on all dissenting media."

Alijiweka vizuri tena kwenye kiti chake cha kuzunguka na kuendelea. "Sioni haja ya kupata hitimisho rahisi wala kumwaga tuhuma kwa vyombo vya habari wakati huu. Pamoja na kuwatupia kila lawama watu wa media, I think in this they are right. Importantly, we need to act vinginevyo tunachoita uongo wa magazeti unaweza kuonekana ukweli kwa wananchi. Na hili siyo jambo jema kwa serikali."Alikohoa na kuendelea. "Inabidi tukumbuke kuwa miaka miwili na ushei iliyobakia siyo mingi. Angalia tunaweza kuumbuka kwenye uchaguzi na mipango yetu ya muda mrefu ikaharibika. Kwanza, kwanini hukunipa true picture of this company? Maana nakumbuka katika briefings zako you just painted a very rosy picture. Na hii ndiyo iliyoni-convince kukubaliana na mpango mzima nikijua kuwa hata tutafanya kama tulivyofanya angalau tutakuwa na cha kuwaonyesha wananchi. Sasa kuna nini cha maana cha kuwaonyesha angalau kuwaridhisha wananchi? Pia tusiendelee kuwachukulia wananchi wetu kuwa ni makondoo. Hata kondoo kuna kipindi hugutuka na kusabisha maafa. Hizi nchi zote zilizosambaratika zilianzia huku tulipo. Kuna haja ya kusoma alama za nyakati kwa makini tena sana sana Bwana waziri."Alikohoa na kuendelea, "Unakumbuka yaliyowapata wenzetu wa nchi jirani ya Mizengwe? Hata sisi yanaweza kutukumba. Maana binadamu ni wale wale na isitoshe hawatabiriki siku zote. Unaweza ukawadhania hivi kumbe wako vile. Unaweza kujidanganya ukadhani nao umewadanganya kumbe nao wakakudanganya kuwa umewadanganya wakati ukweli ni kinyume."Alichomoa leso yake na kupenga kamasi na kuendelea, "Tusifanye makosa kama walilofanya wenzetu wa Mizengwe. Maana kwao kila kitu kilikuwa shwari wakati kwa ndani mgogoro ulikuwa unatokota. Sioni tofauti kwa sasa kati yetu na Mizengwe Bwana waziri hasa nikiangalia suala zima la Richmen."Waziri mkubwa anatingisha kichwa kukubaliana na tahadhari ya bosi wake akiwa anaonekana kukereka na kuchanganyikiwa kabisa japo anajitahidi kuficha silka hizi.

Rais alichomoa miwani yake kwenye bweta lake na kuivaa na kuanza kulisoma gazeti la Chimbuchimbu.

Naye waziri mkubwa alijitenga vizuri kitini mwake na kuvaa miwani yake aliyokuwa ameivua kutokana na kutokwa na jasho haraka haraka alianza kupitia tena gazeti lile huku akimsikiliza bosi wake. Kulikuwa na sehemu ambazo Rais alikukwa amepigia mstari.

Kimya kidogo kilitawala kitambo huku kila mmoja akijaribu kulidurusu vizuri gazeti lake na kuanisha aliyotaka na alivyotaka.

Baada ya kumaliza kusoma lile gazeti Rais alivua miwani yake na kusema. "Umesoma vizuri para ya tisa?" Aliuliza kwa ufupi.Waziri naye ilikuwa ni zamu yake kurudia kusoma gazeti. Ilimchukua muda kuipata para ya tisa. Alichofanya ni kuhesabu para kana kwamba alikuwa hajasoma gazeti. Para ya tisa ilisomeka,

"Majina ya wenye kuhusika na ufisadi huu tunayo. Na mmojawapo ni afisa mwenye madaraka makubwa na ushawishi serikalini na yuko karibu na kiongozi mwingine mkuu. Mkubwa huyu kwa nje hupenda kujionyesha kama mtu safi na mwenye kuwajali wananchi ukiachia mbali kuwa na historia tata tokana na jinsi alivyopata utajiri wake. Na huyu ndiye aliyeasisi mpango huu mzima. Wengeni katika genge hili hatari ni katibu mmoja wa wizara nyeti sana na waziri mmoja anayeshughulika na masuala ya huduma moja muhimu na hali fulani ya kimaumbile." Lilisomeka gazeti ibara ya tisa.

Wakati waziri akihangaika na kuisoma para ya tisa Rais alisema. "Ukisoma kwa makini para hii na kuiunganisha na text nzima utapata hitimisho kuwa hawa watu siyo wababaishaji kama unavyosema. Make no mistake my friend. Maana wameandika kwa kujiamini kuwa majina ya wahusika wanayo. Na jinsi walivyochora picha ya wahusika hakuna mtu asiyejua kuwa anayeongelewa ni wewe, katibu wa wizara ya hazina na mifuko ya pesa na waziri wa maji na upepo. It is as simple as that period."Alivua miwani yake na kuiweka pembeni na kusema, "Je na haya nayo wameya-google?" Alijitenga vizuri kwenye kiti chake. Hakungoja waziri aliyekuwa katumbua macho kama panya aliyenaswa kwenye mtego aseme. Alisema, "Let us be serious. Hawa watu wanaonyesha wanajua wanacho fanya and this is a job well done and researched in the first place. Na je wamejuaje kila kitu au kwenye transactions ulipokuwa Toronto uliingiza watu wasiohusika kwenye msafara wako? You never know. Fikiria siyo kujihami."

"Mheshimwa Rais sikufanya kitu kama hicho. Kama ni kuwa makini huwa nakuwa makini kwenye masuala yetu. Hapa umenipa challenge moja kwamba nisi-draw conclusion bila kuangalia angles mbali mbali. Kwa hili nashukuru umenifumbua macho."Alitabasamu na kuendelea, ""hishimiwa nilikutana na Garo kwenye chumba changu cha hoteli bila ya kuwapo na mtu yeyote."

Rais akiwa amechukia kidogo alisema. "Huu siyo wakati wa compliments. Kinachotakiwa ni umejiandaaje kukabiliana na tuhuma hizi kabla hazijaleta madhara? Pili, je habari hii nyeti ilitokaje hadi kuwafikia wabaya wetu? Je nini yatakuwa madhara yake kwa reputation ya serikali nami binafsi? Je umma utaendelea kusikia habari zetu chafu kila siku na kukaa kimya? Je hawa watu wana habari hatari na nyingi kiasi gani? Kuna maswali milioni na moja. Maana naona wananiingiza kwenye the whole mess!" Alisema kwa kuchukia kidogo huku akinyoosha mikono yake kama mtu aliyeachia bilauri ya maji ikavunjika.

Waziri akiwa anatabasamu kwa aibu alisema, "Mheshimiwa Rais kwa vile hali hii imetokea ghafla, naomba unipe muda nijaribu kufikiri jinsi ya kufanya na kujua ni vipi hawa watu wamepata habari hizi, wana damaging information kiasi gani na naweza kuwazuia vipi. Nakuahidi tutawashinda by hooks and crooks."

Rais hakuridhika na jibu rahisi kiasi hicho alirudia swali lake. Alisema. "Je umcjiandaaje kabla ya habari hii haijaleta madhara? Je nini yatakuwa ni madhara yake kwangu na serikali yangu? These are two things to assure me of bwana waziri kabla ya kufikiria suala la kupeana muda na kutafuta whatever all means possible. Maana kama lolote litatokea atakayewajibika ni mimi ndiye niliyeapishwa. Hujaona former anavyohangaika hadi kuingilia kwa kifua changu? Wasaidizi wake wanaendelea na maisha yao bila aibu wala bughudha. Yeye amegeuka punda wa kubeba mzigo wote simply because ndiye aliyeapishwa hata kama walioiba ni wengi. He was incharge kama mimi. Hili nadhani ni somo zuri na kubwa kwetu if anything."Kumbe na Rais pamoja na kutokuwa na bongo linalowaka kwa kukumbuka mambo alikuwa wamo! Maana alivyorudia swali lake utadhani alikuwa amelinakiri kwenye karatasi.

Waziri alianza kulowa kwa jasho pamoja na kuwa Rais ni rafiki yake na ufisadi huu ulikuwa ukiwanufaisha wote. Alijibu. "Mheshimiwa Rais, haya maswali ni nyeti sana. Si maswali ya kujibu bila kufanya utafiti na tathmini zaidi. Hivyo ningeomba unipe muda angalau nifanye utafiti wangu kwa makini zaidi kwa kufuata mwongozo na ushauri wako wa maana sana."Rais alimpoza rafiki yake baada ya kuona alivyokuwa ameanza kukanganyikiwa kiasi cha kutia shufaka. Hakutaka aendelee kumchanganya zaidi. Maana matokeo yake ingekuwa ni kusahau kila mkakati na kusababisha wabaya wao wawanase kirahisi kitu ambacho kingemsababishia yeye Rais matatizo zaidi ya wasaidizi wake. Maana yeye ndiye aliinua katiba ya nchi na kuapa kuitumikia nchi kwa uaminifu siyo uhalifu.

Huku akitabasamu alisema, "Hebu fanya hivi. Kabla ya kwenda kufanya uchunguzi, hebu nipe sketch ya haraka haraka mambo ambayo ungeyafanya kama jibu lingetakiwa tukitoka hapa mezani ili nione wapi naweza kutoa mchango wa mawazo yangu."Alizidi kutabasamu ili kumpa ithibati waziri wake aliyekuwa anajifuta jasho. Kwani uso ulikuwa umeanza kulowa pamoja na kuwa kwenye ofisi yenye viyoyozi kila pembe. Ile jadi yake ya kujiamini hata pasipostahili ilimkimbia. Maana alijua kuwa kwa jinsi alivyokuwa akiandamwa na kashfa kubwa na zinazonuka mara kwa mara, pamoja na kwamba Rais alikuwa mshirika na rafiki yake, bado angeweza kumvua madaraka. Maana umma ulikuwa ukihanikiza aachishwe uwaziri mkubwa kutokana na kuwa na historia iliyokuwa imejaa mabaka tena mengi na makubwa tu.Waziri mkubwa hakuamini masikio yake. Maana aliishaanza kuonja kibano cha bosi na rafiki na mshirika wake kwenye uhujumu wa nchi yao wenyewe. Pendekezo hili lilionekana kumpunguzia woga na mzigo wa kukanganyikiwa uliokuwa unaanza kumzidi uzito kiasi cha kutokwa na jasho chapa chapa. Alikoroweza ushauri wa Rais, kutabasamu kidogo. Alikohoa na kusema. "Nitawakaribisha wahariri wa gazeti la

Chimbuchimbu baada ya kutoa kanusho haraka sana. Na kanusho hili nitalitoa bila kutishia wala kutaka kubishana nao ili watakapokuja tujaribu jinsi ya kupata kujua wanajua kiasi gani na ikiwezekana nani source wao ili kujua jinsi ya kumshughulikia."

Rais alikuna kichwa na kusema. "Hiyo ni njia nzuri hasa kutobishana na vyombo vya habari. Jitahidi kukanusha. Lakini hili la kuwa mkarimu kwa waandishi wa habari nina wasi wasi sana nalo. Pia usiweke tumaini sana ukitegemea wanaweza ku-cooperate. Sahau. Kama unafikiria kuwa-compromise pia sahau." Alimtazama waziri mkubwa kwa makini na kuendelea. "Hili jamaa tangu lipate wafadhili wa kuli-finance gazeti lake haliwezi kurubuniwa. Gazeti la Chimbuchimbu kumbuka ni tofauti na magezeti mengine njaa njaa. Unakumbuka tulivyowanyamazisha lile gazeti la Oni kwa kulinunua kupitia mshirika wetu Azizi? Kwa hili hata kupenyeza watu wetu ni vigumu. Lakini ni vizuri kujadilina na adui yako kujua anakupangia nini na anakuchukulia vipi."Rais alivuta mtoto wa meza yake na kutoa karatasi nyingine. Alivaa miwani yake na kusoma halafu na kuivua na kusema, "Kumbuka na lile suala nililokwambia wakati magazeti yalipoanza kuandika juu ya kampuni ya Richmen. Unakumbuka jinsi baadhi ya mabalozi walivyokataa kukubaliana na utetezi wetu juu ya kwanini tuliteua kampuni hii? Kimsingi, serikali yangu sasa inanuka sina mfano. Watu wameanza kukata tamaa. Angalia kilimo, elimu, uchumi, mazingira, uongozi bora na mengine vyote viko taabani kama tutakuwa wakweli. Na huu ndiyo ukweli japo tunajitahidi kuuruka au kuwaweka sawa. Hali si nzuri serikali yangu ni inert kusema ukweli, Bwana waziri. We have been talking the talk without walking the walk. Now let us talk the talk and walk the walk Bwana waziri."Alichezesha kidole chake cha shahada kwa kupinda pinda kama wafanyavyo waislamu wakati wanapokaa tahiyatu na kusema, “Hapa lazima nimhamishe waziri wizara ili angalau kujaribu kupoteza ushahidi. Na pia sasa ijulikane kabisa kuwa kama kashfa zitaendelea itabidi nikutakishe orodha mpya ya baraza la mawaziri. Hapa watu wote wenye mabaka lazima nitawapumzisha kuliko kupoteza kabisa imani ya wananchi wetu. Lazima kula tunapuliza badala ya kujikatulia.”

Maskini wasanii hawa hawakujua kuwa walikuwa kwa namna moja ama nyingine wakijisuta. Maana kama kuna kiumbe alikuwa na mabaka ya ufisadi basi alikuwa waziri mkubwa hata Rais aliyemwamini mtu asiyeaminika wala kujiamini. Kama ni uchafu basi waziri mkubwa alikuwa unongo siyo utando.Baada ya waziri kusikia hivyo na kujua kuwa kumbe rafiki yake alikuwa tayari kumuomba orodha ya baraza jipya la mawaziri badala ya kumtimua yeye kinara wa uchafu alijibu haraka. Alisema. “Unajua mheshimiwa hapa kinachogomba ni maslahi. Maana nakumbuka bado tuko na baadhi ya mabalozi wanaotaka tuwape projects. Naamini kama makampuni kutoka kwenye nchi zao yakipata baadhi ya miradi kama uchimbaji wa madini na ujenzi wa barabara watanyamaza.”

Alivua miwani yake kuifuta vumbi na kuivaa na kuendelea, “Hii ni tabia ya wakoloni wote. Hawagombei haki yoyote ya watu wetu hapa bali maslahi ya watu wao. Hivyo kuweza kuwanyamazisha. Nimependekeza kwa waziri wa madini na vito kuhakikisha kampuni za wale wote wanaoonyesha kupiga kelele zinapata upendeleo. Hata kabla sijapata mwaliko wako nilikuwa napanga kuwapigia simu baadhi ya mabalozi ili kuwapima kujua habari hii wameichukuliaje.”Rais alitikisa kichwa kukubaliana na mipango ya waziri wake. Lakini alisema. “Tutauza watu wetu na mali zao zote kwa kila atakayelalamika mpaka lini?

Kwanini tusiwanyime mtama kuku kuliko kumaliza nafaka? Je nafaka ikiisha tutawapa nini?"

Waziri aliendelea, "Kuna hawa mabalozi wa nchi za Scandinavia. Hawa watu ni wagumu sana kuingia kwenye biashara. Hawa ndiyo wagumu kushughulika nao they are as rigid as a hell."Kabla ya kumaliza Rais alimkatiza na kusema."Hawa watu wananisumbua sana hata mimi. They are incorruptible. Pale wizara ya hazina na mifuko ya pesa bado wanadai hawaridhishwi na taarifa zilizotolewa. Juzi walimpigia katibu wa wizara wakimueleza kuwa wanaweza ku-review misaada yao."Rais alipiga mwayo na kuendelea, "In other words, wanataka kupunguza kiasi cha pesa wanachotoa kuchangia bajeti yetu na baadhi ya miradi ya maendeleo wanayoona inasuasua. Inabidi kuwa makini na watu hawa. They are indeed very serious. Na kama ni kushughulika basi hawa ndiyo watu wa kushughulika nao sana. Maana they know what they want. Wananipa wasi wasi sana. Wananinyima usingizi. Si unakumbuka juzi walivyoponda mafanikio ya serikali na kutoa karipio kuwa tumeshindwa kupambana na rushwa. Hivyo hawa wanadhani kupambana na rushwa ni mchezo? Na baya zaidi they are not interested in business like others."

Waziri aliwa amepata faraja kuona kuwa bosi wake alikuwa akiungana naye katika kutafuta suluhu alisema, "Hawa wazungu kuna kipindi wanakuwa wanafiki. Wao wanatusimamia sisi kuhusu uwajibikaji na kupamana na rushwa. Lakini nao kwenye nchi zao wengi wameoza."

Rais hakungoja waziri amalize wala kumruhusu aendelee. Alisema. "Lakini wenzetu tukubali wana kila sababu ya kutusema. Maana wanatimiza angalau baadhi ya haki za watu wao kiasi cha hata kutuchangia sisi tusio wapiga kura wao kwenye bajeti zetu. Leo serikali yangu inalaumiwa kwa makosa ambayo imeyarithi kutoka kwenye serikali iliyopita. Hapa ndipo wenzetu wanakosea."

Anajitenga vizuri kwenye kiti. Anaendelea, "Hawa watu ni wapumbavu. Umesikia wale wapuuzi waliokuwa wakitaka eti tupeleke bungeni mikataba ya uwekezaji. Nani yuko tayari kujivua nguo na kutembea uchi mitaani?"

Waziri mkubwa alitikisa kichwa. Rais aliendelea, "Nani mpumbavu amwage mtama kwenye kuku wengi? Inabidi hili lisifanyike. He who is without sin should be the first to cast the stone. Kwanza wao tumewafanyia hisani kwa kuwapa ruzuku bila hata kuwatakisha marejesho ya mahesabu. Wamesahau kuwa hii ni sirikali siyo serikali kama wanavyodhani!"Alipiga mwayo tena na kuendelea, "Turudi kwenye mada. Lakini pia waziri inabidi niweke wazi kabisa kuwa kuanzia leo nisisikie malalamiko mengine wala miradi yenye kuzusha utata kama huu wa Richmen. Kwanza, kwanini hamkubadilisha hili jina ambalo linaonyesha kabisa utata? Kilichokwishapatikana kinatosha. Maana lazima tuangalie na aina ya watu tunaowaongoza. Na isitoshe mambo yamebadilika sana siku hizi. Zile zama za vita baridi zilizokuwa mazalio ya ukandamizaji zimebaki historia."Aligonganisha mikono yake kama anaifikicha na kuendelea, "Kuna asasi nyingi za kiraia zinazojipenyeza kwa wafadhili na kupeleka majungu ili angalau nazo ziweze kuishi. Hili ni kama pori lenye kila aina ya wawindaji majangili hata wanyama mwitu wote wakigombea wala majani. Na si hilo tu. Hizi Scandinavian countries hawana rushwa ya kuweza kuita rushwa. Kama hiyo itaitwa rushwa basi kwetu itabidi wataalamu wa lugha watutafutie jina. Lazima tuanze kujisuta kuliko kujipendelea na kujiridhisha. Serikali yangu inanuka sana bwana waziri. We have zero credibility. Accountability ndiyo usiseme. Watu wanaiba sana bwana waziri. Watu wanajihudumia badala ya kuwahudumia wananchi. Wanawatumia badala ya kuwatumia. Haya siyo maagano yetu na wapiga kura wetu ambao ni dhahiri tumewasaliti."

Alimkazia macho waziri mkubwa ambaye alikuwa akitahayari kutokana na jinsi bosi wake alivyokuwa anasema ukweli ambao hakutegemea.Waziri alichonga nne yake kwenye kiti kwa furaha na tahayuri akijifurahia moyoni kwa kujua kuwa kumbe kitumbua chake kilikuwa bado kuingia mchanga. Baada ya kukohoa kidogo alisema, "Lakini mheshimiwa Rais ningeshauri tukubaliane kuwa hatufanyi hivi kwa kutaka. Kama tutaridhika na pesa iliyokwishapatikana Kwa kuogopa lawama, tukubaliane kuwa uchanguzi ujao utakuwa mgumu bila ya pesa ya kutosha. Si unawajua watu wetu? Wanalalamika viongozi wanakula rushwa lakini ikifika wakati wa uchaguzi ni hao hao watakao kuwa wa kwanza kuomba pesa. Sasa bila kukusanya nguvu na huu upinzani unaozidi kupata wafadhili unadhani uchaguzi tutauweza?"

Waziri alitoa tahadhali hii huku akirudisha gazeti lake kwenye mkoba akiwa anaonyesha kuwa anaanza kushinda kumshawishi bosi wake ambaye kimsingi kwenye dunia ya rushwa alikuwa anamuongoza Rais wake.

Swali hili liliyeyusha hasira na mashaka aliyokuwa nayo Rais. Lilimtoa kwenye msimamo na kumuacha katikati. Pamoja na kushauriwa na washauri wake avunje serikali na kuwafukuza waziri mkubwa na mawaziri wengine wenye madoa, bado alikuwa anawahitaji kukusanyia mtaji wa uchaguzi ambao ungefuatia. Maana bila ya kufanya hivyo asingetegemea kitu. Kwani ahadi zake alizokuwa katoa kwa wananchi zilikuwa hazijatimizwa hata moja. Wananchi walizidi kuwa maskini. Na hili lingesaidia sana kuwahonga wakati wa uchaguzi ili wamchague. Na isitoshe kwa nchi ya Mafuriko kuhonga kwenye uchaguzi kulikuwa kama haramu iliyokuwa imehalalishwa.

Rais pamoja na kukumbushwa kwanini lazima serikali yake ipokee rushwa na kuingia kwenye mikataba ya kiwizi alisema, "Lakini bwana waziri lazima tuangalie na upande wa pili. Kwani kisingizio cha kukusanya mtaji wa uchaguzi kinatumiwa vibaya na baadhi ya watendaji wetu tena wadogo wasio na jukumu hili mbeleni. Nadhani kutokana na kufanya mambo ama kwa pupa au bila siri, kunawafanya wajue kinachoendelea kiasi cha kufanya wafanyavyo bila kuhofia lolote. Kwani wanajua nasi hatuna udhu wa kuwafukuza iwapo tunashiriki kwenye mambo kama haya. Hivyo ni muhimu kuwa wasiri ili wasijue na wasipojua angalau tunaweza kuwapunguza baadhi ya watakao kuwa wazembe katika mambo yao. Kumbuka jogoo aliwafundisha vifaranga kunya ndani Bwana waziri."

Aliweka vizuri miwani yake kwenye shubaka lake na kuendelea, "Kuna haja angalau ya kuwabana wadogo. Maana wao ndiyo wanaishi na umma maskini karibu kuliko sisi. Kwa mfano polisi, hakimu, mwalimu, nesi na wengine wa kada hii, akigundulika kala rushwa fukuza on the spot. Hii itafanya wananchi wajue kuwa tunawajali angalau hata kama nyuma ya pazia ni vinginevyo. Umenielewa?"

Waziri alitikisa kichwa kukubaliana na Rais. Mpaka hapo habari za gazeti zilikuwa zimeanza kuzoeleka kiasi cha kujadiliwa kama suala la kawaida!Waziri alimuunga mkono Rais na kusema, "Mheshimiwa nafahamu sana kuwa kuna watu wanatumia mwanya huu. Ila ukumbuke kuwa wengi wa watendaji wetu tumewarithi na si rahisi kuwapangua wote na kuweka wapya. Ninachokuahidi ni kuwa msiri zaidi na mkali sana. Hata hivyo nilikuwa nimeishaanza. Maana juzi kwenye ziara yangu mkoani Madodo nilimtimua kazi mwenyekiti wa kijiji bila hata kumsikiliza. Nyuso za wanakijiji ziliwaka kwa furaha. Hata wambea wa magazeti waliniandika vizuri kiasi hata cha kuniandikia makala za pongezi." Alitabasamu na kuendelea. "Mheshimiwa wewe utasikia habari yangu. Nadhani nikishamaliza hili lazima tukutane kuwajadili baadhi ya watu wanaoweza kuwa kikwazo kwa maendeleo ya serikali yetu hasa hawa wanaotoa habari nyeti kama hizi."

Kwa kupeana nadhiri mpya na misimamo, kigwena ndiyo kilikuwa kimekwisha. Na kimsingi kilichokuwa kimemfanya Rais kuitisha kikao hiki cha ghafla hakikuwa chochote zaidi ya woga na kutaka kumpima na kumuonya msiri na mtendaji wake mkuu. Kwa upande mmoja Rais alikuwa amefanikiwa kumtisha na kumtingisha. Kwa upande wa pili alikuwa ameshindwa kukemea uoza kwa vile waziri alikuwa mjanja kumuingiza moja kwa moja kwa kujidai kuwa walikuwa wakiimba kwa ajili ya kusalia madarakani.

Sababu nyingine lilikuwa shinikizo la nchi wafadhili na baadhi ya washauri wake waliokuwa wakimshinikiza amtimue kazi waziri mkubwa wasijue kilichokuwapo nyuma ya pazia.Hawakujua kuwa nyuma ya pazia waziri mkubwa alikuwa siyo waziri mkubwa na msaidizi wa Rais tu bali mshirika mkuu katika kuihujumu nchi! Hakufahamu kuwa wawili hawa walikuwa wanahitajiana sana katika ndoa yao ya dubu na kudu. Maana kila mmoja alikuwa anamtumia mwenzake, walijua kutumiana.

Maana, ukiangalia kwa undani unakuta kama Rais alikuwa akitumiwa na waziri kiasi cha kujipenyeza na kuwa kama ndiye alikuwa akiongoza nchi kutokea nyuma ya pazia huku Rais naye akimtumia waziri mkubwa kufanya biashara haramu na chafu kama ya Richmen.

Mradi wa kuiliibia taifa usingekwama kwa vile kulikuwa na sheria iliyoruhusu wagombea kuwahonga wapiga kura kisheria. Sheria hii iliitwa kirimia.Bunge lilipitisha sheria hii chafu na hatari kwa umma maskini. Haki iligeuzwa bidhaa ya kuweza kuuzwa na kulanguliwa na kila aliyekuwa na pesa na nia ya kuilangua bila ya serikali kuangalia madhara ya ufaski huu wa kimaadili. Watawala walikuwa, chini ya sheria hii, wanaruhusiwa kujilimbikizia utajiri kama waziri mkubwa walivyoweza kiasi cha kuutumia kununulia vyeo.

Wafungwa walikuwa wakiachiwa huru ilmradi watoe chochote kitu. Ilifikia mahali magereza yakajaa wezi wa kuku huku majambazi wakubwa wakiitwa waheshimiwa na kutanua hadharani tena vifua mbele! Majambazi wa wazi wazi ndiyo usiseme. Ghafla, waligeuka wachangiaji na wafadhili wa vyama vya kisiasa hata taasisi za dini na michezo. Haki katika nchi ya Mafuriko ilikuwa imenajisiwa na kubakwa vilivyo! Hata viongozi wa dini hawakubaki nyuma. Kama Yuda, waliwasaliti waumini wao kwa vipande thelathini vya fedha wasijue ni fedheha!

Wahubiri walihubiri haki madhabahuni na kubatilisha nyuma ya pazia. Kwani walikukwa ni matajiri wa kutupwa huku makanisa na madhehebu mapya yakiibuka kama uyoga. Na uganga wa kitapeli wa kienyeji nao ulipanda chati hasa wakati wa uchanguzi. Hata vilabu vya mipira viliacha kufanya mazoezi na kuwekeza kwenye kuroga mechi!

Waziri mkuu pamoja na kumdanganya bosi wake kuwa walikuwa wakikusanya mtaji wa uchaguzi ambao ungefuata, yeye nyuma ya pazia alikuwa anazidi kujirundikia utajiri ambao angeutumia naye kuusaka urais baada ya bosi na rafiki yake kumaliza muda wake wa urais hata mara nyingine kuutumia kujenga ushawishi wa kutaka apigiwe kura ya kutokuwa na imani naye. Kweli siasa ni mchezo mchafu. Kwenye nchi zisizo na adili siasa haina tofauti na kamari. Hivyo, alijijengea himaya mbili. Yaani ile ya nyuma ya pazia ya kuiba pesa nyingi na kuificha nje ya nchi na kujionyesha kama kiongozi mtetezi wa watu na mchapakazi. Alizoea hata kuwazodoa watu wa chini zake kama wakuu wa wilaya na mkoa mbele ya watu wao ili wamuone kuwa alikuwa na uchungu nao wasijue kuwa nyuma ya pazia alikuwa ndiyo mbaya wao nambari wani. Hawakujua kuwa hayo yalikuwa ni machozi ya mamba.

Wakati Rais na waziri mkubwa wakiiba kwa kisingizio cha kushinda uchaguzi, maafisa wa chini nao walikuwa wakiutumia huu upenyo kuiba na kuvuja pesa ya umma. Wengi waliwekeza kwenye magari ya starehe na ufuska. Kuna watu walioweza kununua limousines za hata dola 200,000 kwa ajili ya kujishaua tu mitaaani wakati walikuwa ni watoto wa wawindaji maskini wa kutupwa wa digidigi waliosomeshewa watoto wao na serikali ya nchi wanayoinajisi! Sana pesa ya umma iliwatia nuksi walio wengi. Kwani walipukutishwa na ukimwi kabla hata ya kufikishwa mbele ya vyombo vya sheria.

Idadi ya waliopukutisha na fedha ya ufisadi nchini Mafuriko haikujulikana japo ilifurika vifo vitokanavyo na ukimwi hata ajali za barabarani. Maana kila wezi wakubwa walipokufa walitangazwa kuwa walikuwa wamekufa kwa shinikizo la damu, kisukari hata homa ya ghafla. Walikufa wengi huku serikali ikifanya usiri na unafiki uliokithiri. Pamoja na kufunika kombe, nyuma ya pazia mambo yalikuwa tofauti. Walikuwa wakiipata haswa adhabu ya ufisadi. Kuna kipindi ukimwi ulionekana kama mkombozi wa wanyonge ingawa nao uliwaua lakini siyo kwa wingi na kasi kama wenye nazo.Wapo walioficha utajiri nje na walipokufa mabenki ya nje yakawaruka warithi wao. Yupo waziri mmoja aliyekuwa na mbilioni nje. Alipokufa watoto wake walipigana wao kwa wao kugombea urithi wa wizi na mabenki ya nje yalipojua yaliamua kukataa kuwa baba yao alikuwa na pesa kwenye mabenki hayo. Kuwanyamazisha watoto wa waziri huyo mabenki yaliwawekea sharti la kuita vyombo vya habari na kutangaza utajiri wa baba yao ili umma ujue alipoupata kama ni halali au haramu. Keshi iliishia mezani! Kumbe wezi wanazidiana ujanja!

Baada ya kumaliza kikao chao cha faragha nyuma ya pazia kilichohudhuiriwa na watu hawa wawili, Waziri alimuomba Rais aondoke kwenda kuanza kupambana na gazeti la Chimbuchimbu. Hapakuwa na mbwembwe za picha. Maana siku zote mambo ya nyuma ya pazia huwa yanakwepa jicho kali la kamera. Walikubaliane asitumie nguvu bali rushwa na ushawishi hata kupandikiza watu wa kuweza kufanya kazi gazetini huku wakichunguza vyanzo vya habari mbali mbali za kashfa za serikali zilizokuwa zikifichuliwa na gazeti hili ili baadaye walihujumu hata kwa kuzusha kesi ambayo ingeligharimu mamilioni ya shilingi. Katika hili Rais alimshauri msiri wake awe makini sana ili asije kumrusha njiwa waliyelenga kumnasa.

Waziri mkuu alimpa mkono Rais kwa unyenyekevu na tabasamu na kuondoka tayari kuelekea ofisini kwake kuwashughulikia watu wa gazeti la Chimbuchimbu lililokuwa linachimbua chimbua mambo yao ya nyuma ya pazia.

Baada ya waziri mkubwa kuondoka, Rais aliweka mikono yake uchogoni na kujiegamiza kwenye kiti chake cha enzi huku akitafakari mazungumzo yake na waziri mkuu na kashfa iliyokuwa inazidi kukua. Ghafla, aliajisemea peke yake, "Huyu kama ataendekeza tamaa yake kama fisi yeye na mkewe, hana jinsi hata kama ni rafiki yangu, itabidi nimfukuze kazi bila kujali kuwa ni rafiki yangu au mshirika wangu wa muda mrefu asije kunitia matatani. Maana ameweza kumfundisha hata mke wangu kuanza kupenda pesa." Maskini hakujua kuwa mkewe alikwishavamiwa na pepo la kutaka mali bila kuitesekea! Wakati akiwaza hivyo hakujua kuwa mkewe aliishaunda mkakati wa kujipenyeza kwenye chama yeye na watoto wake ili waweze kuchuma kwa kutumia cheo chake bila kutoa jasho! Aliondoa mikono kichwani na kutaka kupiga simu yake ya mezani lakini akagahamu.

Alitikisa kichwa na kusema, "Hivi huyu na tamaa zake za kutaka utajiri na madaraka nikimaliza muda wangu ataiweza nchi kweli. Maskini hajui kuwa kuongoza nchi siyo mchezo! Je ataweza kunilinda kutokana na haya yanayofanyika nyuma ya pazia? Hakika ningelijua kuwa dhamana hii ni mtihani hivi nisingehangaika na kuusaka urais. Sikujua kuwa kumbe madaraka ni chema usichokuwa nacho ukiwa nacho wema hutoweka! Heri njaa ya haki ya tumbo kuliko ya ubongo."Aliusonya ukuta utadhani ndiyo uliokuwa unamchochea kuwa chaka la wezi na kuendelea, "Tazama kabla ya kuwa Rais sikuwa na wazo kuwa siku moja ningeshiriki kuiibia nchi yangu tena nikiwa mkuu wake!" Alitikisa kichwa tena kwa masikitiko.

Wakati akiendelea kutafakari hili na lile, msaidizi wake wa kike ambaye naye alikuwa moto kuliko hata yule wa kwenye ofisi ya waziri mkubwa, aliingia na kinywaji. Haijulikani kama ilikuwa soda, mvinyo mweupe au whisky.

Alikunja goti na kumkabidhi bilauri yake yenye shingo kama korongo na kutabasamu na kutokomea alikotokea. Aliondoka kwa madaha na mikogo lau amburudishe bosi wake ambaye alikuwa anafahamika kwa kutojiweza mbele ya viumbe hawa pamoja na madaraka makubwa aliyokuwa nayo. Rais naye kama wale makatibu wa wizara na waziri walipokuwa kwa waziri mkubwa, alimkata jicho msaidizi yule wa kike ambalo lilimfuata hadi anatokomea.

Alijisemea moyoni. "Kweli urais una raha zake. Viumbe kama hawa mardadi wanakuhudumia kwa lolote utakalo!"

14
Kashfa Kashfa Kashfa!

Baada ya kashfa kuwa sehemu ya maisha ya vyombo vya habari na wananchi wa Mafuriko ambapo mshukiwa mkuu alikuwa ni waziri mkubwa kuliko hata Rais wake, aliamuru tume ya kuzuia ufisadi ya Mafuriko yaani Tume ya Mafuriko ya kuzuia Rushwa (TUMAKURU), ambayo wananchi waliiona kama tume ya Kusimika na Kuendeleza rushwa, ichunguze kashfa ya Richmen na kumsafisha. Na kweli, bila hata chembe ya aibu, ilimsafisha, kwa wananchi walivyokuwa wametabiri! Kama ni usanii basi ulikuwa ni wa aina yake. Maana ilikuwa ni mara ya kwanza kwa wananchi kujua sura halisi ya watawala wao. Zengeni alizoea kusema kuwa nyoka hata ajivue ngozi yake ya zamani na kuotesha mpya, bado hubakia kuwa ni nyoka tu.

Mkurugenzi wa tume hii, Eddy Horse Zanaki, aliitisha mkutano wa waandishi wa habari na kutoa viapo na vitisho kuwa kila jiwe lingefunuliwa; na wahusika wangekiona cha moto! Aliapia miungu yake yote; kuwa lazima wahusika wangeishia gerezani hata wangekuwa wakubwa kama tembo. Wanafiki kweli walijaliwa kutokuwa na aibu! Maana aliyekuwa akisema hayo hakuwa na tofauti na tambara la kudekia sakafu. Alikuwa ni binadamu kifaa ambacho kingetumiwa na mwenye madaraka yeyote kwa wakati wowote vyovyote atakavyo. Sana sana alikuwa kama nepi izoayo kinyesi bila kugoma! Tangu lini nyenyere na utepetevu wake akamtisha kenge?

Kweli duniani kuna binadamu ambao waliupata ubinadamu na sura yake kwa bahati mbaya. Maana alichokuwa akimaanisha moyoni kilikuwa ni tofauti kabisa na alichokuwa akiropoka. Ile tume ilikuwa ikifanya uchunguzi danganya toto ili kuwafumba macho wananchi ingawa haikuwa. Kwani baadaye wananchi waliikataa ripoti ya tume hii na kuiita ya kimalaya, kisaliti na kitapeli.

Mwanamuziki mmoja alitunga wimbo usemao wizi ndani ya wizi. Huyu jamaa alifuatwa fuatwa kiasi cha kutishiwa kuwa kama angeendelea na "kashfa" zake wangemtangaza kuwa hakuwa raia wa Mafuriko. Walimsingizia kuwa wanafahamu kuwa babu yake hakuwa na asili ya Mafuriko!

Kosa lake ilikuwa ni kusema kuwa zinaibiwa shilingi tano inaundwa tume inayokula shilingi laki tano kuchunguza wizi wa shilingi tano. Hii ni sawa na kuuza ng'ombe ili kuendesha kesi ya kuku! Si kwamba watawala wa Mafuriko hawakujua kuwa mchezo huu ulikuwa wa kipuuzi na wala kuwa madhara yake yasingekuwa makubwa, walijua kila kitu. Kwa vile kwao pesa ilikuwa kila kitu hata kuwa na thamani kuliko utu wao, walifumba macho na kuwaibia wananchi wakidhani kuwa wananchi walikuwa hawaoni wala kujua jinai hii iliyokuwa ikitendekea nyuma ya pazia. Ambacho hawakutegemea ni wananchi kuamua na kuamka kurejesha heshima ya nchi yao.

Kichekesho ni kwamba maafisa wengi wa tume hii walikuwa na utajiri ambao haukuwa na maelezo. Hata mkuu wa tume alipewa cheo hicho kama hongo na mradi wa kuwasafisha wakubwa aliokuwa akiiba na kula nao.

Kadhalika taasisi karibu zote za Mafuriko zilifurika uoza usiosemekana. Polisi, mahakama hata wabunge walikuwa wakiishi kwa rushwa zaidi ya mapato yao halali. Halali iligeuka kuwa haramu na haramu kuwa halali. Uaminifu ulianza kuonekana kama kitu kilichopitwa na wakati huku ufisadi ukionekana kama ushujaa. Rafiki yake Zengeni, Kibaka, alizoea kuonekana mjanja na mwenye busara kuliko yeye kwa sababu alikuwa anaweza kuiba na kuwajengea wazazi wake nyumba kwa pesa yake chafu na asione hata chembe ya aibu!

Ilifikia mahali hata wauza unga wakawa wanaheshimika sawa na wabunge hata kuwazidi kutokana na kuwa na ukwasi usioweza kutolewa maelezo. Ilifikia mahali hata miswaada kupitishwa bungeni lazima waziri aandae hafla ya kuwalisha na kuwanywesha wabunge bila kusahau mabahasha yaliyokuwa yamejaa maburungutu ya fedha. Hii ni mbali na magari ya anasa ya kuwakogea walipa kodi wa Mafuriko. Hii ni mbali na kuingia mikataba ya kufanya biashara na nchi za nje ambayo kimsingi ilikuwa imegeuzwa mali za watawala wa Mafuriko. Kuna kipindi ilisemekana kuwa siku za nyuma mtawala wa zamani wa Mafuriko na jamaa zake walikuwa wakifanya biashara wakiwa serikalini! Ajabu kama mnafiki yeyote, alijionyesha kuwa mtu wa haki wakati nyuma ya pazia alikuwa mtu wa batili kama inzi atuaye kwenye keki na kinyesi!

Mahospitalini wagonjwa walikuwa hawatibiwi bila kutoa chochote. Kila mahali bila chochote hungepata chochote wala kuhudumiwa chochote. Uoza uliiteka na kuikalia nchi ya Mafuriko. Nchi ilikuwa imevamiwa na kunajisiwa si kawaida! Kwani ilifikia mahali hata wabunge wakagundulika kughushi vyeti huku mitihani ikiibiwa kila mwaka. Ilifikia mahali watu wakawa wananunua hata shahada na kuzitumia kupatia ajira! Shahada za kupigia kura ndiyo usiseme. Watawala waliziagiza nje ya nchi wakati walikuwa na viwanda vya uchapaji na kupata chao na kuongeza idadi kubwa ya shahada bandia ambazo ziliwasaidia kusalia madarakani. Hata pesa ya Mafuriko haikunusurika. Kwani ilikuwa inaghushiwa utadhani ni karatasi ya kusokotea bangi au ile ya kuendea uani!

Ilifikia kiwango cha kutisha. Wezi wa kimataifa nao walifurika Mafuriko. Walikuwa wakikopa na kuiba kwenye mabenki kana kwamba yalikuwa yanaendeshwa na kuku au vichaa! Walifikia hatua ya kumiliki pesa nyingi hata zaidi ya serikali! Walishika uchumi wa Mafuriko huku wazalendo wakiishia kuwa watwana na waangaliaji wakati jinai hii chafu kuliko zote ikiendelea chini ya watawala wao wenyewe! Biashara ya mihadharati na kubadilisha pesa za kigeni ndiyo usiseme. Ilikuwa kama imehalalishwa kimya kimya! Baya zaidi mkuu wa upelelezi wa taifa alizoea kuwapa imani wananchi kuwa alikuwa akifuatilia biashara hii hatari na haramu. Kuna kipindi aliwacha hoi waandishi wa habari alipofanya mkutano nao. Aliwaambia kuwa alikuwa ana orodha ya majina ya vigogo wa unga aliyokuwa akiyapokea kupitia simu yake ya kiganjani. Walipotaka awape namba alianza. "haa enhee ahaa unajua!"

Pia cha ajabu kila ilipoikifika wakati wa kuwataja wauza unga na wala rushwa ili kuwakamata, alikuwa akipatwa na kigugumizi hadi watu mitaani kuanza kusema kuwa angemkamata nani wakati wauza unga wenyewe walikuwa yeye na mabosi wake?Jamaa mmoja aliwahi kusema kuwa wakubwa hula viapo kuwatumia wananchi siyo kuwatumikia. Wakati wakipewa madaraka walizoea kusikika wakisema, "Naapa kuwatumikia wananchi wa nchi hii kwa uaminifu bila upendeleo wala uonevu." Lakini matendo yao yalisema na mioyoni mwao ilikuwa hivi:

"Nitawatumia watu wa nchi hii kwa ufisadi, upendeleo na uonevu vya hali ya juu, Ewe Mwenyezi Mungu usinifichue."

Walikuwa wakimshirikisha Mungu kwenye ubahau wao bila kujua kuwa ipo siku angewalipa kama alivyowafanyia wakuu uchwara wa Mafuriko!

Pamoja na kuwa maneno haya yalionekana kuwa utani, mtu angeangalia watawala wa Mafuriko walivyokuwa wakiwaonea watu na kuwatumia, angeamini utani huu. Maana, matendo yao licha ya kunuka yalikuwa yakichefua. Kwani walikuwa ni wezi wenye roho mbaya walioiba si kwa sababu ya uhitaji bali ulafi na roho mbaya vyao.

Hata Zengeni alizoea kuwaita wabunge wabuge kwa jinsi walivyokuwa wanatukana cheo chao cha ubunge kwa kuhongwa magari na serikali kiasi cha kutumikia magari badala ya wapiga kura. Ubunge kwake ulikuwa udohoudoho hata ubuge. Maana magari na pesa hata nyumba ni vitu vidogo kulinganisha na utu wa waliowaamini wakawachagua kushika dhamana kubwa namna hii. Baya zaidi, hata wabunge nao waliingia jinai hii kiasi cha kuwa mateka wa chama na serikali kiasi cha kutunga sheria za kukandamiza wezi wadogo wadogo na vidokozi huku wakitunga nyingine za kuwalinda majambazi wakubwa waliokuwa wamefurika serikalini!

Zengeni aliozea kuwaita watawala wake mafisi na mbweha waliokuwa wakila bila kunawa tena kwa mikono na miguu. Maana ilifikia mahali kukawa hakujulikani tofauti kati ya jambazi na polisi, hakimu na mla rushwa, kasisi na mzinifu. Kulikuwa na visa vingi vya viongozi wa kidini kubaka hata kulawiti watoto wa waumini wao bila kutaja kuwazini waumini wao huku kesi zao zikiishia kuwa siri.

Hakuna kesi iliitikisa Mafuriko kama kesi ya kasisi mmoja aliyepewa jina la utani la Sextous. Huyu kasisi alimlawiti mtoto wa familia iliyokuwa ikimchukilia kama rafiki wa familia. Alizoea kutumia sadaka kuwahonga mashoga na malaya! Wakati watawala walikuwa wakilawiti wapiga Kura wao Kwa kuwaibia, makasisi walikuwa wakilawiti waumini wao kwa kuwahonga sadaka zao wenyewe!

Bibi yake Nengoma alipoona mambo yameharibika kiasi hiki, aliachana na utawa aliokuwa ameutumikia kwa zaidi ya miaka thelathini. Hivyo, hali ya kijamii, kisiasa na kiuchumi ya Mafuriko ilifurika madhambi si kawaida. Wazee wengi walianza kuonya juu ya maafa makubwa kutokea. Maana hata janga la ukame lilihusishwa na kukithiri kwa visa vya ufuska, wizi, ubadhirifu na mabaya mengine lukuki.

15
Walimu Machinga

Baada ya kujaribu kufikia malengo yao bila mafanikio, Nengoma na mumewe Zengeni walianza kufikiria kubadili kazi. Tatizo ilikuwa ni jinsi ya kuanza na nini la kuanza nalo. Kwao haikuwa rahisi japo walijua fika walichokuwa wakitaka kukifanya. Na hali ya mambo ilivyokuwa ikibadilika kwa kasi ilibidi nao wafikirie na kuamua kwa kasi ile ile. Zengeni alizoea kusema kuwa uuwahi wakati kabla wakati haujakuwahi. Kipya kinyemi japo kidonda. Walipiga moyo konde. Lakini kwa sababu maji waliishayavulia nguo, ilikuwa sharti wayaoge. Wakati wao wakipasua vichwa kufikiria la kufanya, kulikuwa na watu tena wezi waliokuwa na mapesa hata waliiyokuwa hawajui jinsi ya kuyatumia. Walitapanya na kufuja bila kujali kuwa kulikuwa na watu tena waliolipa kodi waliyokuwa wakiiba na kutapanya waliokuwa wakifa kwa kukosa madawa ya bei ndogo na huduma nyingine za lazima!

Wapo tena wengi waliokuwa wanakufa kutokana na upungufu wa kinga mwilini si kwa sababu ya ugonjwa wa UKIMWI bali kutokana na kutopata lishe ya kutosha. Wengine walijinyonga kutokana na umaskini hasa madeni au kushindwa kuhudumia familia zao. Hawa walichagua njia hii hafifu ili kuondokana na mateso na aibu badala ya kusimama na kupambana kidete. Maana heri ya kufa umesimama kuliko kuishi umepiga magoti. Japo watapanyaji hawa hawakujua, ni kwamba walikuwa wakiua watu wengi kutokana na ufisadi wao. Zengeni alikuwa akikumbuka jinsi mwalimu mmoja wa shule jirani ya msingi alivyojinyonga kutokana na kuzidiwa na mizigo ya madeni na maisha kwa ujumla.

Zengeni na mkewe walijadiliana kwa muda mrefu wakiangalia madhara na faida za kuachana na kazi ya ualimu ambayo ilikuwa imepoteza heshima yake vibaya sana ukiachia mbali maslahi. Pamoja na kujitahidi kufundisha, bado kulikuwa na wanafunzi walioanza kupuuzia masomo na kujiingiza kwenye starehe wakitegemea kutumia pesa za baba zao kununua mitihani hata ajira. Tatizo jingine lililoongezea mafuta kwenye moto lilikuwa ni kucheleweshewa mishahara yao ukiachia mbali kila mwaka bei za bidhaa kupanda kila baada ya kusomwa bajeti huku mishahara yao ikibakia kuwa ile ile ya masihara. Tatizo na kucheleweshwa mishahara na udogo wake halikuwa la walimu tu. Hata madaktari walipunjwa kiasi cha mishahara ya wanasiasa kuwa mikubwa kuliko yao ilhali wanasiasa hawakuwa wakifanya kazi ya kitaaluma wala ya kitaalamu!Taratibu, lugha ya mzungu wa unga na kuzamia meli kwenda Ulaya ilianza kusikika na hatimaye kuzoeleka! Huku hayo yakiendelea wengi wa walimu walijiingiza kwenye biashara ya kuuza elimu kwa njia maarufu kama tuisheni. Ilifikia mahali mwalimu kuwafundisha wanafunzi wale wale masomo yale yale aliyopaswa kuyafundisha darasani lakini akayabania ili wayanunue kwenye biashara hii ya tuisheni. Kulikuwa na tuisheni hata kwa watoto wa vidudu ambao hawakuwa tayari kufikia umri wa kuanza shule. Bahati mbaya uchafu huu ulipoanza serikali haikuchukua hatua. Maana waliokuwa nacho serikalini walizoea kuwapeleka watoto wa nje ya nchi kusoma shule za kimataifa na zenye hadhi ili warudi wakawatawale wajinga waliozalishwa na mfumo huu nyemelezi. Wengine walianza uayari wa kuuza mitihani kwa wanafunzi waliowakwamisha ili wawaibie kupitia tuisheni na kuwauzia mitihani ya kughushi! Badala ya mwalimu kuwa mlezi na mtume, aligeuka ghafla kuwa kuku alaye mayai yake! Ghafla utume uligeuka utumwa wa pesa!

Nengoma na Zengeni waliamua kuwa hata wamachinga badala kujiingiza kwenye uchafu wa namna hii. Hawakuwa tayari kuendekeza njaa kiasi cha kutumia utumbo kufikiria badala ya ubongo. Walimu walioamua kuwa watuma wa pesa hawakuwa peke yao. Maana karibu kila mwananchi wa Mafuriko alipokuwa hasa wafanyakazi, alianzisha mradi wake. Wapo waliofuma vitambaa. Wengine walianzisha balaa jipya. Mfano magari ya mizigo yaligeuzwa ya abiria huku magari ya abiria yakiongeza nafasi ili kuzidisha kipato kwa kuweka hatarini maisha ya abiria!Wapo walioanzisha biashara ya pombe haramu ambayo ilipata soko sana baada ya bia kupanda bei. Wengine walioanzisha biashara hii walikuwa wake wa polisi ambao waume zao walipaswa kuikamata lakini kutokana na kila mtu kujua mbinu ya kuishi waliwanyamazia wake zao.

Zengeni na Nengoma waliuchukia sana usaliti huu kwa jamii iliyowalea na kuwasomesha. Hawakutaka kugeuka mbwa atapikaye na kulamba matapishi yake. Hawakuwa tayari kufanya huu umalaya wa kimaadili ili kujaza matumbo yao ambayo siku zote, kama moto, hayaridhiki wala kuridhishwa. Walikuwa ni wazalendo kweli kweli. Hawakupenda hata kidogo huu ugendaeka wa kihayawani. Baada ya nchi ya Mafuriko kubariki jinai ya ufisadi kiasi cha mtu kutajirika bila kutoa jasho na asiulizwe, watoto hata wazazi wao walipoteza motisha wa kusoma na kusomesha. Wengi wa vijana walijiingiza kwenye biashara haramu ya mihadarati. Walijikuta wakitekwa na magenge ya jinai hii yaliyokuwa yakihusisha hata watu wakubwa serikalini. Walianza kukamia kwenda Pakstan na kwingineko yalipopatikana madawa ya kulevya kuliko shule! Na hakika, wengi waliumia. Kwani waliishia magerezani baada ya kugeuzwa shehena za mihadarati huku wakiisafirisha kupita njia za aibu za miili yao wasigutuke! Taifa lilikuwa likiangamizwa na watu wake wenyewe!

Wasomi walizidi kudharaulika na kudhalilika huku nafasi yao ikichukuliwa na wanasiasa na wafanyabiashara tena mbumbumbu na waharifu wengine waliokuwa na pesa walioshirikiana namamluki wa kigeni waliowatumia kufichia na kusafirishia nje ya nchi utajiri wao haramu.

Ilifkia mahali ikawa ni rahisi kwa mfanya biashara kukutana na Rais kuliko mwalimu au daktari. Maana kuna kipindi ulitokea mgomo wa madaktari nchi nzima. Walipigwa na kufukuzwa kazi bila kuchelewa wakati wafanyabiashara walipolalamikia kodi au ushuru, serikali haraka haraka iliwasikiliza na kukubaliana na madai yao ya kilafu kwa kuwapa misamaha mingi bila kujali kuwa walikuwa wakiuumiza umma!

Nengoma na Zengeni walikubaliana wasifanye papara bali wafanye utafiti ili kujua hatua ambayo ingefuata. Kilichokuwa kikiwangoza na kuwapa mwanga zaidi ni kujua kuwa uchumi hasa wa kibarua wa Mafuriko aliyeitwa mfanyakazi ulikuwa ukizidi kutetereka huku hujuma na ufisadi vikichukua nafasi yake. Wakati wafanyakazi na wakulima wakizidi kuzama kwenye lindi la umaskini, waliibuka matajiri ambao wengi wao walijulikana kuwa majambazi bila kushughulikiwa. Majambazi hawa walifunga ndoa na wanasiasa kiasi cha kuwadhamini kwenye chaguzi zilizokuwa zikitawaliwa na rushwa na wizi wa kura. Kama kuna shetani alifanikiwa kuiteka Mafuriko si mwingine bali yule shetani wa utajiri na madaraka.

Nchi ilikuwa ikiangamia mchana huku watawala wakiinusuru kwa uongo na visingizio hivi na vile. Maana hata taasisi za umma kama polisi hata jeshi zilihusishwa kwenye mchezo huu mchafu huku maafisa wakubwa wa majeshi wakipewa vyeo mbali mbali vya kisiasa wakati hawakuwa wanasiasa. Siasa na dini viligeuka biashara za kutengenezea utajri wa haraka haraka huku umma ukiangamia na kukata tamaa. Serikali iliunyonya umma na viongozi wa kidini kadhalika wakaunyonya umma wa waumini! Maana mahubiri yao mengi ilikuwa ni juu ya kutoa kwa Mungu aliyekupa bure. Ajabu hawakugusia ufisadi na urongo vilivyokuwa vimetamalaki Mafuriko! Waliridhika kulala kitanda kimoja na serikali chafu chovu na choyo.

Kabla ya kuacha kazi Zengeni na mkewe walianzisha miradi miwili ya majaribio; mradi wa bustani na mradi wa maandazi. Walikubaliana kuanza kubana matumizi ili kuweza kuanza kuwekeza kwa ajili ya badiliko hili la maisha ambalo hawakuwa wamelitegemea wala wamejiandalia. Kwani kwenye nchi ya Mafuriko mtu aliposoma alitegemea kuishi maisha ya kisomi na siyo ya kubabaisha huku na kule katika hili na lile.Bahati mbaya, mambo yalibadilika ghafla kiasi cha kuwafanya wasomi nao wabadilike ghafla. Maana, kabla ya kuingia serikali za kibabaishaji na kiwizi- zilizotokana na rushwa na wizi wa kura, usomi ulikuwa ni nyenzo ya ukombozi na siyo silaha ya maangamizi ya umma kama ilivyokuja kubainika baada ya watawala wasomi kubobea kwenye rushwa na wizi. Ilifikia mahali watu wakawa wanasema wasiwe wanawachagua wasomi maana walikuwa wamesomea wizi na usaliti kwa taifa lao na watu wake! Babu yake Zengeni, Mzee Seshaa aliwahi kumuuliza ni kwanini wasomi maofisini walikuwa wezi kuliko wale ambao hawakuwa na elimu asipate jibu. Hii ni baada ya jirani yao Kibaka kumaliza chuo kikuu na kuajiriwa kufanya kazi kwenye Benki kuu ya Mafuriko alipoibukia kuwa tajiri wa kutupwa ndani ya kipindi kifupi. Kwani ndani ya mwaka mmoja aliweza kuwanunulia gari na kuwajengea wazazi wake nyumba ya kisasa. Hili halikumbabaisha Zengeni wala mkewe.

Kwani alikuwa akijua kilichokuwapo nyuma ya pazia. Alikuwa akijua adhabu ya kuishi maisha ya mashaka na dhambi zitokanazo na mali haramu iliyoibiwa toka kwa umma. Alizoea kusema ni heri ndege aishiye kwenye kiota akalala usingizi mnono kuliko panya au mjusi aishie kwa watu asijue majaliwa yake. Kwake furaha haikuwa utajiri bali kuridhika katika matendo ya mtu. Kwake usalama haukuwa kuta kama magereza wala walinzi wenye bunduki bali jamii yenye kupendana na kuaminiana ikitendeana haki. Na hili ndilo somo alilolipenda kiasi cha kuamua kuacha kazi ya ualimu kwenda kuliishi kama machinga. Pia Zengeni alizoea kujipa moyo kwa kusema penye nia pana njia na hakuna lisilowezekana kwa binadamu ilmradi liwe halali. Pamoja na marafiki zake aliosoma nao kama Kibaka kuwa matajiri wa ghafla, Zengeni hakuamini katika kuiibia jamii. Aliona ni dhambi kubwa isiyo na kitubio wala kustahili msamaha isipokuwa adhabu hata ya kifo. Kwani ni jamii hiyo hiyo ndiyo iliyokuwa imempa fadhila. Ndiyo ilikuwa imemsomesha na kumfikisha alipokuwa amefikia. Kwake kuuibia umma ilikuwa ni sawa na kuwaua wazazi waliomzaa mtu na kumlea kwa mapenzi mazito naye akawalipa mauti. Kwake mtu wa namna hii hakuwa na tofauti na hayawani yoyote hata chakama angelala kwenye hekalu. Aliwalinganisha watu hawa na mbwa wa wazungu walalao kwenye maghorofa na kusafiri kwa magari ya gharama kubwa lakini wakabakia kuwa mbwa. Kwake mbwa alikuwa mbwa hata angevishwa minyororo ya almasi au kula kidari cha kutupiwa na mahanjumati mengine. Kwake kupe alikuwa ni kupe hata angekuwa mgongoni mwa simba! Hakuupenda umbwa na ukupe hata kwa sekunde moja. Hivyo, shukrani zake ilikuwa ni kwake kuwa mzalendo wa kweli kuliko kuwa kibaka msomi na mnafiki kama marafiki zake.

Nyuma ya nyumba yao kulikwa na uwanja mpana uliojaa vichaka. Wazo lilimjia Zengeni kuutumia uwanja huu kwa mradi wake mpya wa mboga mboga. Aliona ni bora kuwa na mazao yanayoweza kuliwa na binadamu badala ya vichaka vilivyoficha nyoka na panya. Isitoshe kwa kufanya kazi kwenye eneo hili angepata uzoefu wa kulima na kusimamia bustani. Maana pamoja na kusoma Zengeni na mkewe walikuwa ni watoto wa wakulima ambao walijivunia asili hii. Hivyo, baada ya saa za kazi, Zengeni alikuwa akifanya kazi ya kusafisha eneo lile tayari kwa kuanza kulima matuta kwa ajili ya bustani ya mboga mboga na mchicha. Hata baadhi ya wanafunzi wake walishiriki kumsaidia mara chache walipopata fursa ya kufanya hivyo. Pamoja na kuanzisha mradi huu bado tatizo la maji lilikuwa likimsumbua. Kutokana na kuwa na uhusiano mzuri na wanafunzi, wanafunzi wengi walijitolea kumsaidia kuwa wanamletea maji toka mto uliokuwa jirani na shule ili kumwagilia miche yake bustanini.

Kwa upande wa mradi wa maandazi aliteuliwa Nengoma kuuanzisha, kuusimamia na kuuendesha. Walikubaliana kuwa inapotokea mmoja akahitajika kumsaidia mwenzeke kwenye mradi wake, awe kama mshauri. Kadhalika, Nengoma naye aliteuliwa kuwa mshauri wa mradi wa bustani. Kwa hiyo kila mmoja alikuwa na kofia mbili. Yaani kuanzisha mradi mmoja na kuuendesha huku akishauri kwenye mradi wa mwenzake.

Walijiwekea lengo pia la kuanzisha mradi wa ufugaji wa kuku kama muda utapatikana. Sharti moja muhimu ambalo walikubaliana liwe kama sheria ni kutotumia pesa yoyote toka kwenye miradi hii miwili nje ya mradi. Jambo usilolijua ni sawa na usiku wa kiza. Na binadamu ni wepesi wa kusema na wavivu wa kutenda. Kwani baada ya Nengoma na Zengeni kuanzisha miradi yao, walimu wenzao walianza kuwasema. Wapo waliosifia utundu na ujasiri wao wa kujaribu kupambana na maisha na wapo waliowacheka kwa kuingilia kazi zisizo za kisomi wala zisizomfaa msomi. Kipindi kile kutokana na mfumo wa elimu uliojaa mapungufu, wasomi wengi waliamini kuwa hawawezi kufanya jambo ambalo hawakulisomea. Lakini pamoja na imani hii, msukumo wa maisha na kubadilika kwa mfumo wa siasa haraka viliwalazimsha kufikiria upya tena haraka zaidi na zaidi. Hivyo, maneno ya wenzake Zengeni hayakumhangaisha wala hakuwashangaa. Kwa vile alijua ni matatizo ya kimfumo ambayo aliamua kuyabadili kwa kujibadili yeye na mkewe. Kwani walichukua yale yaliyolenga kuwapa moyo na kuyapuuzia yale yaliyolenga kuwakatisha tamaa. Bila kutarajia, alianza kusikia utani mitaani ambapo alikuwa akiitwa mwalimu Machinga; kutokana na kuwa mwepesi kufanya jambo lolote; bila kujali watu wanasema nini. Alifarijika na jina hili. Maana ulikuwa ni ukweli usiopingika. Angepingana nalo vipi iwapo hakuwa peke yake? Kwani hata serikali iliyokuwa ikimtawala ilikuwa inafanya mambo mabaya kuliko aliyokuwa akifanya yeye. Umachinga wake uikuwa halali ukilinganishwa na uchangudoa wa serikali ya Mafuriko iliyokuwa imewekwa kinyumba na matapeli wasaka ngawira wa kigeni.

Zengeni aliacha kazi aliyoipenda ili kuepuka kuliibia taifa alilolipenda tofauti na serikali iliyoacha wajibu ulioiweka madarakani na kujigeuza adui wa taifa ililopaswa kulihami na kulijenga. Jina hili alitokea kulipenda hadi hata mkewe mwenyewe kufikia kumtania kwa kumuita mwalimu Machinga. Ila Nengoma alizoea kumtania kuwa asiwe mume Machinga. Maana Machinga hufanya kila linalomjia ili aweze kuishi maisha halali hata kama ni ya kimaskini. Alizoea kumwambia; kwenye ndoa asiwe machinga asije akabeba kila kitu! Kuanzishwa kwa miradi mipya kulikuwa na changamoto yake. Kwani kulibadilisha ratiba yote ya maisha ya Nengoma na Zengeni. Walizoea kufanya mazoezi kila jioni ili kuiweka miili na akili yao vizuri. Lakini baada ya kuwa na ajira mbili yaani ualimu na umachinga, walijikuta wakikosa muda na nguvu ya kufanya mazoezi ya kila jioni. Badala yake waliamua kufanya mazoezi mara tatu kwa wiki badala ya mara sita kama walivyokuwa wamezoea. Hata hivyo hawakuwa wamepata hasara. Maana kazi za kilimo na maandalizi ya mapishi ya maandazi vilikuwa zoezi tosha tena zito lenye faida kimwili na kiuchumi. Kitu kimoja walikubaliana kisiathiriwe; ilikuwa ni muda wa kusikiliza matukio mbali mbali yaliyokuwa yakitokea duniani. Maana vyombo vya habari kwao lilikuwa kama darasa jingine kwa kujinoa na kwenda na wakati duniani. Waliendelea kusikiliza karibu vituo vyote vya redio vya dunia kila siku ili kutoachwa nyuma na matukio duniani. Wao kama wasomi na walimu, waliamini walikuwa ni raia wa dunia. Hivyo, ilikuwa muhimu kwao kujua kila kinachowezekana kilichokuwa kikitokea duniani.

Hakuna kipindi walifaidika na habari kama lilipotokea tukio la kuangushwa kwa mfumo wa kikomunisti. Walijadili dhana mbali mbali na udhaifu wa ukomunisti. Walikubaliana na kuanguka kwa ukomunisti shingo upande pamoja na ubaya wake. Maana walijua athari na hatari ya dunia kutawaliwa chini ya mfumo unaoamriwa na taifa moja tena la kibepari ambalo kwake kilichokuwa kikizingatiwa ni maslahi yake hata kwa kukandamiza haki za wanyonge. Na hili ndilo hasa lilikuwa chimbuko la serikali ya Mafuriko kupokea misaada mingi na kuifuja huku ikijitahidi kutogusa maslahi ya wakubwa wenye uroho kama fisi wa nchi za kipebari. Hata mradi wa Richmen ulikuwa matokeo ya kuanguka kwa ukomunisti. Maana tokana na nchi ya Mafuriko kuwa ya kijamaa, raslimali zake nyingi zilikuwa hazijaguswa. Hivyo kila jambazi wa kimataifa wa kiuchumi alikimbilia Mafuriko kulikofurika neema kama jina la mji wake mkuu.

Hivyo, ulipoingia mfumo wa kibepari, mabepari uchwara wote walifurika Mafuriko kuzoa utajiri huu. Bahati mbaya hata serikali ya Mafuriko iliyokuwa imefurika wezi na wasasi wa ngawira, iliacha kila kitu wazi kiasi cha wezi hawa kuigeuza kichwa cha mwendawazimu mlevi kujifunzia kunyoa. Baya zaidi ilikuwa imefurika watawala waliokuwa wavivu wa kufikiri kiasi cha kujiuza wao kama makahaba na wananchi wao kama samaki mezani! Hali ilifikia pabaya hadi masuala muhimu ya kitaifa kuamriwa mahotelini huko Ulaya badala ya ubalozini!

Hili lilijibainisha wazi. Maana licha ya nchi kuwa na watu wenye mawazo na akili, watawala walipwakia kila amri na uchafu uliotoka kwa wakubwa hawa hasa wa benki ya dunia na shirika la fedha la kimataifa ambalo hakika halikuwa la kimataifa bali la kipebari. Kwa nchi hizi majambazi, dunia ilikuwa ni wao na mambo yao.

Ni wakati huu ambapo Zengeni na Nengoma walipokuwa wakizungumzia mambo mbali mbali ya kijamii na kisiasa. Wawili hawa walikuwa na mapenzi na siasa. Walijadili siasa kiasi cha kubishana hata kufikia kuwa kama wanasiasa wawili wenye milengo miwili tofauti inayokinzana.

Pamoja na kuwa na mitazamo miwili inayopingana - ambapo Nengoma alikuwa mhafidhina na Zengeni mliberali- walikubaliana juu ya kitu kimoja. Kitu hiki ni kwamba wote wawili hawkukubaliana na jinsi nchi yao ilivyokuwa ikiendeshwa kijinga na kijambazi. Pia tofauti zao za kisiasa ziliishia sebuleni. Hazikuingia katu ofisini wala chumba cha kulala. Hali hii ya kuwa na majukumu mapya ilikuwa ikiwapa matatizo sana hasa kitaaluma. Maana wote walikuwa ni walimu wa fasihi na somo la Haki za Binadamu. Siku moja walijikuta wakikesha wakiandaa majibu kwa maswali ya wanafunzi waliotaka kujua falsafa na sera vilivyokuwa vikiendesha nchi yao ya Mafuriko.

Swali hili lilitokana na mwanafunzi mmoja aliyehamia shuleni kwao akitokea nchini Uingereza alikokuwa akiishi na wazazi wake waliokuwa wakifanya kazi ubalozini. Kijana huyu wakati akirejea nchini Mafuriko alikuja na majarida mengi ya kijamii na kisiasa. Mojawapo ya jarida ilikuwa na makala isemayo kuwa Bara la Nuru lilikuwa tajiri wa mali asilia lakini maskini wengi kuliko mabara yote ukiondoa baadhi ya nchi chache kama India ambayo kipindi kile ilikuwa na watu milioni mia mbili na hamsini waliokuwa maskini wa kutupwa.

Mwanafunzi baada ya kusoma makala ile na kuchanganya na uzoefu wake wa kuishi Uingereza alitaka walimu wake wamjulishe ni kwanini hali ilikuwa hivyo na wangewezaje kujikomboa kutoka kwenye kadhia hii bila wananchi wa kawaida kujua sera zinazowaongoza.

Kilichofanya swali hili liwahangaishe ni jinsi mwandishi wa makala hii aliyejulikana kama Richards Watts kujua mambo mengi ya Afrika na kutoa uchambuzi ulioishia kama suto. Kwani hitimisho la makala ile lilikuwa. "Wakazi wa bara la Nuru walio wengi wanaishi kwenye umaskini wa kutupa. Alitumia neno abject poverty au umaskini wa kunuka. Watts aliendelea kusema. "Kitu cha ajabu ambacho kinajenga dhana kuwa huenda wananuru hawaoni vizuri ni ile hali ya viongozi wao kuwa na utajiri usiokuwa hata cha kuufanyia. Ajabu zaidi ni pale wananuru wanapoishi kwenye umaskini na kumtupia Mungu lawama huku wakiwavumilia watawala wao wezi na wadokozi."

Hitimisho la Watts licha ya kuelezea ukweli wa maisha, lilkuwa ni kama suto na tusi hasa kwa wasomi kama Zengeni na Nengoma. Na baya zaidi walijisikia kama wana wajibu mkubwa katika hili kwa kuangalia jinsi wanafunzi walivyokuwa na uchungu na nchi yao kiasi cha kujenga utafiti kama huu.

Licha ya utafiti wa Watts pia kulikuwa na utafiti uliokuwa umefanywa na mtafiti wa kijapani aitwaye Hawa watu Ni majuha na mkewe Watawala Wanawala juu ya utawala wa sheria katika nchi ya Mafuriko. Watafiti hawa waligundua kuwa misaada mingi iliyokuwa imetolewa na nchi yao iliishia kwenye mifuko ya watawala na mawakala wao kutokana na umma kutojulishwa wala kushirikishwa kwenye miradi ya nchi yao. Hitimisho lao lilikuwa ni kwamba kama wananchi wangeendelea kuhujumiwa hivyo ingekuja siku ambapo vita ya wenyewe kwa wenyewe isingeepukika. Maana wenye njaa wangeasi dhidi ya wenye shibe ili wote wakose! Na katika mtafaruko huu, wenye nacho wangepoteza na wasio nacho wangepata na kama siyo kupata wenye nacho wangekosa walichokuwa nacho wakati wasio nacho wanapata waliokuwa nacho kuja kuwa wasio nacho kama wao.

Swali la sera na falsafa iliyokuwa ikitawala Mafuriko lilijadiliwa na wanafunzi na walimu wao kiasi cha kuwa kama klabu ya wasomi. Maana hadi wanahitimisha walikubaliana kuwa nchi yao ilikuwa ni kama mradi wa majaribio wa wanasiasa waliosifika kwa kutumia pesa ya umma maskini kujihudumia bila kujali kuwa maskini wale walikuwa ni binadamu waliostahili kuishi kama binadamu badala ya mifugo. Wanafunzi kama siyo kuzuiliwa na walimu wao, walikwenda hatua mia mbele kuwataka walimu waandike barua ya wazi kwa Rais kumtaka awatajie sera zilizokuwa zikiendesha nchi yao na kwanini ufisadi ulikuwa unaongezeka. Walidai pia kuwa katika barua hiyo watamke wazi kuwa wao kama wasomi wa baadaye walikuwa hawaridhiki na jinsi mambo yalivyokuwa yakienda hasa kuchezewa na kufujwa kwa raslmali za taifa jambo ambalo walisema lingefanya maisha yao baadaye yawe magumu kiasi cha kugeuzwa watumwa na mafukara kwenye nchi iliyokuwa imekaa juu ya utajiri wa ajabu ukisombwa na majambazi ya kigeni yakishirikiana na yale ya ndani yaliyokuwa yamejificha nyuma ya vyeo. Kwa mfano, wanafunzi walihoji maana ya utegemezi wa misaada kwa nchi yao yenye raslimali nyingi. Walihoji pia nidhamu ya matumizi ya pesa ya umma na ukubwa wa serikali huku wakiwalaani watawala kwa kuusaliti na kuunyonya umma. Waligeuka ghafla kuwa wanamageuzi wa kweli kiasi cha kuutia wasi wasi utawala wa shule.

Nengoma na Zengeni pamoja na kuanzisha miradi yao iliyohitaji muda mwingi wa ziada kuihudumia, walikubaliana isiathiri utendaji wao kitaaluma.

Hivyo, mara nyingi, walichelewa kulala au kulala kwa zamu. Muda mwingi wa baada ya kazi za bustani na kupika maandazi ulitumika kuandaa masomo na kusahihisha kazi za darasani kiasi cha kujikuta wanaanza kulala saa saba badala ya saa tano walizokuwa wamezoea. Na kama siyo kutumia kandili walikuwa na uwezo wa kulala hata saa nane. Lakini walihofia kuharibu macho yao. Hivyo kuwa wakilala saa saba. Katika kufanya kazi kwa moyo na bidii na maarifa kuna faida moja kubwa. Mwenye kufanya kazi vilivyo huchoka na kupata usingizi mnono huku muda wake ukitumika kwenye mambo ya maana badala ya kutumika vigengeni kama ilivyokuwa kwa walimu wenzao ambao hawakuwa na shughuli za ziada baada ya masomo. Na hii ndiyo maana walikuwa wakipata hata muda wa kuwasengenya hata kuwakatisha tamaa Zengeni na mkewe kwa hatua waliyokuwa wameamua kuipiga. Ajabu wengi wa waliokuwa wakiwasengenya ni wale waliokuwa wakiharibu muda wao na pesa yao kwenye ulevi huku wakizusha malalamiko na mitafuruko kwenye ndoa zao.

Maisha mapya siku zote siyo lelemama. Yanahitaji kujituma na kuamini katika unachofanya. Zengeni na mkewe walijikuta katika ulimwengu mpya. Walijiandaa kuachana na kazi ya ualimu. Kufungua miradi hii ilikuwa ni fursa ya kupata jinsi ya kuwaeleza wazazi wao uamuzi waliokuwa wamefikia. Maana pamoja na kwamba kazi ilikuwa ni yao, ilichukuliwa kama suala la kifamilia za wazazi wao pamoja na wao kuliko kuwa suala la watu wawili peke yao. Kwa waafrika mtoto huwa hakui hata awe na miaka mia. Bado huendelea kuwa mtoto kwa wazazi wake. Hivyo, uamuzi wao pamoja na kuupitisha tayari lazima wangewataarifu wazazi wao kuhusu hatua hii. Kwa waafrika mtoto kufanya jambo bila kuwahusisha wazazi wake ni jambo baya sana karibu na kuwakana. Hutafsiriwa kama ubinafsi, uchoyo, kiburi, dharau hata dalili za kuharibikiwa. Haina maana kuwa kila jambo lazima mtoto amshirikishe mzazi. Lakini kuna mambo muhimu hasa ya maisha kama kazi, ndoa, biashara, safari za mbali, na mahusiano ya nje kwa ujumla. Hii huwa ni mali ya ukoo husika. Hivyo Zengeni na Nengoma walikuwa wakijiandalia hili. Japo walijua wazi kuwa wazazi wasingeweza kuwakatalia, walifanya hivyo kama ishara ya heshima kwao. Hawakuwa na wasiwasi. Kwani hawakuwa wamewahi kutowashirikisha wazazi wala kufanya uamuzi mbaya katika maisha yao. Na isitoshe wazazi wa pande mbili licha ya kuwategemea walikuwa wanawaamini. Hivyo lilikuwa ni suala la wakati muafaka. Hwakutaka kuwafahamisha wazazi kabla ya kufanya uchunguzi wa kutosha wa uamuzi wao mpya katika maisha.

Hamu ya kuona miradi yao inafanikiwa iliongezeka huku na hofu ya kufikia uamuzi wao nayo ikiongezeka. Waliongeza juhudi katika shughuli zao mpya na za awali.

Aliyekuwa wa kwanza kuweka pesa mezani alikuwa ni

Nengoma. Kwani baada ya kununua unga, mafuta, vikorokoro vya kutengenezea maandazi, kupanga bei na kuamua ni maandazi kiasi gani apike, maandazi ya kwanza yalipikwa kwa utaalamu na uangalifu sana. Mteja wa kwanza alikuwa Zengeni. Alinunua maandazi ya shilingi hamsini ili kutoa baraka kwa biashara ya mkewe.

Kutokana na kutotaka kuajiri mtoto wa kuuza mandazi, siku ya kwanza, Nengoma alikwenda na maandazi ofisini. Kwa vile yalikuwa ni kidogo hakuhitaji kutangaza sana zaidi ya kuweka tangazo dogo kwenye ubao wa shule wa matangazo.

Tangazo lilisomeka hivi:

Ndugu wana jumuia,

Tumeanzisha huduma ya vitafunwa. Ni vitafunwa vilivyopikwa kitaalamu na kwa tahadhari ya usafi na afya ya hali ya juu. Bei zetu ni nzuri. Karibuni nyote.

Wakati wa mapumziko ya asubuhi, walimu walinunua maandazi karibu nusu ya yale aliyokuwa amepika siku hiyo. Nengoma na Zengeni walitazamana kwa mstuko juu ya mwitikio wa biashara yao. Maana siku zote mwanzo mugumu. Kwao haikuwa hivyo.

Mkuu wa shule alimpongeza Nengoma kwa kubuni mradi wa kujiongezea kipato. Pia alifurahia mradi huu kwa vile hakuwa akiwaamini wanawake jirani waliokuwa wanaweka biashara zao kwenye uzio wa shule. Hivyo kwa kuwa na huduma hii ndani ya shule, utoro kwa kisingizio cha kwenda kununua maandazi ungepungua hata kwisha kabisa. Wanafunzi nao hawakubaki nyuma. Baada ya kugundua kuwa kulikuwa na huduma ya maandazi tena toka kwa mwalimu wao Nengoma, walijitokeza kwa wingi kumuunga mkono. Haikuchukua muda maandazi yote yakaisha ilhali wateja wakizidi kuongezeka! Siku hiyo alikuwa amepika maandazi ya shilingi elfu mbili. Hivyo alipania kesho yake kupika mara mbili ya hiyo. Nengoma na mumewe walifurahi sana kuona mawazo yao yakifanikiwa tena kwa haraka. Hii iliwatia moyo sana na kuwazidishia hamasa ya kufanya biashara. Baada ya kurudi nyumbani na kufanya mahesabu, Nengoma alijikuta ana faida ya shilingi elfu moja na mia na hamsini. Hii ni baada ya kutoa gharama zote kuanzia mkaa, mafuta, muda wa kutengeneza na kuuza. Kwa ujumla siku hiyo hapakuwa na hasara. Alizidi kufurahi na kupata hamasa ya kuhakikisha biashara hii haifi.

Biashara ya maandazi iliendelea kiasi cha Nengoma na Zengeni kujilaumu kwanini walichelewa kuianzisha.

Kitu cha ajabu kilitokea. Wake wa walimu ambao hawakuwa walimu hawakubaki nyuma. Nao walianzisha biashara hiyo hiyo ya maandazi kiasi cha wateja wa Nengoma kuanza kupungua. Watu wa Mafuriko kwa kuigizana hasa linapokuja jambo la riziki walikuwa mahiri sana. Maana hata mjini karibu maduka mengi yalikuwa ni matokeo ya kuigizana. Kuna kipindi kwa mfano kulikuwa na maduka mengi ya kuuza madawa kuliko wateja kiasi cha watu kusema kuwa nchi ya Mafuriko ilikuwa na wagonjwa wengi kuliko watu wazima. Hata glosari za kuuza pombe nazo ziliota kama uyoga kiasi cha watu kusema kuwa wanamafuriko walikuwa wakiongoza kwa ulevi kuliko nchi zote duniani. Ajabu walikuwa na baa na glosari nyingi kuliko shule! Kulikuwa na shule nyingi tu maeneo ya vijijini ambazo licha ya kutokuwa na walimu, hazikuwa hata na madawati, mbao hata vitabu wakati nchi ikisifiwa kwa mabaa na maduka ya madawa! Cha ajabu zaidi watawala wa Mafuriko walizidi kuwatia moyo na matumaini kuwa wangewaendeleza. Waliita hii safari ya kwenda peponi wasijue ni jehanam! Kutokana na kupendwa na kuaminiwa na wanafunzi, Nengoma aliendelea kufanya vizuri japo siyo sana kama wakati alipokuwa peke yake. Penye riziki hapokosi fitina. Kutokana na kuuza sana kuliko wanawake wa walimu, ulianza kuzuka uvumi kuwa Nengoma alikuwa akipata biashara sana kutokana na kutumia madawa!

Mke wa Mwalimu Kikwekwe alitaka kuvuka mpaka. Maana alipanga amtokee Nengoma na kumpa vipande vyake kama alivyosema. Lakini kutokana na busara za mume wake aliyejua kuwa hisia zake ilikuwa ni matokeo ya ujinga, ilibidi amzuie kumshambulia mwenzie.

Baada ya mke wa Mwalimu Kikwekwe kuona kuwa alilolitaka lisingekuwa, aliamua kuwa anamnunia Nengoma. Lakini maskini Nengoma mara zote walipokutana alikuwa akimsalimia hadi yule mama kuona aibu na kumweleza mpango aliokuwa nao. Alikiri kuwa kweli ujinga na umaskini ulikuwa umegeuka kuwa shetani aliyemtia majaribuni kumuwazia mwenzie vibaya bure wakati alikukwa na mipango moto moto ya kuwasaidia wanawake waliokuwa hawana ajira pale shuleni!

Nengoma alifurahi na kumpa ushauri wa jinsi ya kufanya biashara na yule mama aliboresha biashara zake.

Kwa vile Nengoma alikuwa hajawahi kuwazia acha kutumia uchafu huu, hakujali. Alizoea kusema kuwa huo ndiyo mzigo wa ujinga. Maana waliozoea kumsema hawakuwa wamefanya utafiti wa ni kwanini alikuwa akiuza sana kuliko wao. Walichofanya ni kutoa hitimisho kuwa alikuwa akitumia ndumba kujiridhisha kutokana na kutotaka kuumiza vichwa vyao kutafiti mambo. Kwao ndumba zilikuwa ni kila kitu. Wakati biashara ya Nengoma ikiendelea vizuri, Zengeni naye alikuwa ameishapanda kila aina ya mboga kwenye bustani yake. Alikuwa akingojea naye siku ya kufungua biashara yake. Na walikubaliana na mkewe kuwa fungu la kwanza la mboga mboga lingenunuliwa na naye kwa bei mara tano ya ile ya watu wengine. Ilibidi mke amuunge mkono mumewe kama yeye alivyofanya wakati alipofungua biashara yake. Ulikuwa kama utani lakini wenye faida. Hauchi hauchi unakucha! Kwani baada ya miezi minne, mazao ya Zengeni yalikuwa tayari. Na kama siyo tatizo la ukame, alikuwa akitegemea kuanza kuuza mazao yake baada ya wiki mbili na nusu.

Kwenye bustani yake alipanda mchicha, bilinganya, Zucchini, tunguja, spinachi, nyanya na vitunguu. Alizoea kuiita bustani yake bustani machinga. Maana ilikuwa mchanganyiko wa kila kitu sana na mchanganyiko wa kila kitu sawa wa na ualimu,ukulima wa bustani,utengenezaji maandazi na uuzaji. Hatimaye siku ya siku iliyokuwa imengojea ilitimu! Zengeni akiwa amevalia kanda mbili kwani hakuwa na mabuti yake ya mvua, aljidamka kwenda kuchuma mboga. Matumaini yalikuwa juu sana. Aliamini kama mkewe angepata wateja wengi. Aliamini kutokana na hali za kipato za majirani kuwa kidogo kiasi cha kulazimika kula mboga za majani. Mwalimu Mahdi alizoea kuwatania kila katika kati ya mwezi kuwa walikuwa wakigeuka mbuzi waliokuwa simba mwishoni mwa mwezi kutokana na kula sana mboga za majani wakati wa ukame mifukoni na nyama wakati wa mafuriko mifukoni yaani mwisho wa mwezi. Maana kwao nyama, pamoja na kuwa waajiriwa waliokuwa wakipata mishahara kila mwisho wa mwezi, ilikuwa ni wakati wa sikukuu na kidogo mwisho wa mwezi walipokuwa wakipata mishahara hasara yao.

Alizidi kuamini kuwa angepata wateja baada ya watu wengi kuwa wanamuulizia ni lini angeanza kuuza mazao yake. Ukiunganisha na kuwa katikati ya mwezi ambapo wengi hawana jeuri ya pesa, alizidi kupata imani ya kupata biashara si haba.

Huku akipiga mbinja na kuimba peke yake, alichuma kiasi cha mboga cha kutosha tayari kwenda nyumbani kufunga mafungu. Hakuuwa mgeni na bustani. Kwani alipokuwa akisoma sekondari, shuleni kwao walikuwa na mradi wa bustani. Hivyo kuchagua ni mimea ipi ya kuvuna na kutovuna halikuwa tatizo. Alikuwa akiimba wimbo wake kipenzi ambao alizoea kuuimba wakati mwingi akiwa peke yake. Aliendela kujiimbia huku akikwanyua majani ya mchicha. Afrika muli bwanji? Itwe kunu tulibwino aaa.

Aliamua kubadili na kuimba wimbo wa kikikuyu aliofundishwa na rafiki yake Ndirangu alipokuwa nchini Kenya wakati akimuuguza baba yake.

Nkoro yakwa n'irakena.
Nkoro yakwa iratumatuma
Nkoro yakwa keigwa ekeigwa
Wega wila niwe muhonokya.
Wendo utumu munu akwe
Wendo waku Nengoma ni muunene
Ni wendo wa amahirania.

Alikuwa akiimba kuisifia kazi na mkewe.
Tafsiri moyo wangu haujasinyaa,
Moyo wangu unadunda dunda
Moyo wangu unajisikia vema.
Kazi ndiyo ukombozi.
Upendo hufanya mtu afe,
Upendo wako Nengoma ni mkubwa,
Ni upendo wa maajabu.

Kabla ya kuendelea anastuliwa na Nengoma. Anasema. "Asante sana mume wangu. Kumbe uko unaniimbia hata bila ya kuniita nisikilize na kuburudika!" Zengeni anajibu. "Nilikuwa naiimbia bustani kwanza. Baada ya kufika nyumbani ningekuimbia wewe. Si unajua mwenembago akipanda." Alimaliza huku akicheka. "Kwa hiyo siku hizi una wake wawili. Una bustani ambaye ni mke wako wa kwanza na wa pili ni Nengoma. Hata mimi nina waume wawili. Wa kwanza ni biashara yangu ya maandazi na wa pili ni Zenge." Nengoma naye aliamua kujibu. Zengeni alijiwahi na kusema. "Kwa taarifa yako maandazi yako na hizi mboga vyote ni vya kike. Hivyo, una jibu la ni nani ni nani katika nini?" Nengoma alisonya na kucheka na kumsaidia mumewe kuchuma mchicha. Zengeni alisema, "Kama unaionea wivu bustani yangu basi ngoja niimbie serikali yetu." Kama utani alianza kuimba wimbo alioupenda sana uliokuwa unaelezea ufisadi na ukwasi wa wezi wa serikalini.

Yetu ni maisha ya dhiki,
Hatuna amani wala haki,
Wamesunda chao kwenye benki,
Utawaona wakitaka,
Utawaona wakitanua.
Wao wala murua sie vibua!
Watuuza na kununua
Tena tunaitwa umma
Kwa uma wanatuuma!
Ajabu twawatazama
Tusijue twazama!
Tusijue ni zahama!

Zengeni aliupenda sana wimbo huu kutokana na kusanifu vizuri sanjari na uoza uliokuwa umefurika Mafuriko. Wimbo ulielezea mengi. Mtunzi alisema, "Usimuone anaendesha gari lake. Muuliza kadi ya gari. Utakuta kaiacha kwa aliyemkopesha,. Usiwaone wakipigiwa saluti. Nyuma ya pazia kuna mengi mazito. Wakati wao wakitanua akina yakhe na wakulima wanakufa kwa jembe. Katika kuukoleza ujumbe video ya wimbo huu ilikuwa na chui akimrarua swala sawa na serikali ya Mafuriko ilivyokuwa ikiwararua wananchi wake.

Mwishoni mwa wimbo huu kuna picha ya nyani anayekula jani. Maana kazidiwa sawa na wananchi wa Mafuriko walivyokuwa wakiishi kwa kubangaiza kama akina Zengeni na Nengoma walioamua kuwa wamachinga badala ya walimu! Nengoma alimtania mumewe, "Naona sasa tuanzishe bendi ya muziki badala ya bustani na maandazi. Ila mwenzangu kwa mawazo yako yalivyo makali watakufunga au kukuzengeni bure." Zengeni alitabasamu huku akianza kupiga mbinja. Kutokana na kuwa muda ulikuwa unasogea na walipaswa waelekee zao madarasani, Nengoma ambaye alikuwa ameishamaliza kupika maandazi alimsaidia mumewe na kuelekea nyumbani tayari kufunga mafungu ya mchicha na kuelekea shuleni.

16
Chimbuchimbu mtegoni

Baada ya waziri mkubwa kumaliza kigwena chake na Rais, aliingia kwenye gari lake aina ya Mercedez Benz C. 800. Thamani ya gari hili kama watawala wa Mafuriko wangelikuwa na akili ya ki utu uzima, ilitosha kuwasomesha chuo kikuu vijana wa Mafuriko si chini ya mia nane. Lakini nani angehangaika na kusomesha vijana maskini wakati watoto wake walikuwa wakipata elimu tena nzuri huko Ulaya kwa kuilipia kwa kodi ya maskini hawa hawa? Msaidizi wake alifunga mlango na msafara wa msururu wa magari kuanza safari kutoka ikulu kuelekea kwenye ofisi ya waziri mkubwa.

Waziri mkuu baada ya kuingia kwenye gari lake tu, alifumba macho na kuanza kutafakari yaliyokuwa yamejadiliwa na Rais na utekelezaji wake. Pia alianza kufikiria jinsi ya kufanya mkutano na wasaidizi wake ili wakanushe ile habari ya gazeti la Chimbuchimbu.

Alibonyea kwenye kiti chake cha nyuma ya Benzi kilichikuwa kinabonyea bonyea kama kitanda na kuzama kwenye tafakuri nzito. Laiti jinsi alivyokuwa akitafakari jinsi ya kuliibia taifa ingekuwa ni kwa ajili ya kulijenga na kuliendeleza mbona angefanikiwa sana tena kwa muda mfupi!

Huko ofisini kwa waziri mkubwa, katibu wa ofisi ya waziri mkubwa na waandishi wake walikuwa kwenye kikao kisicho rasmi kujadili habari iliyochapishwa kwenye gazeti la Chimbuchimbu ili bosi wao akitaka wajibu au kumpa ushauri, wawe tayari wameishaanda la kumwambia.

Ilibidi wafanye hivyo. Maana bosi mwenyewe kwa lawama na kuwafokea wakati mwingine huwafanya wajute kwanini waliteuliwa au kuajiriwa kwenye ofisi yake. Lakini kwa vile nafasi zao ndizo zililikuwa jembe lao la kuchotea pesa na marupurupu, hawakuwa na jinsi bali kumtumikia kafiri. Waziri ni mkubwa ni mtu anayewaona wengine kama hawana akili wala hawakukamilika wakati wa kuumbika. Ni mtu na nyodo zake anayejisikia utadhani watu hawajui kinachoendelea nyuma ya pazia!

Tangu waziri ateuliwe kuwa waziri mkubwa, katibu wa ofisi yake, katibu wake na wasaidizi wengine walikuwa ni kawaida kutoka kazini wakati mwingine usiku wa manane kutokana na kuwepo kwa rundo la kashfa za kukanusha na kazi nyingine za kawaida za kiutawala. Katika kashfa zote hii ya Richmonduli ilikuwa ikila bongo na muda mwingi wao kuliko zote. Tangu asubuhi ya kuchapishwa kwa kashfa ile, simu nyingi zilizokuwa zinajulikana kwa umma ilibidi zizimwe. Maana vyombo mbali mbali vya habari vilikuwa vikipiga simu kutaka ufafanuzi na msimamo wa waziri. Hivyo kukwepa zahama hii idara ya habari ya ofisi ya waziri mkubwa iliamua simu zizimwe ili kuandaa majibu ya shutuma zile.

Wapo waliotaka kujua kwanini waziri mkubwa alifanya kazi ambayo haikuwa chini ya wizara yake. Wengine walihukumu moja kwa moja kuwa kilichomsukuma waziri mkubwa kuingilia wizara za wenzake ilikuwa ni rushwa tu. Wengine walikwenda mbali hata kukumbusha makosa aliyofanya alipokuwa waziri kwenye serikali za zamani. Kila mtu kwa wakati wake na sababu zake alikuwa na lake.

Katika kujisafisha, baadhi ya wachambuzi mahiri ambao hawakuwa na msimamo bali kuuza kalamu zao kwa yoyote kama makahaba, walijulishwa kuandaa majibu na mashambulizi dhidi ya wale waliokuwa wakishinikiza waziri mkubwa aachie ngazi au serikali nzima. Maana ilkuwa imeshindwa vibaya sana kutekeleza wajibu wake uliokuwa umewashawishi wananchi kuichagua.

Magazeti na vituo vya televisheni vilivyokuwa upande wa serikali vilitaarifiwa kuacha nafasi kwenye ratiba zao kwa ajili ya makala za kukanusha na kulishambulia gazeti la Chimbuchimbu. Ulikuwa ni mchezo wa hatari. Maana waandishi wa habari waligeuziana kalamu zao katika kulinda uoza. Kweli penye udhia penyeza rupia. Maana wapo waandishi tena wazee walioheshimika walioweka kando utu wao na kukubali kazi hii chafu! Hakika ulikuwa ni wakati wa mavuno kwa wachumia tumbo wa kalamu ambao mara zote kutokea kwa kashfa kama hizi ilikuwa ni wakati wao wa kuvuna wasipopanda. Wao hawakujali kuwa kalamu zao zilikuwa zinatumiwa vibaya kuihujumu nchi yao wenyewe! Kwao kilichokuwa muhimu ni matumbo yao hata kwa kuhatarisha usalama wa nchi! Kama mikokoteni au taxi bubu walikuwa tayari kubeba mzigo wowote hata uwe kinyesi au bomu ilmradi walipata chao tena malipo yenyewe kidogo kama watoto wapewavyo pipi!

Mkutano usiokuwa rasmi uliweka mikakati yake kwa ajili ya kumtetea bosi wao hata kama walikuwa wanajua fika kuwa kulikuwa na hoja kwa gazeti la Chimbuchimbu. Wangefanyaje iwapo kibarua chao kiliwataka wafanye hata mambo ambayo waliyachukia? Hawa nao pamoja na kupata walichokuwa wakipata, walikuwa wakihatarisha usalama wao na wa nchi yao wenyewe ili kujaza matumbo yao. Walikuwa wameingizwa kwenye mtego wa jinai.

Msafara wa waziri mkubwa haukukawia njiani. Ungekawiaje iwapo piki piki na gari la polisi wa barabarani viliishasafisha njia kwa ajili ya mheshimiwa kupita bila bughudha wala hatari ya kusimamishwa kwenye msongamano? Msafara ulikuwa lango kuu la kuingia kwenye ofisi ya waziri mkubwa limeishafunguliwa. Uliingia kwa mwendo wa kasi kama gari la zima moto au la wangonjwa. Waziri alishuka haraka haraka na kusindikizwa ndani na wasaidizi wake. Alikwenda moja kwa moja hadi kwenye ofisi yake. Alimuita mhudumu wake na kumiminia mvinyo kwenye glasi na kuondoka. Kipindi hiki hakumkata jicho. Maana alikuwa na mawazo na mipango mingi kichwani ya kupambana na kashfa iliyokuwa ikitishia kitumbua chake kichafu. Alichukua nakala ya gazeti la Chimbuchimu na kuanza kusoma upya habari ile iliyohusu kashfa ya Richmen. Naye kama bosi wake aliamua kupigilia mistari maneno yote aliyoona yanafaa kupigiliwa mistari. Aliweka miguu juu ya meza yake na kunywa mvinyo wake taratibu huku akisoma gazeti na kutikisa kichwa. Mara alijisemea, "These goons will know who I am. Hapa lazima nihakikishe baadhi ya waandishi wa gazeti hili wanapangwa kwenye safari yangu ya kikazi ya Hong Kong. Huko najua wasaidizi wangu wanaweza kuwaweka sawa." Alivuta bilauri yake na kunywa mvinyo na kuendelea kusoma gazeti la Chimbuchimbu. Yeye alizoea kuliita gazeti la Chokochoko na udaku.

Baada ya kama dakika arobaini na tano hivi, alimuita katibu wa ofisi yake ili kuweza kujua alikuwa na mipango gani kuhusiana na kashfa ya Richmen. Katibu wa wizara alivunja kikao haraka haraka akiwashukuru wajumbe kwa michango yao na kuondoka kuelekea kwenye ofisi ya bosi wake. Baada ya kusoma na kujihakikishia kuwa alikuwa sasa anaijua ile stori vizuri, waziri mkubwa alitaka asikie mawazo ya katibu wa wizara yake ambaye hakuwa ameshirikishwa kwenye ulaji ule. Hivyo, alitaka aongee yeye kwanza ili ajue jinsi ya kumbana na kuhakikisha anaendelea kutojua kilichokuwa kikiendelea nyuma ya pazia. Katibu aliingia kwa unyenyekevu na kuinama na kusema. "Ndiyo mzee. Nimefika tayari kukusikiliza."

Waziri bila kusema neno alimuashiria akae kwenye kiti

mkabala na chake.

Chokochoko kamchokoe pweza

Katibu alikwenda na kukaa kwenye kiti. Alivua miwani yake na kuifuta futa vumbi kwa kitambaa chake huku akiwa ametega masikio yake kusikia waziri angesema nini. Waziri alijitenga vizuri kwenye kiti chake na kuanza. "Katibu, nadhani umesoma upuuzi wa Chokochoko, I mean, Chimbuchimbu. Hivyo nimekuita hapa kusikia umeuchukuliaje na umeandaa nini kuhusiana na huu umbea. Kwa hiyo nimekuita ili unipe briefings na debriefings."

Alimaliza huku akimkazia macho katibu wa ofisi yake.

Katibu alijikakamua na kuanza. "Mheshimiwa hata mimi nimeshangaa sana. Hadi sasa najiuliza hawa watu huu uzushi wameupata wapi na wanalenga nini. Kusema ukweli bado kuna mambo najaribu kuyachunguza ili kujua msimamo wetu uwe ni upi." Alipekecha pekecha vidole wake na kuendelea. "Mimi nafikiria kwanza ni kukanusha habari nzima na baadaye ni kujaribu kutafuta chanzo na sababu za habari hii. Maana hali hii isipokomeshwa inaweza kutishia mshikamano wa taifa letu."

Kabla ya kuendelea, waziri ambaye alionekana kufurahishwa na mawazo yake alisema. "Hawa pamoja ni kwamba ni watu wa upinzani lakini hapa wamevuka mpaka." Aliiweka vizuri miwani yake na kuendelea. "Nadhani hawa watu wamelewa na kuichoka demokrasia tuliyowapa. Serikali kwa nia nzuri imewapa uhuru wa kujieleza wao sasa wanautumia kama uhuru wa kuchafuana bila sababu yoyote ya msingi." Katibu aliendelea. " Mheshimiwa dawa ya moto ni moto. Ningeshauri tukanushe na kujibu tuhuma hizi. Hapa inabidi tutafute wataalamu wa kukanusha wafanye kazi hii. Tukimaliza hili, tuunde timu ya kuchunguza udhaifu wowote wa utawala mzima wa gazeti la Chimbu chimbu. Kwa mfano nimegundua kuwa maripota wengi wa gazeti hili hawana elimu ya kutosha. Sisi kama serikali kuna haja ya kuandaa mswada wa sheria ya kupambana na watu kama hawa kisayansi."Kabla ya kumaliza pointi yake waziri aliingilia. "Tupambane nao kisayansi vipi?"

"Well." Alijibu katibu wa wizara na kuendelea, "Hapa tunaweza kubadili sura ya taaluma nzima ya habari hapa nchini. Kwa mfano tunaweza kuweka masharti magumu kwa mtu kufanya kazi ya uandishi wa habari. Mimi naona tungetumia kupandisha kiwango cha elimu anachopaswa kuwa nacho mtu ili kukwa mwandishi wa habari. Tunaweza tukataka lazima awe na shahada ya chuo kikuu. Nijuavyo waandishi wengi mahiri hawana muda wa kuwawezesha kuingia chuo kikuu kupata shahada hii."

"Hapa kuna vikwazo vitatu. Kikwazo cha kwanza kwa wale wenye sifa za kuingia chuo kikuu ni muda. Watu wengi hawako tayari kuziumiza familia zao kwa muda watakao kuwa wanasomea shahada zao. Pili hawana uwezo wa kifedha wa kujisomesha. Hivyo watahitaji mikopo toka serikalini. Ili kuhakikisha hawapiti,tunateua bodi ya mikopo yenye watu wa serikali au wanao-sympathize na serikali."

"Kikwazo cha tatu." Alimtazama waziri na kuendelea, "Ni kuhakikisha kuwa makada wetu wanaofundisha chuo kikuu wanawafelisha. Hapa bado hatujaweka kipengele cha kumtaka awe na mdhamini mwenye nyuumba, ardhi au gari kumsimamia mhusika kupata mkopo. Pia tunaweza kutoa sharti kuwa serikali inaweza kuridhia au vinginevyo maombi ya mkopo bila kulazimika kutoa maelezo."

Waziri alizidi kufurahia mawazo mazuri ya katibu wake. Ajabu watu hawa waliokuwa wakitaka kupandisha viwango vya elimu, Rais wao alizoea kuitwa daktari kutokana na shahada za heshima za kupewa na vyuo vya nje ambavyo vilitumia nafasi ya ushamba wa usomi wa wananuru kuwaingiza mjini. Maana viongozi wa nchi kubwa kama Marekani Urusi na Uchina hawakuwahi kupewa shahada hizi kwa vile Vyuo husika vilijua sio washamba wa shahada za kupewa; na isitoshe hawakuwa tayari kuzisaliti nchi zao kwa zawadi au chochote.

Waziri mkubwa alijistukia akisema. "Kweli hili ni jibu la kisayansi. Hili sina pingamizi nalo; si rahisi walengwa kujua kuwa tuna mpango huu." Katibu aliendelea. "Pia kwa kutumia mkono mrefu wa serikali, tunaweza kuhakikisha gazeti la Chimbuchimbu halipati huduma yoyote kama vile mikopo, matangazo ya serikali na tukizidiwa tunaweza hata kutia sumu kwenye kiwanda cha uchapishaji wakawa wanawachelewesha hata kutoa kazi hafifu ambayo itaua soko lao na umaarufu wao."

Katibu alichomoa leso yake na kujifuta jasho na kuendelea, "Mheshimiwa hapa hatujaagiza shirika la umeme kuwa wanawakatia umeme mara kwa mara wala shirika la simu kutegesha vinasa sauti kwenye laini zao za simu."

Waziri alikuwa akitikisa kichwa kwa kila alichokuwa akisema katibu wake. Katibu aliendelea. "Kwa vile wenzetu wanasaidiwa na baadhi ya nchi fadhili, tunaweza kupanga hata kuzilipua ofisi za gazeti. Maana hili halitakuwa jinai kama tunafanya hivi kwa ajili ya kuinusuru nchi kutishiwa usalama wake na uchafuzi na uzushi huu. Pia tunaweza kuongea na wawakilishi wa nchi hizi fadhili kuwaeleza kutoridhika kwetu na jinsi wanavyojihusisha na gazeti linalolenga kueneza chuki miongoni mwa wananchi. Wapo watakaotuelewa hata kutishika na kukpunguza ushawishi wa gazeti." Mkutano ulikuwa mfupi sana. Na isitoshe waziri licha ya kupewa mbinu mujarabu, aligundua kuwa katibu hakuwa anajua mpango mzima.

Kimsingi, mkutano japo ulikuwa unawahusisha waziri mkubwa na katibu wake, kwa ujumla, katibu ndiye aliongea peke yake. Alionyesha wazi kuwa na akili nyingi kuliko bosi wake hata kustahili kuwa waziri mkubwa kuliko katibu wake. Hivyo, alikubaliana na katibu akanushe. Alimpa mamlaka ya kutumia kila aina ya mbinu atakayoona inafaa mradi kuwa makini serikali isiathirike au kuadhirika tena. Waliagana na katibu alirudi kwenye ofisi yake akiwa amefurahi sana. Maana, hali ilivyokuwa ni kwamba aliona kwa mara ya kwanza bosi wake amemgwaya kwa kuwa na akili inayochemka. Moyoni alijisemea: Mshenzi leo kanijua mimi ni nani. Maskini asijue akili yake nzuri ilikuwa ikitumika vibaya kuharibu jamii iliyoisaidia kukua!

Huko nyuma, wakati Rais ameridhika na mikakati na majibu ya waziri wake mkubwa, aliendelea kusoma lile gazeti na kuwaza juu ya mambo mbali mbali.

Siku hiyo alikuwa na hafla ya kumpokea vitambulisho vya balozi mmoja toka nchi ya kiarabu. Hata hivyo, hafla hiyo isingechukua muda mrefu. Baada ya kusoma gazeti na kuchoshwa nalo, alitikisa kichwa na kulirudisha kwenye mto wa meza. Alimuita mwandishi wa hotuba ili amuelezee aliyoandika kwenye hotuba kwa ajili ya hafla husika. Mwandishi hakuchelewa. Aliingia kwa unyenyekevu kama kawaida na kuingia kwenye kumsomea Rais yaliyokuwamo kwenye hotuba ambayo angetoa. Wakati akiendelea mwandishi wa hotuba wa Rais akiendelea kumsomea yaliyoandikwa kwenye hotuba Rais, simu kwenye hotline ya Rais ililia. Ilikuwa inatoka kwa balozi wa nchi moja fadhili.

Balozi aliyepiga simu alikuwa akitaka kusikia mawazo ya Rais kuhusiana na kashfa iliyochapishwa kwenye gazeti la Chimbuchimbu. Hakuishia hapo. Alitaka pia muhtasari wa hatua ambazo serikali ilikuwa imechukua kuzuia wizi wa kughushi wa pesa za kigeni kwenye benki kuu ya Mafuriko ambayo ilikuwa imefurika wizi si kawaida. Alikuwa akimfokea Rais utadhani siyo Rais! Naye Rais alijibu kwa unyenyekevu utadhani hakuwa Rais! Kumbe kila mtu ana kiboko yake! Na isitoshe kumbe amlipaye mpiga zumari ndiye huchagua wimbo.

Kipindi fulani huko nyuma aliwahi kufokewa na balozi huyu. Alisikika akijilaumu. "Hii ndiyo hasara ya utegemezi." Simu hii yenye kufokewa ilimnyima raha Rais. Kwa sababu ubalozi wa nchi hii ulikuwa umepinga mradi mzima wa kujenga mitambo ya maji na jinsi zoezi zima lilivyokuwa limetekwa na waziri mkubwa kinyume cha taratibu na sheria. Kuna kipindi Rais alianza kushuku kuwa huenda gazeti la Chimbuchimbu lilikuwa limeiibua hii kashfa ya Richmen toka ubalozini pale. Maana licha ya kuifahamu ile kampuni feki, ubalozi uliipinga baada ya kupewa mchanganuo wake. Kabla ya kupinga mradi mzima, ubalozi ulikuwa umetoa ushauri kuwa utafutaji wa mkandarasi wa mradi uwe wa makini zaidi ili kupata mkandarasi bora na makini. Ubalozi ulikwenda mbali hata kushauri kuwa uhusishwe kwenye kushauri ni wakandarasi wapi walikuwa wakifaa. Lakini kutokana na ushawishi wa waziri mkubwa na njama nzima ya kuliibia taifa, ushauri wa balozi ulipuuziwa bila hata kutolewa sababu wala maelezo jambo lililomfanya balozi achukie sana baada ya kufumka kwa kashfa ya Richmen. Maana waziri mkubwa na watu wake walitoa uamuzi wa kuipa kandarasi kampuni ya Richmen haraka haraka na kuupuuzia ushauri wa ubalozi tena uliokuwa ukiwafadhili.Wakati huo wanatoa hiyo tenda, ubalozi huu uliombwa uwape mwezi mmoja ili watoe msimamo wa serikali. Hivyo walitumia kisingizio hiki kumaliza mambo yao haraka. Isitoshe muda ulioombwa ulipotimu, hakuna aliyekumbuka wala kuhangaika kuupa maelezo ubalozi. Na ubalozi nao ulinyamaza ili uone mwisho wa kiini macho hiki. Kwani siku zote njia ya mwongo ni fupi. Kwenye suala hili la nini ulikuwa msimamo wa Rais kuhusu kashfa ile, Rais alimuomba balozi ampe muda awasiliane na watendaji wake waliokuwa wakihusika na suala zima.

Balozi alionekana kutoridhishwa na majibu ya Rais. Alichofanya ni kubadilisha swali kwa njia nyingine. Alimtaka Rais amfahamishe ni lini serikali ingetimiza ahadi yake juu ya kupokea ushauri wake kuhusiana na mradi na kandarasi ya ujenzi wa mitambo ya maji.

Rais alijikuta kabanwa. Alisema. "Baada ya mkandarasi kupatikana kwa njia ambazo hazikuwaridhisha baadhi ya watu na haya madai mapya ya rushwa yaliyoibuliwa na magazeti, serikali itaunda tume kuchunguza na matokeo yake yatatoka haraka na kuwekwa wazi." Alisita kidogo kufikiria na kuendelea. Alisema. "Lakini mheshimiwa balozi tukubaliane kitu kimoja kuwa serikali huwa hazifanyi kazi kwa kushinikizwa na magazeti. Nadhani hata serikali yako tukufu haiwezi kuamrishwa na gazeti la The Concord hata kama ni maarufu. Mtukufu balozi lazima tukubaliane kwa hili hata kama tunapishana kwenye baadhi ya mambo ambayo tunaweza kuyaweka sawa." Jawabu hili lilimuudhi balozi. Kwani alisema. "Vyombo vya habari ni sauti ya wasio na sauti-voice of the voiceless. Sasa kama ufisadi mkubwa." Alitumia neno mega corruption. "Unategemea ni wafadhili gani watakaowakamua watu wao kodi kuwaletea watu wachache waichezee huku mamilioni ya watu waliolengwa yakizidi kuumia? Basi, serikali yangu ingefurahi sana kama magazeti hata madogo yataionyesha njia pale inapopofuka au kupagawa?" Rais alikuwa amesahau kuwa balozi aliyekuwa akijibizana nanye alikuwa daktari wa falsafa tena wa somo la falsafa na mwakilishi wa nchi fadhili. Isitoshe balozi huyu Profesa Dietrich Gunter alikuwa ni mwalimu na mtafiti wa masomo ya utawala na uwajibikaji aliyekuwa akiheshimika dunia nzima kutokana na vitabu vyake juu ya miiko ya uongozi vilivyokuwa vimechangia sana kusimika demokrasia na uwajibikaji katika mabara ya Ulaya na Amerika. Wasomi wengi walidiriki hata kumlinganisha na Charles de Secondat Montesqui- yule mfaransa aliyebuni kanuni za utawala bora! Alisahau kuwa kabla ya balozi huyu kuletwa Mafuriko alikuwa msaidizi wa katibu mkuu wa umoja wa mataifa juu ya masuala ya uwajibikaji na uboreshaji wa mifumo na seirkali za nchi maskini. Na isitoshe alikuwa ameletwa Mafuriko kuisafisha. Pia alikuwa kama kiongozi wa mbalozi wote toka nchi fadhili.

Balozi aliendelea kumpa shule Rais, "Mheshimiwa Rais, kusema ukweli tumechoka kutoa pesa ambayo tunashuhudia ikichezewa na kikundi cha watu huku umma ukizidi kuteseka. Kumbuka hii ni kodi ya watu wetu nyumbani." Inaonekana balozi wakati akijibizana na Rais wa Mafuriko hakuwa peke yake ofisini. Maana alikatiza maongezi kidogo huku sauti nyingine zikisikika wazi wazi kwenye simu ya Rais.

Jambo hili lilimstua Rais: alidhani alikuwa akirekodiwa. Lakini hata hivyo angefanyaje iwapo alikuwa akiongea na mfadhili wa serikali yake? Baada ya kitambo kidogo, balozi aliendelea, "Kama hali hii haitatafutiwa jibu sahidhi na haraka na kwa wakati, bila shaka, tutasitisha misaada yetu yote kwa serikali yako na kuipitisha kwenye taasisi zisizo za kiserikali hata kama kuna ulaji, siyo mkubwa kama huu. Pia kumbuka; hata wizi wa Benki kuu haujaushughulikia ukiachia mbali kuwa na simile na ufisadi."Rais hakutoa jibu la swali wala kutoa hoja nyingine zaidi ya kusisitiza kuwa apewe muda awasiliana na watendaji wake. Kutokana na madai haya kuwa mazito, Rais alimuomba balozi ampe muda na ikiwezekana wakutane ili kuweka mambo sawa. Alikata simu na alimpigia simu makamu wake. Alimuamuru akapokee vitambulisho vya balozi toka nchi moja ya kiarabu ambao Rais angeufanya. Hivyo ilibidi taarifa itumwe na mkuu wa itifaki haraka kwa balozi mtarajiwa na vyombo vya habari kuelezea badiliko hilo.Tukio hili la kubadilisha upokeaji toka kwa Rais kwenda kwa makamu wake pia liliiudhi nchi ya kiarabu ambayo nayo ilikuwa ikiifadhili serikali ya Mafuriko kwa kuipa mafuta ya bei nafuu.

Serikali iliomba msamaha baadaye na mambo yakaisha.

17
Jogoo awaharibu vifaranga

Rais aliamua kumuita gavana mkuu wa benki Mafuriko Dadi Balaa Bilali, ili kupata taarifa ya wizi ambao nao kama kashfa ya Richmen, ulifichuliwa na magazeti yasiyo ya serikali na pia ulikuwa umelalamikiwa na balozi. Hali hii ilimchanganya sana kiasi cha kuanza kufikiria kupangua safu ya
tawala wake. Alijisemea, "Now this is too much. Yaani kumbe jogoo aliwafundisha vifaranga kunya ndani! Inabidi nibadilike; nianze kuonyesha njia badala ya kupindisha mambo." Aliendelea kuongea peke yake. "Hawa wasaidizi wangu wanataka kunitumia. Pamoja na kulaumu magazeti, kuna ukweli usiopingika kuwa sasa wanakula bila kunawa. Inabidi niitishe mkutano wa wahariri wa vyombo vya habari na kutoa tishio huenda wanaweza kujirudi. Kumbe urais haupo kama nilivyotarajia!"Akiwa anatafakari, ujumbe wa gavana wa benki kuu uliingia. Kwa vile alitaka maongezi ya faragha na gavana peke yake, alimuamuru katibu wake awataarifu wajumbe waliokuwa wameandamana na gavana wa benki kuu kuwapisha ili aongee yeye na gavana.

Katibu wa Rais alikuwa amewaingiza wote kwenye ofisi yake. Kigwena hiki na gavana kilifanyika kwenye ofisi nyingine iliyoitwa ya Mashujaa. Maana ilikuwa imejaa picha za mashujaa walioifia nchi kwenye kupigania uhuru. Laiti picha zingekuwa zinasema, huenda siku hiyo zingewazaba makofi gavana na Rais. Maana walikuwa wanakutana kwenye chumba cha mashujaa kuubomoa msingi uliokuwa umewekwa tena kwa damu na roho za mashujaa wale. Ajabu! Rais, kila mwaka, alizoea kuweka shada la maua kwenye mnara wa kumbukumbu ya mashujaa kama alama ya kuwaenzi. Lakini nyuma ya pazia, alikuwa akiwadhalilisha na kuwadhihaki si kawaida! Maana, alijitahidi kupinga na kubomoa kila msingi waliokuwa wameuweka kwa ajili ya vizazi vijavyo vya Mafuriko. Kwake Rais, vizazi vijavyo ilikuwa ni tumbo lake, familia yake na marafiki zake! Zilikuwapo picha za mashujaa kama Sokoine, Nyerere, Mkwawa, Mirambo, Nyungu ya Mawe, Kinjekitile na wengine wengi waliokuwa wamepoteza maisha yao kutetea uhuru wa Mafuriko. Hata sura za mashujaa kwenye picha zilionekana kama kuwatazama wale wawili kwa hasira na dharau. Na laiti zingekuwa zinatoka na kutenda, huenda zingewaulia mle bila kujali. Maana, hawakuwa na faida nao wala wanachi waliokuwa wamewatolea damu na uhai wao. Na isitoshe, sehemu kubwa ya mashujaa wale kwenye picha walikuwa ni magwiji wa vita. Gavana kwa kujua tatizo la benki yake na jinsi alivyokuwa ameshiriki kuihujumu nchi, alikuwa amekuja na ujumbe mzito wa watu sita ili kujisafisha na kumdanganya bosi wake kuonyesha kuwa maamuzi mengi ya benki kuu yalikuwa yamefikiwa kwa kushirikisha wakuu wa idara zake ingawa ukweli ni kwamba wahusika walikuwa wanaburuzwa na gavana aliyezoea kuwatisha kuwa yeye alikuwa mtaalamu aliyeagizwa nje ya nchi tena kwa bei mbaya. Kama ni ushauri, washauri wake wakuu walikuwa mkewe, waziri mkubwa na washirika wake wengine katika jinai ya kuifilisi nchi. Alikuwa ameandamana na wakurugenzi wa mikopo, Keni Makeni, uwekezaji, amana za serikali, fedha za kigeni, usalama na naibu gavana Kitomiri Marili.

Wakati wakiwa wametulia kwenye viti vyao, katibu wa Rais alitangaza kuwa mkutano lengwa ulikuwa ni baina ya Rais na gavana. Hivyo, aliwataka wakurugenzi warudi maofisini kwao kuchapa kazi. Hali hii iliwatia wasi wasi wakurugenzi na naibu gavana kiasi cha kuhisi kuwa huenda kungekuwepo mabadiliko kwenye utawala wa Mafuriko.

Kutokana na tukio hili, mkurugenzi wa fedha za kigeni alilazimika kupitia kwa daktari wake, Orton Chikwakwa, ili kumpa ushauri na kupima msukumo wa damu uliokuwa umemshambulia kutokana na tukio hili nyeti. Maana alikuwa akisumbuliwa na kisukari na ugonjwa wa moyo. Daktari wake alikuwa kama Mungu wake wa pili. Maana, asingefanya safari wala shughuli yoyote bila kupata ushauri wake. Na hii ndiyo ilifanya Ng'wanandaja kujua siri nyingi za benki kuu.

Kutokana na kuvurugikiwa kimawazo, daktari wa mkurugenzi wa fedha za kigeni alimshauri apumzike siku hiyo. Hofu yake kubwa ilikuwa ni kudhani kuwa ule mradi wake wa kuvusha pesa za kigeni kupitia duka lake la kubadilishia pesa za kigeni liitwalo Soms Mc, ungenaswa na Rais. Wakati yeye akihofia hilo Bosi wake yaani gavana naye kichwani alikuwa na wasi wasi kuhusu madhambi yake ambayo Rais kutokana na kuwa mpya ofisini alikuwa hayajui vizuri ukiachia kuyasoma magazetini na kuyatetea kwenye baraza la mawaziri alipokuwa waziri wa mambo ya ndani ya Mafuriko.Gavana alikuwa na madhambi magunia kwa magunia. Alikuwa akimilki benki moja iitwayo Delphas ambayo ilikuwa inasimamiwa na mbwindi mmoja aitwaye Chandy au Dencha. Hawa mabwana walikuwa na mali si kawaida. Walikuwa na maduka ya vito na uuzaji wa magari ya bei mbaya, Classic cars na viwanja vya mashindano ya farasi (Race course), kule Monaco na Dubai.

Nchini Uswisi walikuwa na benki yao iitwayo DAAN international. Yaani Dadi na Anna. Majambazi hawa walikuwa na makampuni mengi ya bima, maduka ya kubadilisha pesa za kigeni, makampuni ya ujenzi hata mengine yalisimamiwa na kukendeshwa na watu ambao hawakuwa na ujuzi lakini bado walipata tenda nono nono kupitia mgongoni mwa gavana na mke wa Rais na waziri mkubwa. Watu waliokuwa karibu na gavana na kundi lake la majambazi walidaiwa alikuwa na utajiri kuliko hata bajeti ya Mafuriko! Kila majambazi hawa walipoiibia benki kuu ya Mafuriko, sarafu ya Mafuriko na uchumi vilizidi kuteketea huku Rais naye aliyekuwa mmoja wa majambazi hawa akiwapa moyo wananchi kuwa uchumi ungekuwa.

Walichokuwa wakifanya ni kutoa ripoti za uongo juu ya sarafu ya Mafuriko na muelekeo mzima wa uchumi. Kwenye vitabu mambo yalikuwa safi. Lakini kwa wanachi waliokuwa wakibeba mzigo huu mchafu hali ilikuwa inazidi kuwa mbaya. Hapa ndipo Zengeni alipokuwa akihoji maana na mantiki nzima ya watu waliokuwa wamesomeshwa na nchi huku wengine wakikaribishwa na kuilipa mabaya. Alizoea kuwaita mafisi na malaya wa matumbo. Aliwadharau na kuwalinganisha na kila aina ya kitu duni kuanzia kinyesi hadi maiti bila ya kujali vyeo vyao. Kwake walikuwa ni wanafiki na watu hatari kuliko hata ukoma au mbalanga na mangonjwa mengine yaharibuyo mwili sawa na wao wanavyoharibu jamii. Kwani walikuwa ni gonjwa linaloteketeza watu wengi wasio na hatia. Walikuwa na utitiri wa mali za wazi na sirini. Mbwindi mwingine aliyesimamia himaya hii ya wizi yaani Chandy au Dencha pia alikuwa kaanzisha taasisi ya kujitolea na kutoa misaada kwa watu wa mafuriko aliokuwa akiwaibia. Aliita Cheetah Club. Kweli ilikuwa Cheetah. Maana aliwaibia na kuwasaidia kwa pesa yao wenyewe! Ushirika huu wa majambazi wenye suti ulikuwa na majumba ya mamilioni ya dola karibu kwenye nchi zote tajiri ulaya na uarabuni.

Klabu ya Cheetah ilikuwa ni kama mwamvuli wa kukutanishia wafanyabiashara wa kibwindi na watawala wezi kujadili miradi yao michafu. Ilitumika kama kiini macho kwa wananchi waliokuwa wakiiona kama yenye msaada wakati ilikuwa ni nyoka kwenye debe la unga.

Wananchi wangeshindwaje kuelewa hivyo iwapo Cheetah ilikuwa ikisadia kuchangisha pesa ya gharama za matibabu ya magonjwa yaliyoshindikana nje ya nchi? Kutokana na gavana kuwa na kazi nyingine za kiserikali na kutotaka siri zake kufumka, alijikuta akiwa mateka wa yule mbwindi. Maana katika ujambazi wao huu mhindi licha ya kuleta wahindi wenzake kuendesha biashara ya gavana, alikuwa akitumia anavyotaka. Kuna kipindi gavana alichukia akamtisha kuwa angesitisha uhusiano wao. Mbwindi wala hakustuka zaidi ya kumwambia kuwa angekwenda magazetini na kutubu ili awaombe msamaha watu wa Mafuriko kwa kushiriki kuihujumu nchi yao. Hili tishio lilikuwa ni pigo takatifu lililomziba gavana mdomo hadi leo! Isitoshe, huyu mbwindi alikuwa amejijenga sana kwa watawala. Alifahamiana na mabalozi, wenyeviti wa bodi za mashirika hata wabunge na mawaziri. Alijua kuwachanganya na kupata chake. Maana alizoea kuwaambia wenzake kuwa Mafuriko ilikuwa nchi ya mabwege. Na kweli kwa ilivyokuwa ikinajisiwa ilikuwa nchi ya mabwege.

18
Nyuma ya Pazia

Baada ya wakurugenzi na naibu gavana kuondoka, mkutano wa faragha baina ya Rais na gavana wa benki kuu ulianza. Kama ilivyokuwa kwa mkutano wa kwanza na waziri mkubwa, Rais alitaka kupata maelezo juu ya kashfa ya wizi wa shilingi bilioni 300 kwenye benki kuu uliofanywa na watu wenyc ushawishi mkubwa kwa kushirikiana na maafisa wa benki kuu akiwamo gavana mwenyewe.

Kwanza, gavana alikuwa amenusurika kufukuzwa kazi na kuwekwa ndani baada ya kugundulika kuwa alikuwa amechapisha noti mpya katika nchi moja ya Ulaya kwa pesa kubwa kuliko pesa iliyochapishwa. Kosa lake ilikuwa kuzidisha kiwango alichokuwa ameambiwa cha trilioni tano ambapo tatu zingeenda kwenye kugharimia uchaguzi na zilizobaki kulipa gharama ya uchapishaji. Yeye naye aliongeza zakc mbili! Kibaya zaidi noti zenye zilizokuwa zimegharimu shilingi trilioni saba hazikuwa na ubora uliotakiwa. Zilikuwa siyo imara na pia ilikuwa rahisi kughushiwa. Sasa kabla vumbi halijatua alikuwa na sakata la wizi wa shilingi bilioni 300. Benki kuu ya Mafuriko badala ya kuwa benki kuu ya wananchi iligeuzwa kuwa benki kuu ya wizi mkuu. Badala ya kuwa BoM yaani Bank of Mafuriko iligeuka kuwa Band of Mafia! Pamoja na gavana mkuu wa benki kuu kujua kuwa vitendo kama hivi vilikuwa vikizorotesha uchumi, kwake na wenzake uchumi wao binafsi ulikuwa ni bora kuliko wa nchi. Hivyo, katika nchi ya Mafuriko badala ya kuwa na mashindano na mikakati katika idara na taasisi mbali mbali za umma, kulikuwa na mashindano ya kuuibia umma. Ajabu wengi wa walioongoza ugaidi huu wa kimaadili walikuwa ni watu na taaluma yao! Hawa ndiyo babu yake Zengeni aliwahi kusema kuwa walisomea wizi badala ya kuikwamua jamii.

Wakati sakata la wizi benki kuu likiendelea, wizara mbali mbali hasa zikiongozwa na madini, utalii na wanyama zilikuwa zikisifika kwa wizi. Ripoti ya kila mwaka ya mhasibu na mdhibiti mkuu wa hesabu za serikali (Controller and Auditor General-CAG) zilikuwa zikifichua wizi wa mabilioni hata matrilioni ambayo kama yangetumika vizuri, yangeiondoa nchi kwenye kadhia ya uomba omba na utegemezi. Lakini nani alikuwa anajali iwapo wananchi wa Mafuriko walikuwa wamefurika woga na ujinga? Pamoja na ukubwa wa kiasi hiki na wingi wa watu walioathirika na kuibiwa kwake, hakuna mtu hata mmoja aliyefukuzwa kazi achilia mbali kufikishwa mahakamani! Hii ndiyo amani wakuu wa Mafuriko walizoea kujisifia. Yaani wachache kuiba na kula kwa amani wakati wanaoibiwa wanaambiwa nchi yao ilikuwa ya amani!

Mafuriko kweli ilijaliwa utajiri usio wa kawaida. Maana kama pesa yote iliyokuwa ikiibiwa na kundi dogo la mbweha-watu ingerudishwa, Mafuriko ingeweza kutoa misaada hata kwa nchi jirani maskini ambazo hazikujaliwa kuwa na raslimali kama yenyewe.Taarifa za jarida moja la kimataifa liitwalo "The Financials" iliwahi kufichua kuwa tangu Mafuriko ipate uhuru wake wa bendera zaidi ya miaka 50, zaidi ya dola za kimarekani bilioni 500 zilikuwa zimeibiwa na majambazi hawa wa ndani ukiachia zile zilizokuwa zikiibiwa na washirika wao wa nje. Jarida hili lilibainisha kuwa wizi katika nchi ya Mafuriko ilikuwa ni kama kichaa. Maana utajiri uliokuwa unamilkiwa na watu wachache wasingeweza kuutumia na kuumaliza hata vitukuu, vilembwe na vinying'inya wao.

Gavana wa benki kuu, jamaa wa miaka kama sitini hivi aliyeng'ara utadhani kichanga, aliingia ndani ya ofisi ya Rais bila haraka wala hofu kama waziri mkubwa. Hakuwa na haja ya kuwa na hofu. Kwanza hakuwa ameteuliwa na Rais. Serikali ilimrithi toka serikali ya zamani iliyokuwa nayo ikisifika kwa ufisadi uliokuwa umekubuhu. Zamani, inasemekana, alikuwa akifanya kazi kwenye taasisi za pesa nchi za kikoloni kwenye mji mkuu wa taifa la Nohino. Kuna kipindi ilivumishwa kuwa watu kama yeye hawakufaa kuendelea kuwa kwenye ofisi za umma. Maana walikuwa vibaraka na wapelelezi wa wakiloni. Alikukwa ni mtu mwenye sura ya pesa. Alivalia pete ya almas na saa aina ya Rado yenye kutonwa na vito vya thamani pamoja na almasi na tanzanite. Ilikuwa ni saa ya bei mbaya ambayo kama ingeuzwa na pesa yake kuwagawia maskini,si haba ingewatoa maskini zaidi ya 40 kwenye msiba wa umaskini. Pia, tai yake na vishikizo vya shati lake vilikuwa vya almasi. Hakuishia hapo. Kwani kwenye soli za viatu vyake kulikuwa na ufito wa dhahabu. Viatu venyewe vilitengenezwa kwa ngozi ya chui na chatu huku sori zake zikiwa za pembe za faru. Kweli kwa alivyokuwa amevalia si haba ni ukichaa na uharibifu wa jasho la umma. Ni usaliti karibu na ufuska kwenye ndoa. Maana hauna jinsi ya kuuelezea wala kuusamehe. Ajabu hata Rais hakuona israfu hii! Angeionaje iwapo naye alikuwa limbukeni wa utajiri na usasi wa ngawira? Ajabu Rais yule yule aliposimama majukwaani alijifanya kuwaonea huruma maskini wakati yeye na kundi lake ndio walikuwa chanzo kikuu cha umaskini wa wale maskini aliojitia kuwaonea huruma. Laiti wangejua yaliyokuwa yakiendelea nyuma ya pazia huenda wangelimchoma kama wale vibaka walichomwa Uswekeni kwa kuchomoa simu na vijihereni vya mama maskini. Lakini wangejuaje iwapo kila mmoja alisumbuliwa na kutumikishwa na tumbo lake? Mwenye shibe hamjui mwenye njaa.

Badala ya kumlaani, kumdharau hata kumchoma moto,

wananchi ndiyo walizidi kumnyenyekea. Kila sehemu aliyotembelea alilakiwa kwa nyimbo shangwe na furaha utadhani alikuwa mtu wa maana! Kweli aliyegundua pazia aliuweza ulimwengu kama aliyegundua mlango na pesa. Maana kila alipokwenda alipewa zawadi ya mbuzi, ng'ombe na kuku na mayai yake! Pazia huficha siri zilizoko nyuma yake, huku mlango ukiweka kikwazo. Pesa ndiyo usiseme. Maana kila mtu anaitafuta na hatosheki nayo! Lilipokuja suala la utajiri, huyu gavana hakukaukiwa vituko. Kwani wakati akiingia ofisini kwa Rais simu yake iliita. Alichomoa mfukoni na kupokea. Ilikuwa ni simu ambayo hata Rais mwenyewe ilimshangaza. Kwani alikuwa hajawahi kuona wala kumilki simu kama ile. Ilikuwa ni simu iliyokuwa imeagizwa kiwandani ikiwa imefunikwa na almasi na dhahabu na madini mengine ya thamani ambayo majina yake hata Rais hakuyajua!

Rais aliiangalia sana na hakusema kitu. Kwani kama angeonyesha ushamba wake kwa mtu wa chini yake angejivunjia heshima bure ingawa kimsingi gavana mwenyewe alikuwa anamchukulia kama mjinga na maskini wa kawaida asiyejua kutumia nafasi yake. Rais hakumpenda yule gavana kama ambavyo ana gavana hakumpenda Rais. Lakini kila mmoja alimhitaji mwenzake kutokana na uchafu wao wa nyuma ya pazia.

Gavana alihitaji ulinzi dhidi ya kushitakiwa na kufilisiwa kibarua na sehemu ya kuzidi kuibia wakati Rais alimhitaji kama mtaalam na mtu aliyemsaidia kuchapisha pesa zilizomsaidia kwenye uchaguzi ambapo chama chake kilihonga hadi wananchi wa Mafuriko wakawa wanasema kilimwaga radhi. Hivyo, mkutano huu ulikuwa ni maadui wawili lakini wenye maslahi katika kila mmoja. Kitu kingine kilichokuwa kinamfanya gavana ajiamini hata kuwa na kiburi ni ile hali ya kujua siri za Rais na waziri wake mkubwa na wengine. Hivyo, alikuwa akijua wazi kuwa Rais asingemfanya kitu na akabakia salama. Maana wakati wa kuchapisha zile pesa wakati Rais alikuwa bado hajawa Rais, rafiki yake yaani waziri mkubwa ndiye aliasisi na kusimamia na kutekeleza hujuma hii kwa umma ambayo ilipewa jina la Engaging in pure Advantage (EPA). Na hii ndiyo kete ambayo angeitumia katika lolote baya litakaloelekezwa kwake na Rais.

Hali kwenye chumba ilikuwa ya utulivu kiasi kwamba ilisikika sauti ya kiyoyozi tu. Wajanja wawili mwenye mamlaka ya kisiasa na mwenye mamlaka ya pesa walikuwa uso kwa uso kwenye mkutano ambao mara nyingi ulikuwa nadra. Kitu ambacho kingejulisha kuwa kulikuwa na watu ni harufu kali ya pafyumu aliyokuwa amejipulizia gavana. Maana kama mtu mwenye njaa angeingia mle angetapika hadi kuutapika utumbo kutokana na ukali wa pafyumu ile aghali. Baada ya Rais kuridhika kuwa mgeni wake alikuwa tayari kumsikiliza alimsabahi. "Habari zako Bwana gavana."Gavana alitabasamu kwa kulazimisha na kujibu. "Nzuri mheshimiwa Rais" Gavana alijulikana kwa tabia yake ya kujiona ni msomi na anajua kuliko kiumbe yeyote tokana na shahada yake ya udaktari wa uchumi aliyokuwa akiitumia kinyume kwa kuuvuruga uchumi wa Mafuriko.

Rais akiwa anatabasamu, naye kwa kulazimisha alisema. "Sasa twende moja kwa moja kwenye lengo la kukuiteni."

Gavana alitikisa kichwa kukubali. Na Rais aliendelea. "Gavana nimekuita kutaka maelezo juu ya upotevu wa pesa za wananchi jumla ya bilioni 300. Hiki ni kiwango kikubwa kwa vigezo vyovyote hasa kwa nchi maskini inayoishi kwa kuomba omba kama Mafuriko." Alinyamaza na kumuangalia na kuendelea. "Je kwanza kwanini hujanitaarifu na kwanini wizi huu umetokea?"

Gavana akiwa anatabasamu bila hata ya woga wala

mshangao alijibu. "Mheshimiwa haya maneno yanatoka wapi? Kwanza nikanushe kwa nguvu zote kuwa huu siyo wizi bali ni malipo ya fadhila kwa wafadhili wa uchaguzi. Kumbuka pesa tuliyochota kwenye kasma ya akiba ya nchi kwa ajili ya kuchaguliwa kwa serikali yako tukufu mheshimiwa. Kwa hiyo huu siyo wizi wala hujuma mbele yangu na wewe isipokuwa kwa wananchi ambao hawajui kinachoendelea nyuma ya pazia. Nadhani huu unaonekana kama wizi kutokana na mheshimiwa waziri wa hazina na mifuko na waziri mkubwa kupitisha baadhi ya maamuzi bila kukutaarifu kutokana kuwa na mamlaka juu ya mambo fulani fulani ya moja kwa moja ambayo wanayo toka kwako."Ilibidi ahamishie mzigo kwa waziri mkubwa na katibu wa hazina. Maana kila mwananchi wa Mafuriko alimjua waziri mkubwa kama mtu mwenye tamaa ya fisi.

Rais aliingilia na kusema, "Nisingetaka twende kwenye masuala ya udhamini na ufadhili wa uchaguzi. Kitu ambacho nataka kujua ni kwanini kitu kama hiki kifike kwenye vyombo vya habari? Hii tulikubaliana iwe siri ya wakubwa. Hakuna haja ya kujihatarisha kwa kuwapa faida wapinzani wetu. Na isitoshe suala la uchaguzi sisi siyo peke yetu wala wa kwanza na mwisho. Haya ni mambo ya kawaida ya kiserikali Bwana gavana."

"Mheshimiwa" Gavana alisema na kuvuta mkoba wake kutoa laptop yake na kuendelea. "Katika kuandaa taarifa za mapato na matumizi ya serikali na hali ya uchumi ya kila mwezi, maafisa wangu walifanya kosa kuunganisha taarifa zao na ripoti ya mkaguzi na mthibiti mkuu wa mahesabu ambayo kimsingi siyo nzuri kwetu. Hivyo bila ya wao kujua kuwa CAG angetoa pengo hili ambalo tunaweza kuliziba kwa kuchapisha noti mpya kwenye taarifa yake. Na kutokana na mizania ya matumizi ya serikali kuwa mbaya, tumejikuta hata tukisita kutaja matumizi ya serikali kwa mwezi huu. Tumefanya hivi kwa sababu kuu mbili.

Kwanza kuhakikisha kuwa umma haujui matumizi mabaya ya serikali yako." Alimkazia macho Rais kama kumuonya na kuendelea, "Na pili kuhakikisha kuwa umma ukiishasahau tungeeleza kuwa pengo lilisomekana kuwa wizi kwenye benki yangu siyo wizi bali pesa zilizokuwa zimetumiwa na serikali yao wenyewe. Tungeeleza kuwa yalitokea makosa ya kiuchapaji na mambo yangeisha bila kuleta madhara kwa serikali yako tukufu." Kabla ya kuendelea Rais aliingilia. "Unataka kusema kuwa wananchi hawatahoji serikali inayotumia shilingi bilioni 300 nje ya zilizokubaliwa wakati makusanyo ya kodi ni bilioni 200? Okey wananchi tunaweza kuwafumba macho na nchi fadhili ambazo zimeishaanza kuonyesha kutoridhika na mambo yanavyokwenda?" Gavana alijibu kwa kujiamini. "Hili si tatizo. Nchi fadhili zinatumia watu tena wenye kutaka pesa. Ripoti zao zinaandaliwa na watu. Hao niachie mheshimiwa. Najua jinsi ya kucheza nao mtukufu Rais."

Rais hakuridhika kirahisi. "Hao unaweza kuwanyamazisha kama ambavyo tumekuwa tukifanya. Je mfumko wa bei, kuporomoka kwa sarafu na kushuka kwa uchumi navyo hivi unaviweka wapi?" Gavana alisema, "Mheshimiwa Rais, tutatoa ripoti kuwa uchumi unakwenda vizuri. Hapa nitakachofanya ni kuendaa ripoti ndefu sana kiasi kwamba watu wetu wenye tabia ya kutopenda kusoma hawataisoma yote. Hapa watu wa kushughulika nao ni wafadhili" Alikohoa na kumwangalia Rais aliyekuwa kwa kiasi fulani ameanza kuridhishwa na maelezo ya gavana. "Kawaida wananchi wanaamini taarifa za vyombo vya habari. Hivyo tukichapisha taarifa kuwa uchumi wetu unakuwa kwa asilimia kumi watasherehekea. Maana hawana uwezo wa kufanya utafiti.

Isitoshe ni wavivu wa kusoma volumes kubwa kubwa. Ili kuzidi kuwaua kabisa naweza kushauri marafiki zangu watoe ripoti ya utafiti wa kimataifa juu ya uchumi wa nchi yetu. Wakija na clean report nani atahoji hata awe profesa?"

Gavana aliendelea. "Kiwango cha pesa kinachodaiwa kuwa kimeibiwa nitakipunguza. Hapa vijana wangu maalum watakuja na marundo ya pesa mbovu. Na hii tutatangaza kuwa wananchi wamesababishia taifa hasara ya mabilioni ya pesa kwa kutotunza noti vizuri. Tutaonyesha samples za mabandali ya pesa zilizoharibika. Ili kuushawishi umma kuwa umehusika na hara hii,tutaoa taarifa kwenye vyombo vya habari kuwa yeyote atakayegundulika kutotunza vizuri pesa ambayo ni mali ya umma atashitakiwa kwa kosa la jinai la kuhujumu na kuharibu mali ya umma." Rais alitikisa kichwa kukubaliana na ufundi wa gavana wake wa kuficha maovu yao ingawa moyoni alijilaumu kwa kuwa na gavana jambazi kiasi hiki ambaye alishirikishwa kwenye mambo yake ya ndani na kuyatumia kuihujumu nchi huku akijiamini hivi.

Gavana aliendelea. "Hili la kutochapishwa ripoti ya matumizi ya serikali,tutatoa udhuru kuwa mfumo wetu wa kompyuta ulishambuliwa na kirusi, cyber bug. Hii tutaiitia Y 100 K. Hivyo, kwa kujua unyeti wa ripoti na taarifa hizi, hatukuona sababu ya kutoa taarifa za kubuni. Hivyo tutaomba msamaha kwa hili. Na isitoshe wananchi watashawishika kukubaliana na utetezi wetu. Kwa vile kompyuta zimetengenezwa na binadamu. Naamini this is a logical suggestion your excellency." Rais alitikisa kichwa tena kuonyesha kukubaliana na hoja za gavana wake.

Gavana aliendelea. "Kwa vile mheshimiwa ungejisikia mwenye raha na amani iwapo atakayekurithi baada ya kipindi chako cha kuwa Rais kitakuwa kimetimia, atakuwa rafiki yako na mshirika wako, waziri mkubwa Mheshimiwa Edmond

Ngonyaegg Mpendamali Mwaluwasha, ningeshauri tufanye kila liwezekanalo wakati ule ukifika tuwe na pesa ya kutosha kuliwezesha hili."

Rais aliingilia. "Japo hili ni wazo jema, lisihatarishe reputation yangu na serikali yangu kama inavyoanza kuonekana sasa." Gavana alijibu. "Nafahamu sana. Lakini pia mheshimiwa Rais inabidi tukubaliane kuwa kutokana na mambo yanavyokwenda, ni muhimu kumuachia kiti mtu wako mwaminifu. Maana dunia imebadilika." Gavana alionya. Aliendelea huku akijiamini kama mwalimu anayemfundisha mtoto mdogo asiyejua kitu, "Najua sana. Lakini we need to be extra careful. Maana vyombo huru vya habari navyo vina yake. Nisingependa kusikia kashfa za pesa tena hata kama tunahitaji pesa kiasi hiki. Hivyo nitatumia ujuzi wangu wote kuhakikisha hakuna kinachoharibika mtukufu Rais." Hasira na woga alivyokuwa navyo Rais alistukia vimetoweka kiasi cha kujihisi salama na mwenye furaha.

Mkutano wa Rais na Gavana haukuwa wa muda mrefu. Hivyo baada ya wote wawili kujiridhisha kuwa wamemaliza tofauti zao, walipeana mikono na gavana alimshukuru Rais kwa kuzidi kumuamini na alimpa hakikisho kuwa mambo yote yangekwenda kama ilivyopangwa na madaraka na serikali visingehatarishwa.

Gavana aliondoka kuelekea ofisini kwake na Rais aliamua kwenda kujipumzisha. Alitoa maagizo asibughudhiwe. Aliagiza kuwa atayemhitaji aambiwe Rais ana shughuli muhimu. Hivyo asingepokea taarifa au mgeni yoyote. Pamoja na kwamba Rais alikuwa anakwenda kujipumzisha badala ya kufikiria juu ya masuala muhimu. Hili la kuzuia kupokea mgeni yeyote lilikuwa kama amri na sheria. Maana Rais wa Mafuriko chini ya katiba waliyokuwa wameirithi kwa mkoloni, alikuwa hana tofauti na Mungu mtu. Na huu ndiyo ulikuwa uchochoro uliotumiwa na Rais pamoja na baadhi ya watangulizi wake kuiibia Mafuriko matrilioni ya pesa. Kwani wananchi wa Mafuriko walio wengi hawakujua tofauti baina ya uhuru na ukoloni.

Kwa kutumia uungu mtu wake, Rais wa Mafuriko alikuwa akijifanyia kila alichotaka hata kuingilia uhuru wa taasisi nyingine kama bunge na mahakama bila kizuizi chochote ukiachia mbali serikali yake kuundwa na marafiki na vibaraka wake.

Rais na mawaziri wake walikuwa ni watu wa kutumia na kufuja pesa na utajiri wa Mafuriko bila kuulizwa na yeyote. Maana vyama vya upinzani vilikuwa vimebanwa na kuhujumiwa si kawaida. Vilikuwepo sawa na havipo.

Alitumia pesa ya umma kuwarubuni wapinzani na kuwarejesha kwenye chama chake pale walipotokea watu wakajiunga na upinzani. Wengine walitumwa kwenye vyama ili kuvipeleleza au kuanzisha vurugu ndani ya vyama. Viliposambaratika, walirejea kwao. Kimsingi aliihujumu nchi kwa kutumia pesa ya wananchi kwa faida ya kikundi kidogo cha wezi waliokuwa wamejificha uheshimiwa!

19
Songombwingo wenye vyeo

Baada ya gavana kumaliza kikao chake na Rais, alirudishwa ofisini kwake. Naye utadhani walikuwa wamekubaliana na bosi wake. Alipofika alitoa amri ya kutokuwa tayari kupokea mgeni yoyote au afisa yoyote. Hata naibu gavana alipotaka kwenda kumuona kujua kulikoni kwenye mkutano aliokuwa amemaliza kuufanya na Rais, alipewa maelezo haya ambayo hayakuwa na kipengele cha kuuliza wala kupinga. Gavana alikuwa ofisini mwake akinywa Gin kidogo ili kuondoa uchovu na mawazo kichwani. Kitu kimoja alichofanya ilikuwa ni kumpigia simu msimamizi wake wa biashara zake aliyekuwa ameumuagiza toka bara hindi.

Baada ya kuongea na mshirika wake alianza kurejea picha nzima ya mkutano na kujaribu kufikiria upya juu ya maswali ya Rais na majibu yake. Gavana alikuwa mvutaji mzuri wa cigars toka Cuba. Alivuta mtoto wa meza yake na kutoa sigara moja kubwa na kuiwasha bila kujali kuwa kile chumba kilikuwa na kiyoyozi. Alikupua moshi kwa haraka haraka na kunywa gin yake kidogo huku akiweka miguu yake juu ya meza. Kutokana na kukaa muda mrefu bila kuvuta alikwenda maliwatoni na kutema na kurudi mezani kwake akiendelea kutafakari. Pombe na ukali wa sigara vilichanganyikana kiasi cha kumfanya gavana aanze kuona kama chumba kilikuwa kinaanza kuzunguka. Ikiongezewa na mawazo ya kigwena cha ghafla, alijihisi kama kufurahi kulikochanganyikana na kuchukia. Alishusha miguu yake na kuvuta tena cigar yake kwa taratibu kama mtu anayesikiliza kitu fulani. Alijihisi kupumbaa kwa aina fulani huku akiangalia wingu la moshi mzito likitipaa taratibu chumbani.

Baada ya kumaliza zoezi lake la kuvuta cigar alirudi maliwatoni na kunawa uso huku akiangalia kunyanzi na mvi vilivyokuwa vimeanza kumshambulia. Alijisemea, "Sir Joji Kahami huweka rangi kuficha mvi. Lakini hana rangi ya kuzuia kunyanzi!" Alama za uzee zilikuwa zinaanza kuchukua mahali pake. Aliusonya uzee na kurejea kwenye chumba chake kilichokuwa aghali kuliko hata ofisi ya bosi wake yaani Rais aliyekuwa ndiyo katoka kuongea naye. Kulikuwa na kinyago cha dhahabu cha simba jike na kingine simba dume alivyokuwa amemnunulia zawadi mke wake nchini Hong Kong. Mkabala na kinyago kulikuwa na swala wengi tu ambao walitengenezwa nchini Korea ya kusini alikovinunua Anna Mugando mke wa gavana aliyemuoa baada ya kumfukuza mke wake wa kwanza. Aliuliza Anna."Vinyago hivi vilikuwa alama ya mapenzi na ushupavu wa mume na mkewe. Kwa tafsiri nyingine ni kwamba mke au simba jike ndiye bingwa wa kumtafutia mumewe kama ambavyo Anna alikuwa amefanikiwa kumuingiza mumewe bwege kwenye kashfa la kuliibia taifa huku swala wakiwakilisha wananchi waliokuwa wanawaibia kwa ukatili sawa na simba jike awararuavyo swala. Hakika walijua kujisuta wasijue hivyo! Laiti kwa kinyago cha mkewe angeweka nyoka. Maana hakuwa na tofauti na nyoka kwa sumu yake au cha fisi kwa vile alikuwa na tamaa kama fisi. Kwa upande wake angeweka cha kenge. Maana hakuwa na tofauti na kenge ambaye huikimbia mvua kwa kujizamisha majini.

Ofisi nyingi za Mafuriko zilijaa vinyago. Kwa mtu anayejua maana yake asingeshindwa kujenga dhana kuwa vinyago hivi viliwakilisha uhovyo wa watawala wa Mafuriko ambao hawakuwa na tofauti na vinyago hasa kwa kutumiwa na majambazi toka nje ambao walikuwa wakiwaamrisha kama vibonzo vya kwenye magazeti avifanyiavyo mchoraji.

Alivingalia vinyago vile kwa zamu kana kwamba vilikuwa hai. Baada ya kumaliza kuvivinjari aliegukia upande mwingine alipokuwa ameweka ubao wenye rangi ya samawi ukinakishiwa na maneno yasemayo "Always for the noble service of my country" yaani siku zote utumishi uliotukuka kwa nchi yangu wakati ukweli wa mambo ni kwamba nchi lilikuwa tumbo lake na wezi wenzake! Kwake utumishi wake uliotukuka ilikuwa ni kinyume kabisa. Maana kama ulitukuka ni kwenye ulafi na kuiibia nchi. Katika nchi ya Mafuriko ilikuwa ni jambo la kawaida kukuta vibao kama hivi maofisini.

Gazeti la Chimbuchimbu liliwahi kuandika tahariri juu ya mantiki ya vibao kama hivi. Kwenye tahariri hii gazeti liliuliza nini maana ya kuweka vibao visemavyo "Rushwa marufuku hapa". Lenyewe katika utafiti wake liligundua kuwa kumbe kulikuwa na maana fichi nyuma ya pazia kuwa rushwa maarufu hapa! Kulikuwa na kisa kimoja cha kuchekesha kwenye soko kuu la Mafuriko ambacho kiliandikwa marufuku kukaa hapa. Lakini gazeti la Chimbuchimbu liliwahi kuchapisha picha ikionyesha watu wakiwa wamekaa mbele ya ubao ule. Si hayo tu liliwahi kuchapisha hata picha za watu waliokuwa wakijisaidia haja ndogo mbele au wakati mwingine wakivikojolea vibao vilivyoandikwa usikojoe hapa. Baada ya kuangalia lile tangazo la "Always for the noble service of my country" alirusha ngumi hewani na kusema. "Huyu alidhani mimi ni mtoto mdogo?" Haikujulikana kama alikuwa anaongelea Rais au mtu mwingine. Lakini inavyoonekana alikuwa akiongelea Rais. Maana ndiye alikuwa ametoka kuongea naye. Aliwasha cigar nyingine huku akiimba kwa mguno wimbo maarufu wa By the Rivers of Babylon ambao aliupenda sana. Maana ulimkubusha wakati alipokuwa maskini akienda kusoma Marekani kwa meli badala ya ndege. Alikumbuka alivyokuwa akifanya vibarua vya kudeki vyoo na kuosha vikongwe huku akiosha vyombo vya kulia vya chuo na kufuta vumbi sakatu. Kama siyo kukufuru, gavana hakuwa mtu wa kujisahaulisha kuwa alikuwa ametokea kwenye familia maskini wa kutupwa.

Alikupua moshi na kuendelea kuongea peke yake. "Huyu anaona benki yangu ndiyo chanzo cha kuanguka kwa umaarufu wake. Lakini anasahau kuwa aliingia kwa njia chafu ambazo lazima alipie. Huwezi kuongoza nchi bila sera. Huwezi kuongoza nchi ukiwa umezungukwa na wezi watupu ukaendelea kuwa maarufu. Utakuwaje maarufu wakati watu wanakutumia kufanya mashindano ya kuiibia nchi unayoijenga kwa kuibomoa?" Alikupua moshi tena na kuendelea, "Kwa vile ameonyesha kutojua kitu, lazima nitengeneze pesa kwa bidii ili likitokea la kutokea niwe nimeishachukua changu. Na akiendekeza mawazo ya rafiki yake ya kutaka amrithi anaweza asimalize hata huo muda wake. Maana nchi itakuwa imefilisika kiasi cha kufanya umma ushindwe kuvumilia. Mimi sitahangaika wala kumchafua. Maana ameishachafuka zaidi ya kuchafuka. Nitajiondokea taratibu narejea zangu Washington kwenda kucheza na vijukuu vyangu." Alicheka peka yake na kuendelea, "Inaelekea hawa wapuuzi hawanijui! Kwanza nani amfukuze nani iwapo wote tumeshirikiana. Na isitoshe karibu watoto wao wote wako kwenye pay roll yangu. Waache wambea wapige kelele maana kelele za chura hazimzuii tembo kunywa maji."

Aliangalia saa yake na kuendelea, "Wao wameendekeza tamaa za madaraka na hawana utaalamu yaani mimi nitumike kama kijiko! Impossible."

Alivuta laptop yake na kuifungua halafu na kuandika neno la siri password. Kioo cha laptop mara kiliang'aa kwa maandishi ya dhahabu yaliyosomeka "Time time before time times you." Yaani uwahi muda kabla muda haujakuwahi.

Alianza kuburuza cha kati kwenye sehemu ya kuongozea kompyuta ile ndogo. Ilikuwa ni kompyuta ya bei mbaya sana. Isitoshe yeye kwa ulevi na kichaa cha vitu aghali hakuwa na mpinzani. Kuna kipindi alinunua piki piki mjini Seoul Korea kusini kwa bei aghali kumbe feki! Na isitoshe zaidi ya tamaa hakujua hata kuipanda na uzee ule! Alikuwa akitapanya pesa utadhani zilikuwa zikimuwasha! Wakati yeye anawashwa na kufuja wapo waliokuwa wanawashwa na shida ndogo ndogo tu wasijue pa kupata pesa! Mara simu ililia. Ilikuwa inatoka kwa mkewe Anna Mugando ambaye alikuwa amemuoa kutokana na kushirikiana kwenye ujambazi wa kuiibia nchi. Huyu mama alikuwa akiishi Marekani.

Anna, janajike jeusi toka visiwani Uraka-ukara kwenye ziwa Nyanza lisilo hata pendeza isipokuwa kwa mikorogo, lilibahatika kuwa na ubongo unaochemka. Ni mama aliyezaliwa kuwarubuni wanaume na kuwatumia. Ni shangingi wa kutupwa ambaye kwa hila zake na ghilba angeweza kumnyang'anya hata kigoli mume! Alijaliwa ulimi mtamu uliowanasa wanaume kama chatu amnasavyo mbwa. Kwake wanaume walikuwa kama wanawake na yeye kama mwanaume kwao. Kwani alijua jinsi ya kuwatawala na kuwatumia. Alijua jinsi ya kuwanasa na kuwapagawisha kiasi cha kusahau hata nafsi na familia zao!

Alikuwa kwenye umri wake wa miaka hamsini na ushei. Ni jimama linalojua kumgeuza mwanaume mzima tena msomi kuwa kama mtoto mchanga au hata mbwa. Wanaolijua wanasema hutumia ndumba kuwaweka sawa wanaume. Maana inasemekana kuwa kabla ya kumlazimisha gavana Dadi kumuoa lilikuwa na Bwana liliyekuwa limemgeuza ndondocha hadi ndugu zake walipoamua kumshughulikia na kumtoa kwenye makucha ya mama hili walilozoea kuliita shetani Ann. Na kweli Anna alikuwa shetani tena yule mkubwa karibu na shetani mwenyewe mama wa mashetani. Ni kiumbe aliyeupata ubinadamu kwa bahati mbaya. Maana kwa alivyokuwa amewavuruga wanaume hasa gavana wa Benki kuu ya Mafuriko alifaa aumbike nyoka. Hakuwa na huruma hata chembe linapokuja suala la tamaa ya pesa. Alibuni kampuni iliyoitwa Metameta. Aliitumia kampuni hiyo kuliibia taifa kwa kumtumia gavana mpumbavu. Ilikuwa ni rahisi kumpata. Baada ya kujua gavana huyu bwege alikuwa mlevi wa ngono lakini asiye na ujasiri wa kumkabili mtu, alimuachia mlango wazi na kuuingia mtego kiasi cha kunogewa na kumuoa.

Kwa Anna gavana alikuwa kama inzi kwenye mzoga au kidonda. Kwani licha ya kuhatarisha cheo chake na maisha yake, alikuwa akifanya vitu vilivyokinzana na kiwango na aina ya usomi aliokuwa nao ambao ulimchukua miaka na bidii nyingi. Gavana alikuwa ni msomi aliyetekwa na kupotezwa na mpumbavu wa kawaida tu. Kisa udhaifu wake wa kuendekeza ngono rahisi tena toka kwa jimama ambalo halikuwa na sura. Lakini huwezi kujua aliwahi kujisemea ndugu wa mke wa kwanza wa gavana ambaye alipinduliwa na Anna. Alisema kuwa mara nyingi maua mazuri hayana harufu na maua yenye sura nzuri yana riha nzuri. Alihitimisha kuwa huenda kitu chaweza kuwa kibaya nje kikawa kizuri ndani! Walioana wakiwa watu wazima baada ya kuutumia ujana wao kwenye uhuni. Hawakuwa na shida ya watoto zaidi ya watoto wao kuwa chumo la wizi wa pesa za Mafuriko. Isitoshe ukiachia mbali gavana kuzugwa na mapenzi ya uongo, Anna alichotaka kwa gavana ilikuwa ni kumtumia kuchuma utajiri. Alikuwa na mpango wa kupa sumu afe baadaye ili akafunge ndoga na hawara yake waliyependana tangu shule waliyekuwa wamepotezana Ann alipokimbilia Marekani.

Kwa vile hawara yake huyu alijua utajiri na mapenzi ya Anna,alikuwa ameishampa talaka mkewe aliyekuwa amezaa naye watoto nane tayari kumuoa gavana baada ya gavana bwege kuuawa. Na kama siyo kuingia kwa serikali mpya ya wezi ambayo gavana alijua angeitumia vizuri, angeishasahaulika zamani. Bahati mbaya hakujua kuwa maisha na majigambo yake yalikuwa ya muda tu pale Ann atakapoamua kumfutilia mbali kama alivyokuwa akiifutilia mbali hazina ya Mafuriko. Kweli usilojiua litakusumbua!

Baada ya kuwa wamefanikisha wizi wao, walitangaza kuwa kampuni ya Metameta ilikuwa imefilisika. Nani alilipia madeni yake? Ajuaye Mungu mwenyewe kuwa ni maskini wa Mafuriko! Jamaa yake mmoja mwanasheria aliyekuwa anatumika kusaini mikataba ya ujambazi alifikia ukwasi hadi kuagiza Mercedes Benz ya dola 200,000 toka nchini Japan ambayo aliipakiza kwenye ndege na kuiingiza nchini Mafuriko bila kulipa ushuru. Hakuna mkataba uliomtoa mwanasheria huyu mpinda sheria kama ule wa ujenzi wa minara sita ya jengo la makao makuu ya BoMU yaani Bank of Mafuriko Ulaji. Wataalamu wa ujenzi wa Mafuriko walisema bei ya ujenzi wa jengo ile ilikuwa kubwa kuliko hata ile ambayo ingehitajika kama jengo kubwa mara mbili ya hili lingejengwa mwezini ambapo kila kifaa kingehitaji Shuttle ya kwendea anga za juu kukisafirisha. Wapo waliozoa kuiita minara hii minara ya Babeli. Maana wakati inajengwa, umma wa wanamafuriko ulikuwa umesambaratishwa kiuchumi na mradi huu mchafu unaong'aa kwa juu wakati nyuma ya pazia ulikuwa ni alama ya maovu ya binadamu dhidi ya binadam wenzake!

Mwanasheria huyu habithi na limbukeni aliona fahari kununua Benz la bei mbaya wakati wafanyabiashara wa kihindi walianzisha vitega uchumi vya bei mbaya kule Dubai, London, Washington na Bombay. Yeye maskini aliwekeza kwenye anasa za hovyo asijue mambo yangeweza kubadilika na kuharibika! Na isitoshe hakuwa peke yake. Kwani wakubwa wengi wa Mafuriko waliwekeza kwenye vitu vya hovyo wakati makuwadi wao wa kihindi wakiwekeza kwenye miradi ya maana kiuchumi kiasi cha kuwajengea maisha watoto wao huku mabosi wao wakiyabomoa maisha ya wananchi wao!

Baada ya mama kujua kuwa gavana alikuwa ni bwege, aliwaarika jamaa zake wakaanza kumtumia walivyotaka.

Baada ya simu kuita kama mara tatu hivi, gavana alizima cigar yake haraka maana bi mkubwa alikuwa kwenye laini ya simu. Mara alijibu huku akilazimisha tabasamu la uongo kama mtu aliyekuwa akijifuta futa machozi baada ya kusikia hodi mlangoni. "Hello sugar, Unaendeleaje la Aziz?"

"Sina tatizo. Je huyo bwege wetu alikuwa na jipya gani?" Gavana alijibu kwa mkato "Hana jipya lolote sana sana ni umbea na woga tu vinavyomsumbua." Mke wa Gavana. "Je honey ile safari yetu ya Dubai kukagua miradi yetu bado ipo? Maana ile ndege yetu nimeisha i-summon kutoka London tayari kwa msafara."

"Honey inabidi uende peke yako. Na achana na kuagiza ndege yetu. Maana huyu jamaa alivyoanza kuamka inabidi niwe karibu na nipitie taarifa zake za siri kama atakuja na hatari yoyote nami nimkabili na uchafu wake au nibwage manyanga na kurejea zangu Washington kucheza na wajukuu." Alisema huku akitabasamu peke yake. Anna kusikia akiwataja wajukuu zake ambao walikuwa wamezaliwa na mke wa kwanza alisonya na kusema, "Usinichefue na mapaka wako uliowapata kwa huyo malaya wako wa zamani." Gavana kujua alikuwa amekosea alijitetea haraka, "Honey nisamehe. Ulimi unajua aaa hauna mfupa sitarudia sugar wangu." Mke wa gavana hakujibu zaidi ya kuendelea kutokota na hasira zake. Ili kuua mada hii gavana aliendelea, "Ila ukitoka Dubai ningeshauri upitie Argentina angalau ulete japo kondoo watatu. Si unajua pasaka imekaribia honey." Anna kwa kujua udhaifu wa mumewe na hali aliyokuwa anapambana nayo hakutaka kuendeleza hasira juu ya wajukuu wa mume wake bwege. "Honey pia kumbuka kuwa yale madini tuliyotuma kule Brussels hajawa counter-checked. Hivyo nimeamua yule mtoto wa kaka yangu aliyemaliza kusomea jiolojia kwenye chuo kikuu cha Roughborough awe wakala wetu wa Brussels. Je wewe una ushauri gani?" Aliuliza Anna. "Okey Oke hamna tatizo. Je hana mdomo mpana? Maana kwa hali ilivyo hawa kondoo wetu wameanza kuamka hasa hivi vijigazeti vya uongo na umbea. Hivyo inabidi umuonye kuwa akisema hovyo hovyo anaandaa kifo chake. Okey." Gavana alijibu huku akishusha pumzi na kumshukuru Mungu kwa mkewe kuingia mambo ya biashara badala ya wivu. Gavana alikumbuka jambo na kuendelea kwenye simu, "Hiyo safari uliyonitaarifu ndiyo hivyo kwa hali ilivyo sitaweza kwenda. Nitakaa angalau vumbi litulie. Na wewe ukienda huko Dubai hakikisha huandamani na wasaidizi wako. Maana watu hawaaminiki siku hizi. Na isitoshe kikulacho siku zote ki nguoni mwako."

Alisogeza Laptop yake vizuri na kuendelea, "Au unaonaje badala ya kutafuta mtu tusiye na uhakika naye tumhamishe Rechwo akasimamie miradi yetu?"

"Lakini Rechwo hapendi kuishi Uarabuni si unajua anasimamia pia hisa za Meta meta kwenye mabenki ya hapa. Hatuwezi kumhamisha maana hawa jamaa zetu siwaamini wanaweza kutuibia." Alijibu mke wa gavana.

Maskini wakati gavana akiwahofia wasaidizi wa mkewe hakujua kuwa kimlacho yeye kilikuwa nguoni mwake! Laiti angejua mipango ya mkewe wala asingekufuru kusema aliyokuwa akijiropokea! Aliendelea, " Mimi ningeshauri uchukue ndege hadi Nairobi. Usiku nitaongea na rubani wa ndege yetu binafsi ile Gulf stream namba five aje aku-pick pale na kukupeleka kwanza hadi Athens kuelekea Uppsala Sweden then uelekee Dubai ambapo utaingia na kutoka usiku. Miji yote utakayokwenda hakikisha unavaa mascarade na kutembelea miradi yetu usiku. Okey?" Mawasiliano hayakuwa mazuri hivyo hakusikia vizuri alichokuwa amesema mkewe. Aliendelea, "Utafikia kwa shehe Makhtoum badala ya hotelini kwetu ili kuepuka hawa wambea wa media kama watakuwa wamekufatilia au kum-alert mtu wao. Najua wana mtandao mkubwa kuliko hata wa Rais wetu."

"Okey dear." Mkewe gavana alikata simu. Anna alikata simu na kumpigia mke wa waziri mkubwa ambaye ndiye aliyemuunganisha na gavana aliyekuja kumuoa baada ya biashara yao kunoga. Licha ya mke wa waziri mkubwa yeye na mke wa Rais wa zamani walikuwa ni marafiki na washirika wakubwa kwenye biashara zao za nyuma ya pazia. Aliheshimiana sana na mke wa waziri mkubwa kuliko hata mke wa Rais. Maana naye ndiye aliyemuunganisha na mke wa Rais wa zamani wakati waziri mkubwa alipokuwa waziri wa kawaida. Kwenye harusi ya binti mkubwa wa waziri mkubwa, Gavana alitoa zawadi ya pete ya emerald pamoja na kuleta asusa zote kwa kuagiza kondoo kutoka kwenye shamba lake la Argentina.

Pia aliagiza mvinyo aina ya Sangiovese Rubicone toka nchini Ufaransa uliogharimu dola za kimarekani milioni moja. Pia ulikuwapo mvinyo aina ya Campanelli 177na Giacondi rouge toka Utaliano uliogharimu Dola za kimarekani laki saba.

Harusi ile ilikuwa si ya kawaida. Wataalamu wa uchambuzi na masuala ya matanuzi walisema kuwa hata wafalme wanaochezea mafuta wa nchi za kiarabu hawakuwa na jeuri ya pesa kama ya watawala wa Mafuriko. Maana hata majumba yao yalikuwa ni makasri ya bei mbaya ambayo yangetokea mashindano ya nchi gani yenye nyumba aghali basi Mafuriko ingefurika medali za ushindi. Pia kama yangefanyika mashindano ya ufisadi na matumizi ya hovyo na uchafu mwingine kama huo, bila shaka Mafuriko ingenyakua medali zote. Gavana na mkewe mfanya biashara ya wizi, walikuwa wakitumia muda mwingi kwa mwaka kusafiri kwenda kuficha pesa yao na kukagua miradi yao nje ya nchi huku safari zote hizi zikigharimiwa na hazina hiyo hiyo waliyokuwa wakiibia!

Walikuwa wakiingiza pesa kuliko hata nusu ya bajeti ya Mafuriko. Ama kweli walijua kuiba. Watu hawa, Zengeni alizoea kuwaita vichaa. Maana walikuwa wana pesa ambayo wasingeweza kuitumia na kuimaliza hata asilimia moja! Walikuwa ni wagonjwa wa tamaa na roho mbaya ambao wao kuona masifuri yamejaa kwenye vitabu vyao vya akiba ilikuwa ni raha kuliko kuona maskini angalau mmoja akiondokana na umaskini.

Zengeni alizoea kusema wana mashetani malafi miilini mwao. Maana kama ni umaskini waliujua zaidi ikizingatiwa kuwa gavana na mkewe walikuwa watoto wa masikini tena wale wa kunuka. Na kama siyo siasa safi ya Rais wa kwanza wa Mafuriko, huenda wasingesoma na badala yake wangeishia kuwa makahaba na majambazi. Maana walisoma bure ingawa elimu hii waliyoipata bure waliitumia kuihujumu nchi hiyo hiyo iliyowaondoa kwenye umaskini wa kunuka! Kweli wahenga walisema tenda wema uondoke na heri kumfadhili mbuzi maana mwanadamu ana maudhi.

Kuonyesha jinsi viumbe hawa ambavyo walikuwa wanyama, kila jumapili hawakukosa kanisani! Walikuwa wakitoa pesa nyingi kama sadaka. Na hii ilifanya hata viongozi wa kanisa lao kuwapenda na kuwapa upendeleo maalumu ili hali wakijua fika kuwa zile sadaka zilitokana na dhambi ya kuua umma kwa umaskini! Kuna siku mchungaji aliwaomba waumini kuwaombea watu hawa kwa mchango wao wa kueneza neno la Mungu! Maskini hawakujua kuwa Mungu siyo kipofu kama wao! Mchungaji hakujua kuwa alikuwa amejigeuza chui awalaye kondoo wake! Hakujua kuwa alijigeuza mtoza ushuru akalitumikia tumbo badala ya Mungu wake!

20
Mwalimu azindua umaskini!

Baada ya Zengeni kuzindua mradi kama alivyokuwa akisema, mauzo hayakuwa mabaya ukiachia mbali baadhi wa wateja kuja na maombi ya mikopo. Kama mkewe, biashara ilianza vizuri. Kwani siku ya ufunguzi, mkuu wa shule alipendekeza mboga zote zinunuliwe ili kuwa chakula cha siku hiyo cha wanafunzi ambao kama kawaida ya watoto watundu walimuongezea jina jingine la Chinga mboga mboga na mkewe mwalimu Vitafunwa.

Pamoja na kwamba wanafunzi walikuwa wakichukia mchicha, siku hiyo walifurahi kula mboga iliyokuwa imezalishwa shuleni kwao na mtu waliyekuwa wakimfahamu. Hawakuwa wakichukia mboga kwa sababu zilikuwa chakula kibaya. Bali walizichukia kutokana na kutokuwa na uhakika wa jinsi zilivyozalishwa. Mwalimu wa somo la bailojia alizoea kuwaambia kuwa wao kama wasomi ilibidi waepuke kula ili mradi wamekula. Alikuwa sahihi. Maana mboga nyingi zilikuwa zikizalishwa kwenye vijito na chemi chemi zilizokuwa zimechafuliwa na viwanda vilivyokuwa vimejengwa hovyo huku vikitiririsha kemikali mbali mbali hatari kwenye vijito na chemi chemi hizo.

Jambo la ajabu lilitokea. Kwenye ubao wa matangazo mwanafunzi mtundu alikuwa ameweka tangazo lililoanidkwa. "Tumeona vitu vyako Mwalimu Chinga Mboga mboga na mama Vitafunwa wapendwa, endelea na utundu na ujasiliamali huo si haba." Zengeni alishangaa jina la Machinga lilivyokuwa limesambaa hadi hata kwa wanafunzi. Tangazo hili pamoja na kuwa la kitoto na utani lilimfariji kugundua kuwa kumbe jumuia ya pale shuleni ilikuwa ikitambua mchango wake kwake. Kwa upande wa Nengoma alikuwa hata ameanza kunenepa si haba. Maana ndani ya miezi mitatu alikuwa ameishafungua akaunti ya biashara kwenye benki ya taifa ya biashara kabla haijabinafsishwa akitegemea kuwa kama angekuwa mteja mzuri baadaye angeweza kupata mkopo. Alikuwa ameishajiwekea takribani shilingi laki moja baada ya kuondoa matumizi ya kawaida na gharama za kuendesha mradi. Mume wake alizoea kumtania kwa kumuita mama Vitafunwa au Bi. Tajiri. Miradi hii pamoja na kuleta changamoto, ilileta faraja ya aina yake ukiachia mbali masikitiko kuwa hali ilivyokuwa ni kwamba wangeachana na ualimu. Hili liliwasononesha. Kwa sababu kwa kuacha kwao kazi ya kitaaluma na kwenda kwenye kazi zisizo za kitaaluma taifa lingepata hasara. Maana kila alipokumbuka pesa iliyotumika kuwasomesha walisikitika. Lakini hawakuwa na jinsi. Isitoshe Nengoma alipokuwa akiangalia jinsi wanawake wa walimu wenzake ambao hawakuwa na elimu wala ajira aliishia kusikitika na kujiona kama mwenye bahati. Hivyo kwao kuacha walimu ilikuwa ni kama usaliti. Lakini waliliwazwa na ukweli kuwa hawakufikia uamuzi ule kwa kutaka bali kulazimika. Maana ushikwapo shikamana wahenga walisema.

Ilibidi mapenzi ya taifa yasiwakwaze. Isitoshe wakati wao wakifikiria taifa kuna watu walikuwa wameishalisahau na kulihujumu. Tena watu waliokuwa na maisha na nyadhifa bora kuliko wao.

Siku moja kwenye kikao cha mke na mme kulijadili suala la taifa na maisha ya kimachinga, walifikia hatima kuwa hata kama wao wangeendelea kufunga mkanda ili walitumikie taifa ingekuwa ni bure. Maana kulikuwa na watu tena wenye kauli na madaraka waliokuwa wameamua kulibomoa. Hivyo kuendelea kushikilia utaifa ilikuwa sawa na kujaza maji kwenye pakacha. Zengeni alizoea kusema kifo cha wengi ni harusi. Nengoma naye alizoea kusema, kila ilipojitokeza hofu hii, kuwa hakuna haja ya kujenga taifa ambalo wajanja walikuwa wakilibomoa bila sababu zaidi ya uroho wao.

Biashara ya Zengeni na mkewe iliendelea vizuri huku maandalizi ya kuacha kazi yakiwa ndiyo yamepamba moto yamekamilika. Walionea fahari kujiajiri badala ya kuajiriwa ambako katika nchi ya Mafuriko hakukuwa na tofauti na utumwa. Walikuwa wameamua kuachana na ukuku na kukumbatia ukanga hata kama mbele kulikuwa na changamoto nyingi na kubwa. Ndani ya miezi mitano, walikuwa wameishafanya tathmini na kuamua kuandika barua za kuacha kazi. Maana pesa waliyokuwa wameishaweka kibindoni haikuwa haba ikilinganishwa na kiduchu walichokuwa wakipata kila mwisho wa mwezi baada ya suluba nyingi na kubwa. Kutokana na kuwa na mahusiano mazuri na mkuu wa shule, aliwakubalia kuacha kazi kwao bila masharti wala vikwazo. Lakini aliwaomba angalau wamsukume hadi kwenye likizo ya katikati ya mwaka ili awe amepata walimu wa kuchukua nafaisi zao. Nao kwa heshima yake walimkubalia kuendelea hadi muda aliotaka. Hivyo wangeendelea kufanya kazi nje ya mkataba hadi mwezi wa sita.

Wakati wakingojea kuacha kazi ya ualimu, pigo lilitokea. Kutokana na ukosefu wa maji uliokuwa unalikabili taifa la Mafuriko, ugonjwa wa kipindupindu uliibuka kiasi cha serikali kupiga marufuku biashara ndogo ndogo zote. Mabwana afya nao waliutumia mwanya huu kuwakamata na kuwaomba rushwa wale waliovunja amri hii ya serikali. Makali ya kwanza ya amri hii yalimkumba Zengeni. Kwani afisa wa afya wa eneo lao aliandika barua rasmi kumfahamisha amri ya serikali kupiga marufuku biashara ndogo ndogo. Hivyo barua hii ilihitimisha ufanisi wa Nengoma na Zengeni. Kwani aliiona biashara yake ikizama. Zengeni alizoea kusema kuwa mbuzi wa maskini hazai na akizaa basi huzaa dume. Maana alikuwa amekataa kusomea sheria kwa kuupenda ualimu. Wenzake waliokuwa wamesomea sheria walikuwa wakiingiza pesa kutokana na wingi wa kesi za uhujumu wa mali ya umma na kusaini mikataba ya wizi ya wakubwa wa serikali ya Mafuriko. Mmojawapo alikuwa ndugu wa hawara mke wa gavana aliyekuwa akiendesha gari la thamani ya dola 200,000 ambaye walisoma wote na alikuwa akimshinda darasani. Alikuwa na utajiri usio wa kawaida. Ingawa alikuwa bingwa wa kufuja pesa bado hakuweza kuufanya kitu utajiri wake ambao mwingi ulitokana na kusaini mikataba ya kuuza machimbo ya madini ya serikali kwa wafanyabiashara binafsi walioshirikiana na watawala wa Mafuriko kwenye biashara hii chafu. Zengeni, alimuomba mkuu wa shule kununua mboga mboga zake zote na ukawa ndiyo mwisho wa miradi hii miwili ya wawili hawa. Tukio hili liliongeza hasira kwa Zengeni na Nengoma dhidi ya serikali ya Mafuriko ambayo waliita ya kijambazi bila kuficha. Walijawa na hasira na chuki kiasi cha kuanza kuwahamasisha watu wa karibu yao kuichukia serikali. Waliwahimiza wasichague tena chama kilichokuwa kimetawala. Maana badala ya kuwaletea utajiri kama kilivyowaahidi kwenye kampeni za uchaguzi,kiliwaletea umaskini huku viongozi wake wakitajirika kwa mgongo wa wananchi.

Baada ya kuona kuwa mipango yao imeingiliwa na serikali ambayo siku zote Zengeni aliita ya kikoloni na kijambazi, aliamua kuanza kuandika makala za kuikosoa kwenye gazeti la Chimbuchimbu. Bahati nzuri hata utawala wa gazeti la Chimbuchimbu ulipenda sana makala zake kiasi cha kumteua kuwa mchambuzi wake maalumu. Alipata wasomaji na mashabiki wengi kiasi cha mauzo ya gazeti kuongezeka. Kama ulikuwa ni mchuzi basi Zengeni hata baadaye Nengoma walikuwa ndiyo viungo. Kama chao, basi wao sukari. Kutokana na Zengeni kuwa mwalimu wa fasihi, makala zake nyingi zilivutia wasomaji kiasi cha kuongeza wasomaji wa gazeti la Chimbuchimbu hasa siku ya jumatano zilipokuwa zikitoka makala zake kwenye safu yake ya Darubini. Hii ilimpa faraja hasa ukichukulia kuwa hata uongozi wa gazeti haukuwa wezi wa fadhila. Ulimtaarifu rasmi kuutambua mchango wake. Hili lilimpa faraja sana kuona kuwa naye ni sehemu ya timu ya kudai mabadiliko katika kuendesha nchi yake ambayo makali ya ulafi na ufisadi wa utawala wake mbovu licha ya kuwakumba wananchi wote, yalikuwa yamemkumba yeye na mkewe kwa namna ya pekee. Maana kama siyo ufisadi na upogo wao biashara zao zisingeuawa. Kwao, chanzo cha kipindupindu hawakuwa wadudu waitwao vibrio cholerae bali watawala wa Mafuriko. Aliandika makala nyingi kuutaka umma uiponde badala ya kuikubali. Maana kitendo hiki kilikuwa kinaugeuza umma mataahira hata wapumbavu wasioweza kupima mambo. Aliita ripoti hii unajisi mkubwa kwa taifa la Mafuriko. Hakusita kumshauri Rais aache ubabaishaji na kujidanganya kuwa angeweza kufanikisha malengo machafu ya kutawala kwa uongo badala ya kanuni na sheria. Pamoja na kuutambua mchango wake kwa maneno, utawala wa Chimbuchimbu ulikuwa ukichelewesha kumlipa pesa yake kutokana na mauzo mabaya yaliyokuwa yakisababishwa na hujuma na vikwazo vya serikali. Ilifikia mahali akaanza kutishia kuigeuzia kalamu yake kwa gazeti. Maana, alizoea kusema kuwa huwezi kupigana na adui yako iwapo una tabia na matendo kama yeye. Alikuwa akiudhika kutokana na gazeti kuwa mwiba kwa serikali juu ya uwajibikaji lakini lenyewe lisiwajibike kwa watendaji wake.

Kashfa ya Richmen ilikuwa inaendelea ingawa nyuma ya pazia kila juhudi zilikuwa zinafanywa ili kuhakikisha kashfa hii inauawa na waziri mkubwa anasafishwa.

Tume iliyokuwa inangoja kutoa ripoti yake hatimaye ilitoa ripoti hiyo. Ilikuwa ni ripoti ambayo Zengeni aliita ya aibu na msiba kwa taifa. Siku ya kutolewa ripoti juu ya kashfa ya Richmen, mkuu wa kikosi cha kuzuia wizi alikuja na ripoti ya kurasa nne ambayo kimsingi haikuwa na chochote cha maana bali kuwasafisha wezi waliokuwa nyuma ya pazia. Maana ripoti haikuelezea kuwahoji washukiwa wala vyanzo vyake vya ushahidi. Ilikuwa ni ripoti ya kisiasa zaidi iliyolenga kuhalalisha haramu na kuharamisha halali yaani malalamiko ya umma kuonekana kama umbea! Ilikosa hata chembe ya taaluma! Ripoti hii ilikuwa inaudhi. Kwani hata magazeti mengine yaliyokuwa yakilala kitanda kimoja na serikali yalionekana kuchukia kiasi cha kuandika tahariri zenye kuponda ripoti hiyo. Ila yalifanya hivyo kwa ujanja na umakini mkubwa kuepuka kuukata mkono uliokuwa ukiwatupia makombo. Kwao mkate wao ulikuwa bora kuliko taifa. Walikuwa tayari kuliangamiza taifa kwa malipo machafu yatokanayo na damu za ndugu zao hata wao! Kashfa ilikuwa imezimwa. Lakini tatizo la ukame lilikuwa linaendelea. Hili hawakulizima. Wakati wakubwa wakiendelea kusafishana na kupanga mikakati ya kuzima uovu wao, tatizo nalo lilizidi kujiweka wazi. Hali ilianza kuwa mbaya kiasi cha kuwaumbua. Taarifa za kusambaa kwa kipindupindu,watu kukesha wakisaka maji bila kwenda kufanya kazi, kuzimwa kwa mitambo ya umeme na kuporomoka kwa uchumi ulikuwa mtihani ambao ulikuwa umewaelemea watawala.

Katika nchi zenye kutawaliwa na matumbo na kufikiri kwa njaa, watawala walitumia msemo wa kufa kufaana. Kwani kwao hiki kilikuwa ni kipindi cha neema cha kuutumia umma kuvuna wasipopanda huku wakivuna pesa na kupanda umaskini na mateso kwa watu wasio na hatia waliokuwa wametenda kosa la kuwaamini watu wasioaminika na kuwategemea watu wasiotegemeka. Kweli shukrani ya punda siku zote ni mateke. Maana mtu aliyewaona watawala wakati wa uchaguzi wakijifanya watu halafu angewakuta wakifanya unyama waliokuwa wakiufanya, asingeamini! Lakini ndivyo ilivyokuwa.

Pamoja na Rais kujiridhisha kutokana na ushauri na taarifa vya uongo alivyokuwa akipewa na wasaidizi wake, na hakikisho la uongo toka kwa waziri wake mkubwa, hali ilikuwa mbaya kiasi cha kuufanya umma uanze kuamka na kuachana na woga na kuonyesha hasira zake kwa serikali japo kwa maneno. Watawala hawakutikisika. Maana maneno matupu hayavunji mfupa na isitoshe maji ya moto hayachomi nyumba. Hapa ndipo Zengeni kwenye makala zake alizoea kuwalinganisha watu wa Mafuriko na kondoo hata kuku kwa kukumbatia uoza bila kujitokeza mitaani kuuondoa. Zilianza taarifa na makala magazetini. Baadaye mjadala wa Mafuriko na hatima yake ulihamia kwenye vijiwe vya kahawa, migahawa ya mama ntilie, mabaa hata kwenye mabasi ya umma. Umma ulianza kuotesha dhamira na mbegu ya kuuasi mfumo wa ukondoo na uganga njaa. Hata hivyo watawala wa Mafuriko walikuwa na bahati ya mtende. Maana umma ulichelewa kuamka na kuchukua hatua madhubuti mapema. Umma ulianza kukengeuka taratibu na kufikiria kuasi viapo vya uaminifu kwa watawala ambao kimsingi walikuwa si watawala wala viongozi bali watu wala watu. Umma ulianza kutaka kujua kilichokuwa kikiendelea nyuma ya pazia. Ulianza kutaka viapo vitekelezwe kwa vitendo na siyo maneno. Ulianza kuviita viapo vya uhalifu badala ya uaminifu! Hakika umma ulianza kujenga hoja nzito ya mabadiliko. Maneno kama "Mageuzi sasa", "Tumeuchoka ukondoo" na mengine mengi makali yalianza kuwa msamiati wa kila siku kwenye vinywa vya umma. Kuvunjika moyo kulianza kujitokea wazi wazi katika nyanja zote za chini za maisha nchi nzima. Wanafunzi wa vyuo vikuu walianza kuandamana na kugoma kupinga madhira waliyokuwa wakipata wao na wananchi wengine. Taasisi zisizo za kiserikali zilianza kuondoa blanketi la woga na uganga njaa na kusema wazi kuwa nchi ilikuwa imevamiwa na viwavi watu. Barua za wasomaji kwenye magazeti mbali mbali zilianza kuchukua mwelekeo mpya wa kuliita koleo kwa jina lake badala ya kijiko kikubwa. Umma ulianza kuhoji na kuhoji na kuhoji kila jambo. Umma ulianza kujaribu kulifunua pazia ili kilichokuwako nyuma kionekane na kila jicho la wananchi. Kwa kiasi fulani vyama vya upinzani vilianza kupata nguvu na imani na umma uliokuwa umedanganywa na kuvichukulia kama adui wakati adui ilikuwa ni serikali.

Wakulima vijijini walizidi kupoteza matumaini. Maana baada ya hali kuwa mbaya, serikali ilijichimbia mijini huku ikiwasahau watu wa vijijini. Ilifikia mahali watu wakawa wanasema kuwa Mafuriko ilikuwa ni mkusanyiko wa nchi mbili tofauti yaani mijini na vijijini! Wakulima walianza kugomea mazao yao kukopwa na serikali na mawakala wake. Wapo hata walioanza kuhoji uhalali wa kuilipa kodi serikali fisadi. Wengine walienda mbali kiasi cha kutaka bunge lipige kura ya kutokuwa na imani na Rais. Na kama siyo chama tawala kuwa na wabunge wengi waliozoea kuwaita misukule, mbona serikali ingeanguka mapema!

Katika historia ya nchi ya Mafuriko, haikuwa imewahi kutokea kwa watu wa vijiji kupata ujasiri wa kushuku ithibati ya serikali. Lakini hali ilivyokuwa ikienda hii haikuwa siri tena. Wanatu wa mashambani walikuwa wamesema imetosha. Maana wakati watu wa mijini wakilalamika angalau walikuwa na ahueni ikilinganishwa na watu wa mashambani ambao siku zote walikuwa kama shamba la chama tawala kujizoelea kura na kushinda kwa kishindo.

Wapo wanaosema waliupata ujasiri baada ya kusikia kilichokuwa kimetokea nchi jirani ya Mizengwc ambapo chama tawala kilipoteza serikali na viongozi wake kuishia kufungwa na kufilisiwa mali walizokuwa wamejilimbikizia toka kwenye taasisi za umma. Moto ulioanzia Mizengwe ulianza kusambaa taratibu kuelekea Mafuriko. Pia ujirani ulichangia sana pamoja na serikali ya Mafuriko kuwa fisidi. Maana watu wengi wa Mafuriko hasa wa mipakani wana udugu wa damu na nchi jirani. Maana kabla ya kugawanywa na wakoloni nchi hizi zilikuwa nchi moja yenye falme ndogo ndogo ndani mwake. Wanakijiji waligeuka wanasiasa ghafla wengine kufikia hata kutaka wabunge wao wajiuzulu. Maana walipotaka maelezo ya mateso yao walijibiwa ukame. Walipouliza juu ya wizi wa pesa na miradi hewa baadhi ya wabunge walipiga siasa badala ya kuwaeleza ukweli. Ukame uligeuka kuwa sababu ya kila kitu hata kile kilchokuwa kimetokea kabla ya huo ukame. Watu walianza kudai hapakuwa na ukame wa kimazingira bali kimawazo na visheni!

Wengine walikwenda hatua mia mbele kudai kuwa tatizo la Mafuriko haukuwa ukame bali upofu na ulafi wa watawala waliokuwa wamefurika kila pembe ya nchi kwenye ngazi za chini za juu. Katika jimbo la Kemete ambalo ni jimbo la Zengeni, mbunge alikosa la kuwambia na kusingizia upinzani. Watu walianza utani wa kusema" akifa mtu upinzani au ukame, isiponyesha, mvua upinzani."

Wakati wanasiasa wakiendelea kupiga siasa, uchumi ulizorota na kuporomoka huku bei za vitu zikipanda hovyo hovyo huku wafanyabiashara wa kigeni wakiwalangua wazalendo. Maana licha ya viwanda vingi kumilkiwa na wageni, vilifungwa kutokana na kukosekana umeme. Umeme ulianza kuwa wa mgawo. Ila wakubwa hawakuwa na mgawo!

Walichofanya ambacho kilichochea hasira za wananchi ni kuleta mita za umeme zilizoitwa BUKU yaani Bania Umeme Kadri Unavyopaswa. Mita hizi zilileta malalamiko na migomo. Maana zilifungwa kwenye majumba ya watu maskini huku matajiri na watawala wakiendelea kutumia umeme vibaya tena bila kulipia.

Shirika la umeme la Mafuriko National Electrical Company (MANESCO) nalo halikusalimika. Lilijikuta likifilisika kutokana na serikali na wakubwa kutolipia umeme waliokuwa wakiutumia. Kuwazuga wananchi walisingizia menejimenti ya shirika. Hivyo walileta nyingine ya kigeni iliyoliulia mbali kabisa shirika hili ambalo kama siyo wakubwa na serikali kutolipia umeme waliokuwa wakitumia lisingefilisika. Kuongeza chumvi kwenye donda hata hii menejimenti ya kigeni iliyoletwa na kuingizwa kwa mtutu wa bunduki, ilivuna pesa na kuliacha shirika lijifie kama ng'ombe aliyekosa malisho wakati wa kiangazi. Ilikuja kujulikana baadaye kuwa kumbe hii menejimenti ya kigeni ilikuwa mradi wa mashemeji zake mtawala wa zamani wa Mafuriko.

Hata hivyo, MANESCO ishukuru Mungu. Kwani uhai wake ulitegemea kuwapandishia watu maskini ankara kiasi cha kuwachanganya na kusababisha malalamiko. Bahati mbaya watu wa Mafuriko walikuwa wamelewa sifa za watawala. Walizoea kuwaambia kuwa walikuwa ni taifa la upendo. Hivyo imani ya upendo ilikua na kuwa sugu mioyoni mwa wananchi kiasi cha kuliwa wakijiona. Walikuwa kama kondoo mbele ya mbwa mwitu. Ajabu waliowaaminisha kuwa Mafuriko ilikuwa nchi ya upendo, hawakuwa na upendo na taifa wala watu wake. Kwao upendo ulikuwa ni ukondoo wa wananchi kushuhudia nchi ikiangamia. Waliogopa kuchukia mwanzoni. Kwani kwa kufanya hivyo wangechafua rekodi yao ya kuwa taifa la upendo. Wakati maskini wakileweshwa na sifa hizi za uongo, kama mbwa mwitu kwenye mzoga wa tembo,watawala waliendelea kuliibia taifa wao wake,watoto na marafiki zao waliotokea kuwa matajiri wa kutupwa huku wananchi wakiendelea kuwa maskini wa kutupwa!

Ajabu maskini kwa maskini walikuwa hawapendani. Maana kama wangelikuwa na upendo wa kweli siyo wa imani wasingewachoma vibaka na vidokozi huku wakiwanyenyekea majambazi wakubwa kwa vile walikuwa ama na pesa au madaraka. Kuleta menejimenti ya kigeni kuliongezea chumvi kwenye kidonda. Maana kampuni la kigeni liitwalo Net Problem Group lililetwa kukuweka miundo mbinu mpya kumbe ilikuwa siyo kuweka miundo mbinu mipya bali mbinu na miundo mipya ya kuuibia umma! Kampuni hili ndiyo liliongezea machungu. Maana mwaka mzima liliofanya kazi ilikuwa ni kazi ya kutorosha pesa na kutokarabati miundo mbinu ya shirika la MANESCO kiasi cha kuliacha likiwa limefilisika na kutaniwa kwa kuitwa Mkangafu! Baya zaidi baada ya mwaka mmoja kampuni hilo kufanikisha wizi wake, iligundulika kuwa kumbe wakubwa walikuwa wamelileta ili kulitumia kujitajirisha! Na hali hii ilikuwa karibu kwenye kila sekta iliyokuwa na kipato kilichoishia kwenye mifuko ya kundi dogo la watawala. Hali ilikuwa mbaya.

Katika tathmini binafsi iliyowahi kufanywa na Zengeni wakati akiandika makala zake, aligundua kuwa:

Raia wa kawaida wa Mafuriko alikuwa akiibiwa takribani dola 86 kwa mwaka katika sekta ya nishati.

Raia huyu huyu wa Mafuriko alikuwa akipoteza zaidi ya dola 56 kwa mwaka kwenye huduma ya maji.

Katika elimu alikuwa akipoteza si chini ya dola 40 kwa mwaka bila kuingiza maeneo mengine kama afya, usafari, chakula na mengine. Katika kuangalia kipato cha jumla cha mwananchi wa Mafuriko ambacho kilikuwa dola 160 kwa mwaka, Zengeni aligundua kuwa kumbe hii dola 160 ilikuwa ni hasi ya mapato. Maana mzigo aliokuwa amebebeshwa raia wa Mafuriko ulikuwa ni mkubwa kuliko nchi yoyote duniani. Wakati mambo yakizidi kuharibika, Rais na maafisa wake walizidi kuwachafua watu kwa kuwaahidi kuwa wangebadili maisha yao na kujihisi wako peponi. Lakini ukweli ulikuwa ni kwamba pepo iliyokuwa imeahidiwa haikuwa pepo kitu bali jehanamu. Na kweli maisha ya wananchi yalibadiliika kutoka peponi walipokuwa! Kwa jinsi watawala walivyojua kukufuru mtu angehoji utimamu wa vichwa vyao. Maana waliwachukulia wananchi kama vipofu kiasi cha kujiamani na kuwaaminsha kuwa usiku ulikuwa mchana! Ni watawala walioota ndoto za mchana na kuzichukulia kama ukweli!

Rais wa zamani wa Mafuriko Denjamani Makapi aligundulika kuwa yeye na mkewe walikuwa wamilki wa makampuni ya wizi ya ANDE yaani Anna and Denjamani na ManPower consortium lililokuwa na makampuni mengine madogo yakimilkiwa na watoto marafiki hata wakwe zao. Kampuni hili lilikuwa na hisa karibu katika kila mradi wa maana uliokuwa umeanzishwa chini ya siasa za Ubinafsi.

Mtoto wa rais aitwaye Nicas na mkewe aitwaye Forester walikuwa na kampuni lao liitwalo Fosnic.

Hadhi ya Rais aliyekuwa madarakani ilishuka kiasi cha kuanza kuitwa kibaka wazi wazi na baadhi ya wachambuzi wa mambo. Naye kwa kujua ukweli hakuweza kuchukua hatua zozote zaidi ya kutoa vitisho mara kwa mara. Maana aliogopa kuzidi kuutibua umma uliokuwa umemchoka yeye na marafiki zake aliokuwa amewajaza kwenye nafasi za juu hata bila ya kuwa na sifa! Angechukua hatua gani wakati mbele ya umma alikuwa mheshimiwa lakini nyuma ya pazia alikuwa ameishiwa kiasi cha kuonekana kama kibaka hata jambazi? Hakupenda kuwaamsha simba waliokuwa wamelala tena njaa. Alijitahidi kila alivyoweza kukaa kimya ingawa hatimaye halikuwa jibu. Waziri wake mkubwa kwa unafiki alijitia kutembelea mikoa mara kwa mara akihimiza maendeleo wakati nyuma ya pazia alikuwa mhujumu mkubwa na kikwazo cha maendeleo hayo hayo aliyokuwa akihubiri kwa mdomo na kuyazuia kwa matendo yake machafu. Kama kuna kitu alikijua sana hakikuwa kingine bali unafiki. Maana hata marehemu baba yake alikuwa amemchoka kiasi cha kumwambia kuwa alikuwa mwizi hata kama alikuwa akimsaidia. Asiyesikia la mkuu huvunjika guu. Maana baada ya kifo cha baba yake siku alipoteuliwa kuwa waziri mkubwa watu wengi walihoji ni lini alikuwa ameokoka na kuachana na wizi. Walizidi kuhoji hata kama alikuwa ameokoka je alikuwa amerejesha mali za umma alizokuwa ameiba kwa mujibu wa shutuma za baba yake ambaye alimjua kuliko mtu yeyote. Kila swali hili lilipojitokeza alijitahidi kulipuuzia huku akijifanya hasikii. Aliendela kujionyesha kama mchapa kazi wakati ukweli ulikuwa ni kwamba alikuwa na jambazi aliyekuwa amejificha nyuma ya madaraka ambayo alifuja nyuma ya pazia akihoka kwa kila mbinu hili lisijulikane. Hata hivyo umma uliendelea kuuliza swali lake huku ukishinikiza atimuliwe kazi na kuchunguzwa na wenzake waliokuwa wanajulikana kwa ufisadi na ulafi wao.

Pamoja na kujibaraguza na kujifanya kiongozi anayefaa, magazeti ambayo yalikuwa hayakufunga ndoa na ujambazi uliokuwa unaendelea yaliendelea kumsakama lakini alikaa kimya. Maana yeye kama bosi wake hakuwa na jinsi ya kujitetea bali kujaribu kuzusha hili na lile ili mambo yapoe lakini hayakupoa bali kuzidi kuchemka.

Siku ilipofumka kashfa kubwa ya wizi kwenye benki kuu ya Mafuriko hali ya mambo ilianza kuwa mbaya na kuwagumia watawala. Kama ngawa aliyeiba maziwa, walianza kuogopa hata vivuli vyao. Magazeti ya upinzani yalivalia kibwebwe suala hili. Serikali ilikuwa imenasa kiasi cha wakubwa kuzikimbia ofisi zao ili wasikumbane na patashika na kizaazaa cha waandishi wa habari. Wakati serikali ikitafuta jinsi ya kuuficha uso wake, timu ya taifa ya la Mafuriko iliyoitwa Mafuriko warriors ambayo nayo ilikuwa imetelekezwa na watawala kiasi cha kutegemea ufadhili wa wafanyabiashara wezi, iliishinda timu ngumu ya nchi ya Sofanakibu. Serikali haraka haraka ili kuwaziba macho wananchi iliandaa hafla kubwa kiasi cha wachezaji kukaribishwa chakula cha mchana na Rais na mkewe na mawaziri wake wote! Watunzi wa muziki walijua mambo haya. Maana walitunga wimbo wa vijembe ulioitwa waso haya wana mji wao na mji wao hakika ulikuwa Mafuriko. Maana mtu aliyejua tabia za Rais alishangaa alivyokuwa akikenua meno yote thelathini mbili utadhani alikuwa akiipenda timu ile! Angeipenda angeacha iishi kwa hisani ya watu wachafu?

Serikali ya Mafuriko ilikuwa bingwa wa mizengwe kama jina la nchi ya jirani yake. Wananchi waliozoea kuiita serikali sanii. Baadaye iligundulika kuwa kumbe mtoto wa waziri mkubwa kwa kushirikiana na mke wa Rais walikuwa wameingiza majenereta kutoka Uchina. Hawakuwa wameyalipia ushuru na waliyauza kwa bei mbaya. Kashfa hii ilinyunyuta kiasi cha waziri mkubwa kwenda nchini Poland kutibiwa shinikizo la damu. Alipokwenda kutibiwa watu waliomba arudi kwenye jeneza lakini haikuwa. Maana, dua la kuku halimpati mwewe.alipoanguka jukwaani wakati wa sherehe za ushindi wengi walitamani angetokea pale kwenda Makaburini. Viongozi wa upinzani waliwataka wananchi kuacha ndoto za alinacha zakutegemea kudra kutatua matatizo yao. Badala yake waliwataka kusimama na kupambana na utawala mchafu na mchovu uliokuwa unawacheleweshа.

Kwa upande mwingine nao wananchi waliwaambia wapinzani kuacha uchoyo na kutegemea kudura vile vile. Kwani kwao nao walikuwa kikwazo japo si kikubwa kama watawala. Wananchi walianza kuwatania watawala wao kuwa walikuwa magaidi na majambazi wa kisiasa. Wengine waliwaita malaya na wengine waliwaita kila aina ya majina machafu walilojisikia kuita. Nchi ilianza taratibu kujiendea kama haikuwa na msimamizi. Karibu kila mradi wa umma ulioanzishwa ulikuwa na wingu la kashfa za wizi juu yake ukikaa miaka mingi bila kukamilika huku kila mwaka ukitengewa pesa kwenye bajeti ya nchi iliyokuwa ikitokana na misaada kwa zaidi ya asilimia 50. Maana kutokana na kutokuwa na mipango na visheni, Mafuriko ilifilisika kimya kimya kiasi cha kutegemea hisani ya wafadhili karibu kwa kila kitu hata kuchimba vyoo vya mashule na mahospitali! Kuna kipindi waziri mkuu wa zamani aliwahi kujisifu kuwa serikali yake ilikuwa imeleta maendeleo kwa kuchimba vyoo ambavyo navyo vilichimbwa na wafadhili! Barabara nyingi zilizokuwa zimejengwa hata majengo ya shule au zahanati viligundulika kuwa vya kiwango cha chini kutokana na wakandarasi kutoa rushwa. Hivyo walibana matumizi kwenye kujenga ili kuokoa pesa yao waliyohonga. Wengine hata hawakufanya hivyo kurejesha pesa yao. Bali walikuwa wanajua jinsi watawala wa Mafuriko wasivyo wafuatiliaji. Hivyo, vyovyote ambavyo wangefanya hakuna ambaye angejisumbua kuwakagua au kuwachukulia hatua. Kulikuwa na msemo mchafu kuwa mali ya umma haiumi! Hivyo, iume haikuumi! Hali ilikuwa mbaya sana. Ilifikia mahali wakandarasi wakawa wanapunguza ukubwa wa barabara kwa mita moja ili kujipatia pesa chafu haraka haraka na serikali haikustuka! Ingestukaje wakati watendaji wake ndiyo walikuwa vinara wa jinai hii?

Mafuriko ilifikia pabaya kiasi cha kutegemea hata

wafadhili kufikiri! Maana kila kitu ilikuwa wafadhili ambao nao taratibu waligeuka miungu na wanyonyaji wakubwa wa Mafuriko. Ilifikia hata kujenga vyoo vya shule vilitegemea wafadhili huku baadhi ya mawaziri wakijisifu kwa hili badala ya kuhuzunika!

21
Wateule na ukoo wao

Baada ya Zengeni kusimamishiwa biashara zake na kuwa ameishakata shauri kuachana na ualimu, ilibidi aanze kufikiria shughuli nyingine ya kufanya yenye kuweza kumletea kipato. Hakukata tamaa licha ya kuchukia serikali ambayo mara nyingi aliifananisha na kuku anayekula mayai yake. Maana alishaona jinsi kipato cha biashara hii ndogo kilivyokuwa kikubwa kuliko cha ualimu. Kilichomfurahisha zaidi ni kugundua kuwa biashara ingempa uhuru zaidi badala ya kutegemea mwisho wa mwezi ambao kutokana na hali ya nchi kudorora, haukuwa hata na uhakika. Maana kuna kipindi walilipa mshahara baada ya miezi miwili hata mitatu. Ili kupambana na hali hii ya kuzuiwa kufanya biashara ya vyakula, alianza kubuni biashara isiyohusiana na vyakula wala vinywaji. Alianza kufanya utafiti wa kuuza vyuma chakavu, kuanzisha machimbo ya mchanga au kokoto na nyingine nyingi.

Kabla ya kufikia uamuzi wa wapi kuelekea, walikubaliana na mkewe kwanza wafanye utafiti kuona ni biashara gani ingewaepusha na adha za serikali. Alifikiria kwenda kijijini kwao kulima. Lakini alikataa wazo hili baada ya kugundua kuwa licha ya serikali kutowahudumia wakulima kwa kuwapelekea wataalamu wa kilimo waliokuwa wamelowea mijini kusiko na kilimo, ilikuwa ikiwakopa mazao yao. Hivyo, hii aliita biashara kichaa ya kutwanga pili pili na kuambulia kupiga chafya na kupofuka. Japo kwake kilimo ilikuwa ni kazi ya heshima, hakuipenda kwa vile ilikuwa imenyang'anywa heshima yake. Alikuwa amechagua kilimo cha mboga mboga kwa vile ilikuwa na soko la uhakika.

Zengeni hakuwa peke yake kwenye suala la kilimo. Kwani hata kwenye bajeti ya kila mwaka ya nchi ya Mafuriko kilimo kilitengewa pesa kidogo kuliko hata ofisi ya Rais. Kimsingi, wakulima walikuwa kama watoto yatima waliokuwa wamesahauliwa na serikali waliyoiita yao. Serikali iliwakumbuka tu wakati wa uchaguzi na kukusanya kodi. Zengeni alizoea kusema kuwa kama kilimo kingekuwa hakikutelekezwa, angeweza kuwa mkulima mkubwa kama wakuliwa wa Ulaya. Lakini kila alipoangalia bei za pembejeo na mbolea na bei ya mazao, roho ilikunjika kiasi cha kubaki akitamani mambo yangebadilika bila mafanikio. Pamoja na kilimo kusalitiwa na kuuawa, Zengeni alifarijika sana kipindi kidogo alichojaribu kukuza mboga mboga. Maana walimu wenzake walizoea kuja kwake kuomba mboga ambazo alikuwa hawanyimi. Aliweza kujifunza jinsi ya kuishi na watu wenye shida na uhitaji bila kujali kama wanatumia mwaya huo kunyonya au walikuwa wakilazimishwa na shida tokana na kucheleweshwa mishahara yao. Aligundua ubaya wa kuwanacho wakati wenzio hawana hasa kama mwenye kuwa nacho hana roho mbaya wala kuwa mlafi na mnyama. Maana ni lawama sana. Alishangaa ubinadamu wa watawala wa Mafuriko ambao waliweza kununua migari ya bei mbaya na kujilipa mishahara mikubwa huku nyuma ya pazia wakiibia na kuihujumu nchi bila kuwaonea huruma wananchi maskini waliokuwa wakiwakamua kama ng'ombe. Hata ng'ombe alikuwa na nafuu maana hulishwa kwanza ili atoe maziwa au nyama. Hali hii iliongeza hasira zake dhidi ya mfumo mzima wa Mafuriko ambao alizoea kuuita mfumo wa kifisi na kimbwa mwitu. Mfumo mchafu na katili kuliko mifumo yote michafu iliyowahi kuwapo. Maana kabla ya Mafuriko kupata uhuru wake wa bendera watesi walikuwa wageni na siyo watu wenye nasaba na yeyote. Kwake ilikuwa ni dhambi isiyostahili msamaha kwa mtu kumtesa na kumnyonya mtu wa mbari yake na taifa lake. Na kweli watu wa Mafuriko walikuwa wakiteswa na watu waliozoea kuwahadaa na kuwazuga kuwa walikuwa ndugu na viongozi wao. Hakuna kipindi Zengeni alishangaa watu wake kama kipindi walichoishi bila umeme kwa mwaka mzima bila ya kulalamika huku watawala wezi wakiutumia mwanya huo kutengeneza utajiri kwa kule kampuni kama Richmen, ambayo alizoea kuiita Richmonduli, kuingiza majenereta na kuyauza kwa bei ya kuruka, kupandisha bei ya umeme na hata kujiongezea pesa kwa kisingizio cha mgao!

Kuongezea chumvi kwenye donda, bado walikuwa wakiibia benki kuu ya Mafuriko ukiachia mbali matumizi mabaya na machafu ya pesa ya umma kila mwaka wa pesa kwenye karibu kila wizara ya serikali. Wizi wa wakubwa ulisimamiwa na watoto wao waliokuwa wameajiriwa benki kuu kusimamia maslahi ya wazazi wao badala ya taifa. Walilipwa mirupurupu mingi na mishahara mikubwa na makandokando mengine kutimiza jinai hii! Lilikuwa ni jambo la kawaida kukuta kwa mfano mfagiaji kwenye wizara kama ya fedha, mamlaka ya kushughulikia mapato na kodi, viwanja vya ndege na bandari akiwa ni milionea wa kutupwa aliyeweza kumiliki majumba na magari na utajiri mwingine wa ajabu kwenye maeneo aghali ya mijini

Ilifikia mahali Mafuriko ikiwa inasifika kwa matumizi ya magari ya bei mbaya kwenye ukanda mzima wa mawio. Watawala wote wa Mafuriko wakubwa na wadogo walitumia migari ya bei mbaya kuliko hata ya mawaziri katika baadhi ya nchi zilizokuwa tajiri kuliko yenyewe. Ilifikia mahali hata polisi wa Mafuriko kutumia magari kama Mercedes Benz kufukuzia vibaka mitaani au kufanyia doria kwenye mitaa michafu kama ile ya akina Zengeni iliyokuwa imegeuzwa makazi ya kudumu na kipindupindu ukiachia mbali kutopimwa na kukosa karibu huduma zote alizostahili mwananchi wa nchi iliyokuwa ikijisifia kuwa huru.

Wakati wakubwa wakiiagamiza nchi kwa matumizi na maamuzi mabaya, wizi na ufisadi kila aina, kujuana hasa katika nafasi za masomo nje ya Mafuriko na ajira sehemu zenye mishahara mikubwa na marupurupu, watoto wa wakubwa nao walikuwa wameanzisha serikali yao ndani ya serikali! Hata kashfa ya wizi wa mabilioni kwenye benki kuu ya Mafuriko haikumtisha gavana kwa vile alikuwa akijua uchafu wa wakubwa wenzake hasa kuajiri watoto wao kwenye benki hii. Benki ya Mafuriko iligeuka ghafla kuwa benki ya wakubwa. Zengeni alizoea kuwaita watoto wa wakubwa waliokuwa wameajiriwa na Benki kuu matunguli aliyokuwa akiyatumia gavana kulinda uchafu wake na mkewe na ndugu zao. Katika jinai hii ya ajira za kujuana Zengeni alizoea kuita kundi la watoto wa wakubwa waliokuwa wamejazana benkini humo, Belly of Tembo (BOT II), huku gavana na wezi wakubwa wenzake akiwaita a Bunch of Thugs au BOT I! Zengeni alizoea kuwaita wananchi wa Mafuriko mataahira na wapumbavu ambao walijua uchafu huu bila kuchukua hatua! Kwenye makala moja aliyoiita kurejesha Mafuriko kwenye enzi zake aliwahimiza wananchi kuandamana na kuigomea serikali ili itimuliwe. Maana ilikuwa imeshindwa vibaya sana. Nani angeamini kuwa mtoto wa kwanza wa kike na mumewe walikuwa wameajiri benki kuu? Binti huyu aliyeitwa Pammie Eddie mwa Luwasha, mtoto wa waziri mkubwa wa zamani aliyeitwa Filie Freddie Sumuye, mtoto wa mkuu wa ofisi ya Rais aitwaye Hariet Martie Lumbango, mtoto wa katibu wa chama wa zamani, Zalia Kavava, Mtoto wa Rais wa Zamani, Salama Ali Nyimwi, mtoto wa Rais wa zamani wa awamu nyingine Blasie Blass Bonnie Mkapu, mtoto wa mkuu wa zamani wa jeshi la polisi Sylivia Omaria Mahuta, mtoto wa waziri wa mambo ya ndani, Justina Jimmie Muigai, mtoto wa mwanasiasa mashuhuri mkuu wa chama tawala Kennie Johnnie Nchimbu wote hawa na wengine wengi walikuwa waajiri wa benki kuu ya Mafuriko wakishika nafasi nyeti ilhali kazi yao ilikuwa kuiibia Mafuriko!

Wengine katika Belly of Tembo kampuni tanzu ya Bunch of Thieves walikuwa, Viola Phil Luhanjoa mtoto wa mkuu wa utumishi, alikuwapo Kuli Kate Kambi mtoto wa waziri wa zamani, Tom Mongellani mtoto wa waziri wa zamani, Mica Maleali mwizi mtoto wa chifu wa zamani wa kabila la gachawa, Jabbie Abdy Kigodani, waziri aliyeiingiza Mafuriko kwenye matatizo alipokuwa akisimamia mipango, pia alikuwapo mtoto wa kufikia wa gavana mwenyewe, Rachael Mugando! Zengeni alizoea kuwaita hawa wezi na watoto wa wezi tunguli la gavana ambalo humuwezesha kuiba bila kuogopa kitu. Kwa kujua uchafu huu alikuwa akijua hata Rais asingeweza kumfukuza akawa salama! Ukiachia benki kuu, hata mabenki ya kigeni yenye kulipa vizuri, bandari, mamlaka ya mapato, viwanja vya ndege na mipakani walipopitisha madawa ya kulevya ya wazazi wao na washirika wao nako walikuwa wamejazana! Mbuga za wanyama, madini, misitu, forodha, ubalozini na hata kwenye serikali za mitaa walijazana ndugu wa wakubwa! Ajabu bado Rais alikuwa akiwakejeli wanamafuriko kuwa alikuwa ikulu kwa ajili yao ilhali alikuwapo pale kulinda maslahi ya kundi dogo la wezi! Watoto hawa waliokuwa wamesomeshwa nje ya Mafuriko kwa kodi ya mwananchi mvuja jasho na maskini wa kutupwa licha ya kutofaulu vizuri, walipewa kazi nzuri huku watoto wa wakulima na wafanyakazi maskini wa Mafuriko wenye viwango vikubwa vya kushinda wakiwa wanafanya kazi hafifu hata kukosa kazi! Ilifikia mahali sifa ya kupata ajira ilitegemea sana jina la mtu badala ya sifa za usomi wake! Yaani hali ikuwa ni mbaya kiasi cha kutisha. Maana hata wakwe wa wakubwa ambao walikuwa wakitoka kwenye familia zisizo na majina nao walijikuta wakilala maskini na kuamka matajiri kisa wameoa kwa wakubwa!

Kwa kujua matokeo ya mfumo huu mchafu, wakubwa waliua elimu ili kuhakikisha watoto wao waliosoma nje ya nchi kuchukua nafasi zao baada ya kuwaandaa vilivyo na kuwakabidhi nchi. Benki ya Mafuriko, hazina, bandari, viwanja vya ndege, taasisi ya mapato na kodi, wizara nyeti kama fedha biashara, madini, mambo ya nchi za nje, na nyingine nyeti zilikuwa ndiyo mazalio ya kazi kwa watoto wa wakubwa. Hata hivyo, ilikuwa ni nadra kwa mtoto wa maskini kuoa kwenye tabaka hili la wateule wachache wachafu waliokuwa wamepata ukwasi kwa kunyonya watu kama kupe. Afadhali hata ya kupe, maana kupe hamnyonyi kupe mwenzie!

22
Shem, First lady

Waziri mkubwa aliporejea ofisini kwake haraka haraka alimpigia simu mke wa rais maarufu kama First lady aliyeitwa Salanna ambaye naye alikuwa anafahamika kwa tamaa ya pesa huku akitumia madaraka ya mumewe kuwavutia wafanyabiashara wezi waliokuwa wakimtumia kupata tenda na kukwepa kodi. Kulikuwa na ndoa kati ya mbuzi mpumbavu na fisi mjanja. Kama ni urafiki basi ulikuwa ni urafiki wa mashaka tena makubwa sana. Hapa ilikuwa ni kutumiana mtindo mmoja huku kila mmoja akijiona mjanja kuliko mwenzake. Kitu ambacho mke wa Rais hakujua ni kwamba katika mchezo huu mchafu yeye ndiye alikuwa mwenye hasara. Maana wakati mumewe akichaguliwa na kuapishwa, hawa wafanyabiashara fisi hawakupiga hata kura. Na isitoshe kama lingezuka tatizo lolote, jamii yao ilijulikana kwa tabia yake ya kukimbia matatizo na kurejea yalipokuwa yamekwisha na hali kurejea kwenye ushwari. Wao walikuwa ni marafiki wa mwisho wa mwezi. Maana kabla ya mumewe kuingia madarakani, wezi hawa walikuwa na usuhuba na mke wa Rais aliyewatungulia ambaye naye yalipomkuta yaliyomkuta hakuna hata mmoja aliyekwenda kwake hata kumsalimia hadi alipokufa kwa kihoro. Madaraka yalipomkimbia nao walimkimbia kadhalika. Hawakuwa na hamu wala haja ya kununua picha au pete yake. Nani angepoteza muda kulifuata ganda la muua alilokuwa amekwisha kulikamua na kulikausha halafu akalitupa?

Mke wa Rais alikuwa na shirika lake lisilo la kiserikali la kushughulikia yatima. Akishirikiana na mke wa waziri mkubwa. Shirika hili liliitwa MAWA yaani Maulaji ya

Wakubwa. Na kweli wananchi wa Mafuriko walikuwa ni ulaji wa wakubwa. Hivyo, kama shirika lake lingezingatia maana ya neno ulaji, basi wananchi wengi walipaswa kuliogopa na kulichukia shirika hili chafu na fisadi.

MAWA ilianzishwa kama njia ya kufanyia biashara kwa kutumia cheo cha Rais. Na hii kwa Mafuriko haikuwa mara ya kwanza kwa cheo cha Rais kutumika kuiibia nchi. Rais aliyekuwa amemaliza muda wake alikuwa ameshirikiana na mkewe chini ya shirika lisilo la kiserikali la mkewe lililoitwa Economic Opportunity for the First Lady (EOFL) pamoja na kampuni yake na mkewe iitwayo BENA vifupi vya majina ya Bwana na bibi ambayo Zengeni alizoea kuiita Benefit Economically on National Accounts. Waziri mkubwa alipiga simu kwa mke wa Rais kutaka kumtaarifu kuwa mumewe yaani Rais, alikuwa akishauriwa vibaya dhidi yao.

Alisema. “Halo Shem, salama?”Mke wa Rais alijibu. “Halo salama shemeji. Habari za majukumu?”

Waziri mkubwa, “Siyo nzuri Shem. Maana kuna watu wanamshauri vibaya mzee. Leo ameniita na kuniuliza maswali ambayo si ya kawaida. Je jana usiku alikuwa na maongezi na nani katika washauri wake?”

Mke wa Rais. “Ngoja nifikirie.” Kulipita kitambo kidogo huku mke huyu wa Rais akijaribu kukumbuka watu waliokuwa na mumewe usiku wa jana yake.

Baada ya kukaa kimya kwa muda, mke wa Rais aliita, “Halo shemeji. Jana nilikuwa kwenye pati ya kuchangisha pesa ya watoto yatima wa kule Kisamvule. Nilichelewa kurudi. Lakini nitacheki na mkuu wa usalama wa ndani. Maana ndiye huwa anaondoka usiku hapa. Si unajua tulivyompa hiyo kazi ya kuangalia watu wanaokuja kuongea na mume wangu?”

Kikulacho ki nguoni mwako siku zote. Kwani waziri mkubwa kwa kumtumia mkewe alifanikiwa kumrubuni mke wa bosi wake yaani Rais, kumchunguza mumewe kwa ajili ya faida ya mtandao wa kijambazi wa wakubwa majambazi. Isitoshe, mke wa Rais alikuwa mama mwenye huruma na adili kabla ya mumewe kuukwaa urais. Lakini baada ya mumewe kuingia madarakani mke wa waziri mkubwa na mke wa Rais wa zamani walimuingiza kwenye jinai ya kusaka ngawira kiasi cha kuanzisha taasisi yake isiyo ya kiserikali ingawa mumewe alikuwa ndiyo serikali yenyewe! Mke wa Rais ambaye kitaaluma ni mfagizi yaani janitor, hakutegemewa kujiingiza kwenye ujambazi wa kutumia madaraka ya mumewe kutokana na kashfa iliyokuwa imemkumba mtangulizi wake. Kwa vile hakuwana na elimu wala busara alinaswa na mtego ambao aliujua vizuri akashindwa kuukwepa kwa tamaa na upogo wake. Kweli binadamu hubadilika. Pamoja na kuwa Rais alikuwa naye akishiriki uchafu wa kuihujumu nchi na serikali yake mwenyewe, kishawishi kikubwa ilikuwa ni songombwingo waziri mkubwa na mke wa Rais mwenyewe. Maana hawa watu walikuwa na tamaa si ya kawaida.

Wakishirikiana na mkuu wa usalama wa ndani, walihakikisha kila mshauri wa Rais waliyemshuku kutopenda kushiriki uchafu wao, aliwekewa walinzi waliokuwa wakiripoti moja kwa moja kwa mkuu wa usalama ili kufuatilia nyenzo za washauri wa Rais waliowahofia kumshauri dhidi ya uoza. Walikuwa tayari hata kumtoa roho yeyote aliyetishia maslahi uoza yao.

Mmoja wa washauri wa Rais aliyekuwa akifuatiliwa sana, alikuwa ni jaji mstaafu ambaye alikuwa anachukia vitendo vya rushwa. Mwingine alikuwa ni katibu wa wizara ya nishati ambaye naye licha ya kutoka kwenye ukoo tajiri alikuwa ni mtu safi na mzalendo aliyechukia uoza huu. Alikuwa ni msomi vya kutosha. Huyu aliuchukia uchafu wa kuliibia taifa lake mwenyewe. Hata Rais alilijua hili vizuri kiasi cha kumheshimu sana. Nyuma ya pazia alimhusudu katibu huyu mwenye kuona mbali. Baada ya Rais kuonyesha wasi wasi juu ya mstakabali wa uchumi wa nchi na ubadhilifu katika benki kuu, waziri mkubwa, kwa kumtumia mke wa Rais maarufu kama First Lady, alianza kusuka mpango wa kuhakikisha katibu huyu mwiba anahamishiwa kwenye wizara ambayo haikuwa na maslahi kama adhabu. Kwa roho mbaya ya waziri mkubwa, hata kumuamisha wizara ilikuwa ni bahati. Na huenda hii ilitokana na baba yake kuwa maarufu nchini Mafuriko. Hivyo waziri mkubwa na wezi wenzake waliogopa kumfukuzisha kazi ili baba yake asiutumie ushawishi wake kuwaangusha na wao.

Baada ya kukata simu, mke wa Rais alimpigia mkuu wa usalama wa ndani,balozi mstaafu mwenye cheo cha Brigedia Jenerali aliyeitwa Ommy Mahiti. Alikuwa ni pandikizi la mtu katili na mlafi ambaye licha ya kupenda kujipendekeza kwa wakubwa, alikuwa naye mwingi wa tamaa ya utajiri mnuko kama waziri mkubwa na mke wa Rais. Maongezi yao yalikuwa hivi. Mke wa Rais, "Halo Roger, kwanza uko wapi?" Mkuu wa usalama wa ndani, "Niko ofisini kwangu nasoma ripoti ya LTPI." Huu ulikuwa ni mradi bomu kama Richmonduli ambao uliingiza nchi ya Mafuriko hasara isiyo ya kawaida baada ya mwanasheria mkuu wa zamani, waziri wa fedha wa zamani ambaye alikuwa marehemu tayari, waziri wa mipango na uchumu mwenye shahada ya udaktari aliyoipata ughaibuni, mfanyabiashara tapeli aliyekuwa ameacha kazi kwenye benki kuu ya Mafuriko, wabunge na mwaziri mbali mbali, walikuwa wameingiza nchi ya Mafuriko kwenye mradi mchafu uliokuwa umeikamua zaidi ya dola za kimarekani milioni 200. Huu ulikuwa ni mradi wa kutengeneza nishati mbadala na rafiki wa mazingira. Lakini kutokana na wakubwa kutumia lugha hii, nyuma ya pazia mradi huu ulikuwa wa zama za mawe lakini aghali ulioligharimu taifa la Mafuriko zaidi ya dola milioni tano kila mwezi kununua nishati hii mfu na ya kizamani!

Mke wa Rais aliendelea. "Je tunaweza kukutana leo jioni?"

Mkuu wa usalama wa ndani alijibu, "Vipi na wapi?"

Mke wa Rais. "Nipe muda ngoja niongee na …" Alitaja jina la waziri mkubwa.

"Okey mama" Alijibu mkuu wa usalama wa ndani.

Baada ya kukata simu alimpigia waziri mkubwa kuandaa hafla ya ghafla ambayo yeye mke wa Rais angehudhuria ndani ya siku mbili au kabla hata ya hapo kadri ambavyo ingewezekana.

Maongezi yao yalikuwa hivi. "Shemeji, tafadhali wasiliana na Chandy aandae hafla ya kutoa msaada kwa watoto yatima kupitia shirika langu ili tupate fursa ya kukutana na mkuu wa usalama wa ndani kujua nani alikukuwa na mzee usiku wa jana. Fanya kila liwezekanalo. Na umwambie Chandy afanye hivyo haraka. Unaweza kum-brief. Ni kwa usalama wetu sote. Okey." Mke wa Rais alikata simu haraka na kuanza kufikiria kama angekuwa na njia nyingine ya kukutana na mkuu wa usalama wa ndani haraka sana.' Yeye kutokana na elimu yake ndogo hakutaka akutane na mkuu wa usalama wa ndani peke yake. Maana hakuwa na jinsi ya kumbana na kupata ukweli uliotakiwa. Angeweza hata kumuita chumbani mwake yakaisha. Lakini kwa vile alikuwa hana cha kumwambia aliona ni vizuri kukutana naye wakati akiwapo waziri mkubwa ili iwe rahisi kumshawishi la kufanya kama ingebidi afe mtu.

Baada ya kuongea na mke wa Rais, waziri mkubwa alimpigia mfanyabiashara wa kihindi aliyekuwa mkuu wa taasisi ya Cheetah aliyeitwa chandy pia. Huyu alionekana mtu wa heshima na huruma nje. Lakini nyuma ya pazia alikuwa ni jambazi na shetani si wa kawaida. Hata kunguru na vyura wa Mafuriko walimjua kuwa alikuwa habithi ambaye hakustahili kuitwa mtu bali hayawani. Naye pamoja na kujifanya mwema rohoni alizoea kujisuta kwa jinsi alivyokuwa fisidi na mnafiki wa kutupwa. Baada ya Chandy kuongea na waziri mkubwa, simu yake ilikuwa bize akiwataarifu majambazi wenzake juu ya ulaji mwingine na sifa za kupiga picha na mke wa Rais ambaye wangemtumia hasa wale ambao walikuwa bado hawajawahi kuwa karibu naye au mumewe. Alitumia misaada shirika lake liliyokuwa likiitoa kwa watu maskini kama mwamvuli wa kufichia uovu wake na majambazi wenzake. Kwani ukilinganisha kiasi walichokuwa wakitumia kwenye shughuli za "kuwasaidia" maskini wa kutengenezwa na utawala mchafu wa Mafuriko, ilikuwa ni sawa na tone la mkojo kwenye bahari. Nyuma ya pazia walikuwa wakijiingizia mabilioni kwa matrilioni ya pesa toka kwenye hazina na raslimali za hao hao waliojifanya kuwasaidia! Maana kama Mafuriko ingekuwa na watawala wenye akili timamu, wananchi wake hawakuwa wakusaidiwa tena kwa makombo ya wizi. Waliokuwa wakiwasaidia watu wa Mafuriko wengi wao walikuwa ni wezi, wakwepa kodi, wafanyabiashara haramu na uchafu mwingine mwingi tu. Walichofanya ilikuwa sawa na kumkamata mtoto wa mbwa ukampika na kumpa mama yake ale tena kwa furaha asijue alikuwa akila damu yake mwenyewe.

Ili kumhadaa Rais, na umma, waziri mkubwa alimshauri Chandy aandae hafla ambapo mgeni rasmi angekuwa mke wa Rais. Hafla hii ilikuwa na lengo la kumsaidia waziri mkubwa kumbaini mbaya wake na siyo kuwasaidia wananchi au yatima. Kwani ni katika hafla hii angeweza kuongea vizuri na mke wa Rais pamoja na mkuu wa usalama wa ndani bila kustukiwa na Rais. Wananchi walitumika tu kama walivyozoeleka kutumia wasijue kilichokuwa kinaendelea nyuma ya pazia. Chandy hakuwa na kizuizi. Kwani alishazoea vitu kama hivyo.

Alikuwa amefanikiwa kutumia ujanja huu kuwa karibu na kila serikali iliyoingia au kutoka madarakani. Ukiondoa picha za mwanzilishi wa taifa la Mafuriko ambaye hakuwa mtu mchafu, Chandy ana karibu pete, saa, picha na vitu mbali mbali vya marais wa Mafuriko ambavyo yeye na kundi lake la majambazi walivinunua kupitia minada hadaa ya kuchangia watu maskini wa Mafuriko. Kivitendo na kinadharia utawala wote wa Mafuriko ulikuwa mikononi na mifukoni mwa kundi hili la chini chini la kigaidi. Kundi hili ndilo lilimilki, kuendesha, kunyonya na kufaidi raslimali na uhuru wa bendera wa Mafuriko. Lilijipenyeza karibu kwenye nyanja zote za kiuchumi, kisiasa hata za kijamii. Kila lilipochuma vyakutosha au kuogopa kustukiwa, lilihamishia pesa zake za wizi kwao au nchi nyingine za Ulaya. Ni jamii ya watu maskini kiasili lakini wenye utajiri wakujikomba na unafiki wa hali ya juu. Ni watu wasiojiamini lakini wabaguzi na mabingwa wa wizi na ufisadi. Wako tayari hata kuwauza wake zao ilmradi wapate utajiri. Ni watumwa wa vitu na maskini wa utu. Ajabu hata wakati wa uchaguzi walikuwa hawapigi kura zaidi ya kukaa pembeni wakingojea atakayeshinda uchaguzi wamtumie. Walichofanya ni kuandaa hafla za kumpongeza pindi alipochaguliwa.

Baada ya Rais kutangazwa walimteka kwa hila zao kiasi cha kumtenganisha na kumsahaulisha wale waliomchagua. Naye Rais kwa ulevi wa madaraka aliiingia mkenge asijue hawa ndio wangekuwa chanzo cha kuporomoka kwa madaraka yake! Ama kweli usilolijua ni usiku wa kiza, tena kinene! Kwa kutumia unafiki na urafiki wake na wa watawala, lilifanikiwa hata kujipenyeza kwenye siasa ukiachia. Ukiachia mbali kuwatumia watawala wachovu na wachafu wa Mafuriko, lilijipenyeza kwenye siasa kiasi cha kudhamini vyama vyenye nguvu na kunyakua hata nafasi za ubunge.

Kundi hili chafu lilividhamini vyama vyote vilivyoonekana kuwa tishio ili kama kimojawapo kitapata madaraka lisiachwe nyuma kwenye shughuli za kuliibia taifa. Maana kwa kundi hili kila aliyeingia alikuwa ni mlaji na siyo kiongozi. Na dhana hii ilikuwa ni kweli. Kwani Mafuriko ilikuwa na viongozi kwa maneno tena kwenye majukwaa, nyuma ya pazia ilikuwa ni vigumu kutofautisha kati ya vibaka na viongozi. Nyuma ya pazia kulikuwa na majambazi kila aina waliokuwa wamejazana karibu kila wizara na ofisi ya umma.Kundi hili la kigaidi lilianza taratibu kwa kudhamini vilabu vya mpira wa miguu na kutoa misaada mbali mbali hadi kuwateka hata wananchi ambao liliwahonga wakati wa uchaguzi na kupitisha makuadi wake au wenzao. Ilisemekana kuwa wakati wa uchaguzi lilikidhamini chama tawala kiasi cha kukiteka na kukitumia lilivyotaka.

Hapa ndipo uchafu kama wa Benki kuu ya Mafuriko na miradi mingine michafu ilipochipuka na kuwaacha wananchi wa Mafuriko wakiwa maskini wa kutupa licha ya nchi yao kufurika utajiri lukuki!

Baada ya Chandy kukata simu, akiwa amehakikisha kila kitu kilikuwa kamili, alimpigia tena waziri mkubwa kumpa muhtasari wa shughuli nzima.

Mazungumzo yao yalikuwa hivi.

"Bwana Kuba. Pango yote kwisafanyika. So function tafanyika kumbi ya Murikajee na watu yote maarufu na tajiri sana takuwepo. Yote nahesimu wewe sana sana na pesa mingi tatoa. Aha ha ha ha." Aliangua kicheko Chandy.

Waziri mkuu alijibu. "You are as smart as always. Pia nashauri uhakikishe unadhibiti nyendo za gavana na bosi. Maana hali ilivyo ni kwamba kuna watu hawataki maendeleo yetu. Si unaijua nchi yetu ilivyokuwa na kila aina ya watu wenye roho mbaya?"

Chandy alijibu kwa kujiamini. "Mimi iko jua yote na tasugulikia yote kama una-consent Bana Kuba."

"Tumalize kwanza na Bi. mkubwa ili tuone ushawishi wake kwa bosi utatoa matunda gani. Lakini najua hana ujanja. Kwani nimeishamzamisha vilivyo aha ha ha!" Waziri mkubwa aliangusha kicheko cha kuridhika na kufanikiwa kwa hila zake hatari kwa nchi yake akishirikiana na wageni ambao walikuwa kama ndege kwenye mti. Maana walikuwa wakichuma na kutajirika halafu kuhamia nchini kwa au nchi nyingine tajiri kwenda kutumbua chumo la wizi toka Mafuriko. Chandy alijibu, "Bwana kuba haiko tatizo. Bibi yake iko memba aminifu kwa organization yetu. Yeye zee haiko na big say. Say iko kwa bibi kuba yake."

"Okey hakikisha mambo yanakwenda kama yalivyopangwa otherwise we will be in trouble." Waziri mkubwa alikata simu. Chandy na magaidi wenzake walikuwa wakiliibia taifa la Mafuriko pesa nyingi kuliko hata bajeti yake. Walitumia pesa hiyo kuagizia bidhaa mbali mbali za kiwango cha chini toka nchini mwao na nchi nyingine za bara Asia. Pia mtandao huu ulihusika na wizi wa magari, mbao, madini, nyara za serikali, ulanguzi wa pesa, magendo na uuzaji wa madawa ya kulevya. Pamoja na mihadarati kuharibu vijana wengi wa Mafuriko, serikali iliifumbia macho kama ufisadi kwa vile wakubwa wake walikuwa wakinufaika nayo nyuma ya pazia huku hadharani wakijidai walikuwa wana dhamira ya kupambana nayo. Mtandao huu ulitumia maduka ya kubadilishia pesa za kigeni kuhamishia utajiri wake nje ya Mafuriko. Nchini mwao ulikuwa na taasisi iliyoitwa Non-residential Citizens (NRC), iliyokuwa ikichangia zaidi ya dola za kimarekani bilioni 35 kwa mwaka. Pia ulikuwa ukiingiza nchini Mafuriko wahamiaji haramu ambao uliwatoza pesa na kuwaajiri kwa ujira mdogo. Pia ulidhibiti biashara ya kutorosha binadamu ima kuwatumia kufanya biashara ya ukahaba au kuwatafutia pasi za kusafiria za Mafuriko kuondokea kwenda nchi tajiri. Bahati mbaya walipofika kwenye nchi tajiri walijihusisha na jinai hata ugaidi huku sifa mbaya ikiliangukia taifa la Mafuriko. Wengi wao walikuwa matapeli watoroshaji pesa na mabosi wa magenge ya kutorosha watu na mihadarati. Lakini nani angewagusa iwapo walikuwa wanakula na serikali? Nani angewagusa iwapo walikuwa ni serikali ndani ya serikali tena iliyowekwa mikobani?Pamoja na uchafu huu wakuu wa Mafuriko walikuwa wakijua jinai hii. Kwao hii haikuwa jinai. Kwani iliwaingizia pesa nyingi kiasi cha kufumbia macho maslahi ya nchi yao wenyewe! Kuna kipindi fulani kwenye kikao cha siri cha magaidi hawa peke yao bila kuwa na mwananchi wa Mafuriko hata mmoja, walipokuwa wakijisifu kuwa lazima waitajirishe nchi yao kwa kuinyonya Mafuriko ambayo ilikuwa ina watawala vipofu na wapumbavu waliokuwa wakifikiri kwa utumbo badala ya ubongo. Bahati yao taarifa hizi hazikuwafikia wapumbavu wao. Hata kama zingewafikia wangefanya nini iwapo walikuwa wamejigeuza mateka wa hiari wa magaidi haya na matumbo yao?

Kwa kundi hili la manyang'au watawala wa Mafuriko hawakuwa na tofauti na malaya wa kawaida ambaye utu wake aliishauuza kwa ajili ya kupata tonge la kuzamisha tumboni. Kama shimo la choo au la taka taka, watawala wa Mafuriko walikuwa tayari kumeza kila aina ya uchafu ilmradi wapate pesa! Kuna waziri tena msomi aliyehongwa tripu ya ndege kwenda na kurudi Hong Kong na akatoa tenda ya mabilioni ya shilingi huku akiambulia kununuliwa uwanja na kujengewa kijumba ambacho kilikuwa ni kaburi la haki za wananchi. Hali ilikuwa mbaya. Ilifikia mahali mambo ya serikali yakawa yanafanyika mahotelini tena Ulaya. Hakuna tukio lililowaudhi wananchi kama waziri wa ulinzi kusaini mkataba wa ununuzi wa silaha bila kutangaza tenda akiwa hotelini Ulaya. Wapo waliouliza kama alikuwa akitembea hata na mihuri ya taifa yenye nembo ya taifa katika utapeli huu wa kisiasa.Wananchi walizoea kuwaona na kuwamilki viongozi wao wakati wa kampeni. Kipindi hiki lilikuwa jambo la kawaida kushikana mikono na watawala walioonekana wa watu wa kawaida. Baada ya kuchanguliwa waliegeuka wateule ghafla kiasi cha kuwatupa mkono! Ilifikia mahali wananchi wa Mafuriko wakaanza kuona siasa kama usanii hata utapeli wa kawaida. Kwao siasa badala ya kuwa maisha iligeuka kuwa tishio na balaa kwa maisha yao!

Badala ya siasa kuwa chombo na taasisi ya ukombozi iligeuzwa na watu wachache kuwa chanzo cha maangamizi tena kwa gharama ya jasho na pesa yao! Siasa iligeuka kuwa nyenzo na dhana ya usaliti kwa umma. Iligeuzwa kuwa silaha ya kuwateka, kuwanyonya, kuwadhulumu, kuwanyanyasa na kuwapuuza kiasi cha kutoona umuhimu wa uwepo wa taasisi za kisiasa. Wananchi walifikia hatua ya kuona kama asasi za kiraia zilikuwa bora kuliko serikali pamoja na zenyewe kuwa na mtatizo yake. Tangu serikali ilipoanzisha sera za ubinafsi zilizopewa jina zuri la ubinafsishaji, ilikuwa ni kama ilikuwa likizo kiasi cha kila tapeli kujitengenezea utajiri binafsi kwa kutengeneza umaskini kwa watu wa chini. Kikundi cha watu kama hiki cha waziri mkubwa na Chandy kilichofanya ilikukuwa ni kuhamishia umaskini wao kwa umma. Na kama kikundi hiki kingetafuta utajiri kwa ajili ya wana kikundi tatizo lisingekuwa kubwa. Lakini hawa majambazi wa kigeni walikuwa wakiiba kwa ajili ya kuneemesha raia wa nchi zao kwa kuwafukarisha raia wa Mafuriko. Zengeni alizoea kuwambia wanafunzi wake kuwa democracy kwa Mafuriko ilikuwa demon-class au tabaka la mashetani. Tabaka la mashetani waliokosa uzalendo kwa watu wao hata Mungu wao huku wakizidiwa maarifa na wapumbavu waliokuwa wakiwaabudu ng'ombe kama miungu yao! Aliwaona watawala wa mfauriko kama hayawani waliokuwa wamevishwa sura ya binadamu. Alizoea kuwaita mizoga inayotembea ikichafua jamii kwa uoza wao. Alizoea kuliita kundi hili wapenda vya dezo kama maiti. Maana nchini Mafuriko asasi za kiraia hazikunusurika. Zilivamiwa na matapeli na wasasi wa ngawira ambao nao kama serikali waliwatumia wananchi kujipatia riziki huku wale walioitwa walengwa wakihenyeka na kuteseka.

Moja ya asasi hii ambayo haikujulikana kama ilikuwa ya kiserikali au kiraia iliitwa Mafuriko Commission Against Aids (MACAIDS). Hii ni taasisi iliyojinaki kuwa ilikuwa ikipambana na ukimwi ambao uligeuka kuwa muuaji mwingine ilhali ilikuwa ikiueneza. Kama kuna kitu ilikuwa imefanikisha si kingine bali kununua magari ya bei mbaya aina ya Toyota VX na kuwalipa watumishi wake mishahara mikubwa na marupurupu yaliyotokana na semina, makongamano na warsha za mara kwa mara. Yote haya ilikuwa ni sababu ya kupatia pesa lakini siyo kupambana na ukimwi. Hii taasisi mbali na kuwa kidhabu ilikuwa ni tajiri sana. Ilikuwa kama kitendawili. Kwani ilianzishwa na serikali na kujiita asasi ya kiraia! Hii nayo ilihusishwa kwenye ghilba ya waziri mkubwa, mke wa Rais na taasisi ya mwizi Chandy. Maana kutokana na kutokuwa na kauli juu ya miili yao, wanawake wengi wa Mafuriko walikuwa wameambukizwa ukimwi kutokana na kubakwa na waume zao. Kwenye ripoti za mkaguzi wa mahesabu kila mwaka ilikuwa ikipata hati chafu sawa na wizara za serikali ambazo wakubwa wake waligeuza bajeti kuwa chanzo cha pesa ya utajiri binafsi! Kila mtu katika Mafuriko aliiba ofisini kwake sawa na mbuzi kula kwa urefu wa kamba yake! Hafla ilifanyika baada ya siku mbili na Chandy alimkabidhi mke wa Rais kitita cha pesa na zawadi nyingine. Pesa ziliingizwa kwenye akaunti yake binafsi na zawadi kupewa watoto yatima.

Kwa vile lengo la hafla hii lilikuwa kumbaini aliyekuwa anamshauri vibaya, haya mengine yalikuwa ni visingizio tu. Mkuu wa usalama alimtaja jaji Hose Waryuba.Baada ya kumjua mbaya wao, walipanga jinsi ya kummaliza. Pamoja na kutokuwa na uhakika hapo mwanzo, walikuwa wanamuhisi yeye. Maana ndiye aliyekuwa mshauri wa Rais kati ya wengi waliyekuwa wamemjaribu kumrubuni bila mafanikio. Hivyo, waziri mkubwa alimuomba mke wa Rais aliyezoea kumuita shemeji yake aanze kumwekea mtima nyongo huku naye akitafuta jinsi ya kumkabili Rais kumshauri amfukuze kazi. Hii haikuwa mara ya kwanza kwa waziri mkubwa kumtumia mke wa Rais kuwafukuzisha kazi watu aliowaona kama walikuwa wakiingilia maslahi yake. Mwaka mmoja kabla ya hapo alishirikiana na mke wa Rais hata kurudisha baadhi ya mabalozi waliokuwa wakiwakilisha Mafuriko ughaibuni baada ya kuonyesha kutokubaliana na baadhi ya miradi aliyowataka waitetee. Wakati akimtafuta aliyekuwa na Rais siku hiyo, pia alikuwa anapanga mpango wa kumshari Rais ambadilishe waziri wa maji mvua na upepo ili kuficha madhambi ya Richmonfuli. Maana bila kuwapo mbuzi wa kafara si ajabu mambo yangeweza kufichuka na wazee wazima kuadhirika. Pamoja na kwamba kwa hali ya ufisadi ilivyokuwa imeongezeka Rais na mawaziri wake walikwishaumbuka ukiachia mbali kusitiriwa na uvumilivu wa wananchi na utii wa majeshi yaliyokuwa nayo yananyanyaswa sawa na wananchi, bado walijiona kama waheshimiwa. Hivyo hawakutaka waendelee kuumbuka. Walikuwa tayari kwa lolote kuepuka vyombo vya habari kuuzindua umma. Isitoshe kwa hali ilivyokuwa ni kama waziri mkubwa ndiye aliyekuwa akiendesha nchi nyuma ya pazia. Maana Rais alikuwa kama kinyago kinachoweza kusafirishwa popote bila kuulizwa wala kupinga. Maana karibu madhambi mengi yaliyokuwa yakiiyumbisha nchi ya Mafuriko yalikuwa yameasisiwa na kusimamiwa na waziri mkubwa.

Kwa upande wake, Waziri mkubwa alikuwa mtu wa ajabu. Alikuwa sawa na nyani asiyeweza kuona kundule na kuona ya wenzie. Maana siku moja akiwa kwenye ziara ya kichama kwenye mkoa wa Madodo aliwahi kumfukuza kazi kiongozi mmoja wa ngazi ya chini kutokana na kukiibia taasisi ya umma mali ya shilingi kama laki saba. Ulikuwa ni wakati wa kashfa ya Richmen. Walio kuwa wanaojua kuwa Richmonduli alikuwa ni yeye, walimshangaa kwa unafiki wake. Walishangaa alipokuwa akipata mshipa wa kuweza kumfukuza mtu aliyegaga wakati yeye alikuwa ameoza kabisa! Hawakujua kuwa wanasiasa wababaishaji ndivyo siku zote walivyo! Hawakujua kuwa tofauti yao na matapeli waliokuwa wamejazana kwenye mji wa Neema ilikuwa ni jinsi walivyopata kazi zao wakati matokeo yalikuwa sawa kuchuma kwa kuwaumiza wengine! Na huu ulikuwa mtihani mkubwa uliomuumbua. Maana kwenye ziara zake karibu zote mikoani na wilayani hakuwa akiongelea ufisadi. Yeye alipenda kuwahimiza wananchi kufanya kazi ilitafsiriwa kama kuwambia wazalishe sana yeye na wenzake wachume. Hakupenda kabisa kuongelea ufisadi. Maana roho yake ilizoea kumsuta ndani kwa ndani. Hata wananchi wa Mafuriko walijua hili. Hivyo, alivyolalamikiwa kuhusu afisa mdogo alikuwa akitiwa majaribuni kama vyombo vya habari vilivyoelezea tukio hili la kinafiki. Kweli bila hata chembe ya aibu, aliamuru afisa yule mdogo akamatwe mara moja na kufunguliwa mashtaka. Chimbuchimbu lilitoka asubuhi iliyofuata na kijembe kuwa kweli nyani haoni kundule.

23
Chimbuchimbu na mchimvi!

Wakati waziri mkubwa na mke wa Rais wakimtafuta mbaya wao aliyekuwa akimshauri vibaya Rais, katibu wa ofisi ya waziri mkubwa chini ya maelekezo ya bosi wake, aliitisha mkutano wa waandishi wa habari kukanusha habari iliyochapishwa na gazeti la chimbuchimbu kuhusiana nani walikuwa nyuma ya kashfa ya Richmen.

Wengi wa waliohudhuria mkutano huu walikuwa maarufu kama mbwa mwitu au vyangudoa ambao wakati wa kampeni za kuwania urais, walikuwa wakijikomba kwa wagombea ili watakaposhinda wapewe mabaki ya vyeo kama ukuu wa mkoa au wilaya na kazi nyingine za hovyo kwenye ofisi ya rais. Wengi walijikomba wachache wakapewa vyeo ambavyo Nkweo Nkhwazi, mhariri mwandamizi wa Chimbuchimbu, alizoea kuviita aibu na usaliti kwa umma. Baada ya kuwasalimia waandishi wa habari kwa bashasha, katibu wa ofisi ya waziri mkubwa alianza kusema., "Pamoja na vyombo vya habari kuwa na haki ya kupata na kutoa habari, pia vina haki na wajibu wa kuandika habari sahihi. Vina jukumu la kuhakikisha kuwa wasomaji wake hawalishwi uongo au uchafu." Alitoa leso yake na kujipenga kamasi hewa kidogo na kuendelea.

"Sikuwaiteni hapa kulaumiana bali kukanusha kuwa habari zilizoandikwa kuhusiana na kampuni ya Richmen si za kweli."

Baada ya kumaliza utadhani alichokoza nyuki! Nkhwazi hakumkopesha. Isitoshe ukumbi mzima wa mikutano ulikuwa unategemea kuwa lazima Nkhwazi angeuliza licha ya waandishi wengine kunyoosha mikono kwa ajili ya kutaka kuuliza maswali. Kama ilivyotazamiwa na wengi aliuliza, "Ndugu Katibu ni kwanini na kitu gani kimefanya ofisi ya waziri mkubwa ijibu tuhuma badala ya wizara ya maji mvua na upepo wakati mtuhumiwa mkuu ni wizara hii ambayo mradi mzima uko chini yake?"

Katibu wa wizara alisita kidogo akacheka na kupiga siasa, "Mmea huzaa mbegu na mbegu huzaa mmea. Je hapa kipi ni kipi?" Waandishi walipigwa na butwaa hata wale wa magazeti ya serikali. Maana hawakuelewa alichokuwa akimaanisha katibu wa ofisi ya waziri mkuu! Wale makanjanja bingwa wa kujipendekeza badala ya kustuka walianza kukenua meno ili bosi awaone aweze kuwatupia lau mabaki ya vyeo vilivyokuwa havijatolewa kama maafisa wa propaganda wa chama na upuuzi mwingine kama huo utokanao na usaliti wa umma.

Wakati waandishi wakiwa wamebung'aa, katibu wa wizara alijijibu mwenyewe kwa kufanunua, "Kimsingi uamuzi wa kuleta kampuni ya Richmen ulifikiwa na baraza la mawaziri. Na hii ndiyo serikali yenyewe. Sasa hawa Richmen wana pesa kiasi gani kuihonga serikali nzima? Na je serikali nzima inaweza kuwa fisidi? Bila shaka jibu ni hapana" Alichomoa leso yake mfukoni na kujifuta jasho. Maana alikuwa anatiririka jasho utadhani alikuwa kwenye mbio za marathoni!' Aliendelea, "Kimsingi serikali nzima haiwezi kufanya mambo yaliyoandikwa na magazeti. Tukubaliane kwanza kwa hili." Kabla ya kuendelea Nkhwazi alionekana kuudhika na kuuliza maswali mengine kabla ya kungoja katibu wa wizara aendelee na maudhi yake. Alisema, "Kwa hiyo ndugu katibu unataka kuuambia umma kuwa msiba huu umetengenezwa na serikali? Hilo moja. Pili je bunge lilishirikishwa? Kama ndiyo vipi? Na kama hapana kwanini? Pia uelewe kuwa mmea mmoja una matawi tofauti na kila tawi lina majani yake ingawa vyote ni wamoja." Waandishi ilibidi wampigie makofi Nkhwazi kwa kufumbua kitendawili.

Katibu wa wizara kwa kujikuta amebanwa, aliamua kujitetea kwa kusema, "Mimi nijuavyo hapakuwa na rushwa wala harufu ya rushwa ukiachia mbali rushwa yenyewe. Kitu kingine lazima tukubaliane kuwa pamoja na vyombo vya habari kuwa na haki na uhuru wa kutafuta na kusambaza habari pia vina wajibu wa kuandika na kuripoti ukweli baada ya kufanya utafiti." Alijifuta jasho na kunywa kama tama mbili za maji na kuendelea, "Kuna haja ya kila mwananchi kuwa mzalendo katika kutekeleza majukumu yake. Sambamba na hili, kuna haja ya kila mwanataaluma kulinda maslahi ya umma. Maana mnapoandika mambo kama haya yenye kuchafua jina zuri la serikali na nchi mnafanya hata nchi wafadhili kutunyima misaada. Maana wanadhani kuwa kodi zao zinachezewa tofauti na hali ilivyo." Mwandishi wa gazeti la Mafuriko Leo linalomilkiwa na serikali naye aliuliza swali ili kumsaidia katibu kukwepa kujibu maswali ya Nkhwazi, mhariri mkuu wa Chimbuchimbu. Aliuliza, "Je mheshimiwa mwenzetu wa gazeti la Chimbuchimbu anaweza kutueleza alivyopata habari hizi?" Kabla ya katibu wa wizara kujibu, Nkhwazi alijibu swali bila kujali kama lililengwa kwa katibu wa wizara. Alisema. "Kwanza mimi sijaishiwa kiasi cha kutaka uheshimiwa njiwa. Ndugu yangu wa Mafuriko anachekesha na kushangaza! Maana licha ya kutaka kuvunja maadili inaonekana mwenzetu hajui hata mpaka wa wajibu wake! Miiko ya kazi na taaluma inazuia kutaja sources. Hii ni kanuni ya dunia nzima. Pamoja na mwenzangu kumilikiwa na serikali, ningemshauri aheshimu taaluma na kuwa mzalendo hasa linapokuja suala zima la maslahi ya jamii juu ya maslahi binafsi. Nataka nirudi maswali yangu. "Kwa hiyo ndugu katibu unataka kuuambia umma kuwa msiba huu umetengenezwa na serikali? Hilo moja. Pili je bunge lilishirikishwa? Kama ndiyo vipi? Niongeze jingine ili kusisitiza. Je ni kwanini kila kashfa inayochipuka serikali badala ya kutafuta jibu kwa kuwashughulikia watuhumiwa imegeuka kuwa mtetezi na wakili wa wahalifu? Je huu ndiyo uzalendo anaotaka kutufundisha ndugu katibu wa ofisi ya waziri mkubwa?"

Katibu wa wizara ya ofisi ya waziri mkubwa kuona maji yamezidi unga alisema, "Serikali hufanya mambo yake kwa taratibu, kanuni na utafiti. Hivyo ningemwomba mheshimiwa mhariri." Kabla ya kuendelea watu hawana mbavu. Vicheko na miguno.

Katibu aliendelea, "Ndugu wana habari. Tusikilizane tafadhali. Kwani ulimi hauna mfupa na isitoshe kila raia ni mheshimiwa" Kabla ya kuendelea inasikika sauti ikisema, "Mmenaswa kubalini mmekula." Katibu wa wizara kumbe alilisikia lile neno la kejeli. Alisema, "Hakuna haja ya kupitisha hukumu kabla ya kufanya utafiti. No research no right to speak." Kabla ya kuendelea sauti nyingine inasikika, "No accountability no right to be in public office so to speak." Badala ya kujibu maswali ya msingi, katibu wa wizara alidandia maswali yasiyokuwa rasmi yaliyokuwa yakitolewa kama kejeli. Na isitoshe hayakuwa maswali bali kejeli. Anachomoa tena leso yake mfukoni na kuanza siasa. "Anayesema tumebanwa tukubali anaidharau serikali iliyochanguliwa na wananchi tena kwa kishindo. Namshauri aheshimu serikali. Kuhusu accountability, nani asiyeona kuwa nchi yetu licha ya kusonga mbele kimaendeleo ina amani na mshikamano." Katibu wa wizara akiwa ameishasahau hata yale maswali ya msingi anaendelea, 'Ripoti ya shirika la umoja wa mataifa linaloshughulikia usafi na uadilifu wa serikali zote dunia nzima (Transparent International), hata ikiwemo ya

Marekani mwaka huu limeiweka Mafuriko ya saba toka ya ishirini na tisa kwenye ripoti yake ya usafi wa serikali."

Anakohoa na kuendelea, "Kwanza inabidi wanamafuriko tujipongeze kwa ufanisi huu ambao umetuongezea heshima kwenye mataifa yote duniani. Kwanini wananchi wetu hamuoni haya mafanikio kiasi cha kuzidiwa hata na wageni wanayaona! Nashangaa sana. Kulikoni jamani hata kama ni upinzani kwanini kupinga kila kitu hadi wageni watusifie sisi bila kujisifia!" Sauti kama ada inasema, "Kwanini wageni wasiyaone mema kwenye karibu mgeni mwenyeji aumie inayoendelea hapa nchini kwetu? Kwanini wasiyaone mafanikio iwapo wanachota mali zetu bure utadhani tumepagawa hata kukaukiwa ubongo? Wanaiba hadi mchanga wetu wanaotumia kufichia madini!"

"Du!" Inasikika sauti. Inaendelea, "Jamaa utadhani limekariri. Mbona sanaa!"Katibu kama ada anadakia maswali yasiyo rasmi na kuacha yale yanayolenga kumuumbua. Anaikosoa hii kauli. Anasema, "Kwanini wananchi mnakuwa na mawazo hasi kwa kila kitu? Nani anachota utajiri wetu iwapo huu ndiyo uchumi wa kisasa na wa kimaifa? Hivi jamani hamuoni barabara nzuri, mashule na hata mahospitali?"

Kabla ya kuendelea kupiga siasa Nkhwazi anamrudisha kwenye kikaango. Anasema, "Ndugu katibu mimi ningetaka ujibu maswali yangu badala ya haya ambayo kimsingi ni nyongeza kwa maswali yangu ya msingi." Katibu wa ofisi ya waziri mkubwa naye alitumia mafuta yale yale kumkaanga samaki wake kama alivyotaka kukaangwa yeye na Nkhwazi. Alisema, "Nami ngoja nirudie majibu yangu ya msingi kama wewe ambavyo umerudia maswali yako ya msingi kwako ambayo si ya msingi kwa serikali." Alisema akicheka utadhani alichokuwa anaongelea lilikuwa suala jepesi! Alinong'ona na mwandishi wake aliyekuwa bize akinukuu maswali. Baada ya kunong'ona na kupewa karatasi alisoma na kusema, "Serikali hufanya mambo yake kwa taratibu, kanuni na utafiti. Hivyo, ningeshauri ndugu mhariri utupe muda tufanye utafiti na kuja na majibu ya kisayansi. Isitoshe, mlango wa ofisi yangu uko wazi kwa wanahabari wakati wowote wanapokuwa na masuala ya kujibu. Asanteni naona muda wangu umekwisha."

Wakati akijiandaa kutoka huku miguno ikiendelea, wasaidizi wake baada ya kuhakikisha kuwa kamera za televisheni hazimuliki tena ule mkutano, waliingia na vinywaji baridi na bahasha za khaki ambazo zilishazoeleka kuwa ulikuwa ni mshiko. Baadhi ya waandishi wa habari hawakujivunga. Walichangamkia vile vinywaji baridi na bahasha. Nkhwazi kimya kimya alikusanya vitabu vyake na kuanza kuondoka. Alipokuwa amekatisha ukumbi, katibu wa ofisi ya waziri mkuu alirejea kama alikuwa amesahau kitu. Kumbe alikuwa akimuangalia tokea ndani ya ofisi mkabala aliyokuwa ameingia. Alimpa mkono Nkhwazi na kumvuta pembeni na kusema, "Bwana mdogo, kwanini unahagaika na kupambana na ukuta. Tatizo lako ni nini? Naomba twende ofisini kwangu tukahojiane zaidi." Alitamka tukahojiane zaidi kwa sauti ili kuwazuga waandishi waliokuwa wakisikiliza wasidhani alikuwa anataka kwenda kumhonga ingawa ilikuwa hivyo. Nkhwazi, kwa vile hakuwa mgeni kwa watawala fisidi wa Mafuriko, wala hakuwa na pingamizi. Waliingia kwenye ofisi mkabala huku katibu akijifanya mchangamfu wakati kila mmoja moyoni alikuwa na lake. Moyoni Nkhwazi alijiambia asile wala kunywa chochote maana asingejua upande wa pili ulikuwa unataka nini. Hakujua kuwa nyendo zake zote tangu alipingia kwenye ofisi ya waziri mkubwa zilikuwa zikifuatiliwa. Maana baada ya kuketi tu, katibu wa ofisi ya waziri mkuu alimuuliza mbona hakunywa soda wala kuchukua bahasha yake? Nkhwazi alijibu kwa ufupi. Alisema, "Sikuwa na kiu wala sikuja kwa ajili za mshiko bali habari." Katibu wa ofisi ya waziri mkubwa alicheka na kutikisa kichwa na kusema, "Umekataa ukidhani ni inducement? Siyo. Si wote wamepewa. Tunajua mazingira yenu ya kazi ni magumu na wengi wenu hawana hata usafiri. Hivyo usihofu hiyo ni kwa ajili ya nauli ndugu yangu." Nkhwazi alijibu, "Ndiyo mazingira ni magumu. Kama kungekuwa na sera nzuri na uadilifu nadhani yangekuwa mazuri kama nchi za wenzetu hata hivyo hakuna haja ya kujidhalilisha na kuidhalilisha taaluma hata taifa kwa sababu ya ugumu wa maisha. Hapa jibu ni kutafuta jibu badala ya njia chafu za mkato."

Kabla ya kujibu hoja hii, mwandishi mwingine mwandamizi aitwaye Charles Kizigo aliingia huku amechukia. Aliwasalimia akijifanya hajuani na katibu wa ofisi ya waziri mkubwa na kuanza kuuliza, "Katibu nimekuja kukusumbua samahani. Nahitaji ku-cross check tuhuma zinazoikabili serikali. Maana, nikiandika bila kuwasikiliza hamkawii kunipachikia uchochezi wakati mambo yanavyoonekana kuna mshikeli wa wazi." Maskini Kizigo, hakujua kuwa janja yake ya nyani na uovu wake vilikuwa vikijulikana. Kwani, licha ya kusaidia kueneza uovu na ufisadi wa serikali, alikuwa ameishawaumiza wengi kwa kuwashawishi wachukue pesa chafu ya rushwa halafu wakakamatwa. Alikuwa mwandishi malaya aliyeisaliti taaluma yake kwa kulala kitanda kimoja na waovu huku akijifanya alikuwa upande wa pili. Katibu wa ofisi ya waziri mkubwa kuficha uovu wao, alijifanya kumfokea Kizigo. Alisema kwa hasira, "Sasa kama umeishahitimisha kuwa kuna mshikeli wa wazi umeijia nini hapa?" Aliamka kwenye kiti chake na kuanza kuzunguka zunguka huku akifoka, "Kama umetumwa na hao waliokutuma umepotea. Kwanza, elewa kuwa nimeishafanya briefings nawe hukuwapo kwenye mkutano. Sasa kosa langu liko wapi? Anyway in short tuhuma zote si za kweli." Pamoja na katibu wa ofisi ya waziri mkubwa kujibu kwa hasira ili kumzuga mhariri Nkhwazi, hakujua kuwa yeye na muovu mwenzie wakati wakijua huu wenzao walijua ule! Walijiona wajanja wasijue kuwa mhariri mkuu alikuwa anaujua upumbavu wao wa kumtegeshea bomu ili waliaibishe gazeti lake na kuushawishi umma kuwa halikuwa na ithibati. Katibu wa ofisi ya waziri mkubwa alizidi kufoka, "Kwanza, nani kakuruhudu uingie humu. Yaani hata kama ni kutafuta habari hujali faragha za wenzio. Sasa ni kwamba hakuna habari." Alimgeukia Nkhwazi na kusema, "Nitawasiliana nawe baadaye ndugu mhariri ili nikupe ufafanuzi zaidi. Kwaheri na samahani kwa kuvamiwa." Ilikuwa kama mchezo wa kuigiza.

Moyoni, katibu wa ofisi ya waziri mkubwa alijifariji kuwa angalau alikuwa anaanza kumnasa ndege wake. Hapa ndipo kitendawili cha ajabu kilizuka. Maana, aliyepaswa kuilinda na kuitekeleza sheria, alikuwa anaiteketeza kwa maslahi uchwara binafsi! Maana, Nkhwazi hakupinga Pendekezo lake. Alizidi kufarijika zaidi kuwa kibaraka wao, Kizigo angemnasa mhariri hata kabla yake. Hivyo, alikuwa ametega mitego miwili ima wake au wa Kizigo kachero mchafu aliyejulikana kwa uchafu na roho mbaya yake dhidi ya wanataaluma wa habari nchini Mafuriko. Waliomjua walioea kumuita nepi. Maana alikuwa akifanyishwa kazi chafu kama nepi ibugiavyo vinyesi vya watoto.

Kizigo pamoja na kujificha kwenye kuuvamia mkutano usio rasmi wa katibu wa ofisi ya waziri mkubwa na Nkhwazi, alikuwa na mpango mbaya wa kumshikisha pesa ya rushwa mhariri ili kumchafua yeye na gazeti lake na harakati za umma za kupambana na uoza katika nchi.

Waliondoka ofisini kwa katibu wa ofisi ya waziri mkubwa

huku Kizigo akimlaumu katibu ili kumvutia Nkhwazi kwenye nyavu zake tayari kumkwaza ili amharibie. Kizigo alianzia mazungumzo. Alisema, "Mzee umeonaje hawa wezi wetu? Nadhani tukimbana sana huyu bwana kinaweza kueleweka. Au unasemaje?" Nkhwazi alijibu, "Of course kila kitu kiko wazi kuwa hii hujuma inahusisha mtandao mkubwa unaoendesha serikali."

Kizigo aliuliza, "Je mmemalizanaje? Unaona kweli huyu jamaa anaweza kuweka sawa mambo?" Nkhwazi, "Kuweka sawa mambo ni kutoa sababu kwanini waziri mkubwa alijihusisha na masuala ya tenda wakati hayako chini ya wizara yake? Na kwanini atoe tenda kubwa namna hii na kupoteza pesa ya umma kwa kampuni isiyo na sifa?"

"Sasa mmepanga kukutana lini kutoa maelezo zaidi?" Aliuliza Kizigo. Nkhwazi alijibu, "Mimi sihitaji mkutano naye. Nakwenda kuandika ukweli kama atakuwa tayari kukubaliana na ukweli sina neno naye."

Kizigo alizidi kuuliza, "Una maanisha nini mbona umeniacha njia panda?"

Nkhwazi alijibu,"Wa-admit kuwa wakubwa wameshiriki mchezo huu mchafu na warejeshe pesa ya umma na kufuta tenda na kuitangaza upya na kuteua kampuni yenye sifa bila ya kutumia kujuana na kupeana rushwa."

"Wakikataa kufanya hivyo?" Aliuliza tena Kizigo.

Nkhwazi, "Wakikataa tutauachia umma uamue. Maana sisi kama media tutakuwa tumetimiza wajibu wetu. Lakini siamini kama wananchi wetu wanaweza kuendelea kugeuzwa asusa ya upuuzi na uchafu wa wakubwa wasio na maana wala maadili. Kwani hii nchi ni yao peke yao? Kwani pesa wanayotoa ni ya mama zao? Umma lazima utatoa adhabu kwa uchafu huu kwa njia ya kuwafagia wahusika wote toka kwenye ofisi za umma. Hili sina wasi wasi nalo. Maana alama za nyakati zinaonyesha kila dalili kuwa wananchi wanataka kurejeshewa nchi yao toka mikononi mwa wezi."

Kizigo, "Lakini angalia wasije wakakumaliza kama Stan Kataa waliyemuua baada ya kufichua ubadhirifu kwenye mbuga za wanyama." Alitahadharisha Kizigo.

"Kufa si jambo la kuogopwa na isitoshe siyo jibu. Kwani tangu Stan auawe wamekufa vigogo wangapi tena kwa ukimwi huku wakijifanya wamekufa kwa presha?"

Alipiga chafya na kuendelea, "Kuogopa kuawa ni upuuzi. Mbona kama ni kufa tunakufa kila siku kutokana na shida wanazotusababishia?"

"Hapa ndugu yangu umenena na umenipata. Kwanza, nina mpango wa kuhama gazeti la serikali. Maana tunazibwa midomo na kulazimishwa kutetea upuuzi. Je uko tayari kunipa kibarua kwenye gazeti lako ili tuchape kazi pamoja. Hawa lazima tuwashughulikie.....eh tuwaumbue waumbuke vilivyo. Nina usongo nao sina mfano." Alisema Kizigo.

"Ongea na utawala. Mie siko kwenye idara ya ajira. Ukitaka recommendations nitatoa wholeheartedly."

Kizigo, "Asante kaka. Muhimu, wakati tunapanga hii transition naona tuunganishe vichwa kwanza tupambane na hawa washenzi mbwa, wezi waliojificha nyuma ya utukufu. Isitoshe, kuna mambo yao mengi nayajua. Lazima Chimbuchimbu iwachimbe chimbe na kuwashikisha adabu."

Kabla ya Nkhwazi kujibu, simu ya Kizigo ililia. Baada ya Kizigo kujua kuwa aliyekuwa upande wa pili ni katibu wa ofisi ya waziri mkubwa, alimuomba mhariri mkuu alijibu simu na kujifanya mawasiliano ni mabaya. Hivyo alitumia mwanya huu kwenda chemba kusikiliza simu yake.

Nkhwazi kwa kujua mnyama aliyekuwa mbele yake alirefusha masikio yake kujua kulikoni.

Maongezi ya Kizigo na katibu wa ofisi ya waziri mkubwa

yalikuwa hivi;

"Halo bosi, naona unipigie baadaye. Maana ndege anakaribia kutua mtegoni. Hivyo nashauri usimrushe."

"Okey. Hata mimi sikuwa na jipya zaidi ya kutaka kujua umefikia wapi. Make sure tunamnasa na kumchinja. Okey. Good luck and God bless." Katibu wa ofisi ya waziri mkubwa alikata simu.

Kizigo aliporudi alimdanganya Nkhwazi kuwa mkewe alikuwa akipiga simu kutaka kujua alikuwa wapi asijue kuwa masikio ya mhariri yalikuwa kazini wakati akipanga uchafu wake! Kizigo alisema, "Hawa ndugu zetu kwa wivu! Sisi tuko tunahangaika kulikomboa taifa ili nao wawe huru waondokane na kupewa nafasi chafu za kuteuliwa na kuachwa nyuma katika kila nyanja, yeye anafikiria niko chemba nakula maraha wakati nipo napambana na viumbe hatari kuliko hata shetani mwenyewe!" Nkhwazi hakujibu kitu. Alijifanya kuwa bize akibofya simu yake kama kuandika ujumbe mfupi. Mara ghafla alisema, "Utadhani viumbe hawa nao wana mtandao wa wivu kama mtandao wa ujambazi wa wakubwa zetu! Maana nami wakati ukiongea nimepokea ujumbe mke wangu akitaka kujua niko wapi nafanya nini na niko na nani! Nimemwambia niko gerezani kwani nimekamatwa. Wacha ahahe asijue niko na swahiba na mwana mapinduzi mwenzangu!"

Maneno haya yalimfurahisha Kizigo akaanza kuona kama ndege ndiyo kajiingiza mtegoni kwake! Kizigo alitabasamu na kusema, "Ndiyo maana ndoa ni halali kwa watu wazima. Maana kama watoto wangeoa utotoni si ajabu mauaji na talaka vingeongezeka. Lakini tusilaumu sana. Maana, mapenzi bila wivu ni sawa na chumvi iliyochujuka."

"Lakini wakati mwingine na chumvi ikizidi kwenye chakula nayo hukiharibu." Alijibu Nkhwazi. "Fikiria isipokuwapo kabisa kitalika?" Kizigo aliendelea kurefusha hadithi ya mapenzi. Nkhwazi alifanikiwa kuvishinda vishawishi na mitego vya kupewa rushwa ili anyamaze na kulisaliti gazeti lake. Kizigo alimkaribisha kwenye hoteli moja huku akiwa ameishasuka mpango na mamlaka za kuzuia rushwa bila mafanikio. Maana alikataa zile pesa.

Pia aliahidiwa angepewa ukuu wa wilaya hata ukuu mkoa angetaka ilmradi aache kuishambulia na kuichimbua chimbua serikali. Kadhalika alikataa kata kata na kuwaambia makuadi wa serikali kuwa hakuwa tayari kuwa msaliti kwa wananchi na malaya wa cheo huku akiendekeza tumbo lake kupalilia maangamizi wa jamii iliyomsomesha. Badala ya serikali kutumia raslimali vizuri kuwaendeleza wananchi, ilizitumia raslimali nyingi pesa na muda mwingi kuwatafuta watu wa kuipamba ili iendelee kuumiza umma jambo amabalo Nkhwazi alikuwa ameapa kupambana nalo kwa uwezo na vipaji vyake kadri alivyoweza.

24
Arobaini ya mwizi

Wakati Rais akiwa amejichimbia kwenye harakati za kuokoa serikali yake iliyokuwa inaanza kuporomoshwa na kashfa za mara kwa mara, upinzani ulitumia upenyo huu kurekebisha makosa yao. Upinzani ulianza kupanga mikakati ya kufanya migomo na maandamano nchi nzima kushinikiza kuondolewa na hatimaye kutimuliwa kwa serikali usijue kuwa chama cha wafanyakazi kilikuwa kimeishamaliza maandalizi ya pigo takatifu! Pia kulianza kujengeka upinzani ndani ya chama na serikali ya Rais mwenyewe. Kuna wanachama wa chama tawala walioanza kupaza sauti zao wazi kuitaka serikali ijisafishe au kujing'atua baada ya kuona chama na serikali vimekosa udhu wa kutawala nchi. Kwa kiasi fulani, upinzani nao ulikuwa na mafyongo yake. Ulikuwa umewaangusha wananchi kutokana na uroho na ubinafsi wa baadhi ya viongozi wa vyama ambao kwao siasa ilikuwa ni kwa wao kuchukua dola ili kupatia hati ya kuiibia umma na kujitajirisha sawa na wale waliokuwa wakiwapinga na kutaka kuwatimua madarakani. Wengine walivitumia vyama vyao kama makampuni ya mfukoni kuweza kujipatia vijipesa mbuzi vya kula na kupitisha siku. Kwa hawa siasa ilikuwa haina tofauti na biashara ndogo ndogo au umachinga ambapo mhusika huranda mtaa hadi mtaa.

Wengine nao walikuwa kama vyangudoa. Walidandia chama hiki na kile ilmradi wapate riziki yao na siku zisogee bila kujali kuwa walikuwa wakijichuuza wao, utu wao na watu wao! Hii ikichangiwa na mbinu chafu za serikali zilizofanya upinzani uwe sawa na hakuna. Kama ulikuwapo basi yake ilikuwa ni makelele, kugombea ruzuku, wafuasi na malalamiko mengine ambayo hayakuwa hata na msingi kwa umma uliokuwa tayari kuwaamini kwa kuwachagua.

Wananchi walikuwa tayari kuuamini upinzani. Lakini upinzani haukujiamini wala kuwapa wananchi matumaini kutokana na ulivyokuwa ukifanya mambo yake. Maana vita ya wao kwa wao ilikuwa ndiyo sala ya kila siku. Walikuwa wakilana kama wadudu huku wakiisaidia serikali hafifu na chafu kuendelea kuwatesa wananchi wa Mafuriko maskini!

Ajabu katika uchafu na usaliti huu wa upinzani walikuwamo wanasiasa wasomi wenye hata shahada za udaktari wakifanya mambo ambayo hata msukuma mkokoteni asingejaribu kuyaafanya achilia mbali kuyafanya. Zengeni alizoea kuwaita wana siasa wa namna hii vyangudoa wa kisiasa waliokuwa wakitumia utumbo kufikiri badala ya ubongo sawa na maafisa wezi na fisidi wa serikali ya Mafuriko iliyokuwa imepoteza mwelekeo kiasi cha kuanza kujimomonyoa yenyewe.

Kimsingi, kama siyo upinzani kugawanyika kiasi cha kuwa dhalili, serikali ya Mafuriko isingetawala hata miezi sita. Kilichoifanya itawale ni ombwe na udhaifu wa upinzani ambao licha ya kuwa dhaifu ulikuwa umegawanywa na serikali kwa kuingiza vidudu watu waliouzuga na kuusambaratisha huku wakirejea "nyumbani" yaani kwenye chama chao tawala. Hivyo, baada ya vyombo vya habari kushupalia uoza katika ngazi zote za utawala, wapinzani walitia akilini waliungana na kuzika tofauti zao zote tayari kushinikiza serikali itimliwe. Rais akiwa anahangaika na kupambana na jinsi ya kufunika mianya yake, ndani ya chama chake yalizuka makundi yakaanza kumalizana. Mwanzoni aliichukulia hali hii kama ghubari ambalo lingepita naye kuendelea kutesa kama kawaida asijue siku ya kufa Mungu hakuandikii barua wala kukupigia simu!

Nyuma ya pazia alikuwapo waziri mkubwa na watu wake ambao lengo lao ilikuwa ni kuhakikisha Rais hamalizi muda wake. Walipanga kumuangusha kwa kuzidi kuitia doa serikali yake. Maana baadhi ya ufisadi walioufanya haukuwa na sababu zaidi ya kumharibia Rais ili watu wamuone ameshindwa kutawala nchi kama ilivyokuja kubainika baadaye. Walizidi kujichimbia kwenye wizi huku waziri mkubwa akijitahidi kujionyesha kama kiongozi mzuri. Ilifikia mahali nchi ikawa inajua kuwa ndiye alikuwa akimtawala Rais. Nyuma ya pazia mambo yalikuwa yanatokota kama volkeno inayongoja kulipuka! Naye kama kipofu yeyote, waziri mkubwa hakujua kuwa kitendo cha usaliti alichokuwa akikifanya kwa Rais na Raia kilikuwa sawa na kukata tawi ulilokalia usichelee kuanguka na kuumia mwenyewe kama ilivyomtokea baadaye. Gazeti la Chimbu chimbu na magazeti mengine huru nayo hayakubaki nyuma. Kashfa ya Richmen ilizidi kufumliwa huku kashfa ya Bank Of MafurikoUlaji (BOMU) kama waandishi walivyozoea kuiita, na ya mwenyekiti wa chama tawala wa zamani, familia yake na marafiki zake zikizidi kuanikwa. Umma nao kwa upande wake ulitoka usingizini na kuanza kuwambia wapinzani waungane haraka uwape madaraka. Bahati mbaya viongozi wa vyama vya upinzani kila mmoja alishikilia yeye ndiye awe mwenyekiti wa muungano wa wapinzani ili awe mgombea wa urais. Hali hii iliwaacha hoi kiasi cha kujidhoofisha wenyewe huku wabunge wao wakifunikwa na wabunge wa chama tawala kiasi cha kupitisha kila upuuzi wa serikali. Mchezo mchafu ulikuwa ukifanyika wazi wazi bungeni kiasi cha bunge kugeuka kuwa nyumba ndogo ya serikali. Serikali iliyokuwa imeingia madarakani ikidai ni ya wananchi ghafla iligeuka ya chama na kundi dogo la marafiki na wapambe wa Rais.

Kuna kipindi bunge lilijigeuza mahakama hata serikali kiasi cha kuwa na utatu-mharibifu ambapo lingeweza kuwasimamisha wabunge, kuhoji waandishi wa habari hata kutoa adhabu kama mahakama!

Wakati haya yakiendelea jumuia ya kimataifa nayo ilimchoka Rais hivyo ikaamua kumtosa kwa kuunga mkono upinzani ambao ulionyesha kuwapo matumaini ya kuweza kuirejesha Mafuriko kwenye enzi zake baada ya taratibu kuanza kuzika tofauti zake. Migomo maandamano na kila aina ya upinzani vilizaliwa ghafla kiasi cha kutikisa misingi dhaifu ya serikali ya Mafuriko. Majeshi na polisi nao hawakubaki nyuma. Waliamka nao usingizini kadhalika na kuunga mkono maandamano kichini chini. Walikuwamo wakubwa wenye hata mapurende. Maana nao waligundua kuwa kumbe walikuwa wakitumika. Kilichokuwa kikifanyika ilikuwa ni kuwapa maafisa wa majesho wa vyeo vya juu vyeo vyenye maslahi wakubwa huku askari wa chini wakiendelea kuteseka sawa na umma! Askari wadogo walifikia mahali wakawa kama chokora. Sare zao zilichujuka na kuzeeka bila kupewa mpya huku majumba waliyokuwa wakiishi yakiwa hata hayafikii uzuri kwa mabanda ya mifugo ya maafisa wa serikali waliyoilinda na kuitumikia kwa moyo na uaminifu wa hali ya juu! Iligundulika kuwa kumbe Mafuriko lilikuwa taifa tajiri kama siyo utajiri wake kuishia kwenye mikono ya watawala wapuuzi na wachafu wachache na familia zao waliokuwa wakishirikiana na wafanyabiashara majambazi toka nje kuliibia.

Wakati watawala wakienda nje kuomba, walikuwa na utajiri usiokuwa wa kawaida. Kashfa zote ziliorodheshwa na kukuta kuwa kama watawala wezi wa Mafuriko wangekuwa waadilifu basi Mafuriko ingekuwa nchi inayoongoza kwa kipato katika bara la Nuru! Kitu kilichowakera wananchi ni ukweli kuwa utajiri wote wa licha ya kutoroshwa na watawala wachafu na maajenti wao wa kigeni, ulikuwa unaozeana nje ukiwafaa watu wa mataifa mengine ilhali waliokuwa wamiliki na wazalishaji halali walikuwa wakifa na kuteseka kwa umaskini wa kunuka! Katika muelekeo wa kudondoka kwa utawala mchovu wa Mafuriko, uchumi ulisambaratika huku serikali ikitoa taarifa za kuvutia wakati nyuma ya pazia mambo yalikuwa tofauti. Ilikuwa sawa na kaburi ambalo hung'ara juu ilhali ndani kuna uoza au kikombe cha mpumbavu ambacho daima huoshwa juu ndani ikitawala nongo.

Rais alizidiwa kweli kweli. Kujaribu kutuliza hasira za wananchi, Rais alivunja baraza lake la mawaziri na kuwatimua wote akiwamo waziri mkubwa isipokuwa makamu wa Rais na mawaziri wawili waliogundulika kutojihusisha na ufisadi. Hawa walinusuriwa na kutonunua kwa mfano nyumba za umma wala kuwa na makampuni ya siri. Hii ilikuwa baada ya bunge kuamka toka usingizini na kuunda tume ya kuchunguza kashfa za uletaji wa kampuni la Richmen ambako waziri mkuu alifichuliwa kuwa ndiye alikuwa nyuma ya kampuni hili ambalo lilikuwa likilipwa dola milioni mbili kwa siku. Uguduzi huu uliwachukiza wananchi wa Mafuriko waliogundua kuwa kumbe walikuwa wakibeba mzigo wa waziri mkuu na marafiki zake!

NGO ya mke wa Rais ilivunjwa na kuamrishwa kurejesha pesa na mali zote ilizokuwa imepokea. Hata heshima ya ofisi ya urais ilirejea pahali pake. Mstakabali wa taifa ulianza kuonyesha miali ya mafanikio. Kama jua la asubuhi nuru mpya katika nchi mpya yenye mikakati na sura mpya vilizaliwa. Baada ya kuunda baraza dogo la mawaziri, Rais alianza kujisafisha ingawa alikuwa amechelewa. Kwani wananchi walikuwa wametokwa na imani naye kabisa. Walimwambia wazi kuwa walikuwa wanampenda lakini wasingeendelea kumuamini chini ya chama chake kilichokuwa licha ya kuzeeka na kuishiwa sera kilishiriki sana kwenye uhujumu na ufisadi wa nchi.

Wapo waliomshauri aanzishe chama kipya ajaribu upya na wale waliomwambia wazi wazi kuwa alikuwa hana udhu tena wa kutawala. Maana alikuwa mtu dhaifu asiye na visheni wala mipango ya kuongoza hata kutawala nchi. Pia alikuwa amehusishwa kwenye baadhi ya kadhia za ufisadi bila ya yeye kujitetea wala kutoa maelezo.

Baada ya kuvunja baraza la mawaziri na kuunda jipya, Rais alitawala kwa kujikongoja kwa miezi mitatu ndipo maandamano yalizuka baada ya kuwa anasita sita kuwachunguza,kuwakamata na kuwafikisha kwenye vyombo vya sheria maafisa wake waliogundulika kuwa wezi wakubwa wakiongozwa na waziri mkubwa, Rais wa zamani,waziri mkuu wa zamani na mawaziri karibia wote.

Vyama vya siasa kwa kutumia kipengele cha katiba kisemacho kuwa kila raia ana wajibu wa kuzuia uhalifu, walipanga wawakamate watuhumiwa kama Rais angeendelea kuwakingia kifua. Bahati mbaya vyama vilitoa tishio vijue kuna watu na akili zao walikuwa wanangojea nafasi na muda muafaka kufanya kweli!Hivyo, Rais hakuwa na chaguo zaidi ya kuamrisha wahusika wakamatwe na kuweka chini ya ulinzi wa nyumbani. Hati zao za kusafiria zilizuiliwa. Bahati mbaya wafanya biashara wengi wa kihindi walitoroka kabla ya kukamatwa. Hata hivyo hii haikuwa dawa maana hati za kukamatwa kwao ziliishatolewa na Interpol ilikuwa ikiwatafuta kwa nguvu zote. Wengi wa waharifu waliojizungusha utajiri na madaraka wakiishi vifua mbele kwa mikogo na tambo walikuwa wakiishi kwa kujificha kama nungunungu. Umma kwa mara nyingine uliirejesha nchi mahali pake huku vibaka na mibaka yote ya kisiasa na kiuchumi ikijikuta pabaya.

Dencha alikamatwa uwanja wa ndege akiwa anajiandaa kukimbia yeye na familia yake. Wakisaidiwa na wafanyakazi wa uwanja wa ndege, wananchi wenye hasira walifanikiwa kumtia mikononi na kumchoma moto.

Hata hivyo, ujanja huu haukufanikiwa. Maana baada ya siku tatu tu umma ulirejea kuishinikza serikali iwashughulikie watuhumiwa wa wizi huu kwenye benki kuu. Bungeni nako wakati wa vikao vyake mawaziri mbali mbali walijitokeza kutoa utetezi wa uoza huu bila mafanikio yoyote ya maana. Nyuma ya pazia mambo yalikuwa moto kweli kweli. Kwani wakubwa walianza kuulizana la kufanya wasipate jibu hadi alipotimuliwa kazi gavana wa benki ambaye alihukumiwa kunyongwa hadi kufa kwa kuhujumu uchumi wa nchi na kudhalililsha kiapo na cheo chake. Mke wake ambaye kimsingi alikuwa mshirika wake alifungwa kifungo cha miaka 50. Gavana na mkewe walikamatwa wakati wakijiandaa kukimbia nchi. Licha ya kunyongwa na mwingine kufungwa, walifilisiwa mali zote zilizokuwa zimeandikishwa kwa majina yao hata zile za marafiki zao. Hakuna jiwe ambalo halilkufunuliwa. Mali zote za nje zilfuatiliwa na kurejeshwa Mafuriko tayari kulijenga taifa.

Jitu na Maleali walivamiwa na majambazi usiku wa siku ya pili ya maandamano na migomo na kuuawa bila kuibiwa kitu chochote. Waliuawa baada ya mtu mmoja mwenye hasira kuwauliza mantiki ya kuwauliza mantiki ya kuwaua vibaka wakati wakiwanyenyekea majambazi.

Hatimaye utabiri wa Zengeni kuwa kuna siku umma ungeacha kuwachoma moto vibaka na kuwarudia mibaka ulitimia bila kutarajiwa. Dunia nzima ilipigwa na butwaa ikakosa la kusema isiamini kilichokuwa kimetokea. Ndiyo hivyo. Historia ilikuwa imeandikwa ili uwe mfano kwa wengine wenye kufanana na Mafuriko. Kwani, wakati bunge,vyombo vya habari , vyama vya kisiasa na serikali vikivutana, ilitokea nguvu iliyoonekana kama ya miujiza iliyosawazisha mambo.

MWIBA chama cha wafanyakazi ambacho kilikuwa hakina historia ya kufurukuta kwenye siasa chafu za Mafuriko iliibuka ghafla na kumaliza mambo kwa namna ya pekee na ambayo haikuwa imetarajiwa na wengi.

Huku Rais akiwa anajipa matumaini nyuma ya pazia kuwa angefanikiwa kuinusuru serikali yake na washirika wake, kwa kubabatiza, MWIBA iliandaa maandamano,migomo na kila aina ya kuipinga serikali dhoofu hadi serikali ikadondoka tena bila umwagaji damu! Hatua hii adhimu ilifikiwa baada ya watawala kuwa wakizomewa kila walipokwenda kuwadanganya wananchi ili kurejesha imani. Watawala walikuwa wamepoteza udhu kabisa!

Mkuu mmoja wa wilaya ya Kinondo alinusurika kuuawa kwa mawe baada ya kuwaamrisha wananchi wa Zowa Hill wahame kupisha mwekezaji apanua mradi wake wa kuchimba mchanga bila kujua kuwa mradi uliopingana na utu usingekubaliwa na watu! Waziri mkubwa naye alikwishazoea kuzomewa kila alipokwenda. Maskini alikuwa na bahati mbaya. Maana zomea zomea ilianzia kwake. Huenda ni kwa vile wananchi walikuwa wakijua uchafu wake kuliko mtawala yeyote. Hakuna siku aliyoina chungu kama ile alipoulizwa swali na mtoto wa darasa la pili juu ya ni kwanini watawala wa Mafuriko walikuwa wakihubiri maji na kunywa divai. Alifedheheka sana. Hali ilikuwa mbaya siku chache baada ya waziri mkubwa kuondoka. Maana watu waliojiita usalama wa taifa waliwaandama walimu na wazazi wa kijana aliyekuwa kauliza swali kwa nia nzuri kabisa.

Wananchi kwa ujumla --wakulima na wafanyakazi wenye

kazi na wasio na ajira mijini na vijijini-- walimiminika mitaani na kusema "BASI" kwa serikali dhalimu kwa herufi na ari kubwa! Yaliyokuwa yamezoeleka kusomwa kwenye historia, majarida na magazetini, ghafla, yaligeuka ukweli usiopingika kwa dunia na wananchi wa Mafuriko! Wafanyakazi walisema wazi wazi kuwa walikuwa wamechoka na kudhalilishwa kunyanyaswa na kudhulumiwa vitendo walivyovilinganisha na kukeketwa kiakili na kunajisiwa kwa haki zao. Walitangaza ukombozi kwa watu wote wakiwamo watesi wao wa muda mrefu yaani watawala dhalimu na wazembe wa Mafuriko. Siku hiyo Zengeni alimwambia Nengoma, "Imetimia arobaini ya mwizi ambapo punda ameamua kumpiga teka mpandaji wake."

Kwa upande wa Zengeni na mkewe Nengoma walipoacha ualimu na kupigwa marufuku kufanya biashara ya mboga mboga na maadazi walisalimu amri kwenye biashara ya kununua na kuuza mazao toka mikoani kiasi cha kufanikiwa kuwasaidia ndugu zao na kujenga banda lao kwenye maeneo ya Uswekeni. Ni eneo lisilopimwa. Kipindupindu na vibaka na kukosekana kwa usalama vina makazi kwenye eneo hili huku kukiwa na ongezeko la watu lisilolingana na ukubwa wa eneo. Waziri mkubwa baada ya bosi wake kulazimika kuwatimua na kuunda serikali ndogo ambayo haikufua dafu kwa madai ya umma dhidi ya ufisadi, arobaini yake na wenzake ilitimia siku yalipofanikiwa maandamano ya wafanyakazi kufichua yaliyokuwa nyuma ya pazia kiasi cha nchi kurejeshwa mikononi mwa umma huku serikali ya mpito ikiundwa ili kufanya kazi mbili.

Mosi, kuandaa uchaguzi huru na wa haki na kuwachunguza wale wote waliojihusisha na ufisadi ili wafikishwe mbele ya sheria.

Pili, kurejesha misingi safi ya utu na ubinadamu

yaliyokuwa yamemomonyoka kiasi cha nchi kugeuzwa kama shamba la wanyama ambapo kila mnyama hujifanyia atakavyo kutegemea na majaliwa yake.

Wengi wa wahusika bado wamo ndani wakingoja tume iliyoundwa kuwachunguza itoe taarifa za utafiti wake. Miradi yote yenye utata imesimamishwa na kampuni la Richmen na mengine yote yako mahakamani kungoja kusikia hukumu ya umma. Bahati mbaya, katika badiliko hili la ghafla, wahusika baadhi wamekufa hapa na pale ama kwa kujiua, kuuawa ama waliobahatika kukimbia huku serikali ya mpito ikishirikiana na Interpol kuwasaka popote walipo. Kitu cha kujivunia ni kwamba maandamano ya wafanyakazi licha ya kuiokoa nchi na kutoa fundisho kwa nchi nyingine, hayakumwaga damu wala kuchukua muda mrefu kuondoa pazia lililokuwapo kwa miongo mingi yakiwaumbua waliokuwako nyuma ya pazia.

Hivyo ndivyo yaliyokuwa Nyuma ya Pazia yalijikuta yakianikwa mbele ya pazia tena jukwaani ambako yalikuwa makazi yake. Hakika, kumbe kila kitu kinaweza kuondolewa Nyuma ya Pazia. Hayo ndiyo ya Nyuma ya Pazia yaliyofunguka na kuishia mbele ya hadhira iliyoamua kuyatumia kutoa funzo kwa waliokuwa mbele na nyuma ya pazia.

Mwisho

Printed in the United States
By Bookmasters